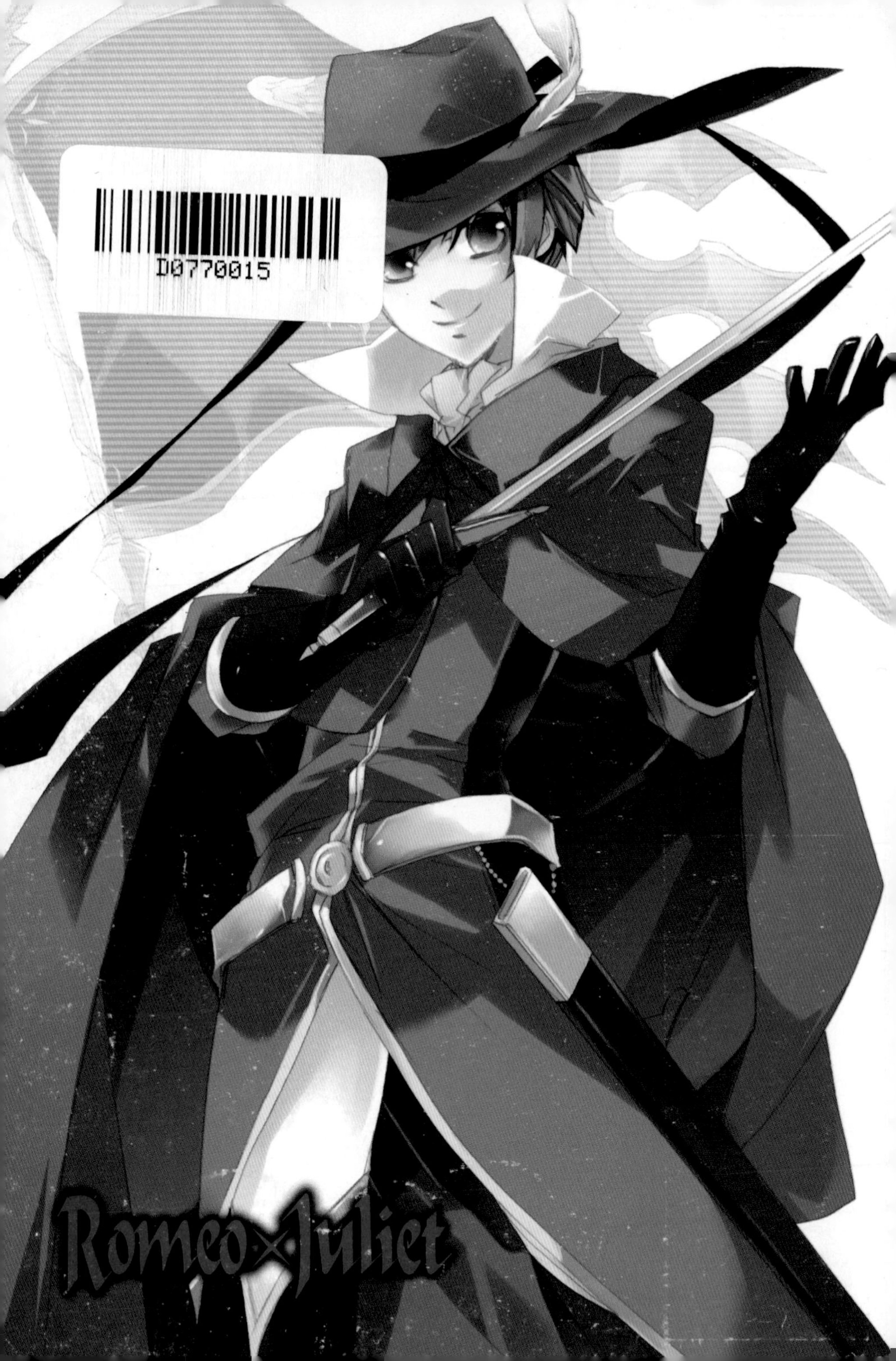
Romeo×Juliet

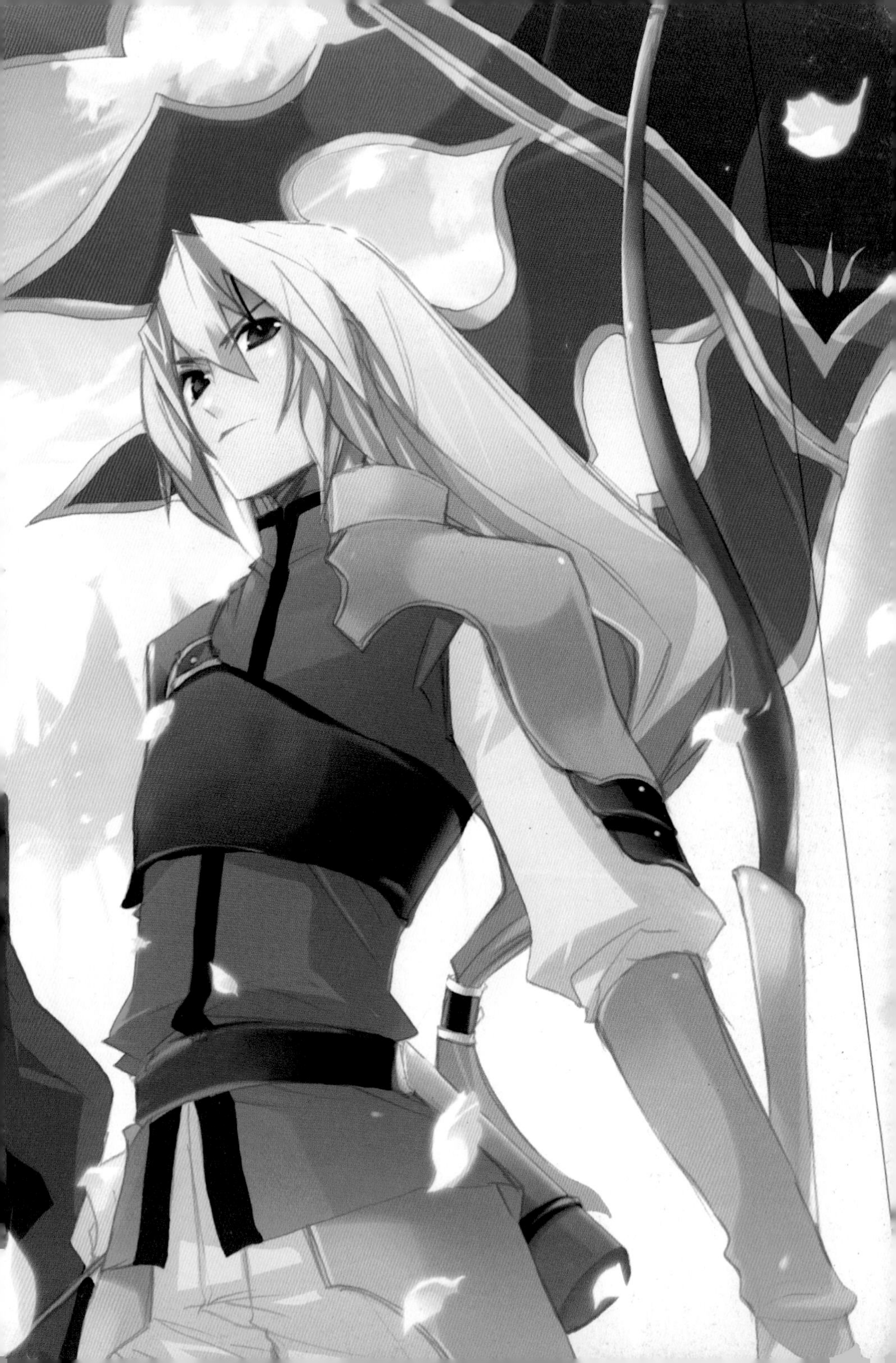

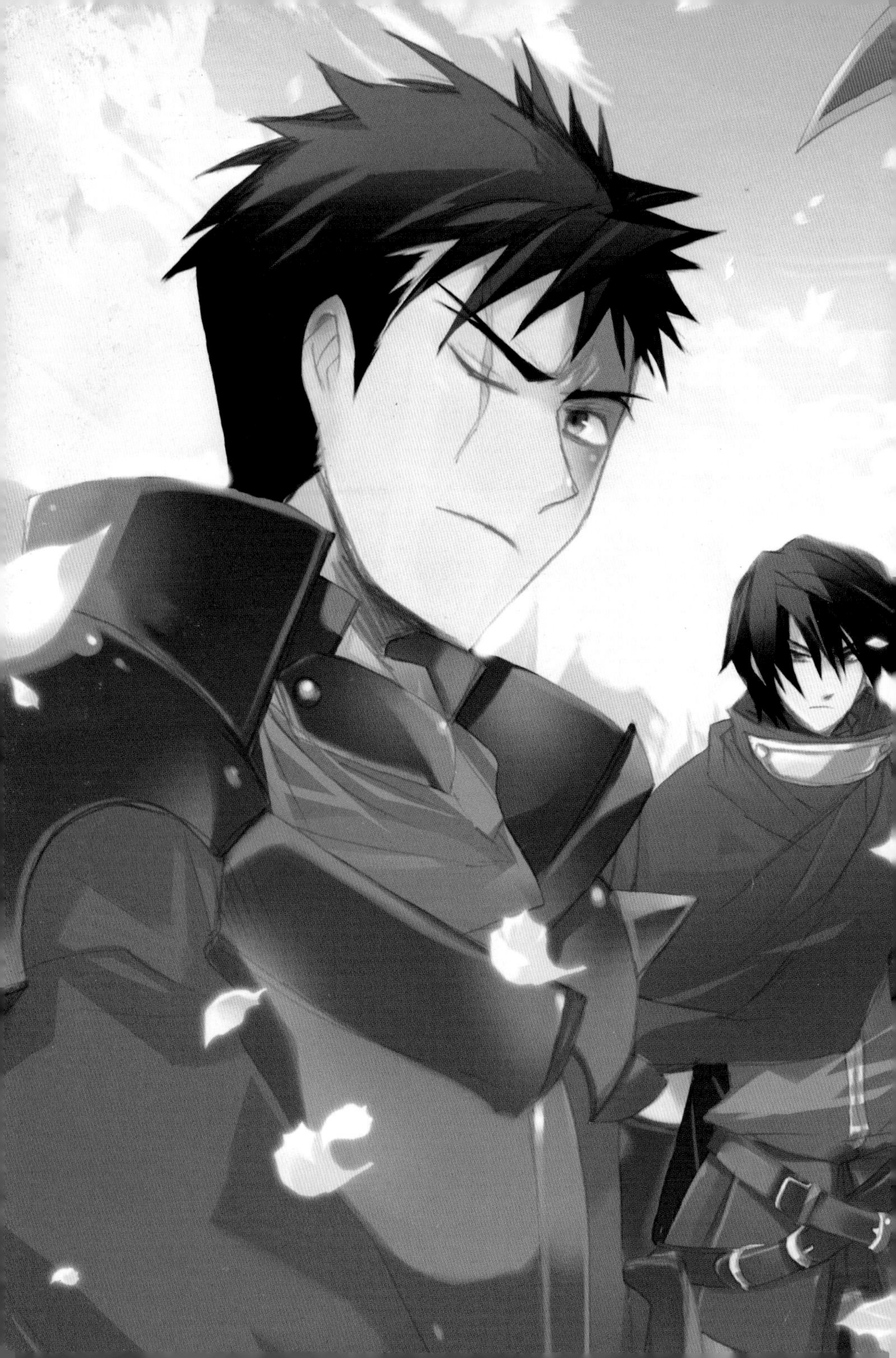

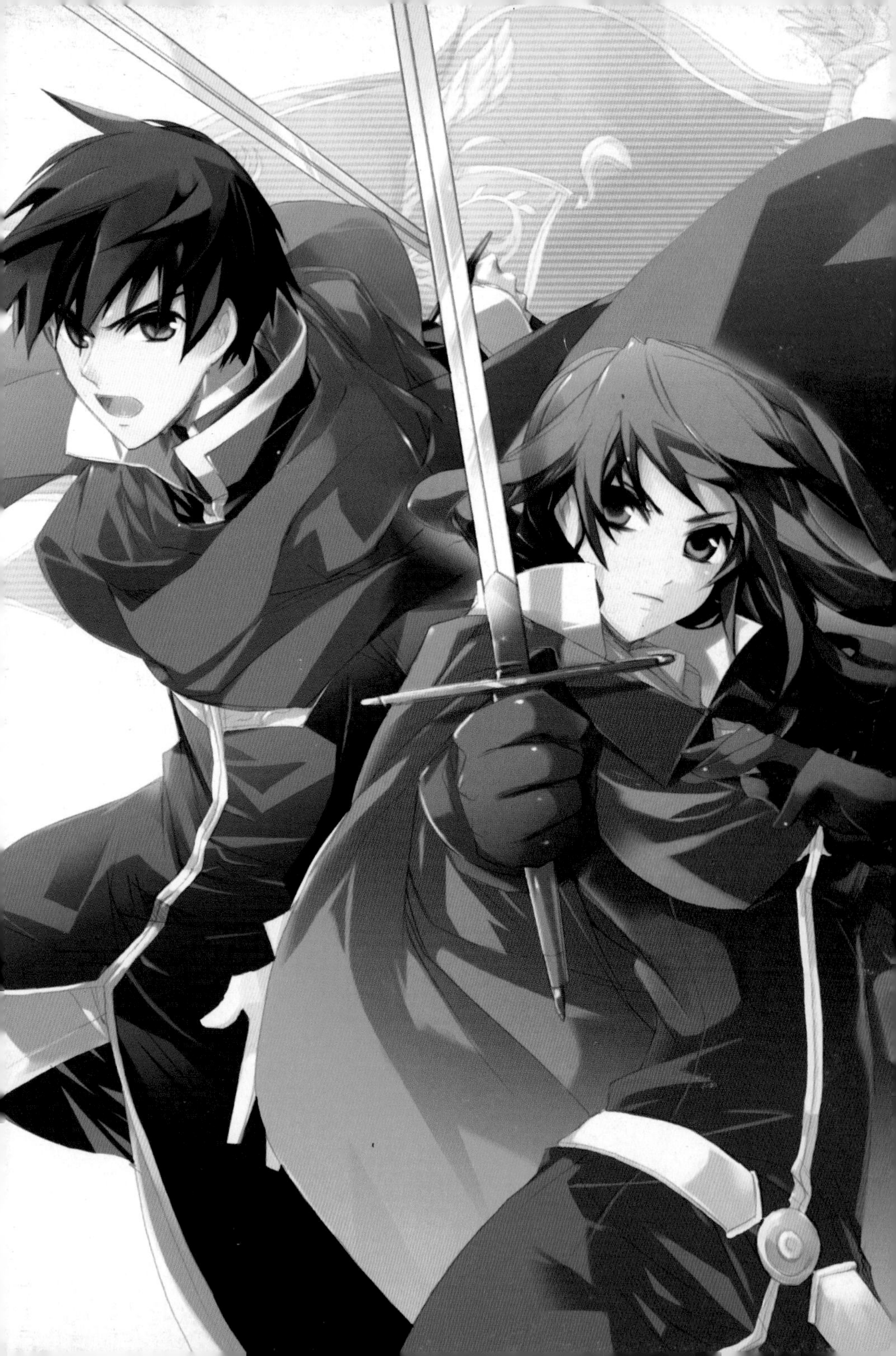

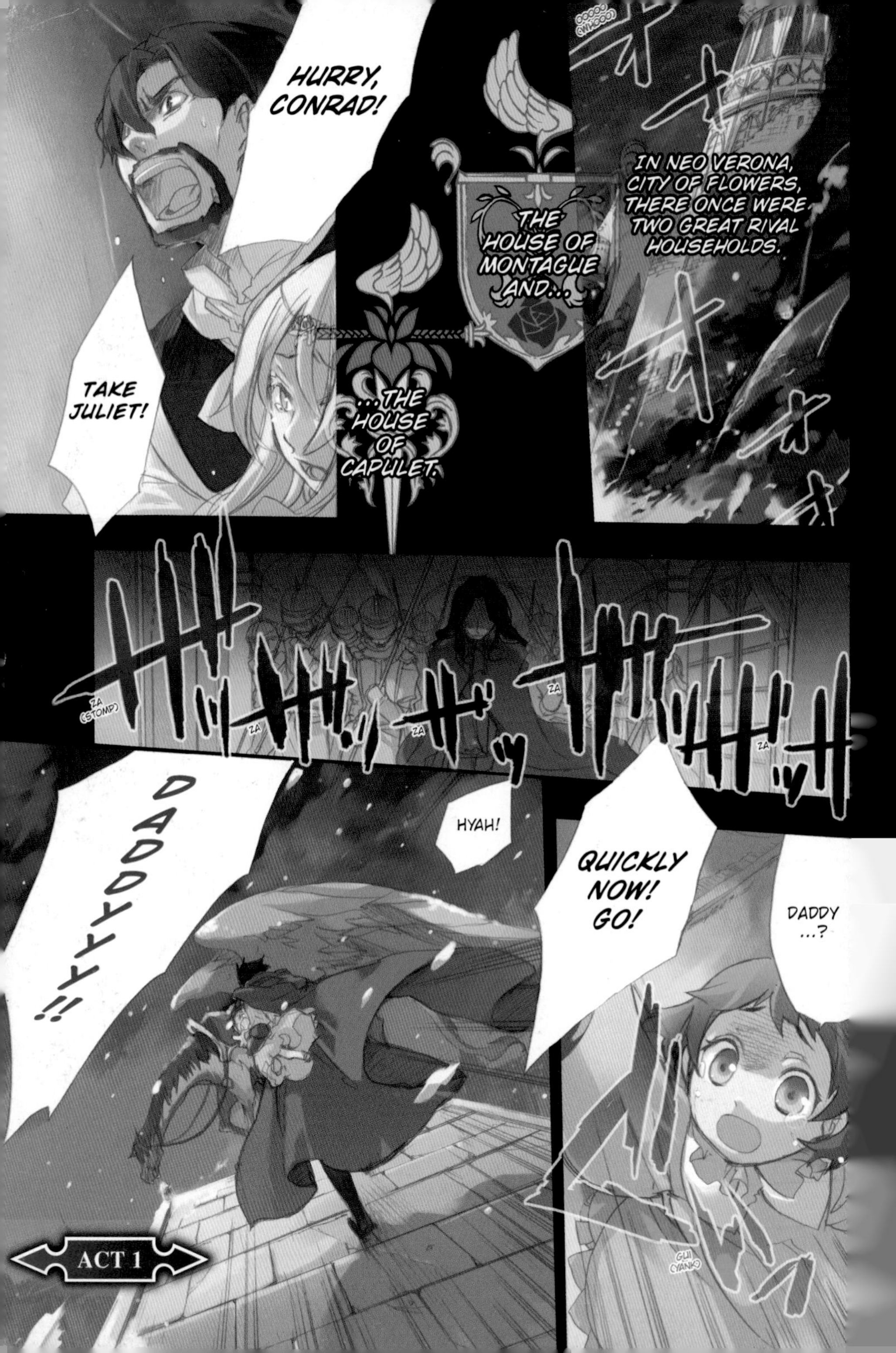
OOOOO (WHOOO)
IN NEO VERONA, CITY OF FLOWERS, THERE ONCE WERE TWO GREAT RIVAL HOUSEHOLDS.
THE HOUSE OF MONTAGUE AND...
...THE HOUSE OF CAPULET.
HURRY, CONRAD!
TAKE JULIET!
ZA
ZA
ZA
ZA
ZA (STOMP)
DADDY ...?
QUICKLY NOW! GO!
GUI (YANK)
HYAH!
DADDYYYYY!!
ACT 1

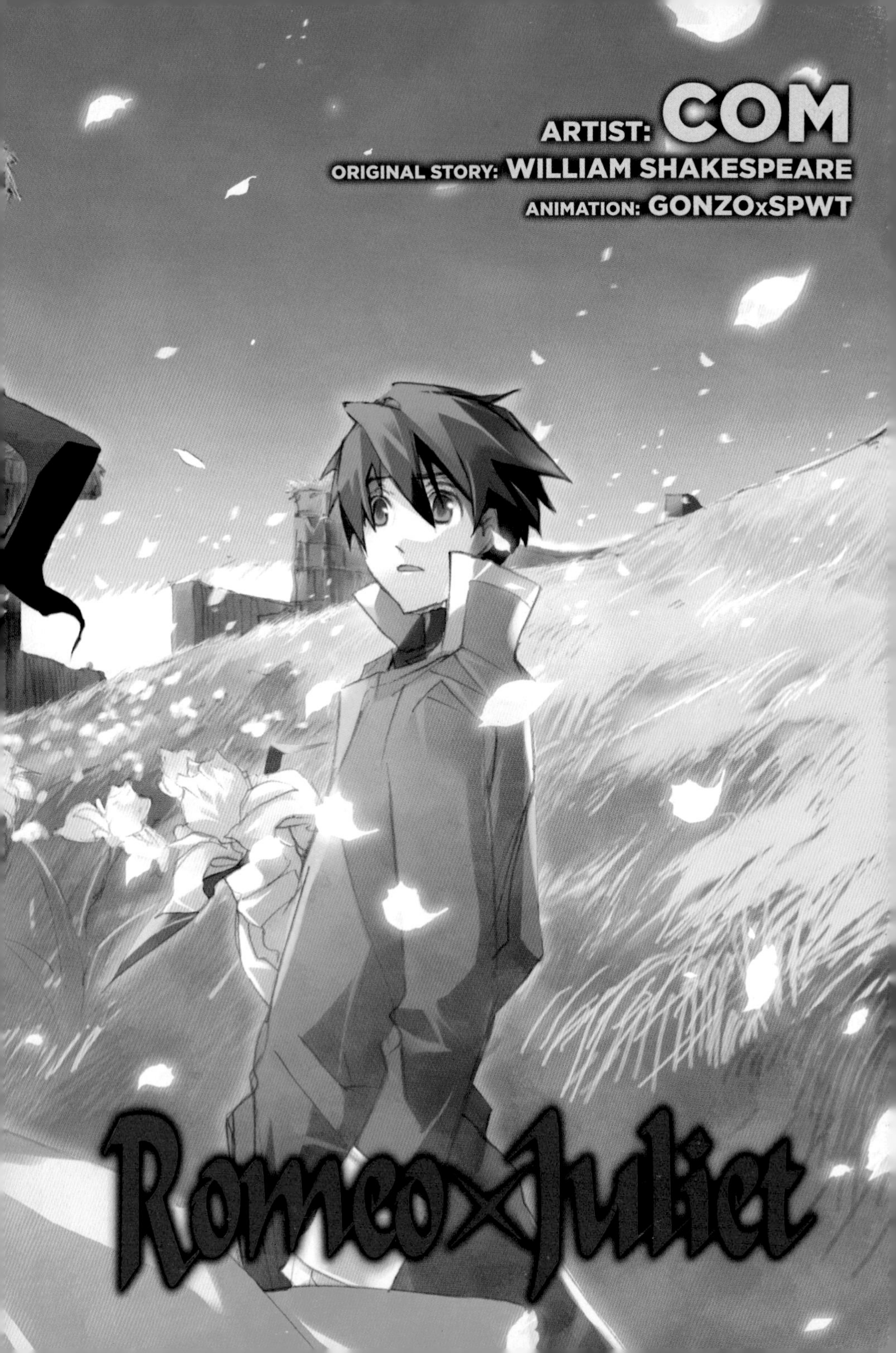
ARTIST: COM
ORIGINAL STORY: WILLIAM SHAKESPEARE
ANIMATION: GONZOxSPWT
Romeo×Juliet

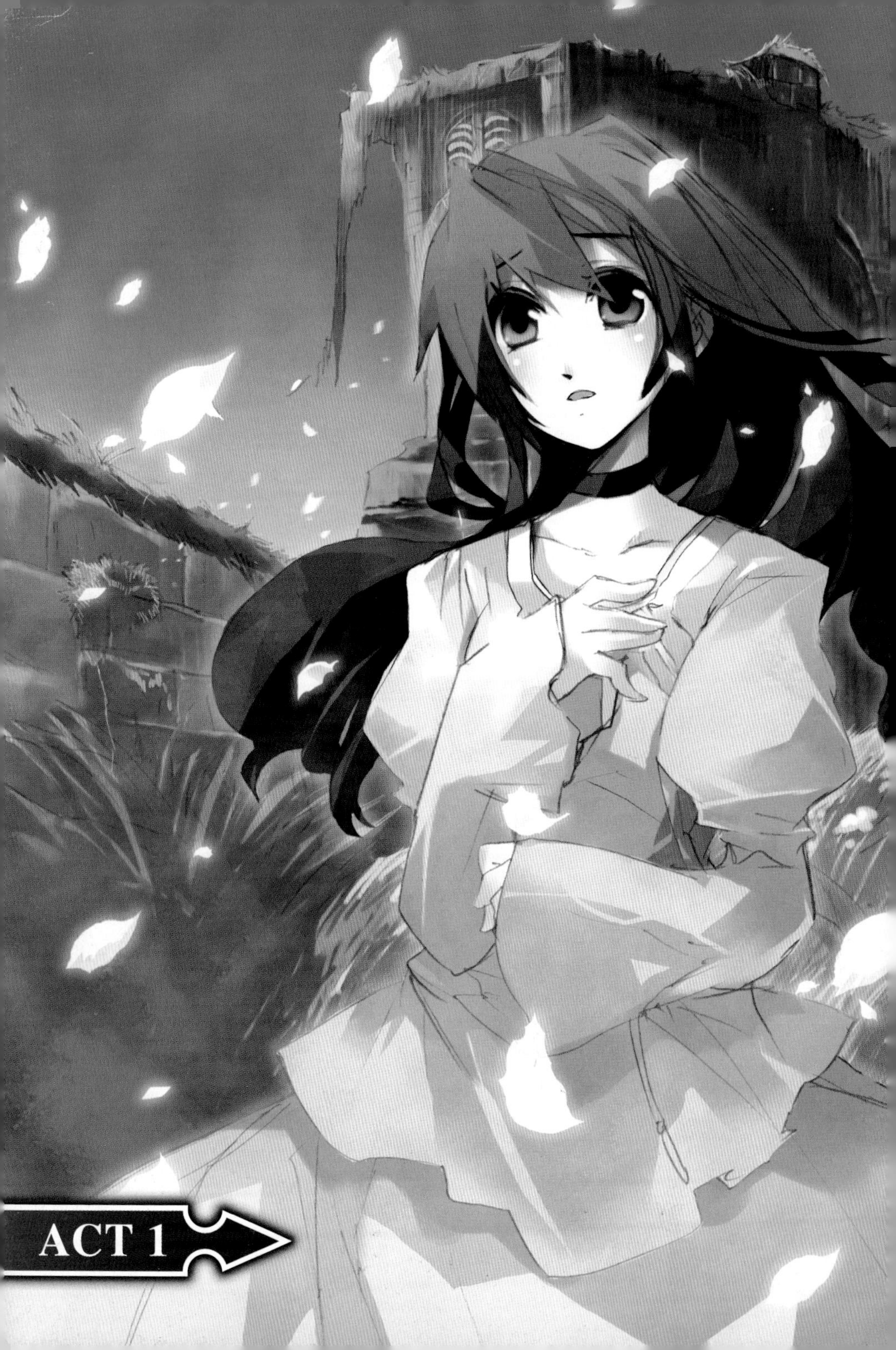
ACT 1

Contents

Romeo×Juliet

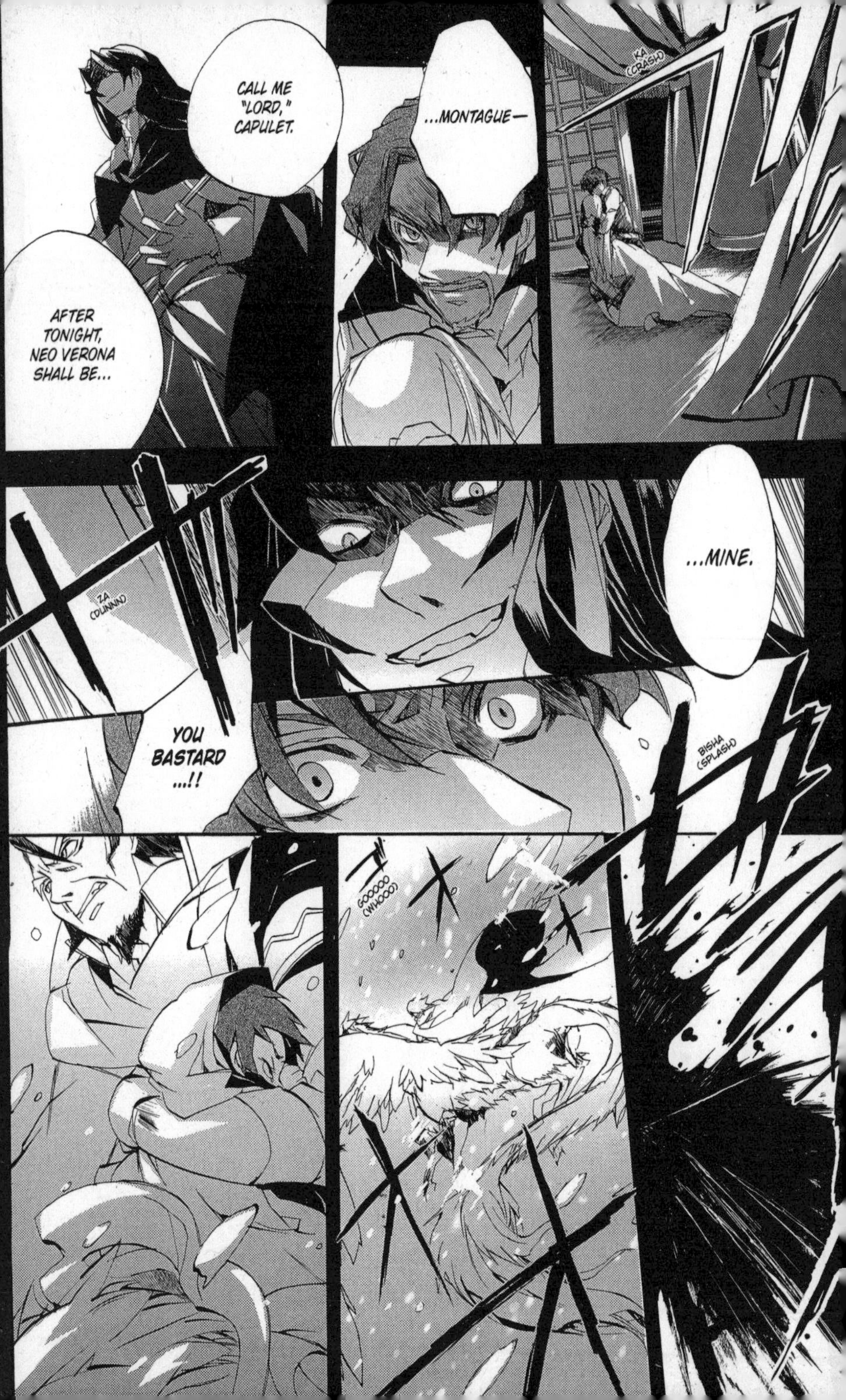
KA (CRASH)
...MONTAGUE—
CALL ME "LORD," CAPULET.
AFTER TONIGHT, NEO VERONA SHALL BE...
...MINE.
ZA (DUNNN)
YOU BASTARD ...!!
BISHA (SPLASH)
GOOOOO (WHOOO)

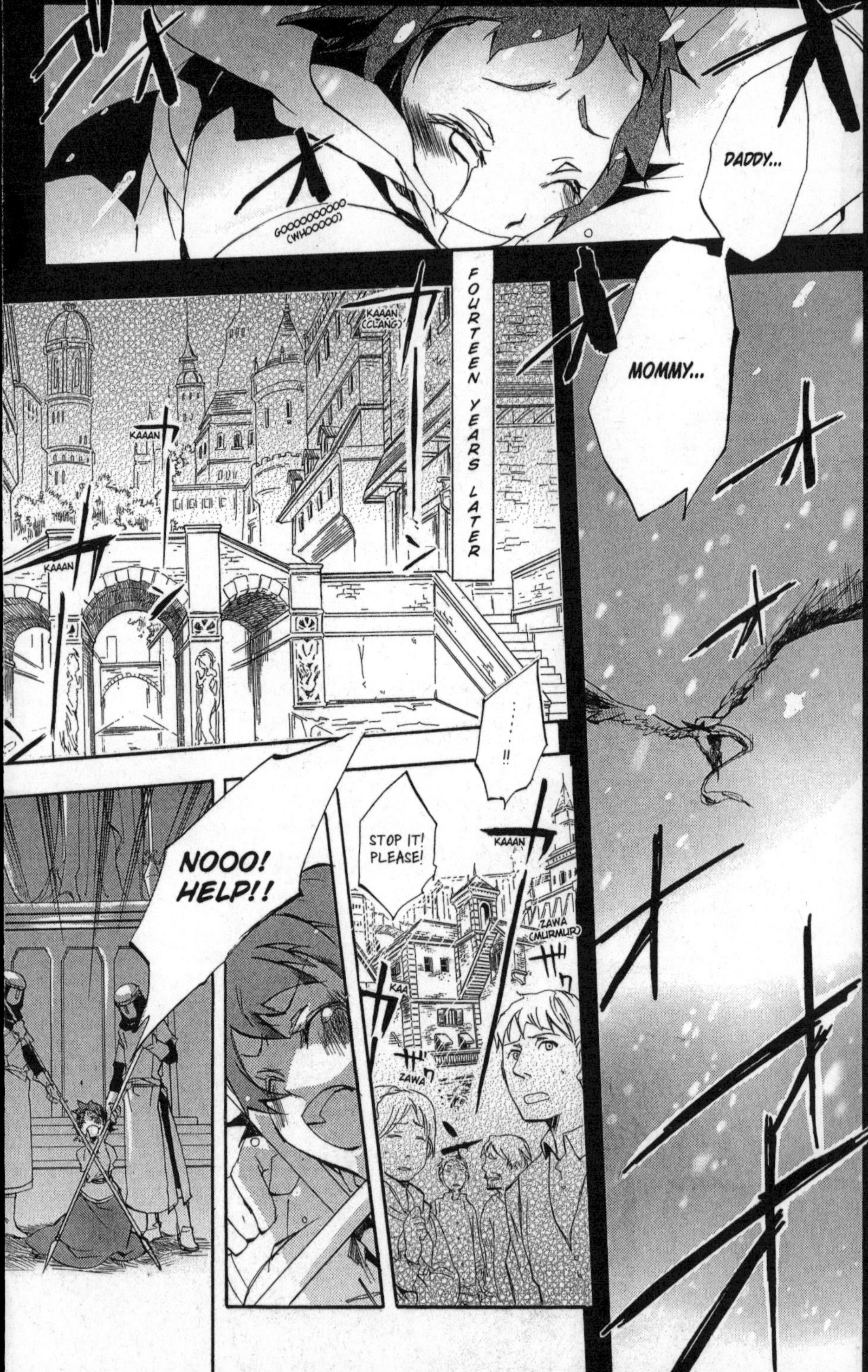

DADDY...
GOOOOOOOOOO
(WHOOOOO)
MOMMY...
FOURTEEN YEARS LATER
KAAAN
(CLANG)
KAAAN
KAAAN
......
!!
STOP IT! PLEASE!
KAAAN
ZAWA
(MURMUR)
KAA
ZAWA
NOOO! HELP!!

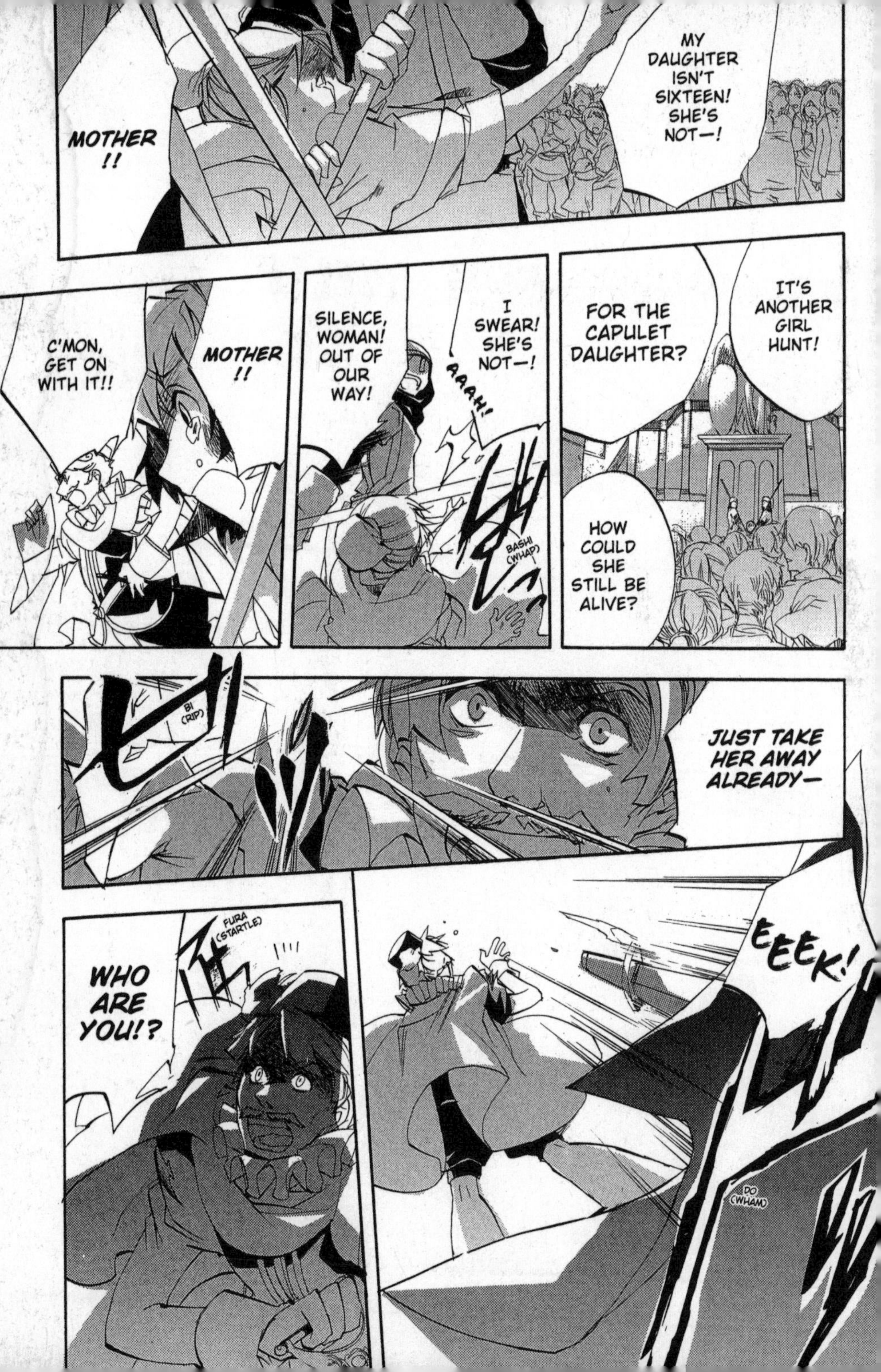
MY DAUGHTER ISN'T SIXTEEN! SHE'S NOT—!
MOTHER !!
IT'S ANOTHER GIRL HUNT!
FOR THE CAPULET DAUGHTER?
HOW COULD SHE STILL BE ALIVE?
I SWEAR! SHE'S NOT—!
SILENCE, WOMAN! OUT OF OUR WAY!
AAAH!
BASHI (WHAP)
MOTHER !!
C'MON, GET ON WITH IT!!
JUST TAKE HER AWAY ALREADY—
BI (RIP)
EEEK!
DO (WHAM)
FURA (STARTLE)
WHO ARE YOU!?

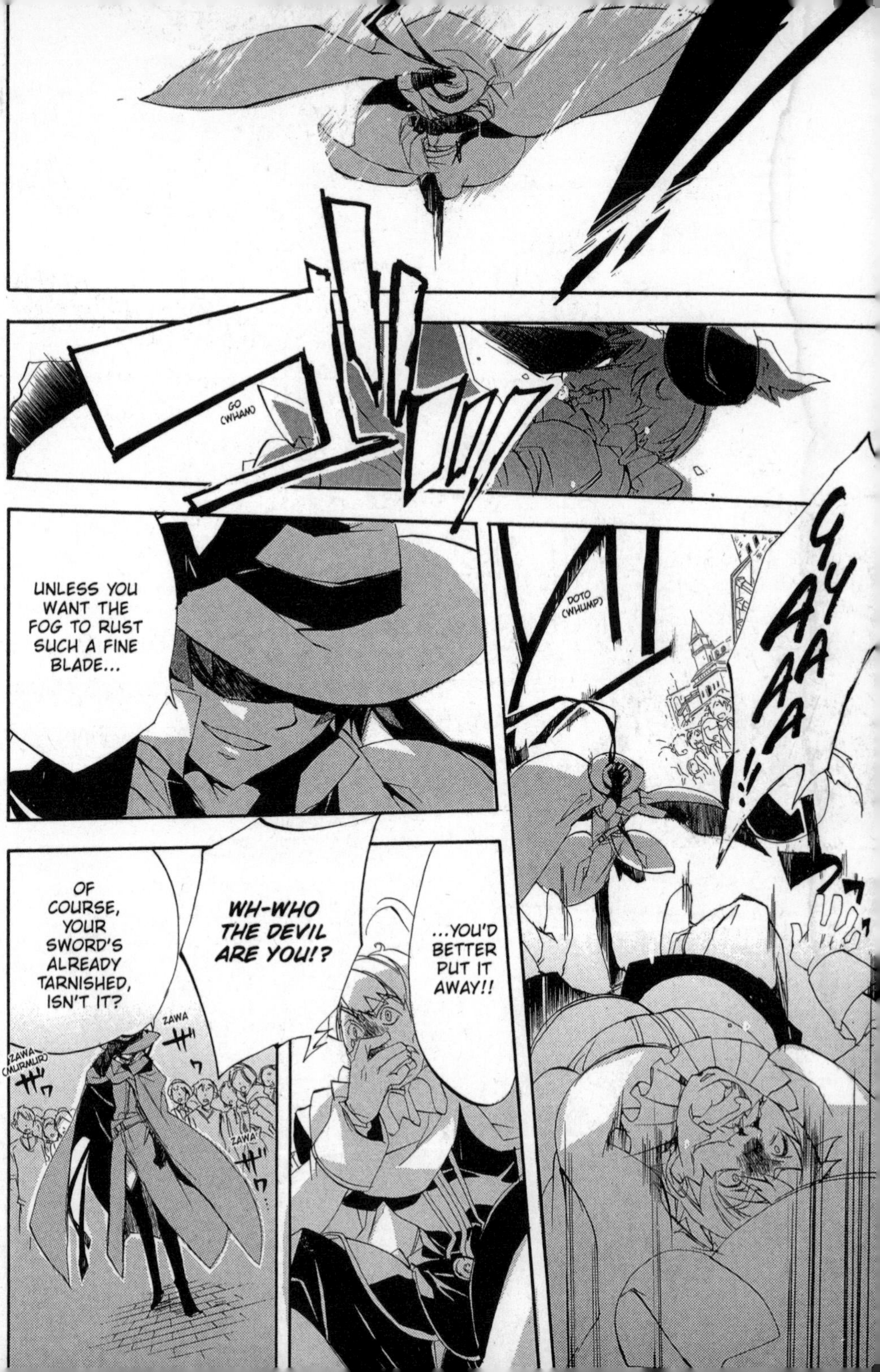
GO (WHAM)
DOTO (WHUMP)
GYAAAAA!!
UNLESS YOU WANT THE FOG TO RUST SUCH A FINE BLADE...
...YOU'D BETTER PUT IT AWAY!!
WH-WHO THE DEVIL ARE YOU!?
OF COURSE, YOUR SWORD'S ALREADY TARNISHED, ISN'T IT?
ZAWA
ZAWA (MURMUR)
ZAWA

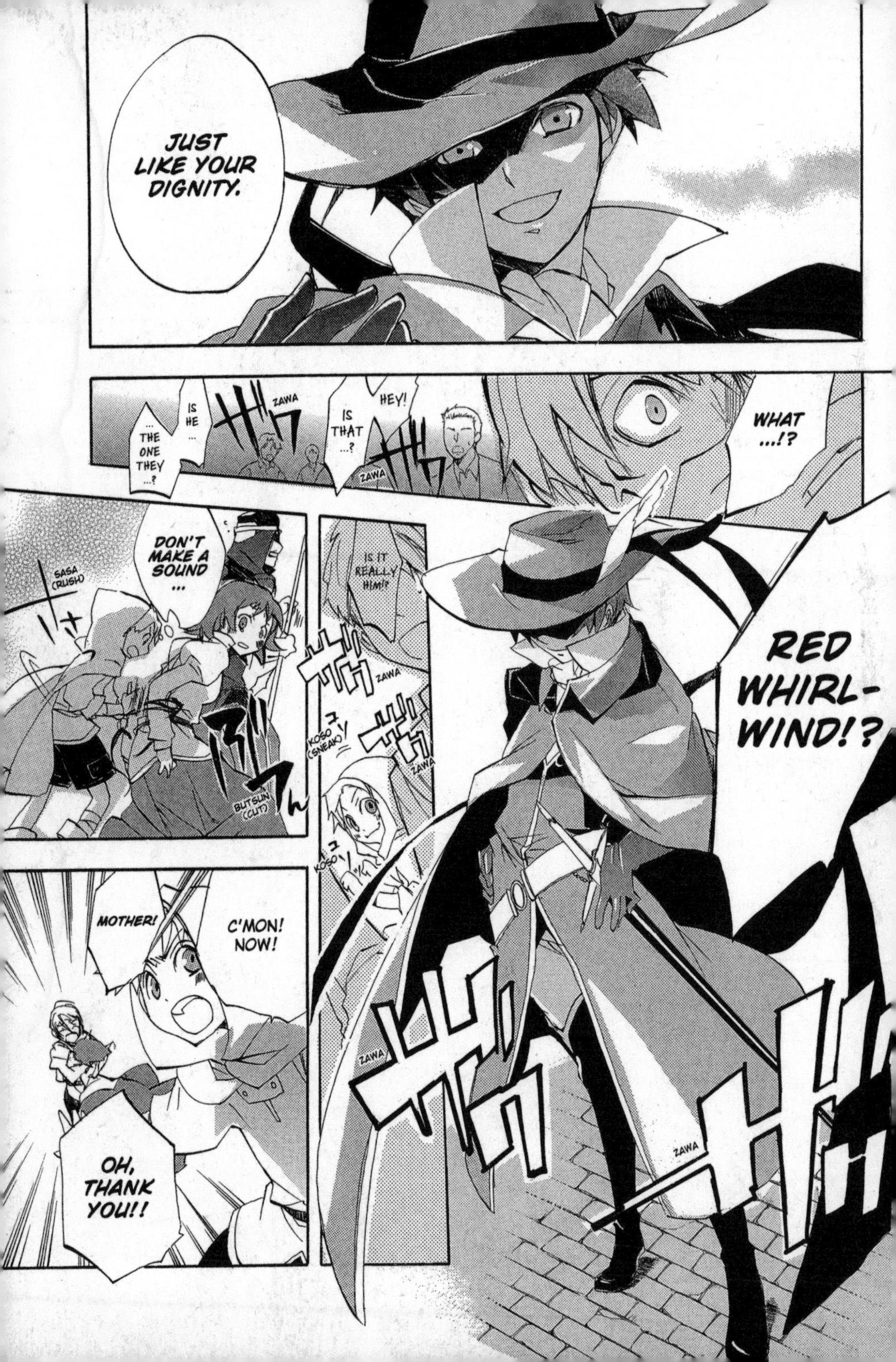
JUST LIKE YOUR DIGNITY.
WHAT ...!?
HEY!
IS THAT ...?
ZAWA
ZAWA
IS HE ...
... THE ONE THEY ...?
RED WHIRL-WIND!?
ZAWA
ZAWA
IS IT REALLY HIM!?
ZAWA
ZAWA
KOSO (SNEAK)
KOSO
DON'T MAKE A SOUND ...
SASA (RUSH)
BUTSUN (CUT)
C'MON! NOW!
MOTHER!
OH, THANK YOU!!

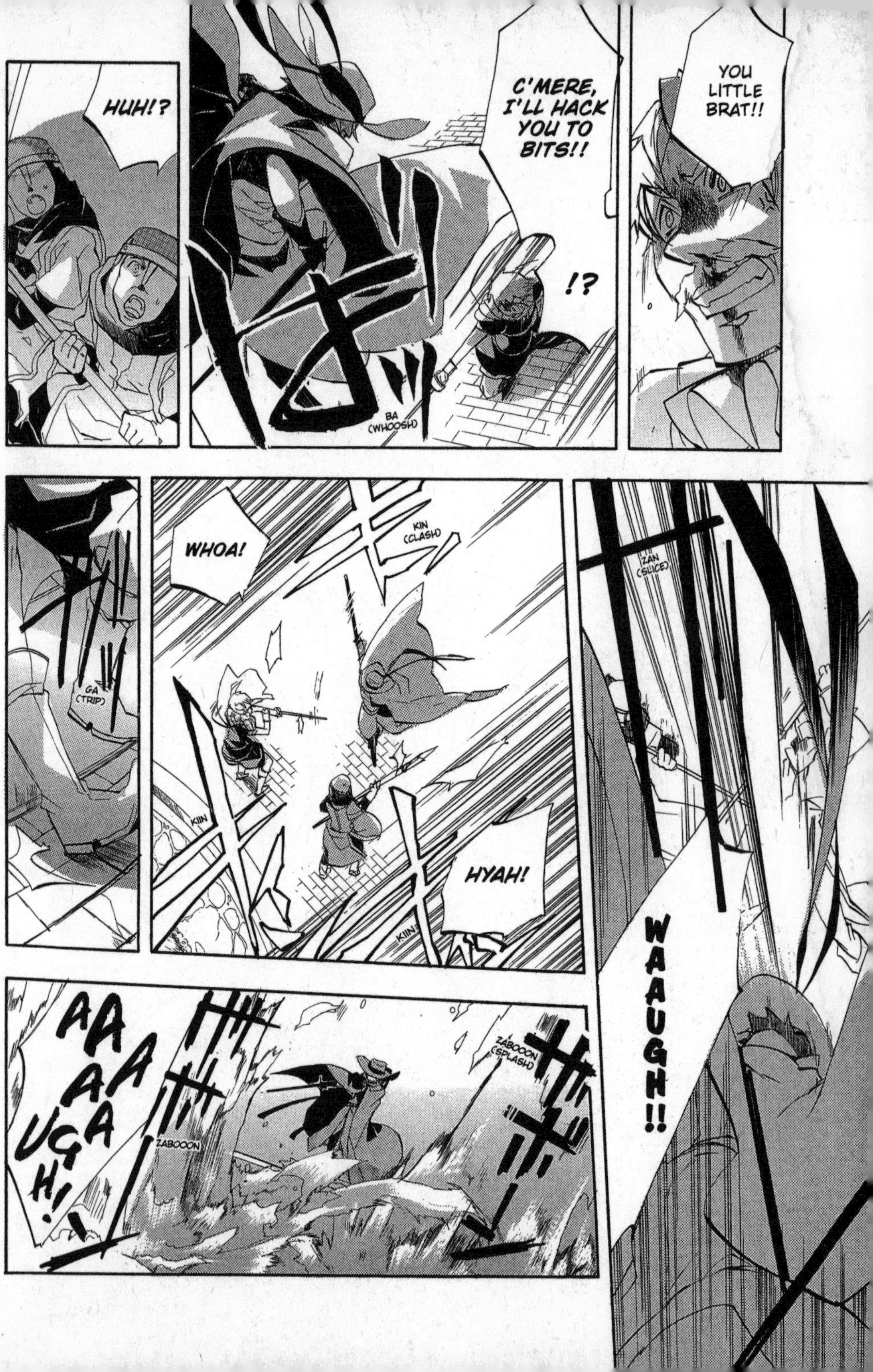
YOU LITTLE BRAT!!
!?
C'MERE, I'LL HACK YOU TO BITS!!
BA (WHOOSH)
HUH!?
ZAN (SLICE)
WAAAUGH!!
KIN (CLASH)
WHOA!
KIIN
HYAH!
KIIN
GA (TRIP)
ZABOOON (SPLASH)
ZABOOON
AAAAAAUGH!!

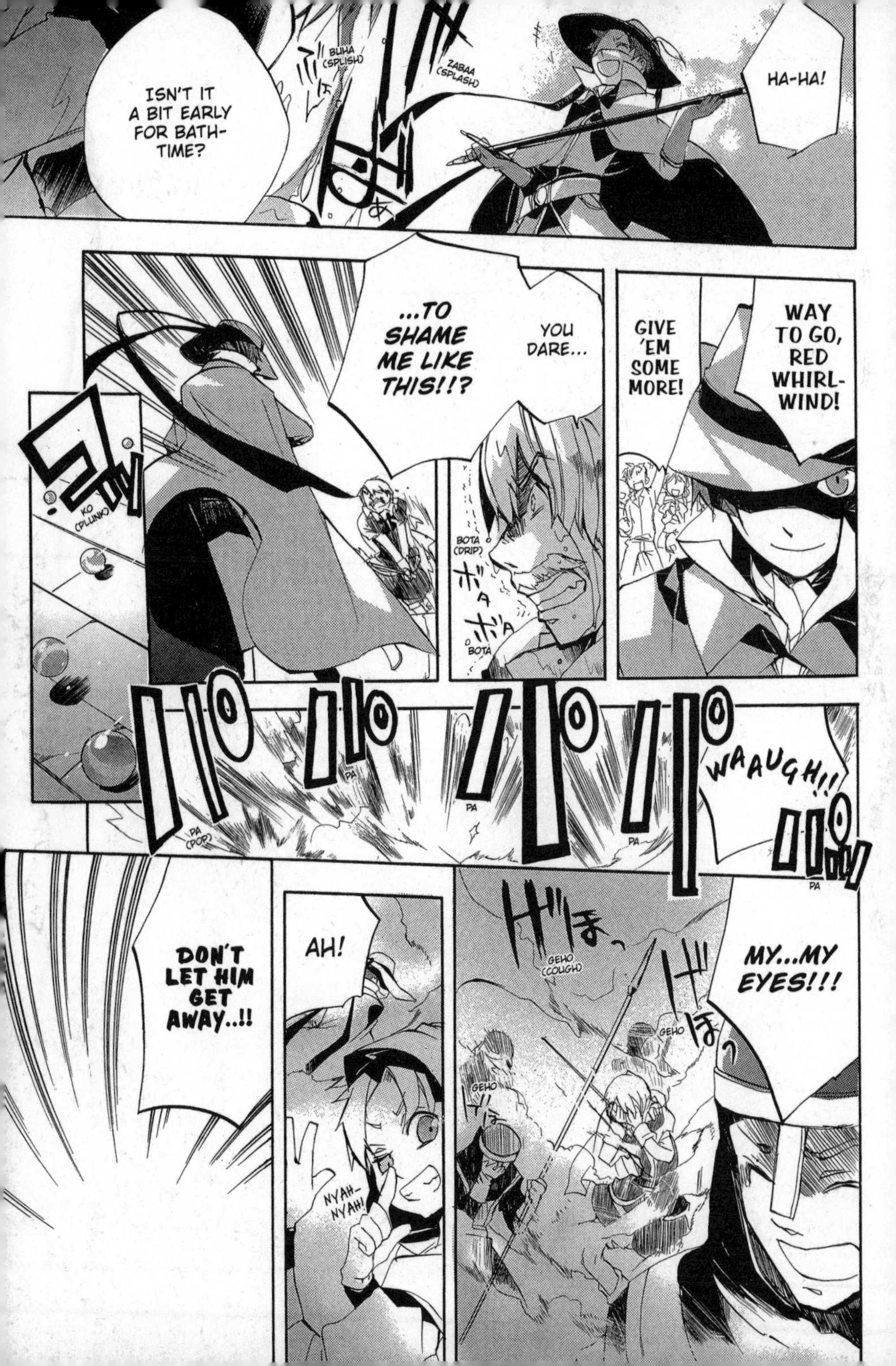
HA-HA!
ZABAA (SPLASH)
BUHA (SPLASH)
ISN'T IT A BIT EARLY FOR BATH-TIME?
WAY TO GO, RED WHIRLWIND!
GIVE 'EM SOME MORE!
YOU DARE...
...TO SHAME ME LIKE THIS!!?
BOTA (DRIP)
BOTA
KO (PLUNK)
WAAUGH!!
PA
PA
PA
PA
PA (POP)
MY...MY EYES!!!
GEHO (COUGH)
GEHO
GEHO
AH!
NYAH-NYAH!
DON'T LET HIM GET AWAY..!!

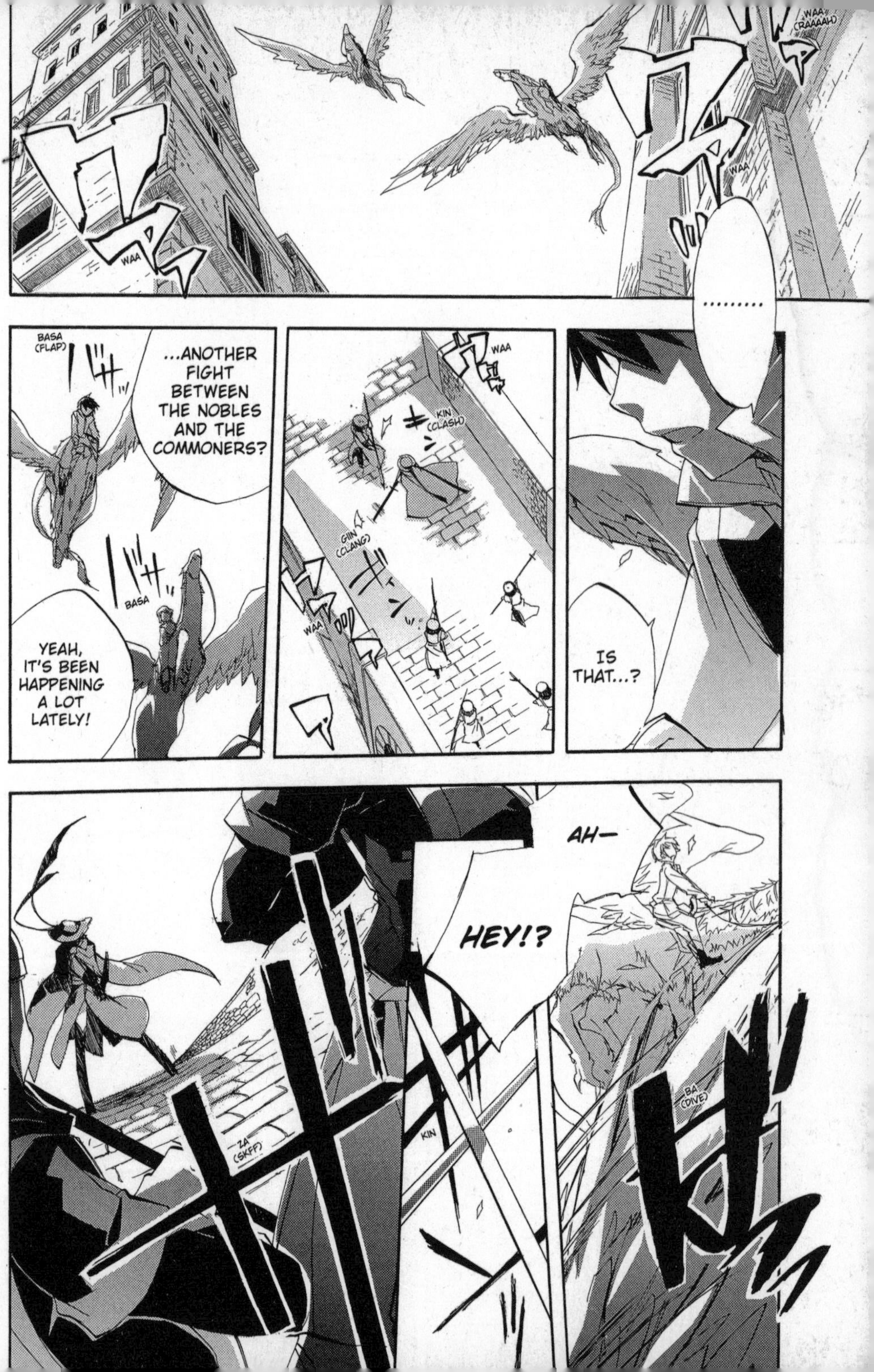

WAA (RAAAAH)
WAA
WAA
....
IS THAT...?
WAA
KIN (CLASH)
GIIN (CLANG)
WAA
BASA (FLAP)
...ANOTHER FIGHT BETWEEN THE NOBLES AND THE COMMONERS?
BASA
YEAH, IT'S BEEN HAPPENING A LOT LATELY!
AH—
HEY!?
BA (DIVE)
KIN
ZA (SKFF)

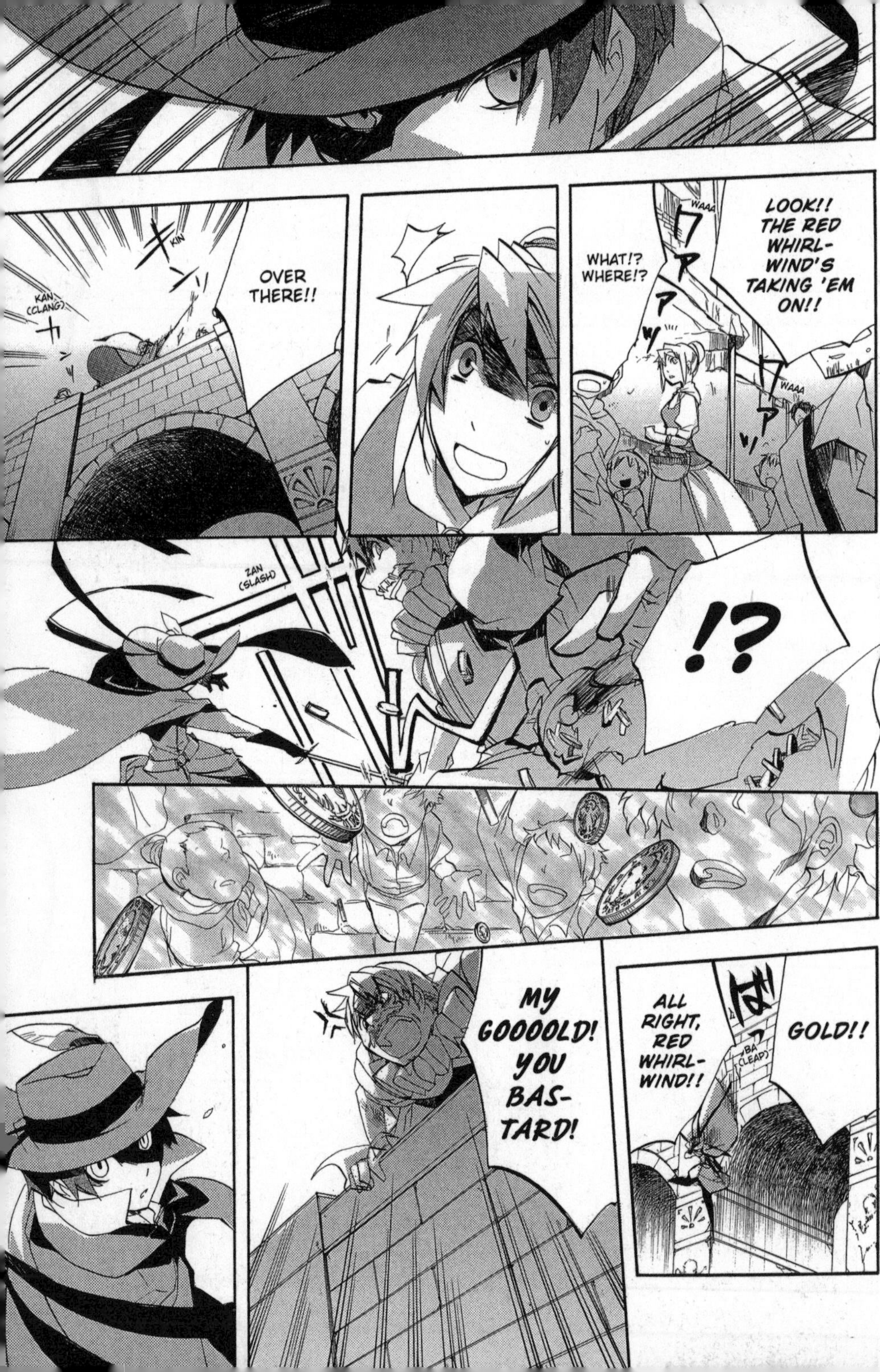
LOOK!! THE RED WHIRLWIND'S TAKING 'EM ON!!
WAAA
WAAA
WHAT!? WHERE!?
OVER THERE!!
KIN
KAN (CLANG)
!?
ZAN (SLASH)
GOLD!!
ALL RIGHT, RED WHIRLWIND!!
BA (LEAP)
MY GOOOOLD! YOU BASTARD!

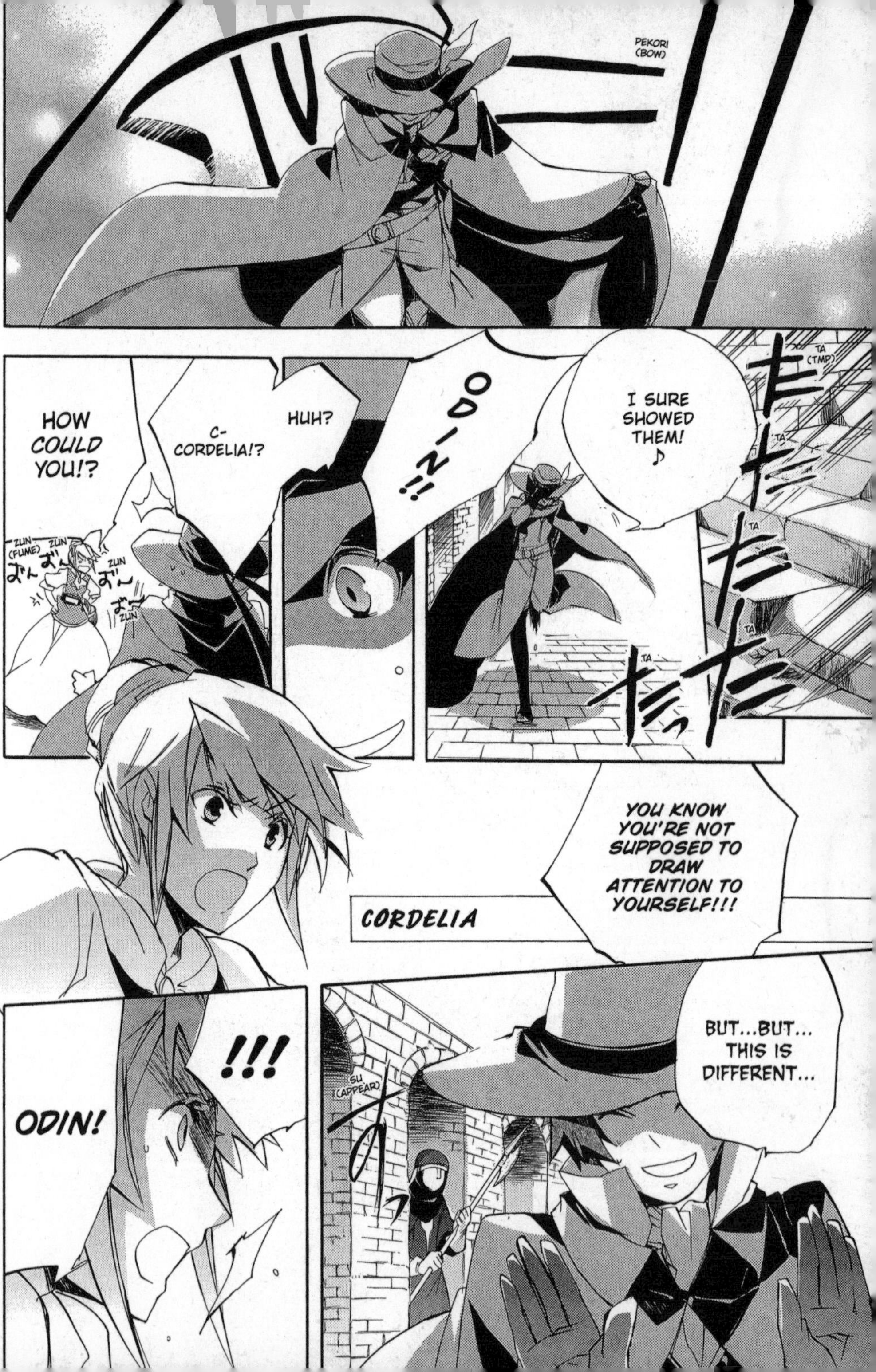
PEKORI (BOW)
TA (TMP)
TA
TA
TA
TA
I SURE SHOWED THEM! ♪
ODIN!!!
HUH?
C- CORDELIA!?
HOW COULD YOU!?
ZUN (FUME) ZUN
ZUN
ZUN
YOU KNOW YOU'RE NOT SUPPOSED TO DRAW ATTENTION TO YOURSELF!!!
CORDELIA
BUT...BUT... THIS IS DIFFERENT...
SU (APPEAR)
!!!
ODIN!

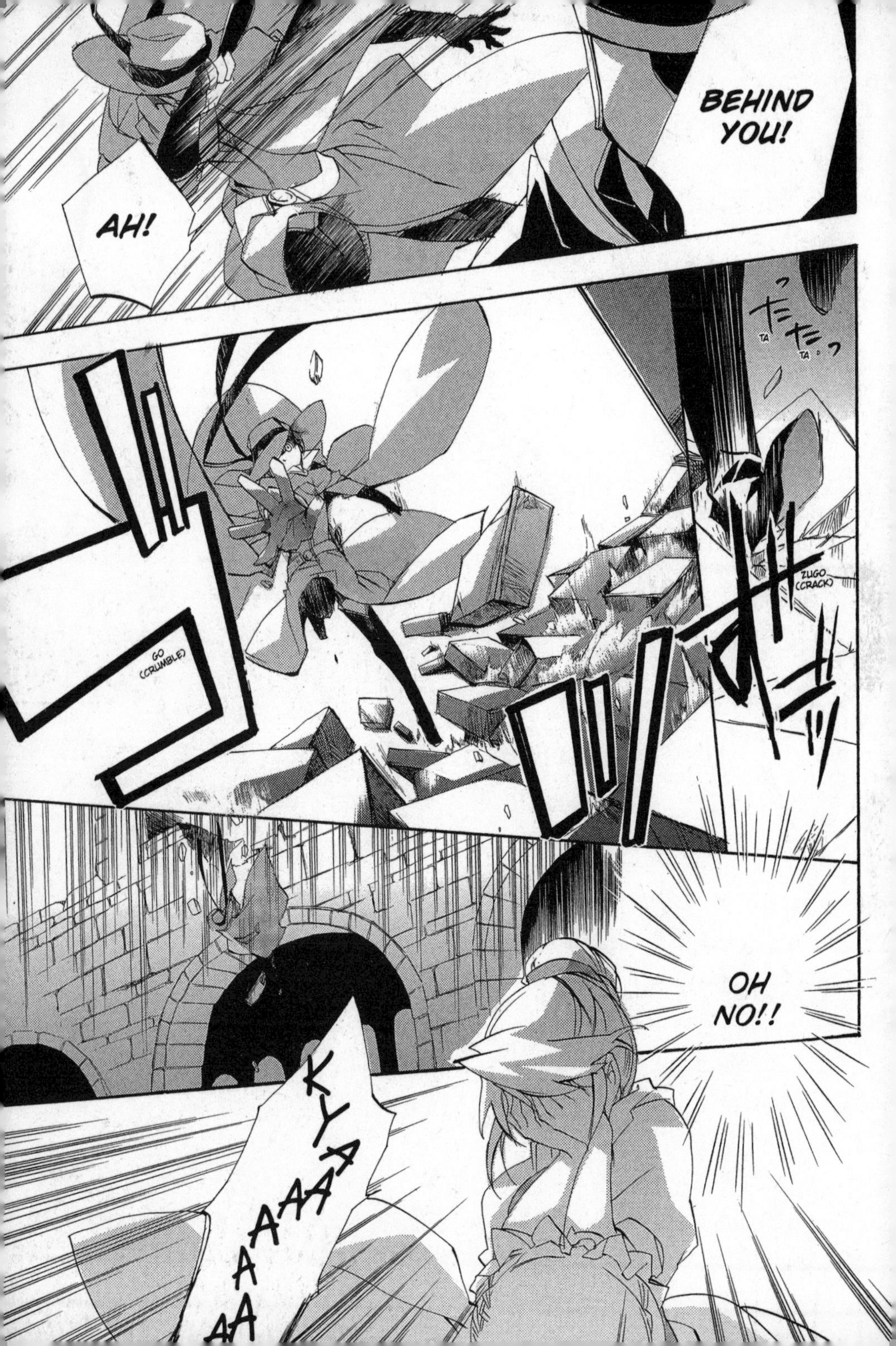
BEHIND YOU!
AH!
TA
TA
ZUGO (CRACK)
GO (CRUMBLE)
OH NO!!
KYAAAAAAAAA

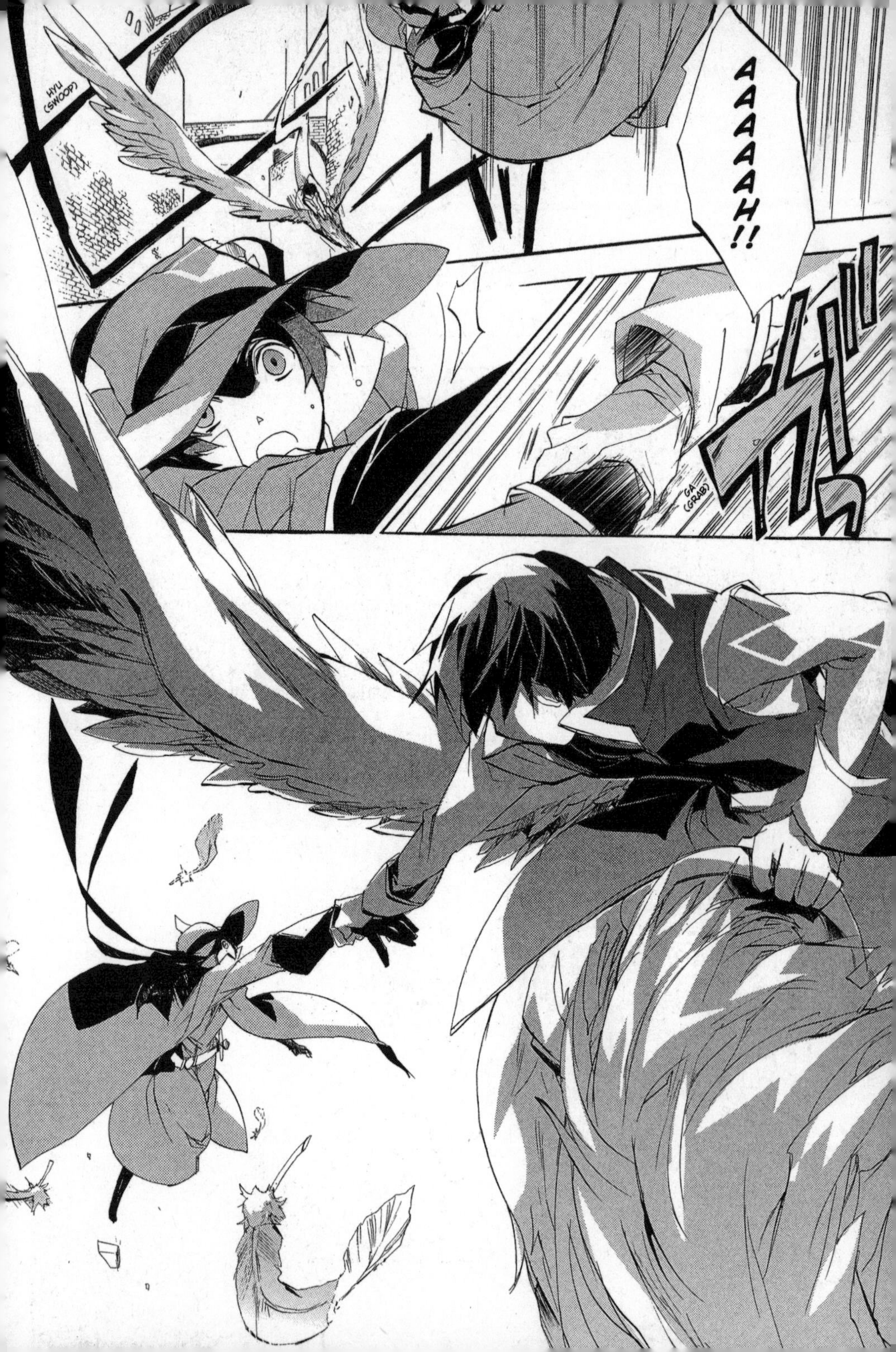
AAAAAAH!!
HYU (SWOOP)
GA (GRAB)

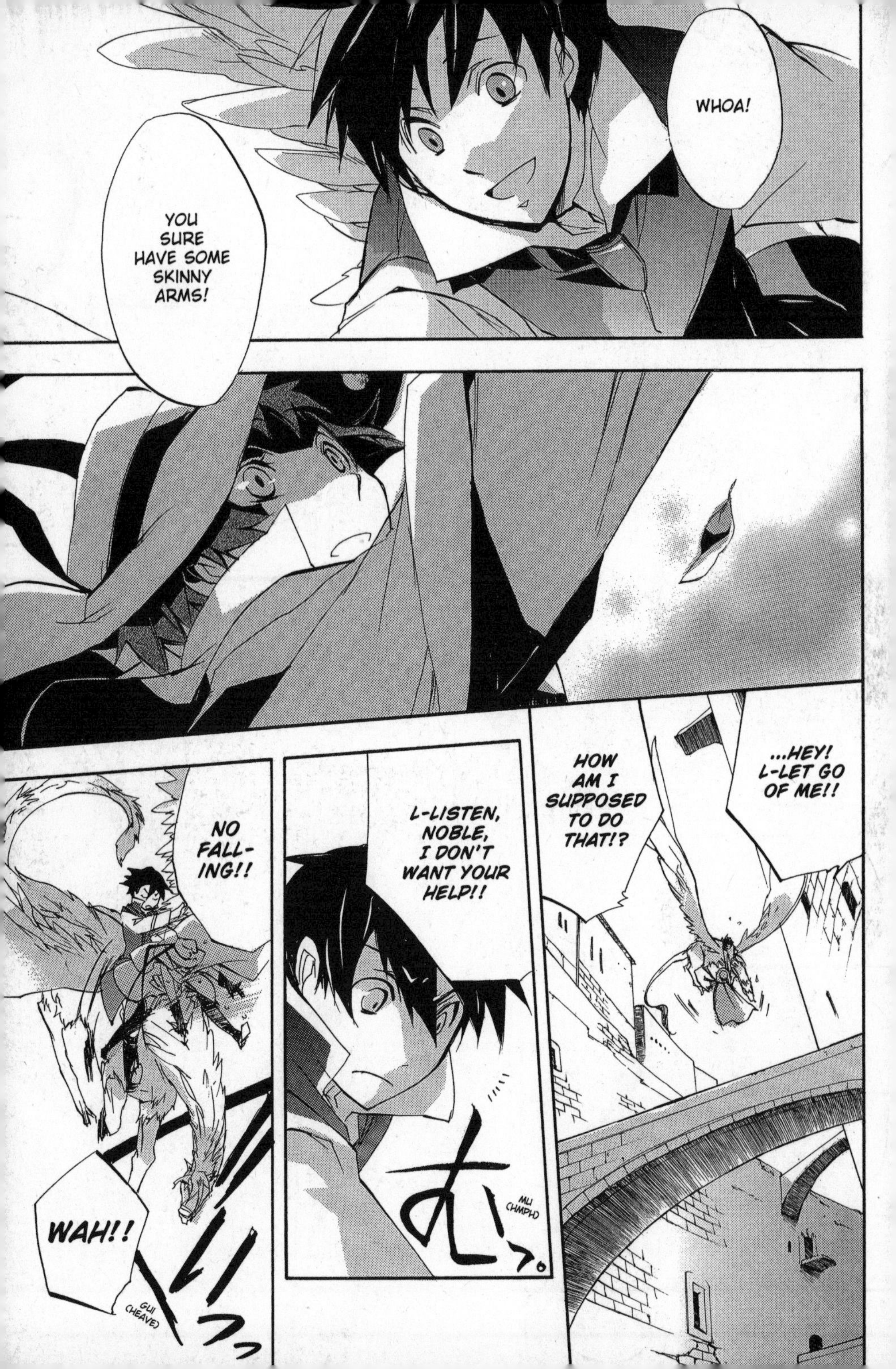
WHOA!
YOU SURE HAVE SOME SKINNY ARMS!
...HEY! L-LET GO OF ME!!
HOW AM I SUPPOSED TO DO THAT!?
L-LISTEN, NOBLE, I DON'T WANT YOUR HELP!!
MU (HMPH)
NO FALL-ING!!
WAH!!
GUI (HEAVE)

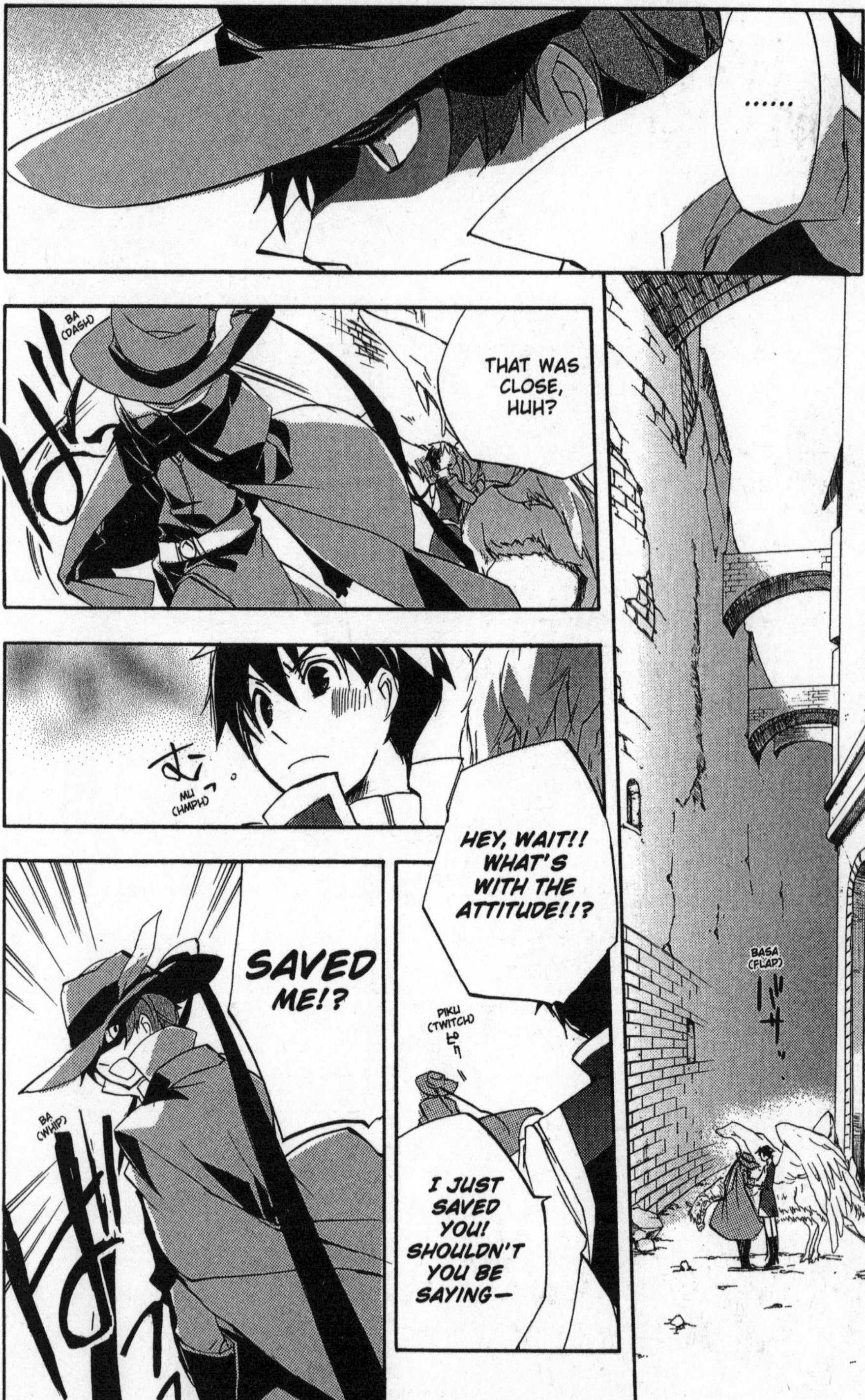
......
BASA (FLAP)
BA (DASH)
THAT WAS CLOSE, HUH?
MU (HMPH)
HEY, WAIT!! WHAT'S WITH THE ATTITUDE!!?
PIKU (TWITCH)
I JUST SAVED YOU! SHOULDN'T YOU BE SAYING—
SAVED ME!?
BA (WHIP)

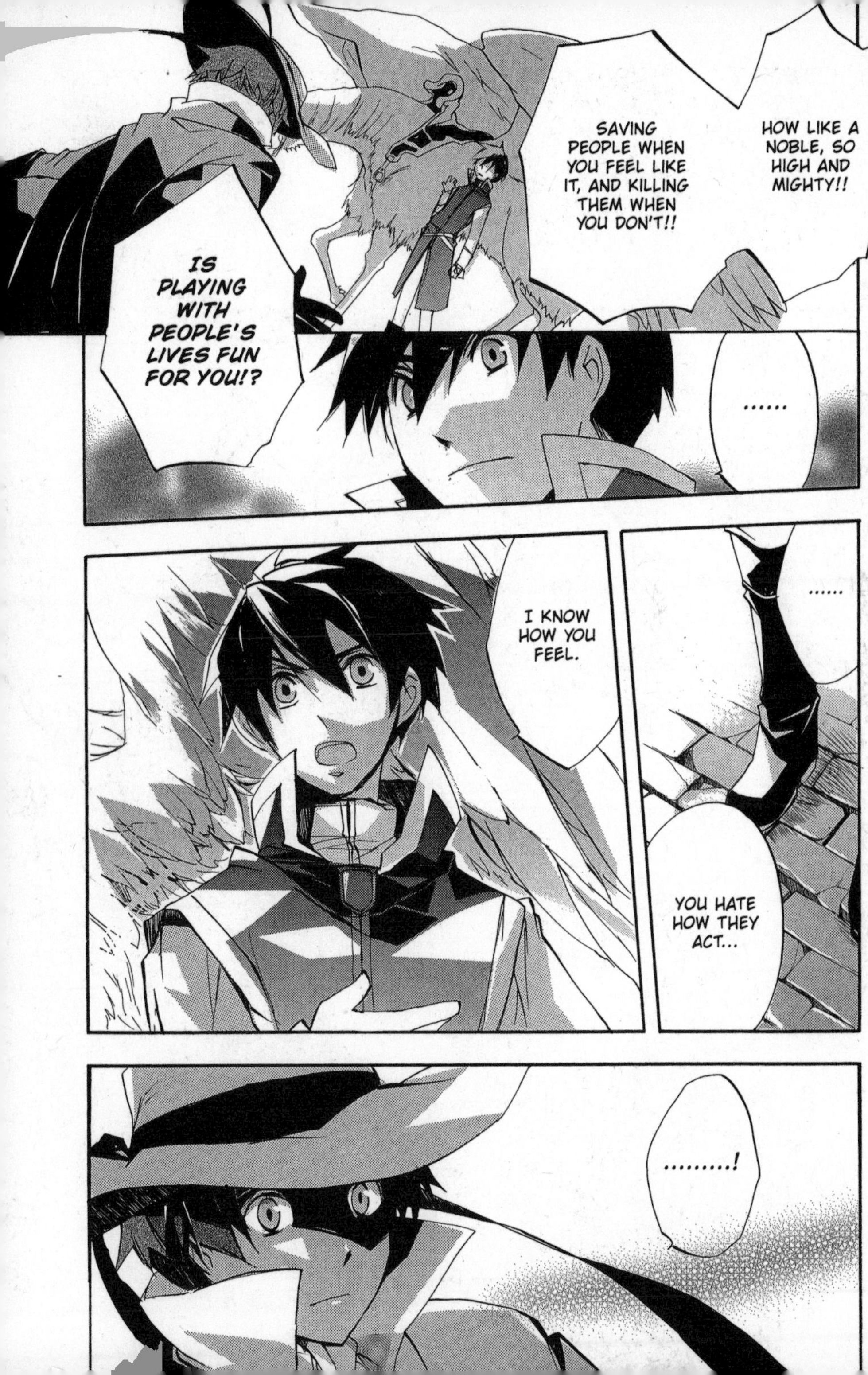
HOW LIKE A NOBLE, SO HIGH AND MIGHTY!!
SAVING PEOPLE WHEN YOU FEEL LIKE IT, AND KILLING THEM WHEN YOU DON'T!!
IS PLAYING WITH PEOPLE'S LIVES FUN FOR YOU!?
......
......
YOU HATE HOW THEY ACT...
I KNOW HOW YOU FEEL.
..........!

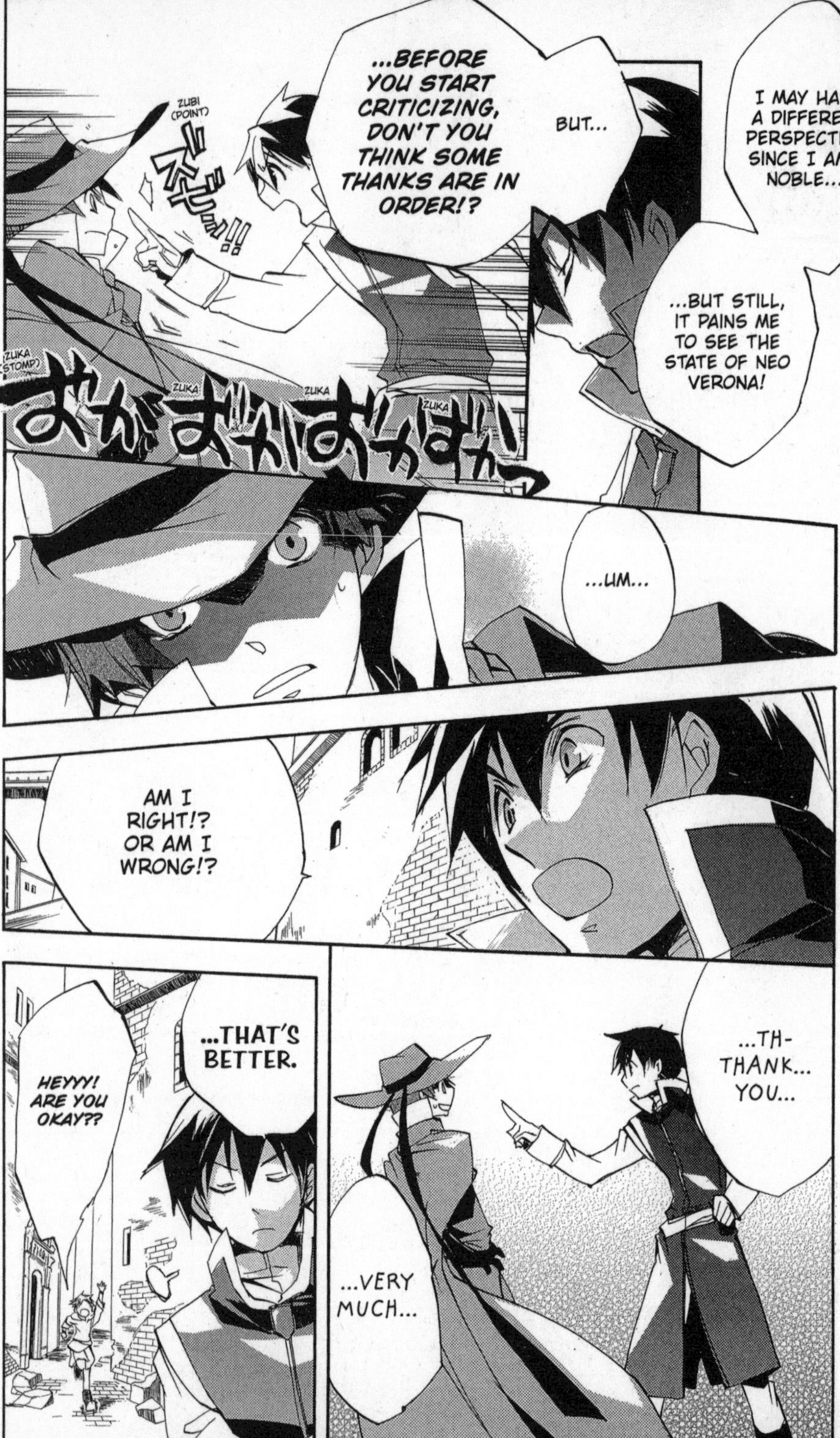
I MAY HAVE A DIFFERENT PERSPECTIVE, SINCE I AM A NOBLE....
...BUT STILL, IT PAINS ME TO SEE THE STATE OF NEO VERONA!
BUT...
...BEFORE YOU START CRITICIZING, DON'T YOU THINK SOME THANKS ARE IN ORDER!?
ZUBI (POINT)
ZUKA (STOMP)
ZUKA
ZUKA
ZUKA
...UM...
AM I RIGHT!? OR AM I WRONG!?
...TH- THANK... YOU...
...VERY MUCH...
...THAT'S BETTER.
HEYYY! ARE YOU OKAY??

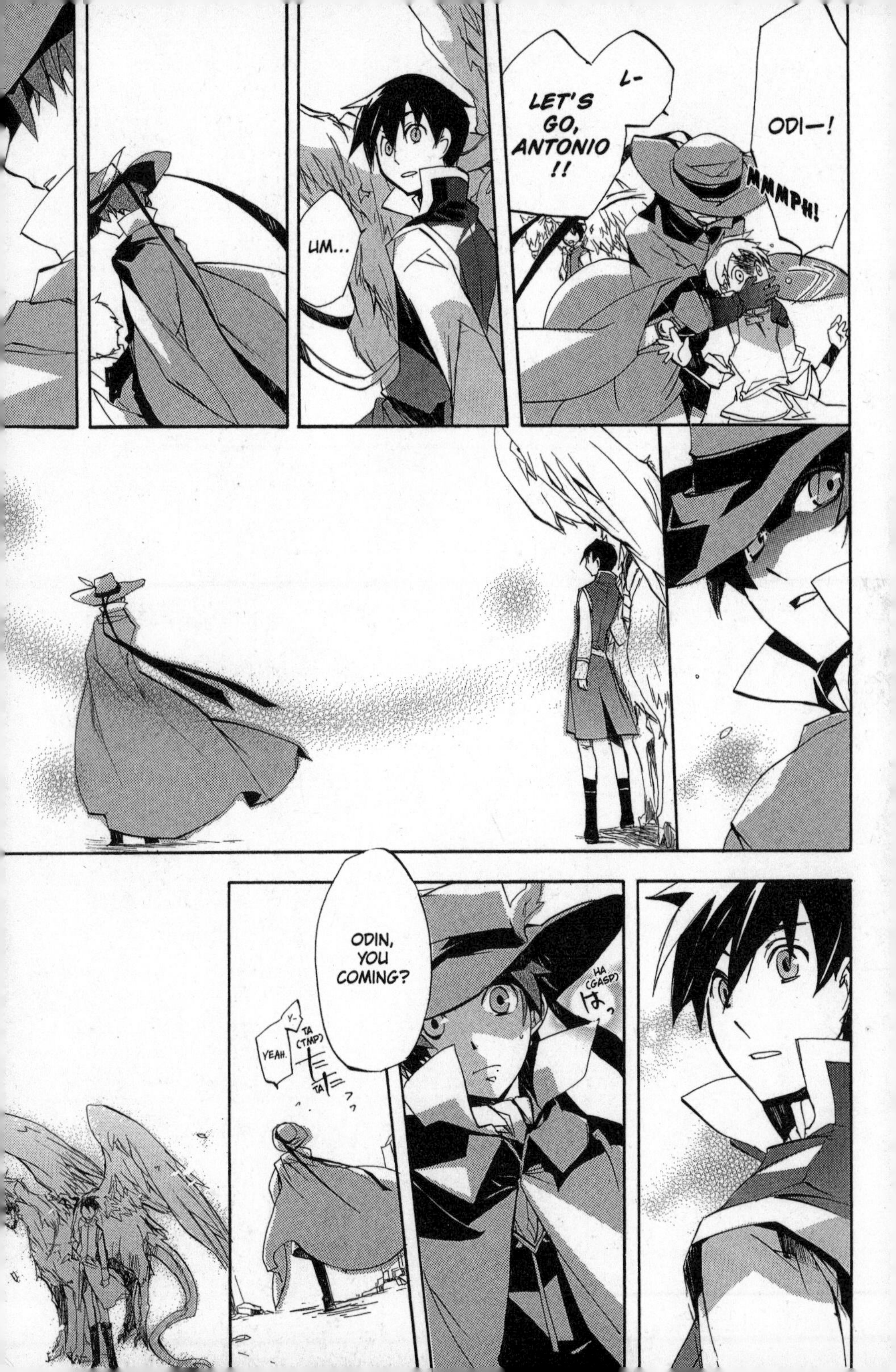
ODI—!
MMMPH!
L-
LET'S GO, ANTONIO!!
UM...
ODIN, YOU COMING?
HA (GASP) はっ
Y-
YEAH.
TA (TMP)
TA

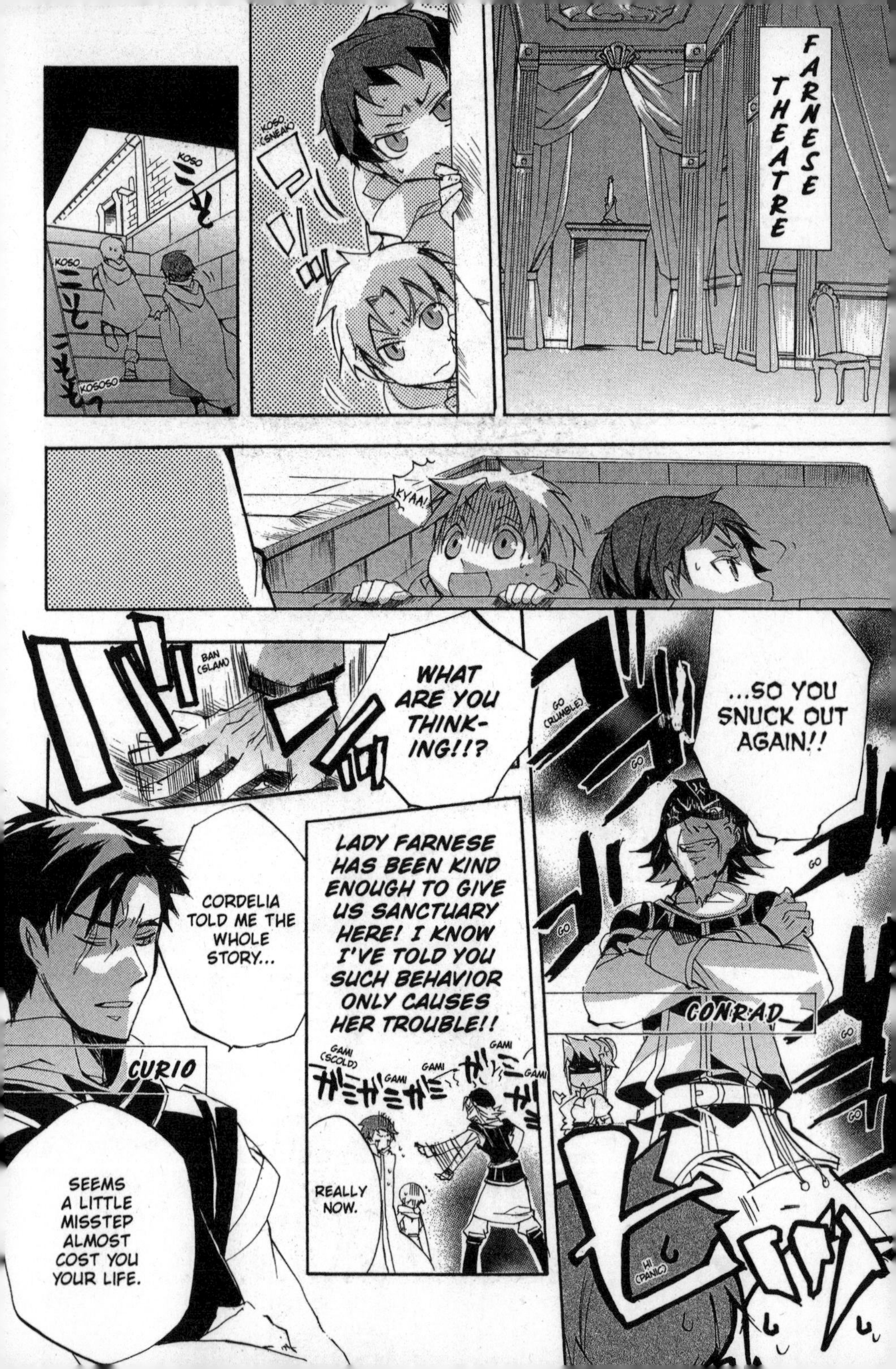
FARNESE THEATRE
KOSO (SNEAK)
KOSO
KOSO
KOSOSO
KYAA!
...SO YOU SNUCK OUT AGAIN!!
GO (RUMBLE)
GO
GO
GO
GO
GO
CONRAD
HI (PANIC)
BAN (SLAM)
WHAT ARE YOU THINKING!!?
LADY FARNESE HAS BEEN KIND ENOUGH TO GIVE US SANCTUARY HERE! I KNOW I'VE TOLD YOU SUCH BEHAVIOR ONLY CAUSES HER TROUBLE!!
GAMI (SCOLD)
GAMI
GAMI
GAMI
GAMI
REALLY NOW.
CORDELIA TOLD ME THE WHOLE STORY...
CURIO
SEEMS A LITTLE MISSTEP ALMOST COST YOU YOUR LIFE.

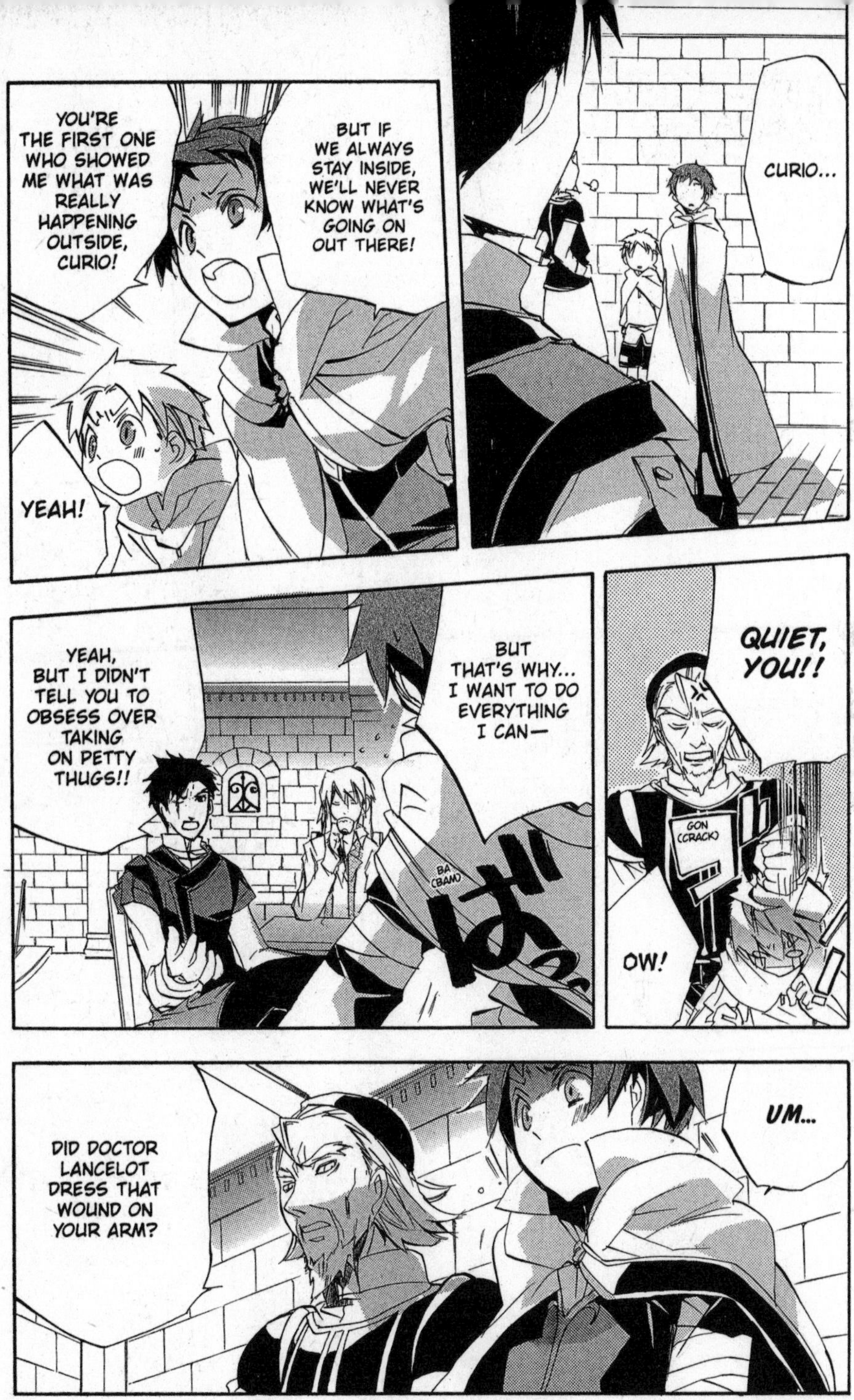
CURIO...
BUT IF WE ALWAYS STAY INSIDE, WE'LL NEVER KNOW WHAT'S GOING ON OUT THERE!
YOU'RE THE FIRST ONE WHO SHOWED ME WHAT WAS REALLY HAPPENING OUTSIDE, CURIO!
YEAH!
QUIET, YOU!!
GON (CRACK)
OW!
BUT THAT'S WHY... I WANT TO DO EVERYTHING I CAN—
BA (BAM)
YEAH, BUT I DIDN'T TELL YOU TO OBSESS OVER TAKING ON PETTY THUGS!!
UM...
DID DOCTOR LANCELOT DRESS THAT WOUND ON YOUR ARM?

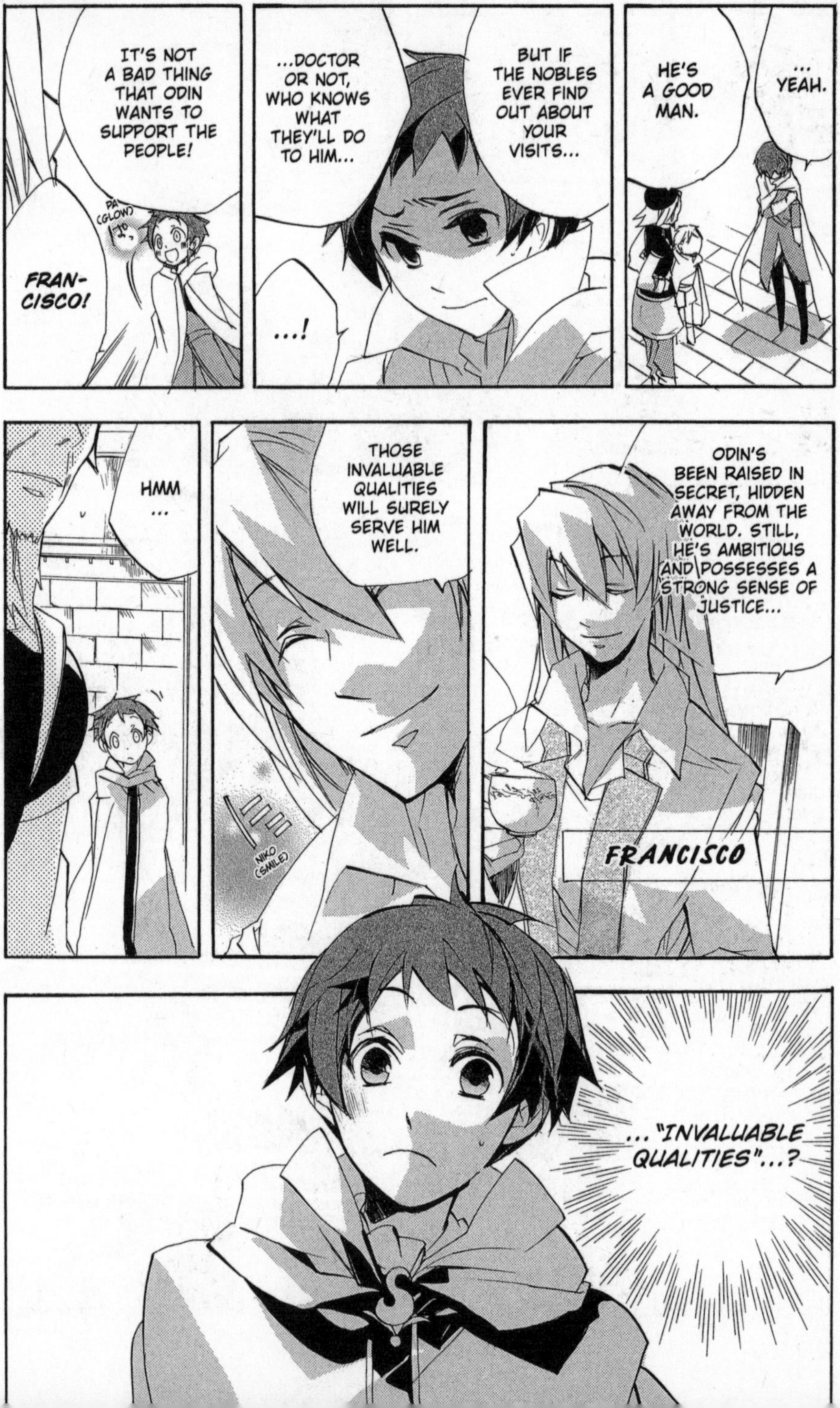
... YEAH.
HE'S A GOOD MAN.
BUT IF THE NOBLES EVER FIND OUT ABOUT YOUR VISITS...
...DOCTOR OR NOT, WHO KNOWS WHAT THEY'LL DO TO HIM...
...!
IT'S NOT A BAD THING THAT ODIN WANTS TO SUPPORT THE PEOPLE!
PA (GLOW)
FRAN-CISCO!
ODIN'S BEEN RAISED IN SECRET, HIDDEN AWAY FROM THE WORLD. STILL, HE'S AMBITIOUS AND POSSESSES A STRONG SENSE OF JUSTICE...
FRANCISCO
THOSE INVALUABLE QUALITIES WILL SURELY SERVE HIM WELL.
NIKO (SMILE)
HMM ...
... "INVALUABLE QUALITIES"...?

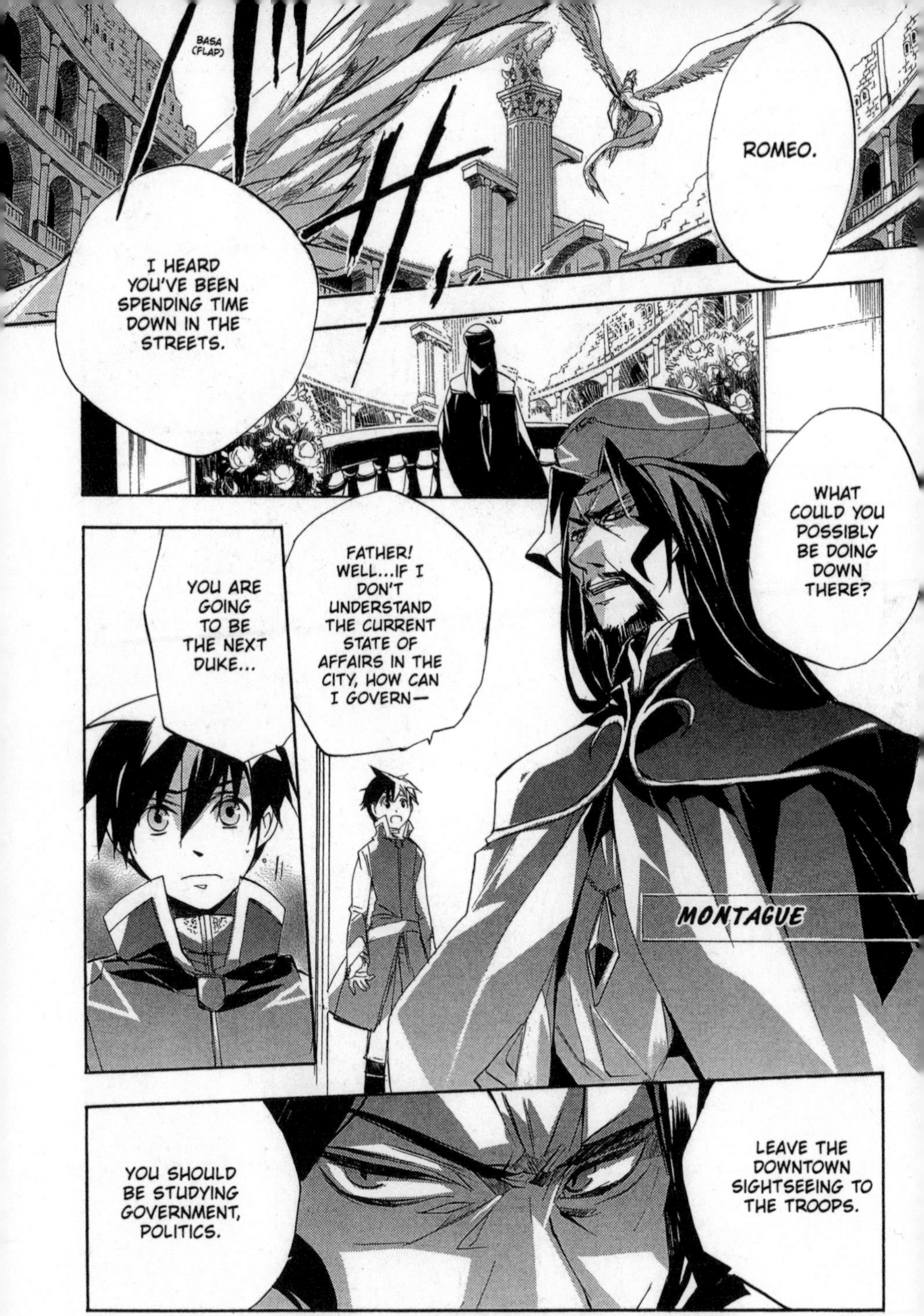

ROMEO.
BASA (FLAP)
I HEARD YOU'VE BEEN SPENDING TIME DOWN IN THE STREETS.
WHAT COULD YOU POSSIBLY BE DOING DOWN THERE?
FATHER! WELL...IF I DON'T UNDERSTAND THE CURRENT STATE OF AFFAIRS IN THE CITY, HOW CAN I GOVERN—
YOU ARE GOING TO BE THE NEXT DUKE...
MONTAGUE
LEAVE THE DOWNTOWN SIGHTSEEING TO THE TROOPS.
YOU SHOULD BE STUDYING GOVERNMENT, POLITICS.

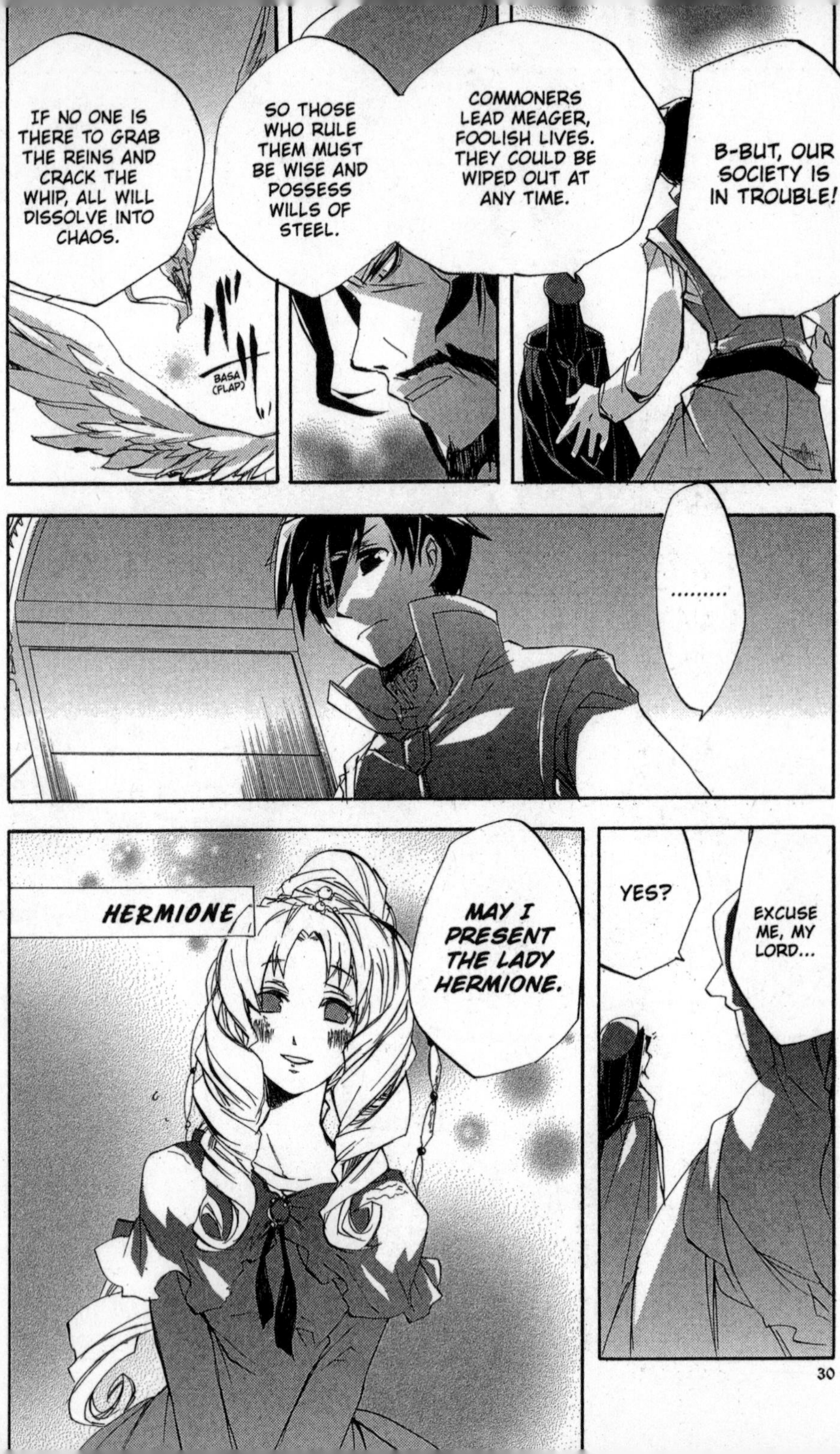
B-BUT, OUR SOCIETY IS IN TROUBLE!
COMMONERS LEAD MEAGER, FOOLISH LIVES. THEY COULD BE WIPED OUT AT ANY TIME.
SO THOSE WHO RULE THEM MUST BE WISE AND POSSESS WILLS OF STEEL.
IF NO ONE IS THERE TO GRAB THE REINS AND CRACK THE WHIP, ALL WILL DISSOLVE INTO CHAOS.
BASA (FLAP)
....
EXCUSE ME, MY LORD...
YES?
MAY I PRESENT THE LADY HERMIONE.
HERMIONE

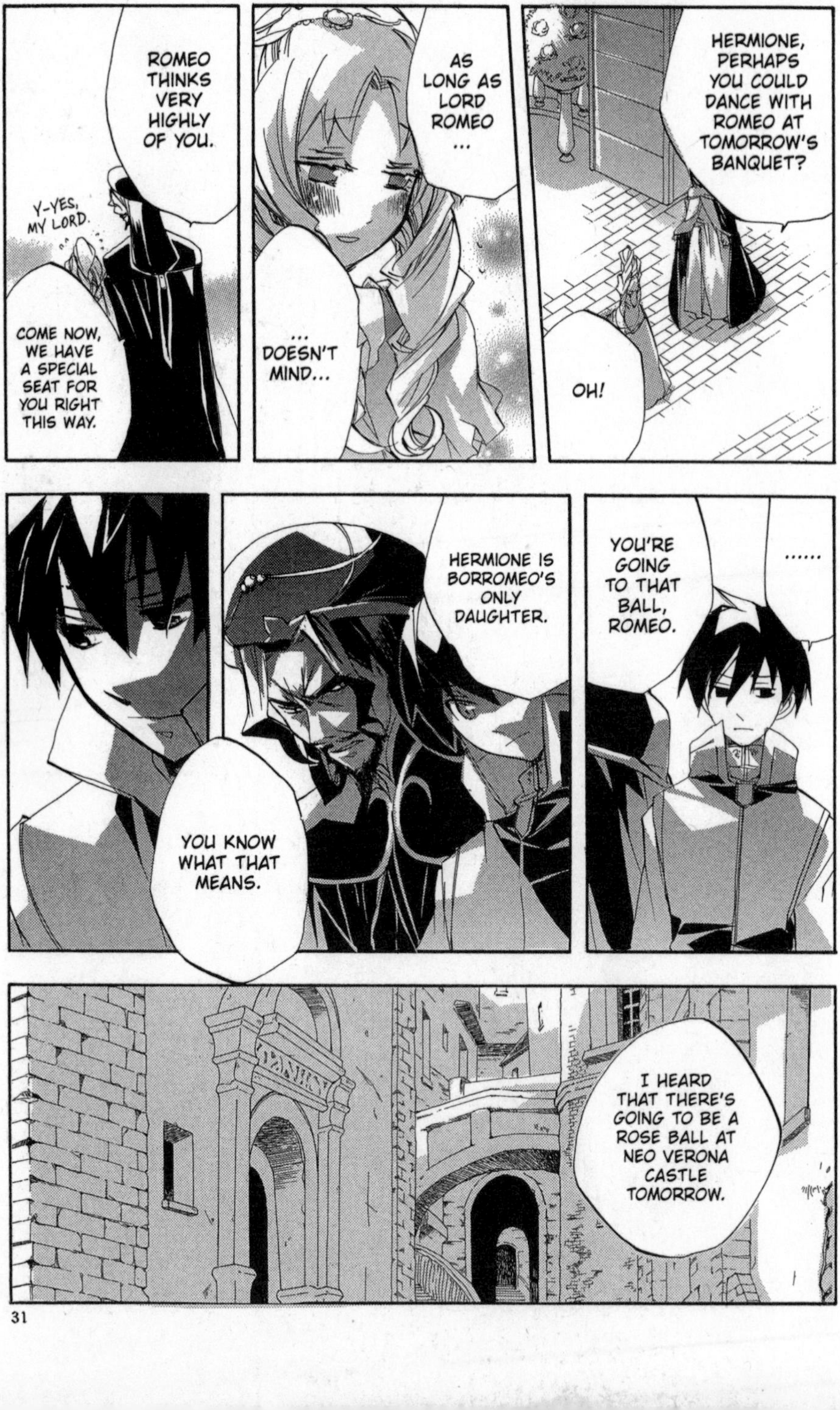
HERMIONE, PERHAPS YOU COULD DANCE WITH ROMEO AT TOMORROW'S BANQUET?
OH!
AS LONG AS LORD ROMEO ...
... DOESN'T MIND...
ROMEO THINKS VERY HIGHLY OF YOU.
Y-YES, MY LORD.
COME NOW, WE HAVE A SPECIAL SEAT FOR YOU RIGHT THIS WAY.
......
YOU'RE GOING TO THAT BALL, ROMEO.
HERMIONE IS BORROMEO'S ONLY DAUGHTER.
YOU KNOW WHAT THAT MEANS.
I HEARD THAT THERE'S GOING TO BE A ROSE BALL AT NEO VERONA CASTLE TOMORROW.

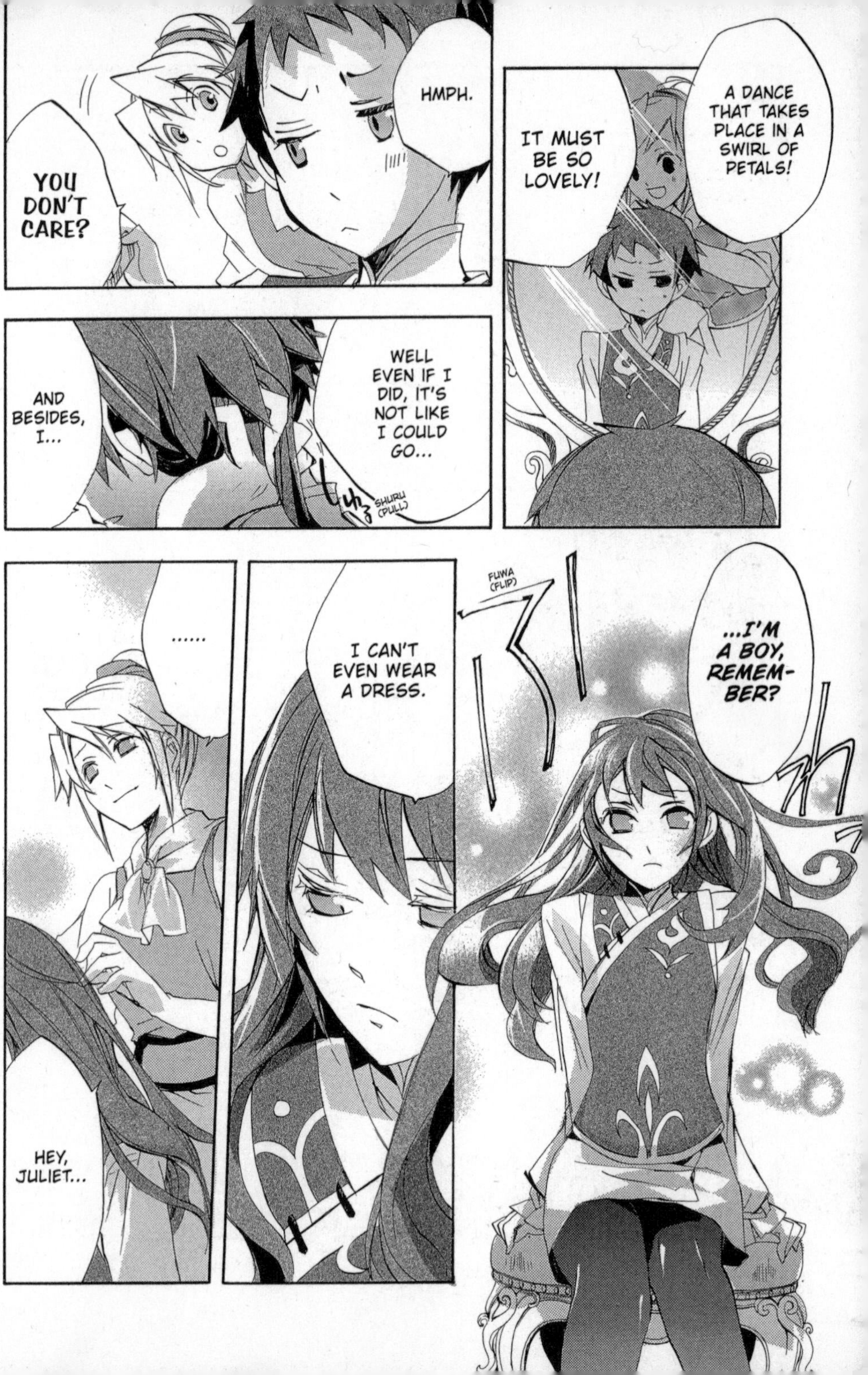
A DANCE THAT TAKES PLACE IN A SWIRL OF PETALS!
IT MUST BE SO LOVELY!
HMPH.
YOU DON'T CARE?
WELL EVEN IF I DID, IT'S NOT LIKE I COULD GO...
SHURU (PULL)
AND BESIDES, I...
FUWA (FLIP)
...I'M A BOY, REMEMBER?
I CAN'T EVEN WEAR A DRESS.
......
HEY, JULIET...

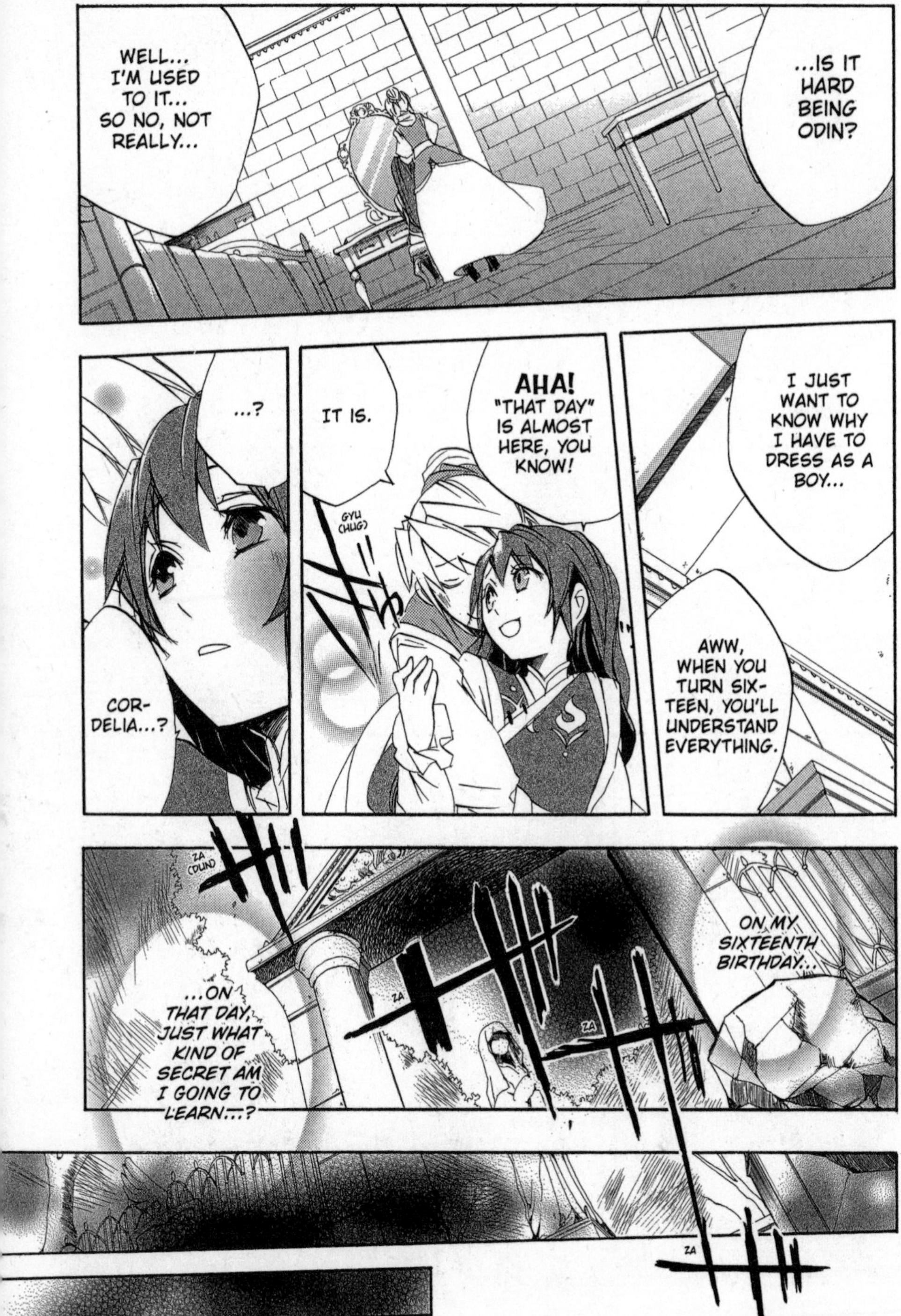
...IS IT HARD BEING ODIN?
WELL... I'M USED TO IT... SO NO, NOT REALLY...
I JUST WANT TO KNOW WHY I HAVE TO DRESS AS A BOY...
AWW, WHEN YOU TURN SIX-TEEN, YOU'LL UNDERSTAND EVERYTHING.
AHA! "THAT DAY" IS ALMOST HERE, YOU KNOW!
IT IS.
GYU (HUG)
...?
COR-DELIA...?
ON MY SIXTEENTH BIRTHDAY...
ZA
ZA
...ON THAT DAY, JUST WHAT KIND OF SECRET AM I GOING TO LEARN...?
ZA (SOUND)
ZA

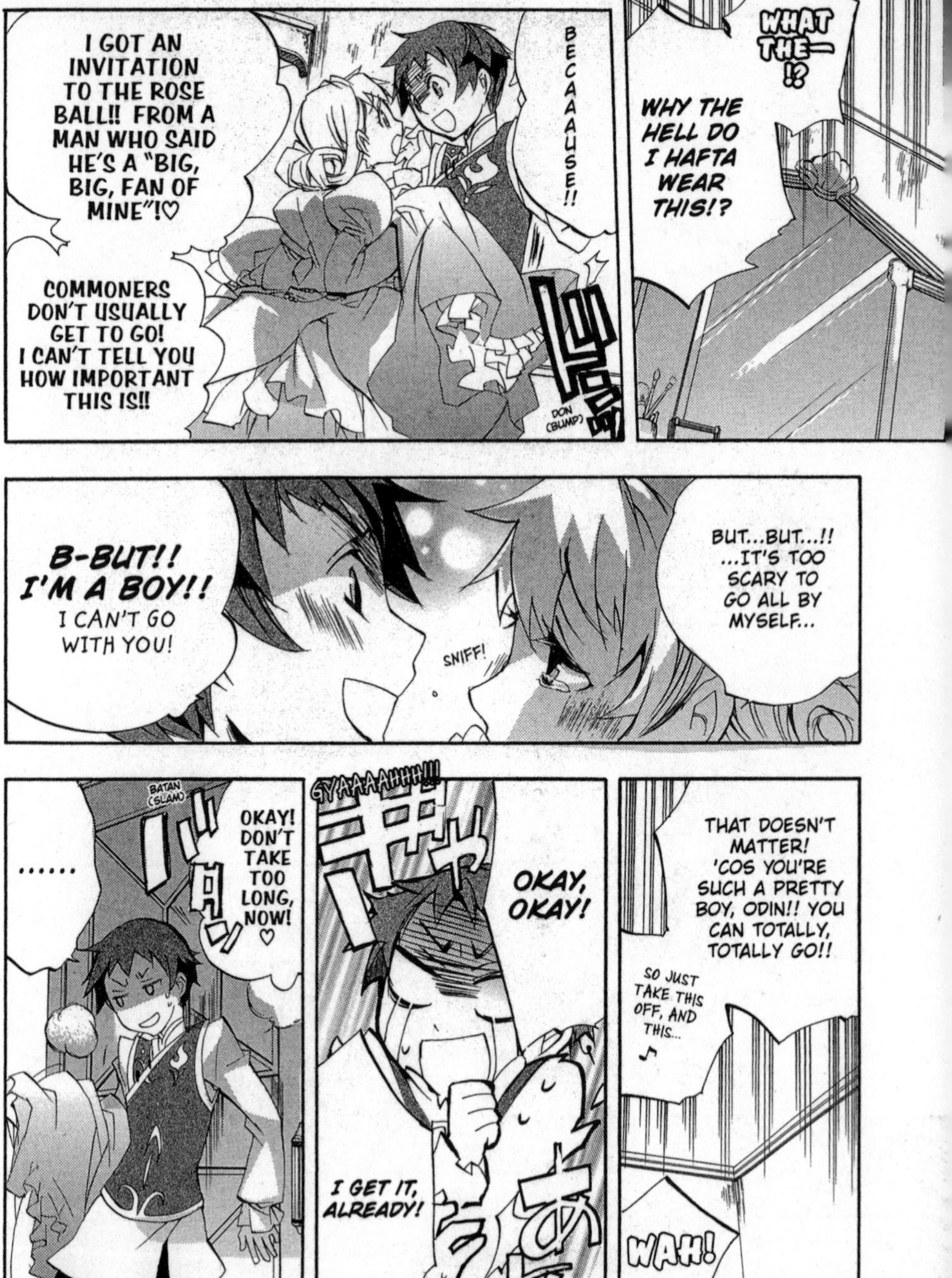
WHAT THE—!?
WHY THE HELL DO I HAFTA WEAR THIS!?
BECAAAAUSE!!
I GOT AN INVITATION TO THE ROSE BALL!! FROM A MAN WHO SAID HE'S A "BIG, BIG, FAN OF MINE"!♡
COMMONERS DON'T USUALLY GET TO GO! I CAN'T TELL YOU HOW IMPORTANT THIS IS!!
DON (BUMP)
BUT...BUT...!! ...IT'S TOO SCARY TO GO ALL BY MYSELF...
SNIFF!
B-BUT!! I'M A BOY!! I CAN'T GO WITH YOU!
THAT DOESN'T MATTER! 'COS YOU'RE SUCH A PRETTY BOY, ODIN!! YOU CAN TOTALLY, TOTALLY GO!!
SO JUST TAKE THIS OFF, AND THIS... ♪
WAH!
GYAAAAHHH!!!
OKAY, OKAY!
I GET IT, ALREADY!
OKAY! DON'T TAKE TOO LONG, NOW! ♡
BATAN (SLAM)
......

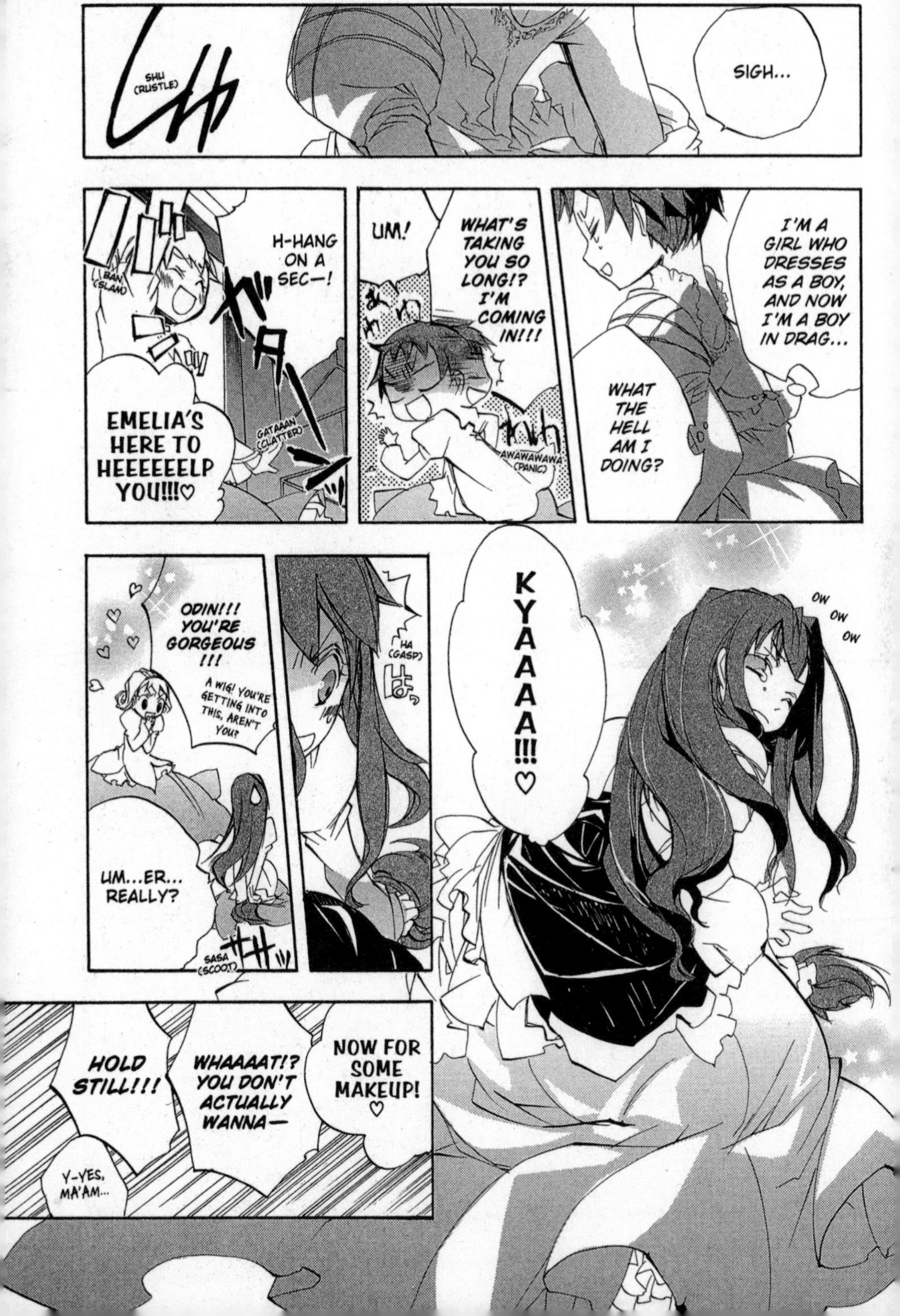
SIGH...
SHU (RUSTLE)
I'M A GIRL WHO DRESSES AS A BOY, AND NOW I'M A BOY IN DRAG...
WHAT THE HELL AM I DOING?
WHAT'S TAKING YOU SO LONG!? I'M COMING IN!!!
UM!
AWAWAWAWA (PANIC)
H-HANG ON A SEC—!
BAN (SLAM)
GATAAAN (CLATTER)
EMELIA'S HERE TO HEEEEEELP YOU!!!♡
KYAAAAA!!!♡
OW OW OW
HA (GASP)
ODIN!!! YOU'RE GORGEOUS!!!
A WIG! YOU'RE GETTING INTO THIS, AREN'T YOU?
UM...ER... REALLY?
SASA (SCOOT)
NOW FOR SOME MAKEUP! ♡
WHAAAAT!? YOU DON'T ACTUALLY WANNA—
HOLD STILL!!!
Y-YES, MA'AM...

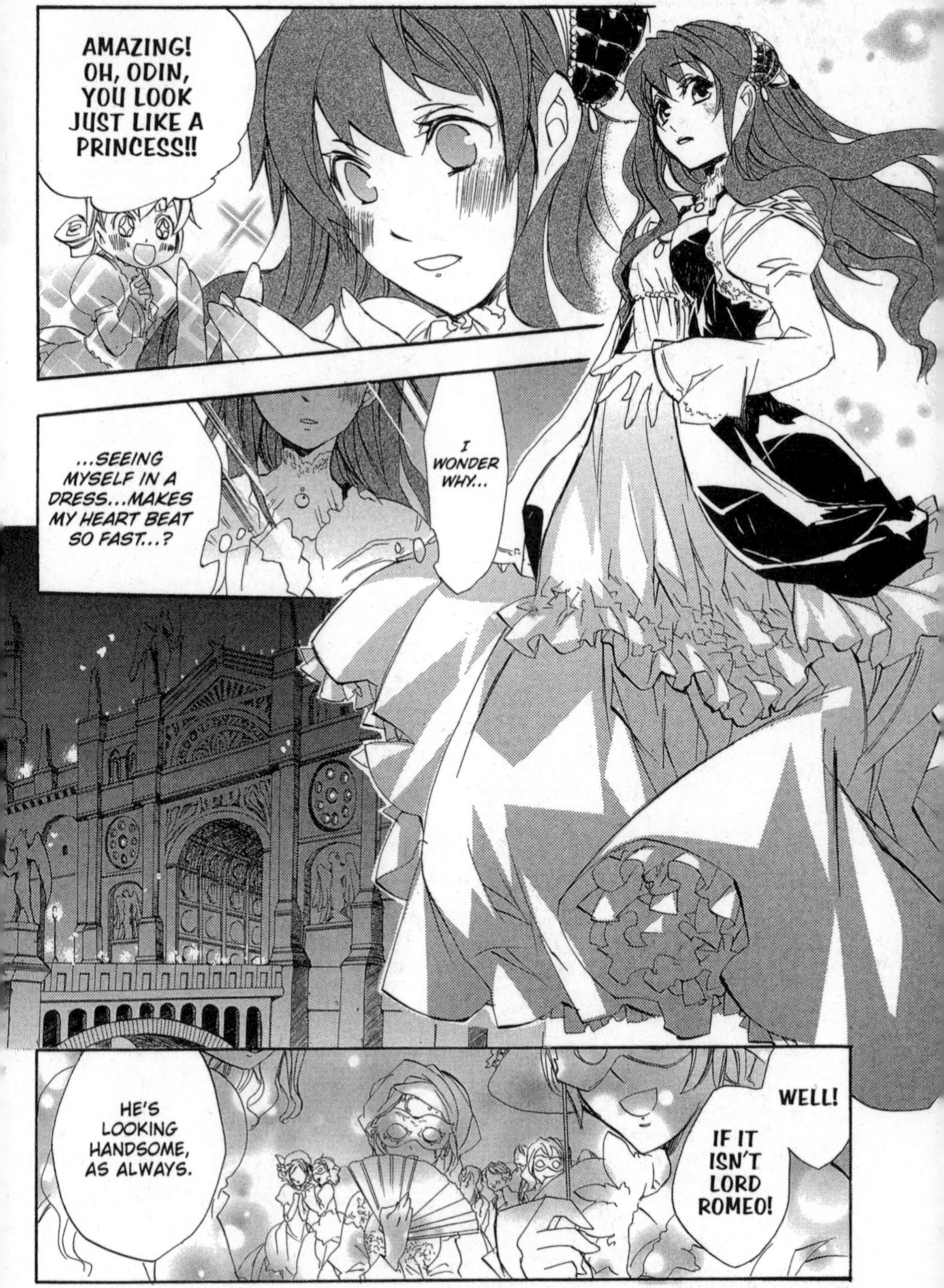
AMAZING! OH, ODIN, YOU LOOK JUST LIKE A PRINCESS!!
I WONDER WHY...
...SEEING MYSELF IN A DRESS...MAKES MY HEART BEAT SO FAST...?
WELL!
IF IT ISN'T LORD ROMEO!
HE'S LOOKING HANDSOME, AS ALWAYS.

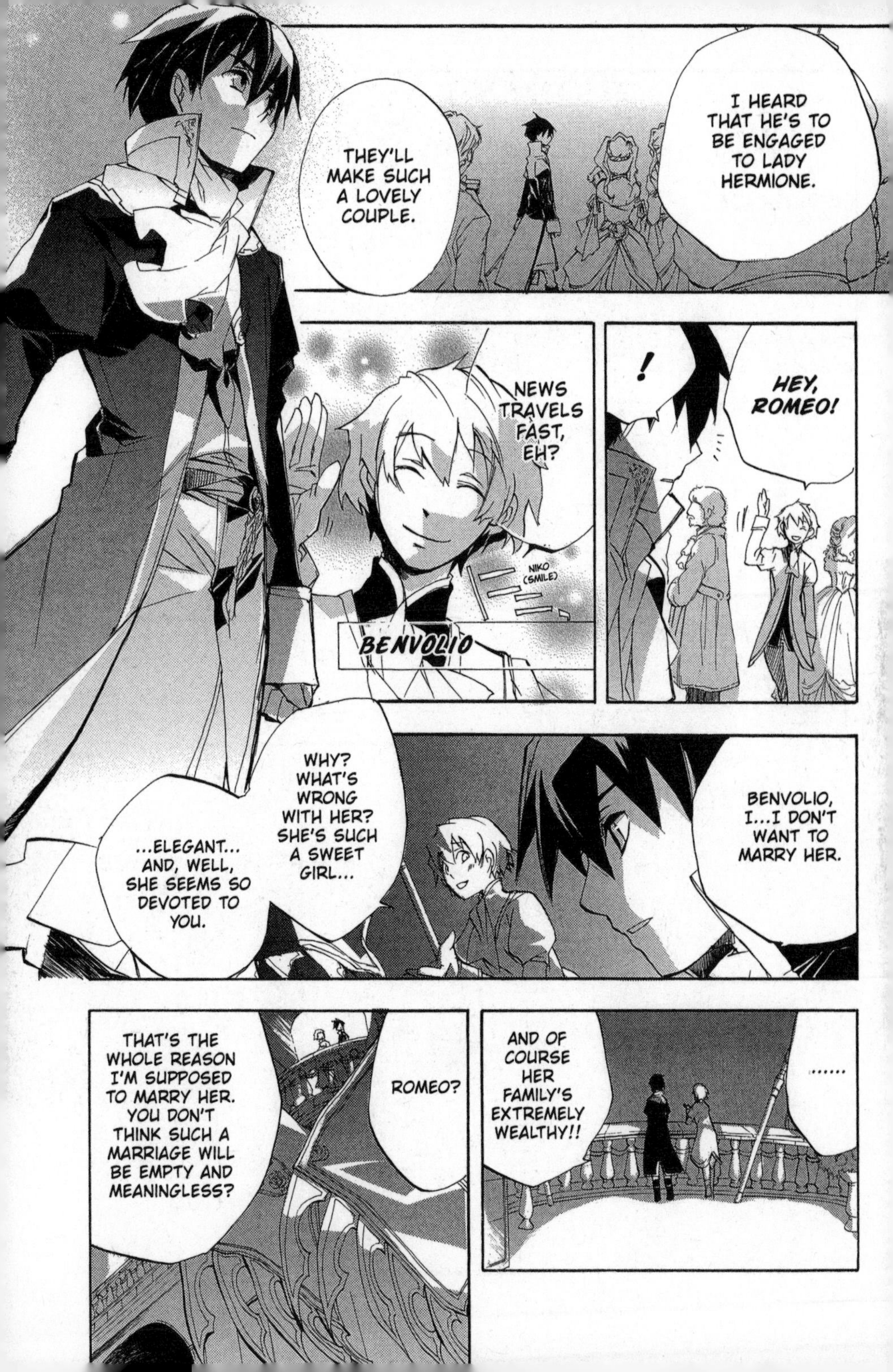
I HEARD THAT HE'S TO BE ENGAGED TO LADY HERMIONE.
THEY'LL MAKE SUCH A LOVELY COUPLE.
!
HEY, ROMEO!
NEWS TRAVELS FAST, EH?
NIKO (SMILE)
BENVOLIO
BENVOLIO, I...I DON'T WANT TO MARRY HER.
WHY? WHAT'S WRONG WITH HER? SHE'S SUCH A SWEET GIRL...
...ELEGANT... AND, WELL, SHE SEEMS SO DEVOTED TO YOU.
......
AND OF COURSE HER FAMILY'S EXTREMELY WEALTHY!!
ROMEO?
THAT'S THE WHOLE REASON I'M SUPPOSED TO MARRY HER. YOU DON'T THINK SUCH A MARRIAGE WILL BE EMPTY AND MEANINGLESS?

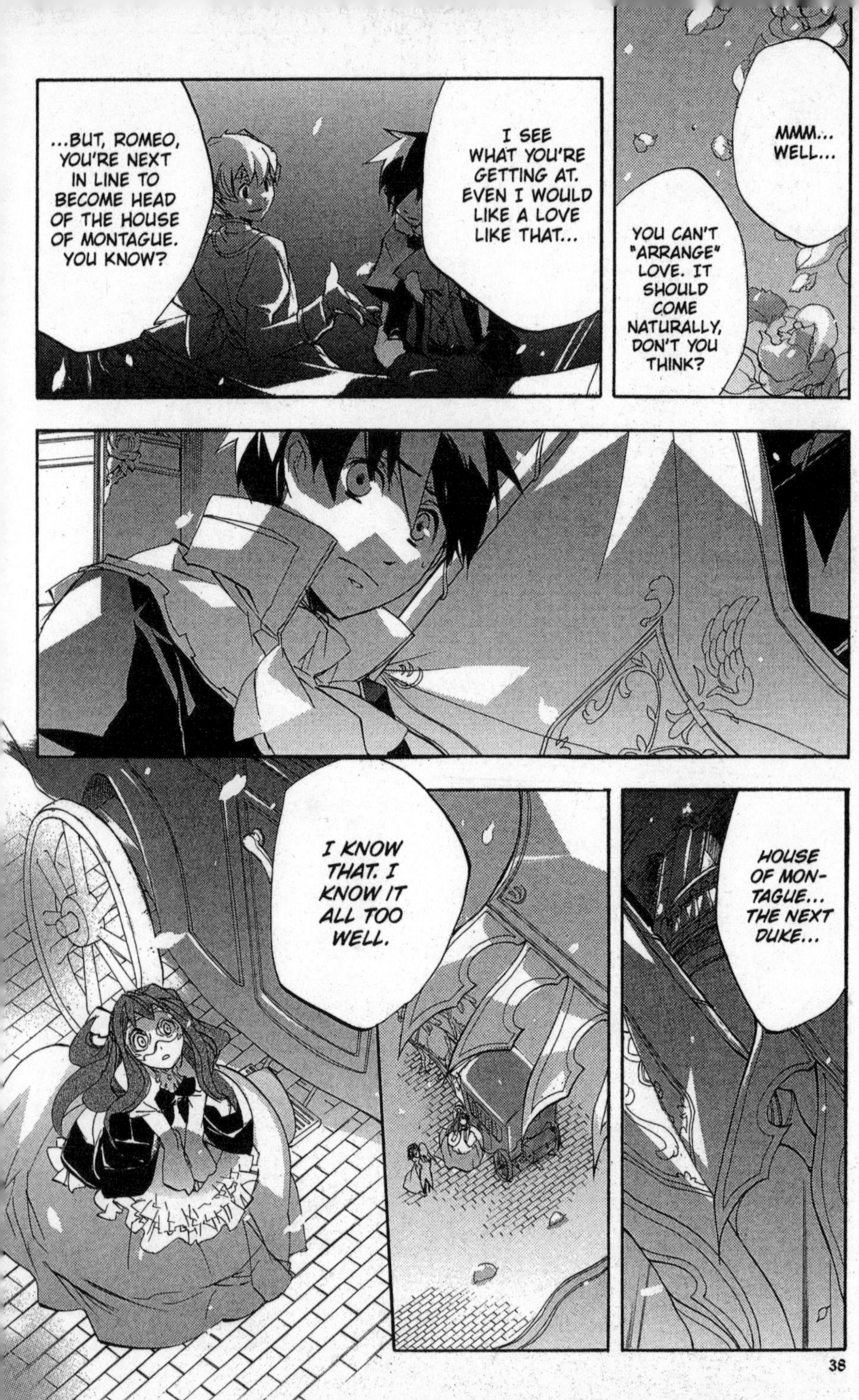
MMM... WELL...
YOU CAN'T "ARRANGE" LOVE. IT SHOULD COME NATURALLY, DON'T YOU THINK?
I SEE WHAT YOU'RE GETTING AT. EVEN I WOULD LIKE A LOVE LIKE THAT...
...BUT, ROMEO, YOU'RE NEXT IN LINE TO BECOME HEAD OF THE HOUSE OF MONTAGUE. YOU KNOW?
HOUSE OF MON-TAGUE... THE NEXT DUKE...
I KNOW THAT. I KNOW IT ALL TOO WELL.

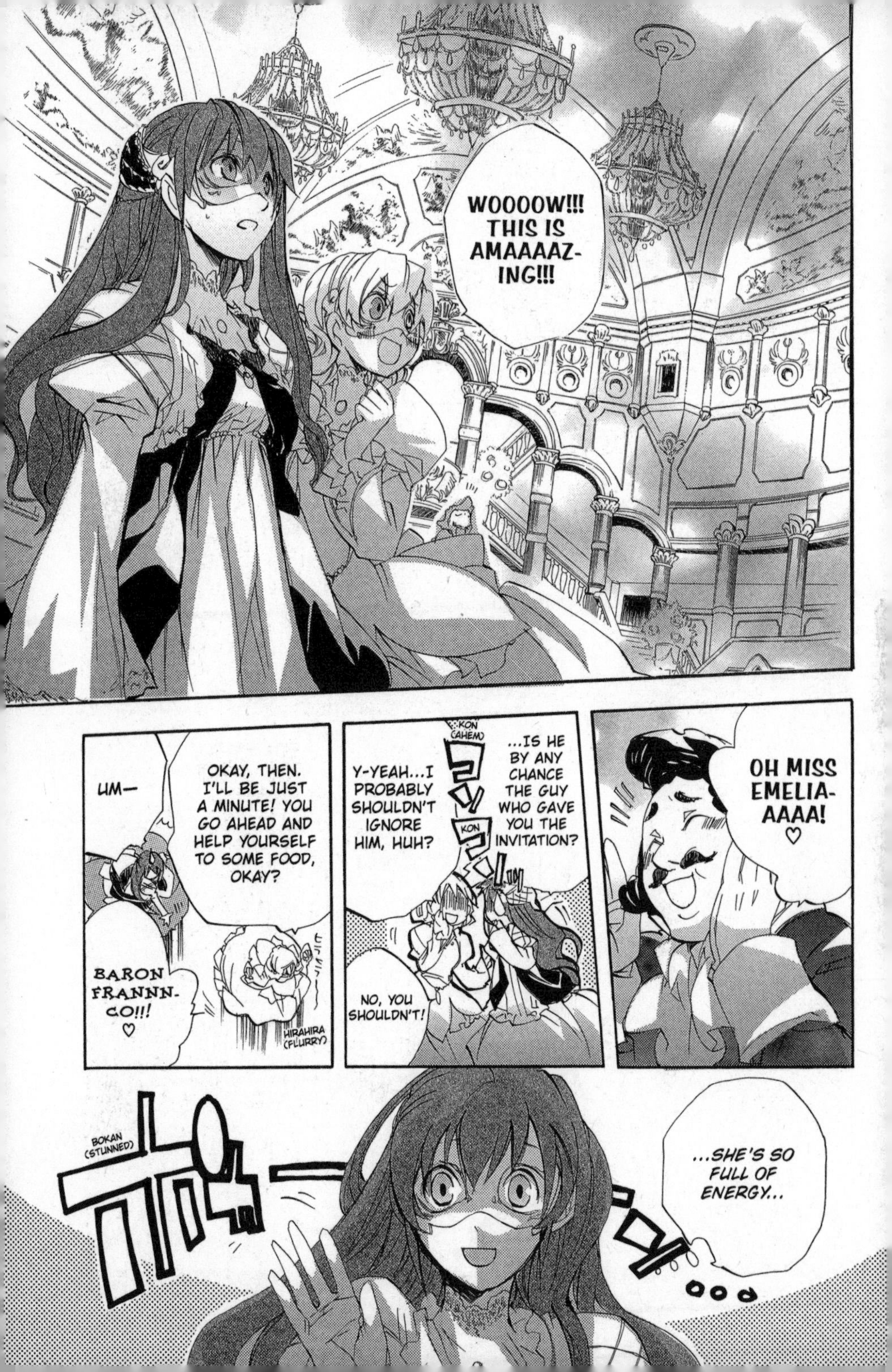
WOOOOW!!! THIS IS AMAAAAZ-ING!!!
OH MISS EMELIA-AAAA! ♡
KON (AHEM)
KON
...IS HE BY ANY CHANCE THE GUY WHO GAVE YOU THE INVITATION?
Y-YEAH...I PROBABLY SHOULDN'T IGNORE HIM, HUH?
NO, YOU SHOULDN'T!
OKAY, THEN. I'LL BE JUST A MINUTE! YOU GO AHEAD AND HELP YOURSELF TO SOME FOOD, OKAY?
UM—
HIRAHIRA (FLURRY)
BARON FRANNN-CO!!! ♡
...SHE'S SO FULL OF ENERGY...
BOKAN (STUNNED)

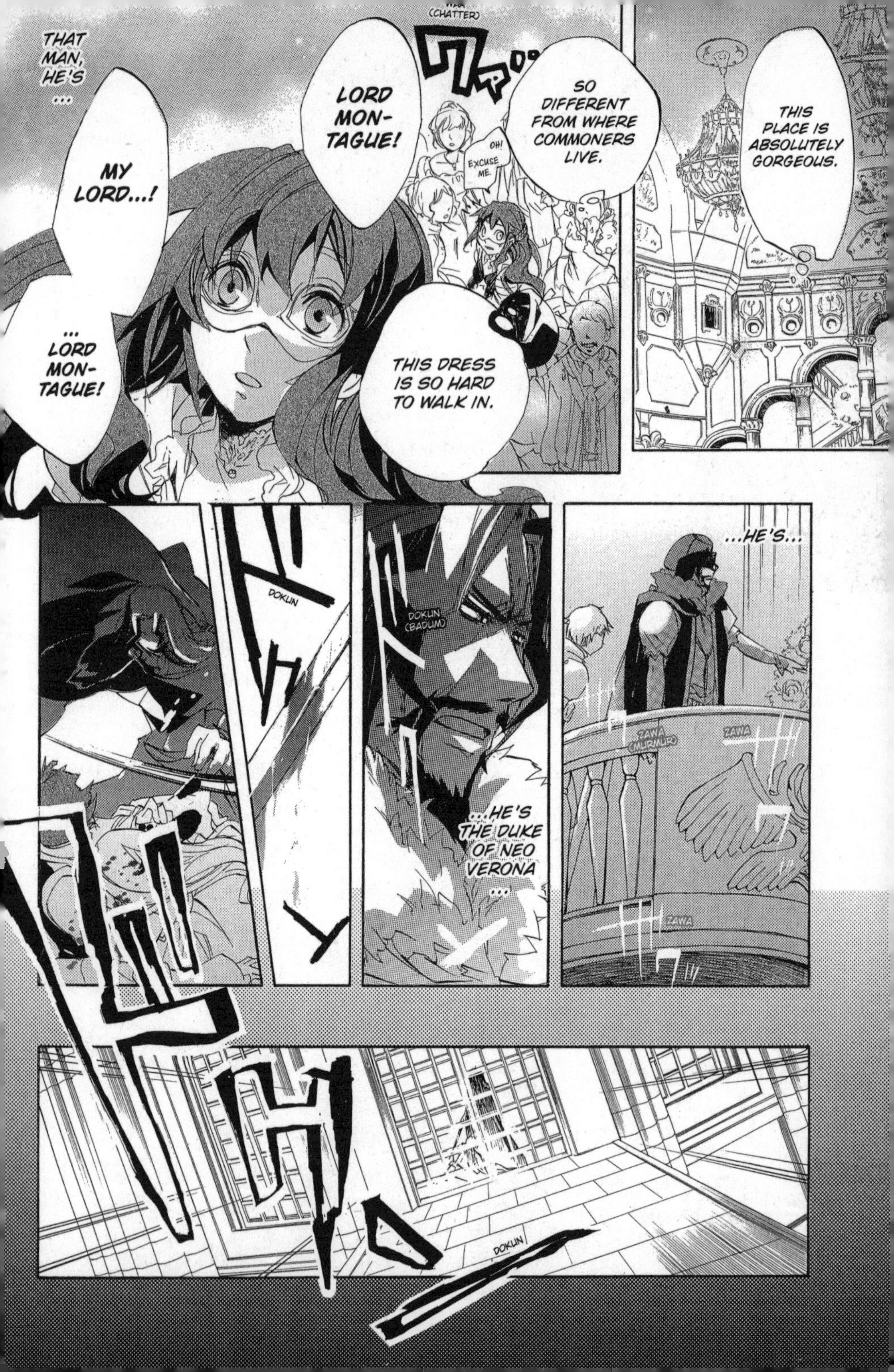
THIS PLACE IS ABSOLUTELY GORGEOUS.
SO DIFFERENT FROM WHERE COMMONERS LIVE.
(CHATTER)
OH! EXCUSE ME.
LORD MON-TAGUE!
THIS DRESS IS SO HARD TO WALK IN.
THAT MAN, HE'S ...
MY LORD...!
... LORD MON-TAGUE!
...HE'S...
ZAWA (MURMUR)
ZAWA
ZAWA
DOKUN (BADUM)
...HE'S THE DUKE OF NEO VERONA ...
DOKUN
DOKUN

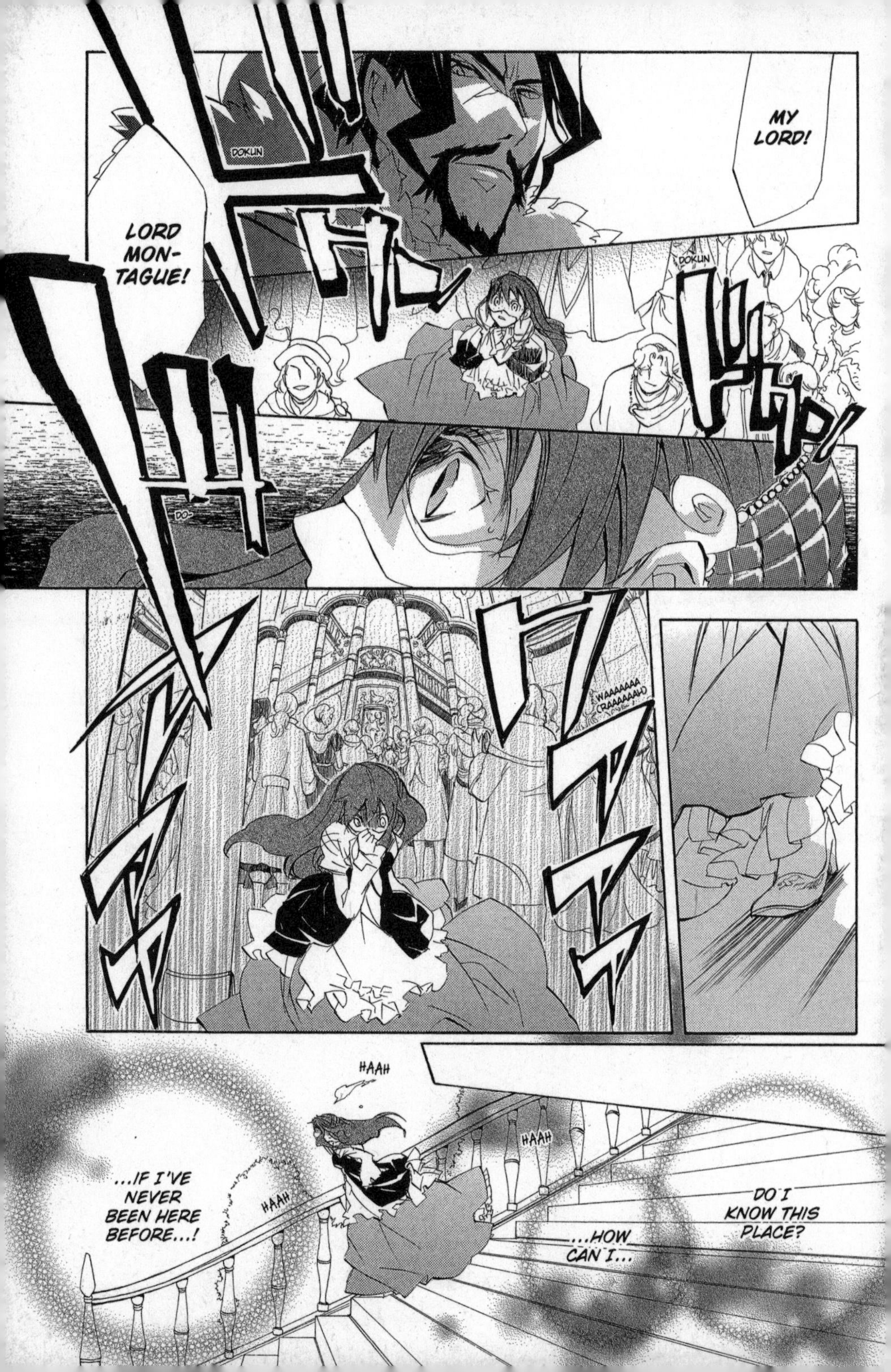
MY LORD!
DOKUN
LORD MONTAGUE!
DOKUN
DO-
WAAAAAAA (RAAAAAAH)
HAAH
HAAH
DO I KNOW THIS PLACE?
...HOW CAN I...
HAAH
...IF I'VE NEVER BEEN HERE BEFORE...!

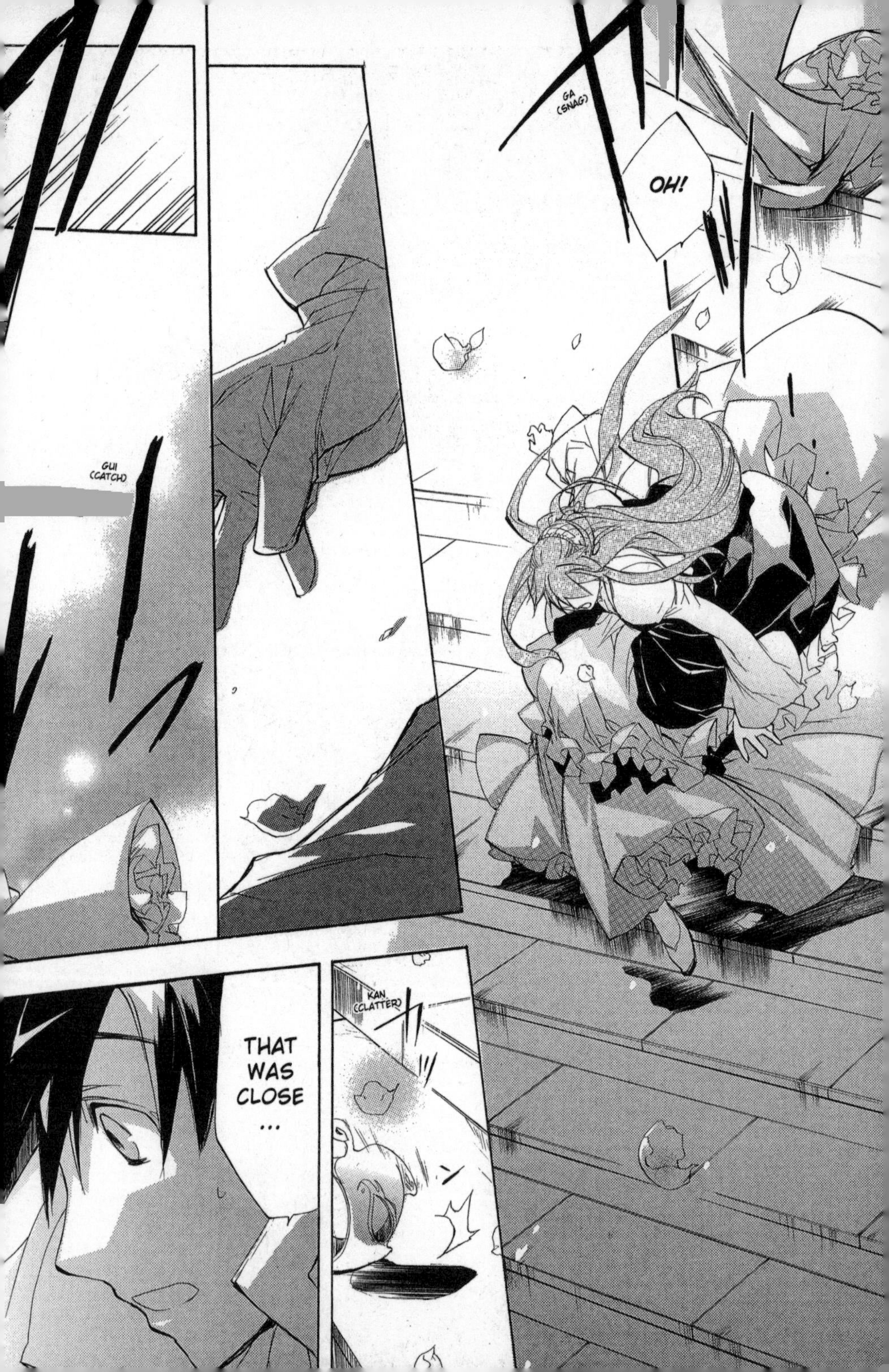
GA (SNAG)
OH!
GUI (CATCH)
KAN (CLATTER)
THAT WAS CLOSE ...

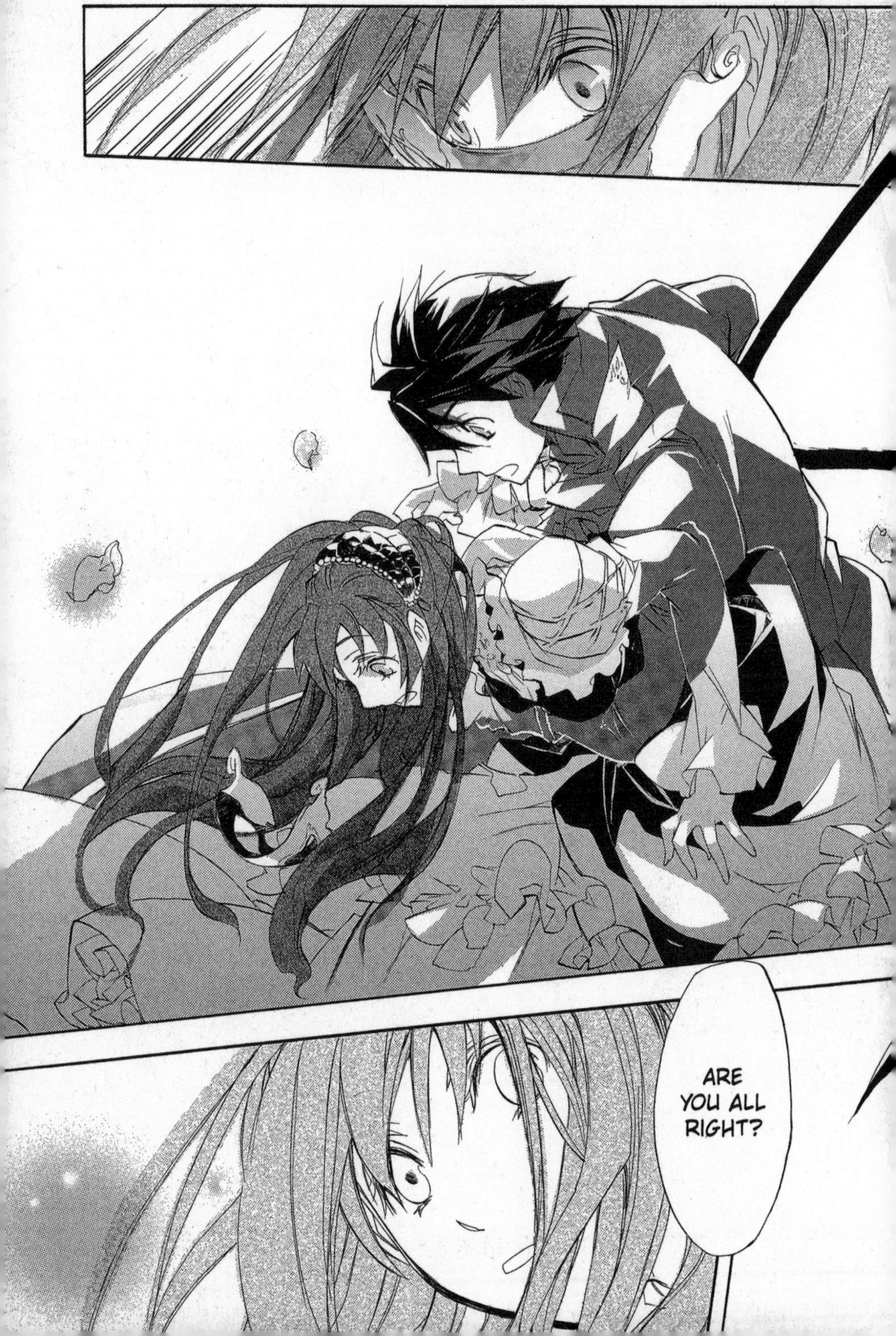
ARE YOU ALL RIGHT?

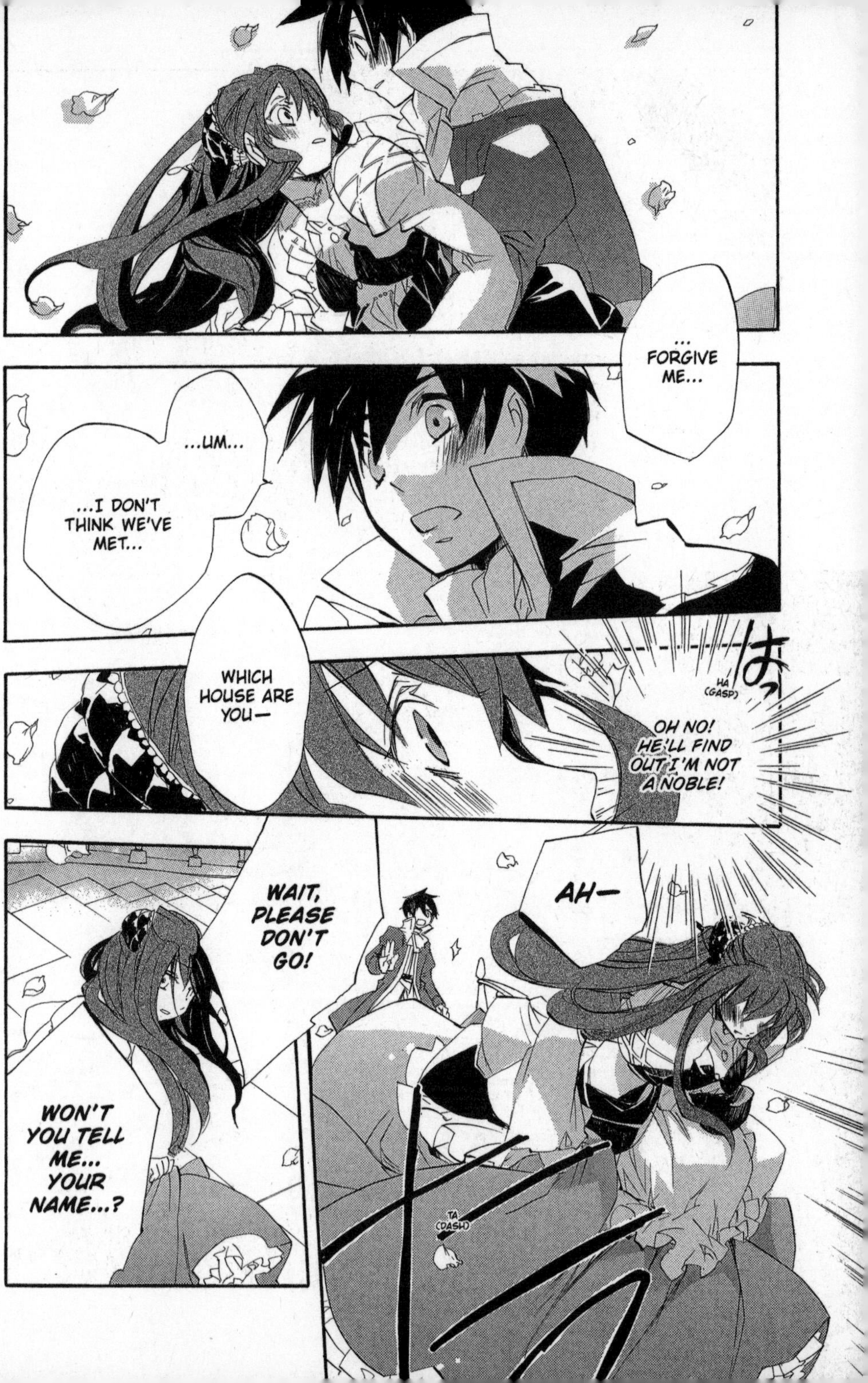

...FORGIVE ME...
...UM...
...I DON'T THINK WE'VE MET...
はっ
HA (GASP)
WHICH HOUSE ARE YOU—
OH NO! HE'LL FIND OUT I'M NOT A NOBLE!
AH—
TA (DASH)
WAIT, PLEASE DON'T GO!
WON'T YOU TELL ME... YOUR NAME...?

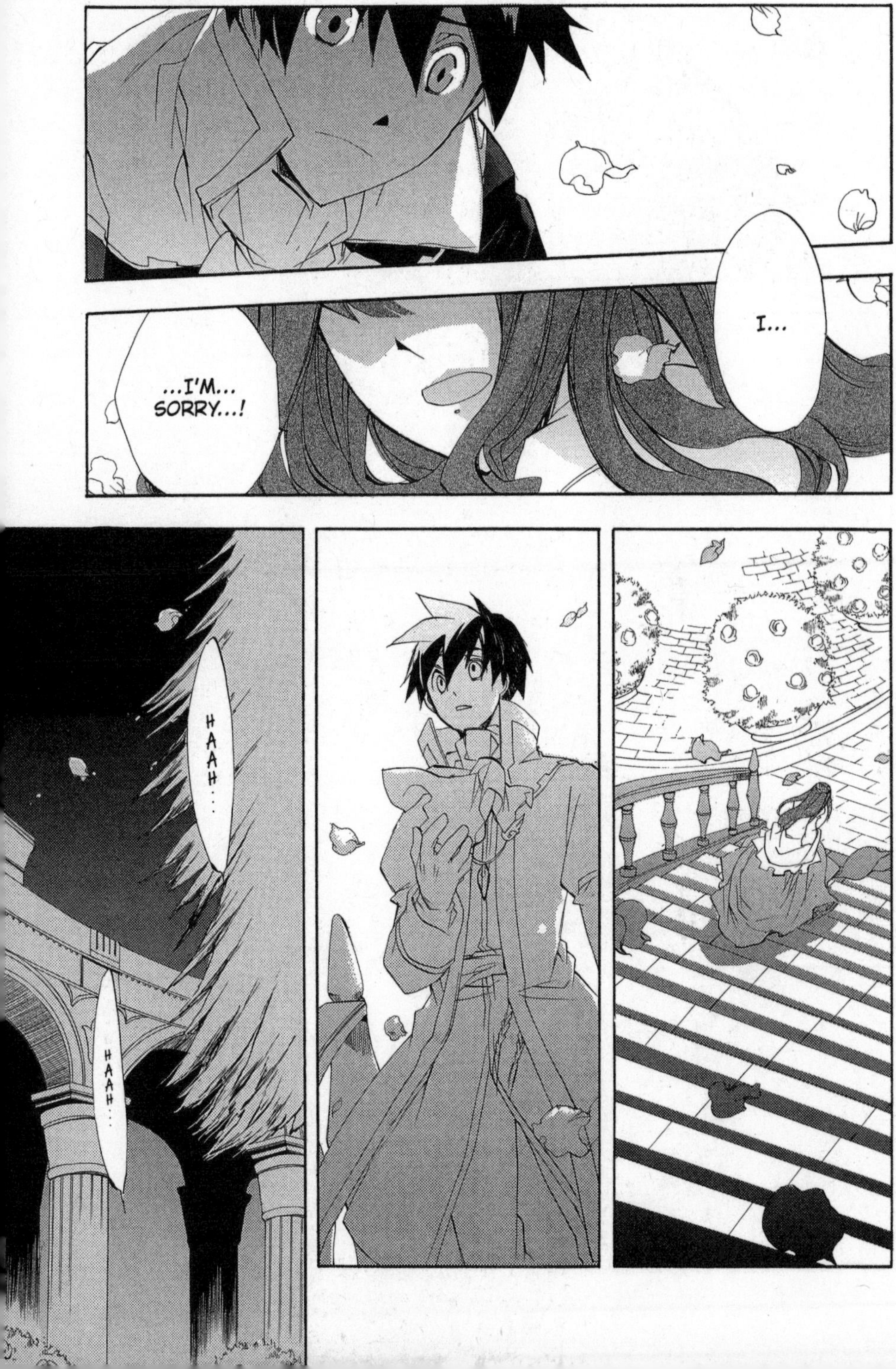
I...
...I'M... SORRY...!
HAAAH...
HAAAH...

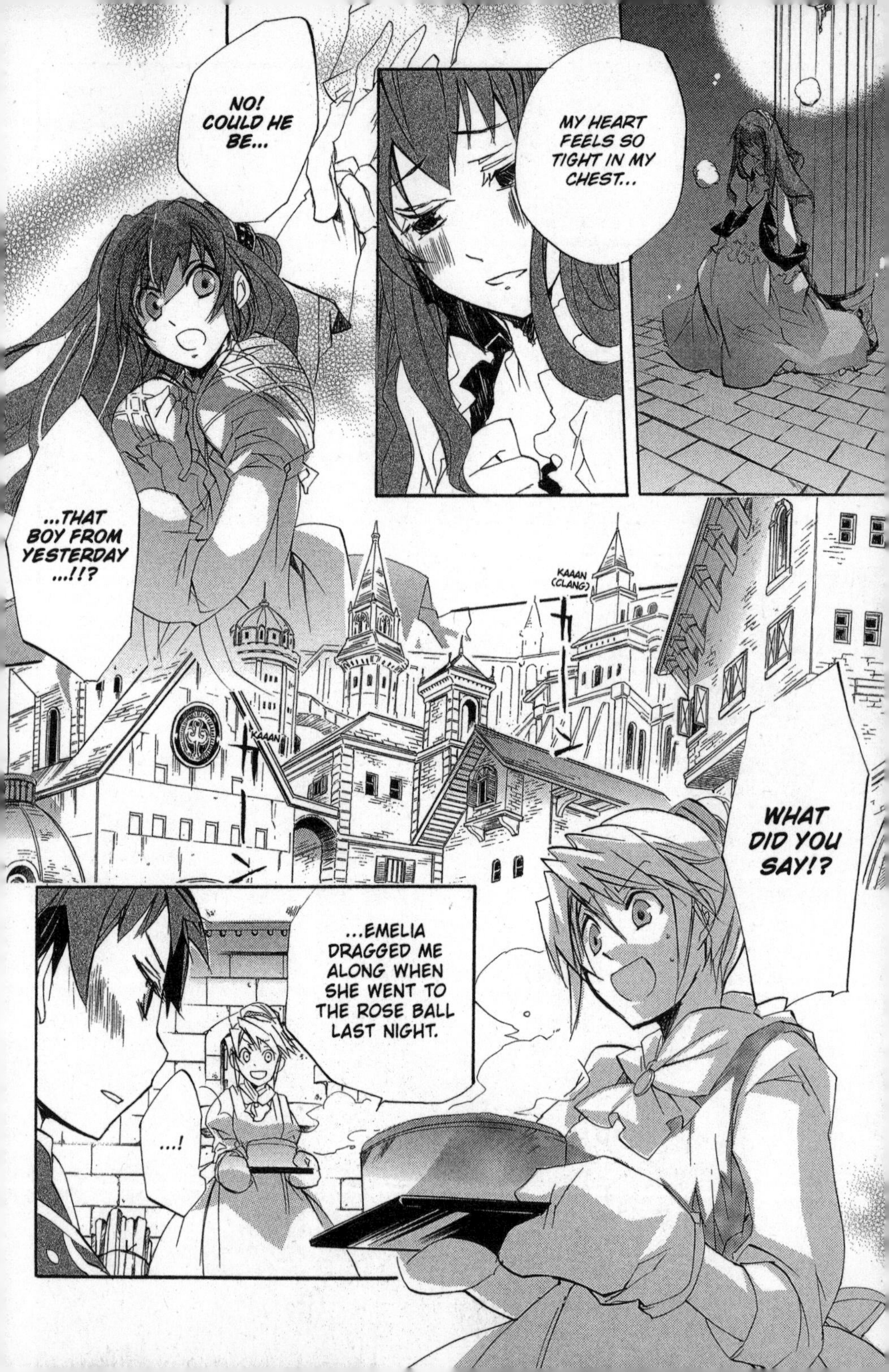
MY HEART FEELS SO TIGHT IN MY CHEST...
NO! COULD HE BE...
...THAT BOY FROM YESTERDAY...!!?
KAAAN (CLANG)
KAAAN
WHAT DID YOU SAY!?
...EMELIA DRAGGED ME ALONG WHEN SHE WENT TO THE ROSE BALL LAST NIGHT.
...!

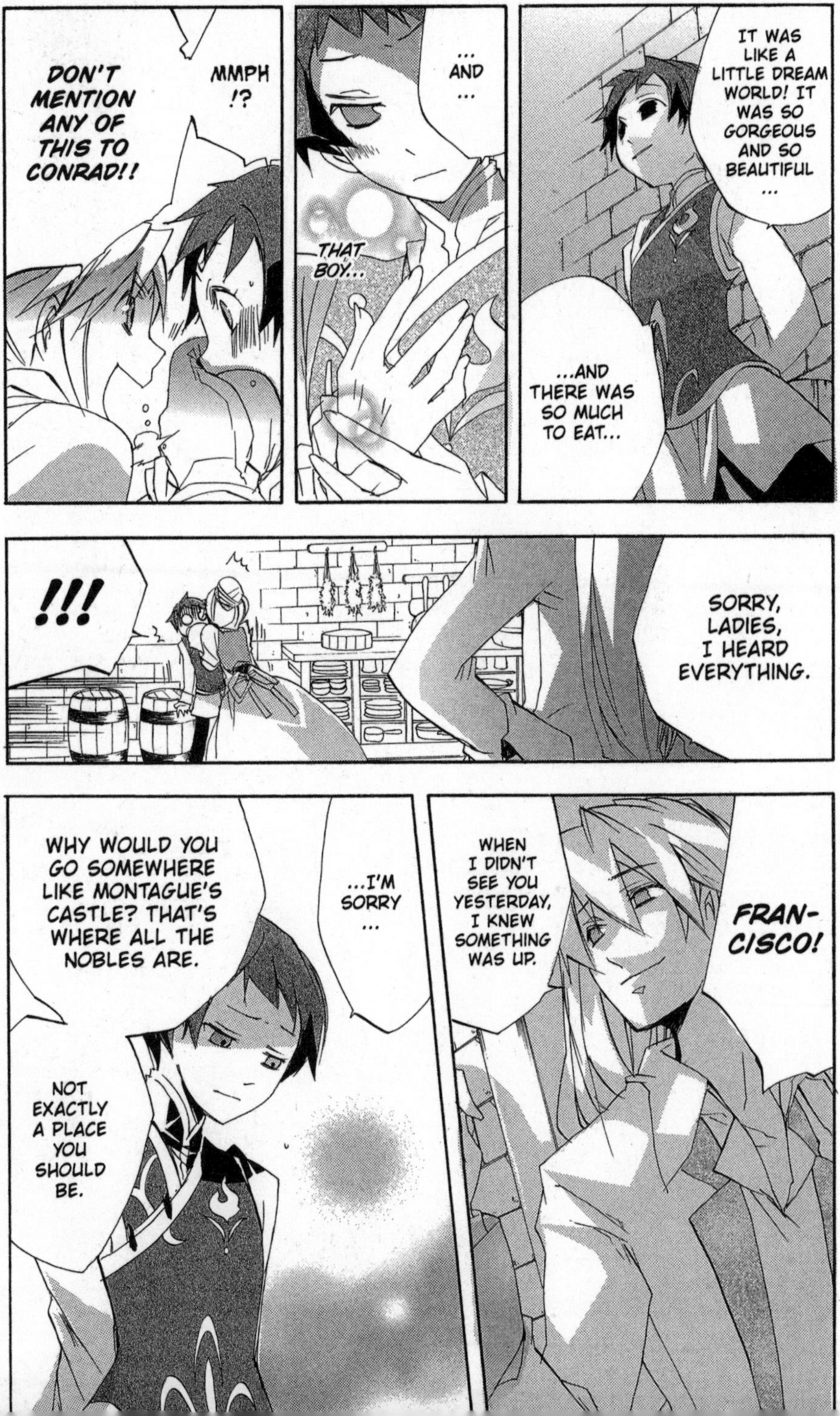
IT WAS LIKE A LITTLE DREAM WORLD! IT WAS SO GORGEOUS AND SO BEAUTIFUL ...
...AND THERE WAS SO MUCH TO EAT...
... AND ...
THAT BOY...
MMPH !?
DON'T MENTION ANY OF THIS TO CONRAD!!
SORRY, LADIES, I HEARD EVERYTHING.
!!!
FRAN-CISCO!
WHEN I DIDN'T SEE YOU YESTERDAY, I KNEW SOMETHING WAS UP.
...I'M SORRY ...
WHY WOULD YOU GO SOMEWHERE LIKE MONTAGUE'S CASTLE? THAT'S WHERE ALL THE NOBLES ARE.
NOT EXACTLY A PLACE YOU SHOULD BE.

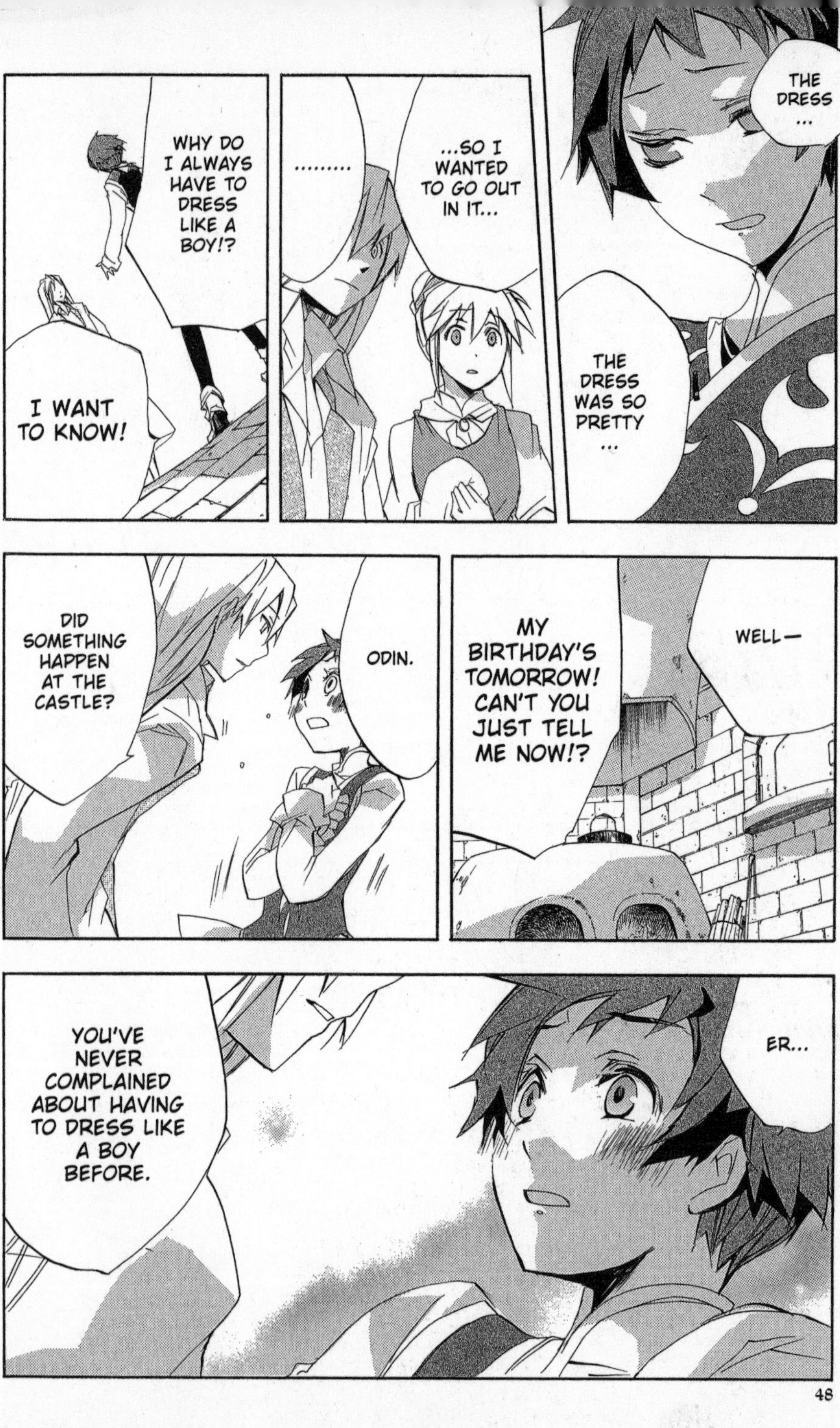
THE DRESS ...
THE DRESS WAS SO PRETTY ...
...SO I WANTED TO GO OUT IN IT...
....
WHY DO I ALWAYS HAVE TO DRESS LIKE A BOY!?
I WANT TO KNOW!
WELL—
MY BIRTHDAY'S TOMORROW! CAN'T YOU JUST TELL ME NOW!?
ODIN.
DID SOMETHING HAPPEN AT THE CASTLE?
ER...
YOU'VE NEVER COMPLAINED ABOUT HAVING TO DRESS LIKE A BOY BEFORE.

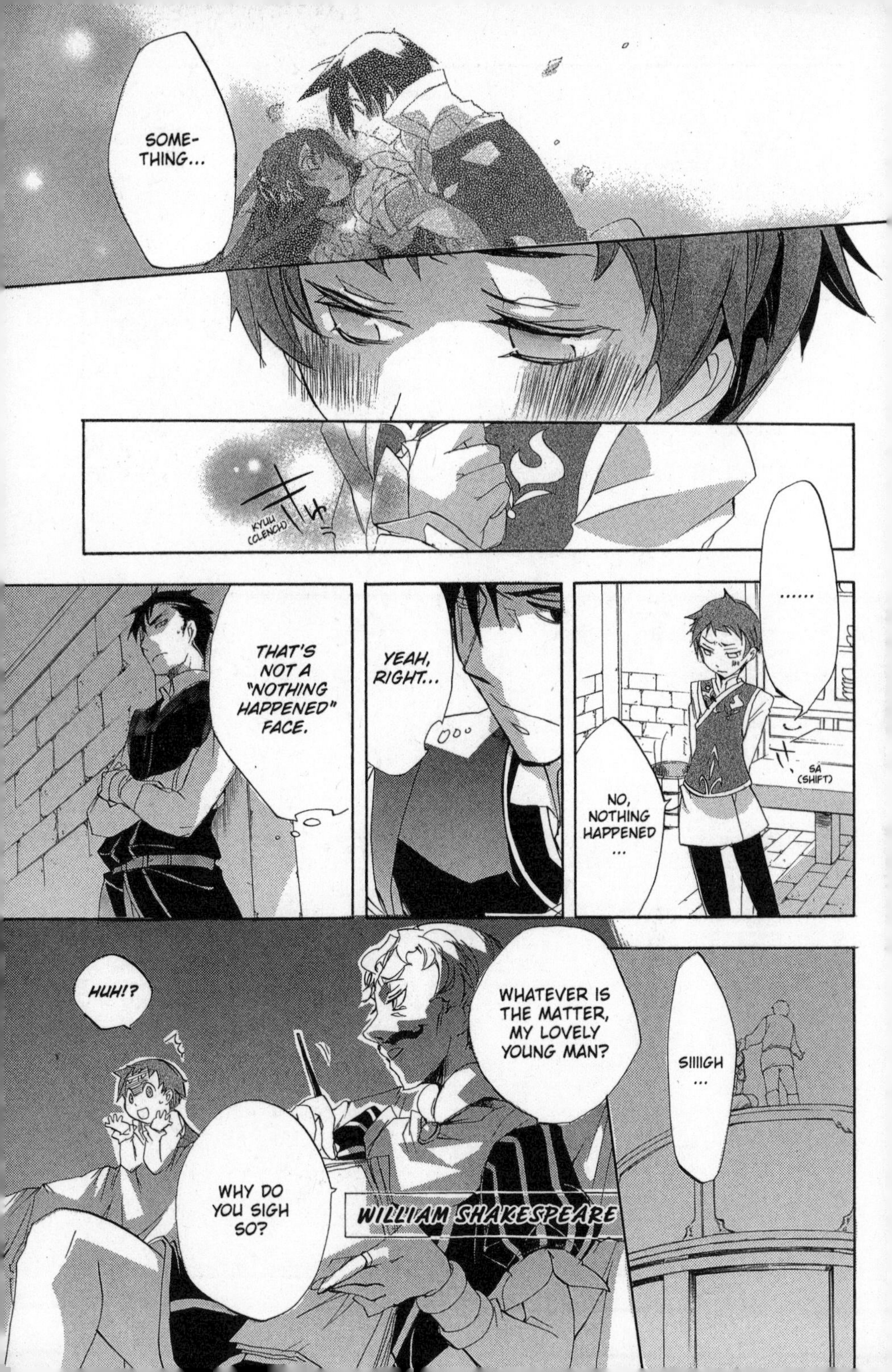
SOME-THING...
KYUU (CLENCH)
......
SA (SHIFT)
NO, NOTHING HAPPENED ...
YEAH, RIGHT...
THAT'S NOT A "NOTHING HAPPENED" FACE.
SIIIGH ...
WHATEVER IS THE MATTER, MY LOVELY YOUNG MAN?
HUH!?
WHY DO YOU SIGH SO?
WILLIAM SHAKESPEARE

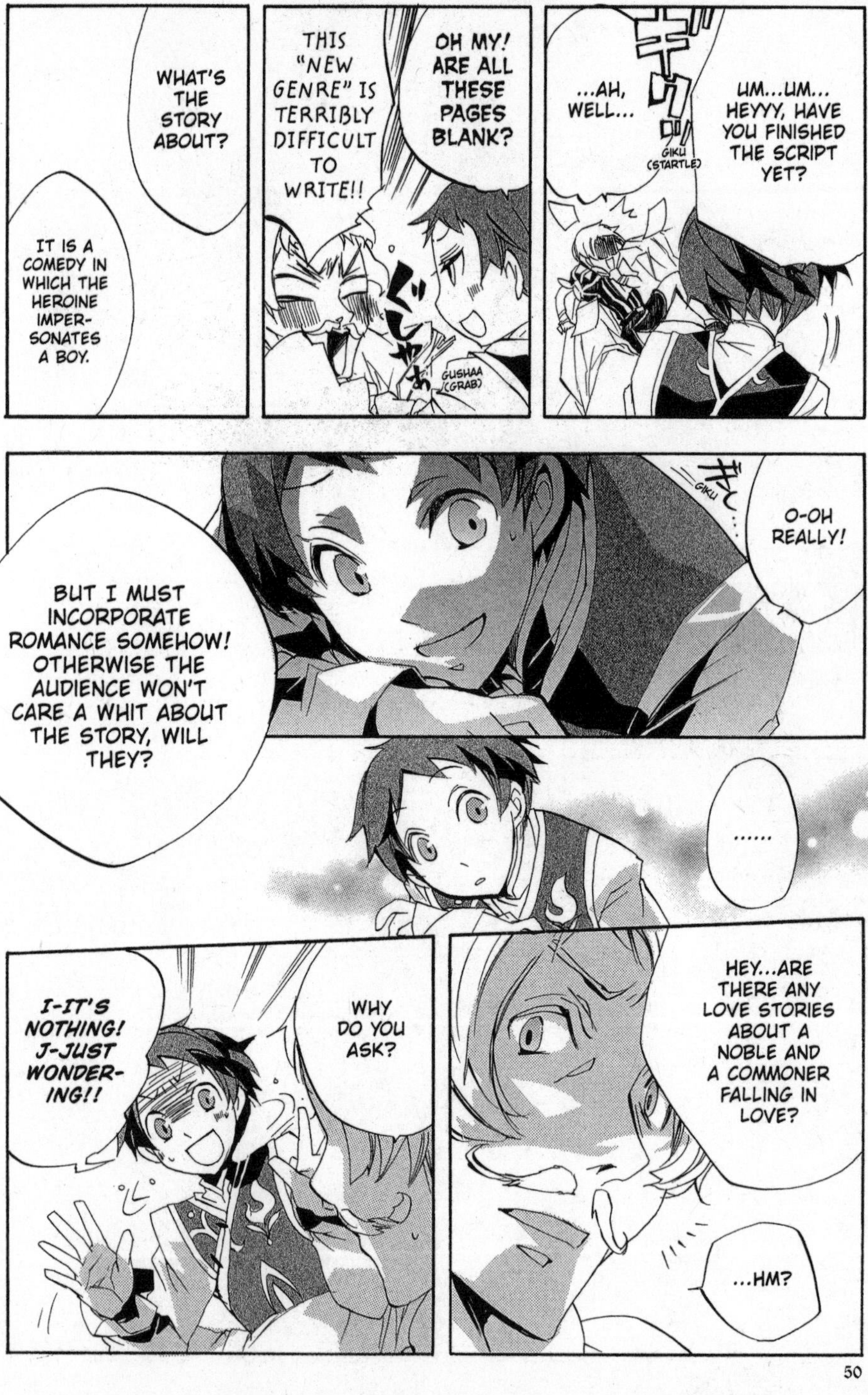
UM...UM... HEYYY, HAVE YOU FINISHED THE SCRIPT YET?
GIKU (STARTLE)
...AH, WELL...
OH MY! ARE ALL THESE PAGES BLANK?
THIS "NEW GENRE" IS TERRIBLY DIFFICULT TO WRITE!!
GUSHAA (GRAB)
WHAT'S THE STORY ABOUT?
IT IS A COMEDY IN WHICH THE HEROINE IMPERSONATES A BOY.
GIKU
O-OH REALLY!
BUT I MUST INCORPORATE ROMANCE SOMEHOW! OTHERWISE THE AUDIENCE WON'T CARE A WHIT ABOUT THE STORY, WILL THEY?
......
HEY...ARE THERE ANY LOVE STORIES ABOUT A NOBLE AND A COMMONER FALLING IN LOVE?
...HM?
WHY DO YOU ASK?
I-IT'S NOTHING! J-JUST WONDERING!!

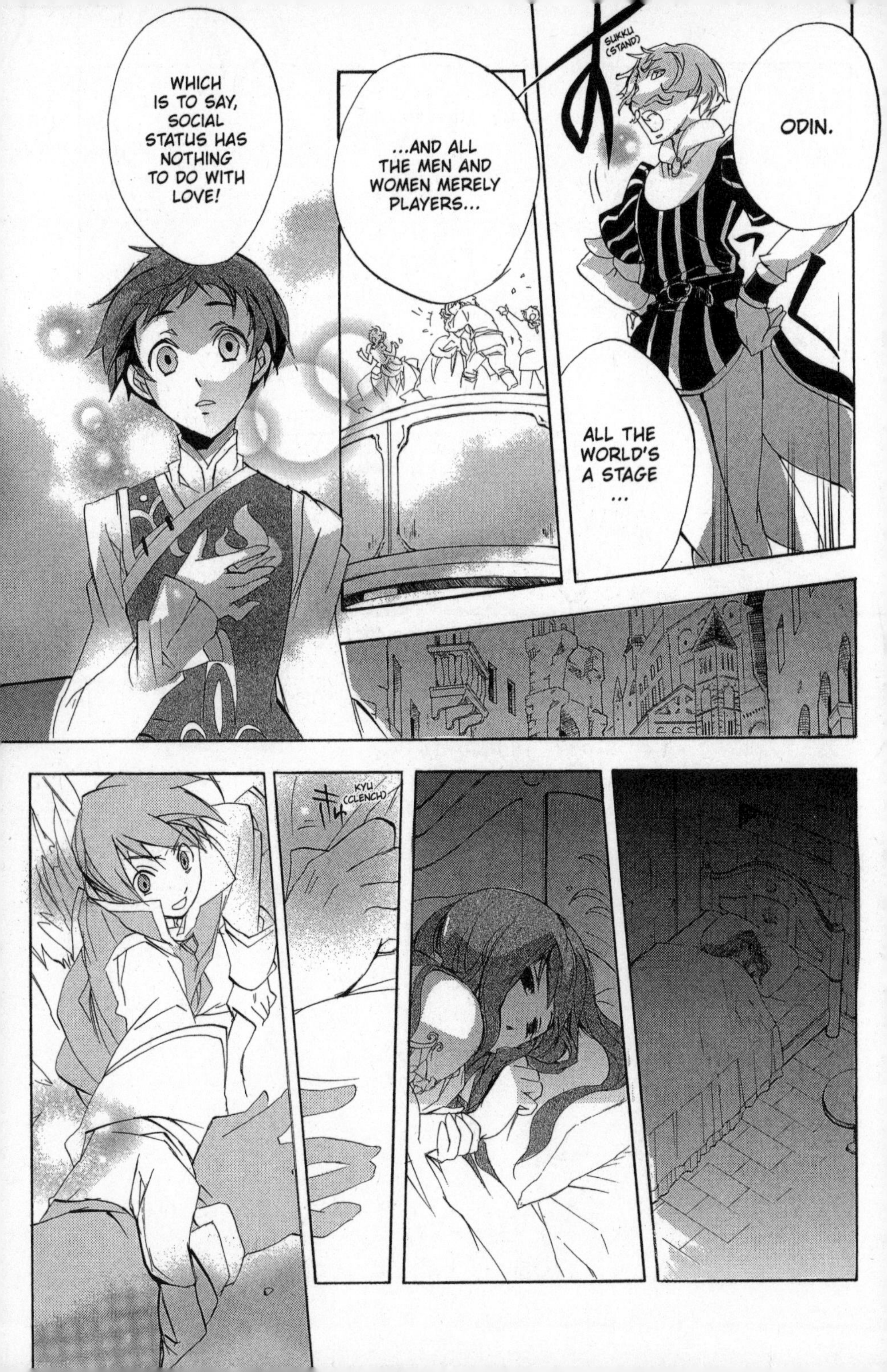
SUKKU (STAND)
ODIN.
ALL THE WORLD'S A STAGE ...
...AND ALL THE MEN AND WOMEN MERELY PLAYERS...
WHICH IS TO SAY, SOCIAL STATUS HAS NOTHING TO DO WITH LOVE!
KYU (CLENCH)

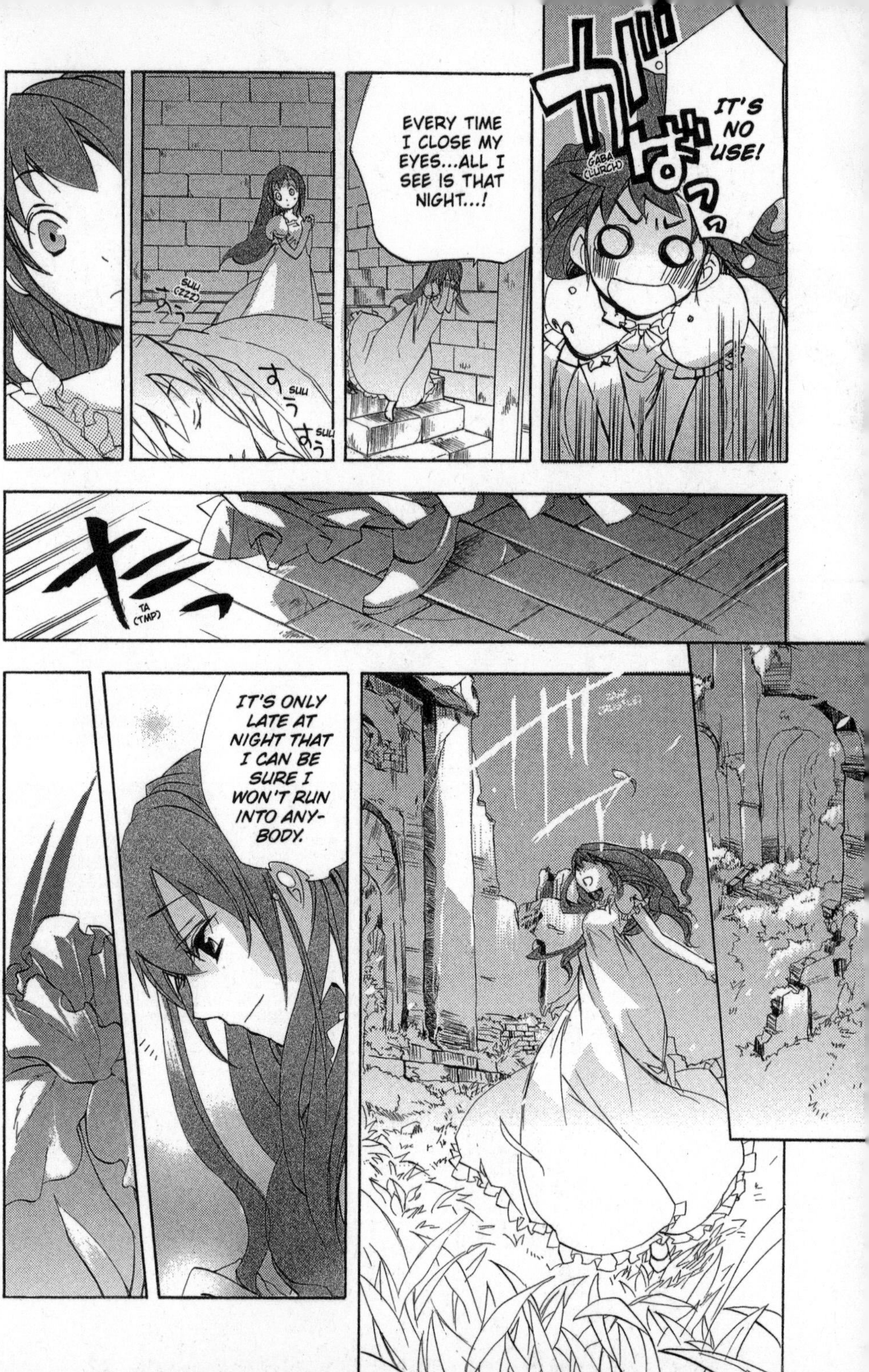

GABA (LURCH)
IT'S NO USE!
EVERY TIME I CLOSE MY EYES...ALL I SEE IS THAT NIGHT...!
SUU (ZZZ)
SUU
SUU
TA (TMP)
IT'S ONLY LATE AT NIGHT THAT I CAN BE SURE I WON'T RUN INTO ANYBODY.

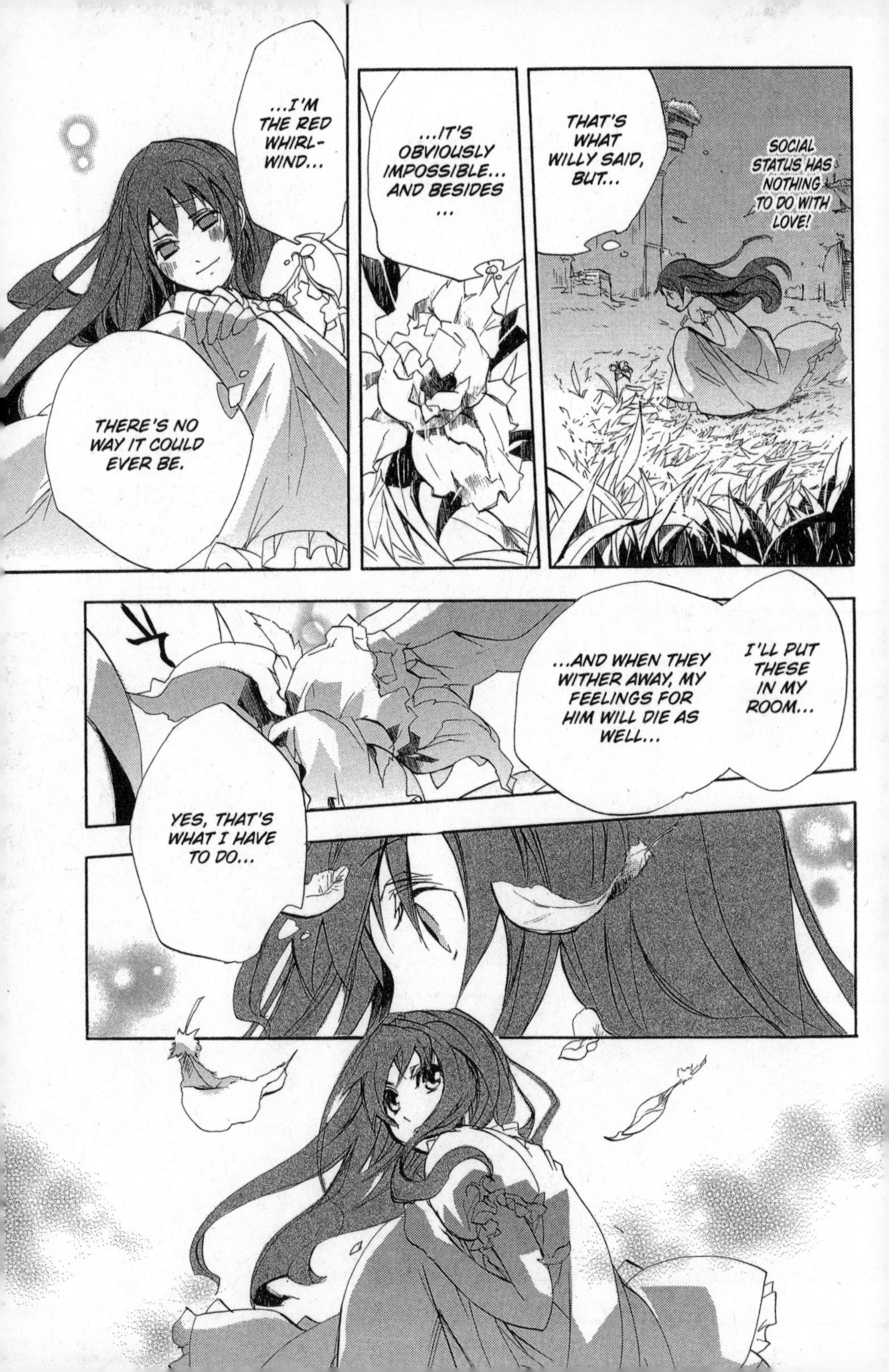
SOCIAL STATUS HAS NOTHING TO DO WITH LOVE!
THAT'S WHAT WILLY SAID, BUT...
...IT'S OBVIOUSLY IMPOSSIBLE... AND BESIDES ...
...I'M THE RED WHIRL-WIND...
THERE'S NO WAY IT COULD EVER BE.
I'LL PUT THESE IN MY ROOM...
...AND WHEN THEY WITHER AWAY, MY FEELINGS FOR HIM WILL DIE AS WELL...
YES, THAT'S WHAT I HAVE TO DO...

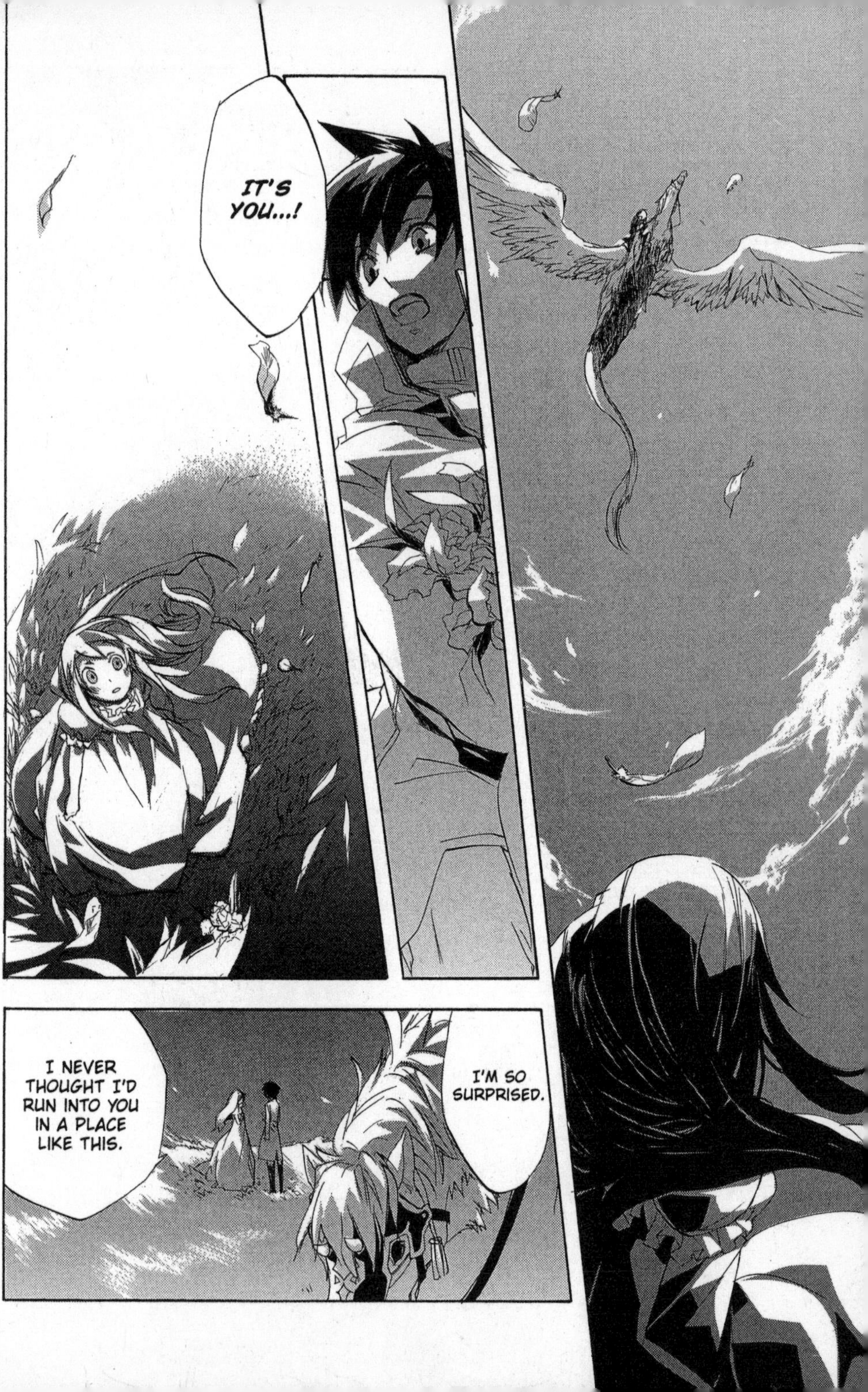
IT'S YOU...!
I'M SO SURPRISED.
I NEVER THOUGHT I'D RUN INTO YOU IN A PLACE LIKE THIS.

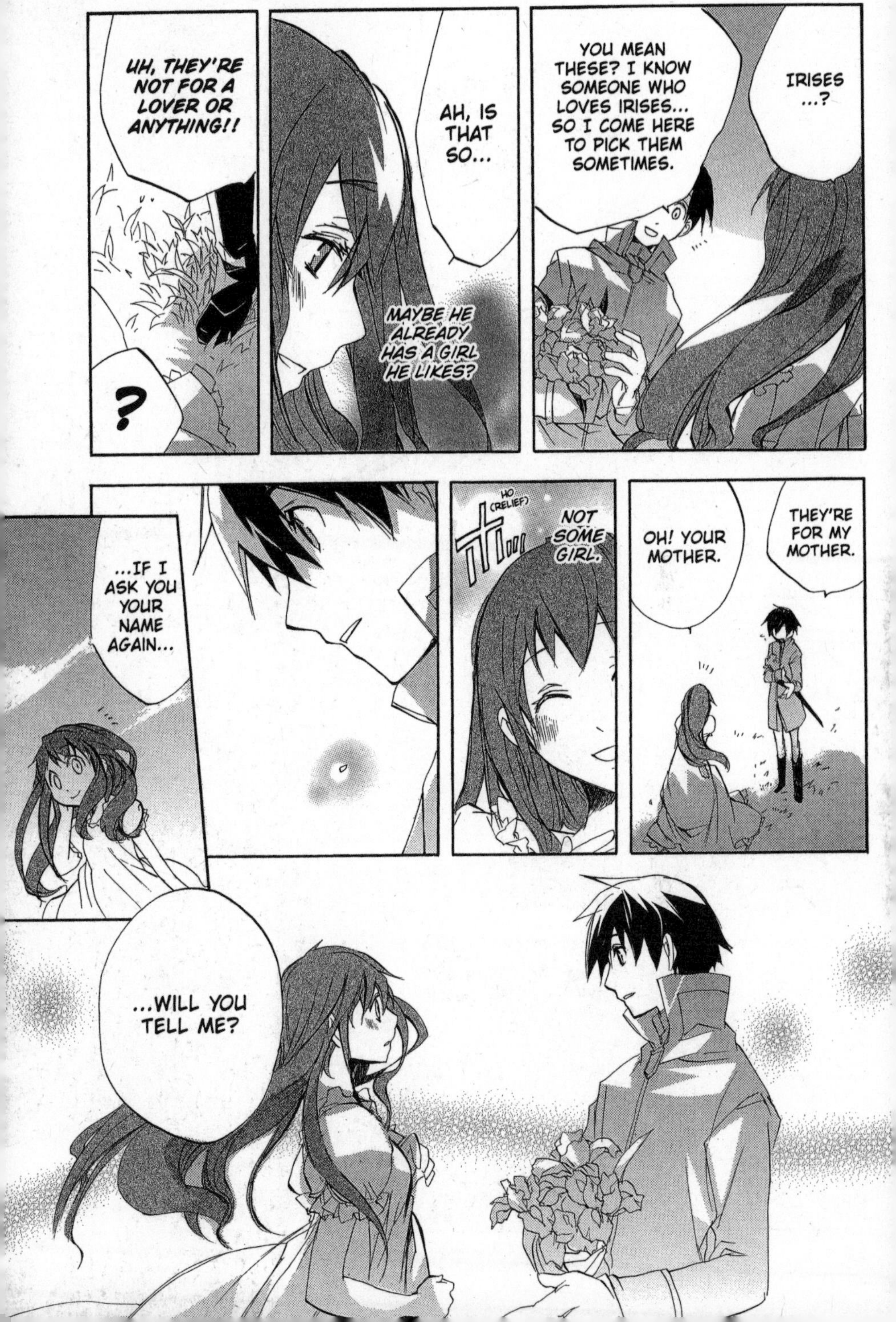
IRISES ...?
YOU MEAN THESE? I KNOW SOMEONE WHO LOVES IRISES... SO I COME HERE TO PICK THEM SOMETIMES.
AH, IS THAT SO...
MAYBE HE ALREADY HAS A GIRL HE LIKES?
UH, THEY'RE NOT FOR A LOVER OR ANYTHING!!
?
THEY'RE FOR MY MOTHER.
OH! YOUR MOTHER.
HO (RELIEF)
NOT SOME GIRL.
...IF I ASK YOU YOUR NAME AGAIN...
...WILL YOU TELL ME?

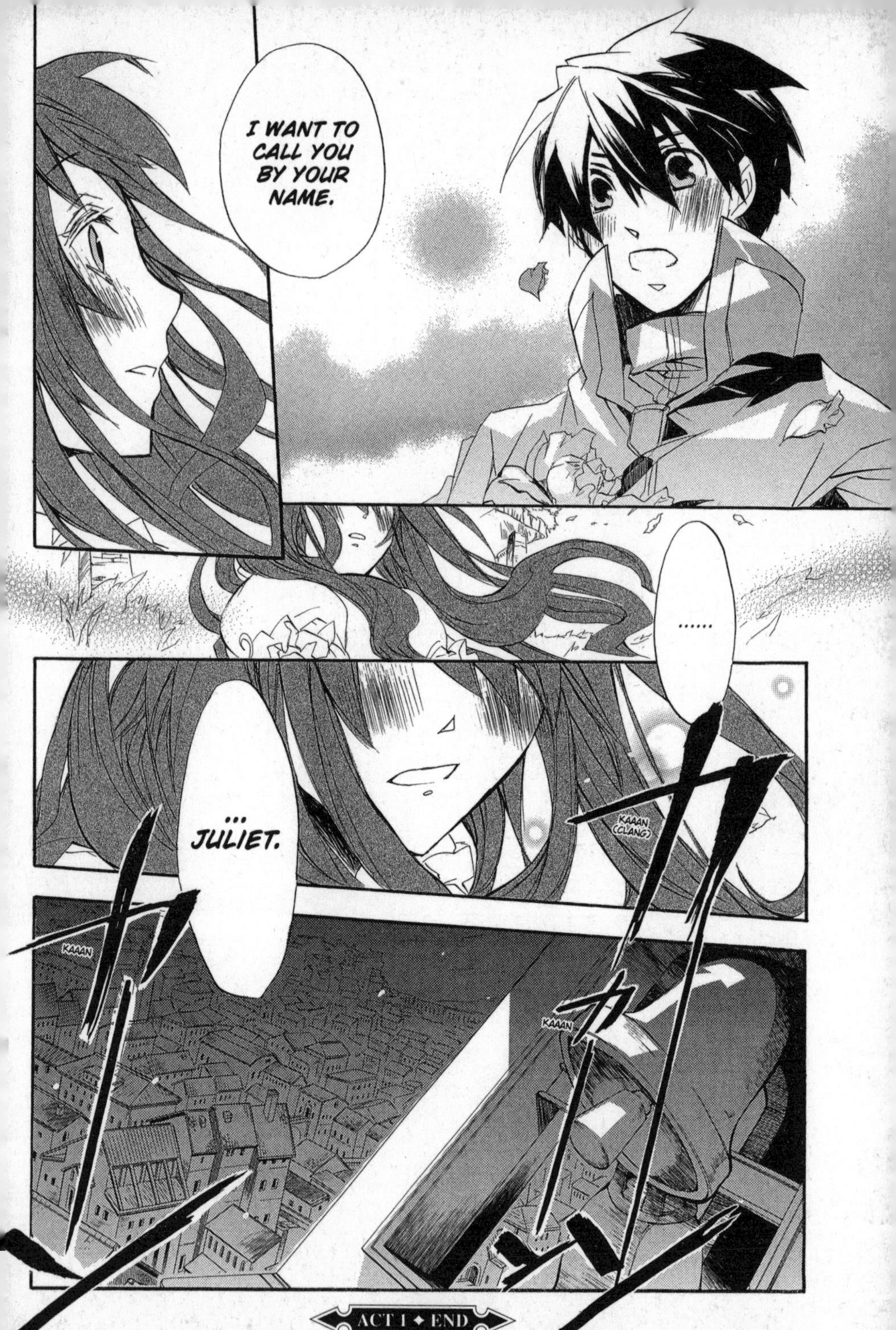
I WANT TO CALL YOU BY YOUR NAME.
......
...JULIET.
KAAAN (CLANG)
KAAAN
KAAAN

ACT 1 ◆ END

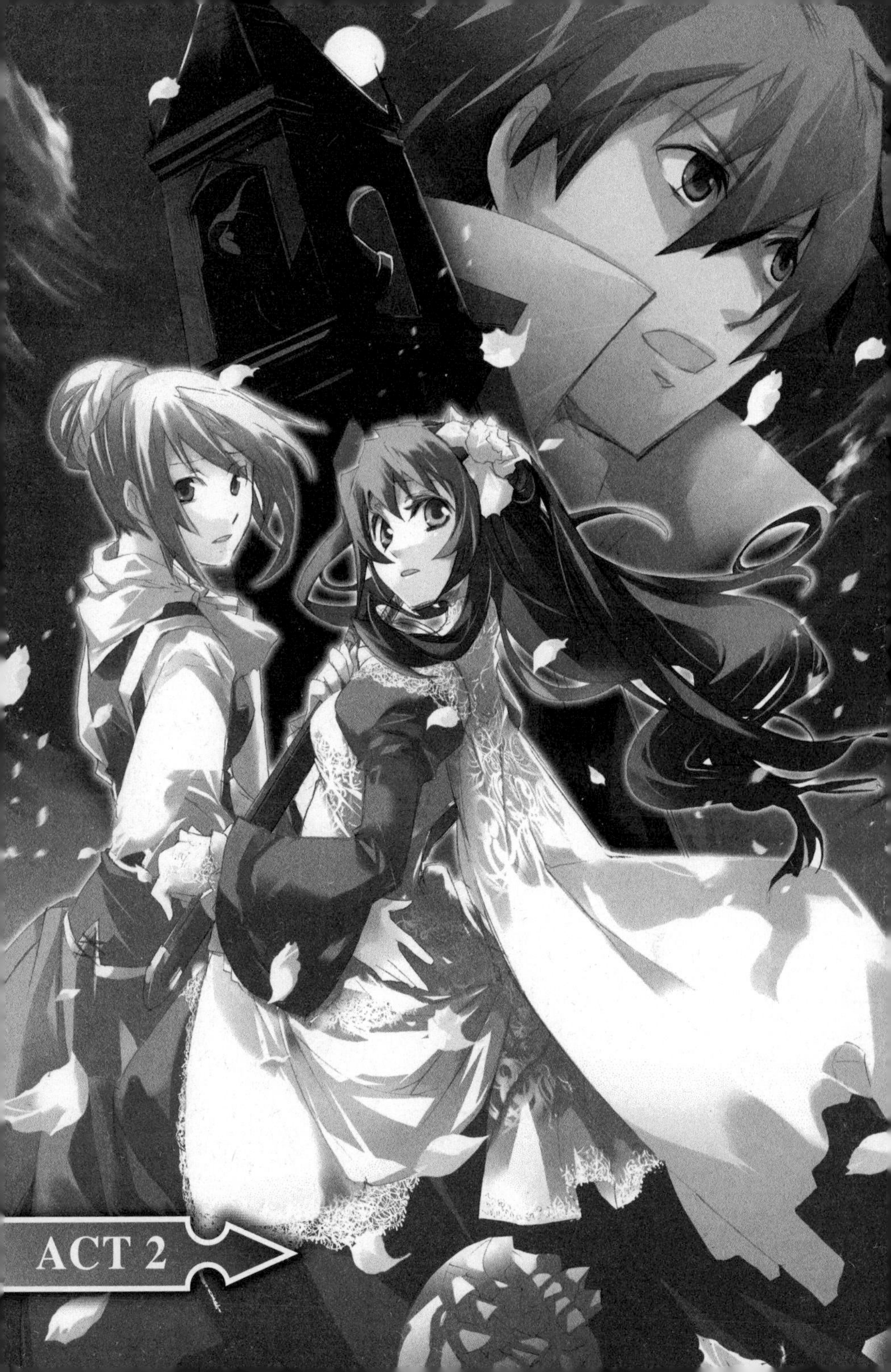
ACT 2

Romeo×Juliet

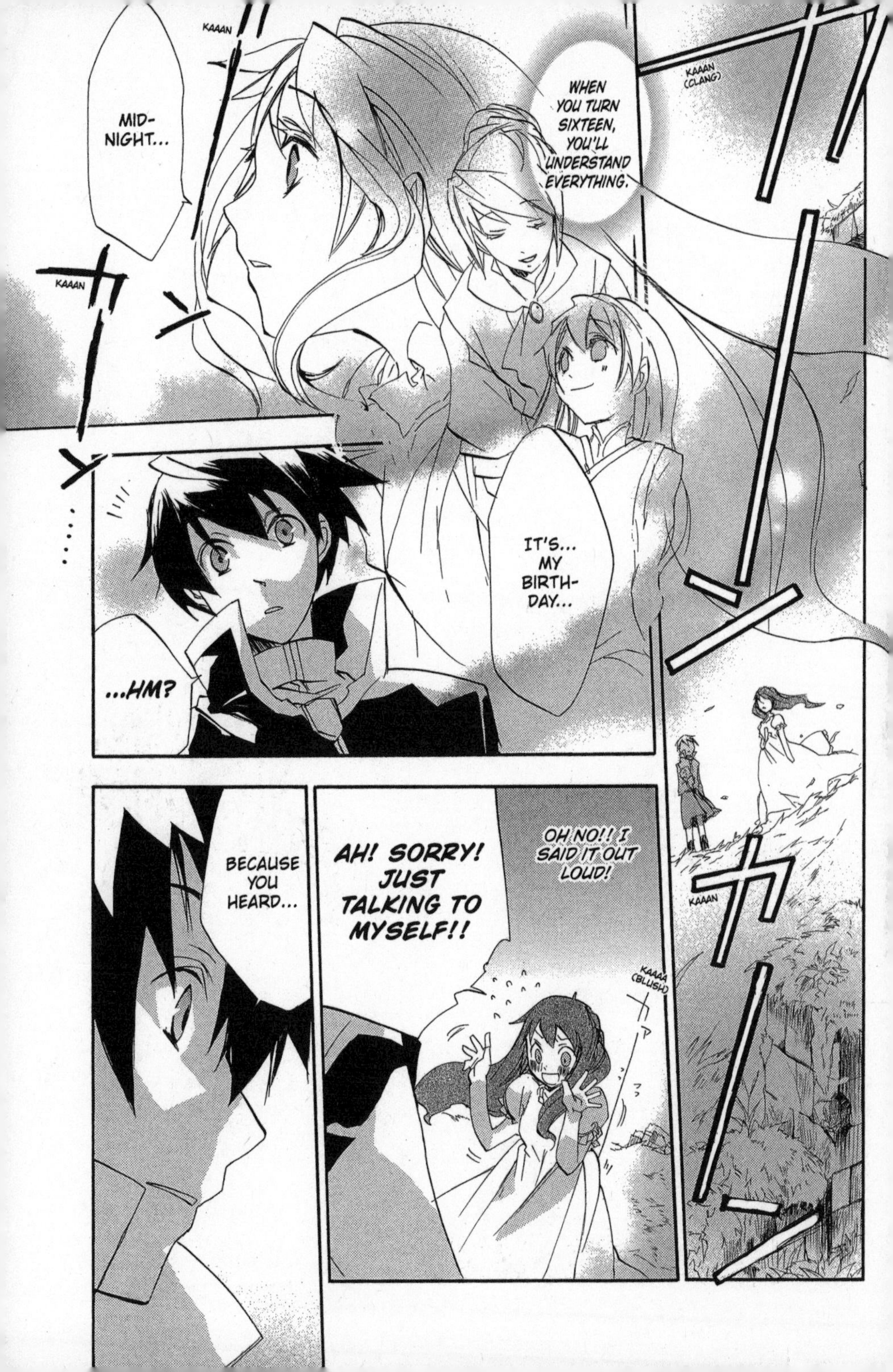
KAAAN (CLANG)
KAAAN
WHEN YOU TURN SIXTEEN, YOU'LL UNDERSTAND EVERYTHING.
MID-NIGHT...
KAAAN
KAAAN
IT'S... MY BIRTH-DAY...
...HM?
OH NO!! I SAID IT OUT LOUD!
KAAAA (BLUSH)
AH! SORRY! JUST TALKING TO MYSELF!!
BECAUSE YOU HEARD...

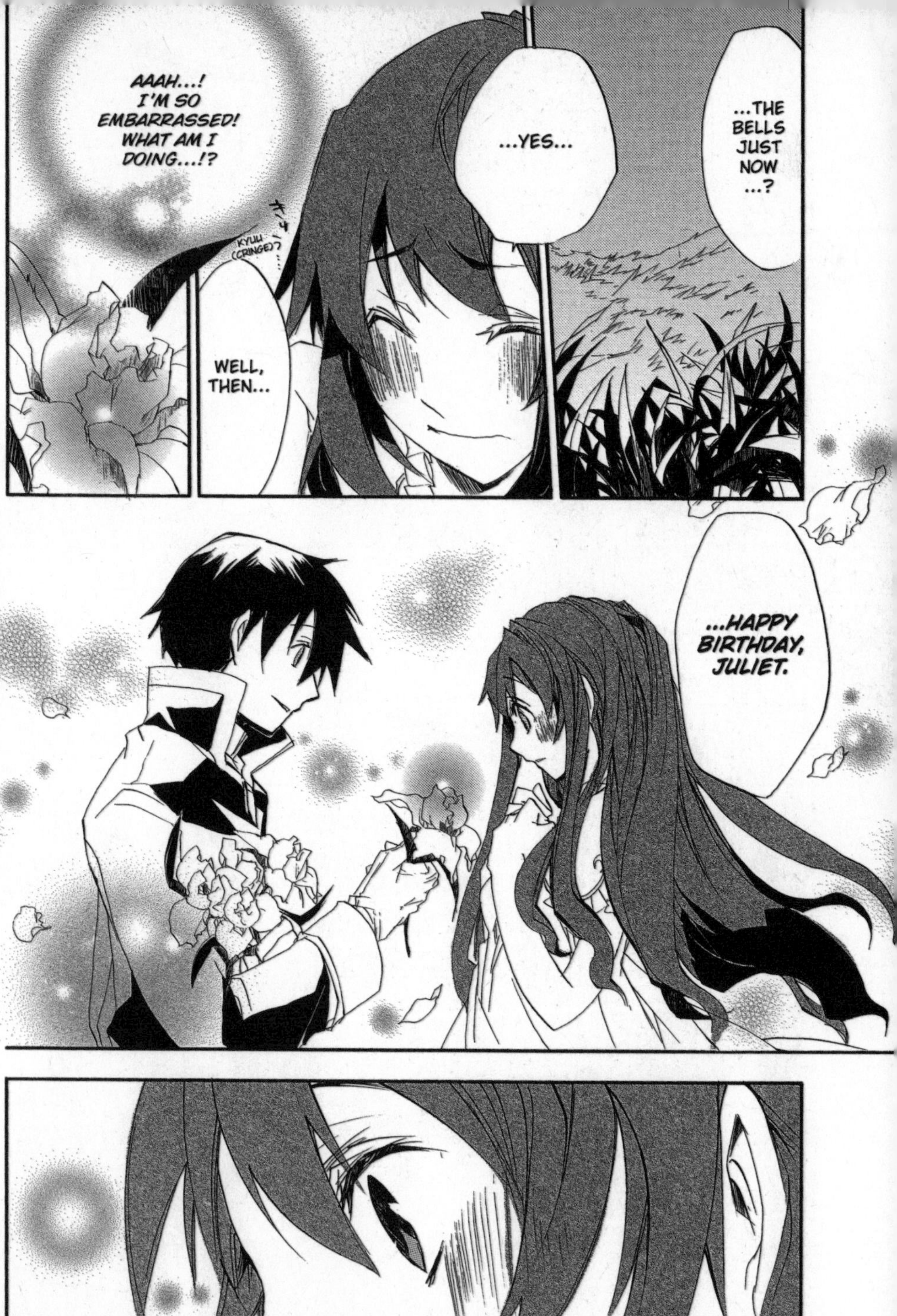
...THE BELLS JUST NOW ...?
...YES...
WELL, THEN...
AAAH...! I'M SO EMBARRASSED! WHAT AM I DOING...!?
KYUU (CRINGE)
...HAPPY BIRTHDAY, JULIET.

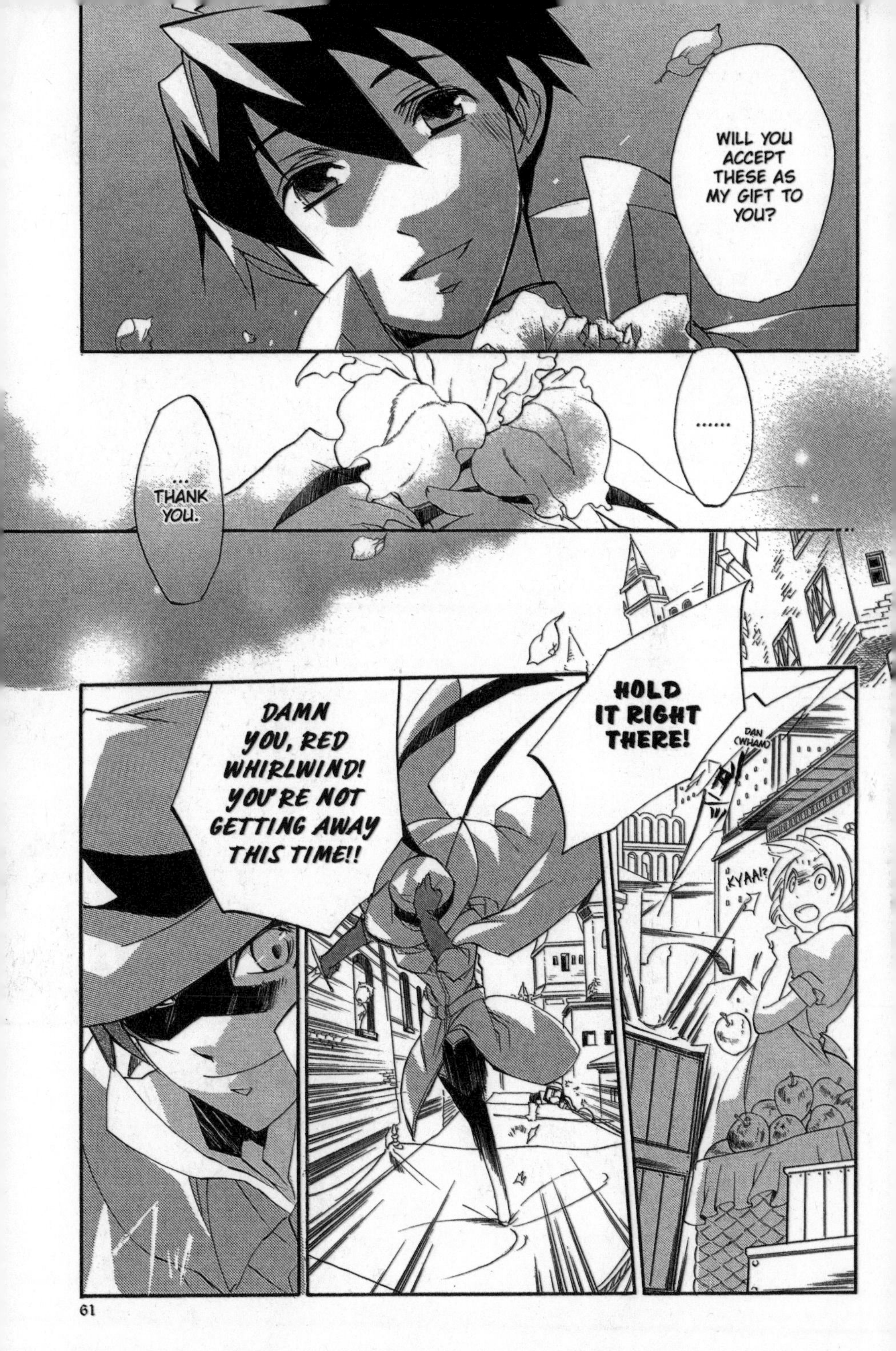
WILL YOU ACCEPT THESE AS MY GIFT TO YOU?
......
...THANK YOU.
HOLD IT RIGHT THERE!
DAN (WHAN)
KYAA!?
DAMN YOU, RED WHIRLWIND! YOU'RE NOT GETTING AWAY THIS TIME!!

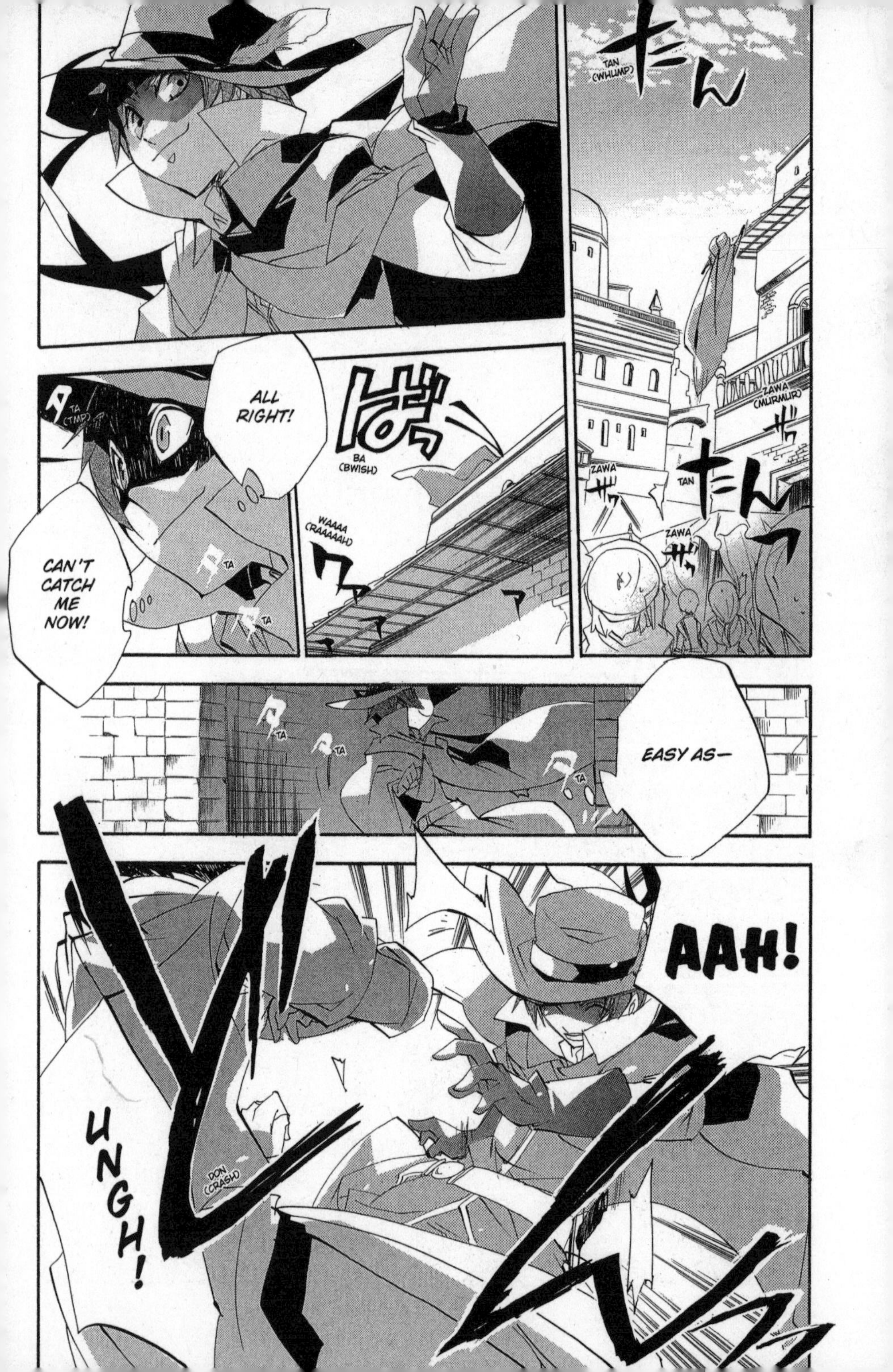
TAN (WHUMP)
ZAWA (MURMUR)
ZAWA
TAN
ZAWA
BA (BWISH)
WAAAA (RAAAAAH)
ALL RIGHT!
TA (TMP)
CAN'T CATCH ME NOW!
TA
TA
EASY AS—
TA
TA
TA
AAH!
UNGH!
DON (CRASH)

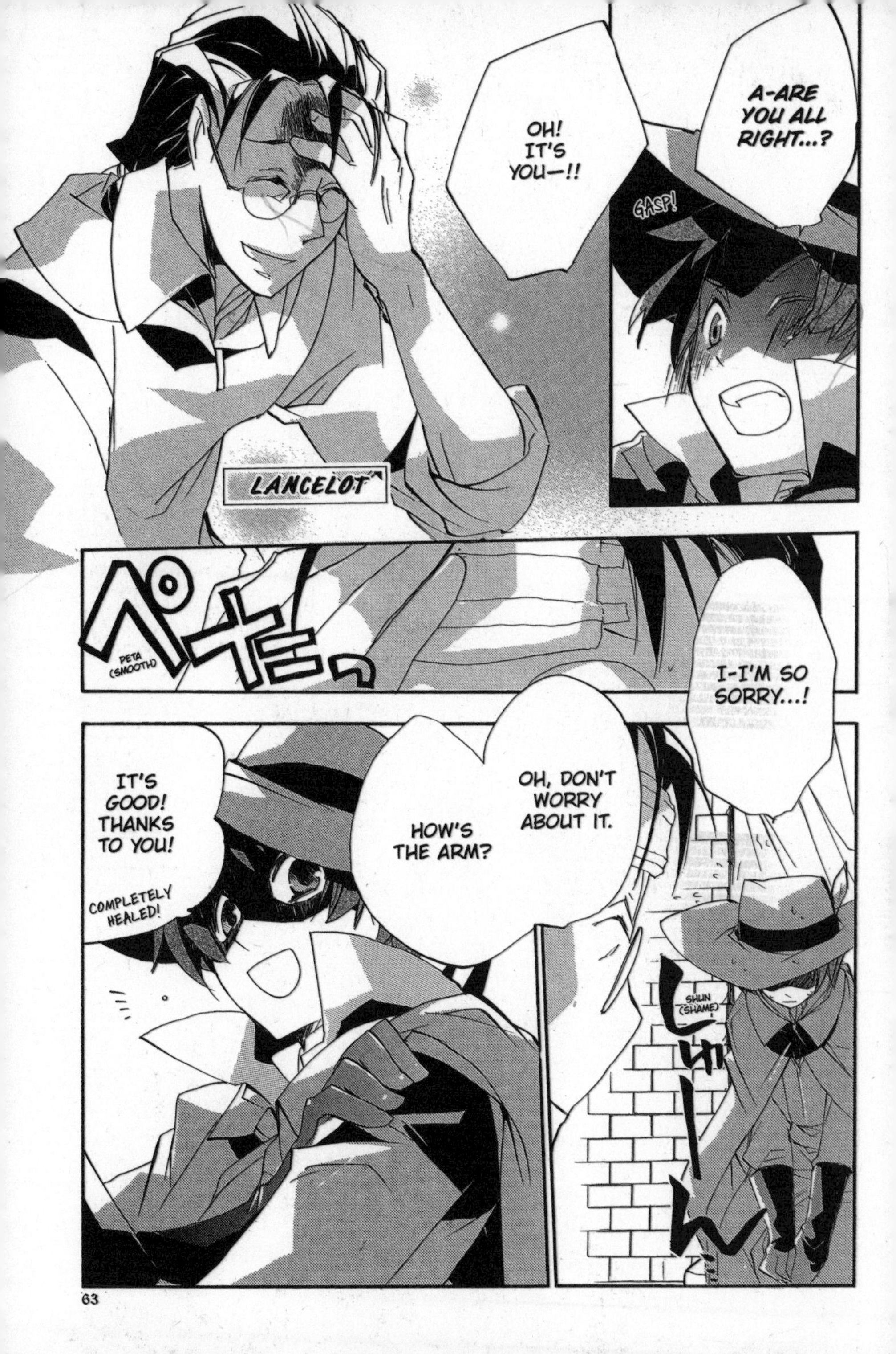
A-ARE YOU ALL RIGHT...?
GASP!
OH! IT'S YOU—!!
LANCELOT
ぺたっ
PETA (SMOOTH)
I-I'M SO SORRY...!
SHUN (SHAME)
OH, DON'T WORRY ABOUT IT.
HOW'S THE ARM?
IT'S GOOD! THANKS TO YOU!
COMPLETELY HEALED!

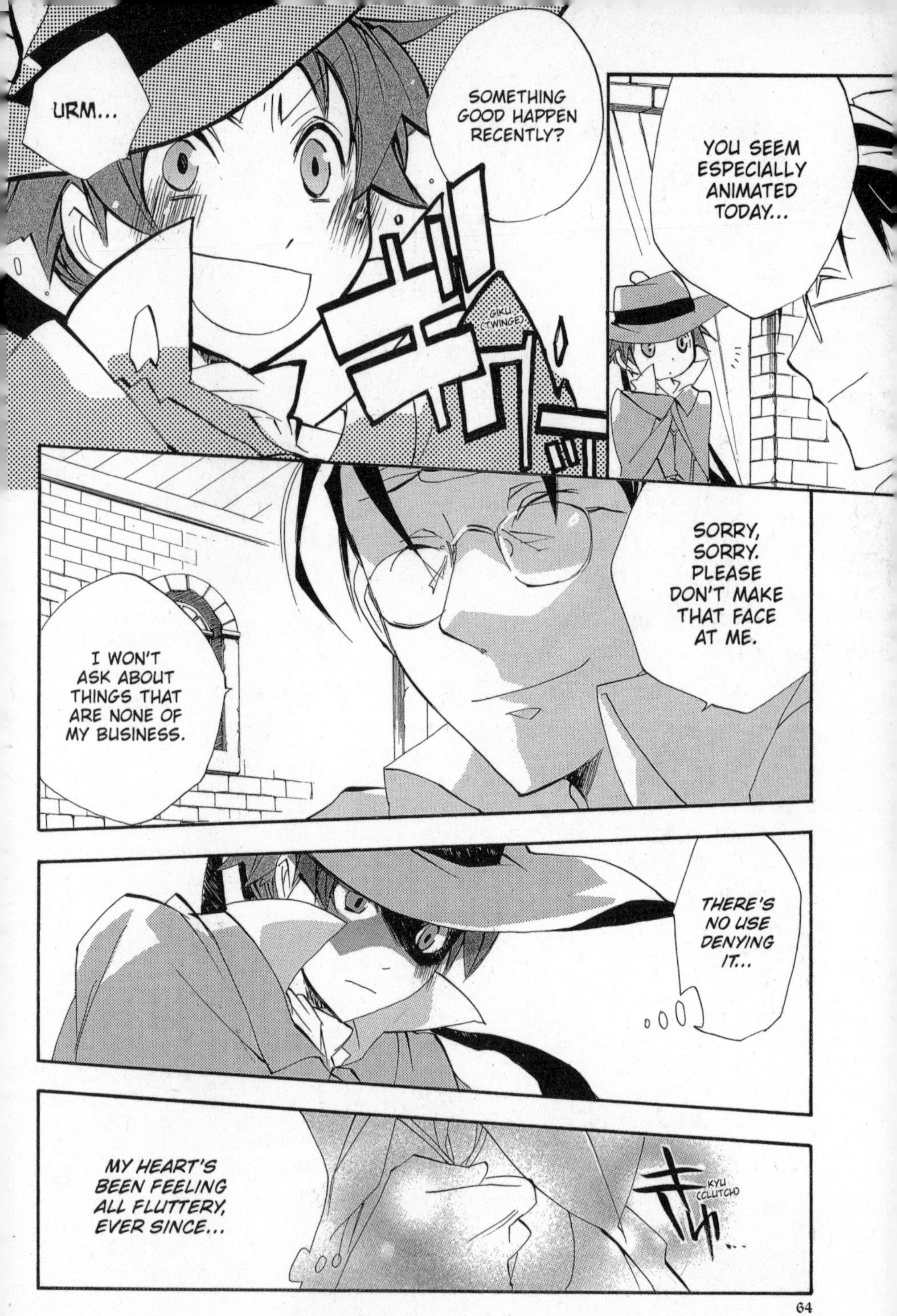
YOU SEEM ESPECIALLY ANIMATED TODAY...
SOMETHING GOOD HAPPEN RECENTLY?
URM...
GIKU (TWINGE)
SORRY, SORRY. PLEASE DON'T MAKE THAT FACE AT ME.
I WON'T ASK ABOUT THINGS THAT ARE NONE OF MY BUSINESS.
THERE'S NO USE DENYING IT...
KYU (CLUTCH)
MY HEART'S BEEN FEELING ALL FLUTTERY, EVER SINCE...

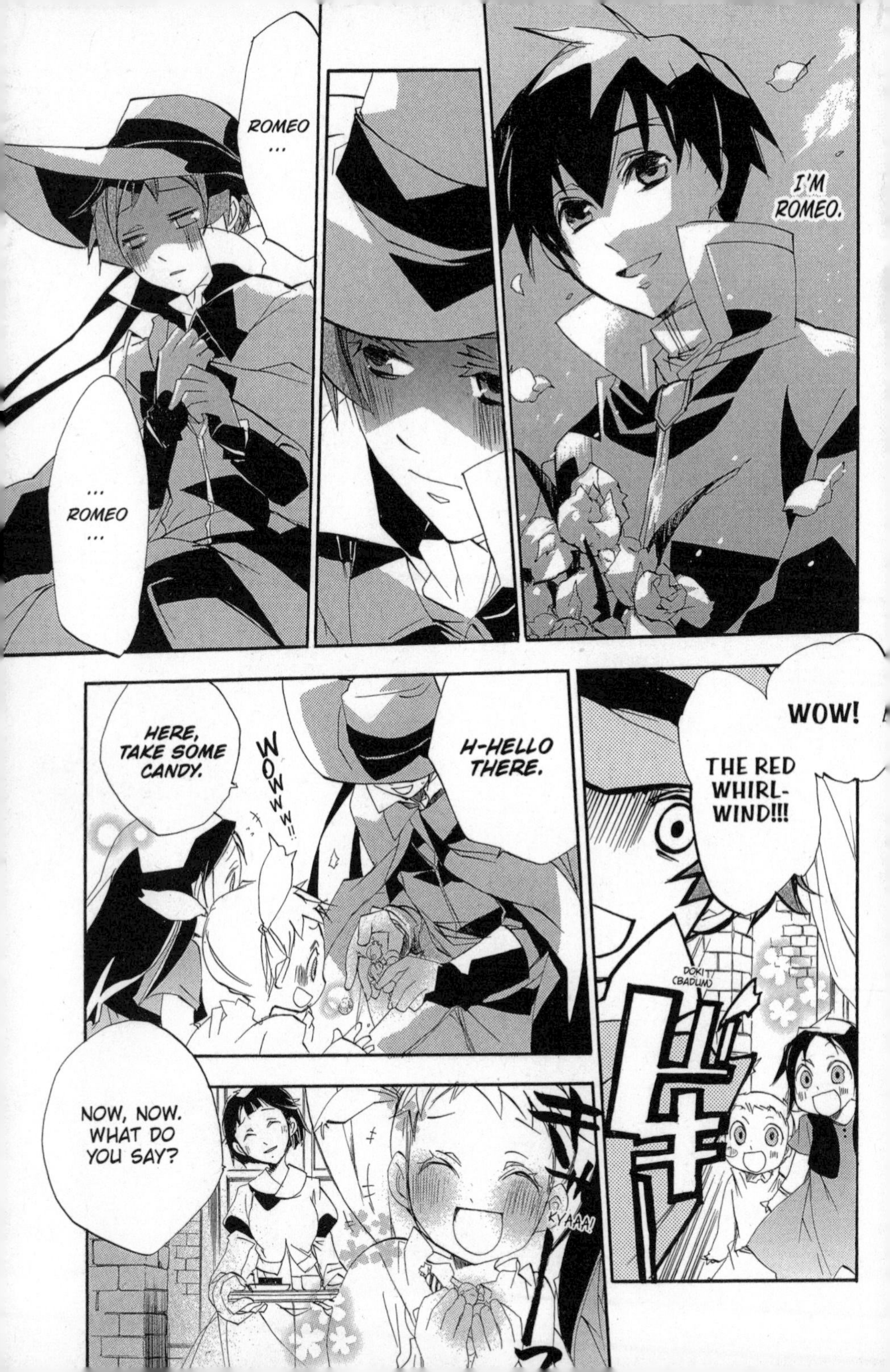
I'M ROMEO.
ROMEO ...
... ROMEO ...
WOW!
THE RED WHIRL-WIND!!!
H-HELLO THERE.
WOWWW!!
HERE, TAKE SOME CANDY.
DOKI (BADUM)
KYAAA!
NOW, NOW. WHAT DO YOU SAY?

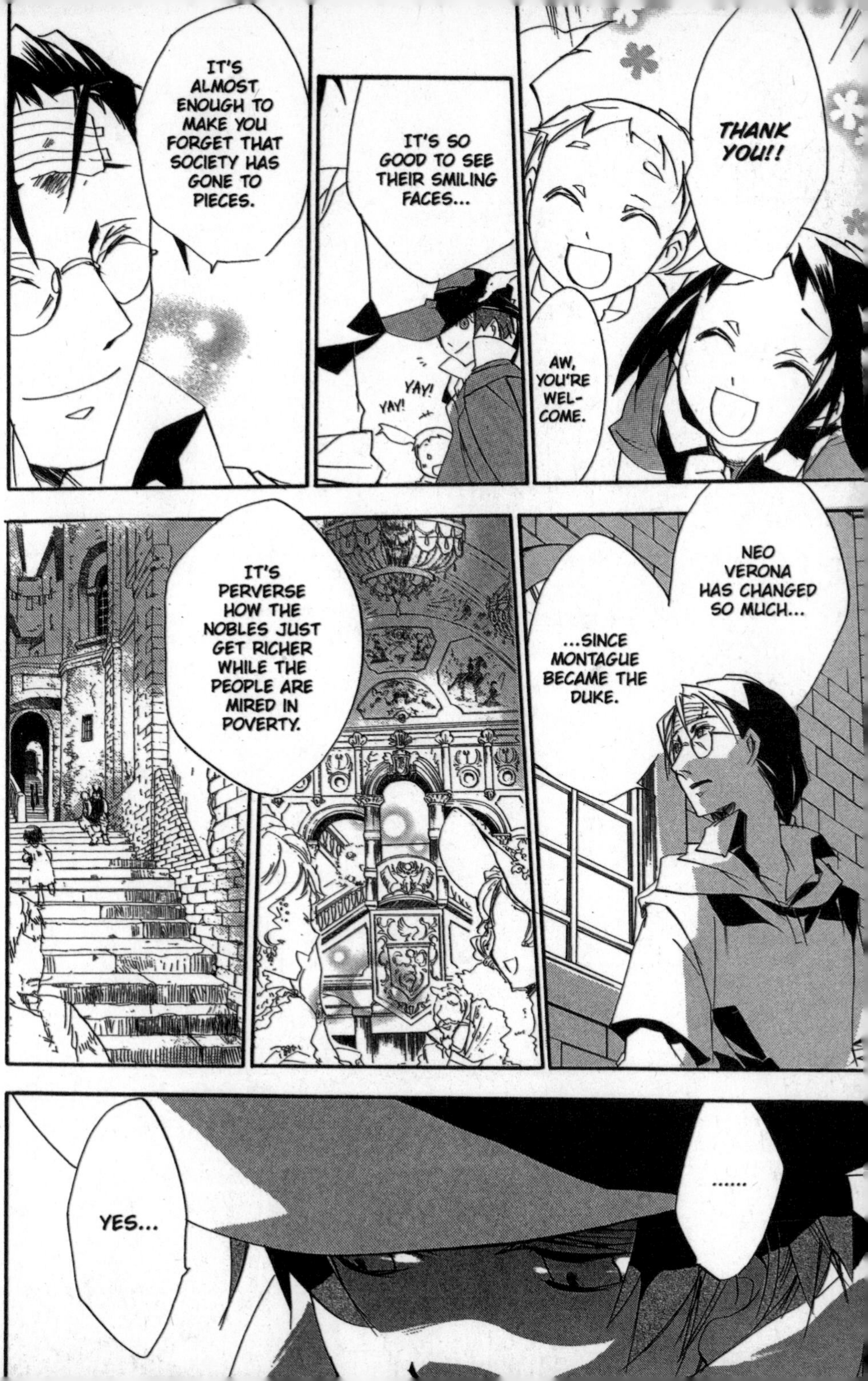
THANK YOU!!
AW, YOU'RE WEL-COME.
IT'S SO GOOD TO SEE THEIR SMILING FACES...
YAY!
YAY!
IT'S ALMOST ENOUGH TO MAKE YOU FORGET THAT SOCIETY HAS GONE TO PIECES.
NEO VERONA HAS CHANGED SO MUCH...
...SINCE MONTAGUE BECAME THE DUKE.
IT'S PERVERSE HOW THE NOBLES JUST GET RICHER WHILE THE PEOPLE ARE MIRED IN POVERTY.
......
YES...

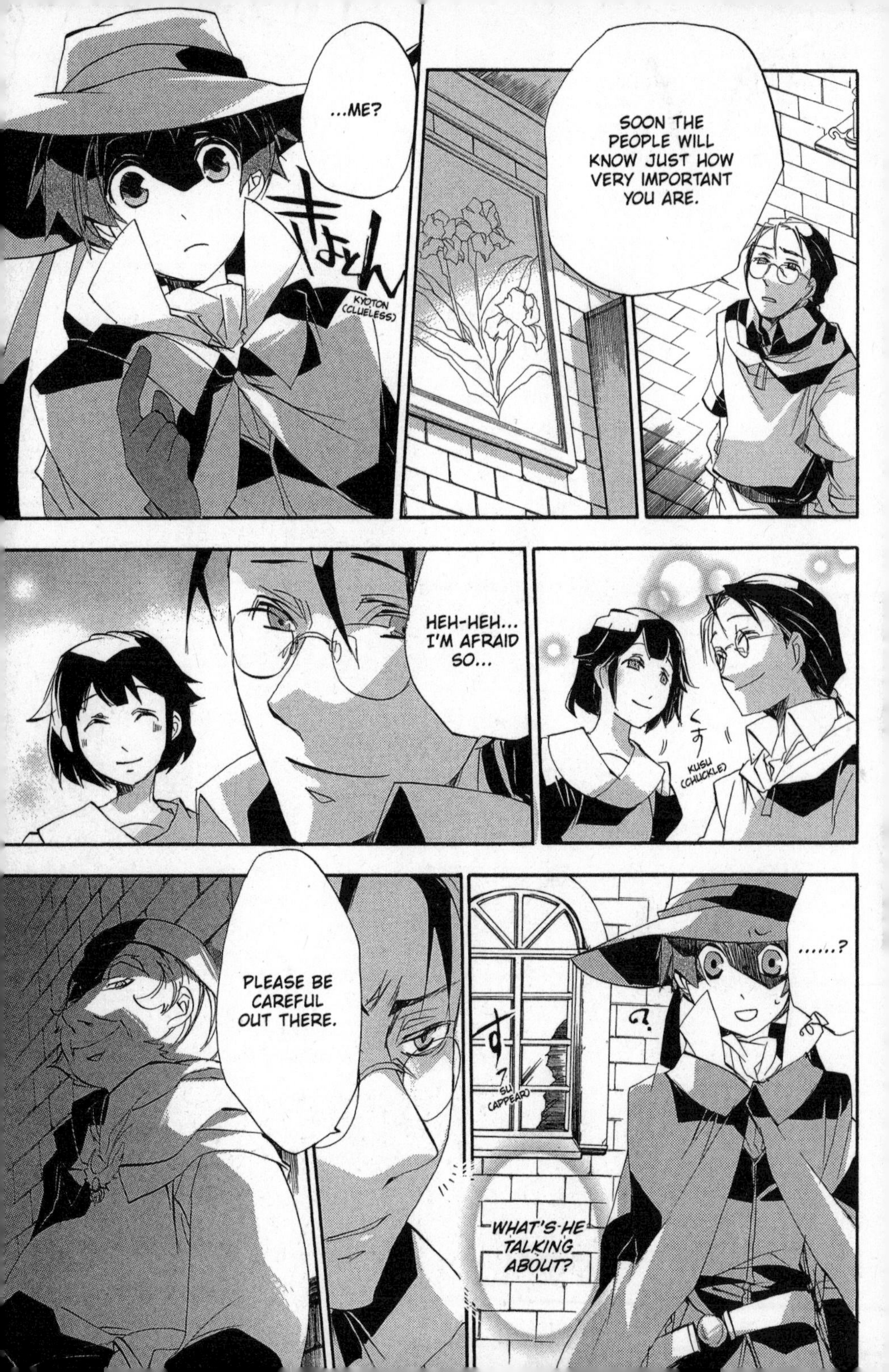
SOON THE PEOPLE WILL KNOW JUST HOW VERY IMPORTANT YOU ARE.
...ME?
きょとん
KYOTON (CLUELESS)
くす
KUSU (CHUCKLE)
HEH-HEH... I'M AFRAID SO...
......?
?
すっ
SU (APPEAR)
WHAT'S HE TALKING ABOUT?
PLEASE BE CAREFUL OUT THERE.

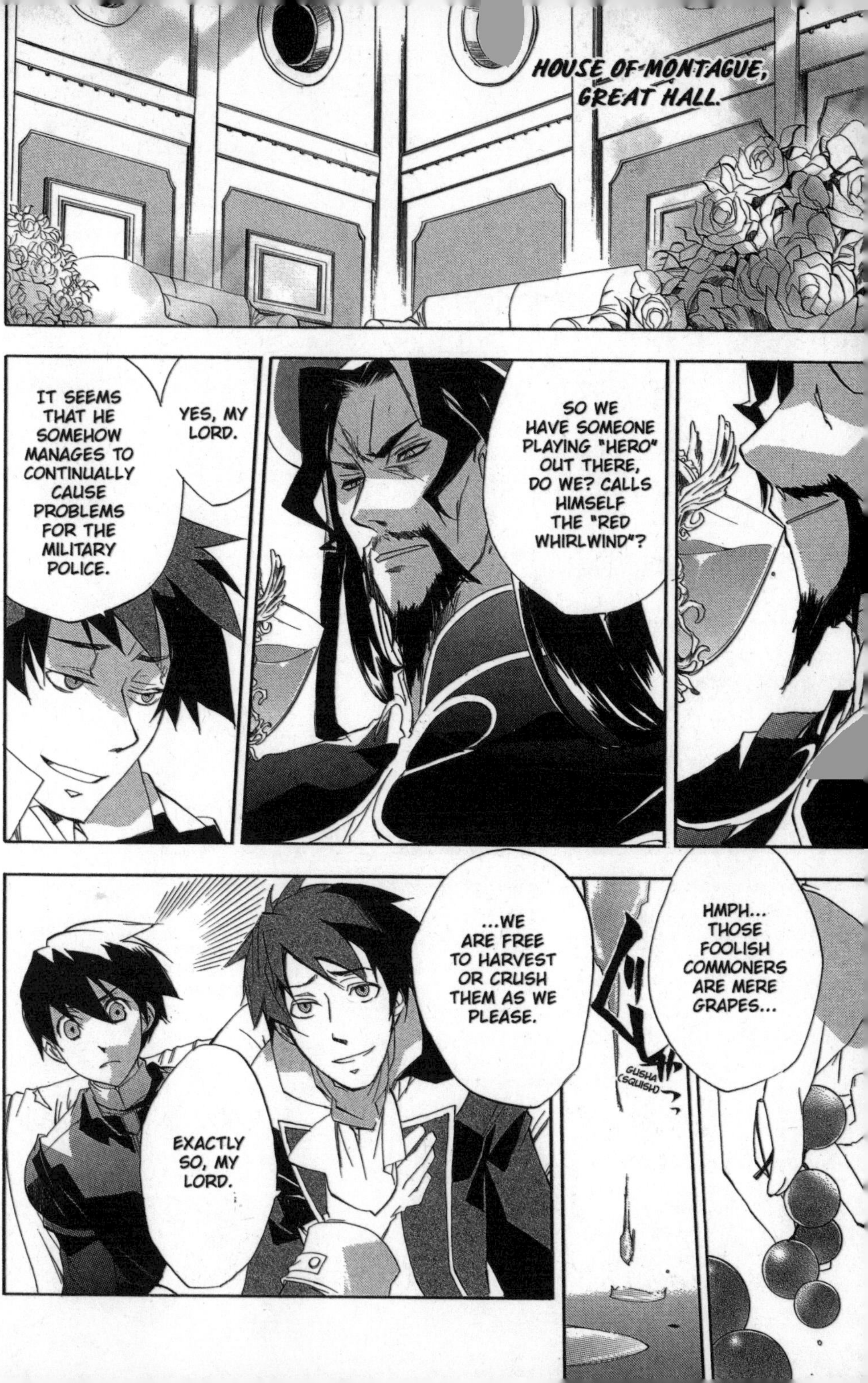
HOUSE OF MONTAGUE, GREAT HALL.
SO WE HAVE SOMEONE PLAYING "HERO" OUT THERE, DO WE? CALLS HIMSELF THE "RED WHIRLWIND"?
YES, MY LORD.
IT SEEMS THAT HE SOMEHOW MANAGES TO CONTINUALLY CAUSE PROBLEMS FOR THE MILITARY POLICE.
HMPH... THOSE FOOLISH COMMONERS ARE MERE GRAPES...
GUSHA (SQUISH)
...WE ARE FREE TO HARVEST OR CRUSH THEM AS WE PLEASE.
EXACTLY SO, MY LORD.

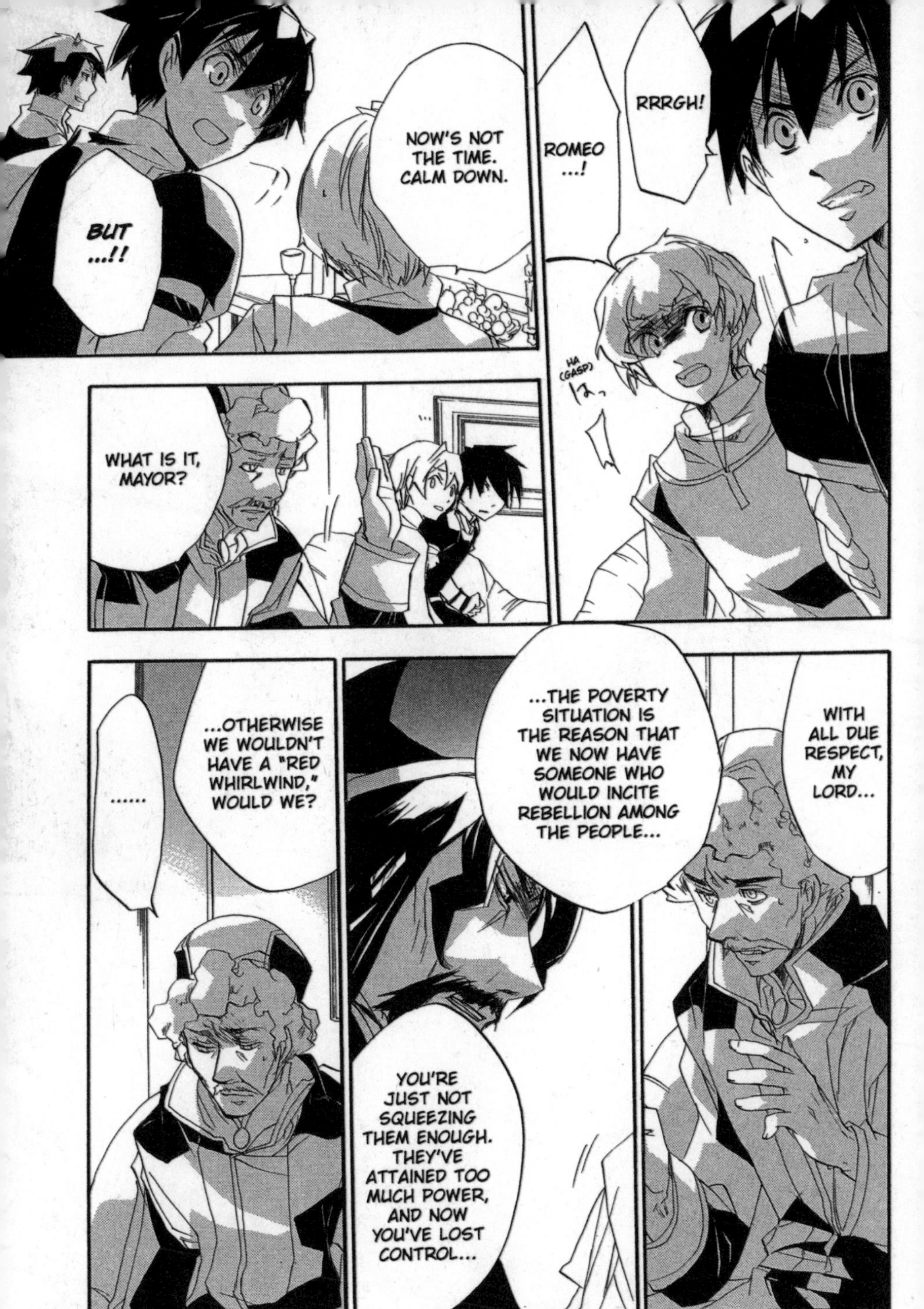
RRRGH!
ROMEO ...!
HA (GASP)
はっ
NOW'S NOT THE TIME. CALM DOWN.
BUT ...!!
...
WHAT IS IT, MAYOR?
WITH ALL DUE RESPECT, MY LORD...
...THE POVERTY SITUATION IS THE REASON THAT WE NOW HAVE SOMEONE WHO WOULD INCITE REBELLION AMONG THE PEOPLE...
YOU'RE JUST NOT SQUEEZING THEM ENOUGH. THEY'VE ATTAINED TOO MUCH POWER, AND NOW YOU'VE LOST CONTROL...
...OTHERWISE WE WOULDN'T HAVE A "RED WHIRLWIND," WOULD WE?
......

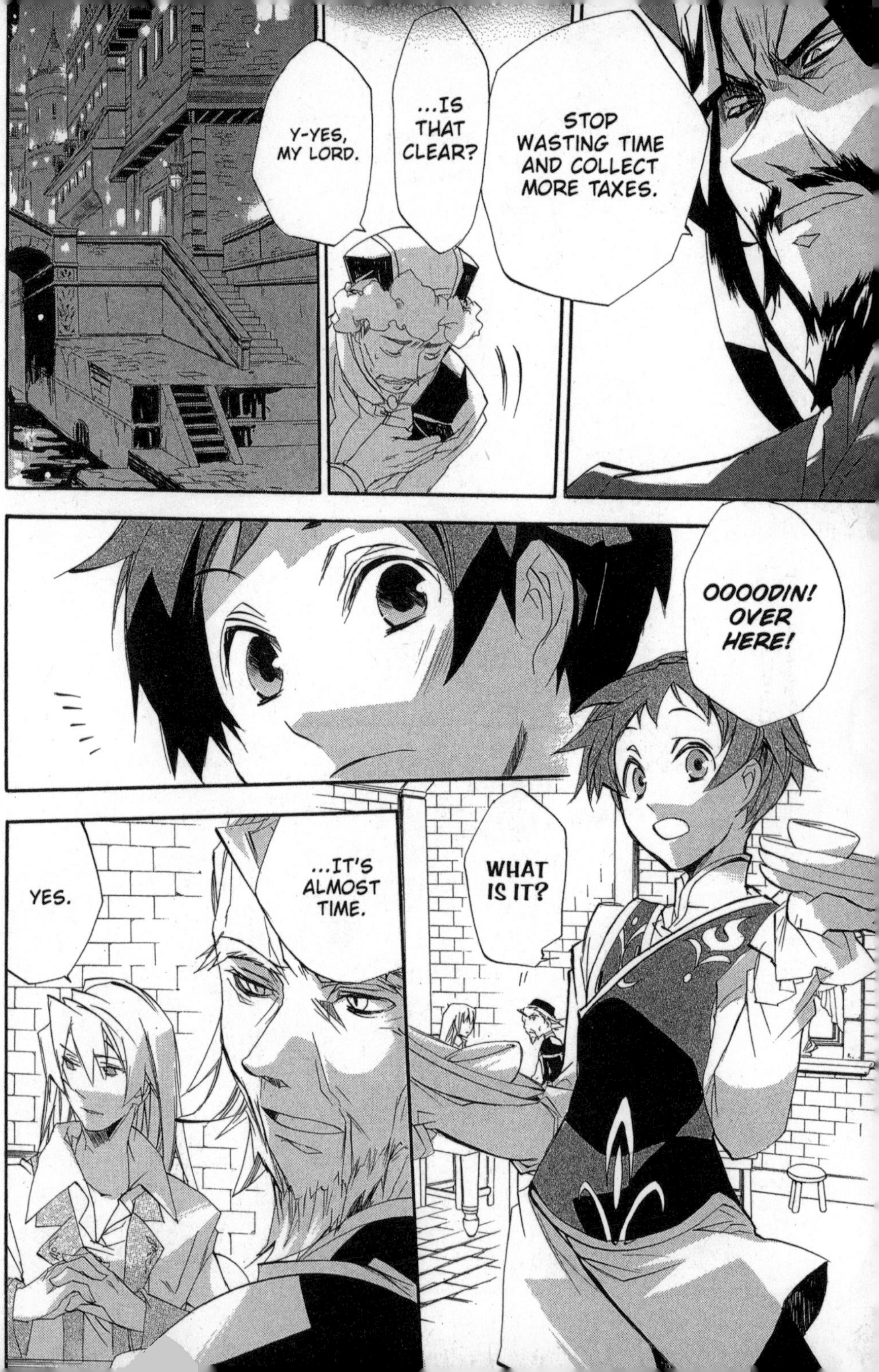
STOP WASTING TIME AND COLLECT MORE TAXES.
...IS THAT CLEAR?
Y-YES, MY LORD.
OOOODIN! OVER HERE!
WHAT IS IT?
...IT'S ALMOST TIME.
YES.

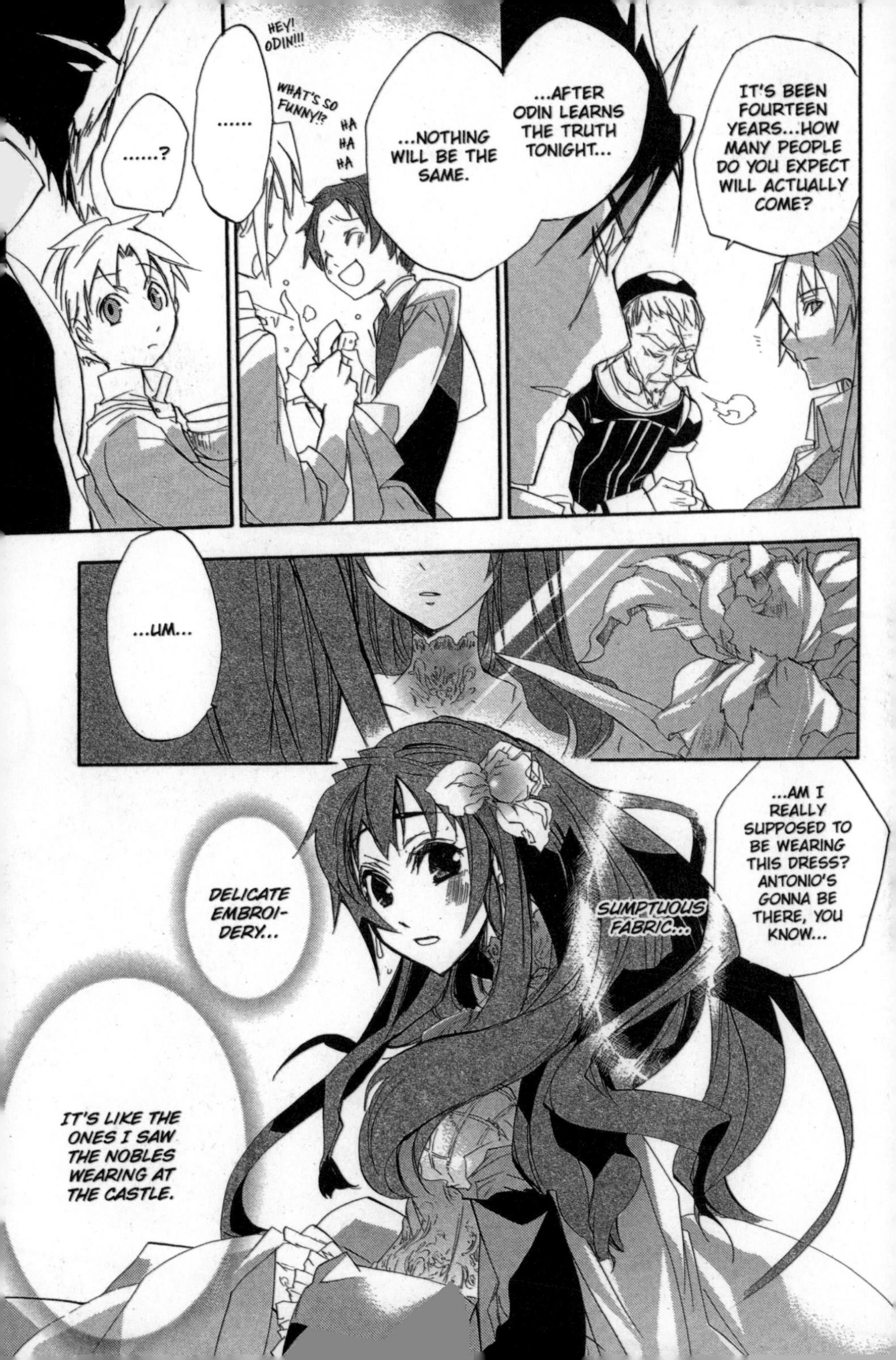
IT'S BEEN FOURTEEN YEARS...HOW MANY PEOPLE DO YOU EXPECT WILL ACTUALLY COME?
...AFTER ODIN LEARNS THE TRUTH TONIGHT...
...NOTHING WILL BE THE SAME.
HEY! ODIN!!!
WHAT'S SO FUNNY!?
HA HA HA
......
......?
...UM...
...AM I REALLY SUPPOSED TO BE WEARING THIS DRESS? ANTONIO'S GONNA BE THERE, YOU KNOW...
SUMPTUOUS FABRIC...
DELICATE EMBROI-DERY...
IT'S LIKE THE ONES I SAW THE NOBLES WEARING AT THE CASTLE.

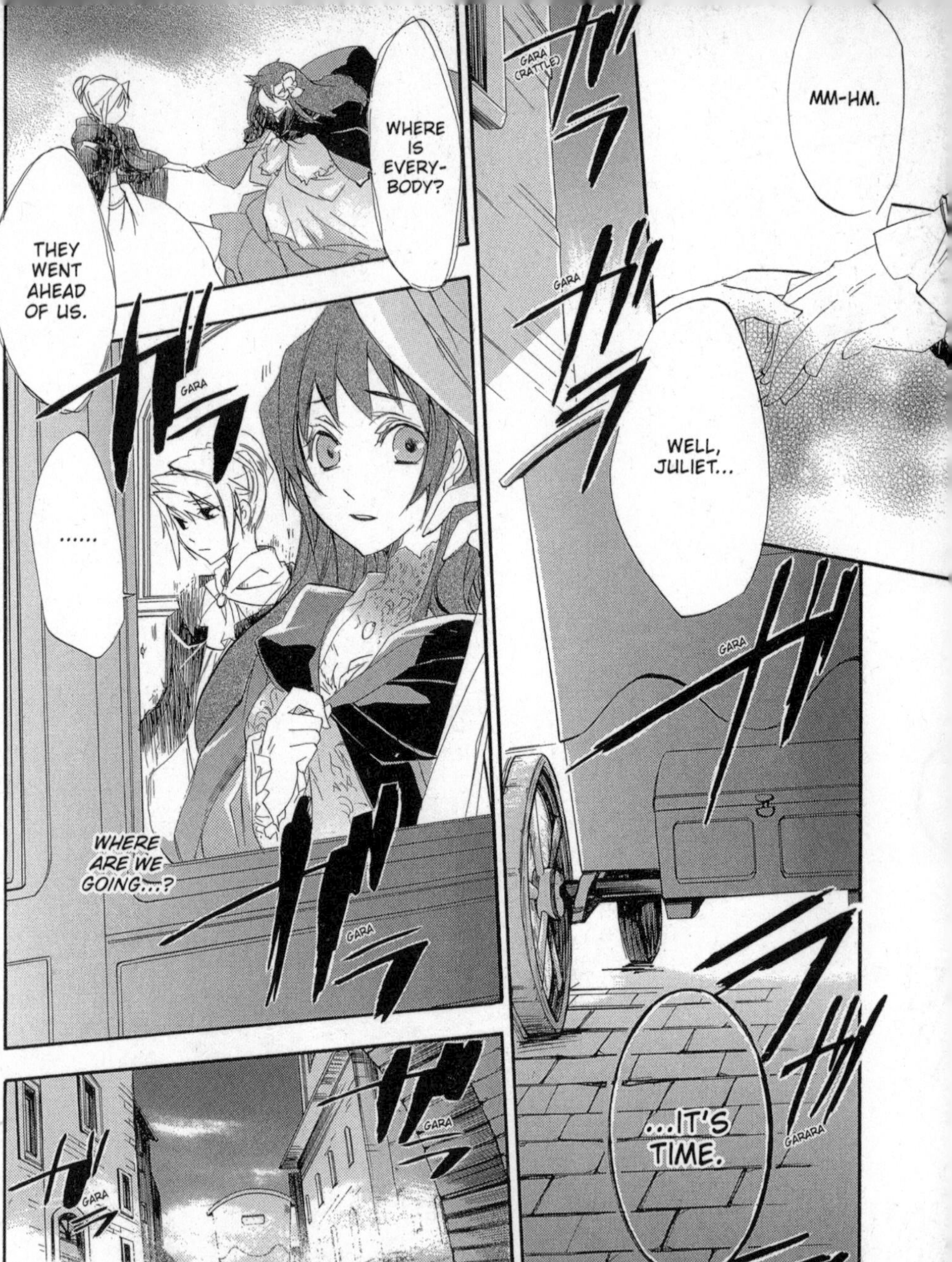

MM-HM.
GARA (RATTLE)
GARA
WELL, JULIET...
GARA
...IT'S TIME.
GARARA
WHERE IS EVERY-BODY?
THEY WENT AHEAD OF US.
GARA
......
WHERE ARE WE GOING...?
GARA
GARA
GARA
GARA

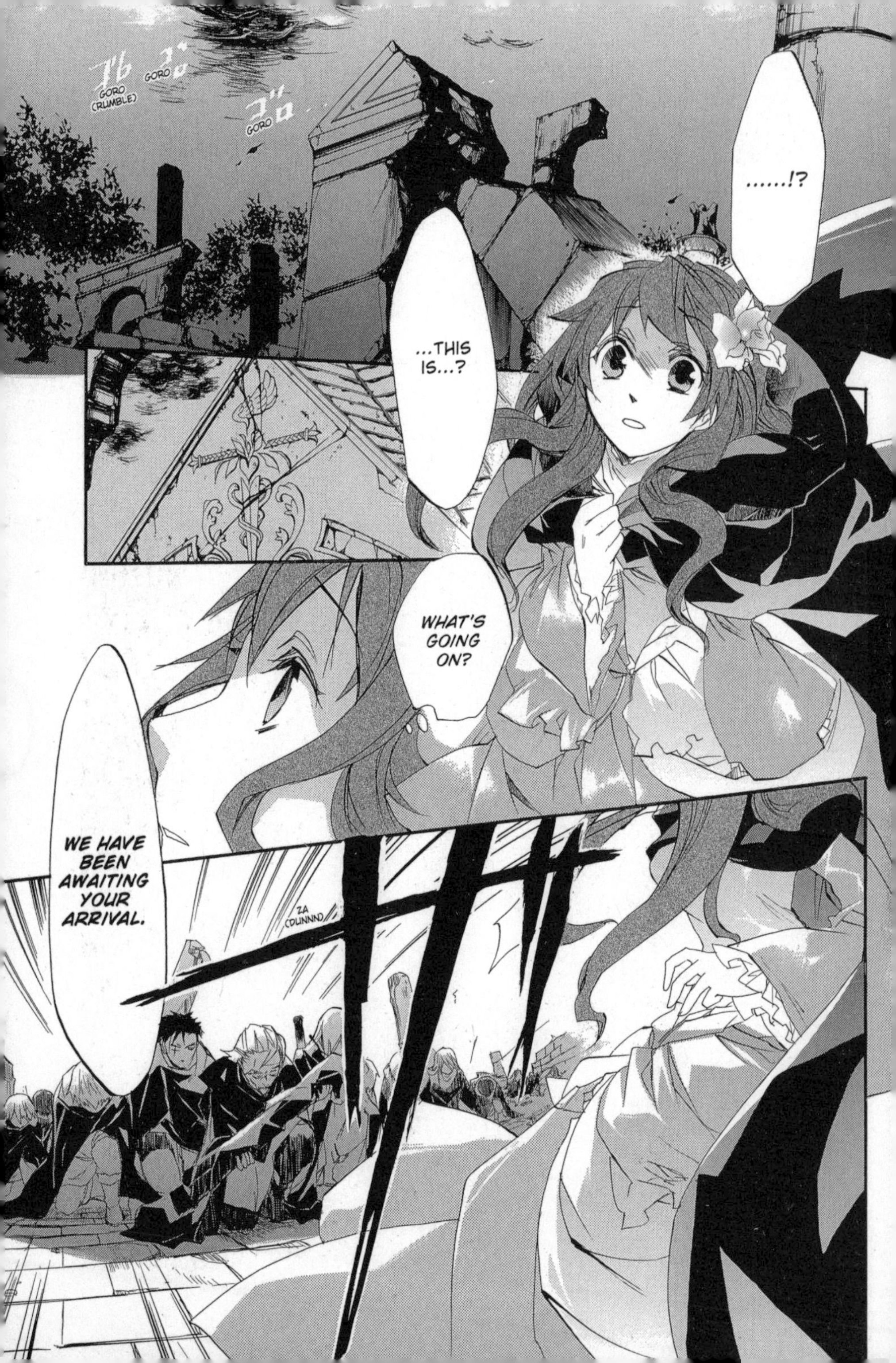
......!?
GORO (RUMBLE)
GORO
GORO
...THIS IS...?
WHAT'S GOING ON?
WE HAVE BEEN AWAITING YOUR ARRIVAL.
ZA (DUNNN)

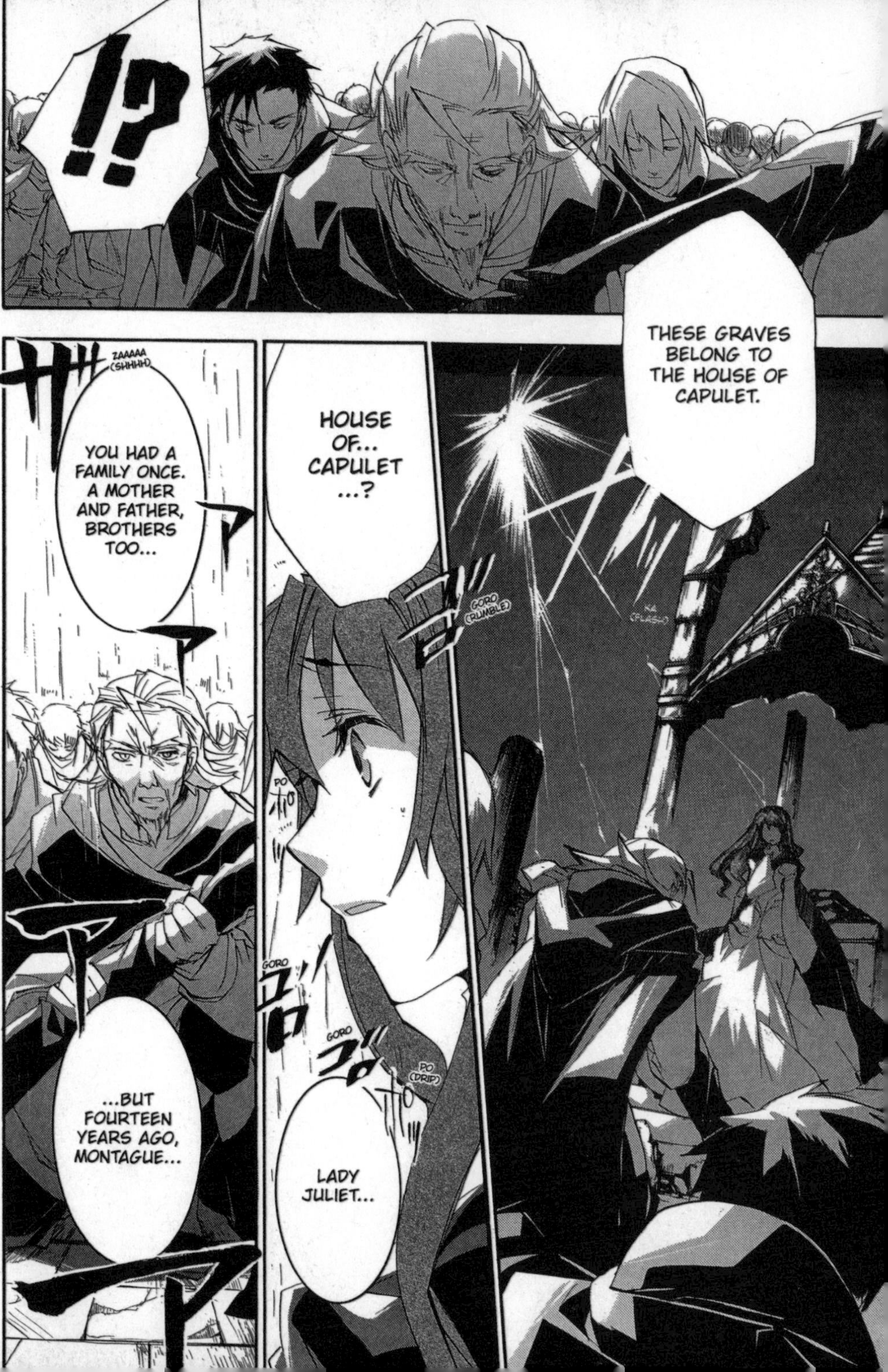
!?
THESE GRAVES BELONG TO THE HOUSE OF CAPULET.
KA (FLASH)
HOUSE OF... CAPULET ...?
GORO (RUMBLE)
PO
GORO
GORO
PO (DRIP)
LADY JULIET...
ZAAAAA (SHHHH)
YOU HAD A FAMILY ONCE. A MOTHER AND FATHER, BROTHERS TOO...
...BUT FOURTEEN YEARS AGO, MONTAGUE...

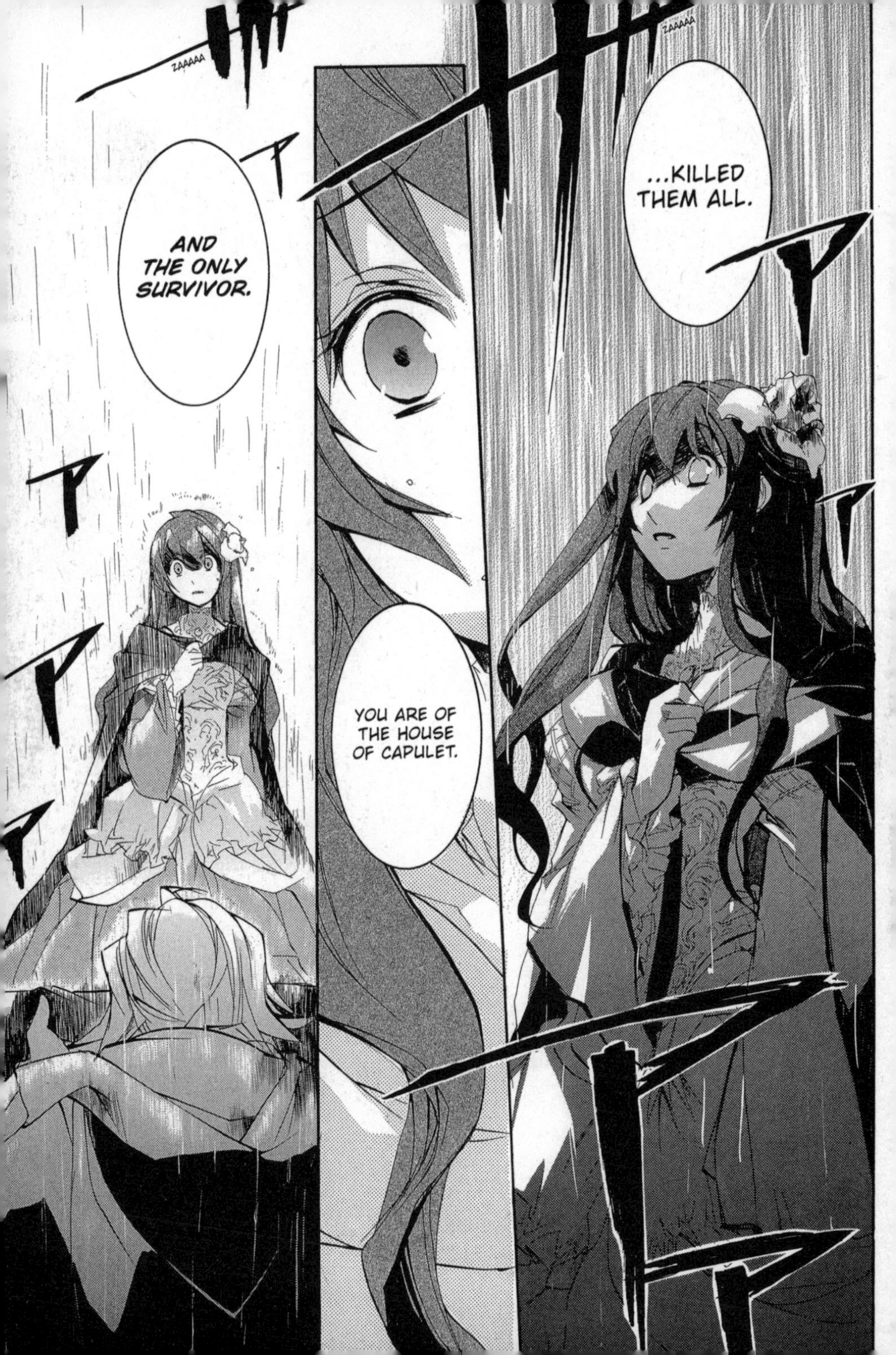
ZAAAAA
...KILLED THEM ALL.
YOU ARE OF THE HOUSE OF CAPULET.
ZAAAAA
AND THE ONLY SURVIVOR.

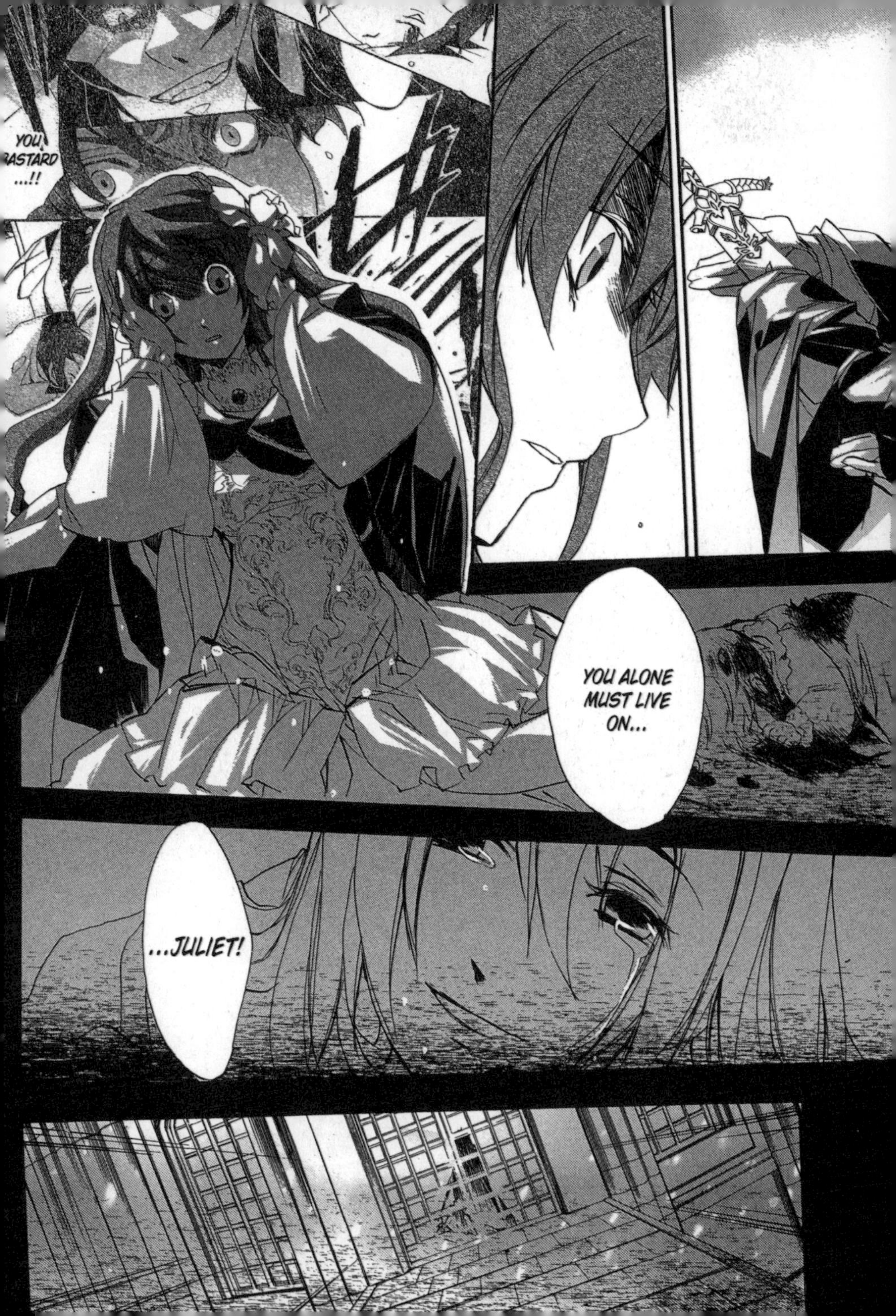
YOU BASTARD ...!!
YOU ALONE MUST LIVE ON...
...JULIET!

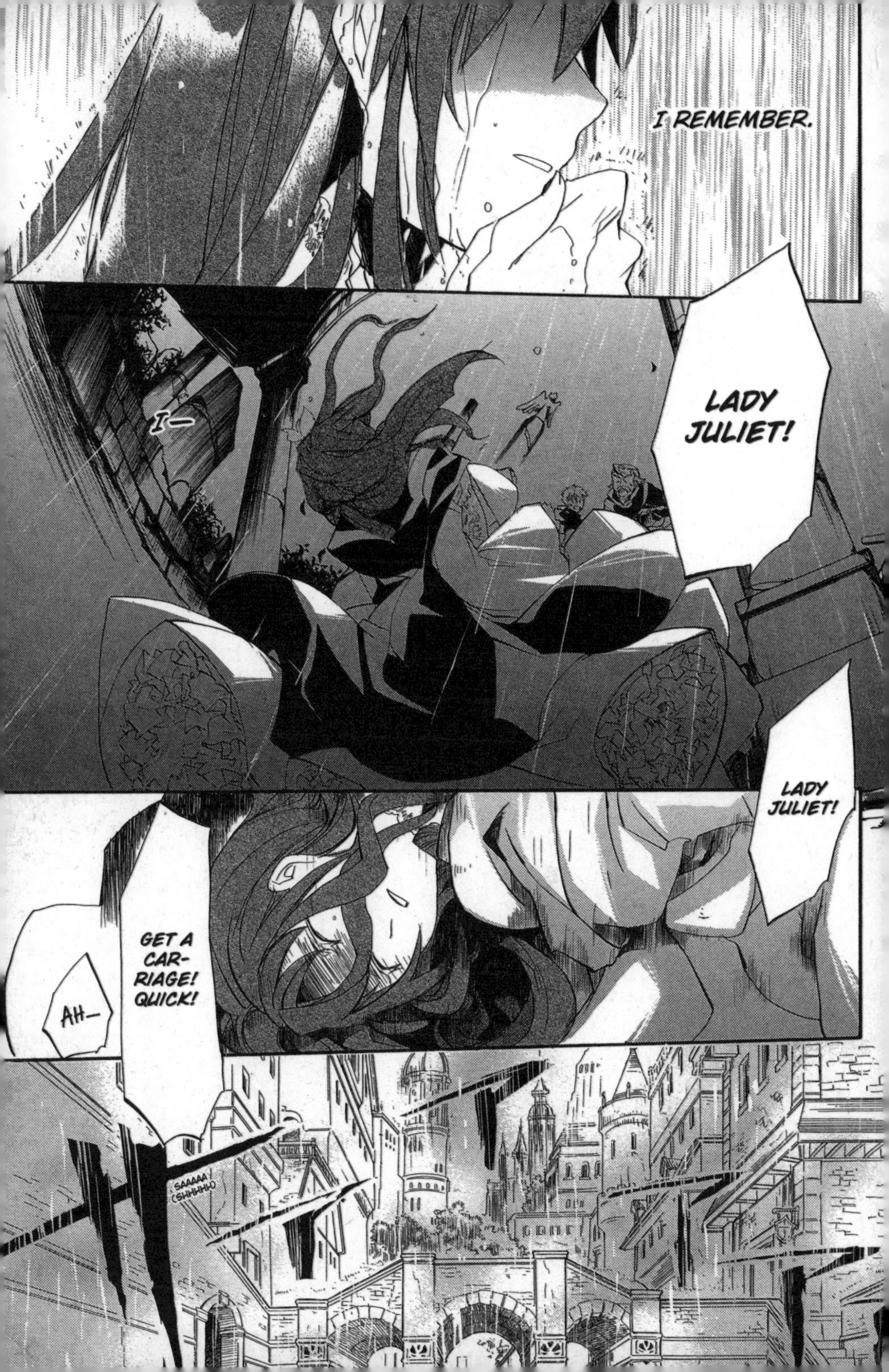
I REMEMBER.
LADY JULIET!
I—
LADY JULIET!
GET A CARRIAGE! QUICK!
AH—
SAAAAA (SHHHHH)

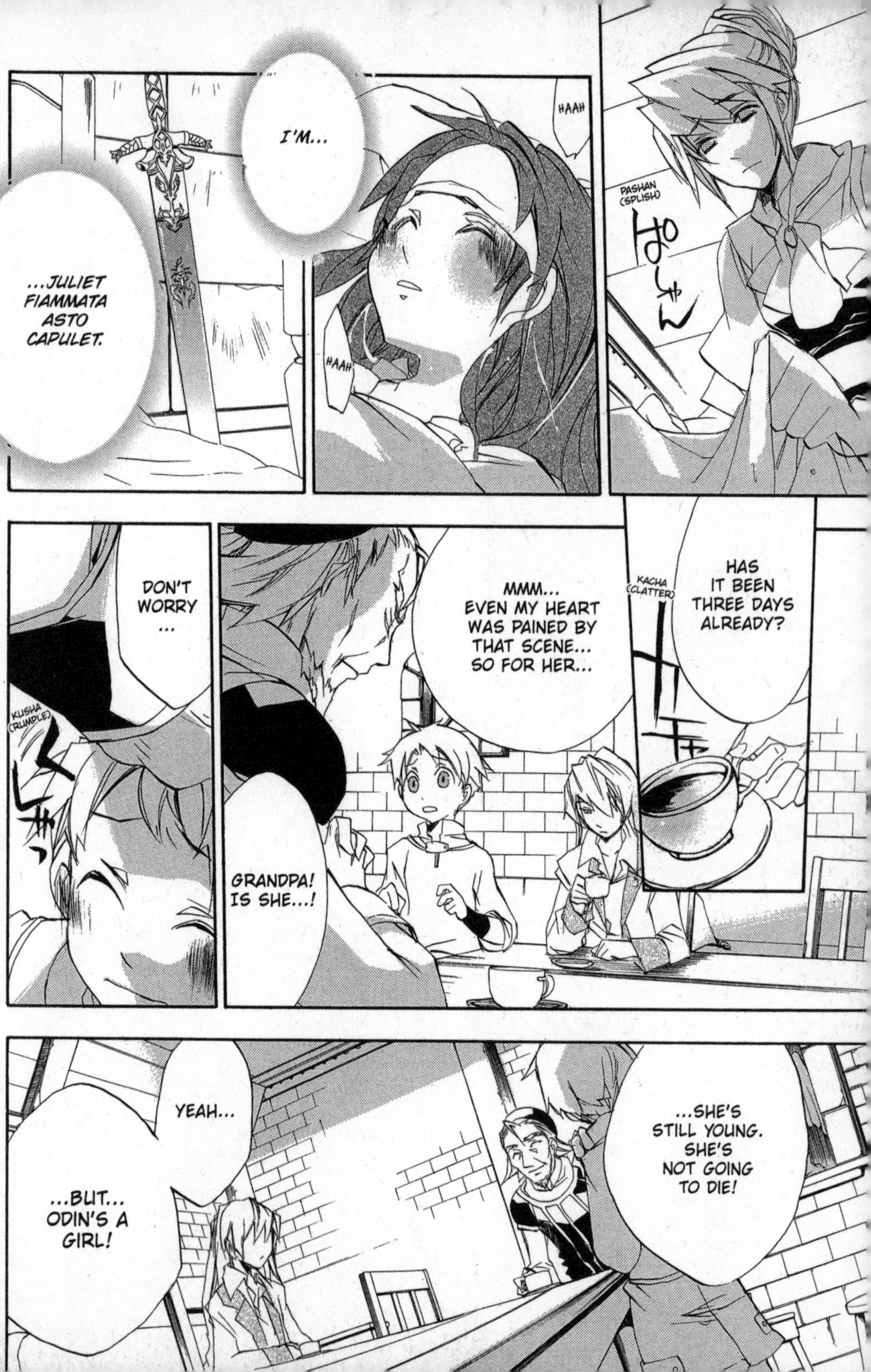
PASHAN (SPLISH)
HAAH
HAAH
I'M...
...JULIET FIAMMATA ASTO CAPULET.
KACHA (CLATTER)
HAS IT BEEN THREE DAYS ALREADY?
MMM... EVEN MY HEART WAS PAINED BY THAT SCENE... SO FOR HER...
GRANDPA! IS SHE...!
DON'T WORRY ...
KUSHA (RUMPLE)
...SHE'S STILL YOUNG. SHE'S NOT GOING TO DIE!
YEAH...
...BUT... ODIN'S A GIRL!

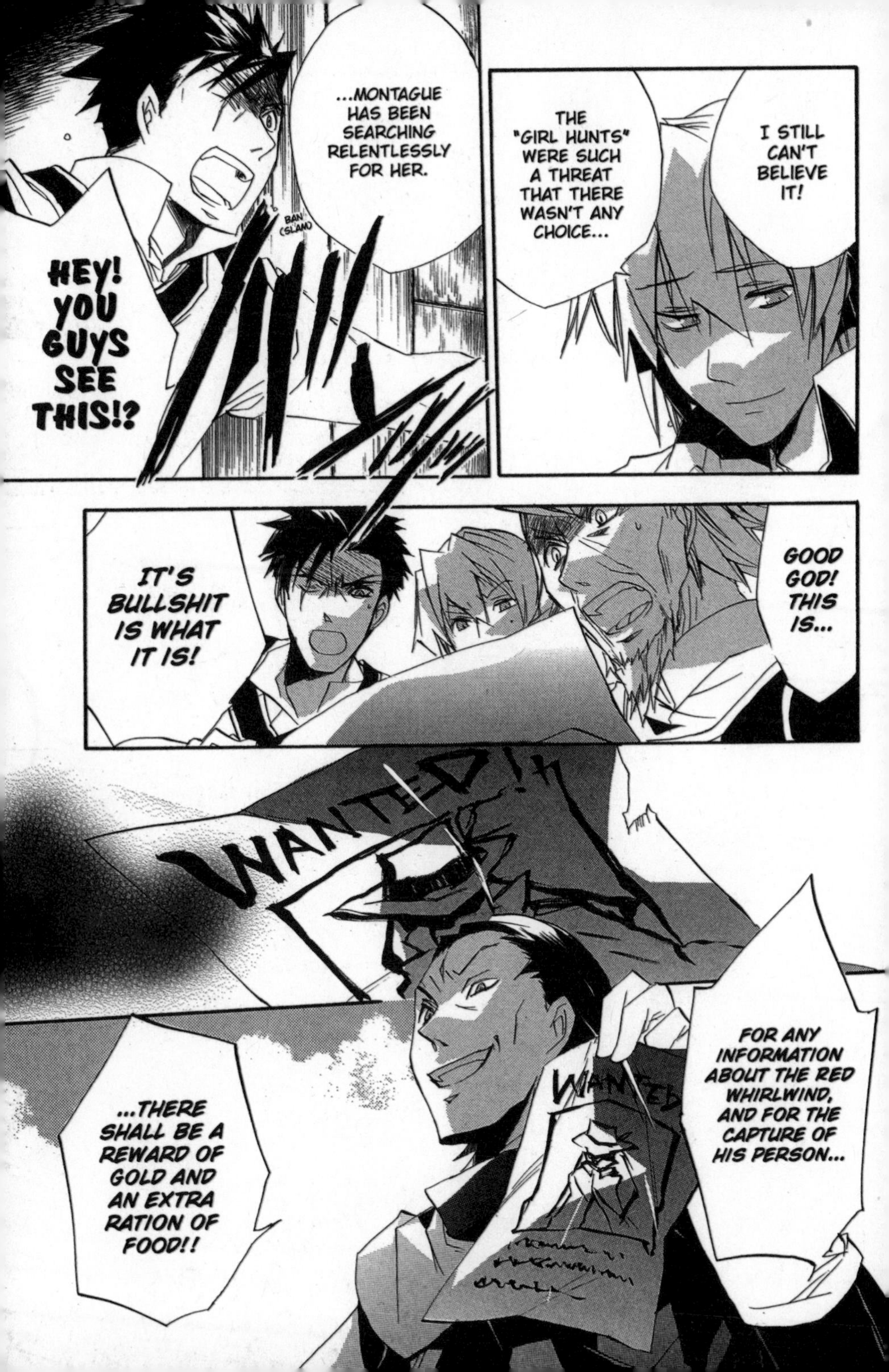
I STILL CAN'T BELIEVE IT!
THE "GIRL HUNTS" WERE SUCH A THREAT THAT THERE WASN'T ANY CHOICE...
...MONTAGUE HAS BEEN SEARCHING RELENTLESSLY FOR HER.
BAN (SLAM)
HEY! YOU GUYS SEE THIS!?
GOOD GOD! THIS IS...
IT'S BULLSHIT IS WHAT IT IS!
WANTED!
FOR ANY INFORMATION ABOUT THE RED WHIRLWIND, AND FOR THE CAPTURE OF HIS PERSON...
...THERE SHALL BE A REWARD OF GOLD AND AN EXTRA RATION OF FOOD!!

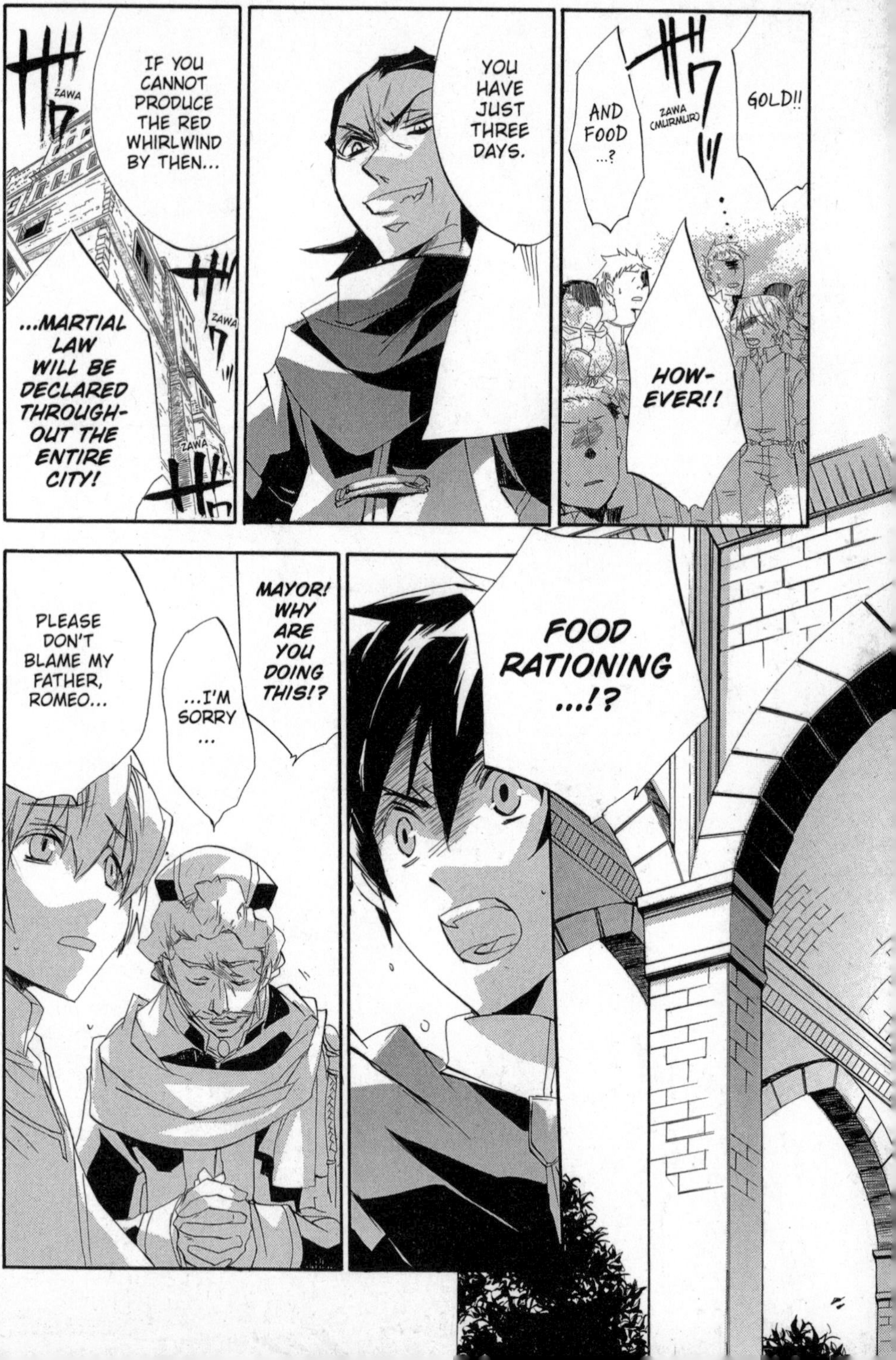
GOLD!!
ZAWA (MURMUR)
AND FOOD ...?
HOW-EVER!!
YOU HAVE JUST THREE DAYS.
IF YOU CANNOT PRODUCE THE RED WHIRLWIND BY THEN...
ZAWA
ZAWA
...MARTIAL LAW WILL BE DECLARED THROUGH-OUT THE ENTIRE CITY!
ZAWA
FOOD RATIONING ...!?
MAYOR! WHY ARE YOU DOING THIS!?
...I'M SORRY ...
PLEASE DON'T BLAME MY FATHER, ROMEO...

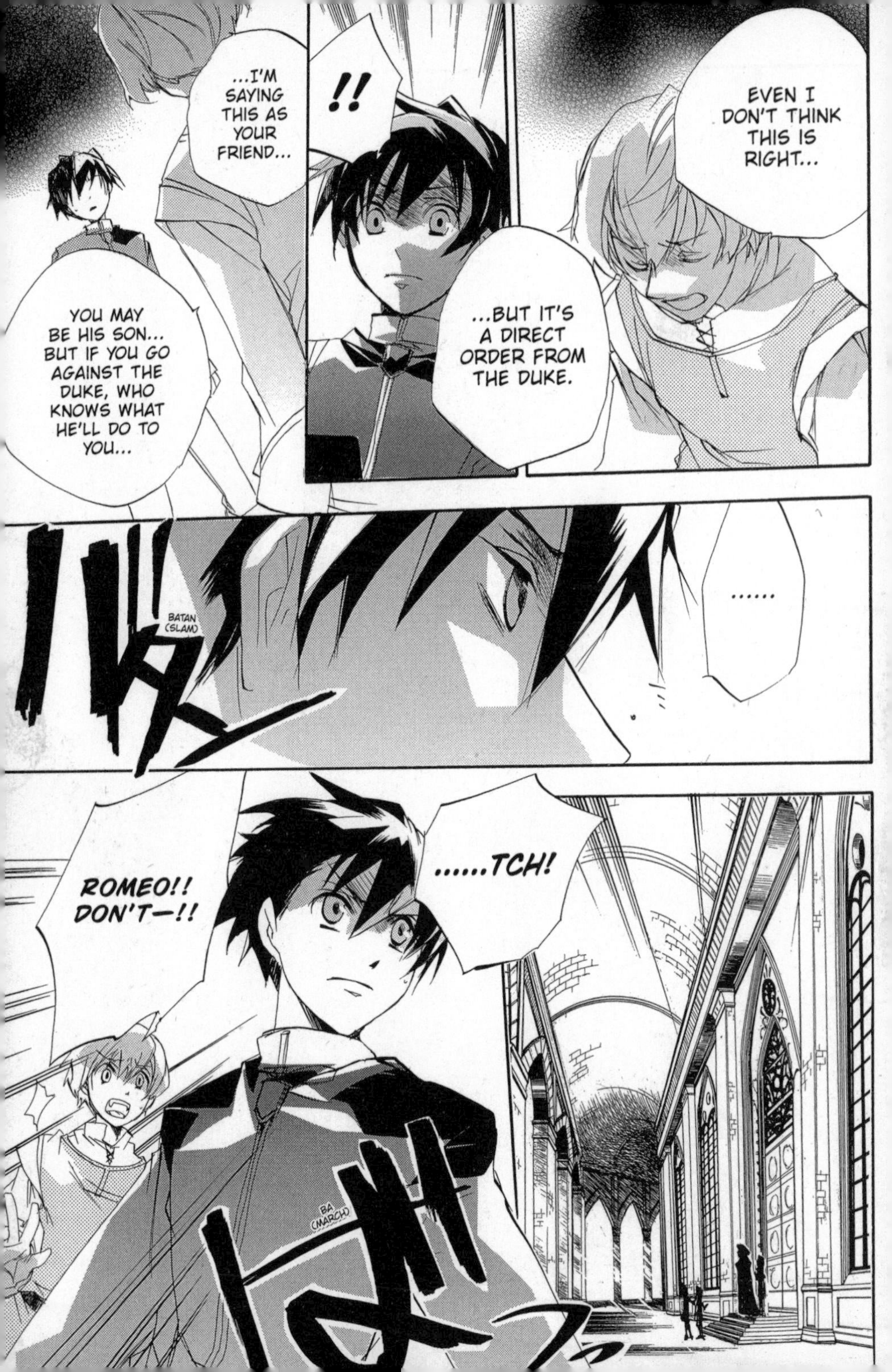

EVEN I DON'T THINK THIS IS RIGHT...
...BUT IT'S A DIRECT ORDER FROM THE DUKE.
!!
...I'M SAYING THIS AS YOUR FRIEND...
YOU MAY BE HIS SON... BUT IF YOU GO AGAINST THE DUKE, WHO KNOWS WHAT HE'LL DO TO YOU...
......
BATAN (SLAM)
......TCH!
ROMEO!! DON'T—!!
BA (MARCH)

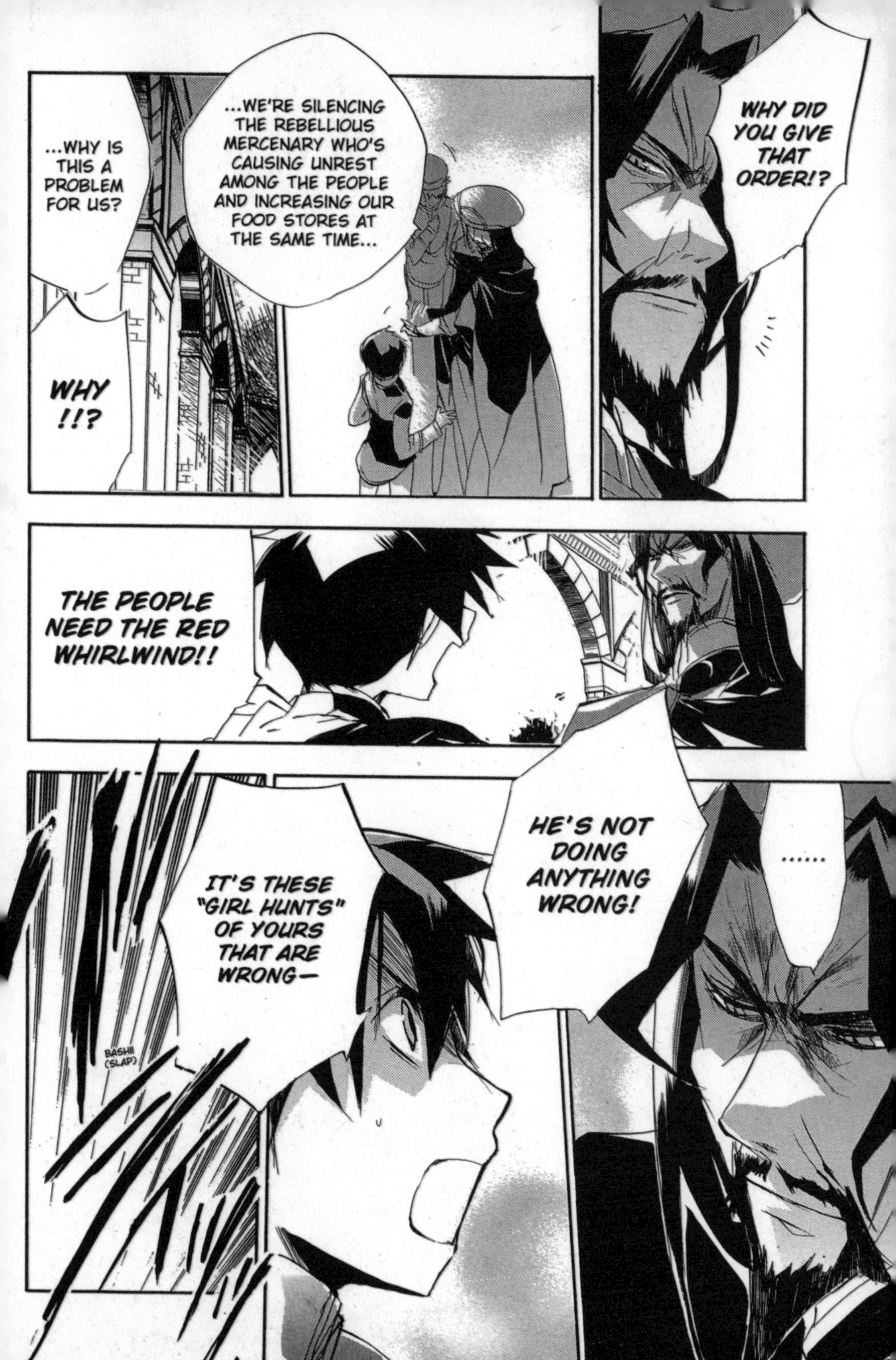
WHY DID YOU GIVE THAT ORDER!?
...WE'RE SILENCING THE REBELLIOUS MERCENARY WHO'S CAUSING UNREST AMONG THE PEOPLE AND INCREASING OUR FOOD STORES AT THE SAME TIME...
...WHY IS THIS A PROBLEM FOR US?
WHY !!?
THE PEOPLE NEED THE RED WHIRLWIND!!
......
HE'S NOT DOING ANYTHING WRONG!
IT'S THESE "GIRL HUNTS" OF YOURS THAT ARE WRONG—
BASHII (SLAP)

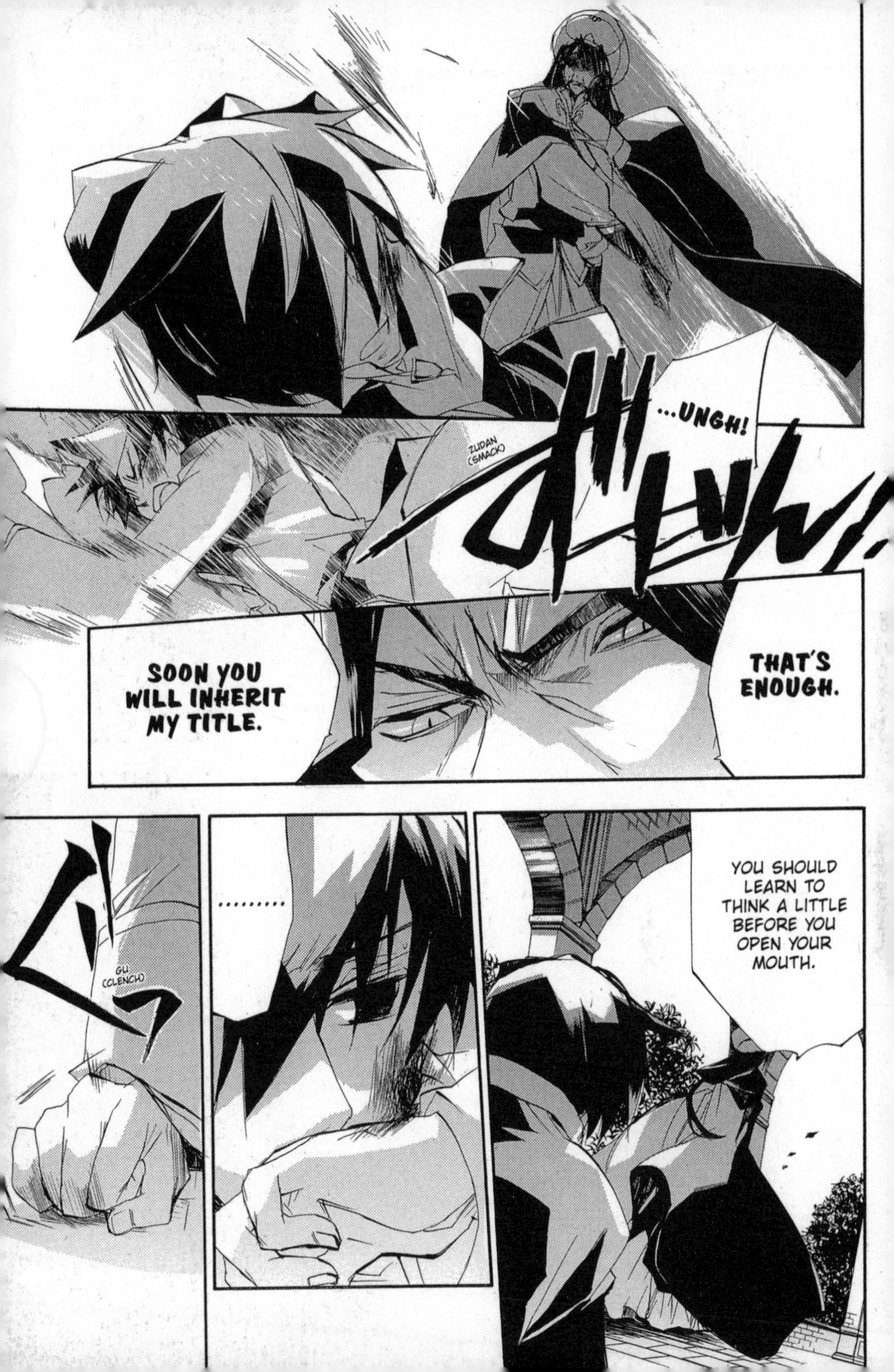
...UNGH!
ZUDAN (SMACK)
THAT'S ENOUGH.
SOON YOU WILL INHERIT MY TITLE.
YOU SHOULD LEARN TO THINK A LITTLE BEFORE YOU OPEN YOUR MOUTH.
....
GU (CLENCH)

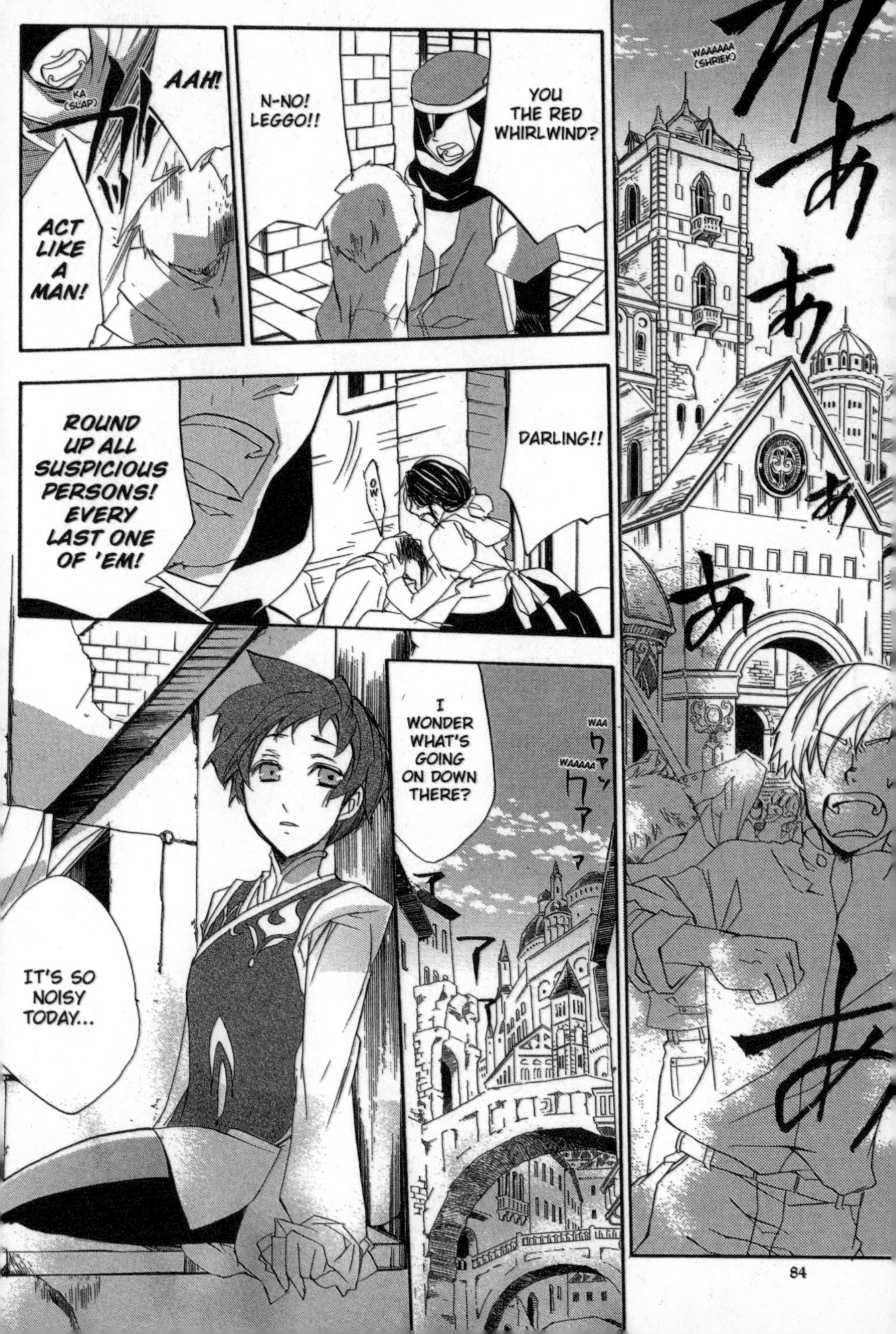
WAAAAAA (SHRIEK)
YOU THE RED WHIRLWIND?
N-NO! LEGGO!!
AAH!
KA (SLAP)
ACT LIKE A MAN!
DARLING!!
OW...
ROUND UP ALL SUSPICIOUS PERSONS! EVERY LAST ONE OF 'EM!
I WONDER WHAT'S GOING ON DOWN THERE?
WAA
WAAAAA
IT'S SO NOISY TODAY...

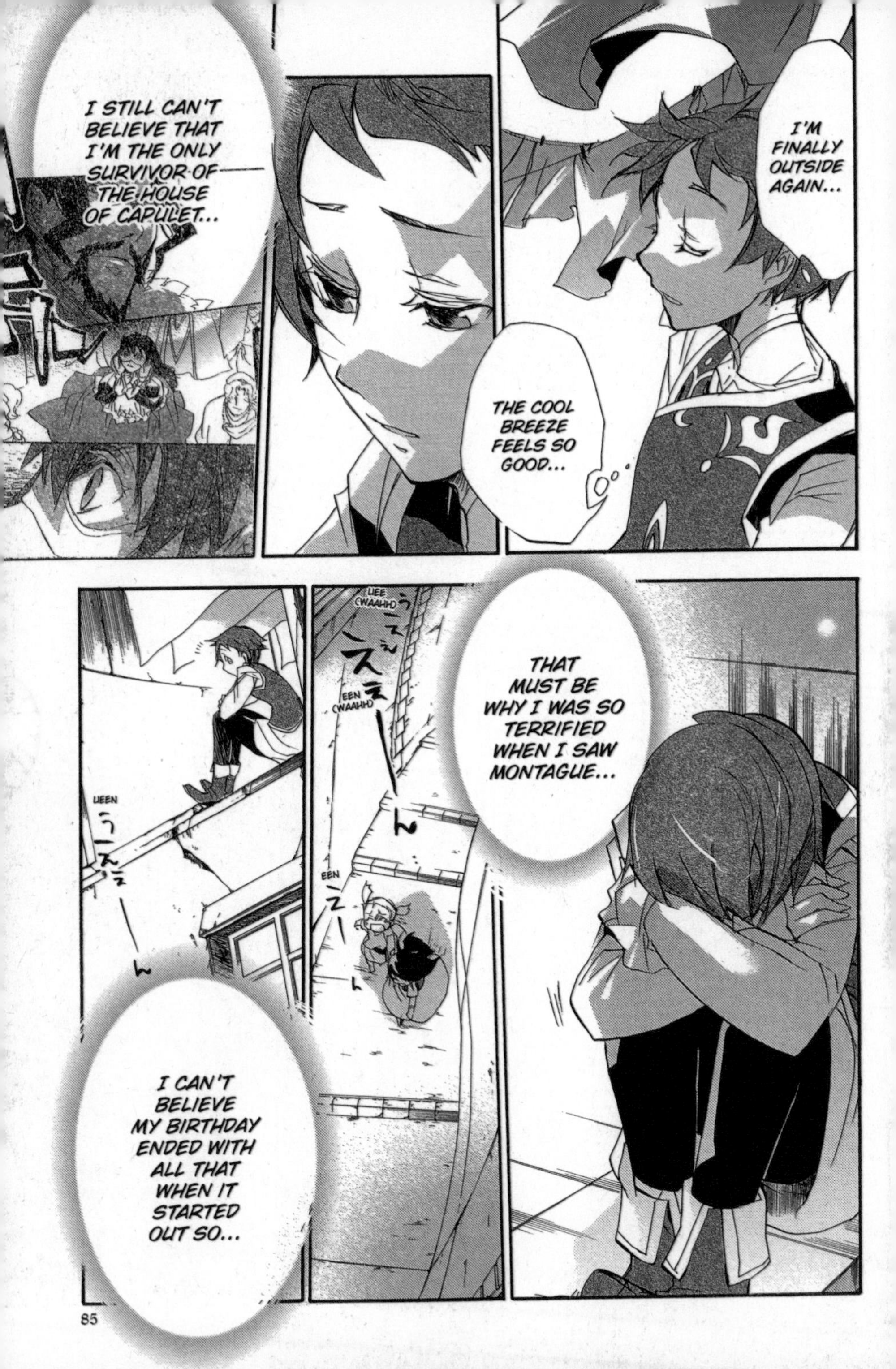
I'M FINALLY OUTSIDE AGAIN...
THE COOL BREEZE FEELS SO GOOD...
I STILL CAN'T BELIEVE THAT I'M THE ONLY SURVIVOR OF THE HOUSE OF CAPULET...
THAT MUST BE WHY I WAS SO TERRIFIED WHEN I SAW MONTAGUE...
UEE (WAAHH)
EEN (WAAHH)
EEN
UEEN
I CAN'T BELIEVE MY BIRTHDAY ENDED WITH ALL THAT WHEN IT STARTED OUT SO...

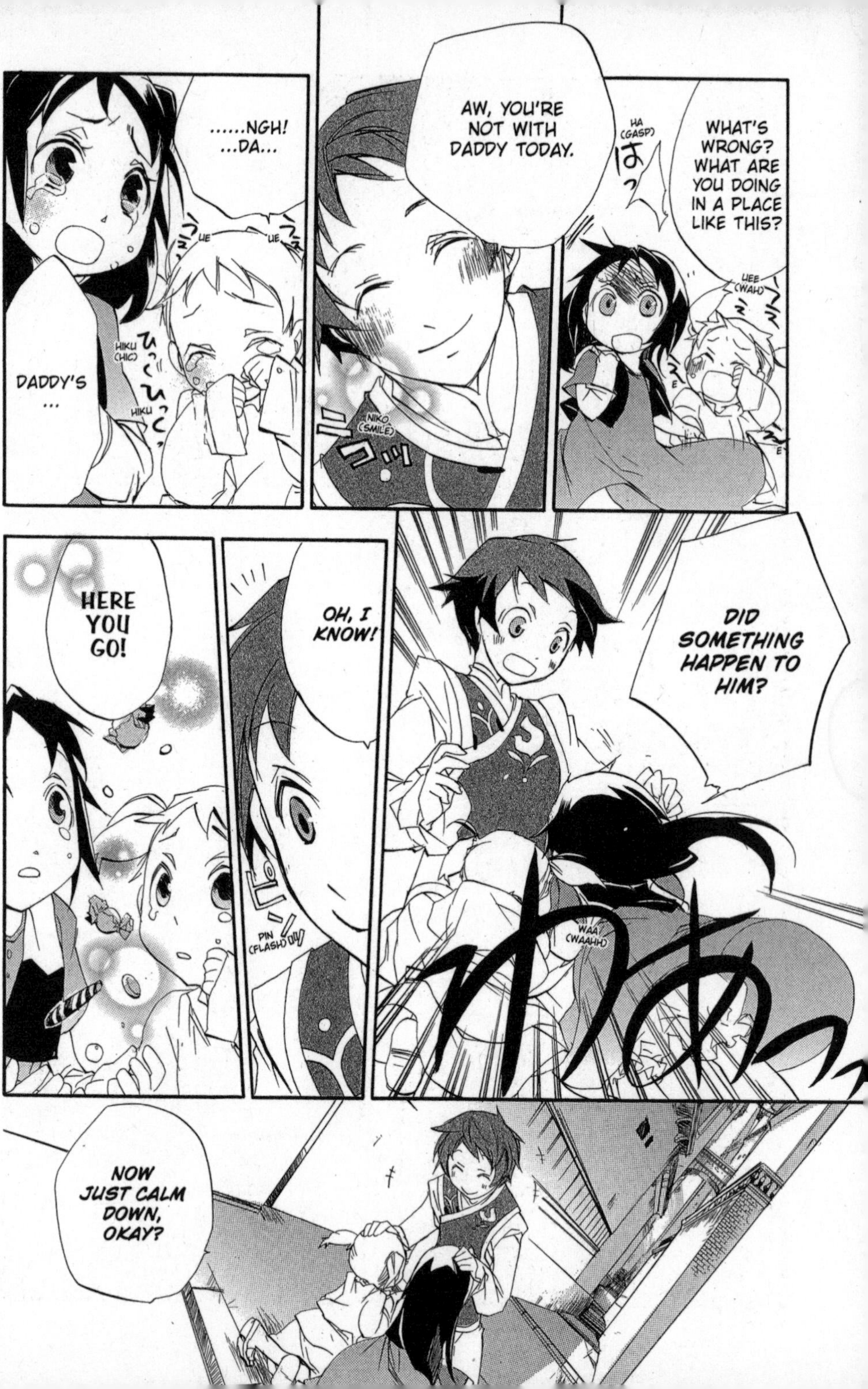
HA (GASP)
WHAT'S WRONG? WHAT ARE YOU DOING IN A PLACE LIKE THIS?
UEE (WAH)
E
E
AW, YOU'RE NOT WITH DADDY TODAY.
NIKO (SMILE)
......NGH! ...DA...
UE
UE
HIKU (HIC)
HIKU
DADDY'S ...
DID SOMETHING HAPPEN TO HIM?
WAA (WAAHH)
OH, I KNOW!
PIN (FLASH)
HERE YOU GO!
NOW JUST CALM DOWN, OKAY?

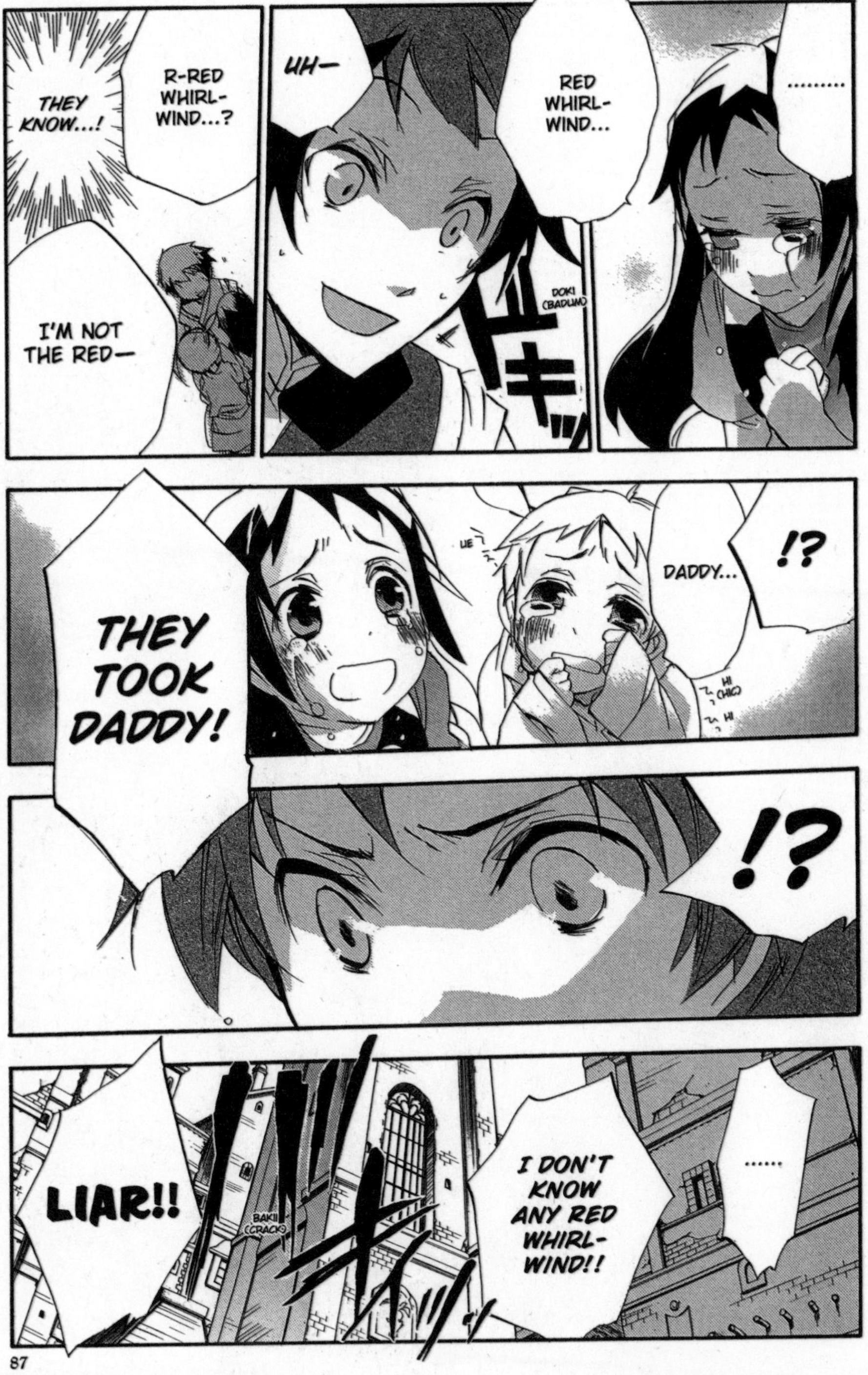
....
RED WHIRL-WIND...
UH—
DOKI (BADUM)
R-RED WHIRL-WIND...?
THEY KNOW...!
I'M NOT THE RED—
!?
DADDY...
HI (HIC)
HI
UE
THEY TOOK DADDY!
!?
......
I DON'T KNOW ANY RED WHIRL-WIND!!
BAKII (CRACK)
LIAR!!

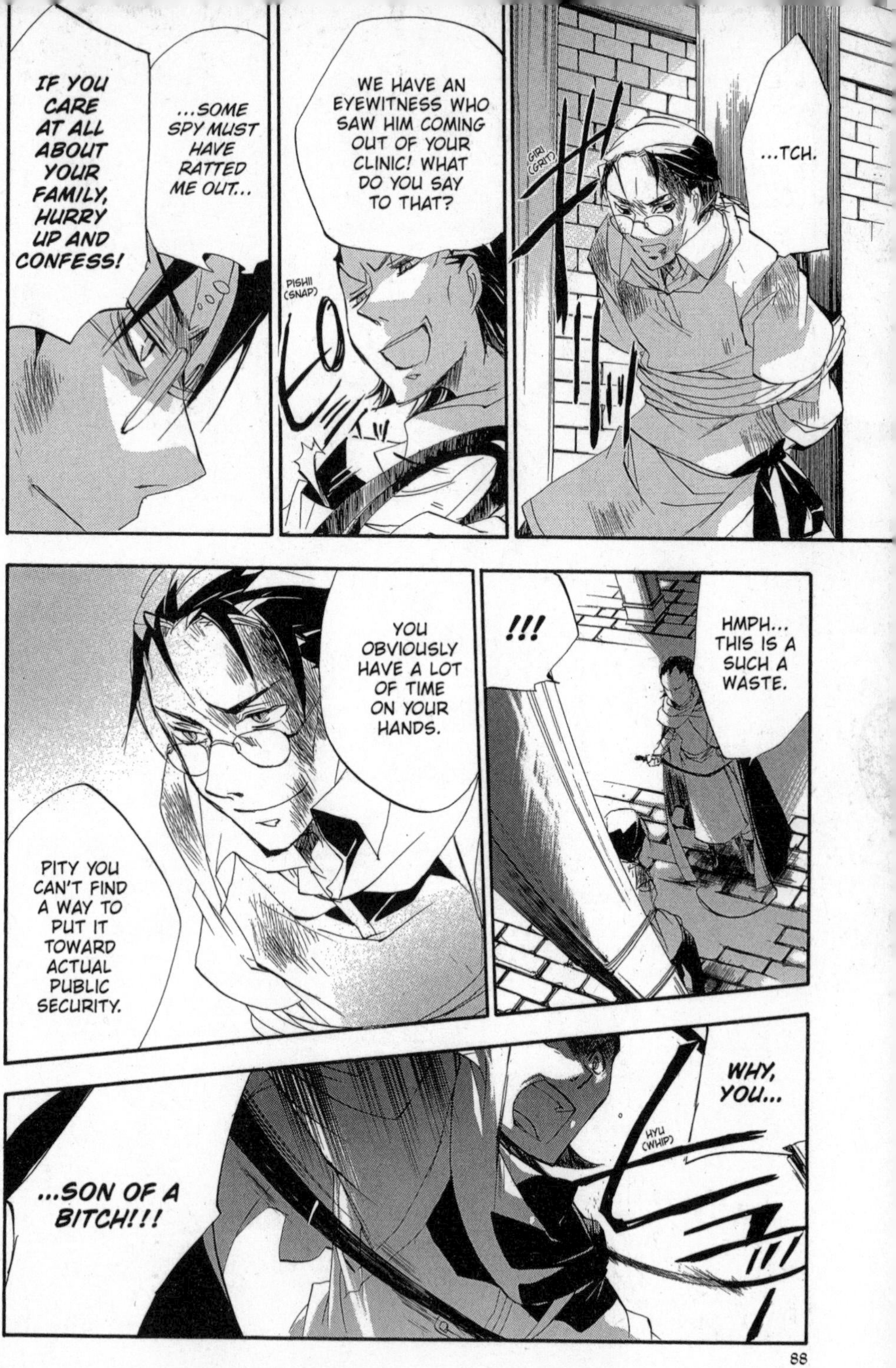
GIRI (GRIT)
...TCH.
WE HAVE AN EYEWITNESS WHO SAW HIM COMING OUT OF YOUR CLINIC! WHAT DO YOU SAY TO THAT?
PISHII (SNAP)
...SOME SPY MUST HAVE RATTED ME OUT...
IF YOU CARE AT ALL ABOUT YOUR FAMILY, HURRY UP AND CONFESS!
HMPH... THIS IS A SUCH A WASTE.
!!!
YOU OBVIOUSLY HAVE A LOT OF TIME ON YOUR HANDS.
PITY YOU CAN'T FIND A WAY TO PUT IT TOWARD ACTUAL PUBLIC SECURITY.
WHY, YOU...
HYU (WHIP)
...SON OF A BITCH!!!

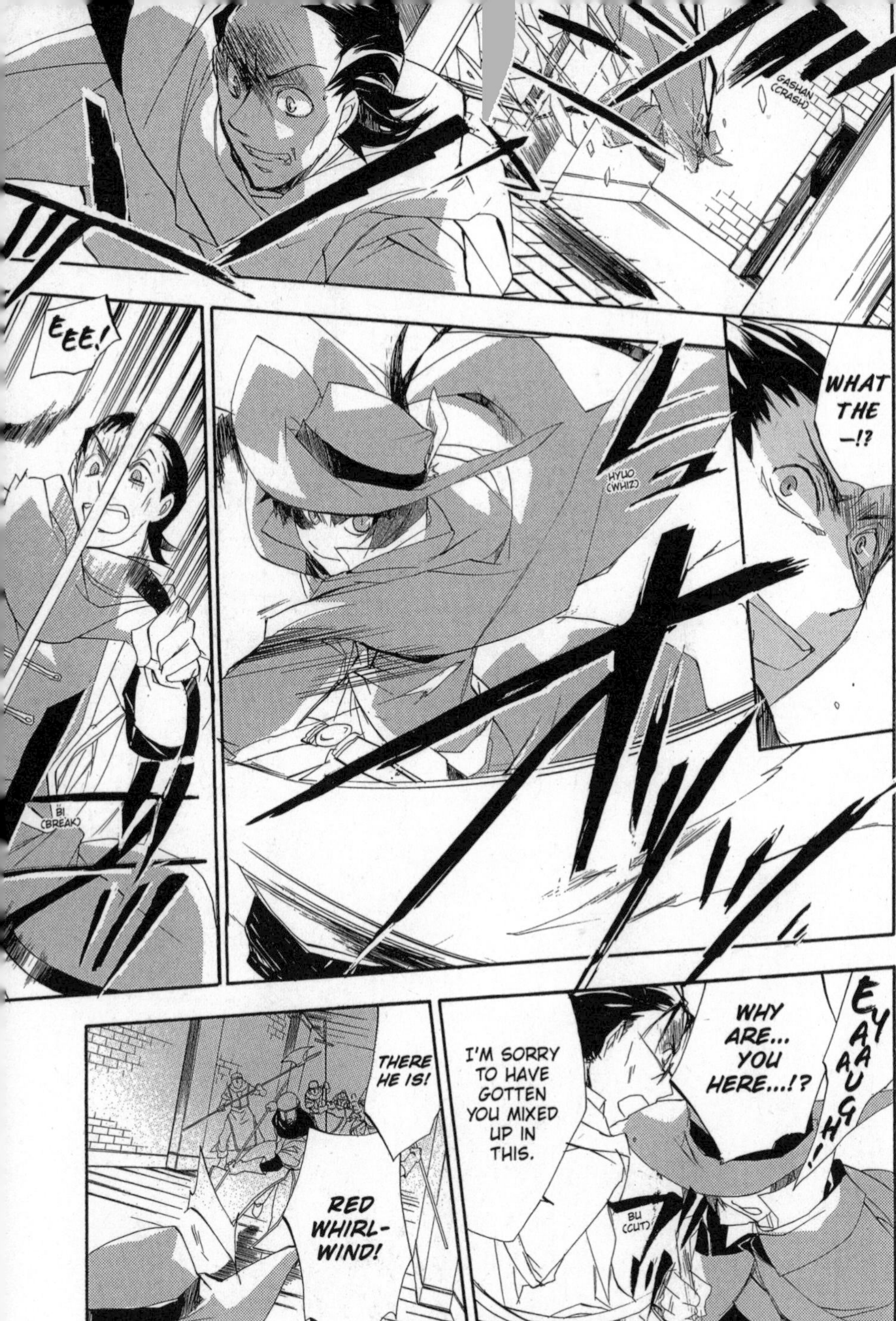

GASHAN (CRASH)
WHAT THE—!?
HYUO (WHIZ)
EEE!
BI (BREAK)
EYAAAUGH!!
WHY ARE... YOU HERE...!?
I'M SORRY TO HAVE GOTTEN YOU MIXED UP IN THIS.
BU (CUT)
THERE HE IS!
RED WHIRLWIND!

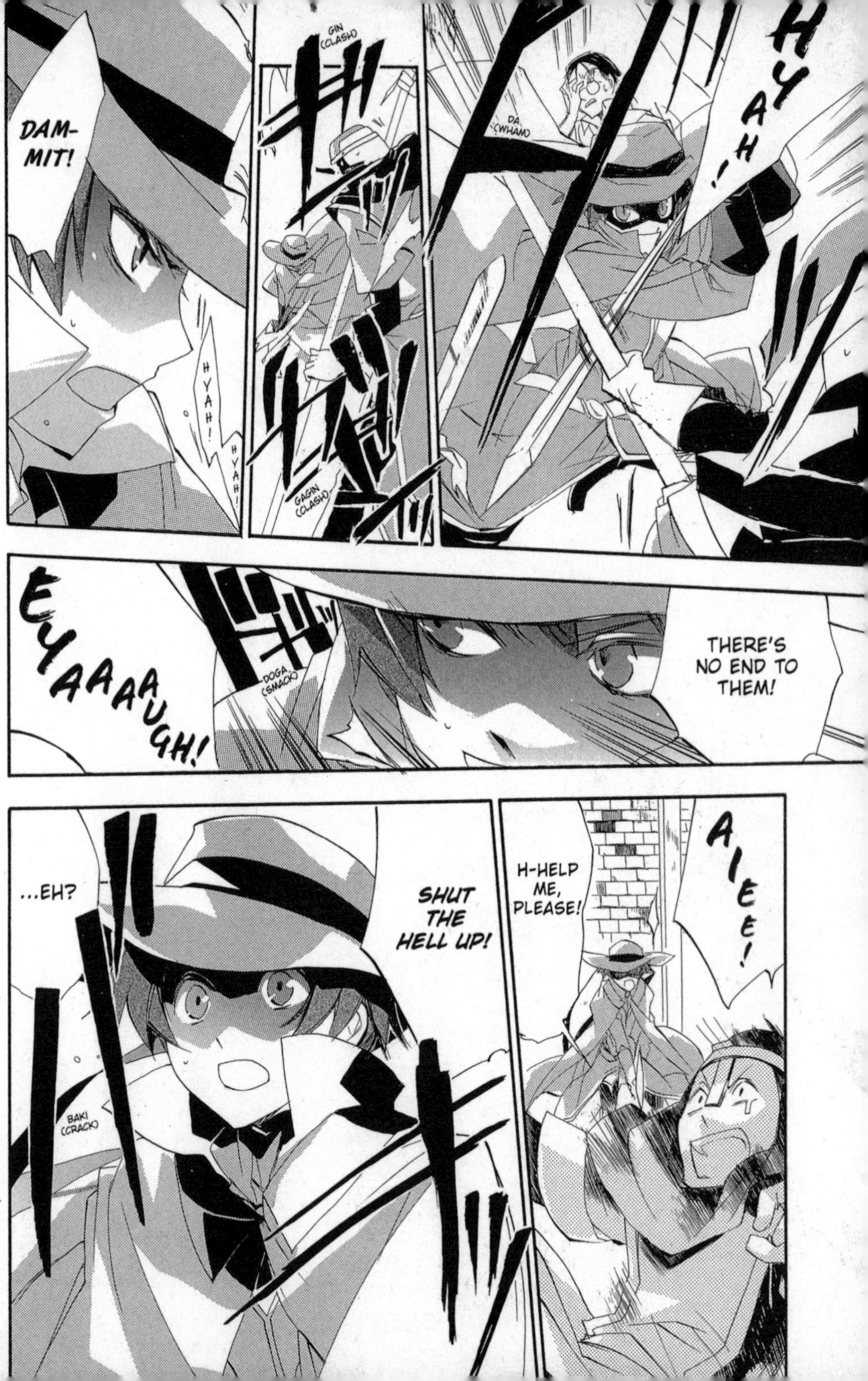
HYAH!
DA (WHAM)
GIN (CLASH)
GAGIN (CLASH)
DAM-MIT!
HYAH!
HYAH!
THERE'S NO END TO THEM!
DOGA (SMACK)
EYAAAAAUGH!
AIEEE!
H-HELP ME, PLEASE!
SHUT THE HELL UP!
...EH?
BAKI (CRACK)

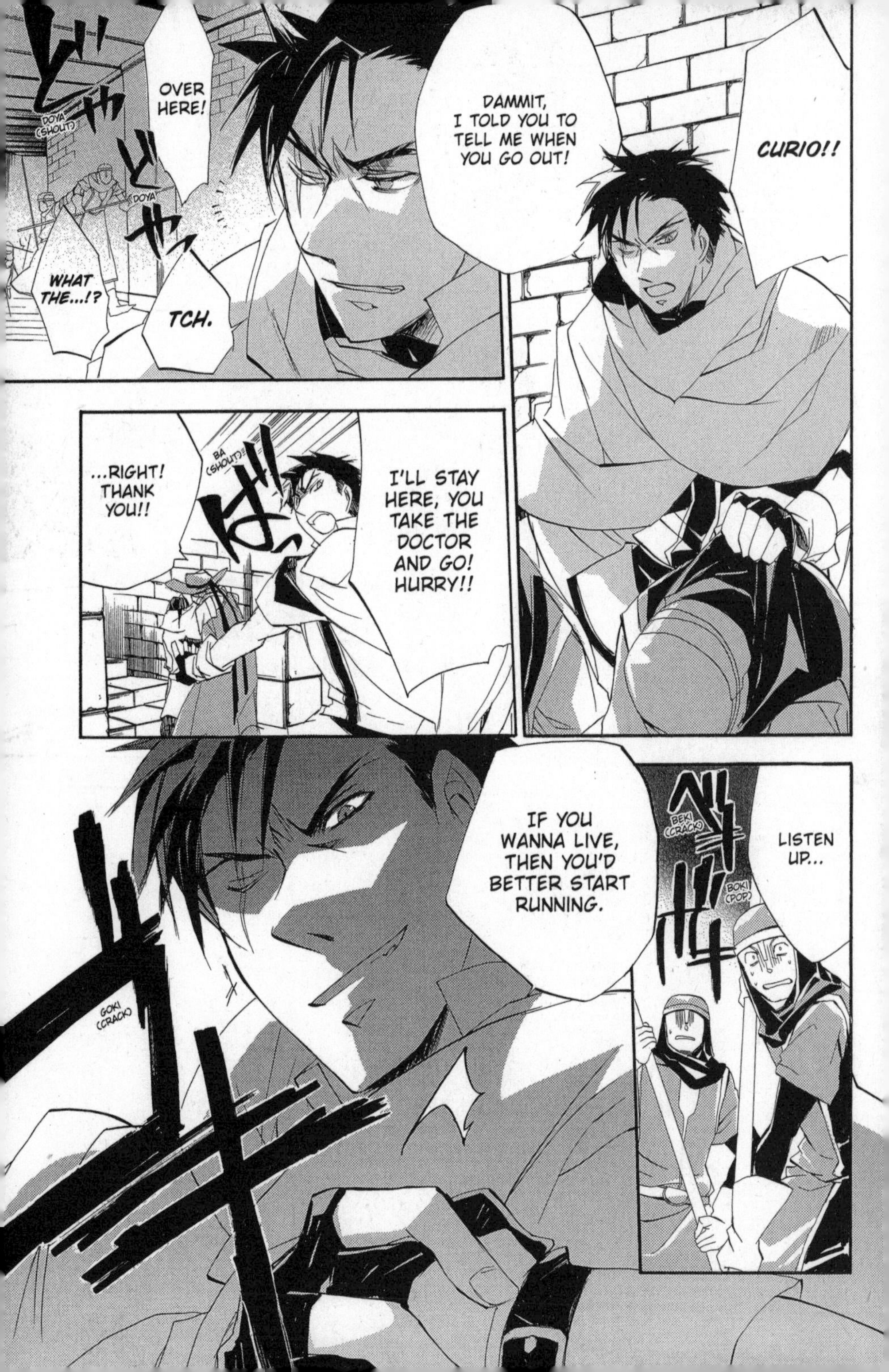
CURIO!!
DAMMIT, I TOLD YOU TO TELL ME WHEN YOU GO OUT!
OVER HERE!
DOYA (SHOUT)
DOYA
WHAT THE...!?
TCH.
I'LL STAY HERE, YOU TAKE THE DOCTOR AND GO! HURRY!!
BA (SHOUT)
...RIGHT! THANK YOU!!
LISTEN UP...
BEKI (CRACK)
BOKI (POP)
IF YOU WANNA LIVE, THEN YOU'D BETTER START RUNNING.
GOKI (CRACK)

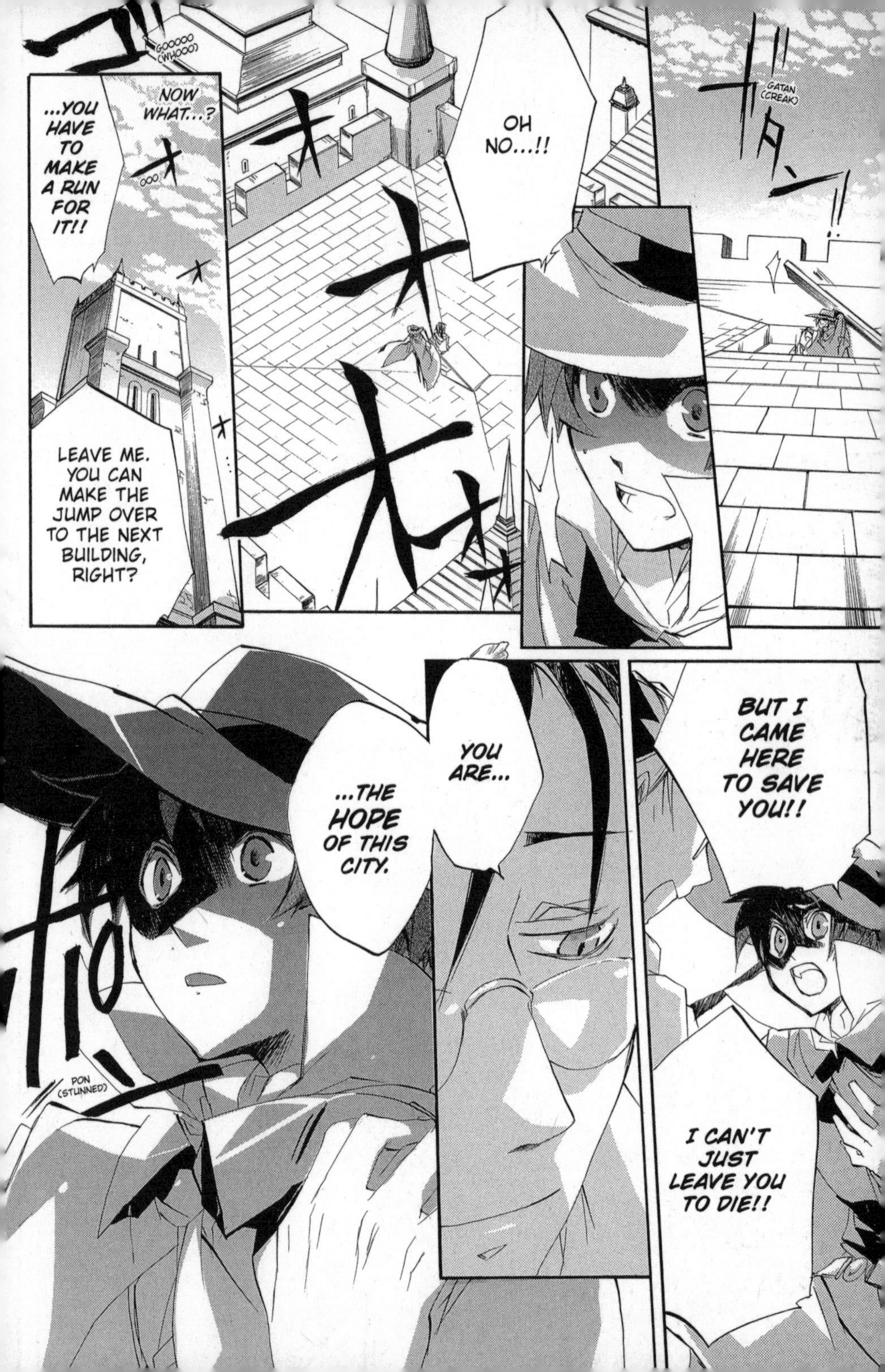
GATAN (CREAK)
OH NO...!!
GOOOOO (WHOOO)
NOW WHAT...?
...YOU HAVE TO MAKE A RUN FOR IT!!
LEAVE ME. YOU CAN MAKE THE JUMP OVER TO THE NEXT BUILDING, RIGHT?
BUT I CAME HERE TO SAVE YOU!!
I CAN'T JUST LEAVE YOU TO DIE!!
YOU ARE...
...THE HOPE OF THIS CITY.
PON (STUNNED)

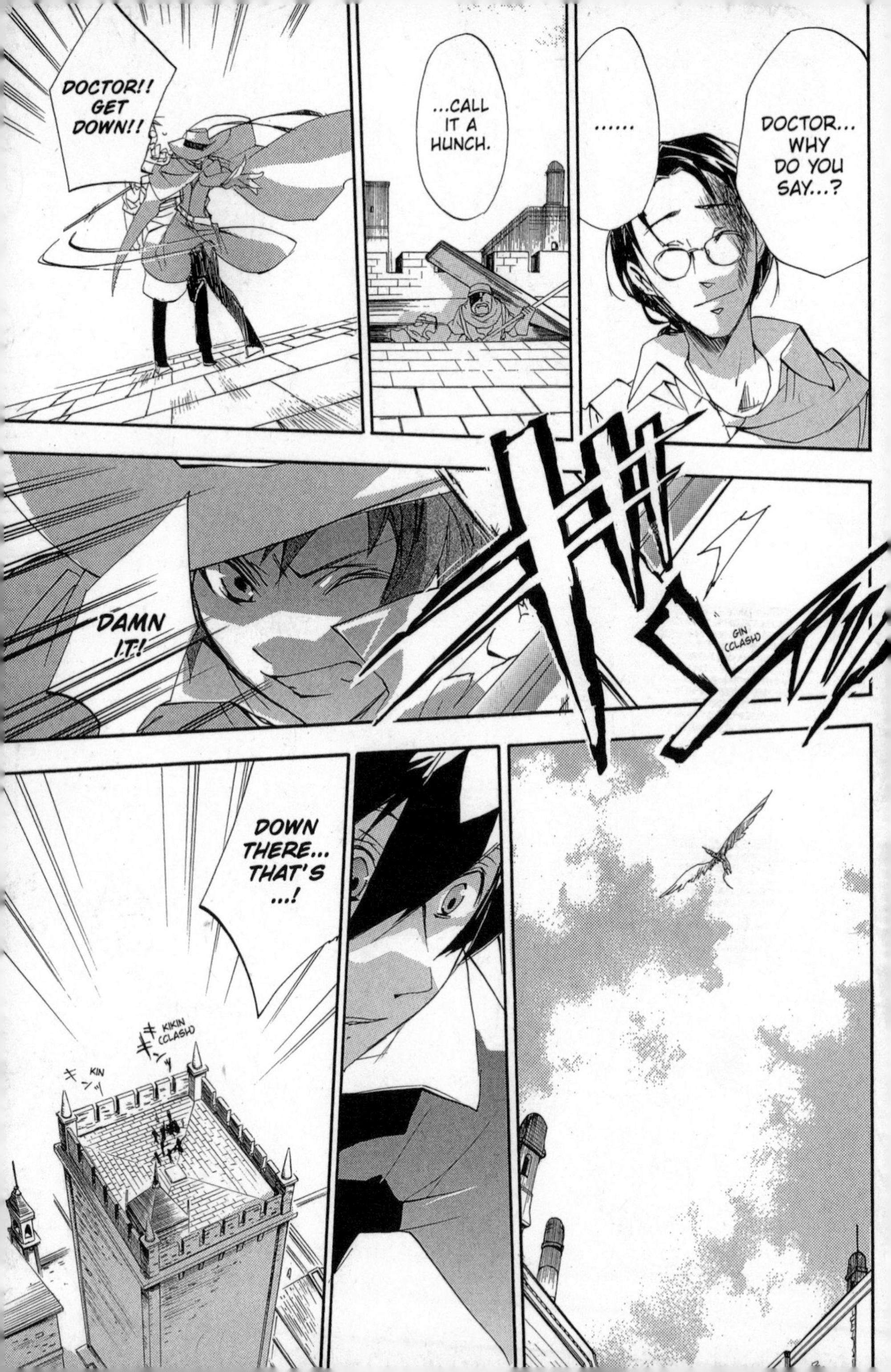
DOCTOR... WHY DO YOU SAY...?
......
...CALL IT A HUNCH.
DOCTOR!! GET DOWN!!
GIN (CLASH)
DAMN IT!
DOWN THERE... THAT'S ...!
KIKIN (CLASH)
KIN

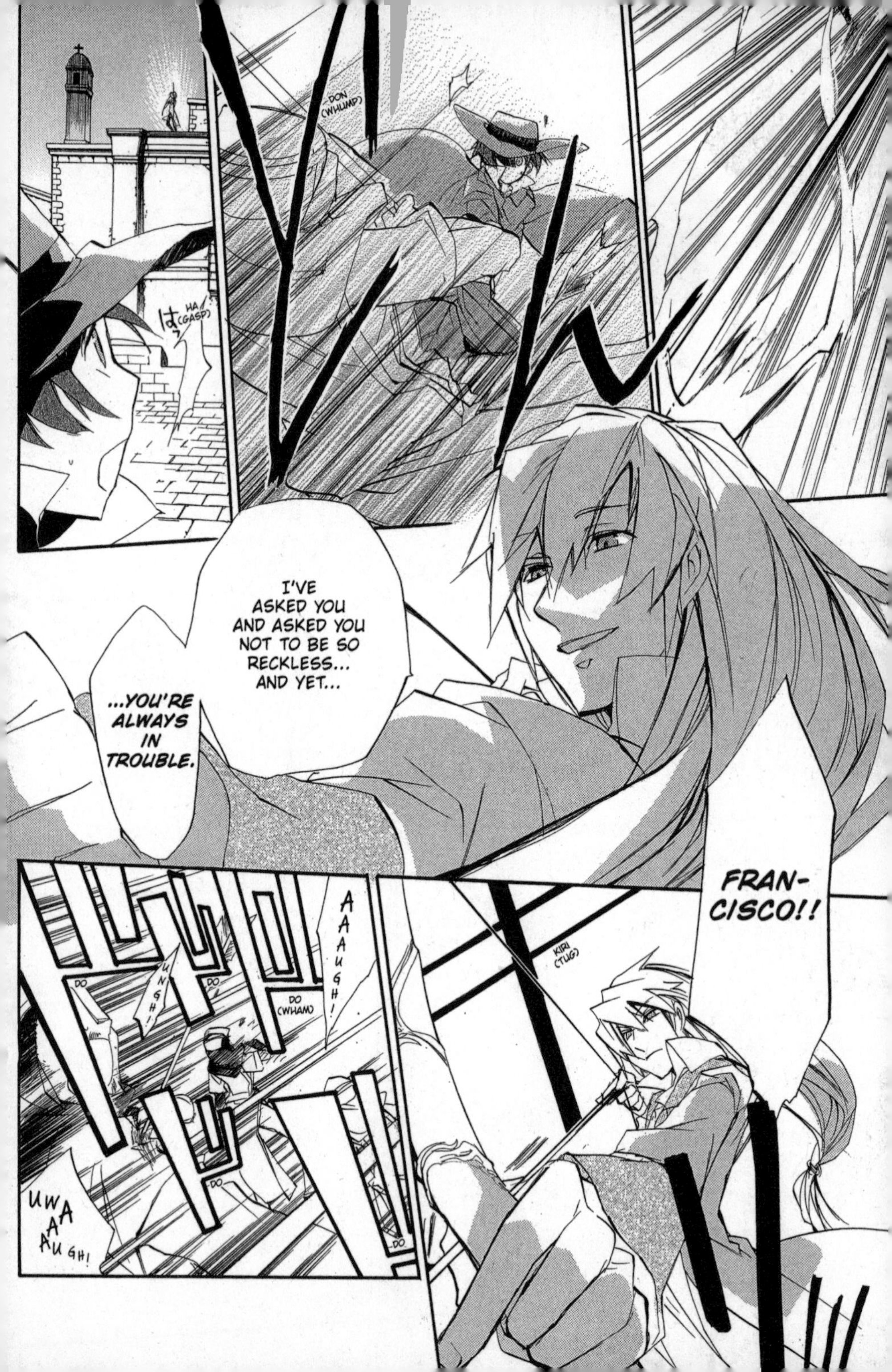
DON (WHUMP)
は HA (GASP)
I'VE ASKED YOU AND ASKED YOU NOT TO BE SO RECKLESS... AND YET...
...YOU'RE ALWAYS IN TROUBLE.
FRAN-CISCO!!
KIRI (TUG)
AAAAUGH!
UNGH!
DO (WHAM)
DO
DO
DO
DO
UWAAAAUGH!

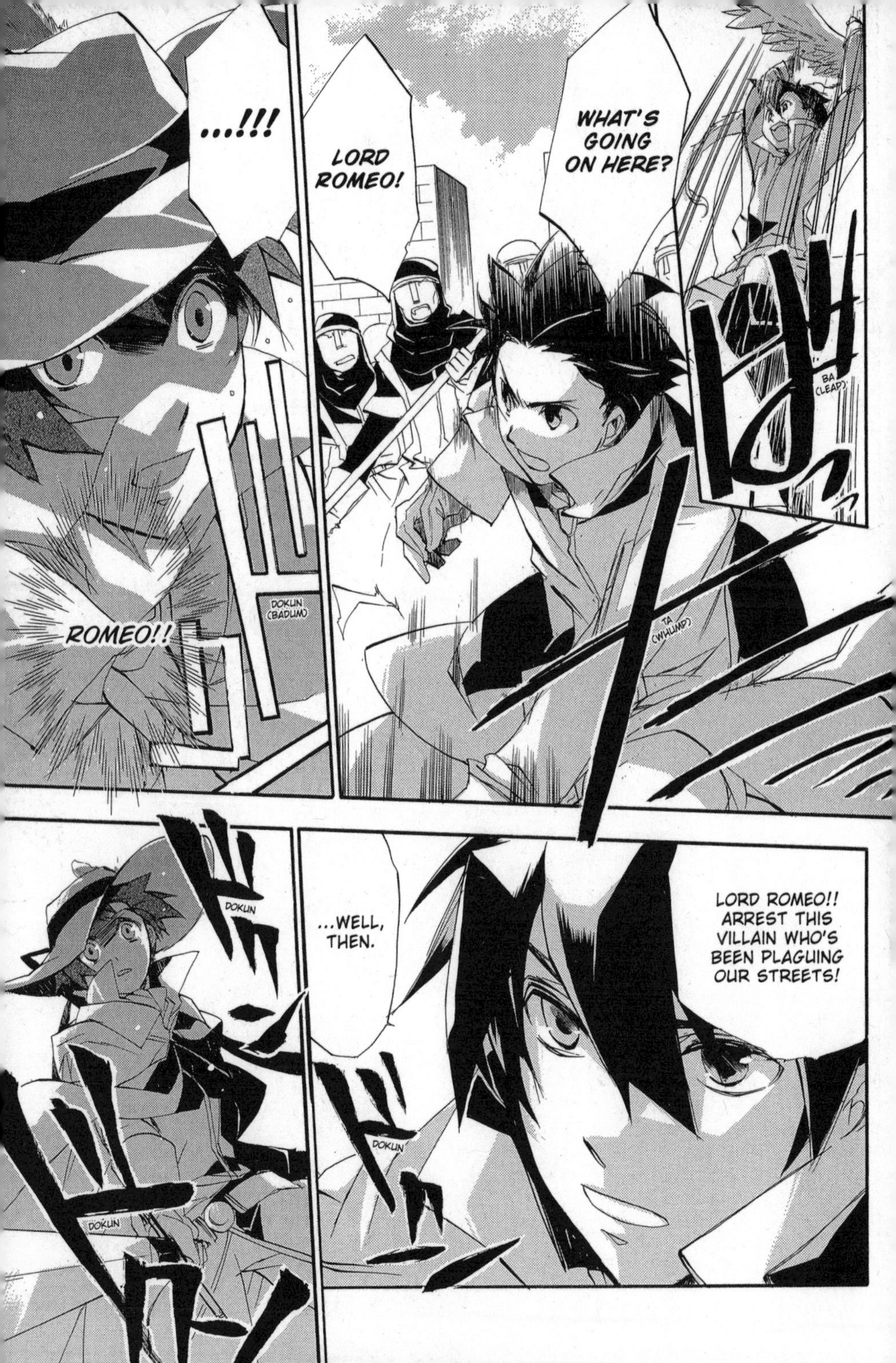
WHAT'S GOING ON HERE?
BA (LEAP)
LORD ROMEO!
TA (WHUMP)
...!!!
DOKUN (BADUM)
ROMEO!!
LORD ROMEO!! ARREST THIS VILLAIN WHO'S BEEN PLAGUING OUR STREETS!
...WELL, THEN.
DOKUN
DOKUN
DOKUN

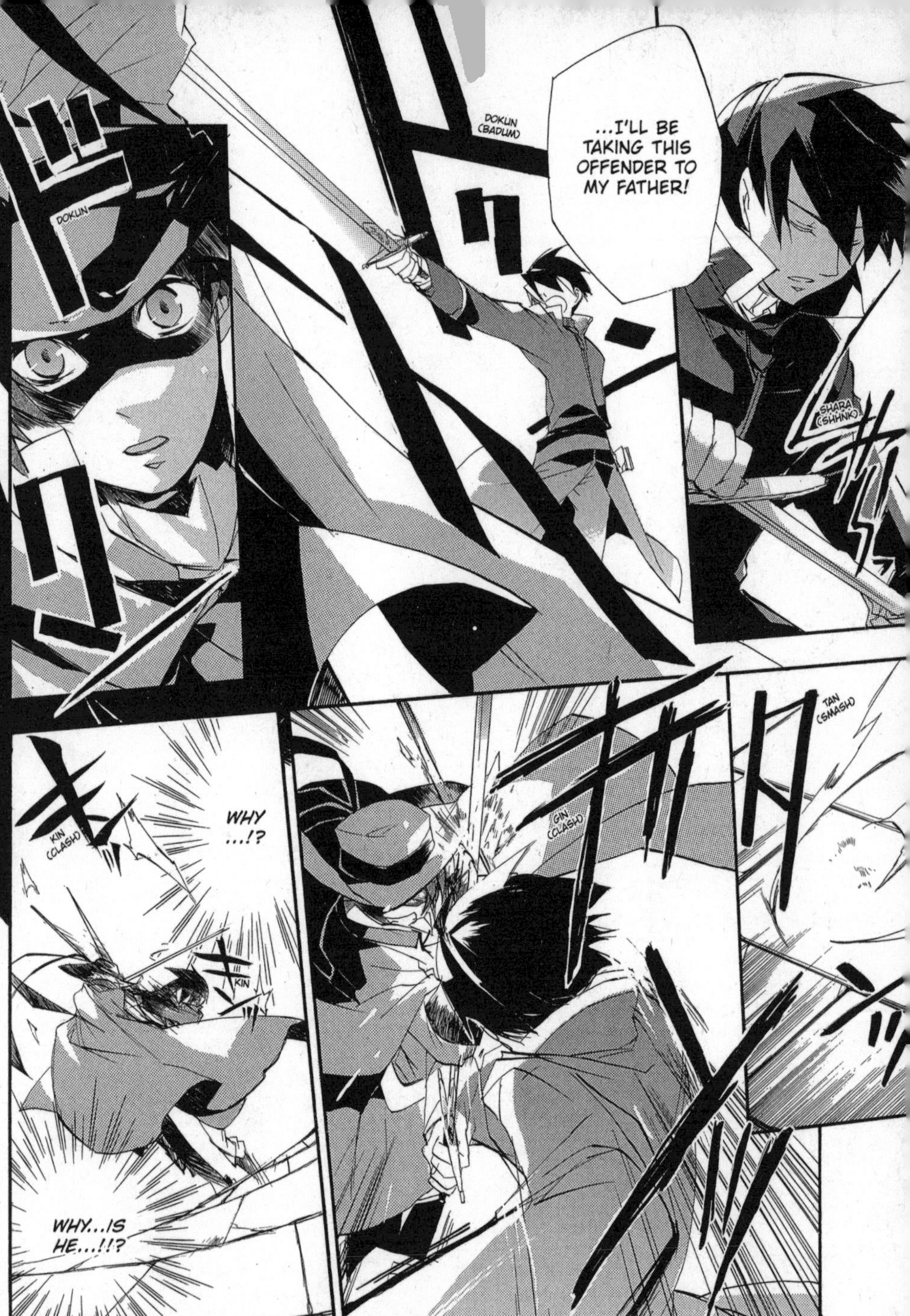
...I'LL BE TAKING THIS OFFENDER TO MY FATHER!
SHARA (SHHNK)
DOKUN (BADUM)
DOKUN
TAN (SMASH)
GIN (CLASH)
KIN (CLASH)
WHY ...!?
KIN
WHY...IS HE...!!?

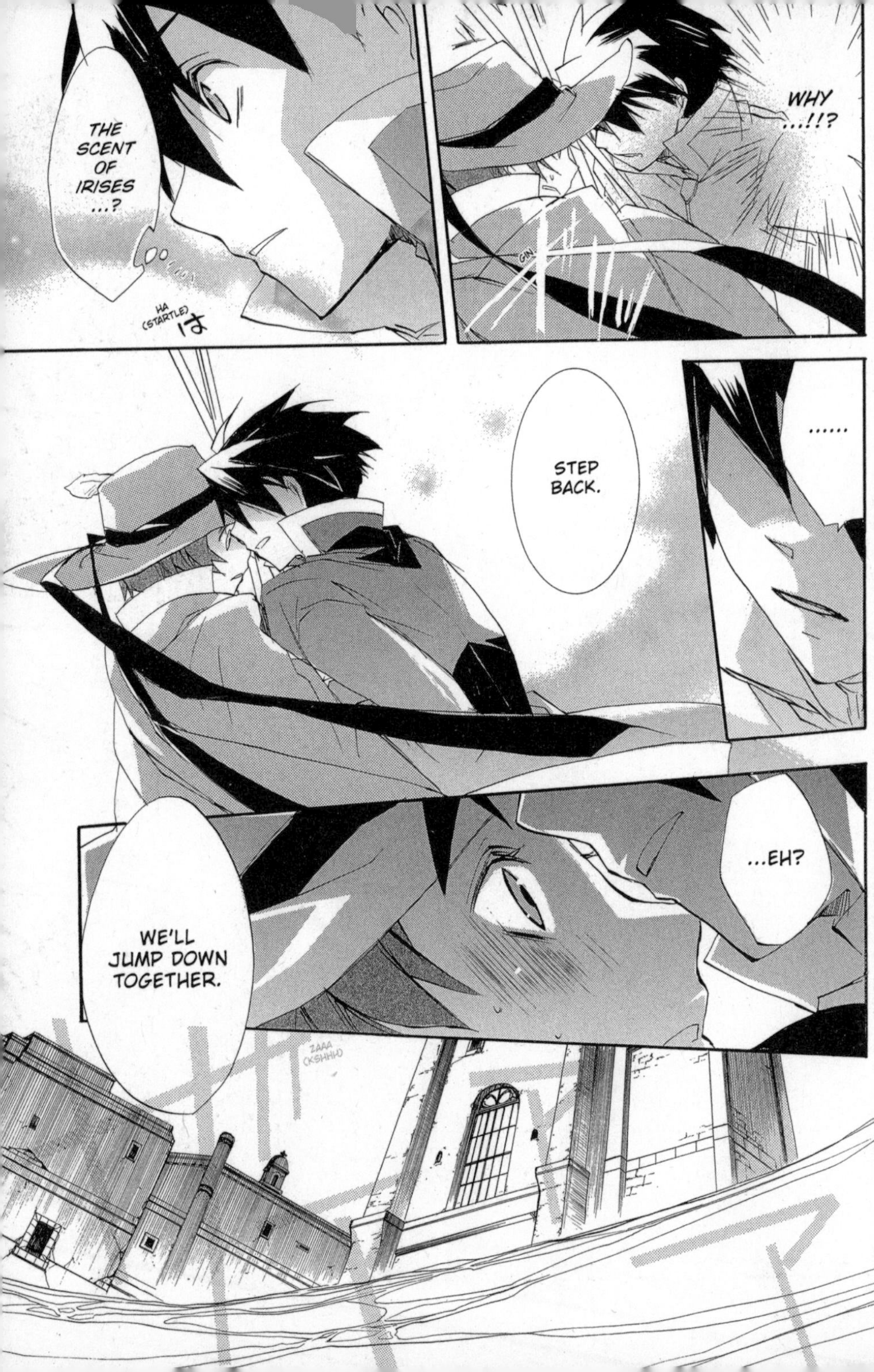
WHY ...!!?
GIN
THE SCENT OF IRISES ...?
HA (STARTLE) は
......
STEP BACK.
...EH?
WE'LL JUMP DOWN TOGETHER.
ZAAA (KSHHH)

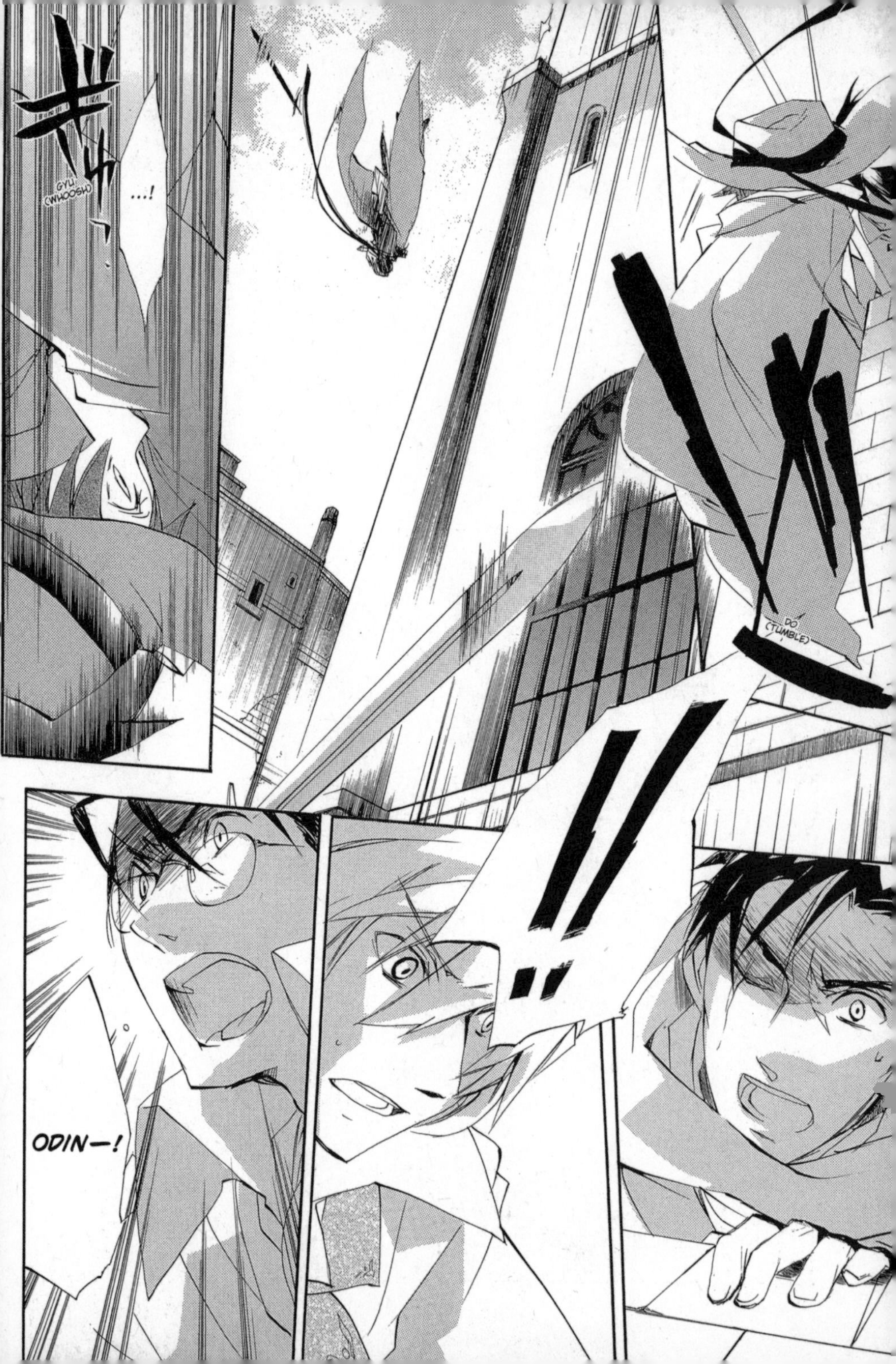
DO (TUMBLE)
GYU (WHOOSH)
...!
ODIN—!

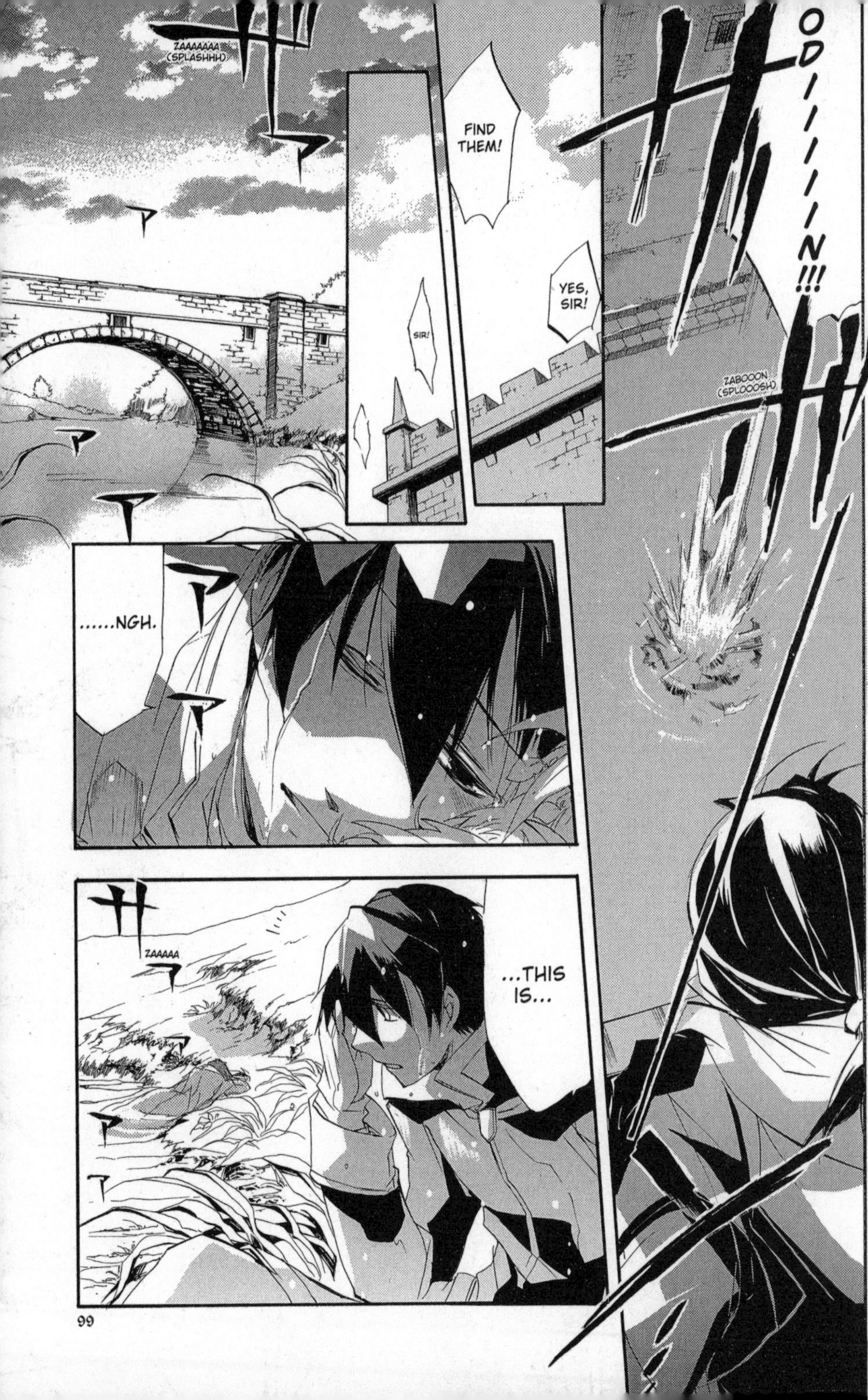
ODIIIIIN!!!
ZABOOON
(SPLOOOSH)
FIND THEM!
YES, SIR!
SIR!
ZAAAAAAA
(SPLASHHH)
......NGH.
ZAAAAA
...THIS IS...

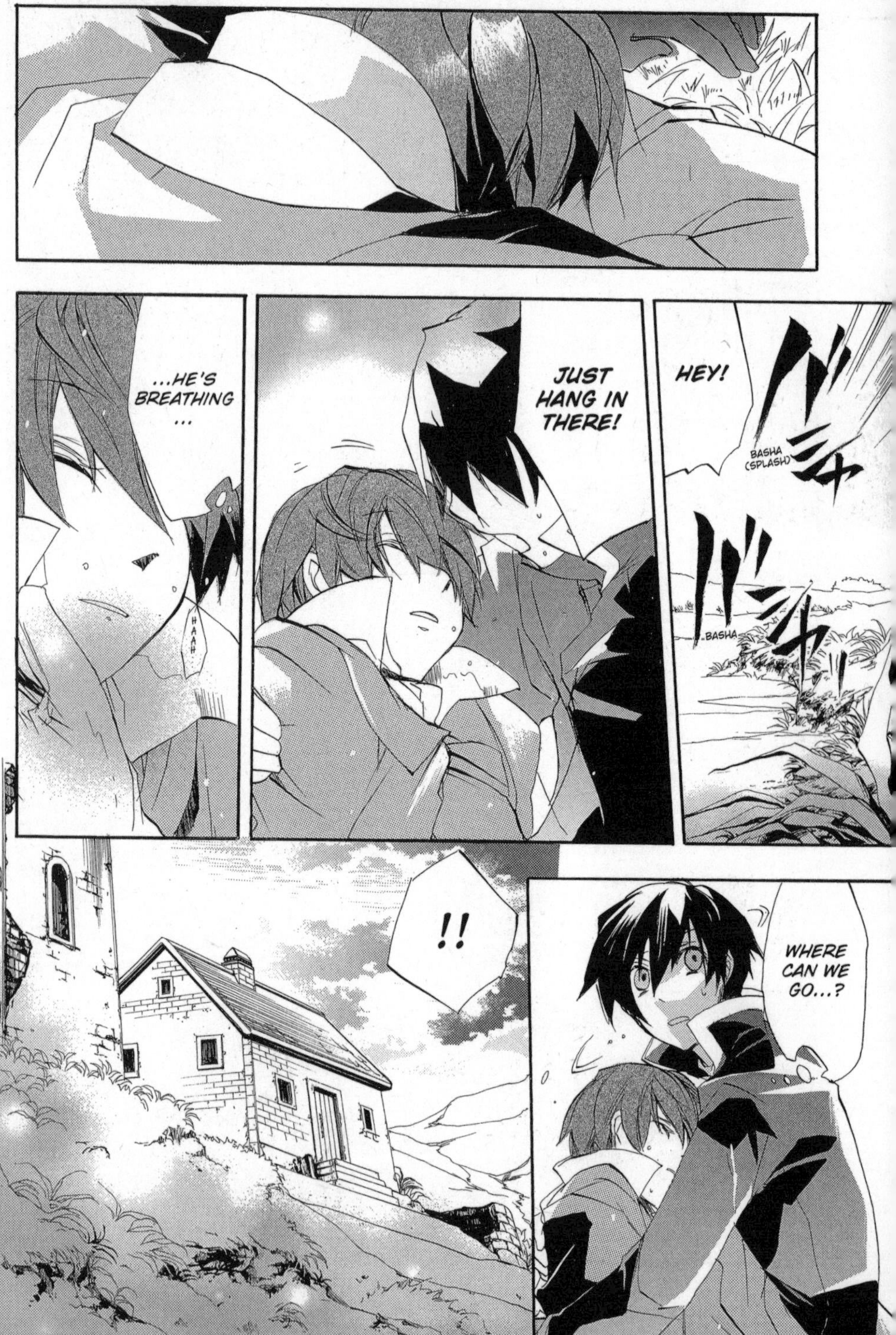
HEY!
BASHA (SPLASH)
...BASHA
JUST HANG IN THERE!
...HE'S BREATHING ...
HAAH
WHERE CAN WE GO...?
!!

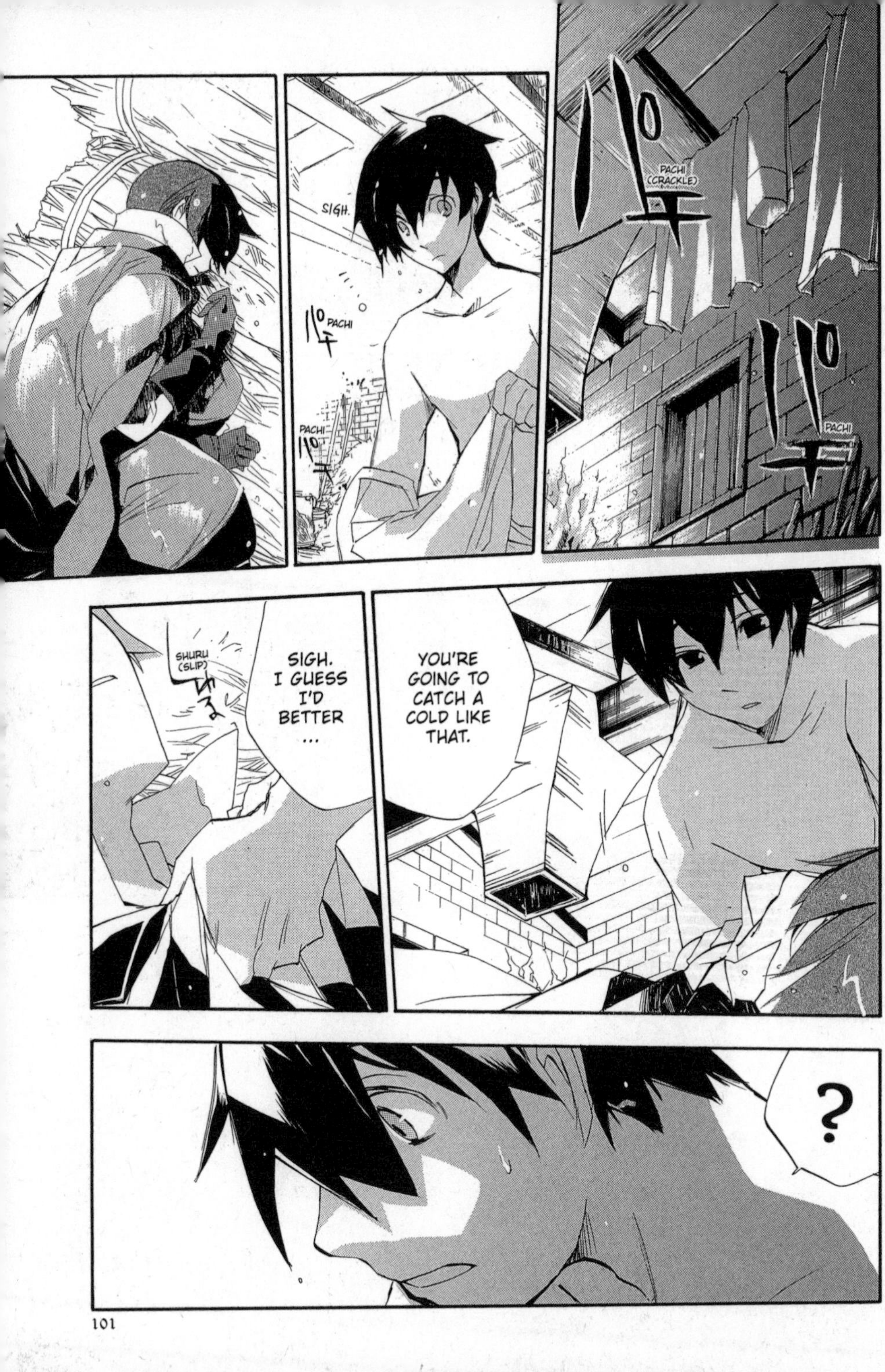
PACHI (CRACKLE)
PACHI
SIGH.
PACHI
PACHI
YOU'RE GOING TO CATCH A COLD LIKE THAT.
SIGH. I GUESS I'D BETTER ...
SHURU (SLIP)
?

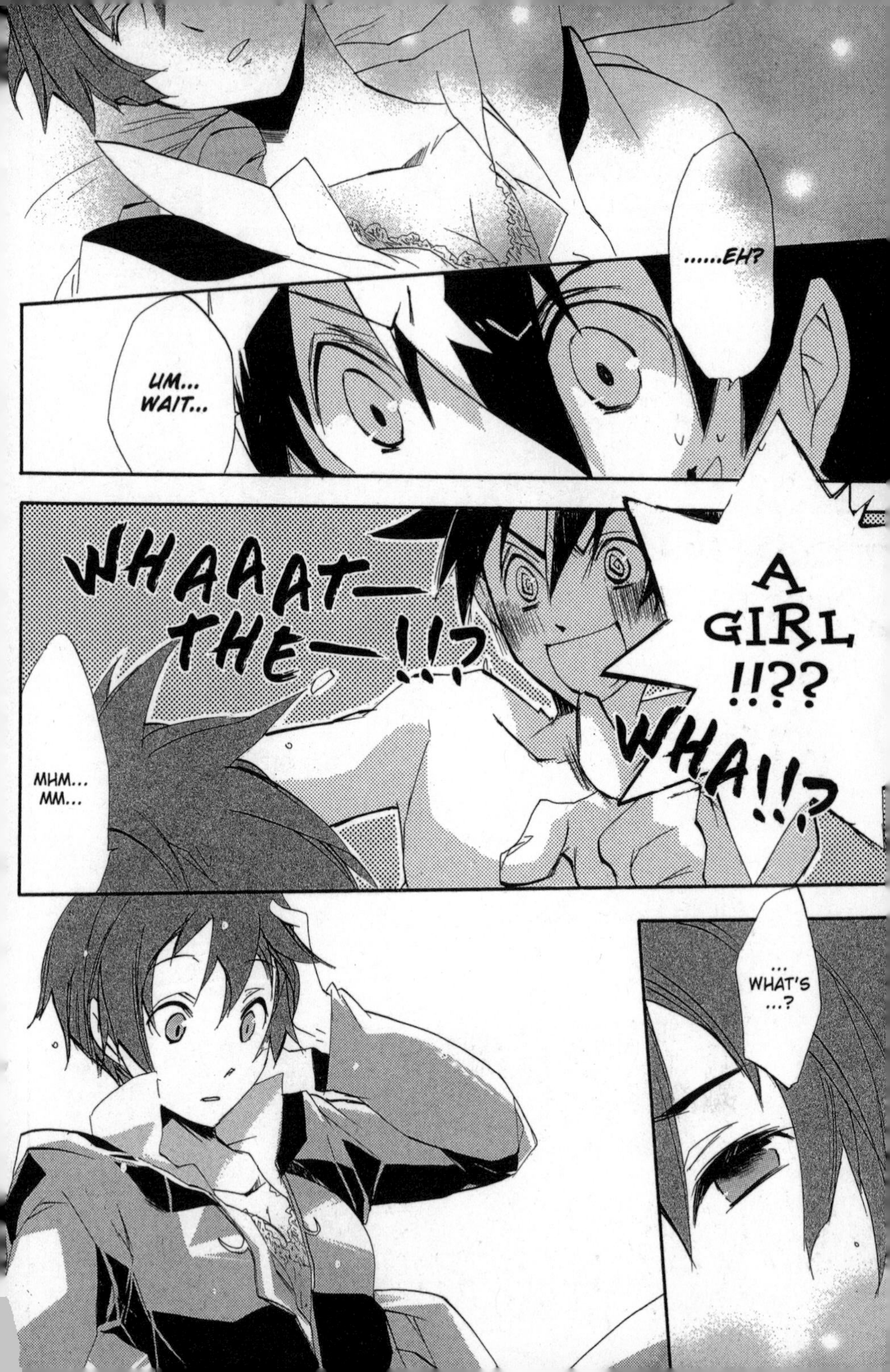
......EH?
UM... WAIT...
A GIRL !!??
WHAAAT— THE—!!?
WHA!!?
MHM... MM...
... WHAT'S ...?

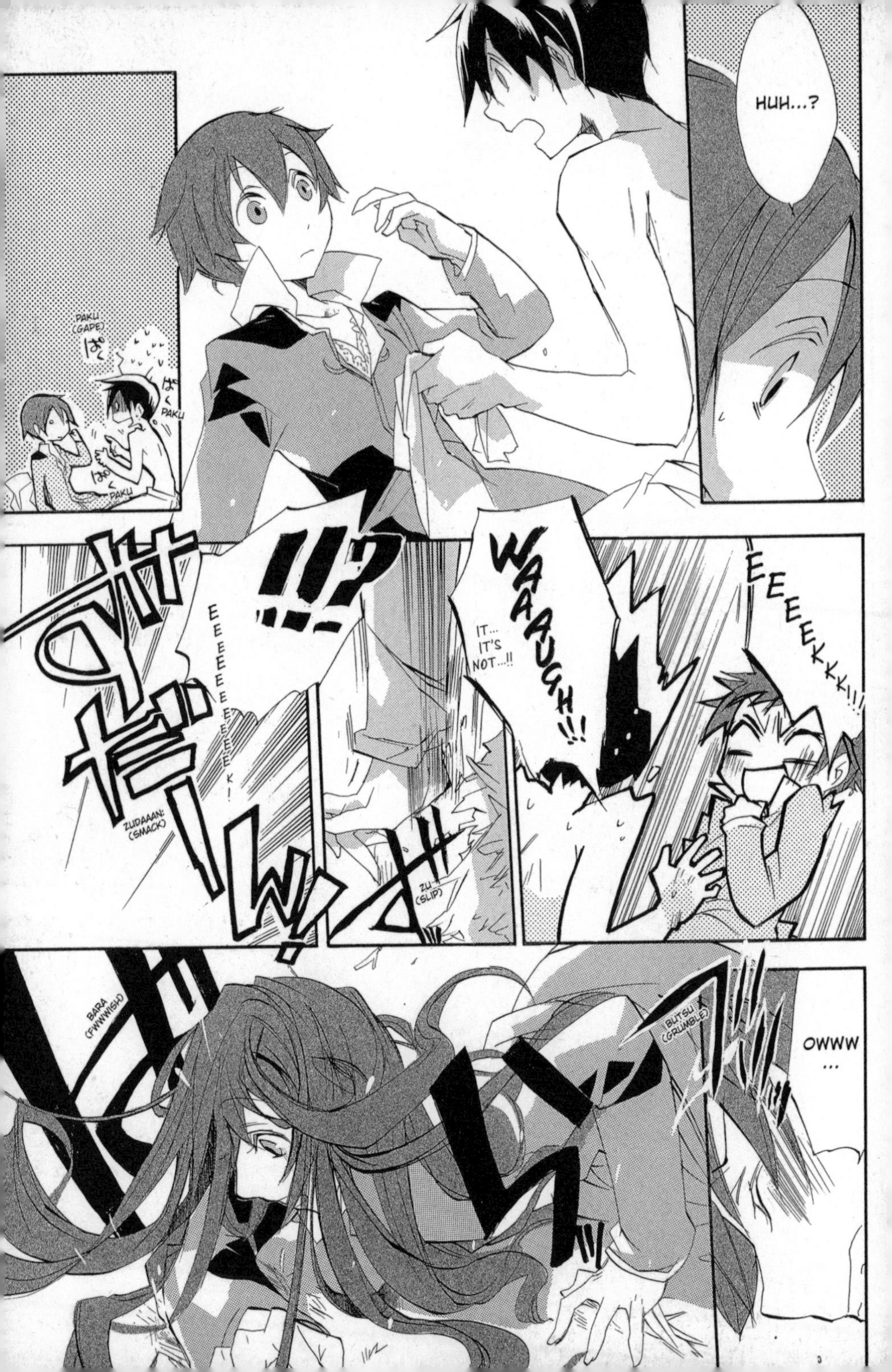
HUH...?
PAKU (GAPE)
ぱく
ぱく
PAKU
ぱく
PAKU
EEEEEKKK!!!
WAAAUGH!!!
IT... IT'S NOT...!!
!!?
EEEEEEEEEEEK!
ZUDAAAN: (SMACK)
ZU (SLIP)
OWWW...
BUTSU (GRUMBLE)
BARA (FWWWIGH)

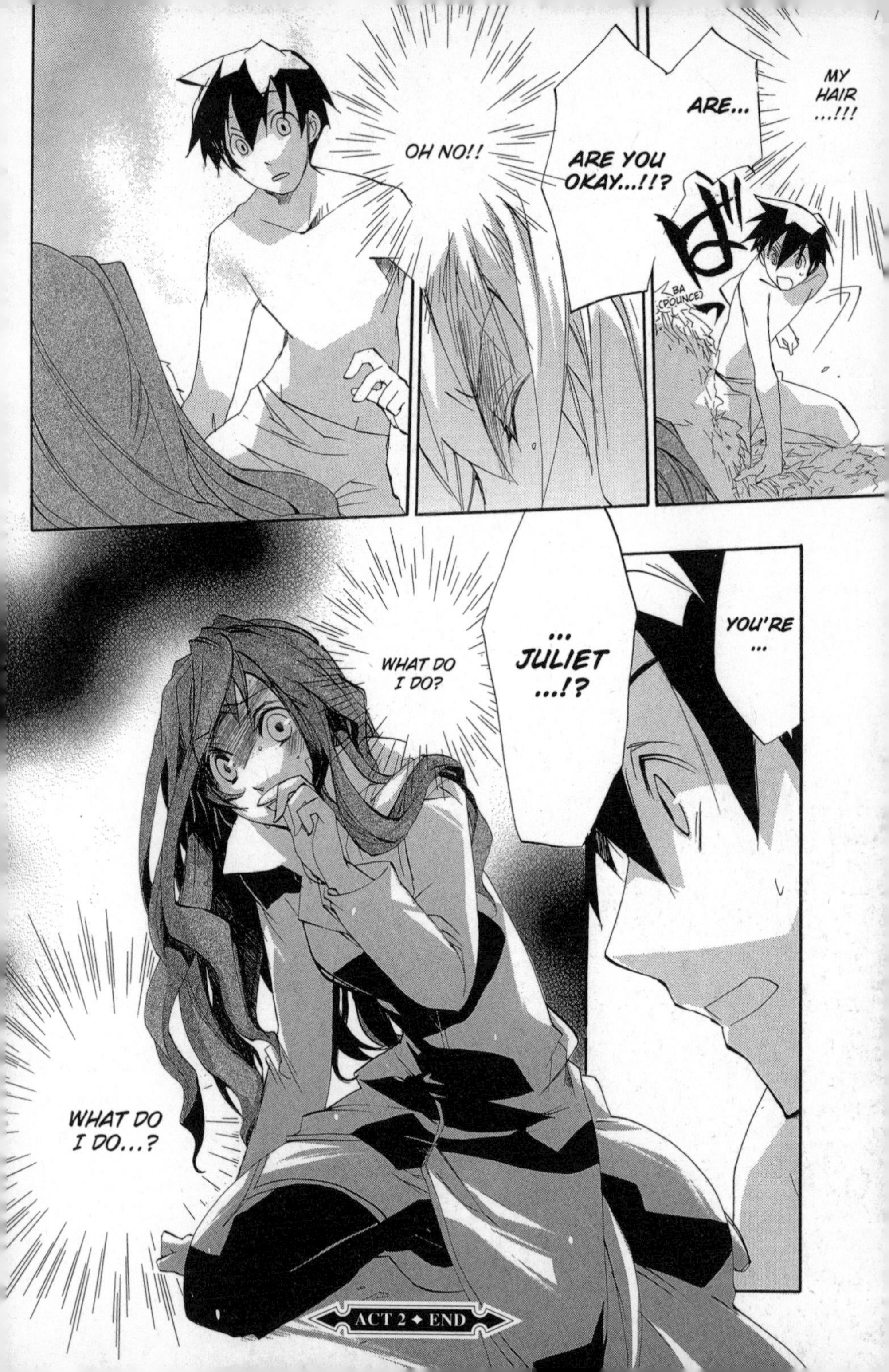
MY HAIR ...!!!
BA (POUNCE)
ARE...
ARE YOU OKAY...!!?
OH NO!!
YOU'RE ...
... JULIET ...!?
WHAT DO I DO?
WHAT DO I DO...?
ACT 2 ◆ END

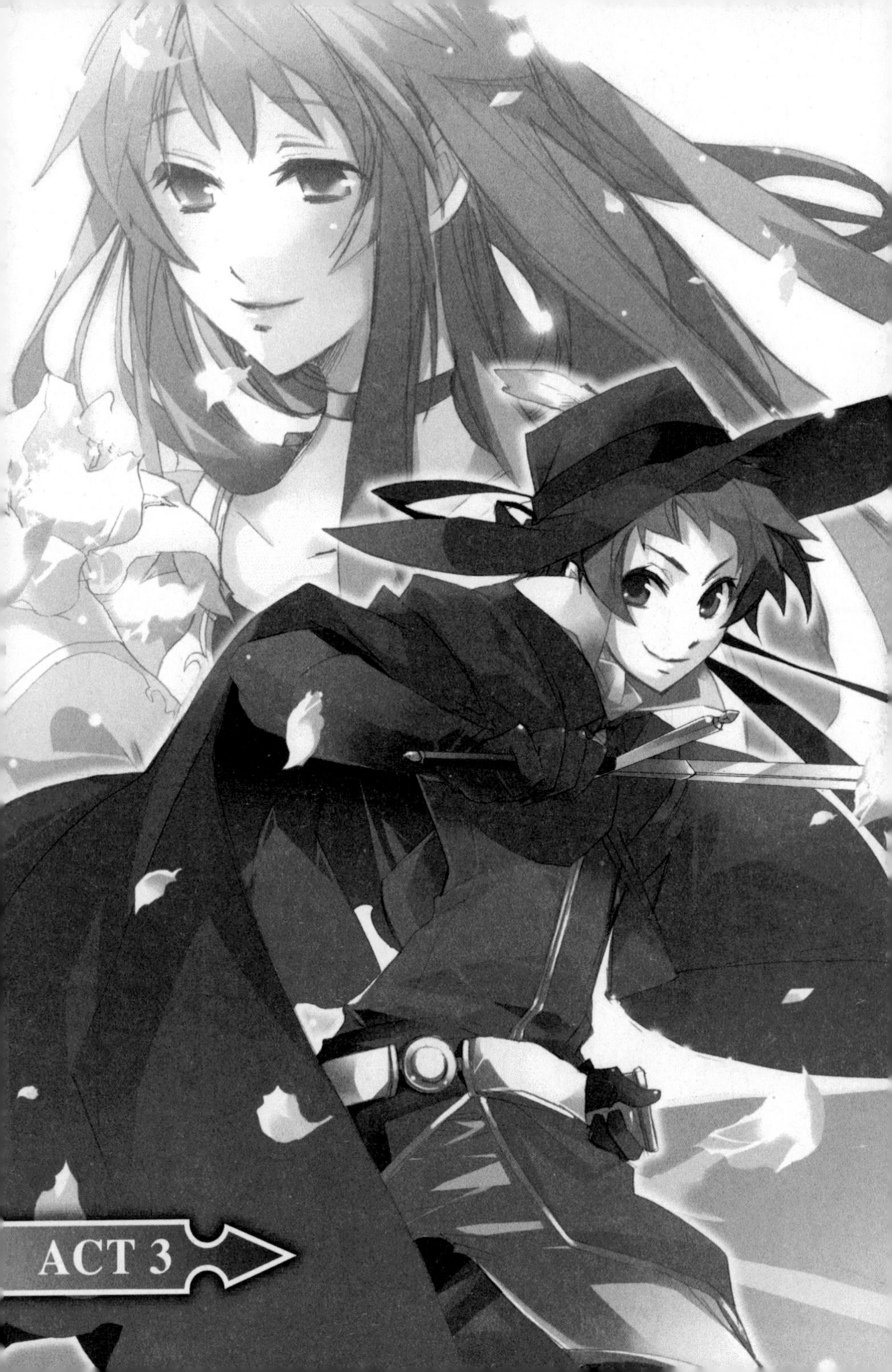
ACT 3

Romeo×Juliet

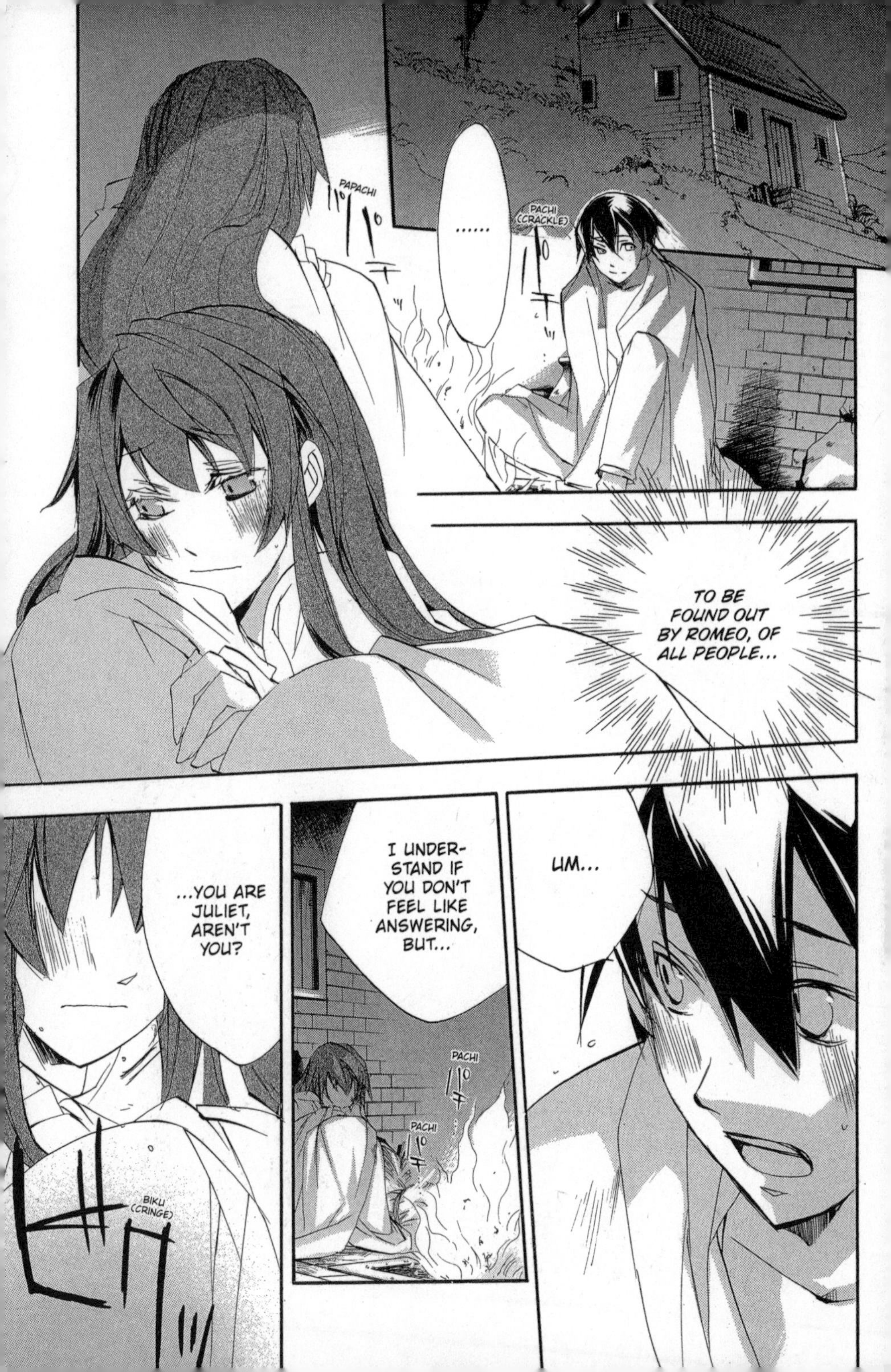
PACHI (CRACKLE)
......
PAPACHI
TO BE FOUND OUT BY ROMEO, OF ALL PEOPLE...
UM...
I UNDER-STAND IF YOU DON'T FEEL LIKE ANSWERING, BUT...
PACHI
PACHI
...YOU ARE JULIET, AREN'T YOU?
BIKU (CRINGE)

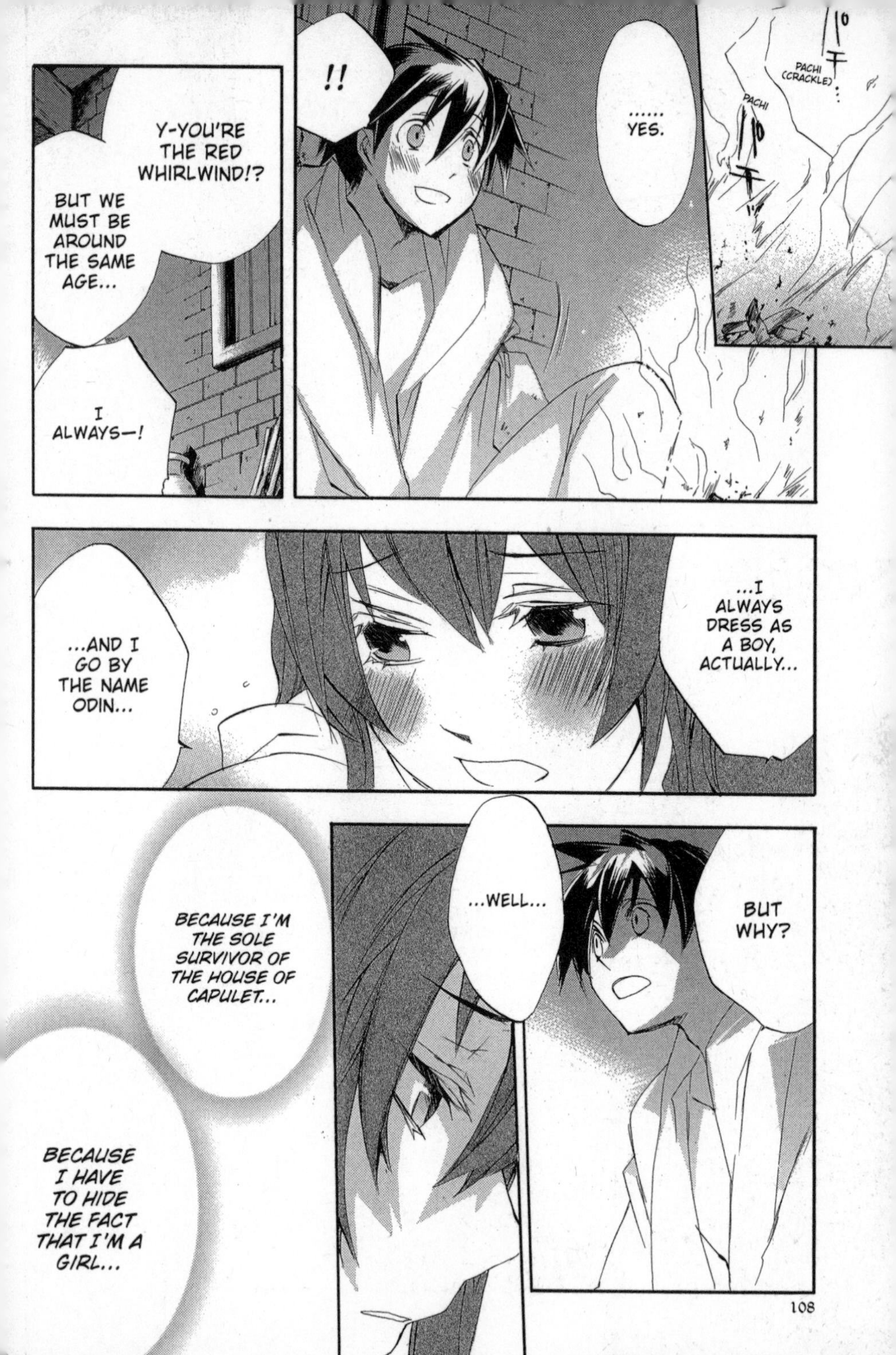
PACHI (CRACKLE)
PACHI
......YES.
!!
Y-YOU'RE THE RED WHIRLWIND!?
BUT WE MUST BE AROUND THE SAME AGE...
I ALWAYS—!
...I ALWAYS DRESS AS A BOY, ACTUALLY...
...AND I GO BY THE NAME ODIN...
BUT WHY?
...WELL...
BECAUSE I'M THE SOLE SURVIVOR OF THE HOUSE OF CAPULET...
BECAUSE I HAVE TO HIDE THE FACT THAT I'M A GIRL...

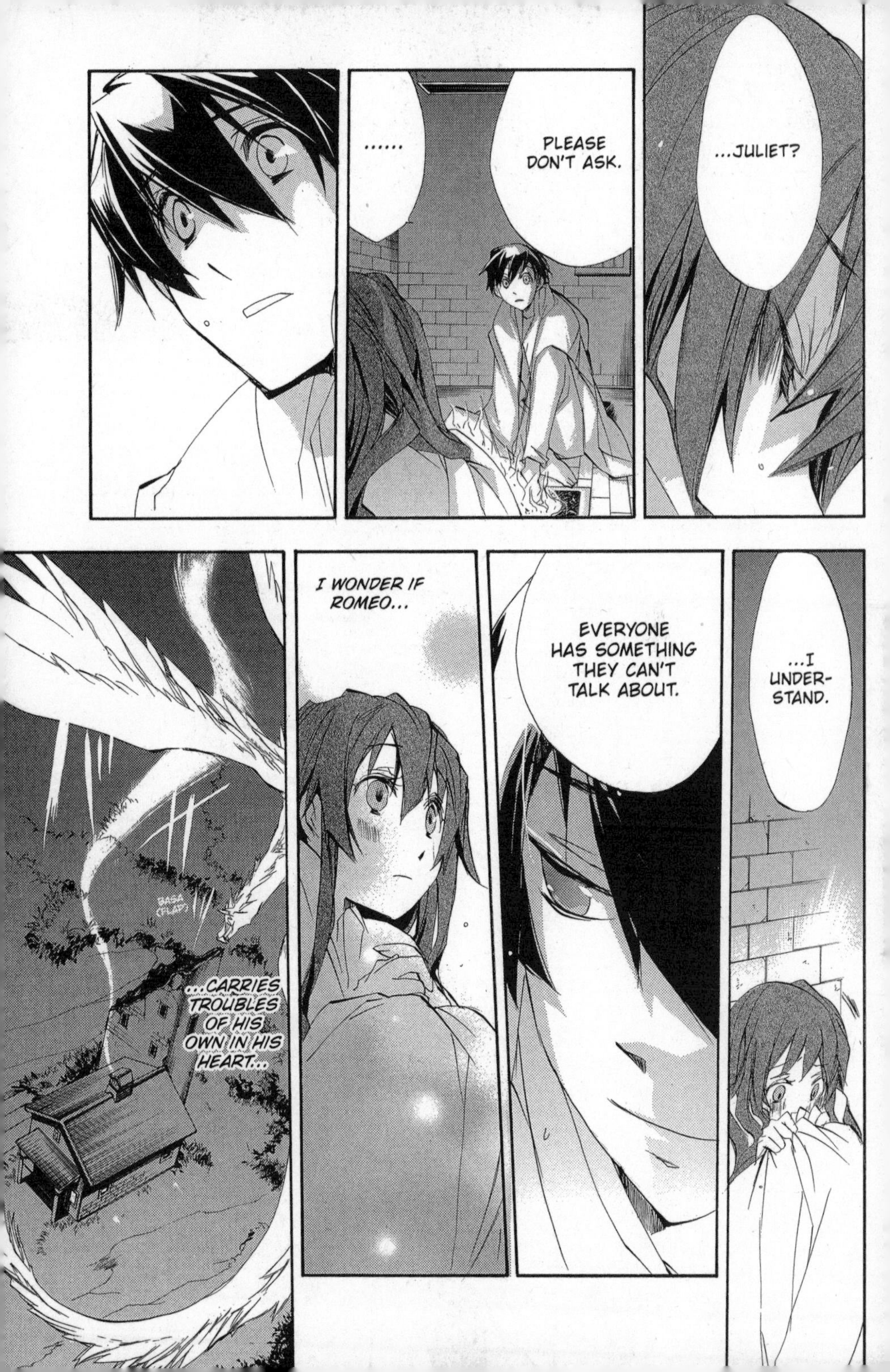

...JULIET?
PLEASE DON'T ASK.
......
...I UNDER-STAND.
EVERYONE HAS SOMETHING THEY CAN'T TALK ABOUT.
I WONDER IF ROMEO...
BASA (FLAP)
...CARRIES TROUBLES OF HIS OWN IN HIS HEART...

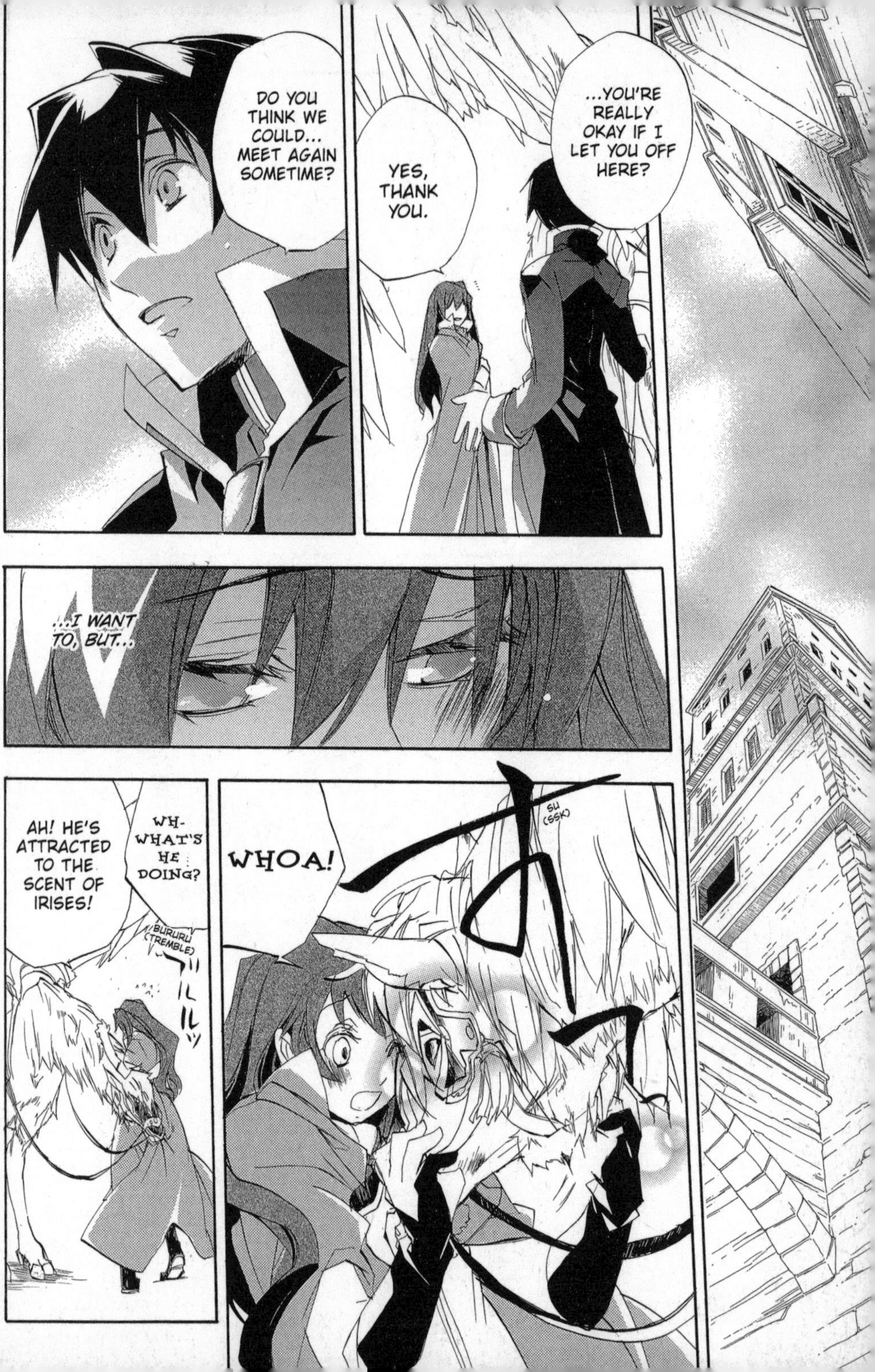
...YOU'RE REALLY OKAY IF I LET YOU OFF HERE?
YES, THANK YOU.
DO YOU THINK WE COULD... MEET AGAIN SOMETIME?
...I WANT TO, BUT...
SU (SSK)
WHOA!
WH-WHAT'S HE DOING?
AH! HE'S ATTRACTED TO THE SCENT OF IRISES!
BURURU (TREMBLE)

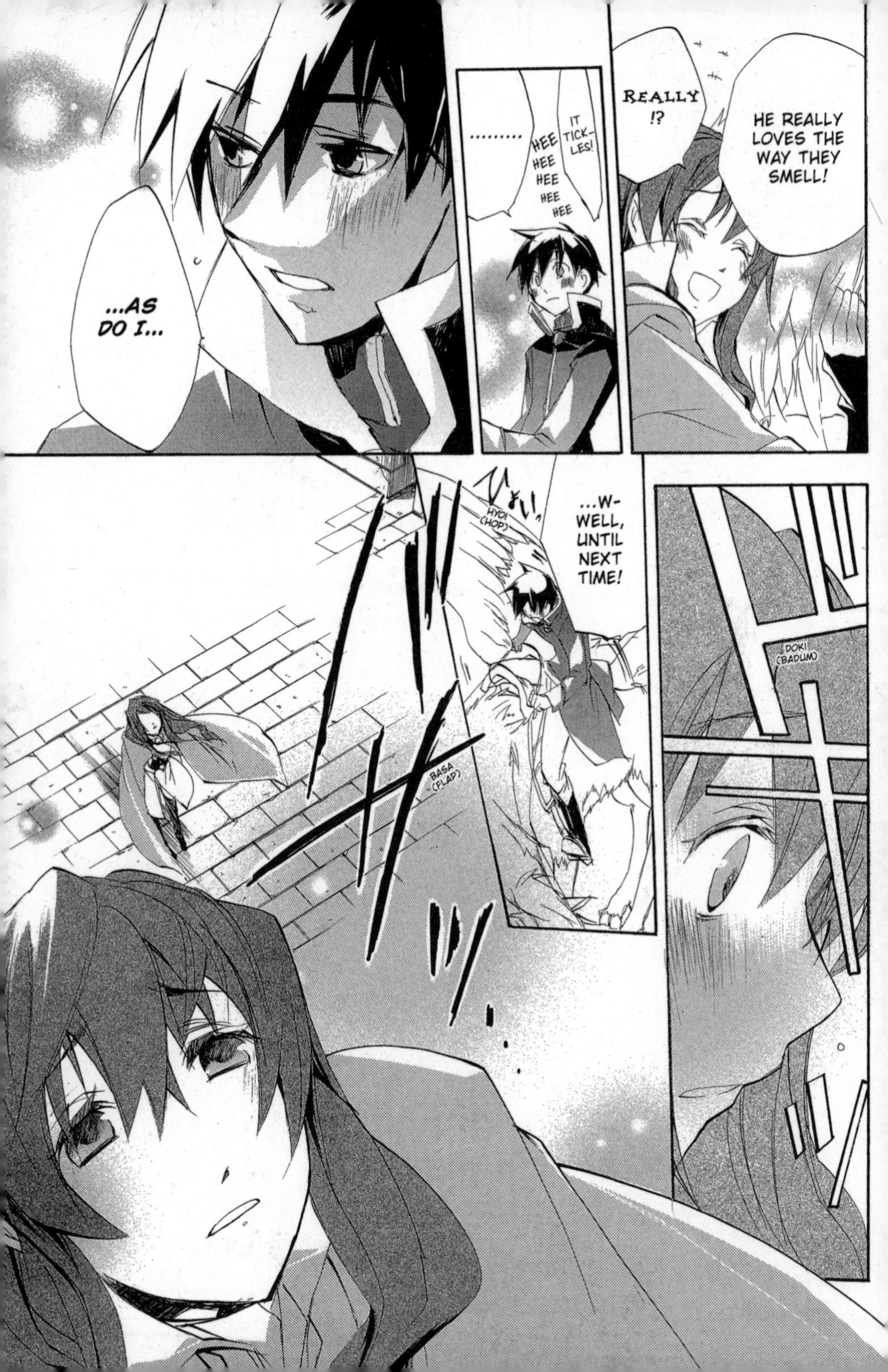
HE REALLY LOVES THE WAY THEY SMELL!
REALLY !?
IT TICK-LES!
HEE HEE HEE HEE HEE
....
...AS DO I...
DOKI (BADUM)
...W-WELL, UNTIL NEXT TIME!
HYOI (HOP)
BASA (FLAP)

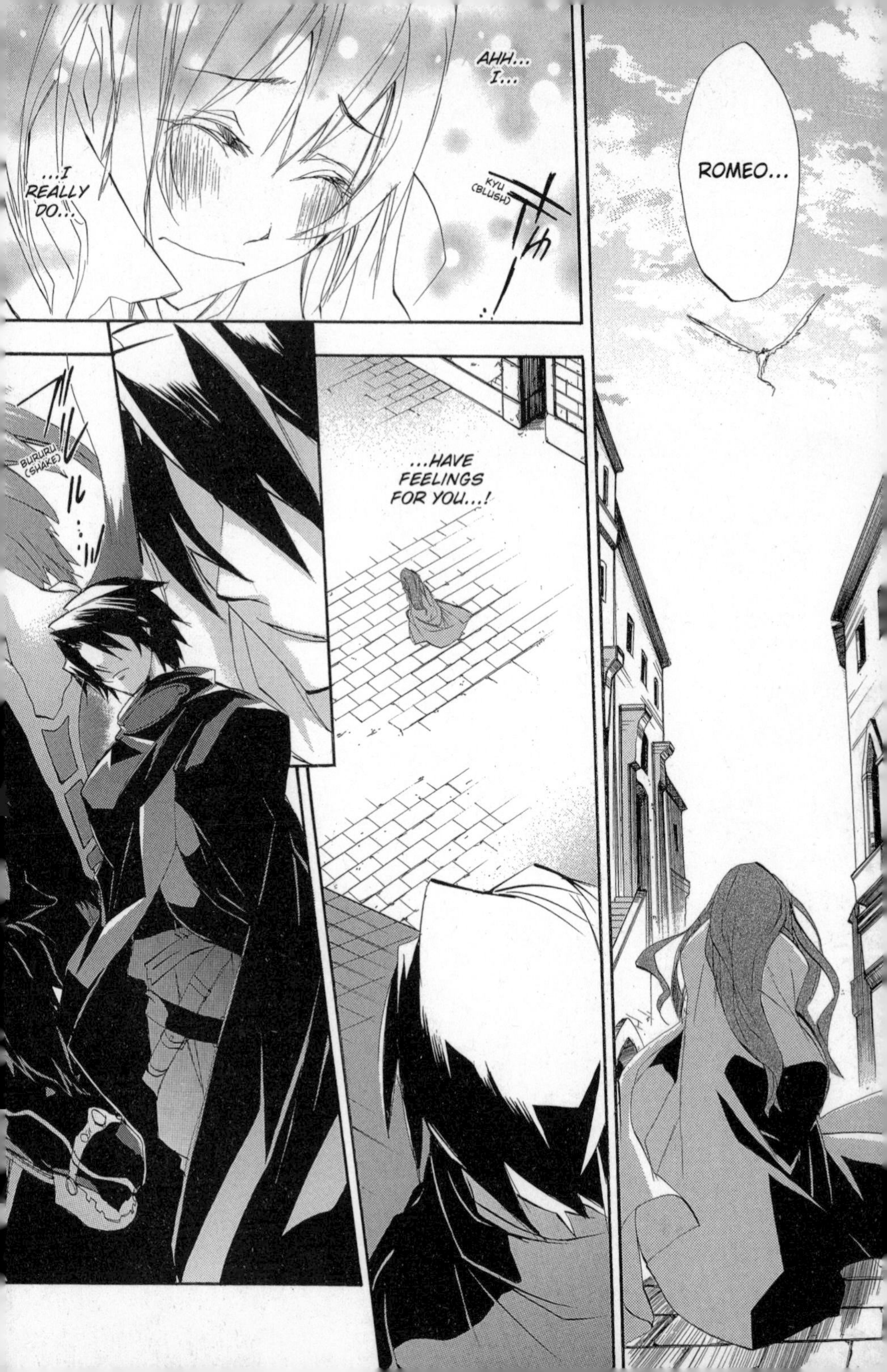
ROMEO...
AHH... I...
KYU (BLUSH)
...I REALLY DO...
...HAVE FEELINGS FOR YOU...!
BURURU (SHAKE)

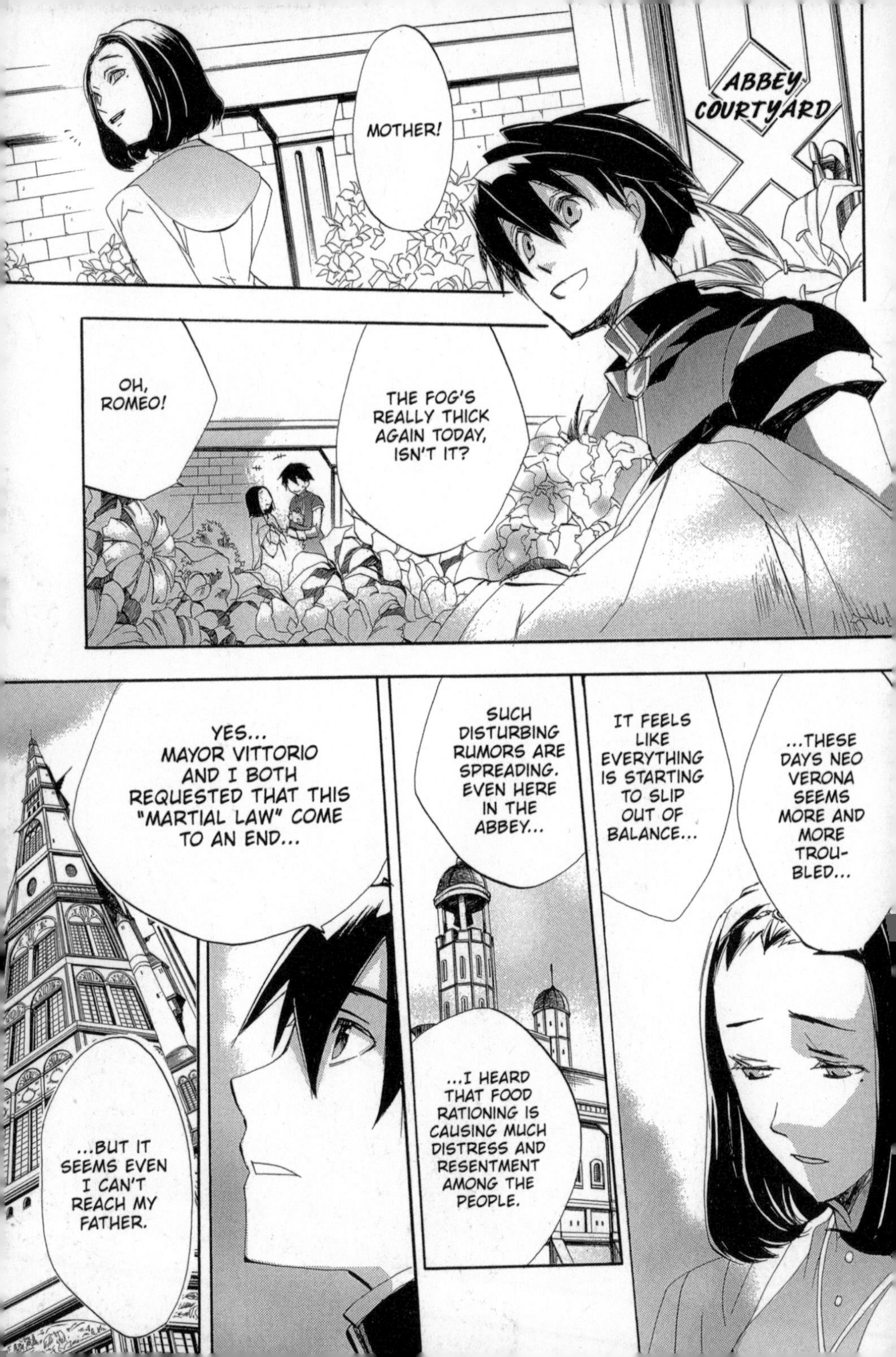
ABBEY COURTYARD
MOTHER!
OH, ROMEO!
THE FOG'S REALLY THICK AGAIN TODAY, ISN'T IT?
...THESE DAYS NEO VERONA SEEMS MORE AND MORE TROU-BLED...
IT FEELS LIKE EVERYTHING IS STARTING TO SLIP OUT OF BALANCE...
SUCH DISTURBING RUMORS ARE SPREADING. EVEN HERE IN THE ABBEY...
...I HEARD THAT FOOD RATIONING IS CAUSING MUCH DISTRESS AND RESENTMENT AMONG THE PEOPLE.
YES... MAYOR VITTORIO AND I BOTH REQUESTED THAT THIS "MARTIAL LAW" COME TO AN END...
...BUT IT SEEMS EVEN I CAN'T REACH MY FATHER.

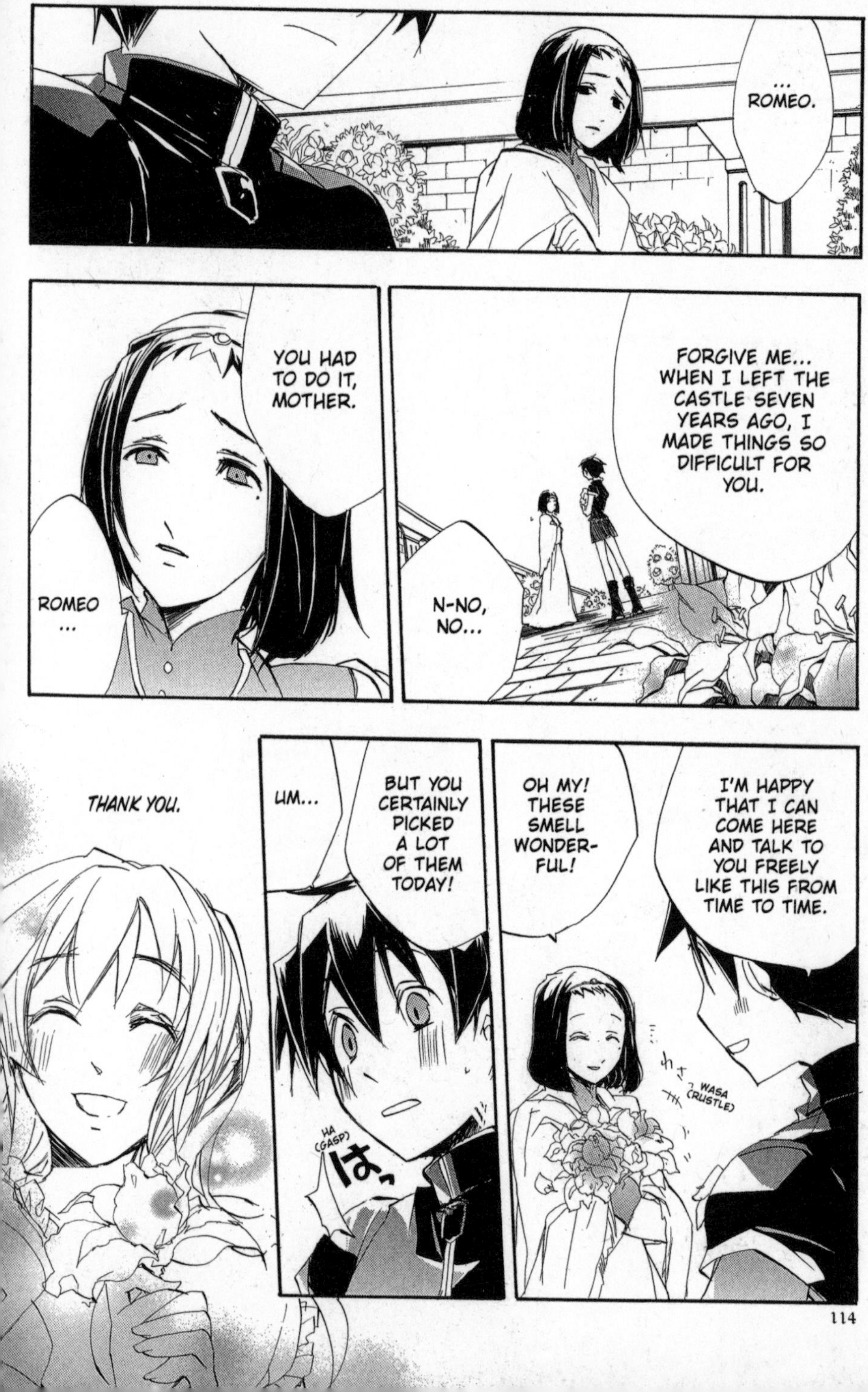
... ROMEO.
FORGIVE ME... WHEN I LEFT THE CASTLE SEVEN YEARS AGO, I MADE THINGS SO DIFFICULT FOR YOU.
N-NO, NO...
YOU HAD TO DO IT, MOTHER.
ROMEO ...
I'M HAPPY THAT I CAN COME HERE AND TALK TO YOU FREELY LIKE THIS FROM TIME TO TIME.
OH MY! THESE SMELL WONDER-FUL!
WASA (RUSTLE)
BUT YOU CERTAINLY PICKED A LOT OF THEM TODAY!
UM...
HA (GASP)
は っ
THANK YOU.

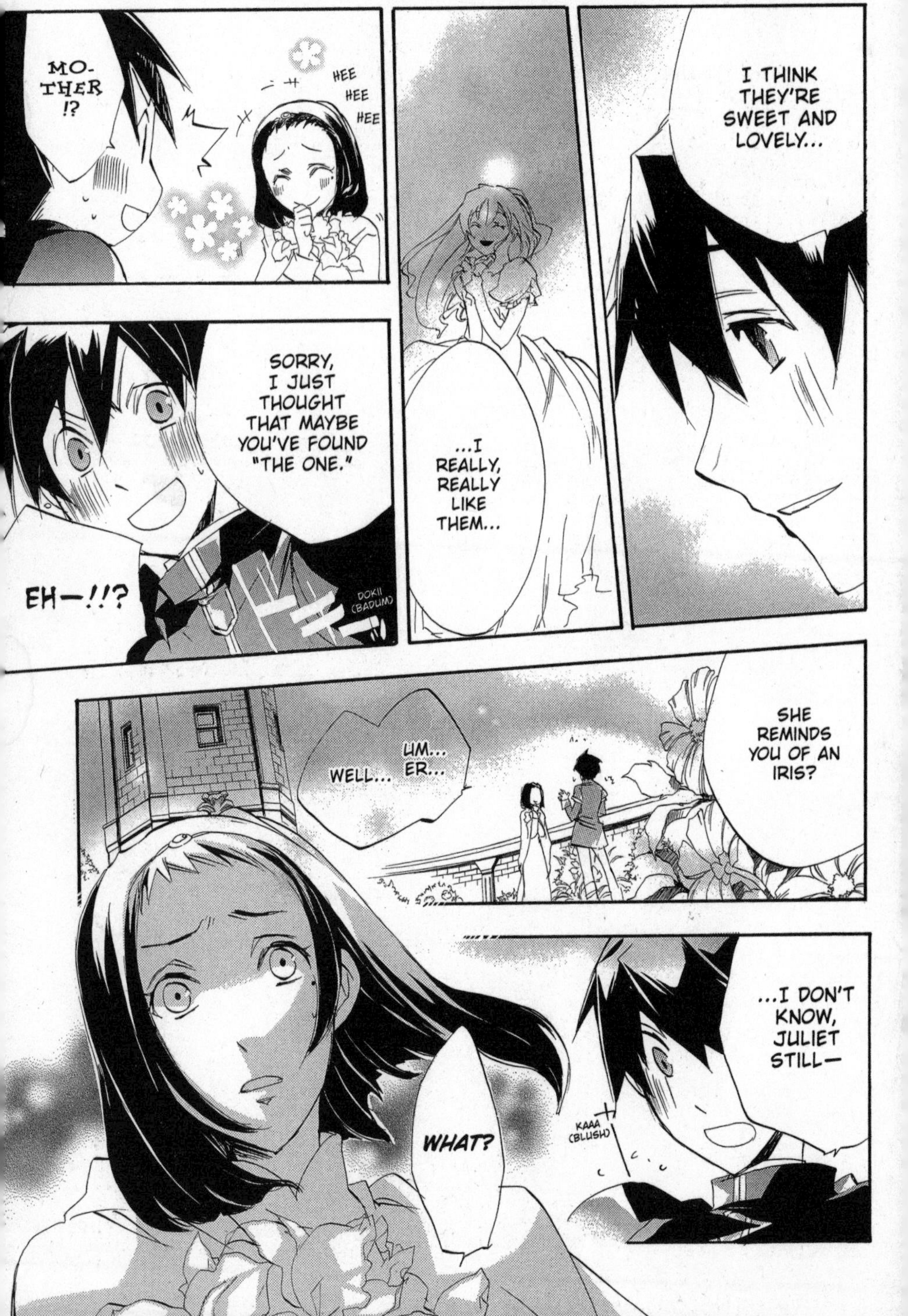
I THINK THEY'RE SWEET AND LOVELY...
...I REALLY, REALLY LIKE THEM...
HEE HEE HEE
MO-THER!?
SORRY, I JUST THOUGHT THAT MAYBE YOU'VE FOUND "THE ONE."
DOKI! (BADUM)
EH—!!?
SHE REMINDS YOU OF AN IRIS?
UM... WELL... ER...
...I DON'T KNOW, JULIET STILL—
KAAA (BLUSH)
WHAT?

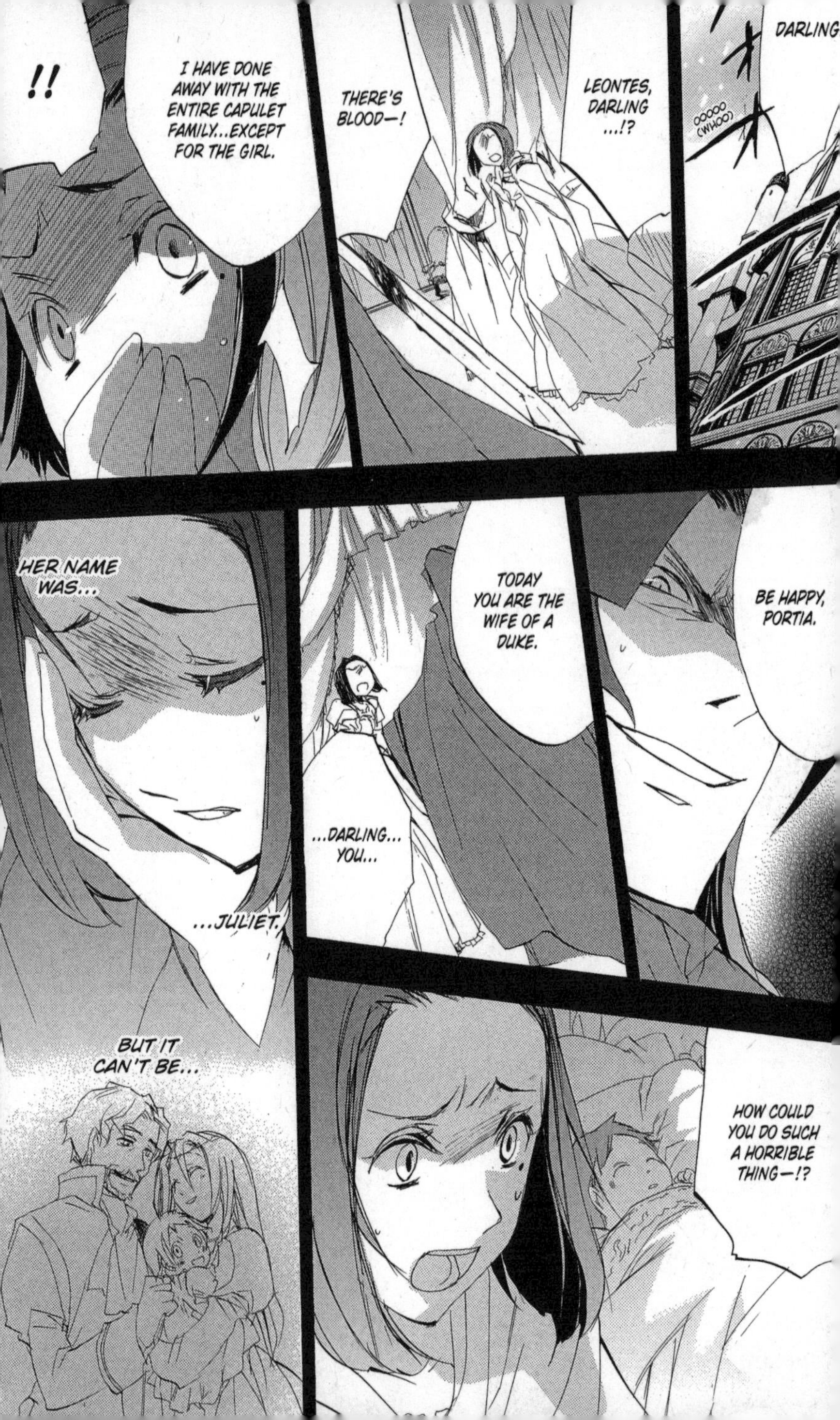
DARLING
OOOOO (WHOO)
LEONTES, DARLING ...!?
THERE'S BLOOD—!
I HAVE DONE AWAY WITH THE ENTIRE CAPULET FAMILY...EXCEPT FOR THE GIRL.
!!
BE HAPPY, PORTIA.
TODAY YOU ARE THE WIFE OF A DUKE.
...DARLING... YOU...
HOW COULD YOU DO SUCH A HORRIBLE THING—!?
HER NAME WAS...
...JULIET.
BUT IT CAN'T BE...

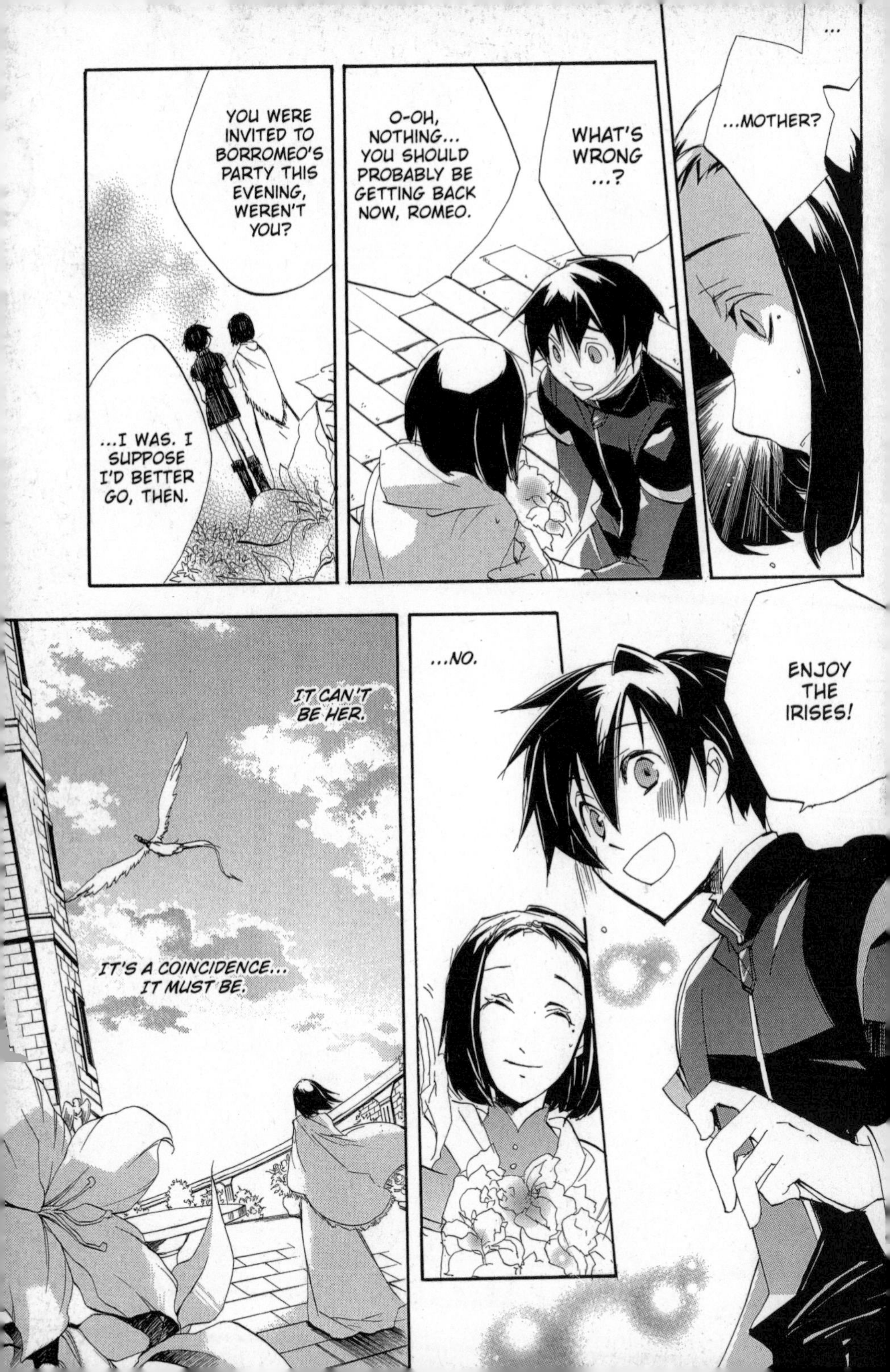
...
...MOTHER?
WHAT'S WRONG ...?
O-OH, NOTHING... YOU SHOULD PROBABLY BE GETTING BACK NOW, ROMEO.
YOU WERE INVITED TO BORROMEO'S PARTY THIS EVENING, WEREN'T YOU?
...I WAS. I SUPPOSE I'D BETTER GO, THEN.
ENJOY THE IRISES!
...NO.
IT CAN'T BE HER.
IT'S A COINCIDENCE... IT MUST BE.

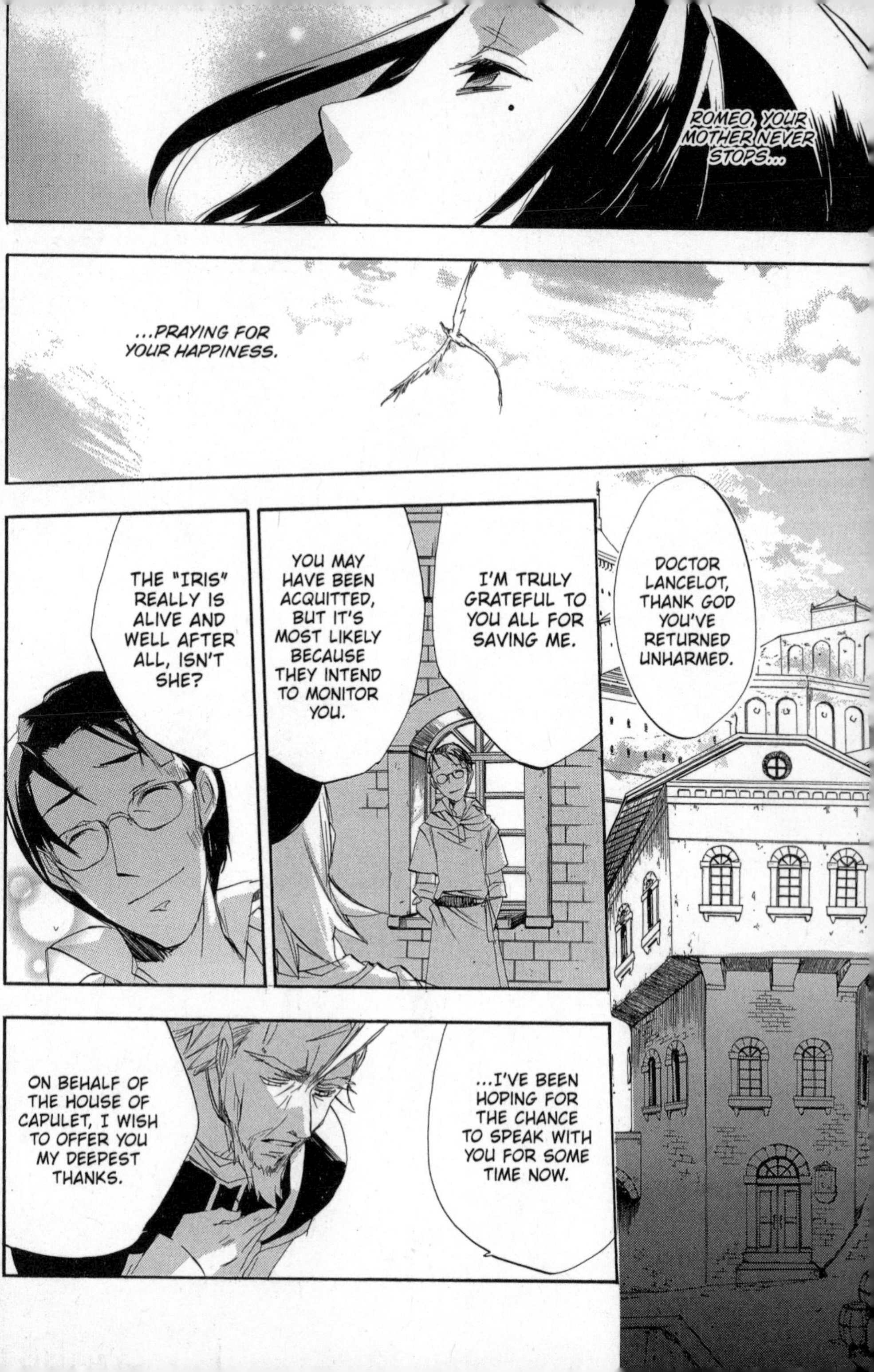

ROMEO, YOUR MOTHER NEVER STOPS...
...PRAYING FOR YOUR HAPPINESS.
DOCTOR LANCELOT, THANK GOD YOU'VE RETURNED UNHARMED.
I'M TRULY GRATEFUL TO YOU ALL FOR SAVING ME.
YOU MAY HAVE BEEN ACQUITTED, BUT IT'S MOST LIKELY BECAUSE THEY INTEND TO MONITOR YOU.
THE "IRIS" REALLY IS ALIVE AND WELL AFTER ALL, ISN'T SHE?
...I'VE BEEN HOPING FOR THE CHANCE TO SPEAK WITH YOU FOR SOME TIME NOW.
ON BEHALF OF THE HOUSE OF CAPULET, I WISH TO OFFER YOU MY DEEPEST THANKS.

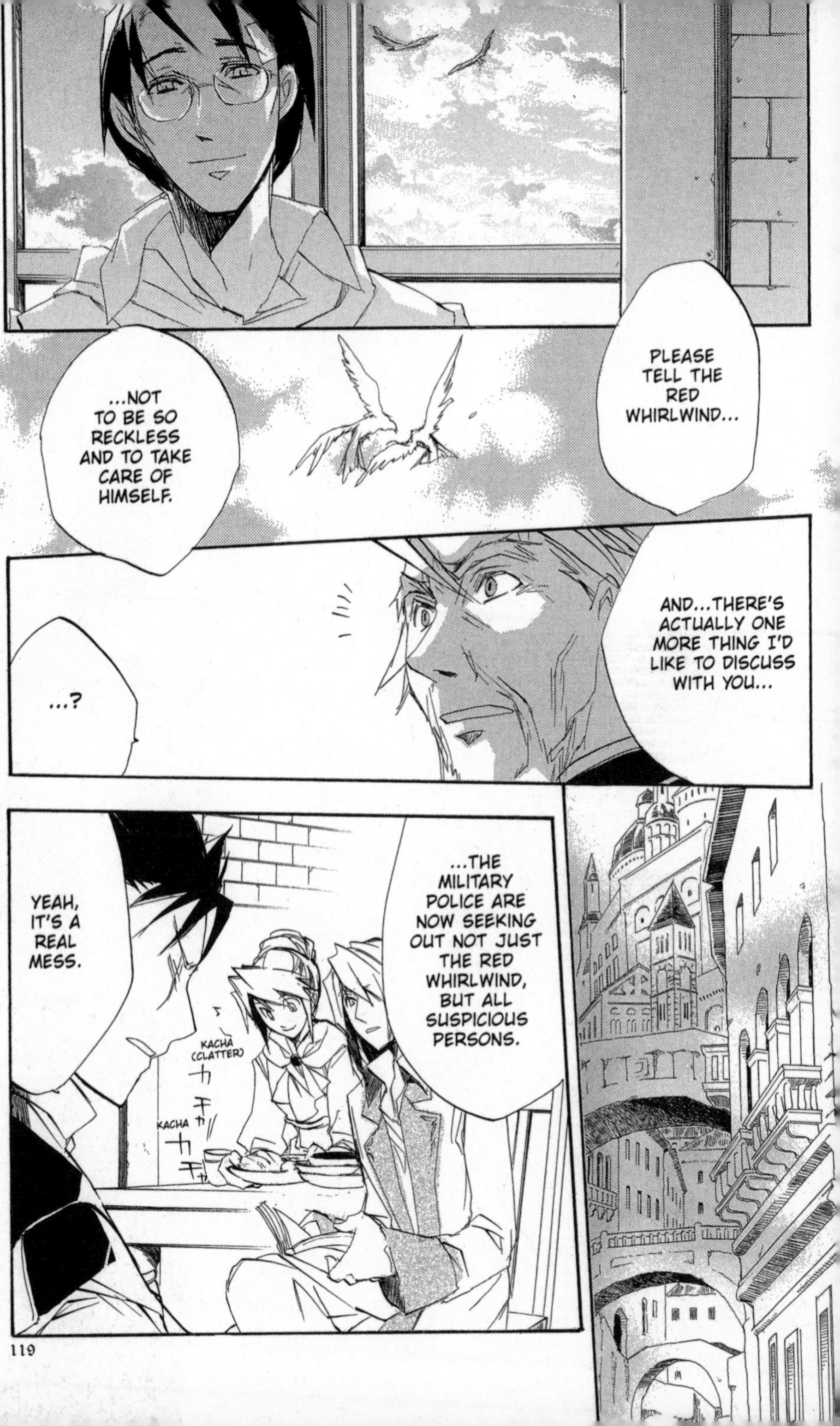
PLEASE TELL THE RED WHIRLWIND...
...NOT TO BE SO RECKLESS AND TO TAKE CARE OF HIMSELF.
AND...THERE'S ACTUALLY ONE MORE THING I'D LIKE TO DISCUSS WITH YOU...
...?
...THE MILITARY POLICE ARE NOW SEEKING OUT NOT JUST THE RED WHIRLWIND, BUT ALL SUSPICIOUS PERSONS.
KACHA (CLATTER)
KACHA
YEAH, IT'S A REAL MESS.

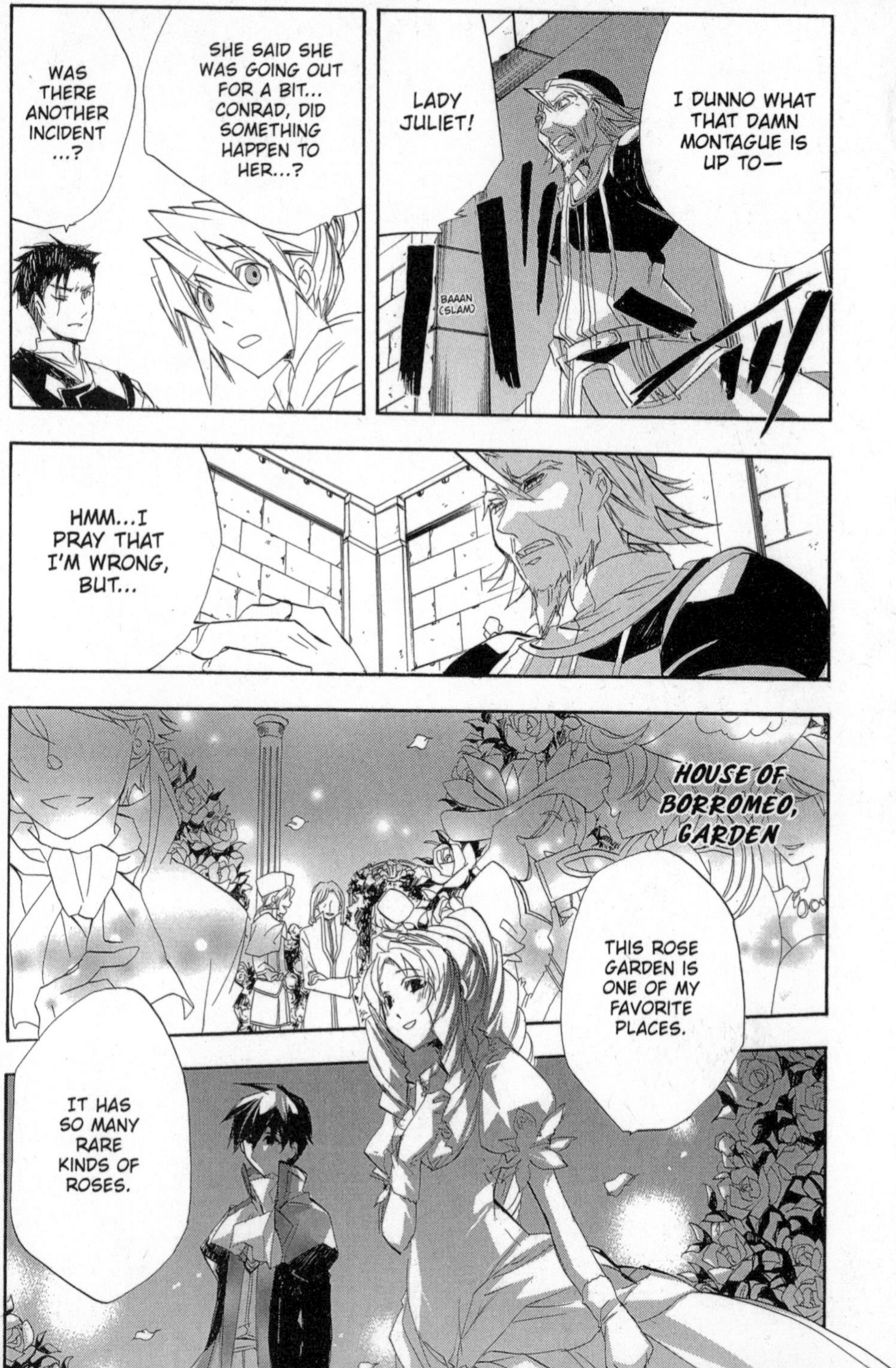
I DUNNO WHAT THAT DAMN MONTAGUE IS UP TO—
LADY JULIET!
BAAAN (SLAM)
SHE SAID SHE WAS GOING OUT FOR A BIT... CONRAD, DID SOMETHING HAPPEN TO HER...?
WAS THERE ANOTHER INCIDENT ...?
HMM...I PRAY THAT I'M WRONG, BUT...
HOUSE OF BORROMEO, GARDEN
THIS ROSE GARDEN IS ONE OF MY FAVORITE PLACES.
IT HAS SO MANY RARE KINDS OF ROSES.

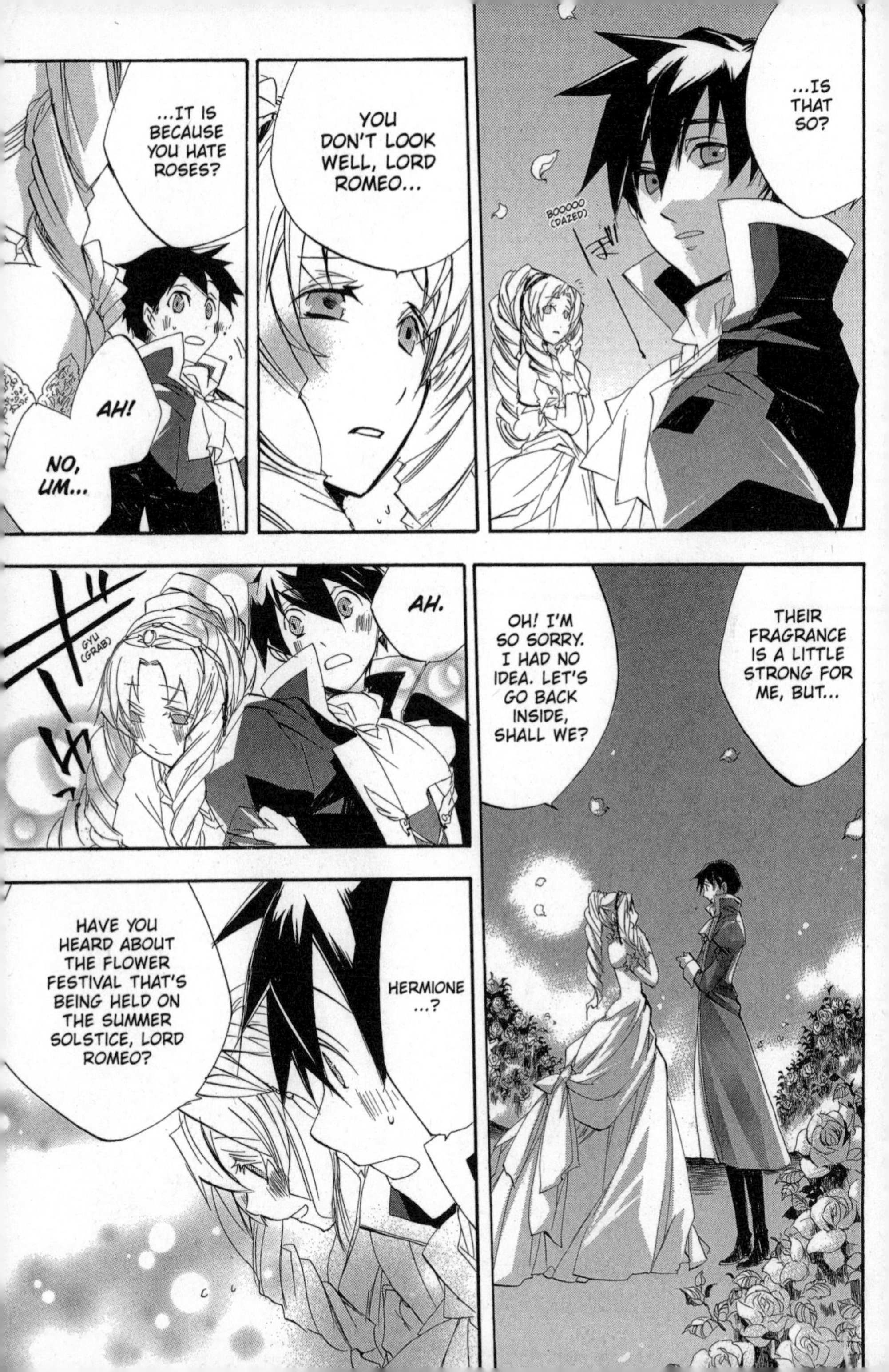
...IS THAT SO?
BOOOOOO (DAZED)
YOU DON'T LOOK WELL, LORD ROMEO...
...IT IS BECAUSE YOU HATE ROSES?
AH!
NO, UM...
THEIR FRAGRANCE IS A LITTLE STRONG FOR ME, BUT...
OH! I'M SO SORRY. I HAD NO IDEA. LET'S GO BACK INSIDE, SHALL WE?
AH.
GYU (GRAB)
HERMIONE ...?
HAVE YOU HEARD ABOUT THE FLOWER FESTIVAL THAT'S BEING HELD ON THE SUMMER SOLSTICE, LORD ROMEO?

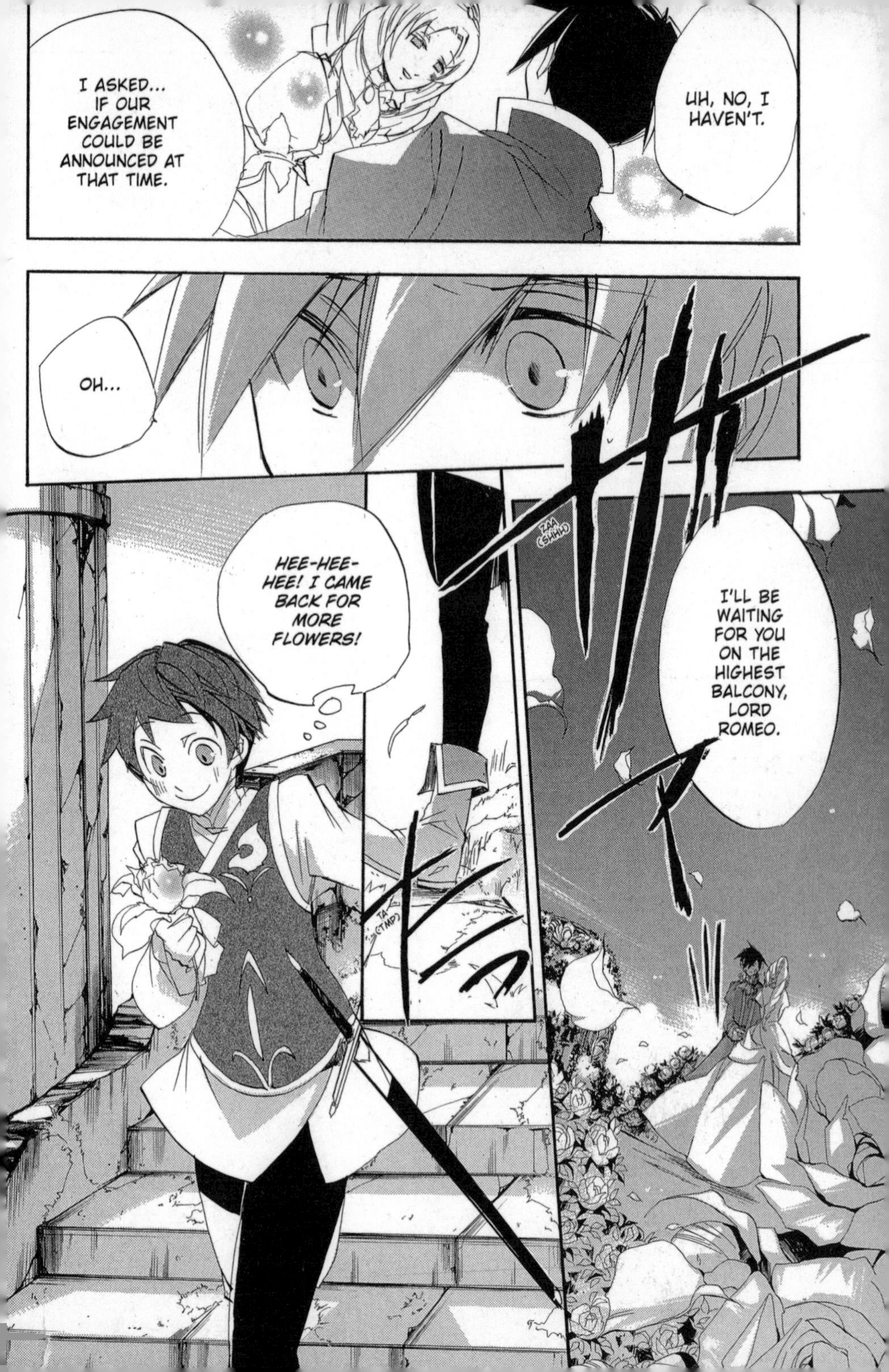
UH, NO, I HAVEN'T.
I ASKED... IF OUR ENGAGEMENT COULD BE ANNOUNCED AT THAT TIME.
OH...
I'LL BE WAITING FOR YOU ON THE HIGHEST BALCONY, LORD ROMEO.
ZAA (SHHH)
TA (TMP)
HEE-HEE-HEE! I CAME BACK FOR MORE FLOWERS!

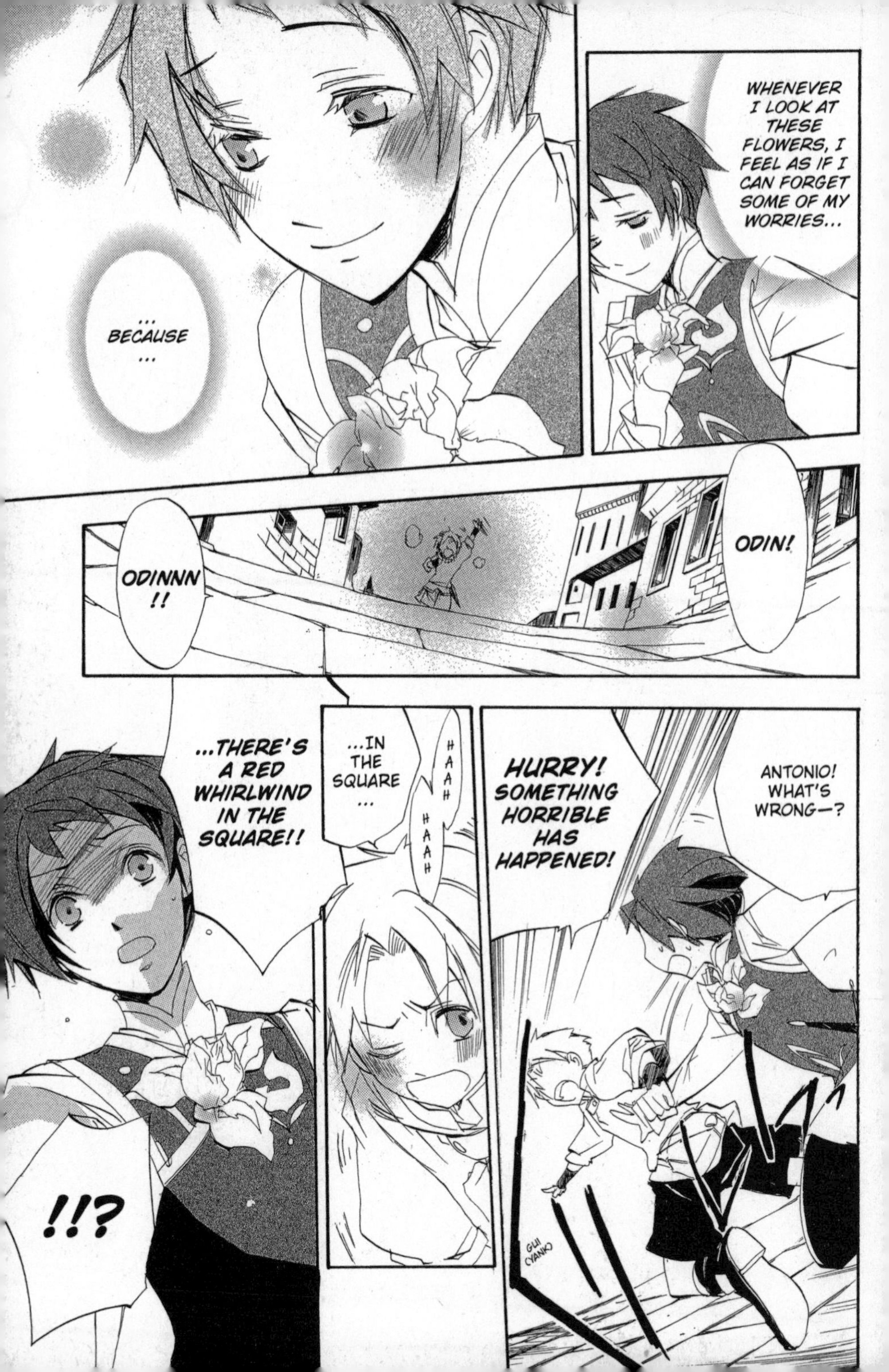

WHENEVER I LOOK AT THESE FLOWERS, I FEEL AS IF I CAN FORGET SOME OF MY WORRIES...
... BECAUSE ...
ODIN!
ODINNN !!
ANTONIO! WHAT'S WRONG—?
HURRY! SOMETHING HORRIBLE HAS HAPPENED!
GUI (YANK)
HAAH HAAH
...IN THE SQUARE ...
...THERE'S A RED WHIRLWIND IN THE SQUARE!!
!!?

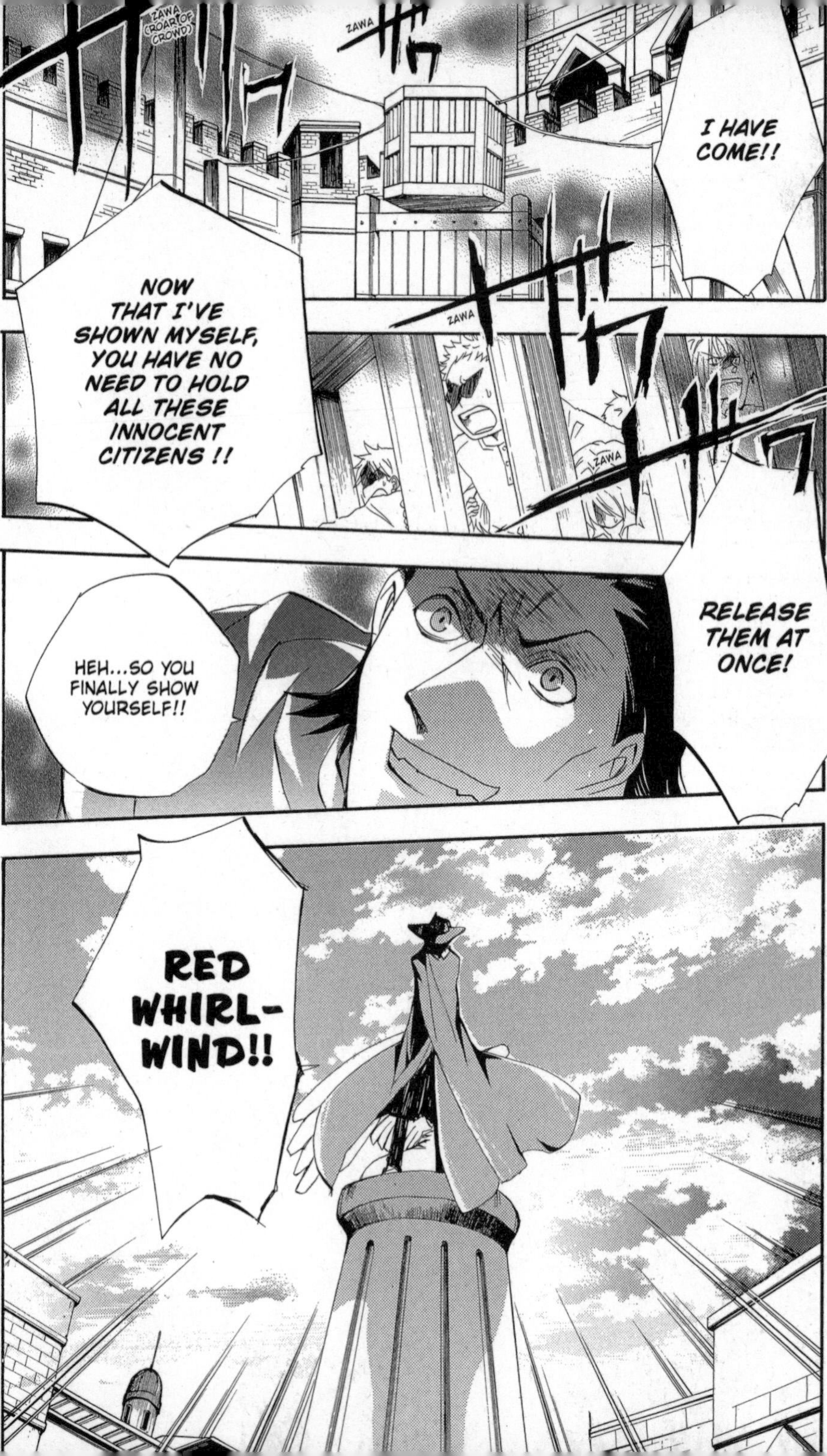

I HAVE COME!!
ZAWA
ZAWA (ROAR OF CROWD)
NOW THAT I'VE SHOWN MYSELF, YOU HAVE NO NEED TO HOLD ALL THESE INNOCENT CITIZENS !!
ZAWA
ZAWA
RELEASE THEM AT ONCE!
HEH...SO YOU FINALLY SHOW YOURSELF!!
RED WHIRL-WIND!!

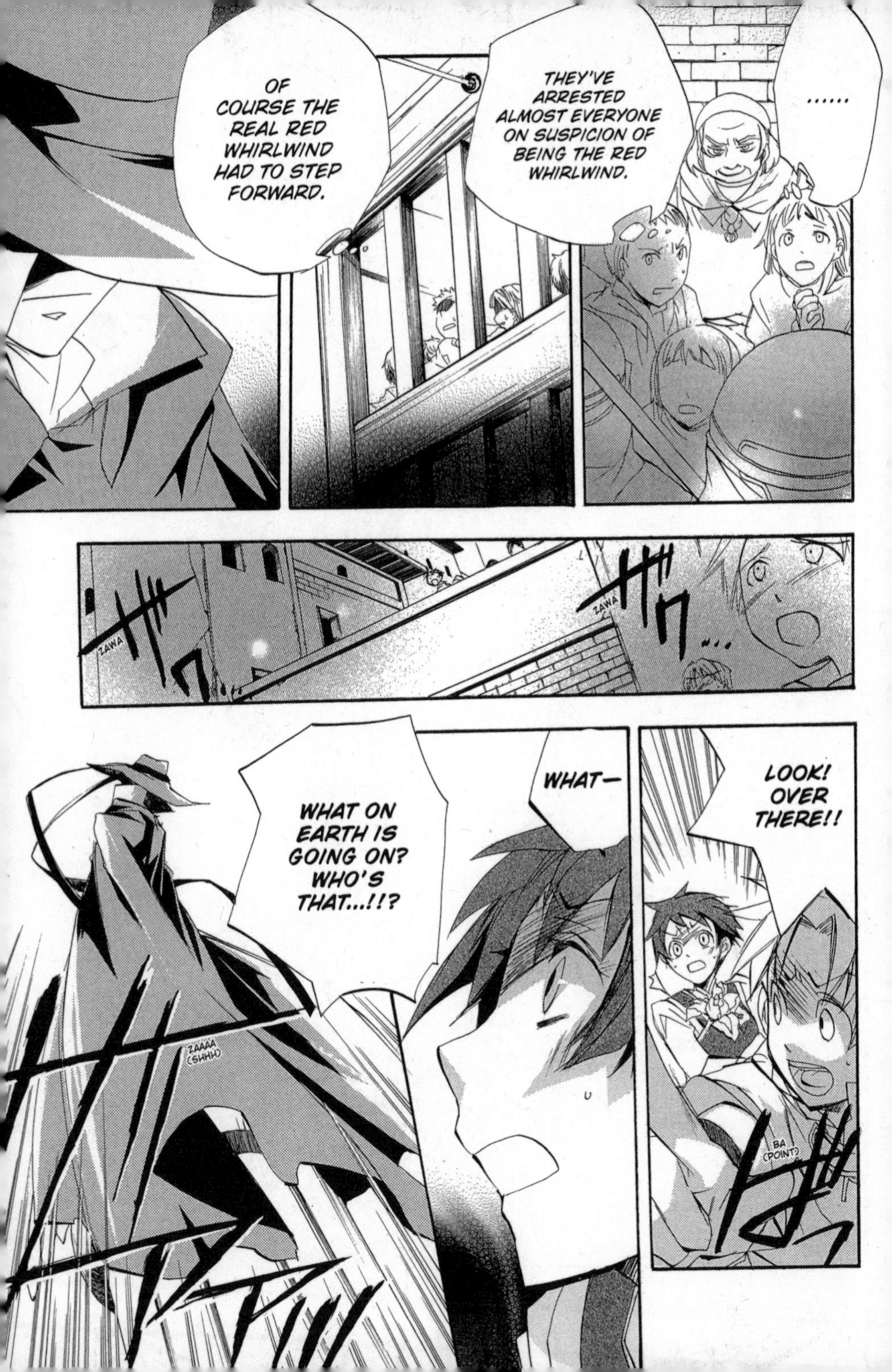

......
THEY'VE ARRESTED ALMOST EVERYONE ON SUSPICION OF BEING THE RED WHIRLWIND.
OF COURSE THE REAL RED WHIRLWIND HAD TO STEP FORWARD.
ZAWA
ZAWA
LOOK! OVER THERE!!
BA (POINT)
WHAT—
WHAT ON EARTH IS GOING ON? WHO'S THAT...!!?
ZAAAA (SHHH)

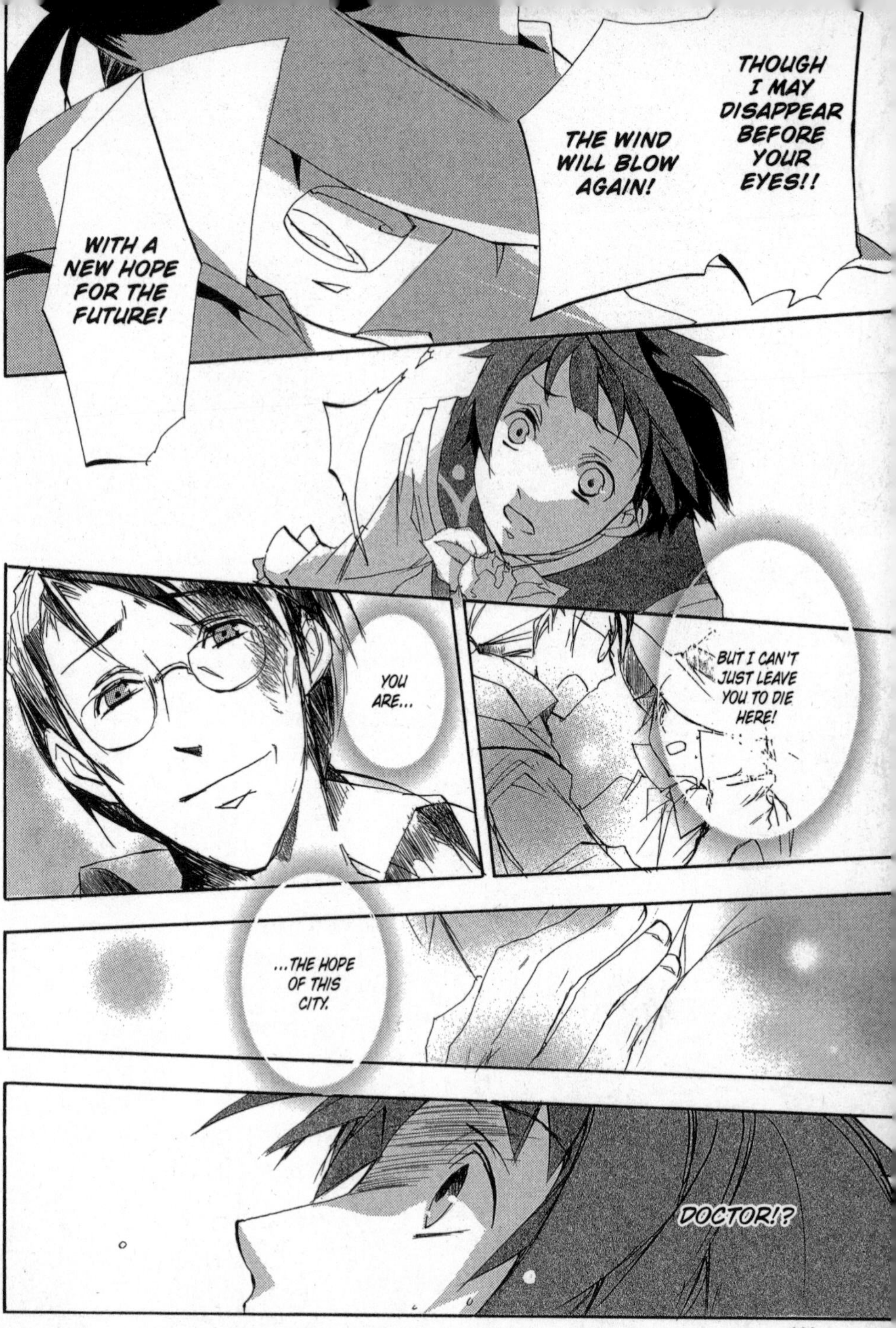
THOUGH I MAY DISAPPEAR BEFORE YOUR EYES!!
THE WIND WILL BLOW AGAIN!
WITH A NEW HOPE FOR THE FUTURE!
BUT I CAN'T JUST LEAVE YOU TO DIE HERE!
YOU ARE...
...THE HOPE OF THIS CITY.
DOCTOR!?

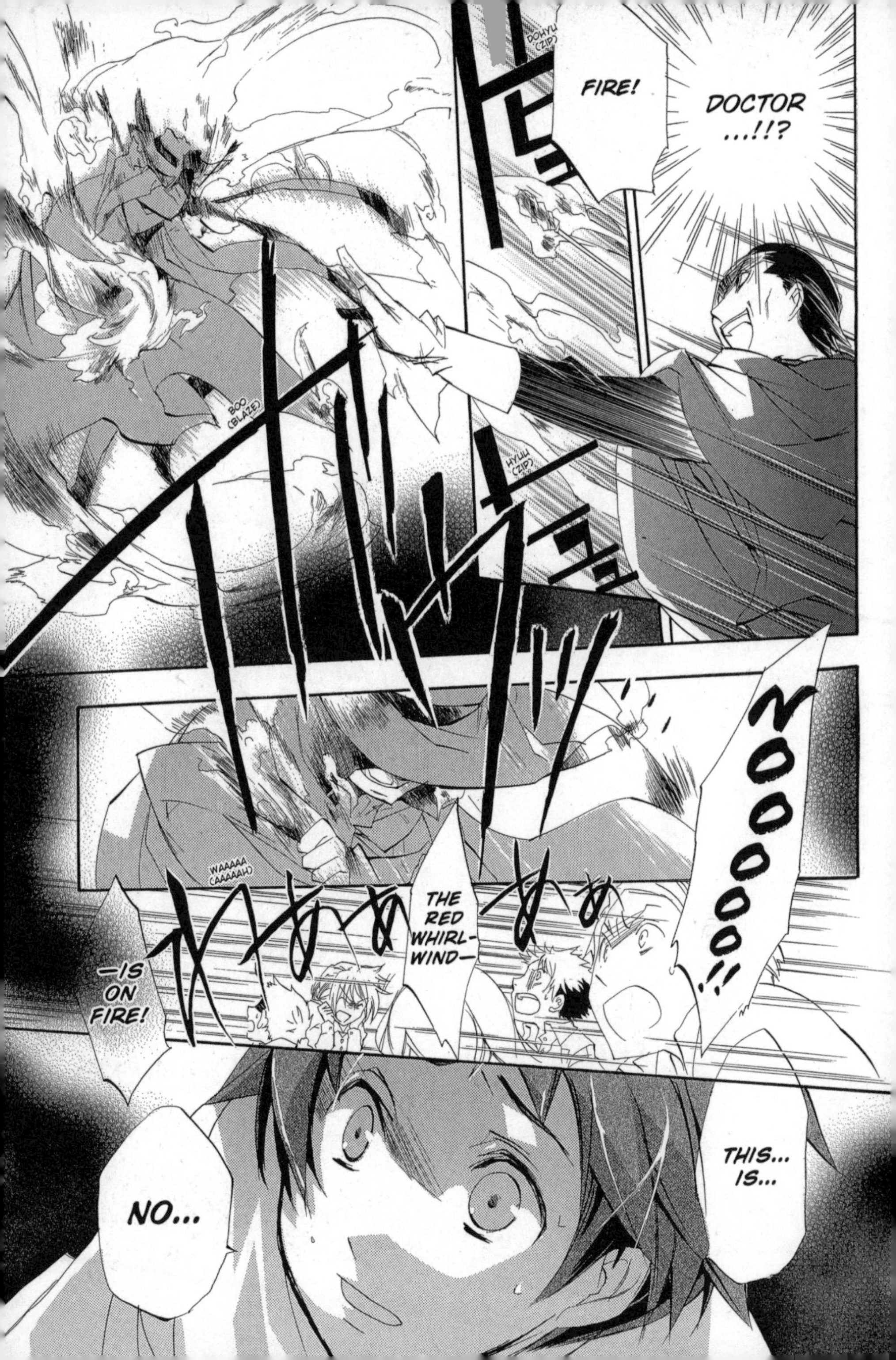
DOCTOR ...!!?
FIRE!
DOHYU (ZIP)
HYUU (ZIP)
BOO (BLAZE)
NOOOOOOO!!
THE RED WHIRLWIND—
WAAAAA (AAAAAH)
—IS ON FIRE!
THIS... IS...
NO...

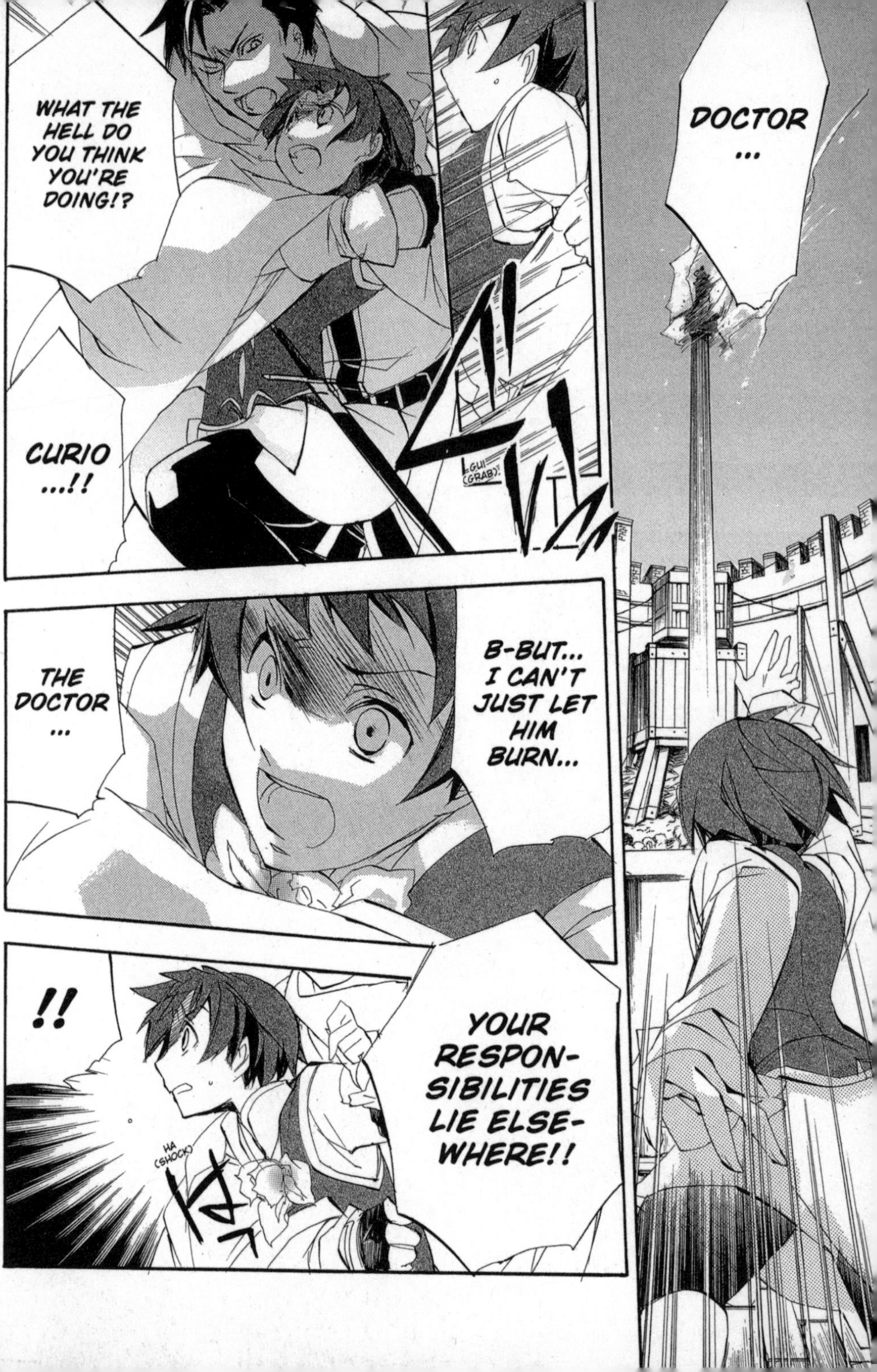
DOCTOR ...
WHAT THE HELL DO YOU THINK YOU'RE DOING!?
GUI (GRAB)
CURIO ...!!
B-BUT... I CAN'T JUST LET HIM BURN...
THE DOCTOR ...
YOUR RESPON-SIBILITIES LIE ELSE-WHERE!!
!!
HA (SHOCK)

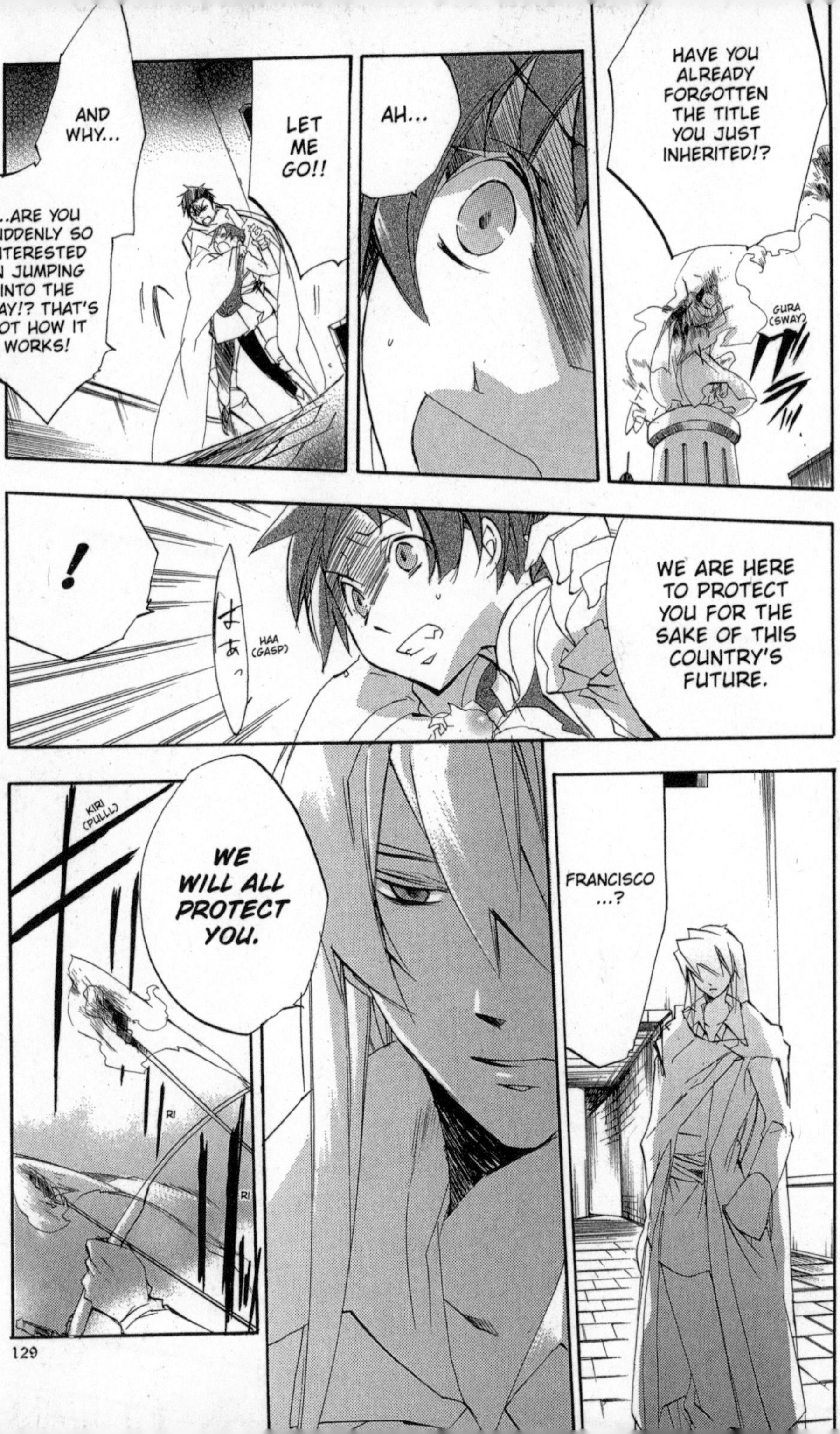
HAVE YOU ALREADY FORGOTTEN THE TITLE YOU JUST INHERITED!?
GURA (SWAY)
AH...
LET ME GO!!
AND WHY...
...ARE YOU SUDDENLY SO INTERESTED IN JUMPING INTO THE FRAY!? THAT'S NOT HOW IT WORKS!
WE ARE HERE TO PROTECT YOU FOR THE SAKE OF THIS COUNTRY'S FUTURE.
はぁっ
HAA (GASP)
!
FRANCISCO ...?
WE WILL ALL PROTECT YOU.
KIRI (PULLL)
RI
RI

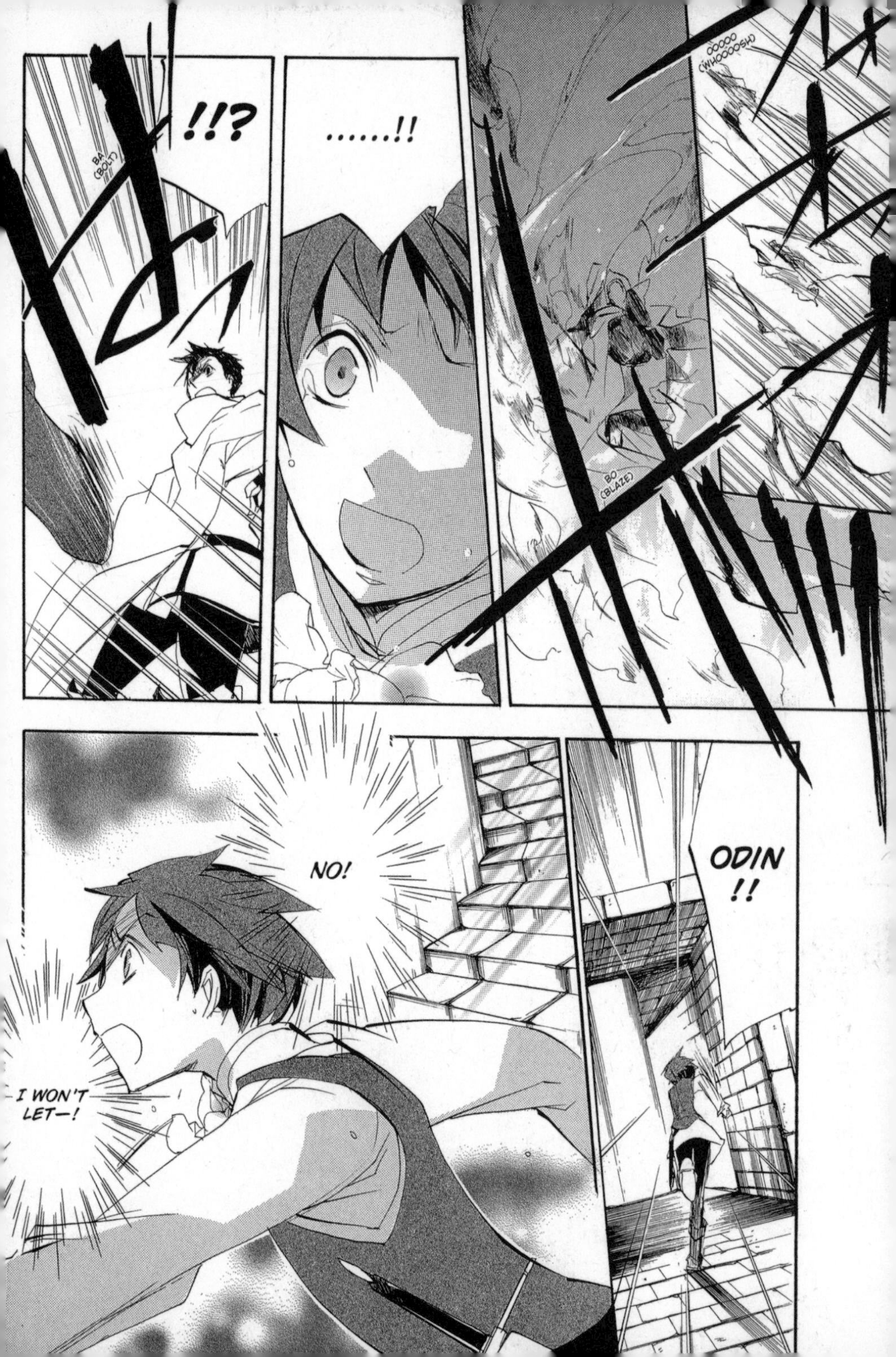
OOOOO (WHOOOOSH)
BO (BLAZE)
......!!
BA (BOLT)
!!?
ODIN !!
NO!
I WON'T LET—!

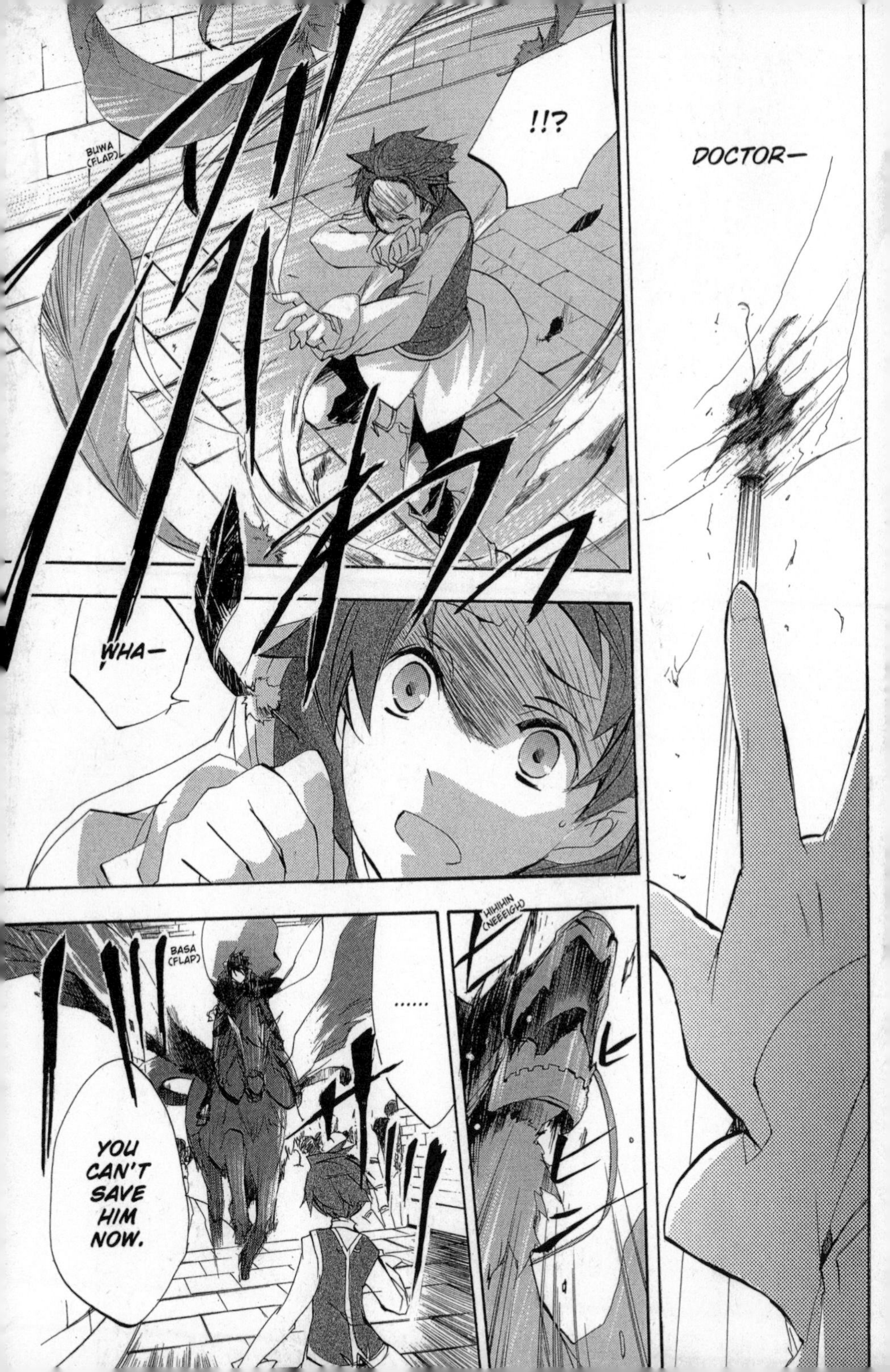
DOCTOR—
!!?
BUWA (FLAP)
WHA—
HIHIHIN (NEEEIGH)
BASA (FLAP)
......
YOU CAN'T SAVE HIM NOW.

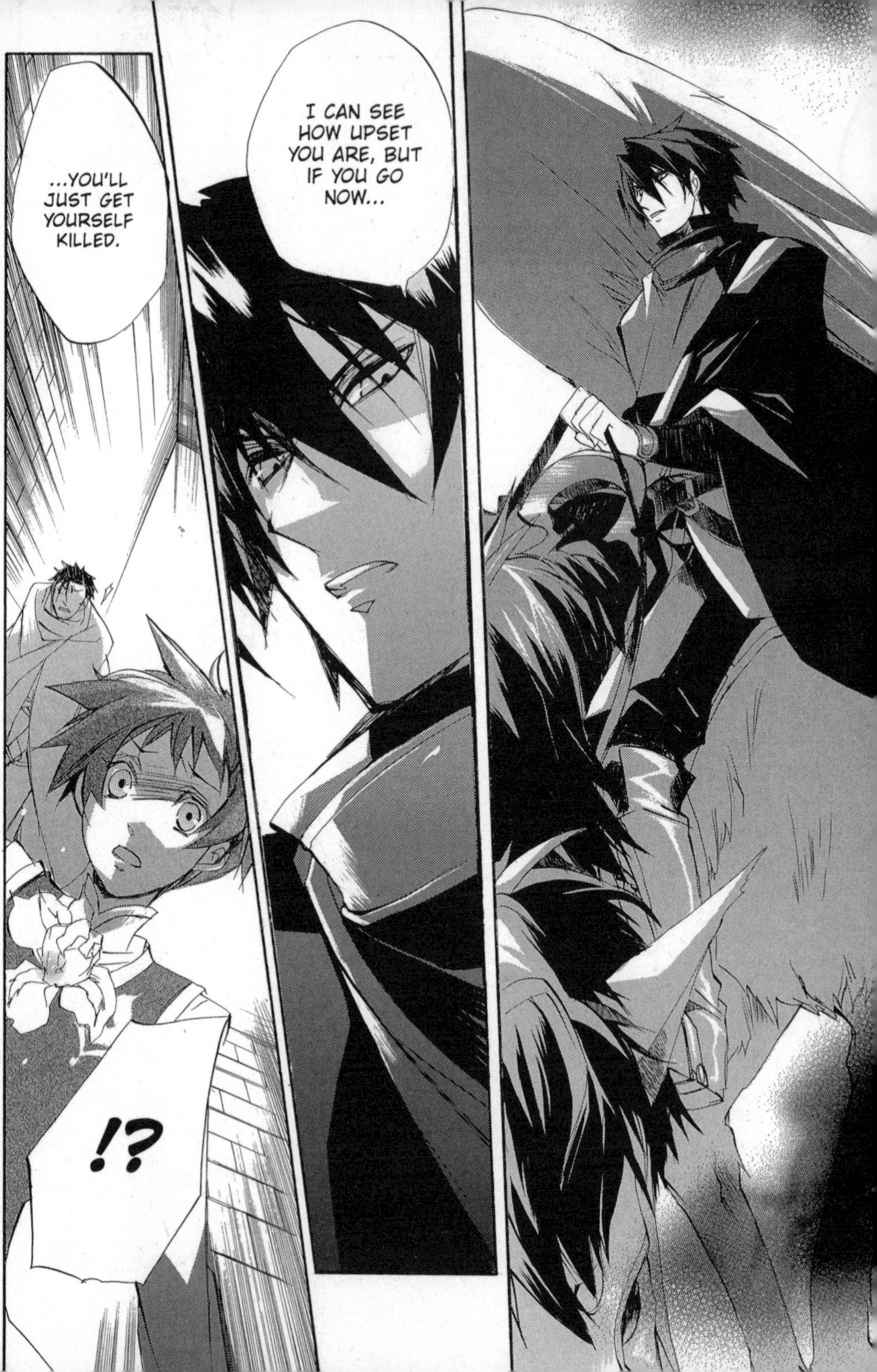
I CAN SEE HOW UPSET YOU ARE, BUT IF YOU GO NOW...
...YOU'LL JUST GET YOURSELF KILLED.
!?

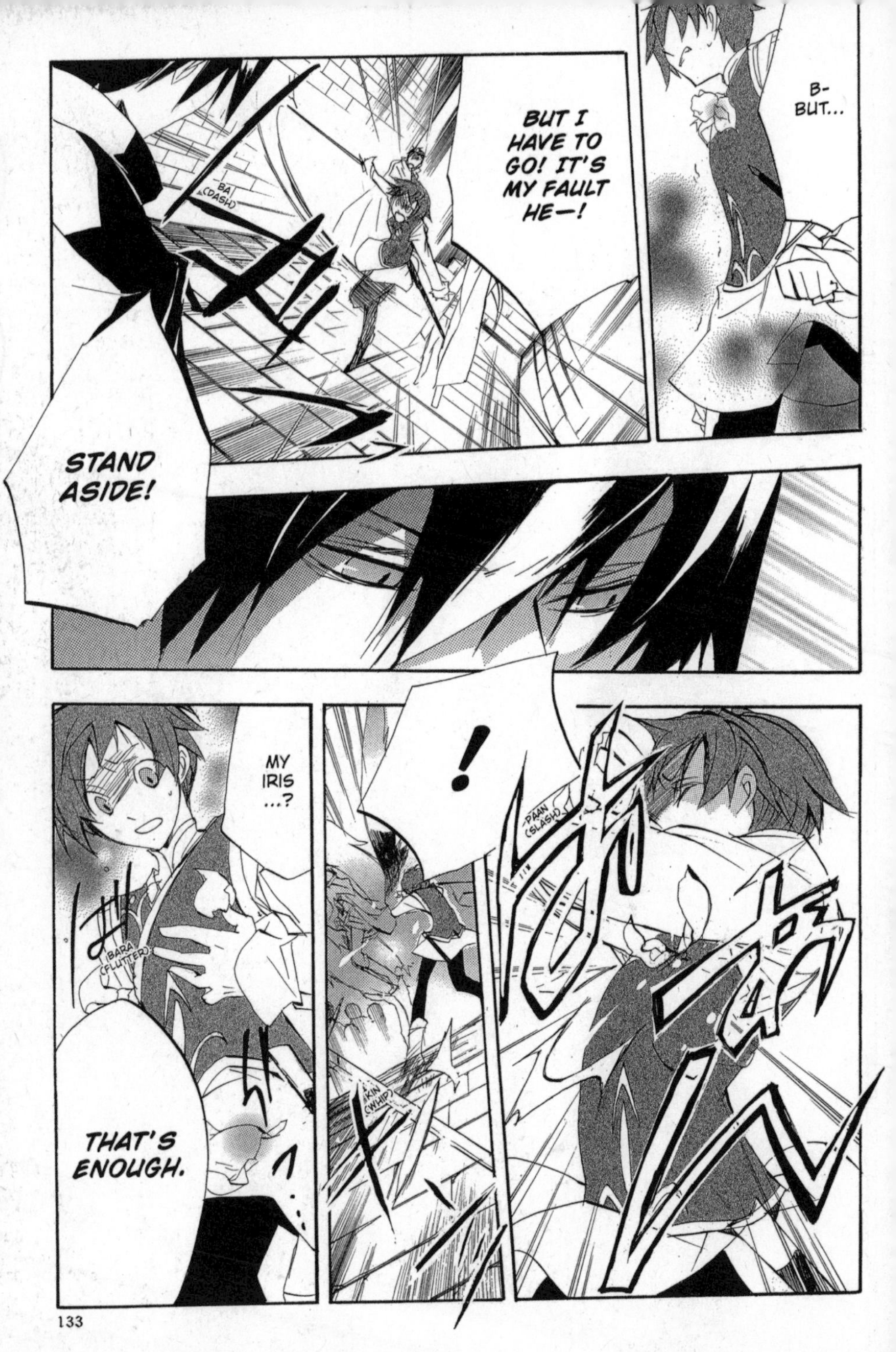
B-
BUT...
BUT I HAVE TO GO! IT'S MY FAULT HE—!
BA (DASH)
STAND ASIDE!
!
PAAN (SLASH)
KIN (WHIP)
MY IRIS ...?
BARA (FLUTTER)
THAT'S ENOUGH.

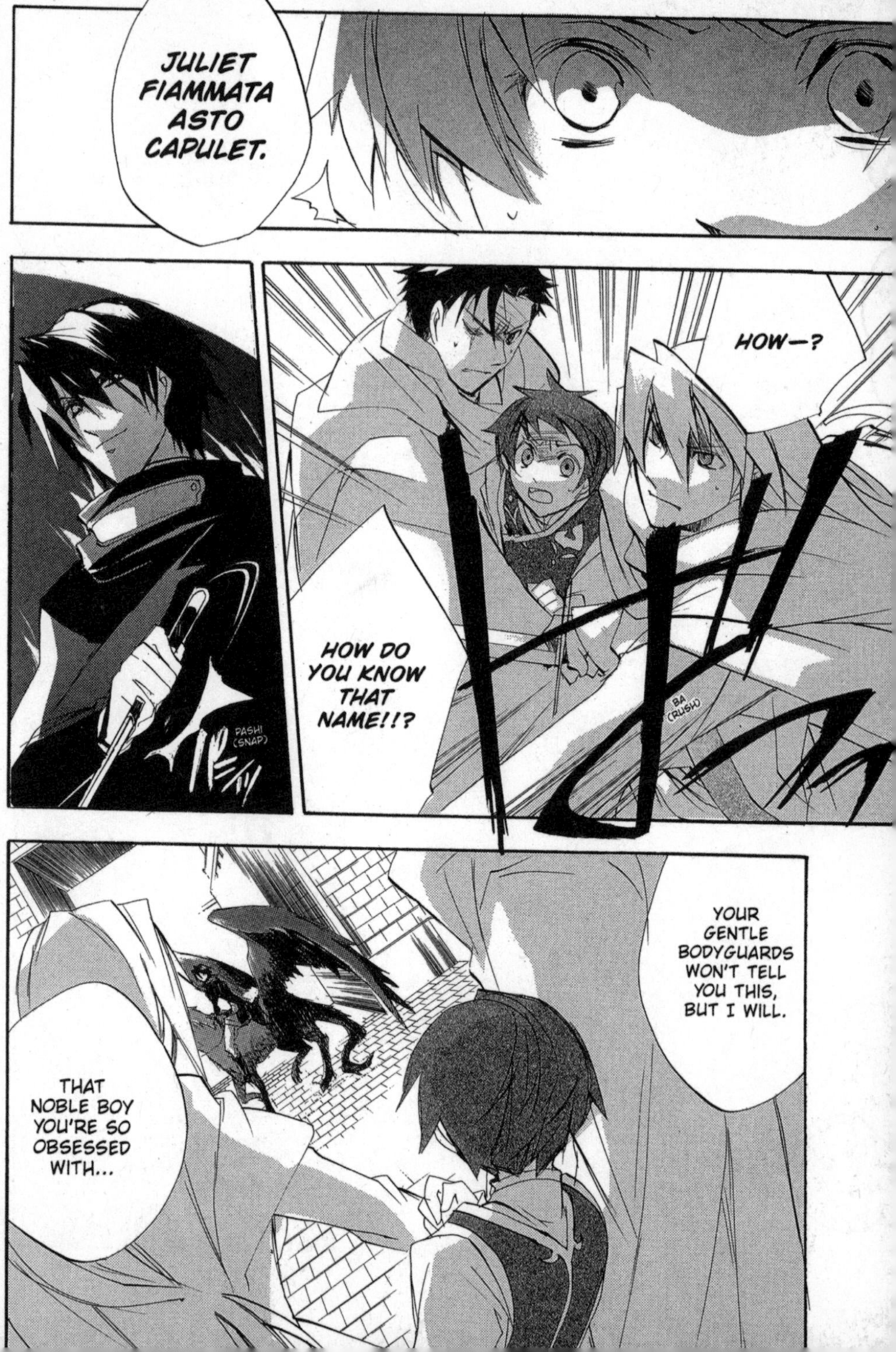
JULIET FIAMMATA ASTO CAPULET.
HOW—?
HOW DO YOU KNOW THAT NAME!!?
BA (RUSH)
PASHI (SNAP)
YOUR GENTLE BODYGUARDS WON'T TELL YOU THIS, BUT I WILL.
THAT NOBLE BOY YOU'RE SO OBSESSED WITH...

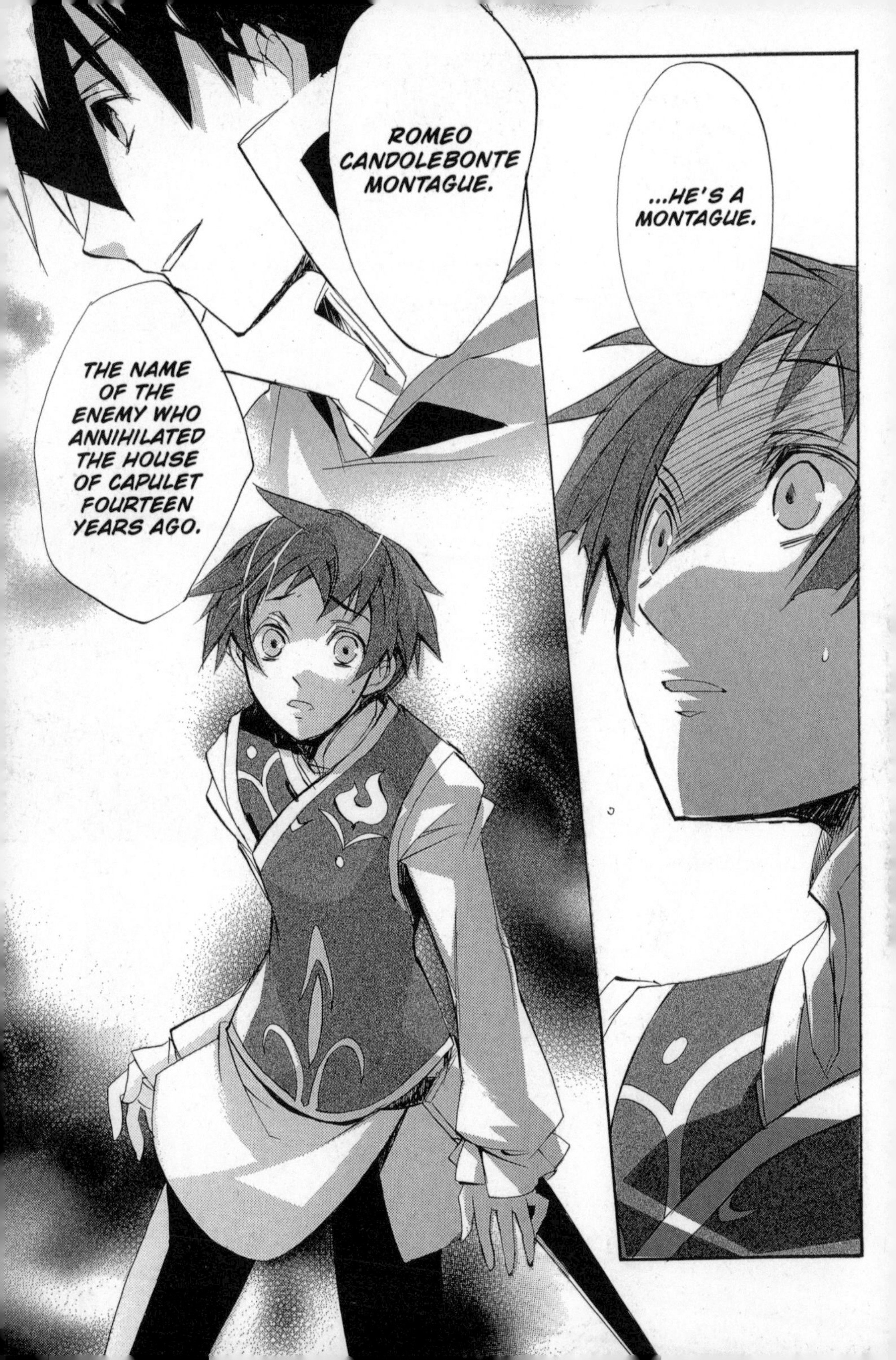
...HE'S A MONTAGUE.
ROMEO CANDOLEBONTE MONTAGUE.
THE NAME OF THE ENEMY WHO ANNIHILATED THE HOUSE OF CAPULET FOURTEEN YEARS AGO.

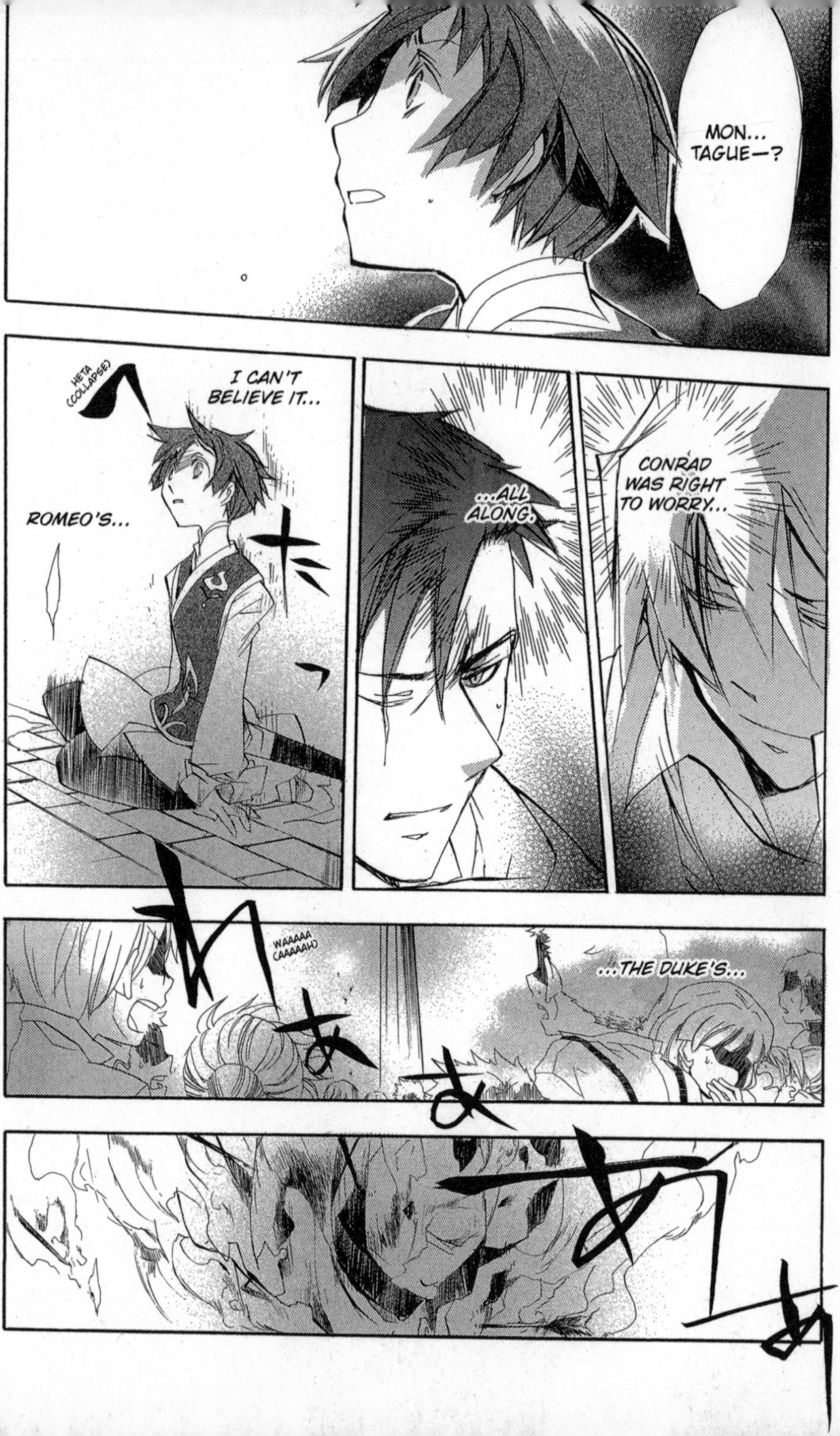
MON... TAGUE—?
CONRAD WAS RIGHT TO WORRY...
...ALL ALONG.
HETA (COLLAPSE)
I CAN'T BELIEVE IT...
ROMEO'S...
...THE DUKE'S...
WAAAAA (AAAAAH)

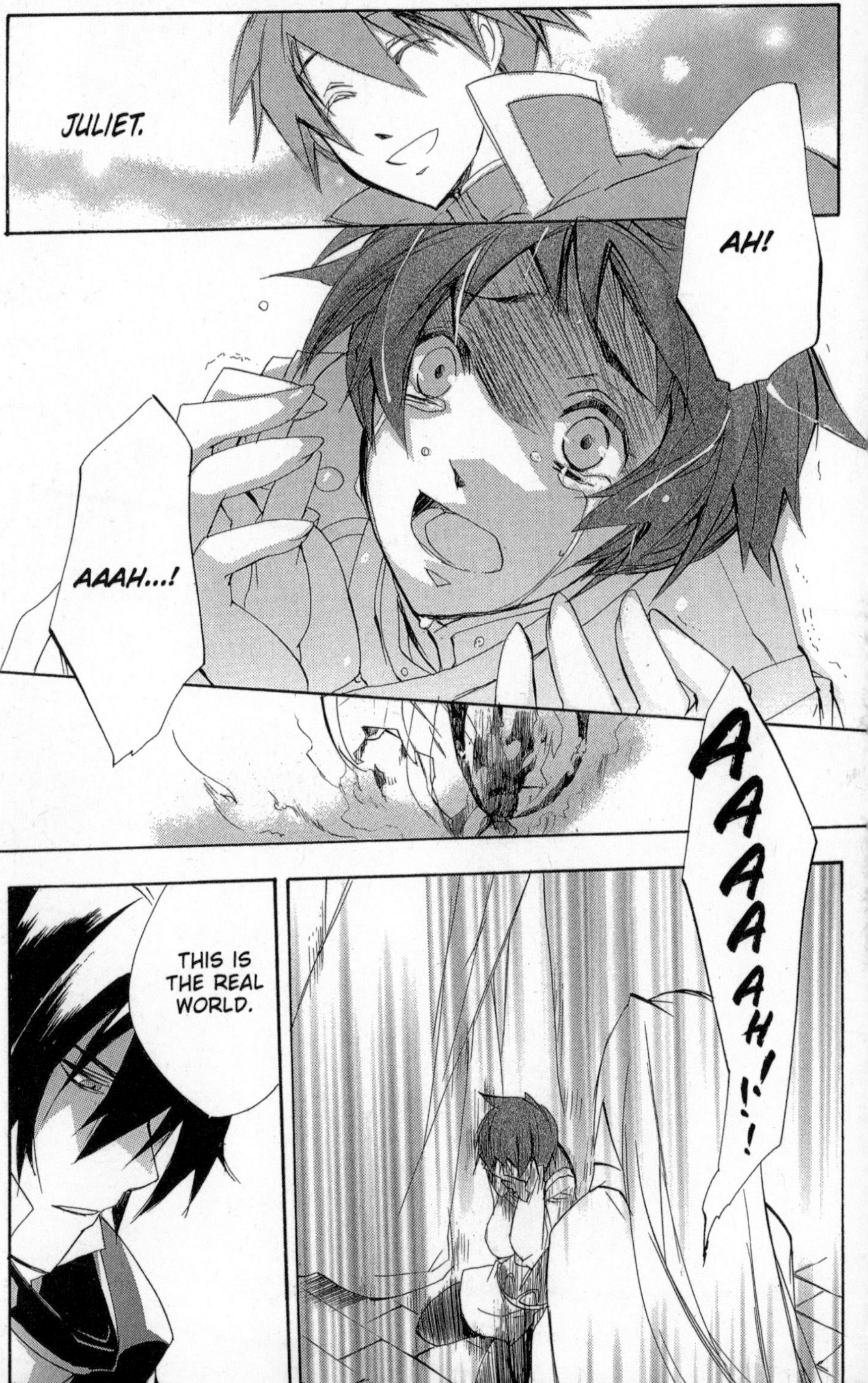
JULIET.
AH!
AAAH...!
AAAAAAH!!!
THIS IS THE REAL WORLD.

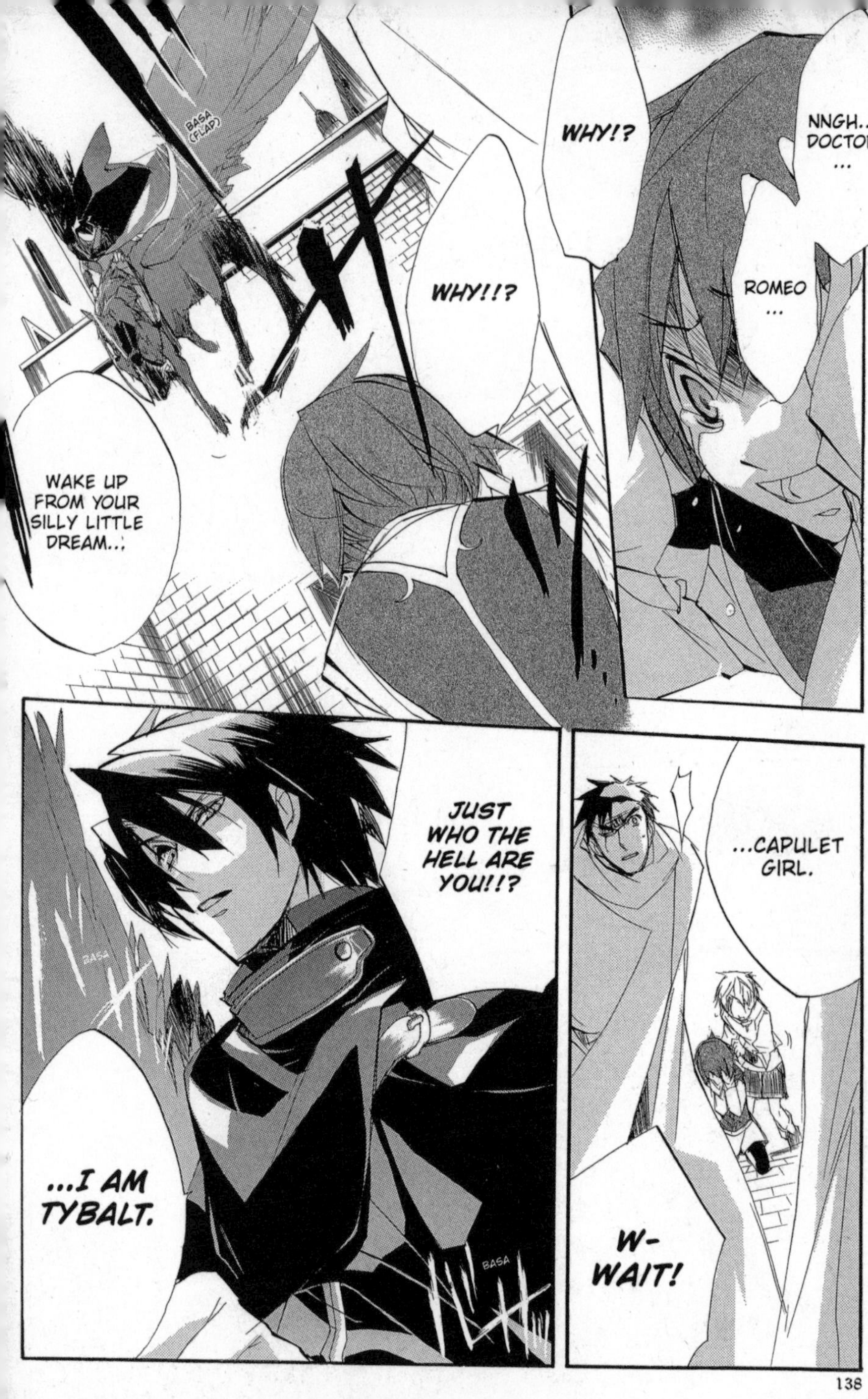
NNGH... DOCTOR ...
ROMEO ...
WHY!?
WHY!!?
BASA (FLAP)
WAKE UP FROM YOUR SILLY LITTLE DREAM...
...CAPULET GIRL.
W-WAIT!
JUST WHO THE HELL ARE YOU!!?
BASA
...I AM TYBALT.
BASA

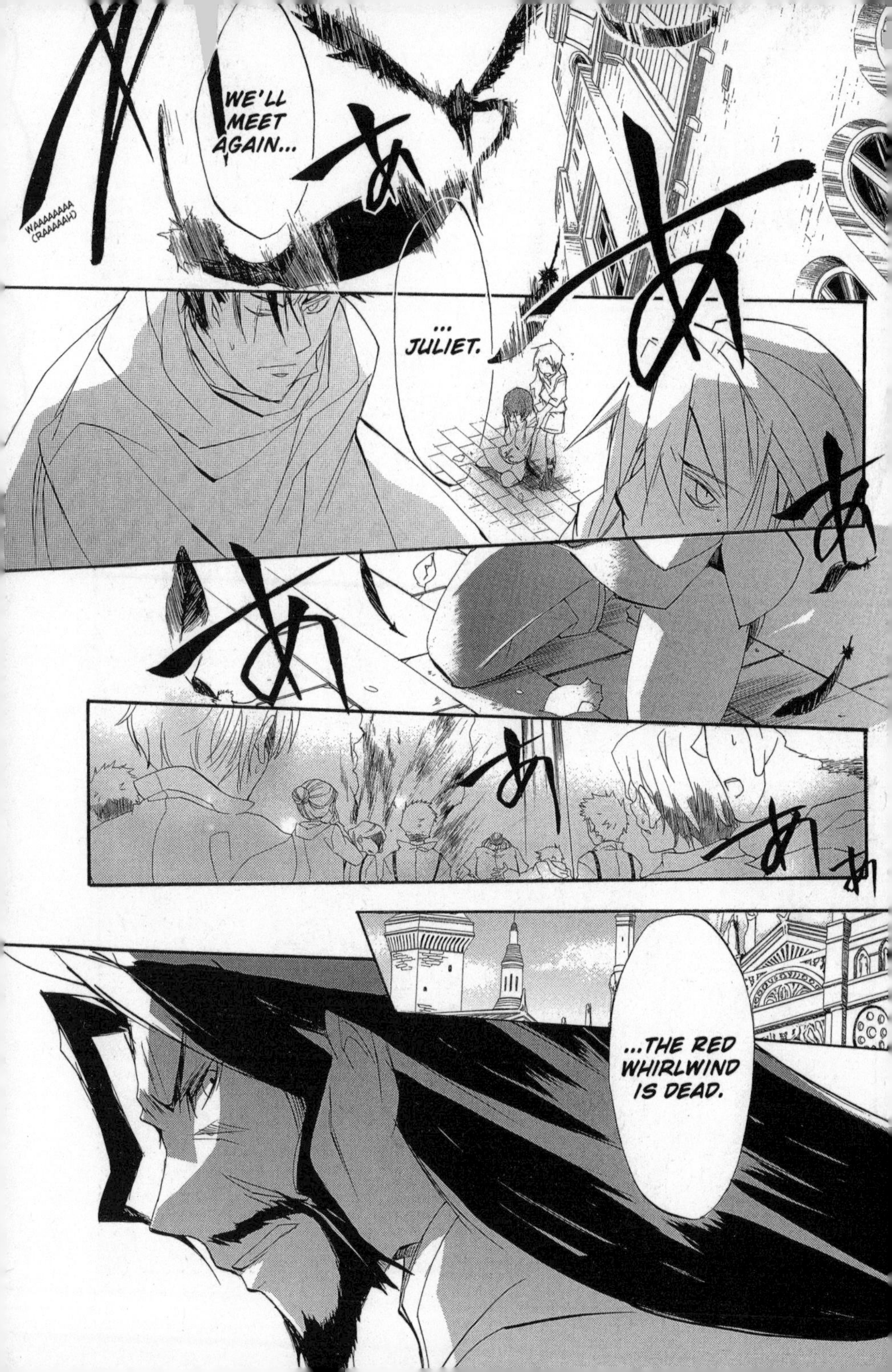
WE'LL MEET AGAIN...
ああ
WAAAAAAAA (RAAAAAAH)
...JULIET.
あああああ
...THE RED WHIRLWIND IS DEAD.

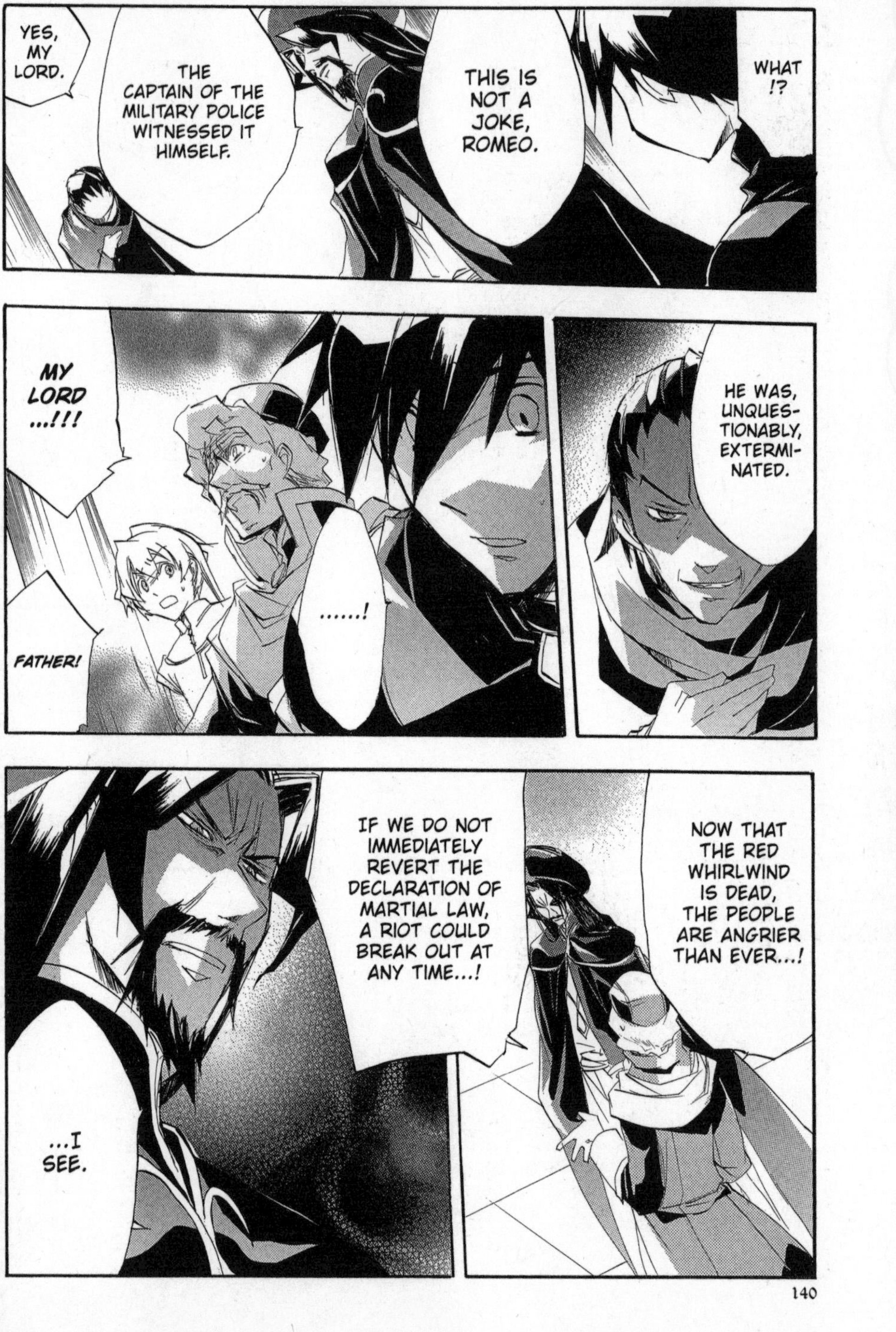
WHAT !?
THIS IS NOT A JOKE, ROMEO.
THE CAPTAIN OF THE MILITARY POLICE WITNESSED IT HIMSELF.
YES, MY LORD.
HE WAS, UNQUESTIONABLY, EXTERMINATED.
......!
MY LORD ...!!!
FATHER!
NOW THAT THE RED WHIRLWIND IS DEAD, THE PEOPLE ARE ANGRIER THAN EVER...!
IF WE DO NOT IMMEDIATELY REVERT THE DECLARATION OF MARTIAL LAW, A RIOT COULD BREAK OUT AT ANY TIME...!
...I SEE.

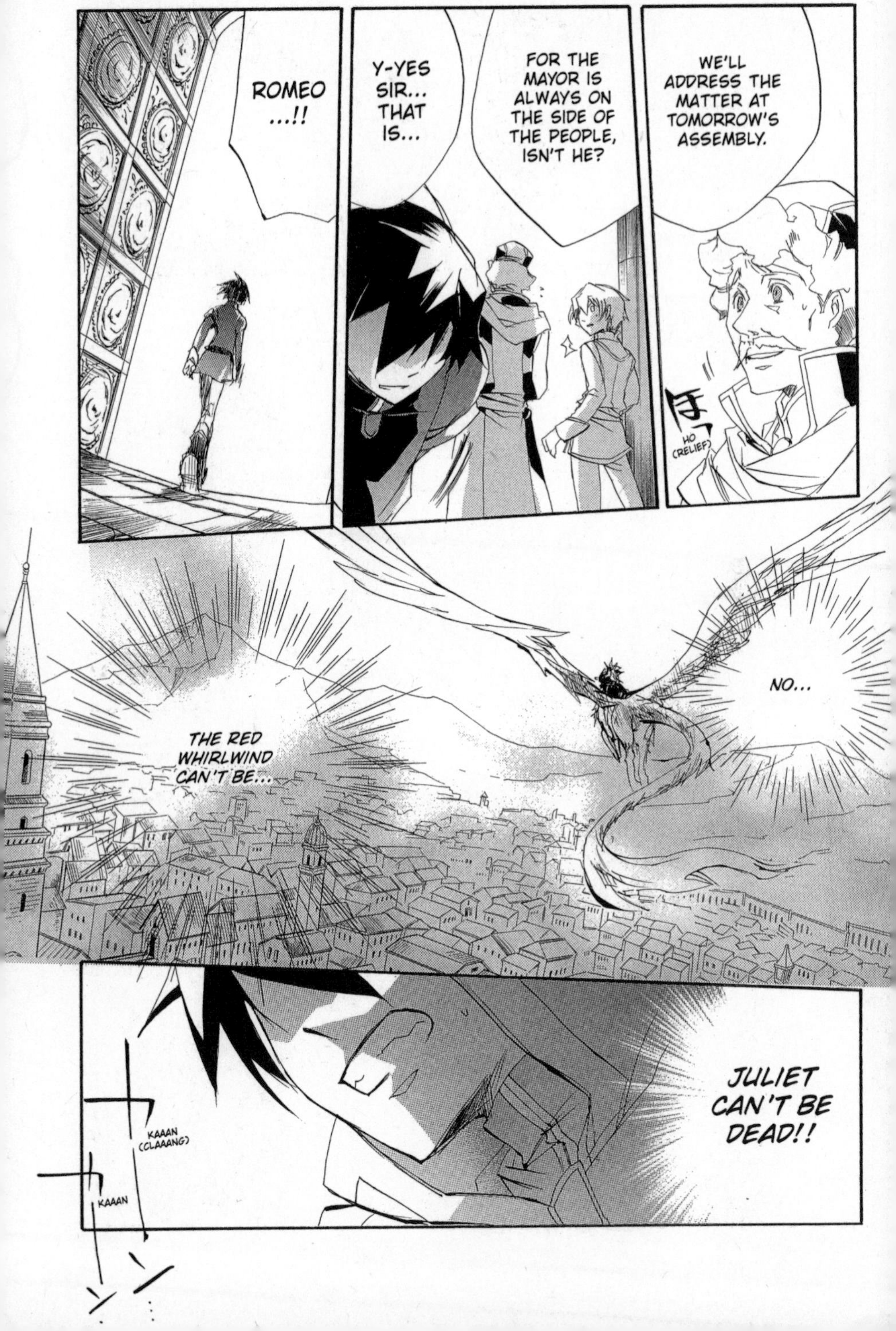
WE'LL ADDRESS THE MATTER AT TOMORROW'S ASSEMBLY.
ほっ
HO (RELIEF)
FOR THE MAYOR IS ALWAYS ON THE SIDE OF THE PEOPLE, ISN'T HE?
Y-YES SIR... THAT IS...
ROMEO ...!!
NO...
THE RED WHIRLWIND CAN'T BE...
JULIET CAN'T BE DEAD!!
KAAAN (CLAAANG)
KAAAN

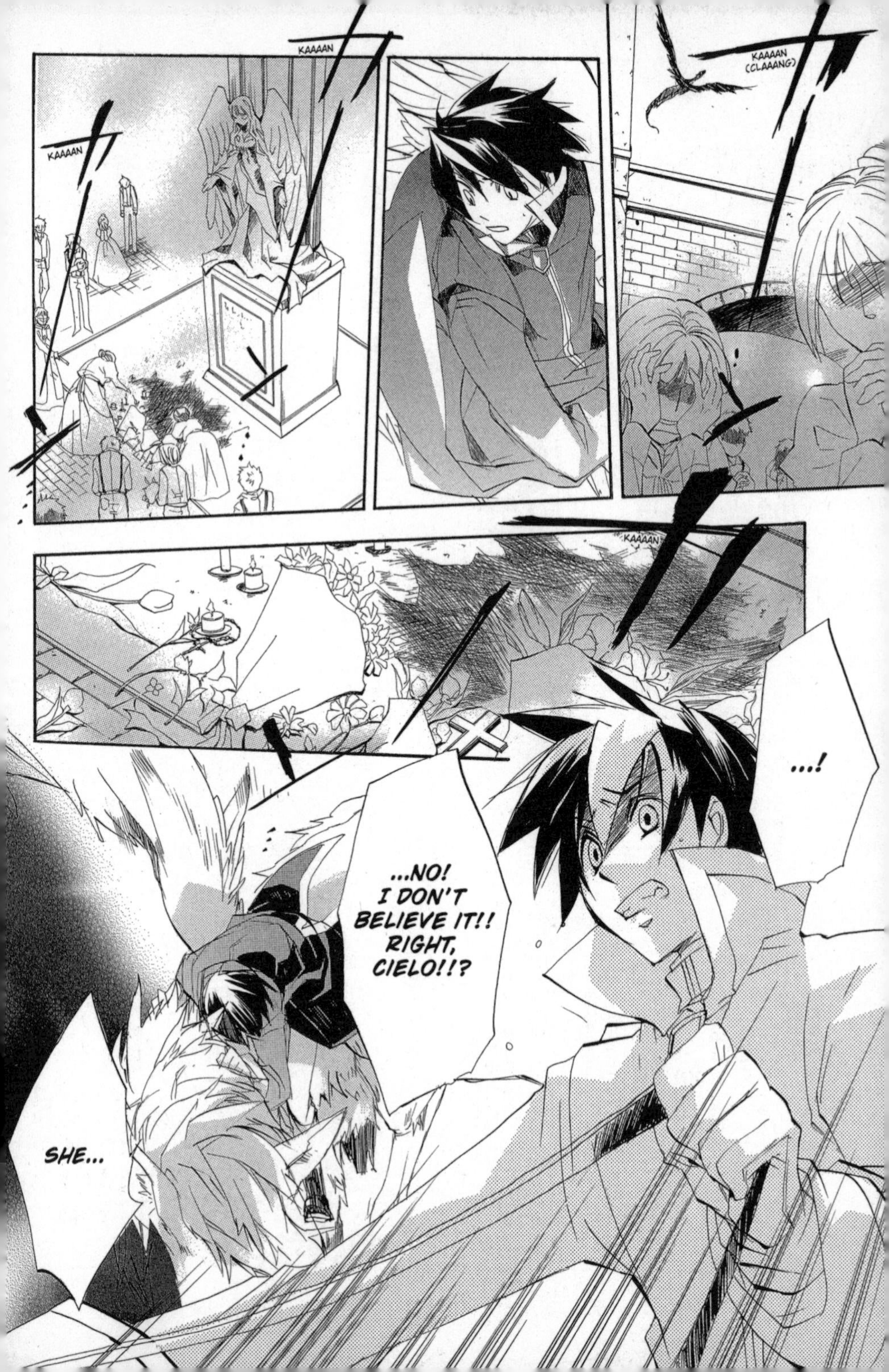
KAAAAN (CLAAANG)
KAAAAN
KAAAAN
KAAAAN
...!
...NO! I DON'T BELIEVE IT!! RIGHT, CIELO!!?
SHE...

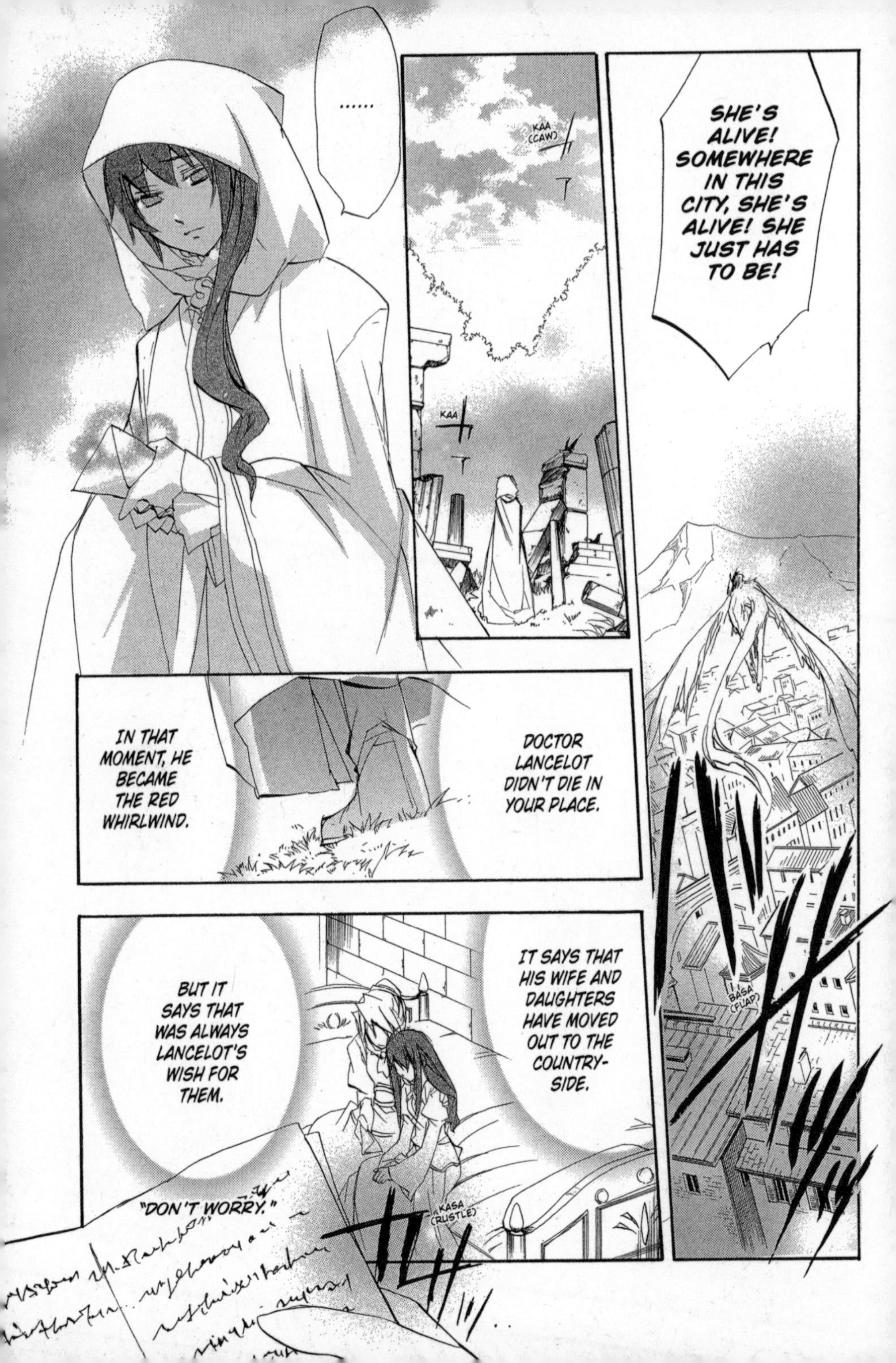
SHE'S ALIVE! SOMEWHERE IN THIS CITY, SHE'S ALIVE! SHE JUST HAS TO BE!
BASA (FLAP)
KAA (CAW)
KAA
......
DOCTOR LANCELOT DIDN'T DIE IN YOUR PLACE.
IN THAT MOMENT, HE BECAME THE RED WHIRLWIND.
IT SAYS THAT HIS WIFE AND DAUGHTERS HAVE MOVED OUT TO THE COUNTRY-SIDE.
BUT IT SAYS THAT WAS ALWAYS LANCELOT'S WISH FOR THEM.
KASA (RUSTLE)
"DON'T WORRY."

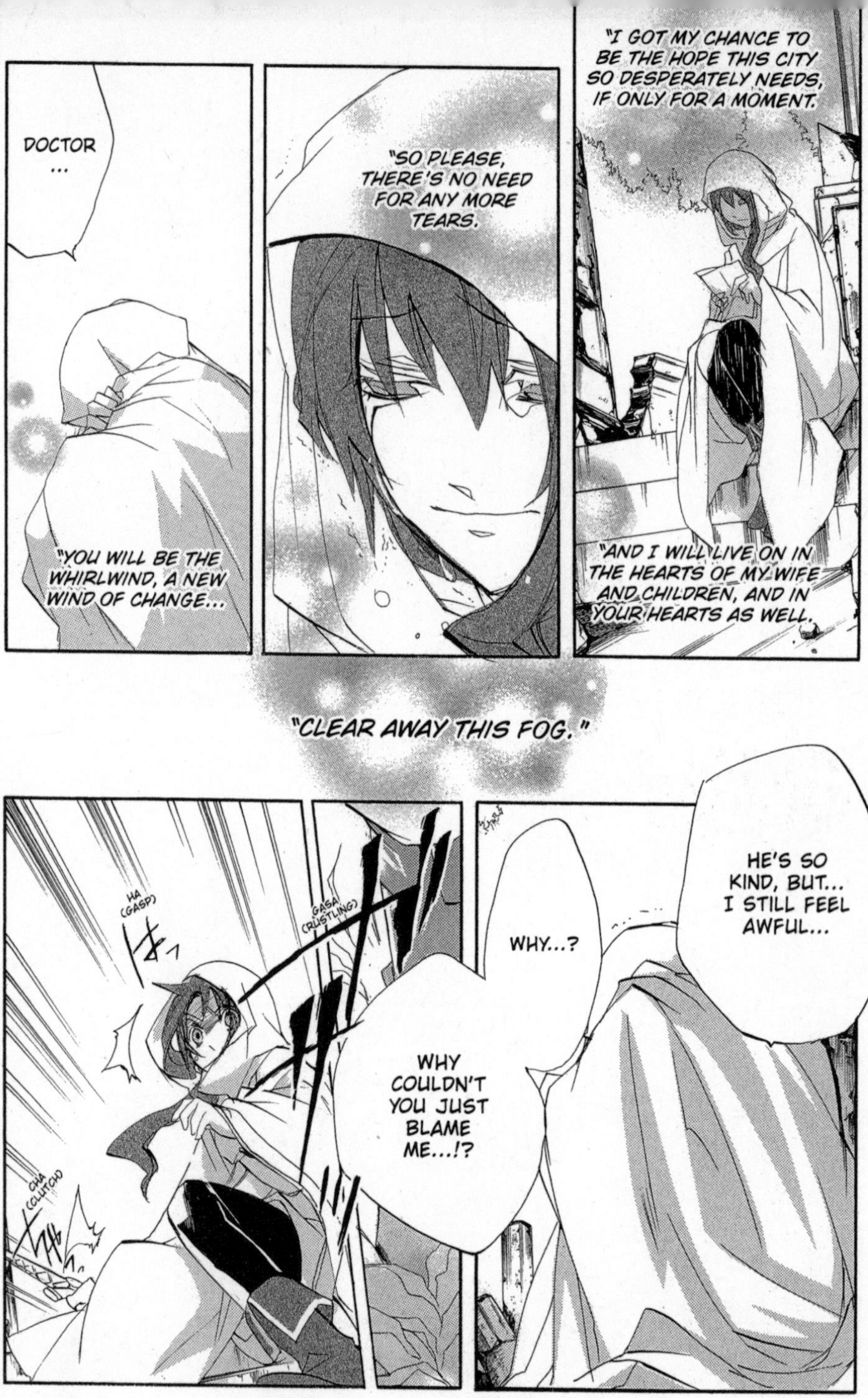
"I GOT MY CHANCE TO BE THE HOPE THIS CITY SO DESPERATELY NEEDS, IF ONLY FOR A MOMENT.
"AND I WILL LIVE ON IN THE HEARTS OF MY WIFE AND CHILDREN, AND IN YOUR HEARTS AS WELL.
"SO PLEASE, THERE'S NO NEED FOR ANY MORE TEARS.
DOCTOR ...
"YOU WILL BE THE WHIRLWIND, A NEW WIND OF CHANGE...
"CLEAR AWAY THIS FOG."
HE'S SO KIND, BUT... I STILL FEEL AWFUL...
WHY...?
WHY COULDN'T YOU JUST BLAME ME...!?
GASA (RUSTLING)
HA (GASP)
CHA (CLUTCH)

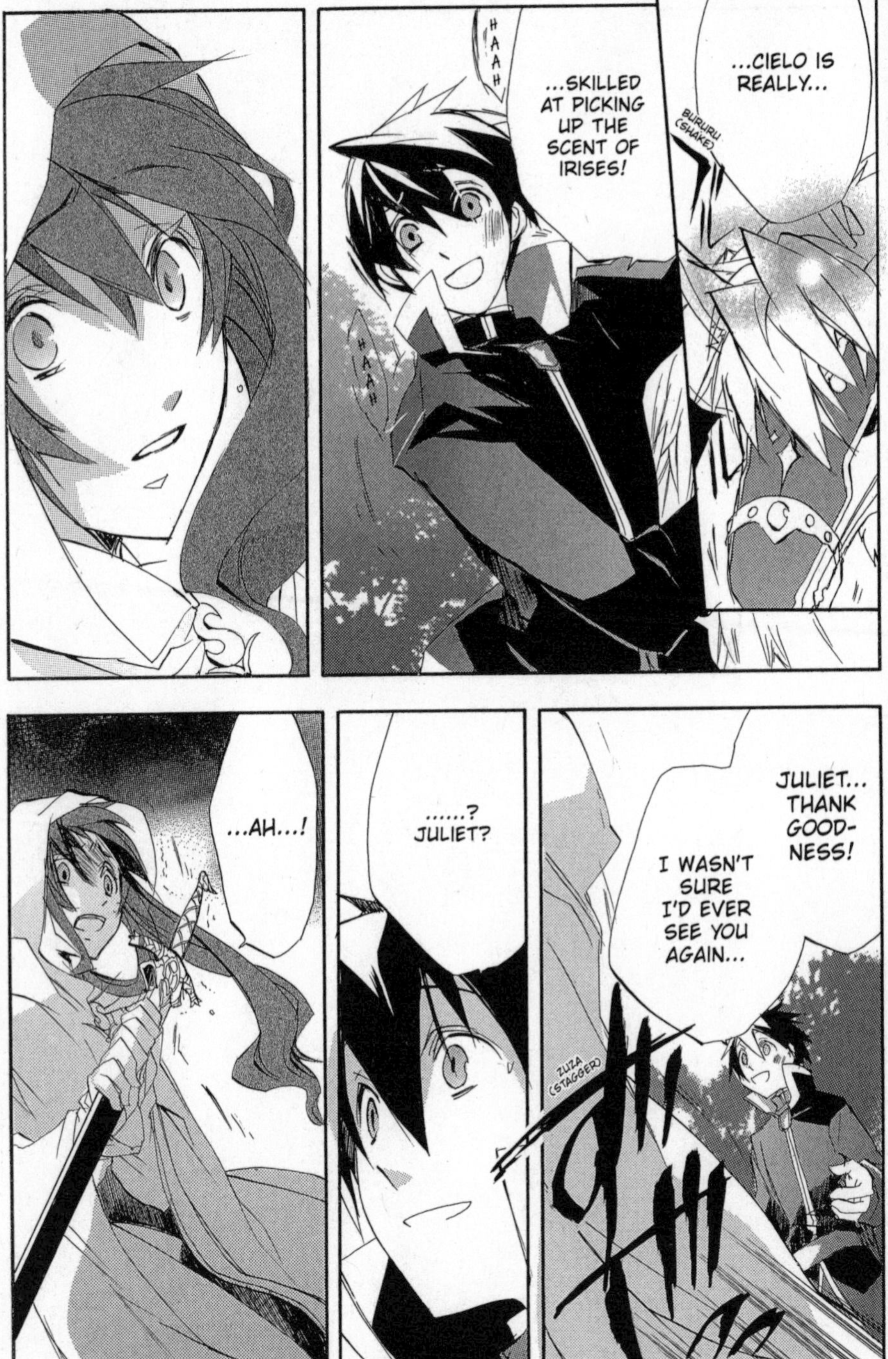
...CIELO IS REALLY...
BURURU (SHAKE)
HAAAH
...SKILLED AT PICKING UP THE SCENT OF IRISES!
HAAAH
JULIET... THANK GOODNESS!
I WASN'T SURE I'D EVER SEE YOU AGAIN...
ZUZA (STAGGER)
......? JULIET?
...AH...!

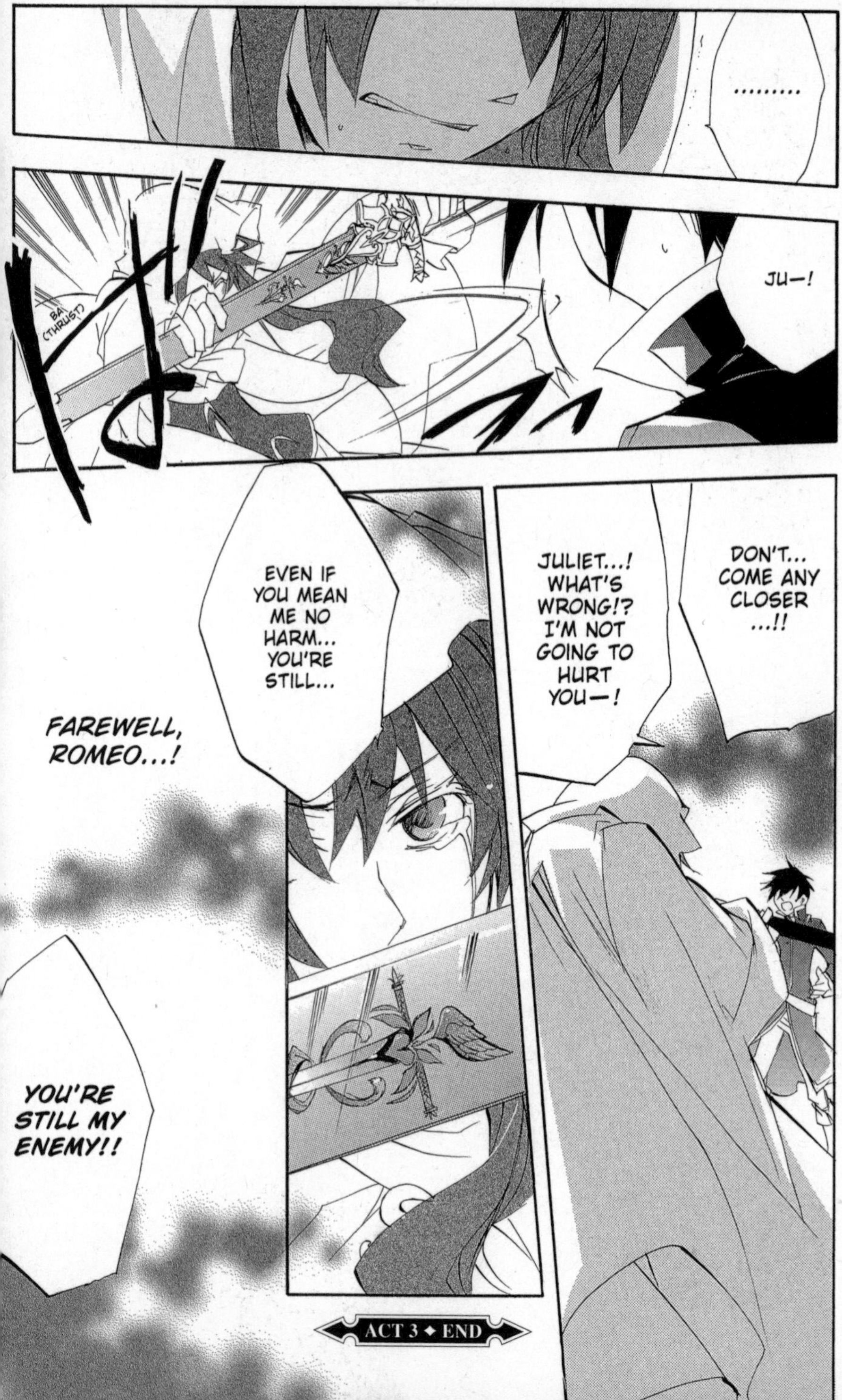
....
JU—!
BA (THRUST)
DON'T... COME ANY CLOSER ...!!
JULIET...! WHAT'S WRONG!? I'M NOT GOING TO HURT YOU—!
EVEN IF YOU MEAN ME NO HARM... YOU'RE STILL...
FAREWELL, ROMEO...!
YOU'RE STILL MY ENEMY!!
ACT 3 ◆ END

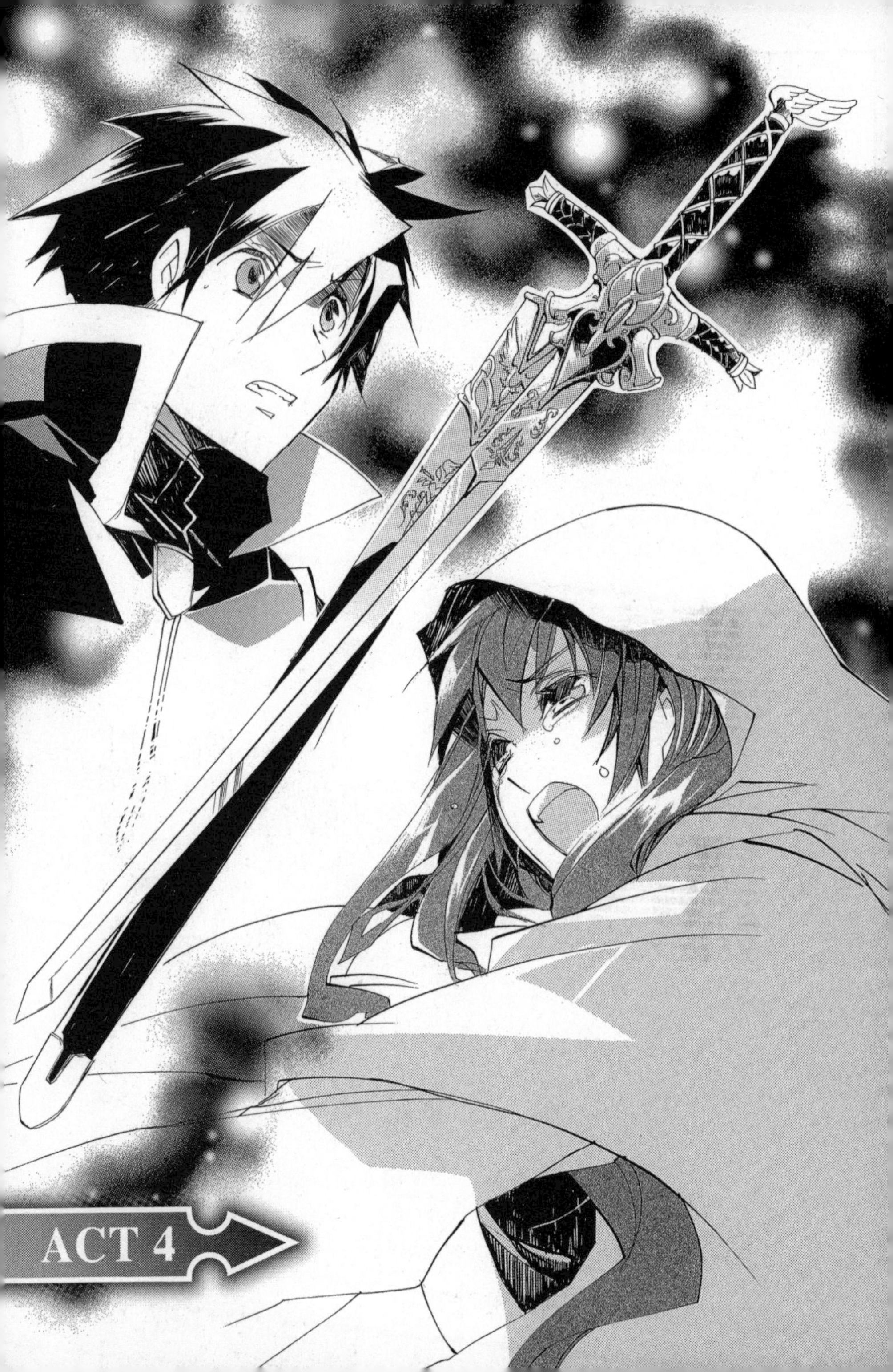
ACT 4

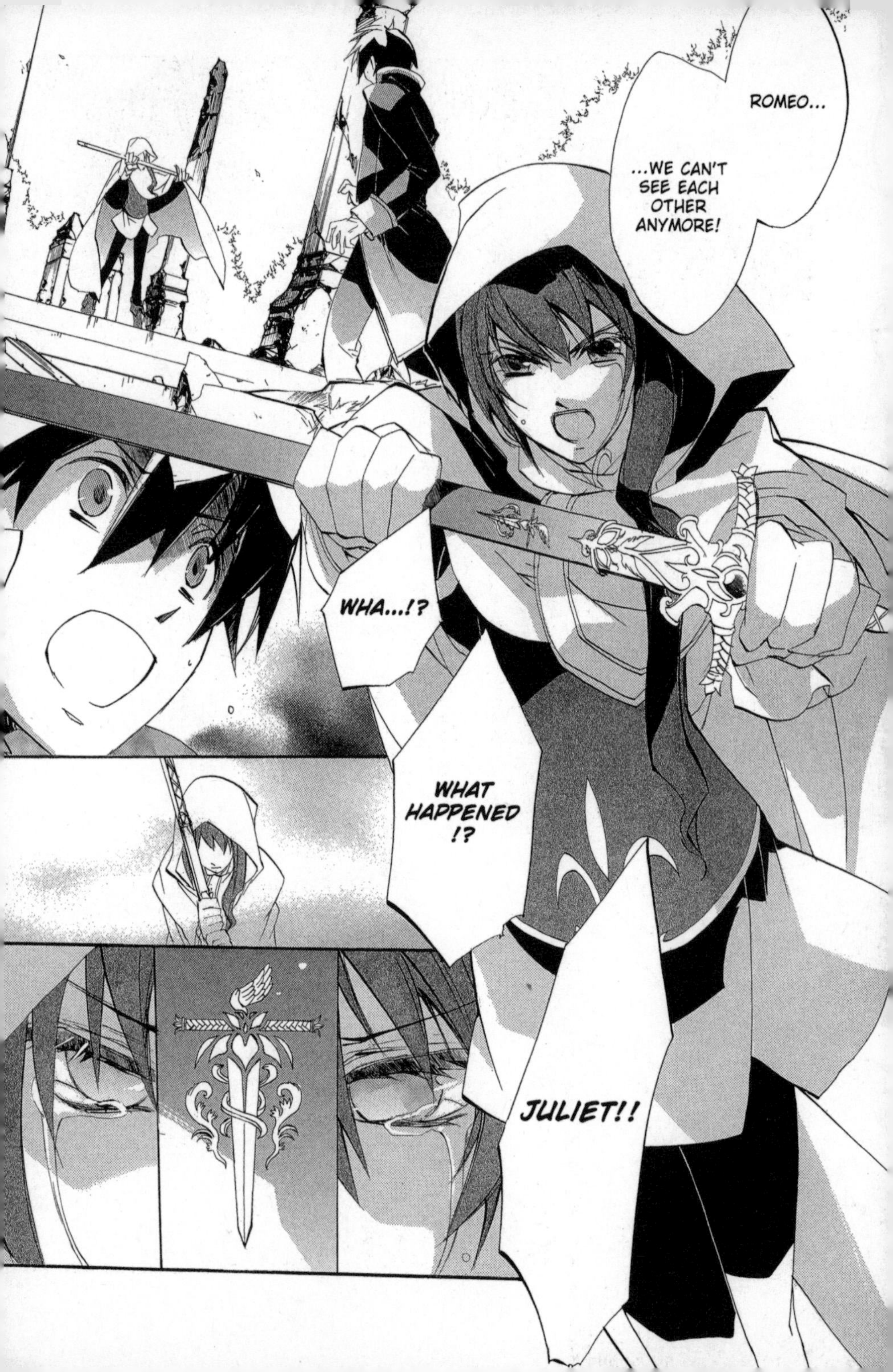
ROMEO...
...WE CAN'T SEE EACH OTHER ANYMORE!
WHA...!?
WHAT HAPPENED !?
JULIET!!

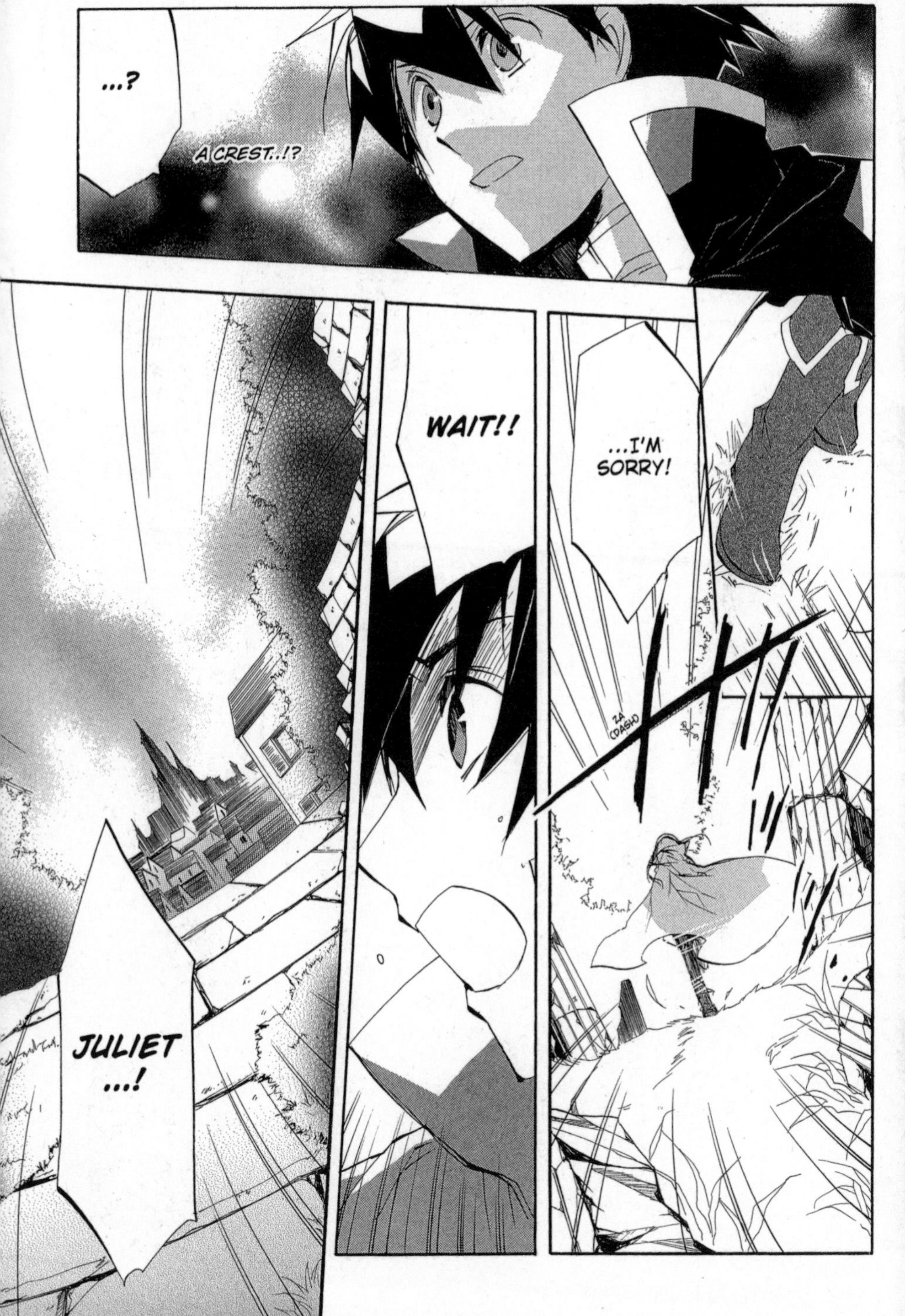
...?
A CREST..!?
...I'M SORRY!
ZA (DASH)
WAIT!!
JULIET ...!

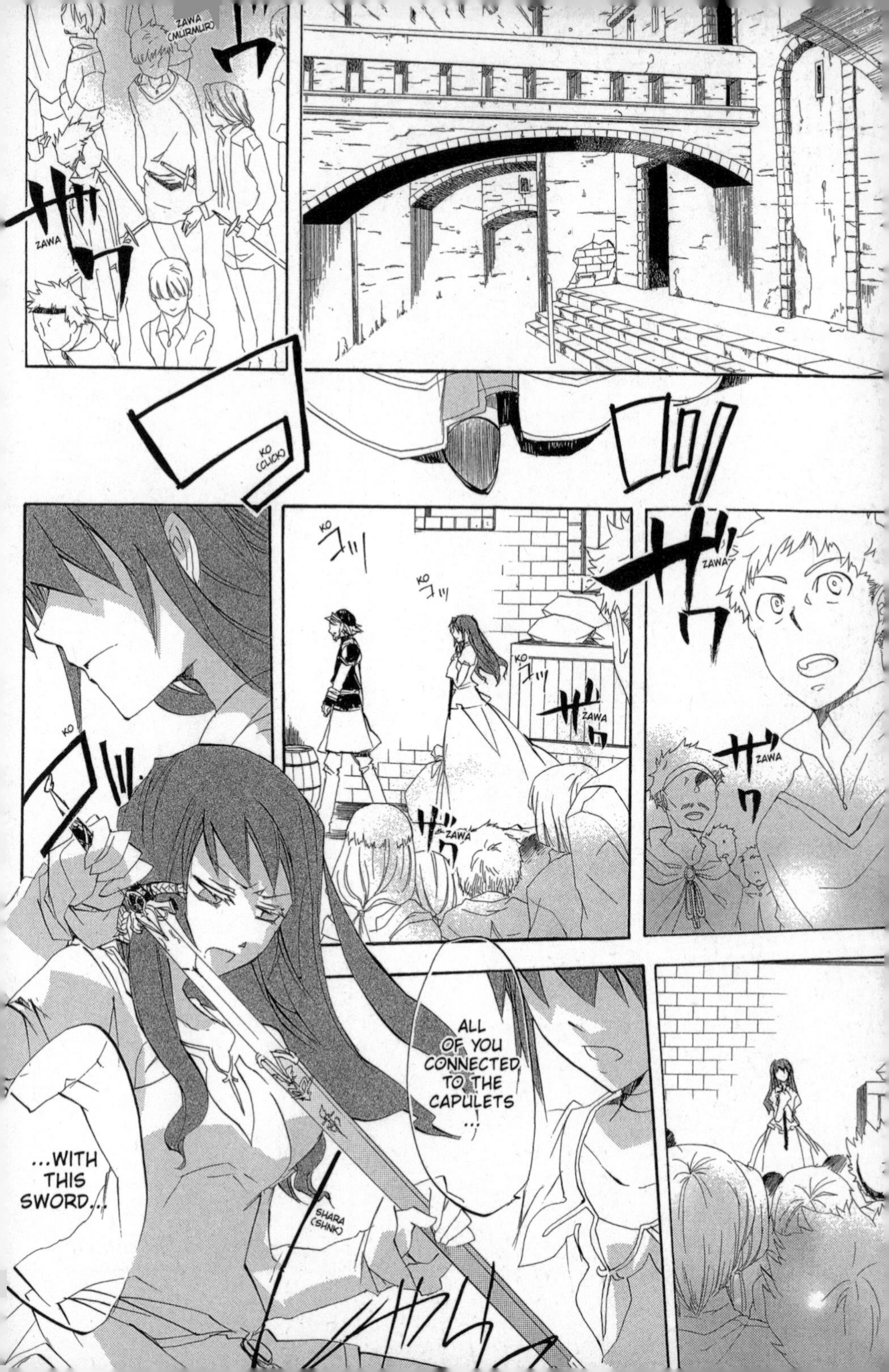
ZAWA (MURMUR)
ZAWA
KO (CLICK)
ZAWA
ZAWA
KO
KO
KO
ZAWA
ZAWA
KO
ALL OF YOU CONNECTED TO THE CAPULETS...!
...WITH THIS SWORD...
SHARA (SHNK)

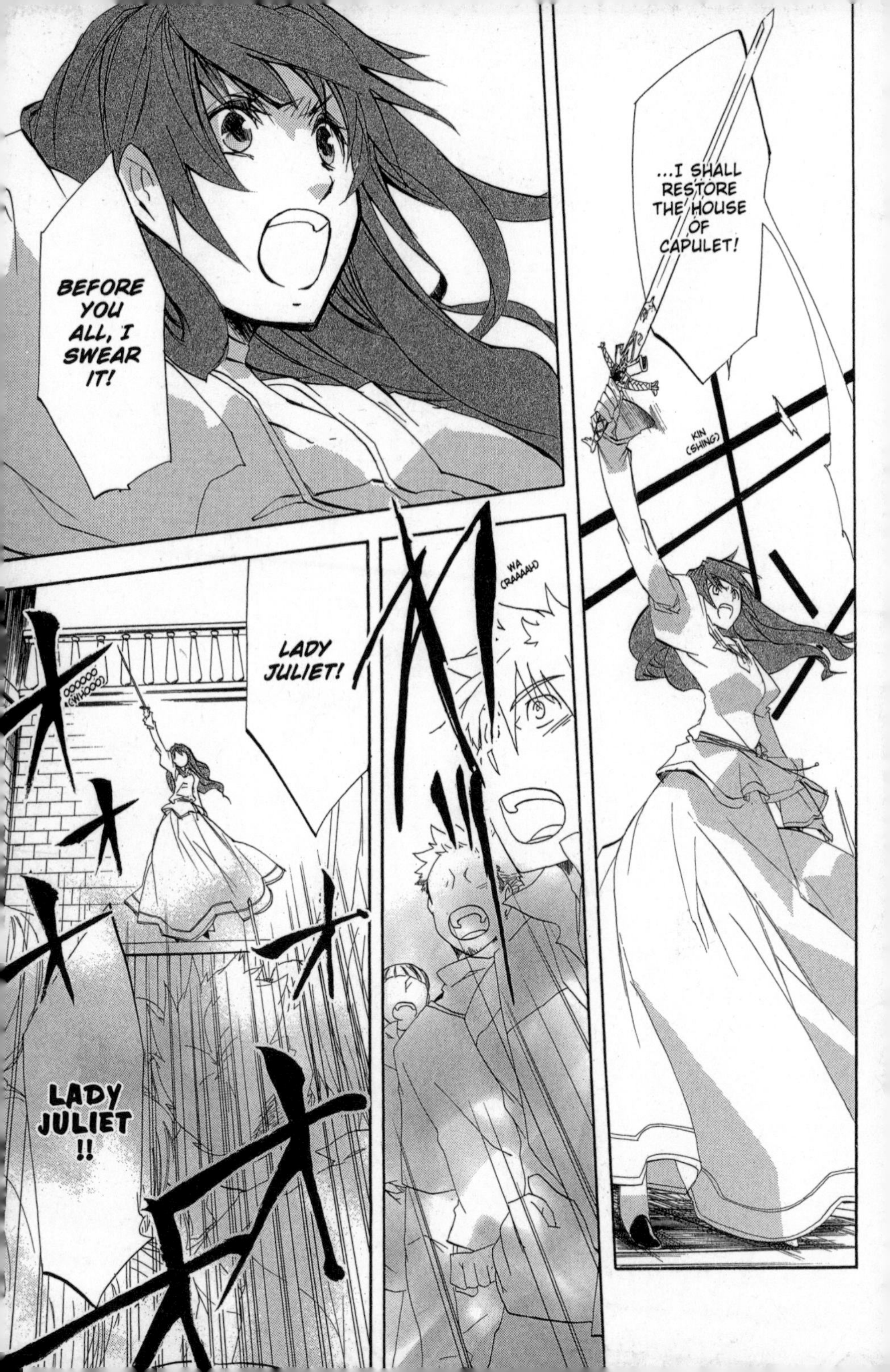
BEFORE YOU ALL, I SWEAR IT!
...I SHALL RESTORE THE HOUSE OF CAPULET!
KIN (SHING)
LADY JULIET!
WA (RAAAAH)
OOOOOOO (WHOOOO)
LADY JULIET !!

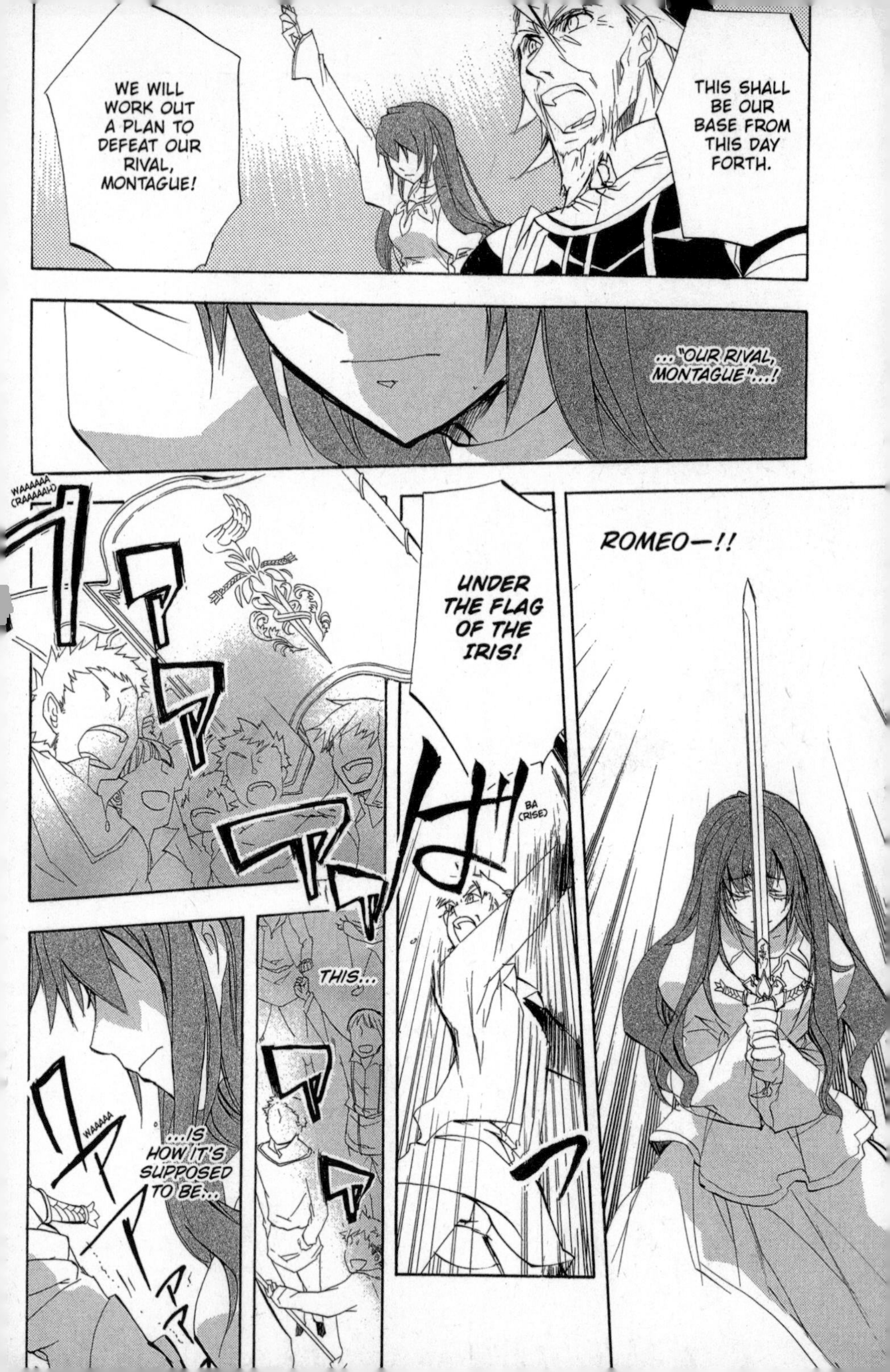
THIS SHALL BE OUR BASE FROM THIS DAY FORTH.
WE WILL WORK OUT A PLAN TO DEFEAT OUR RIVAL, MONTAGUE!
..."OUR RIVAL, MONTAGUE"...!
ROMEO—!!
UNDER THE FLAG OF THE IRIS!
BA (RISE)
WAAAAAA (RAAAAAH)
THIS...
...IS HOW IT'S SUPPOSED TO BE...
WAAAAA

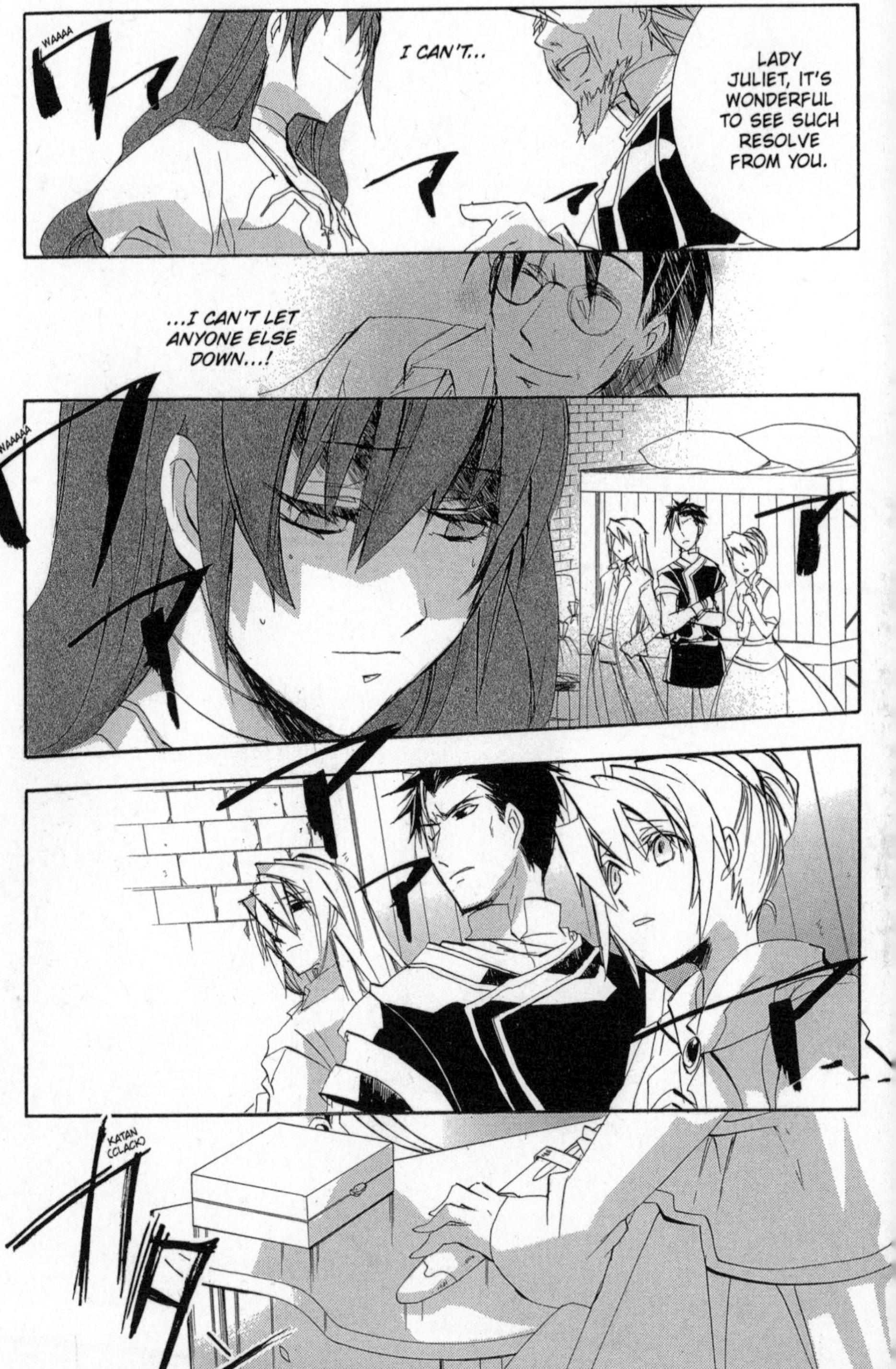
LADY JULIET, IT'S WONDERFUL TO SEE SUCH RESOLVE FROM YOU.
I CAN'T...
WAAAA
...I CAN'T LET ANYONE ELSE DOWN...!
WAAAAA
KATAN (CLACK)

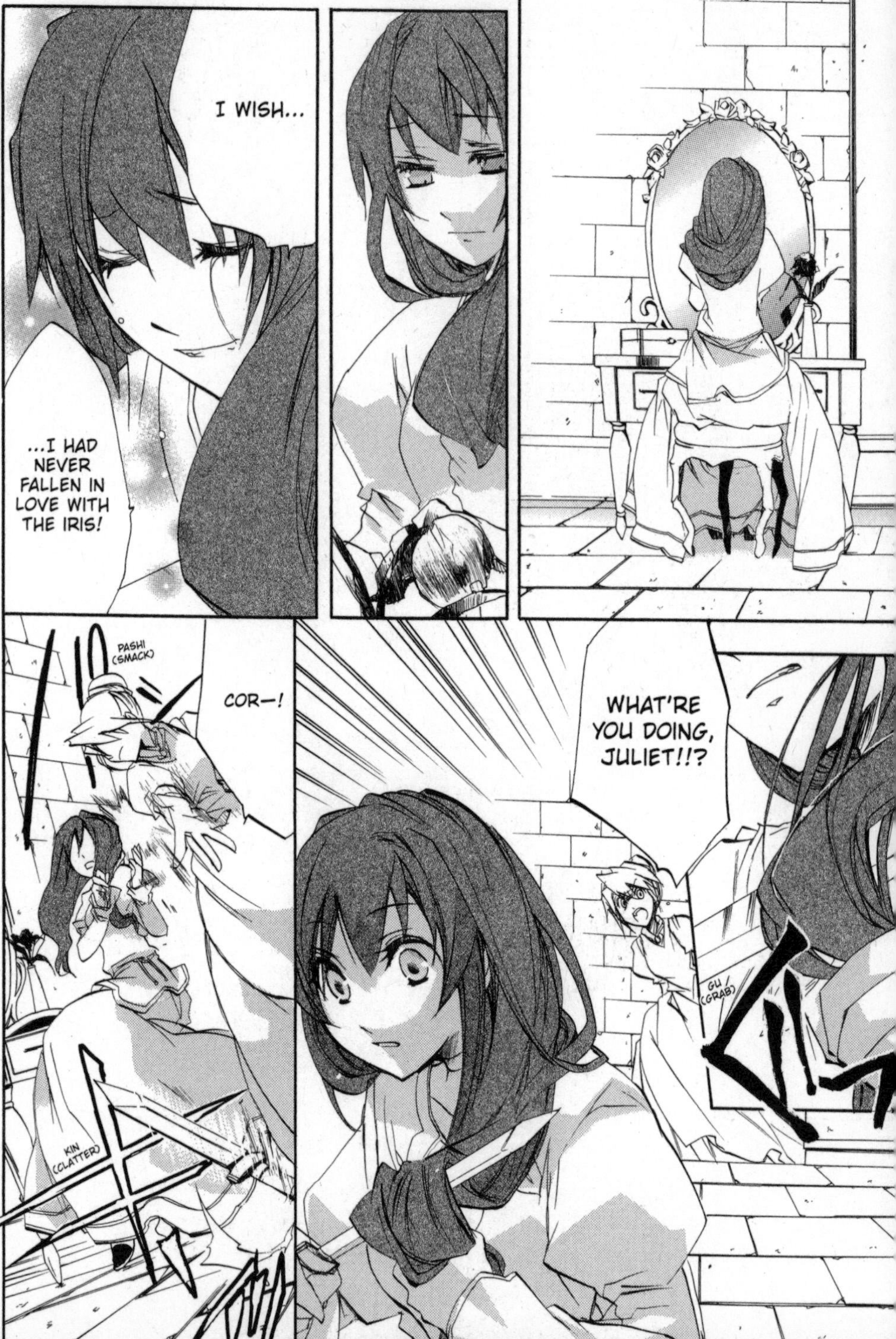
I WISH...
...I HAD NEVER FALLEN IN LOVE WITH THE IRIS!
WHAT'RE YOU DOING, JULIET!!?
GU (GRAB)
PASHI (SMACK)
COR—!
KIN (CLATTER)

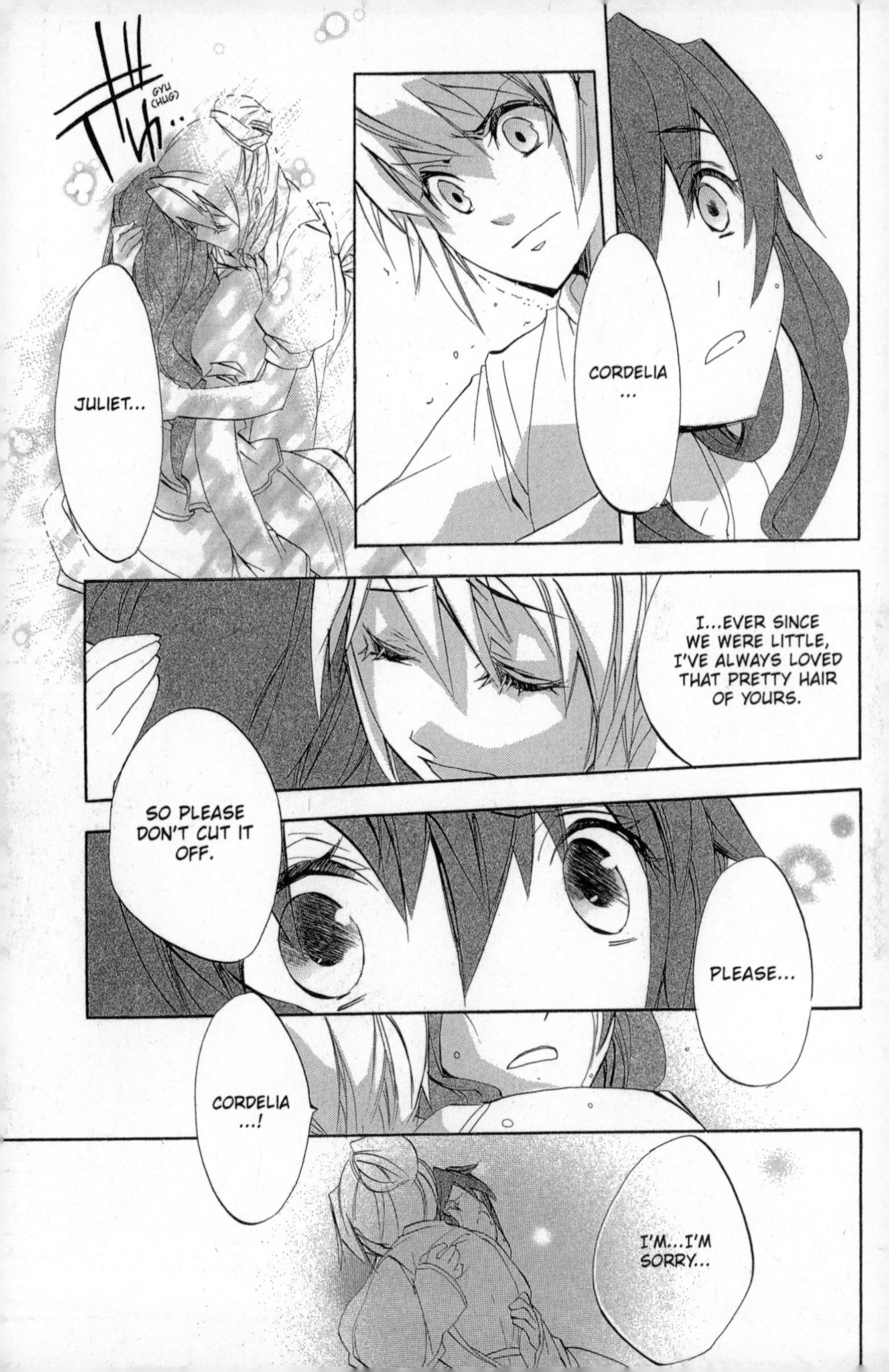
CORDELIA...
GYU (HUG)
JULIET...
I...EVER SINCE WE WERE LITTLE, I'VE ALWAYS LOVED THAT PRETTY HAIR OF YOURS.
SO PLEASE DON'T CUT IT OFF.
PLEASE...
CORDELIA...!
I'M...I'M SORRY...

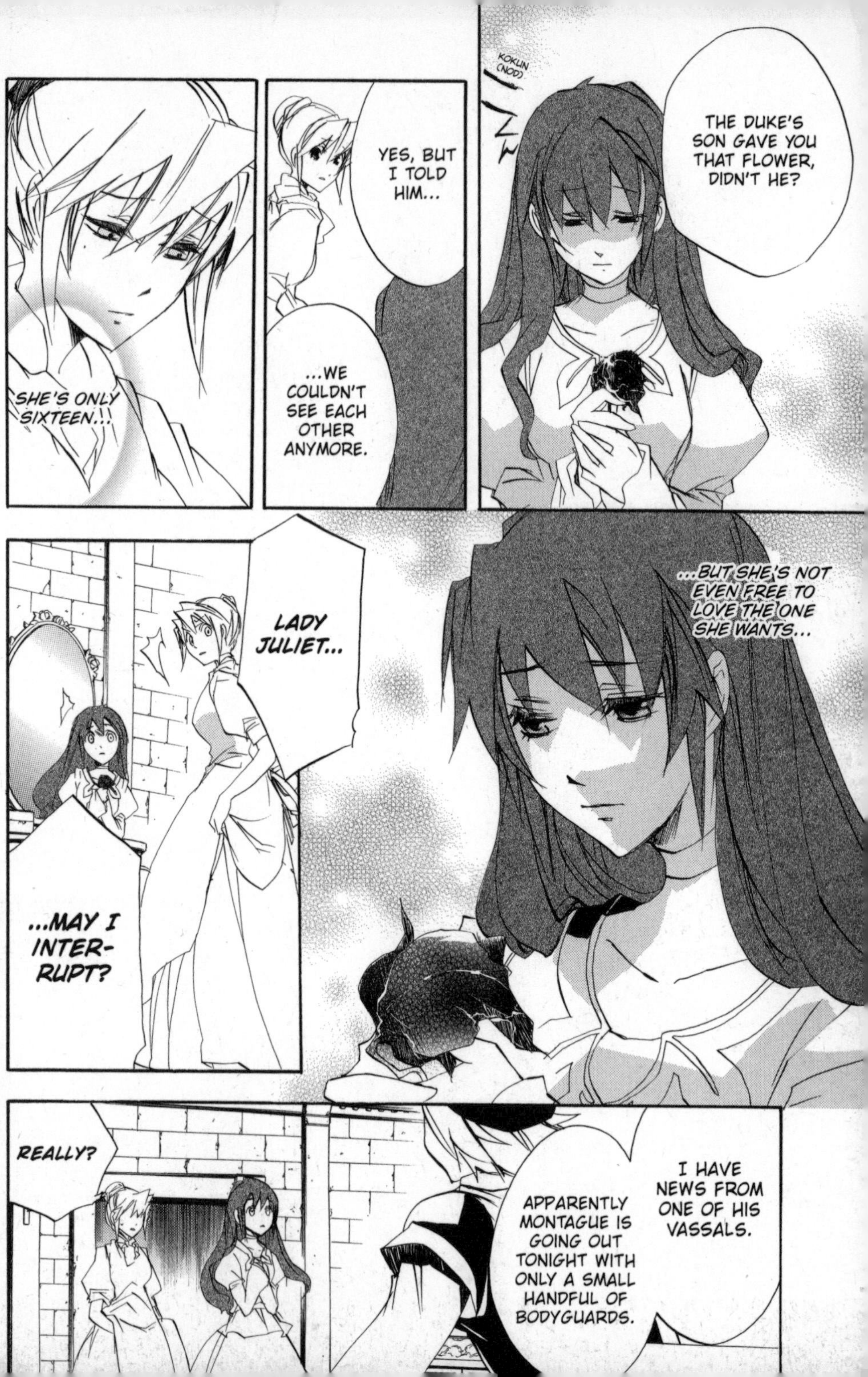
KOKUN (NOD)
THE DUKE'S SON GAVE YOU THAT FLOWER, DIDN'T HE?
YES, BUT I TOLD HIM...
...WE COULDN'T SEE EACH OTHER ANYMORE.
SHE'S ONLY SIXTEEN...!
...BUT SHE'S NOT EVEN FREE TO LOVE THE ONE SHE WANTS...
LADY JULIET...
...MAY I INTER-RUPT?
I HAVE NEWS FROM ONE OF HIS VASSALS.
APPARENTLY MONTAGUE IS GOING OUT TONIGHT WITH ONLY A SMALL HANDFUL OF BODYGUARDS.
REALLY?

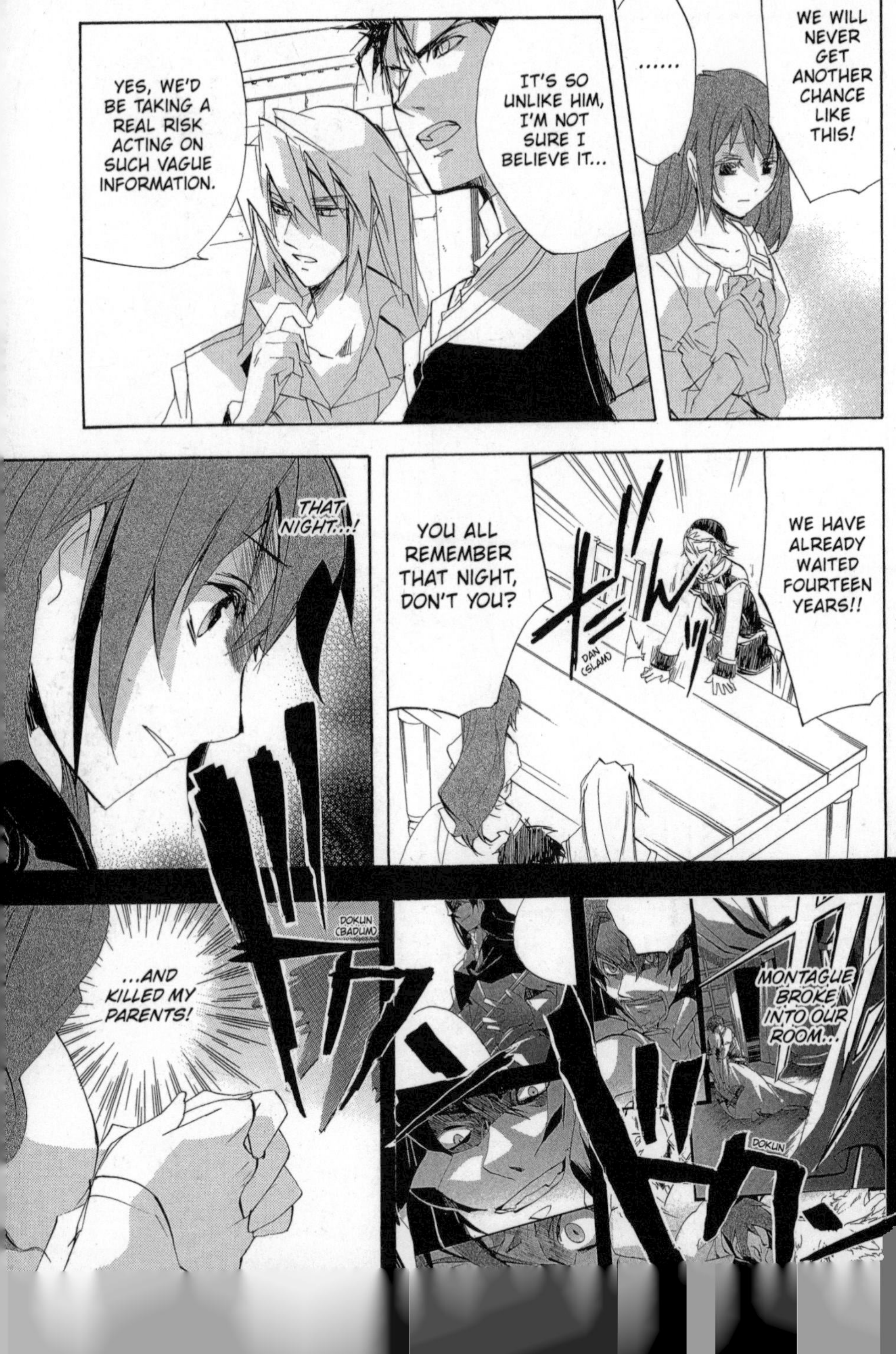
WE WILL NEVER GET ANOTHER CHANCE LIKE THIS!
......
IT'S SO UNLIKE HIM, I'M NOT SURE I BELIEVE IT...
YES, WE'D BE TAKING A REAL RISK ACTING ON SUCH VAGUE INFORMATION.
WE HAVE ALREADY WAITED FOURTEEN YEARS!!
DAN (SLAM)
YOU ALL REMEMBER THAT NIGHT, DON'T YOU?
THAT NIGHT...!
MONTAGUE BROKE INTO OUR ROOM...
DOKUN
DOKUN (BADUM)
...AND KILLED MY PARENTS!

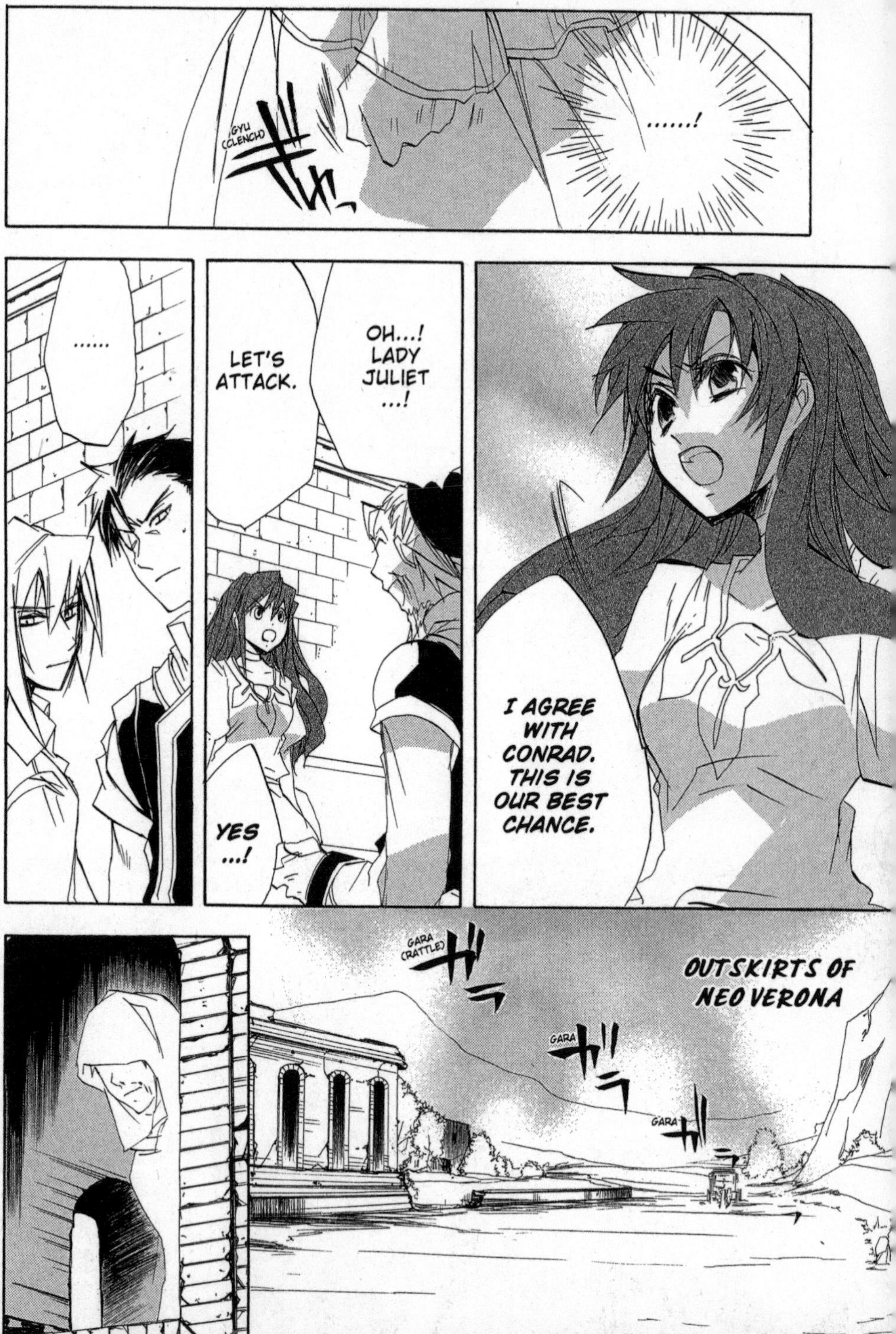
......!
GYU (CLENCH)
I AGREE WITH CONRAD. THIS IS OUR BEST CHANCE.
OH...! LADY JULIET ...!
LET'S ATTACK.
YES ...!
......
OUTSKIRTS OF NEO VERONA
GARA (RATTLE)
GARA
GARA

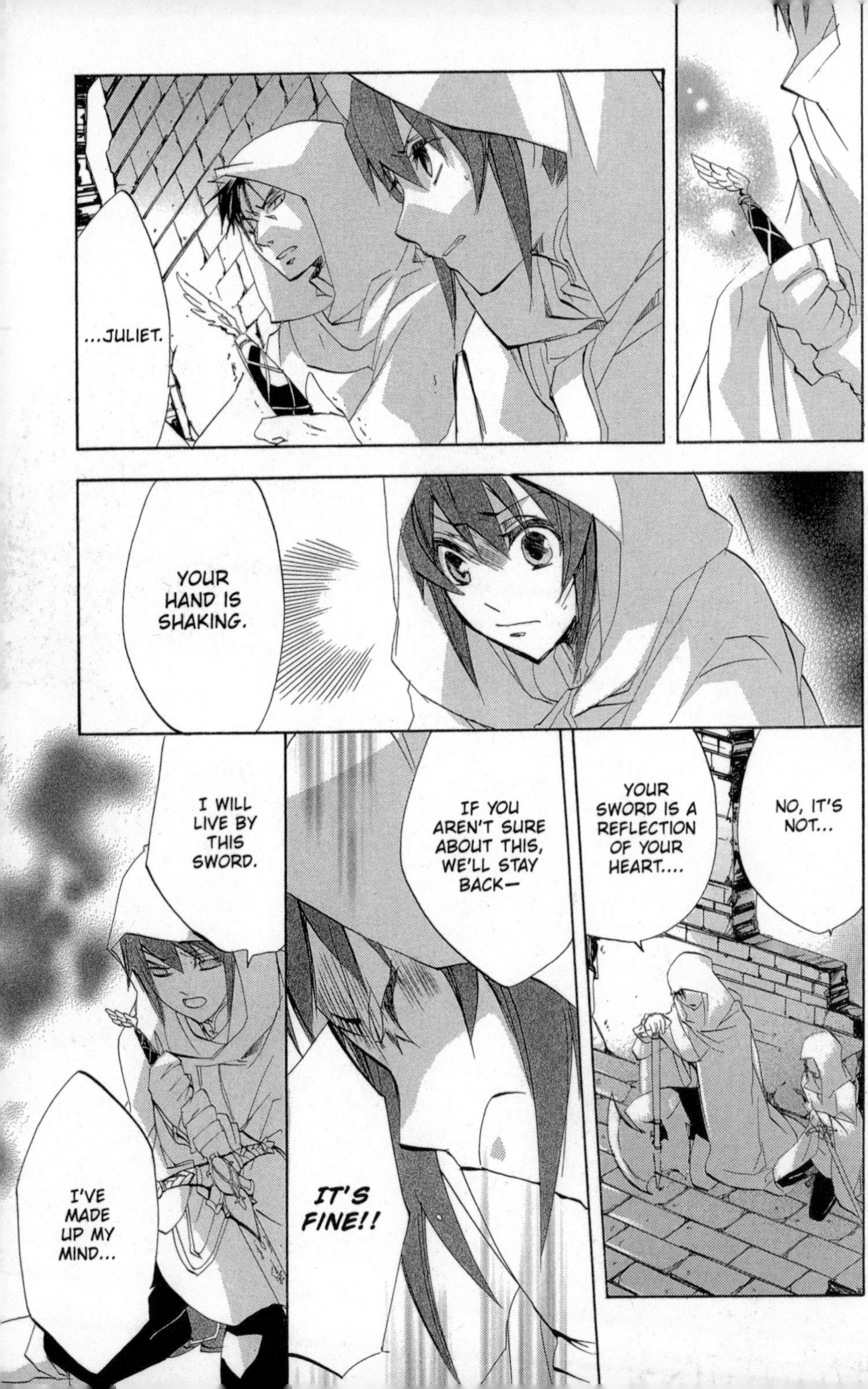
...JULIET.
YOUR HAND IS SHAKING.
NO, IT'S NOT...
YOUR SWORD IS A REFLECTION OF YOUR HEART....
IF YOU AREN'T SURE ABOUT THIS, WE'LL STAY BACK—
IT'S FINE!!
I WILL LIVE BY THIS SWORD.
I'VE MADE UP MY MIND...

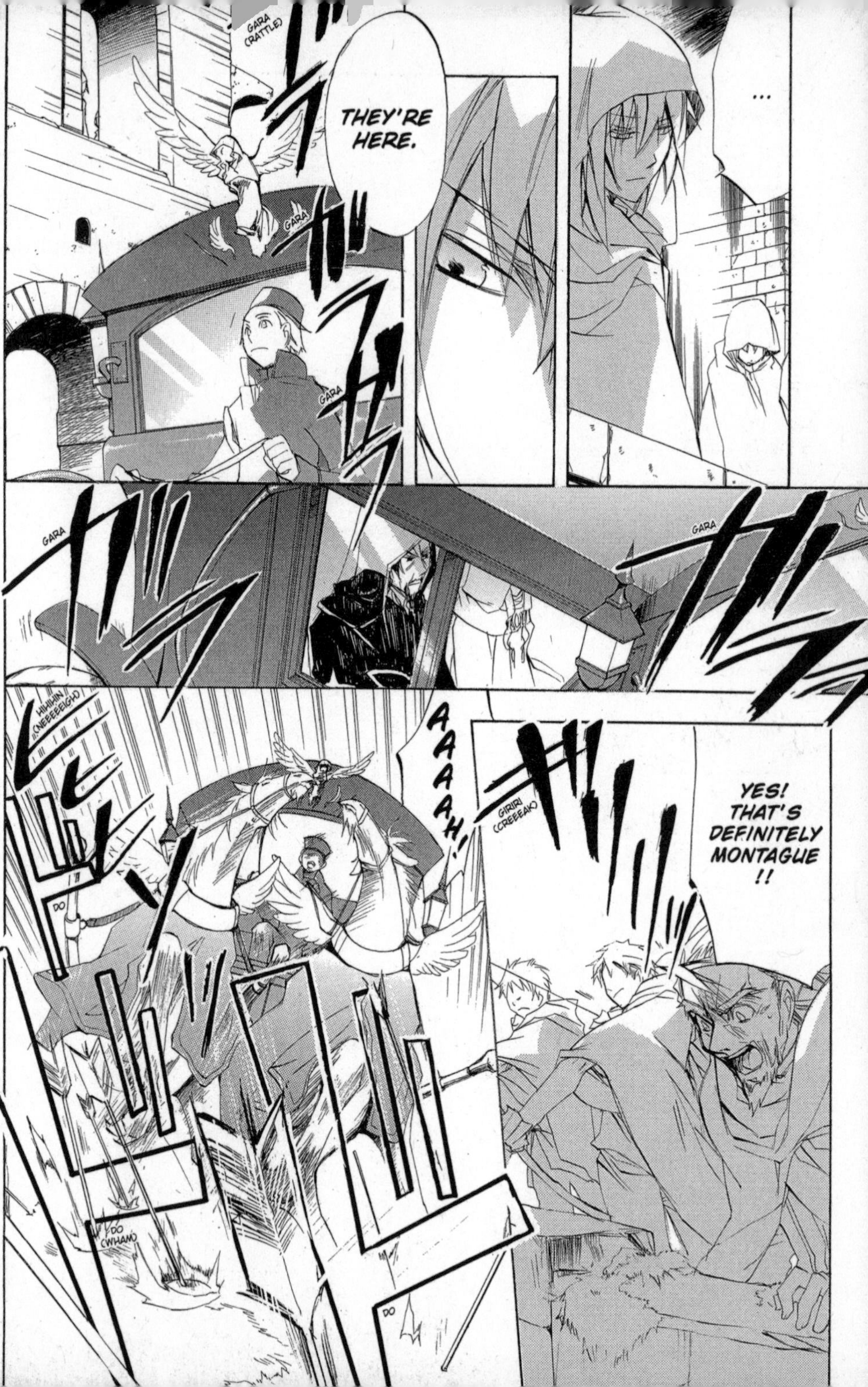
...
THEY'RE HERE.
GARA (RATTLE)
GARA
GARA
GARA
GARA
YES! THAT'S DEFINITELY MONTAGUE!!
GIRIRI (CREEEAK)
AAAAAH!!
HIHIHIN (NEEEEEIGH)!!
DO
DO (WHAM)
DO

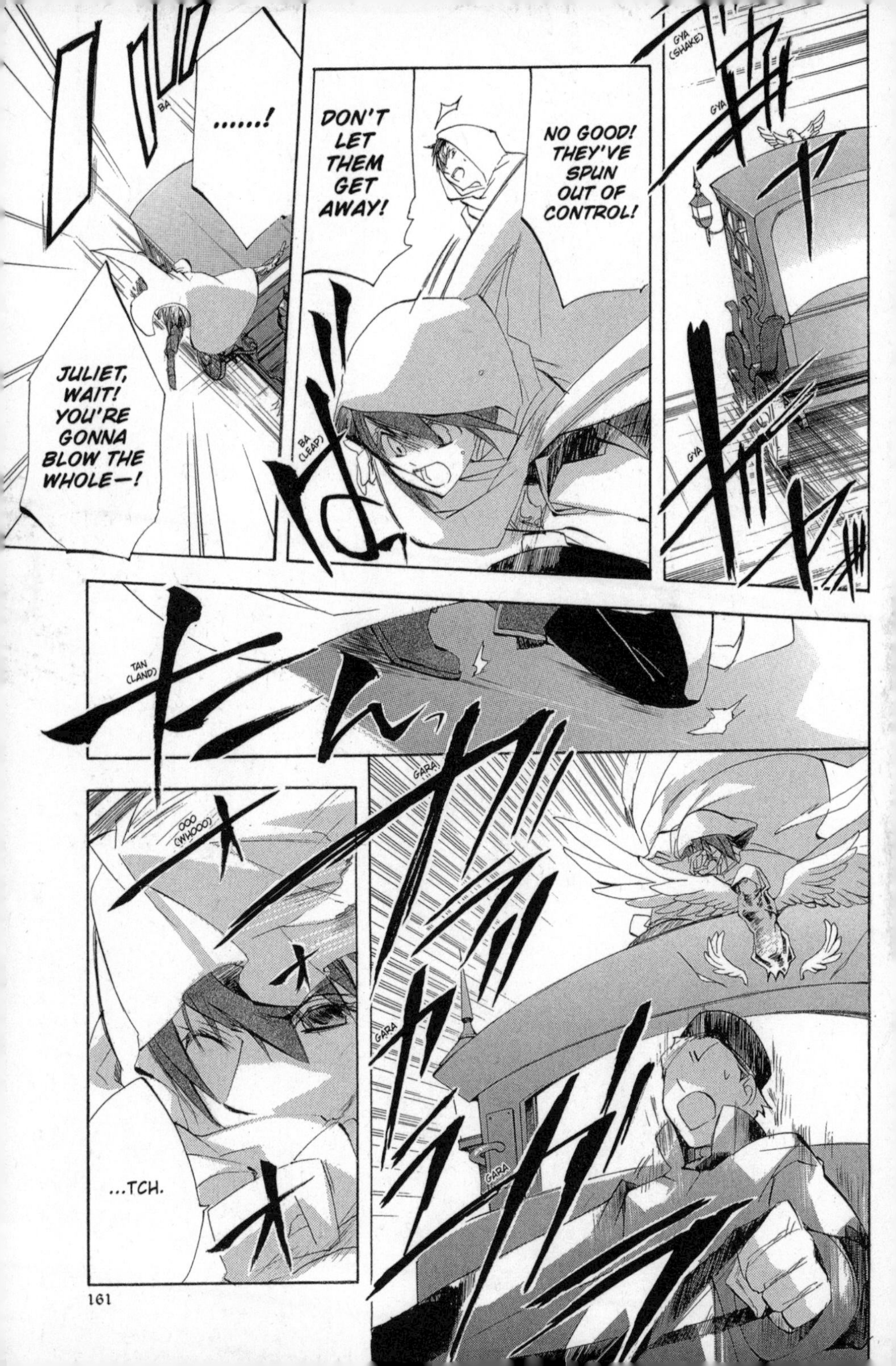
GYA (SHAKE)
GYA
NO GOOD! THEY'VE SPUN OUT OF CONTROL!
GYA
DON'T LET THEM GET AWAY!
BA (LEAP)
BA
......!
JULIET, WAIT! YOU'RE GONNA BLOW THE WHOLE—!
TAN (LAND)
GARA
GARA
GARA
OOO (WHOOO)
...TCH.

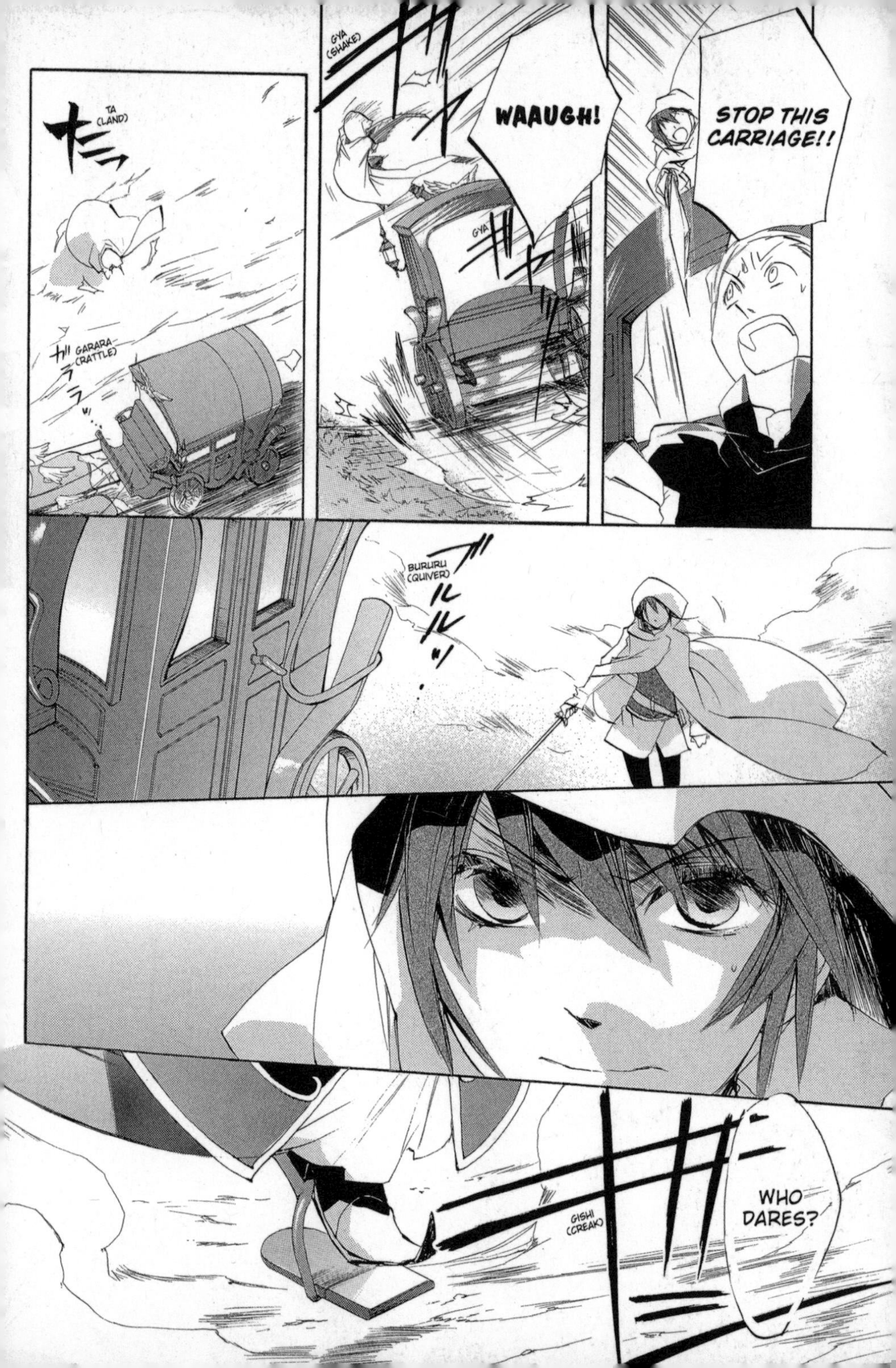
STOP THIS CARRIAGE!!
GYA (SHAKE)
WAAUGH!
GYA
TA (LAND)
GARARA (RATTLE)
BURURU (QUIVER)
WHO DARES?
GISHI (CREAK)

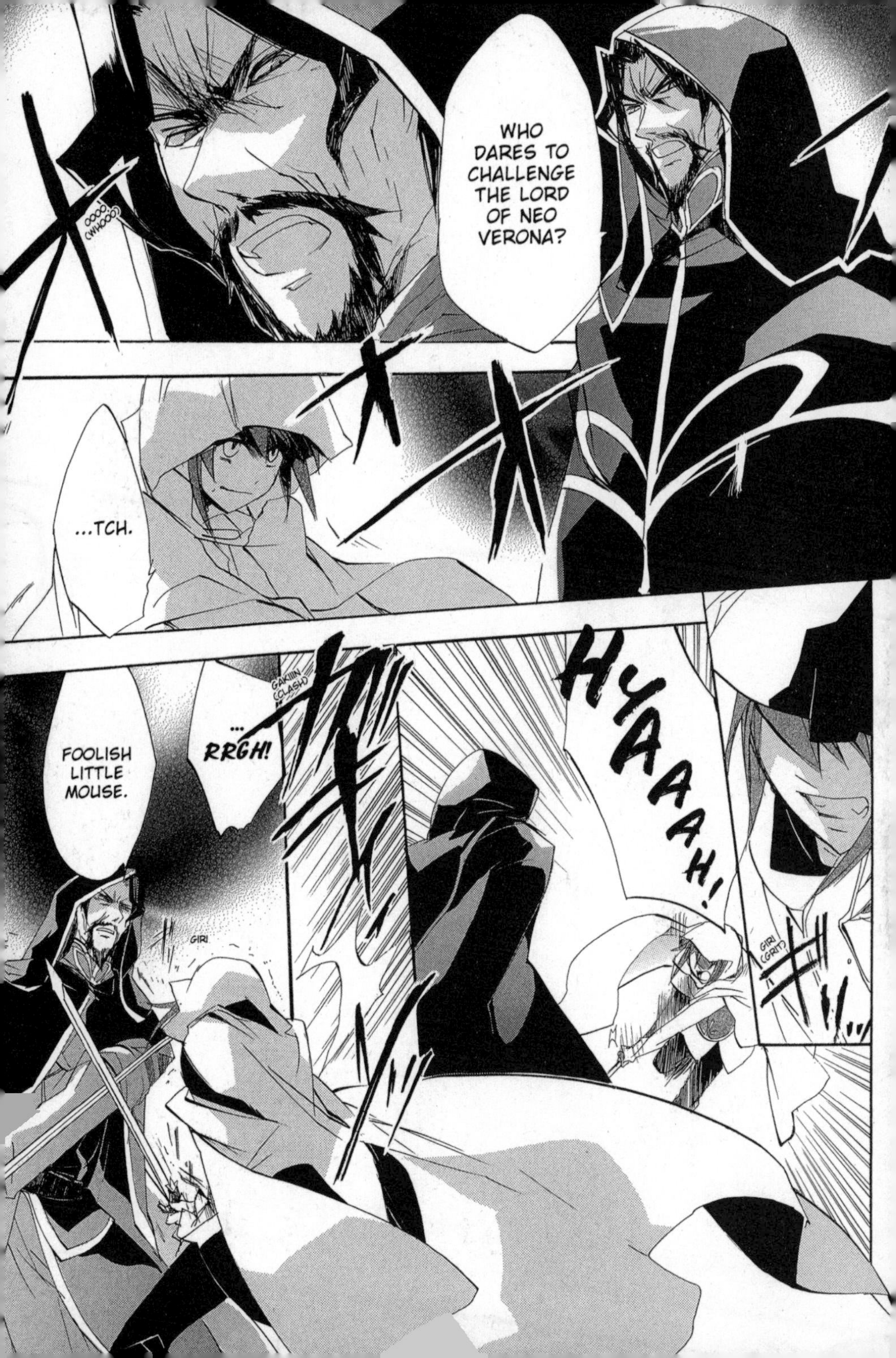
WHO DARES TO CHALLENGE THE LORD OF NEO VERONA?
OOOO! (WHOOO)
...TCH.
GIRI (GRIT)
HYAAAAH!
GAKIIN (CLASH)
... RRGH!
FOOLISH LITTLE MOUSE.
GIRI

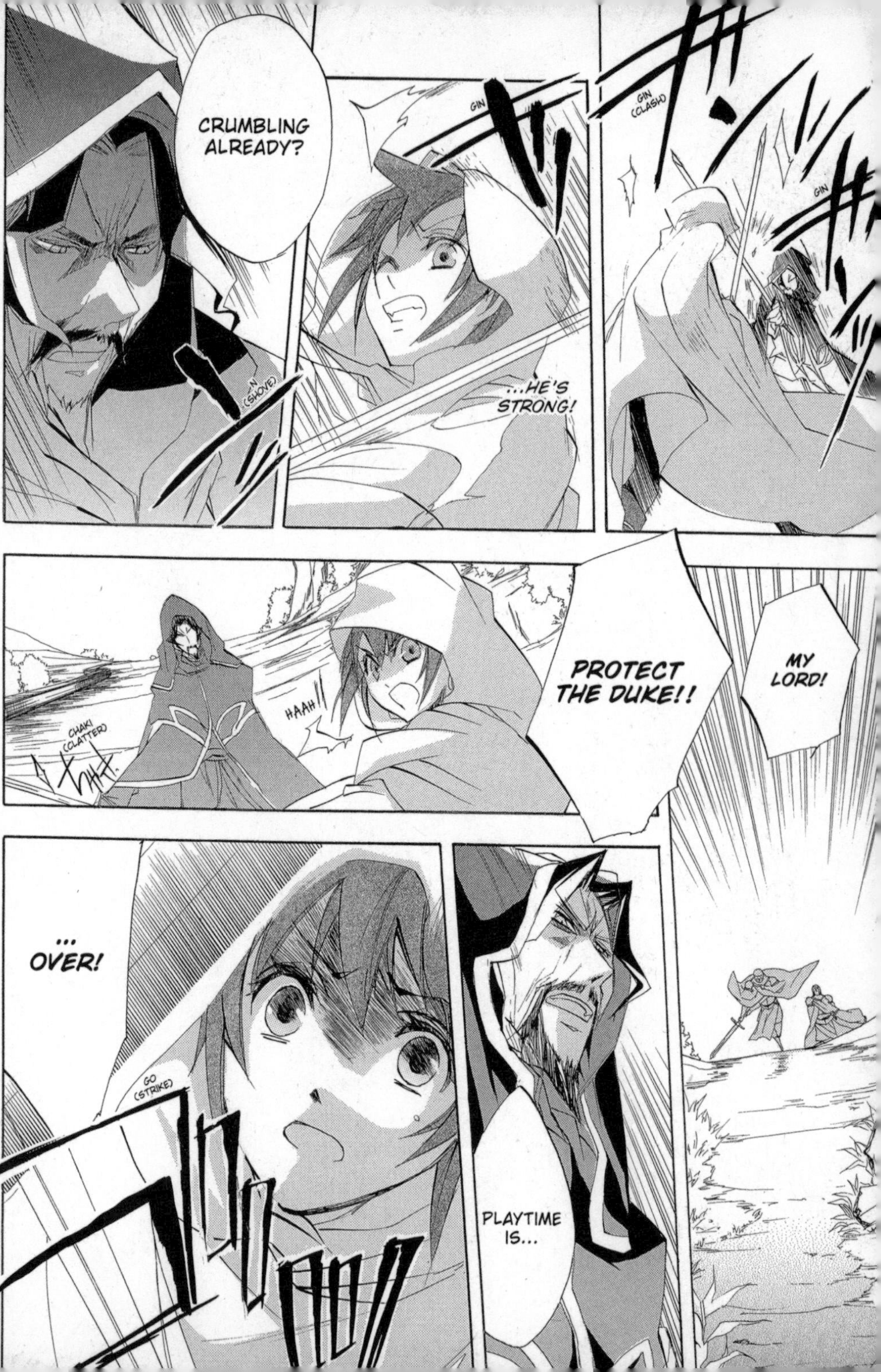
GIN (CLASH)
GIN
GIN
...HE'S STRONG!
N (SHOVE)
CRUMBLING ALREADY?
MY LORD!
PROTECT THE DUKE!!
HAAH!!
CHAKI (CLATTER)
PLAYTIME IS...
...OVER!
GO (STRIKE)

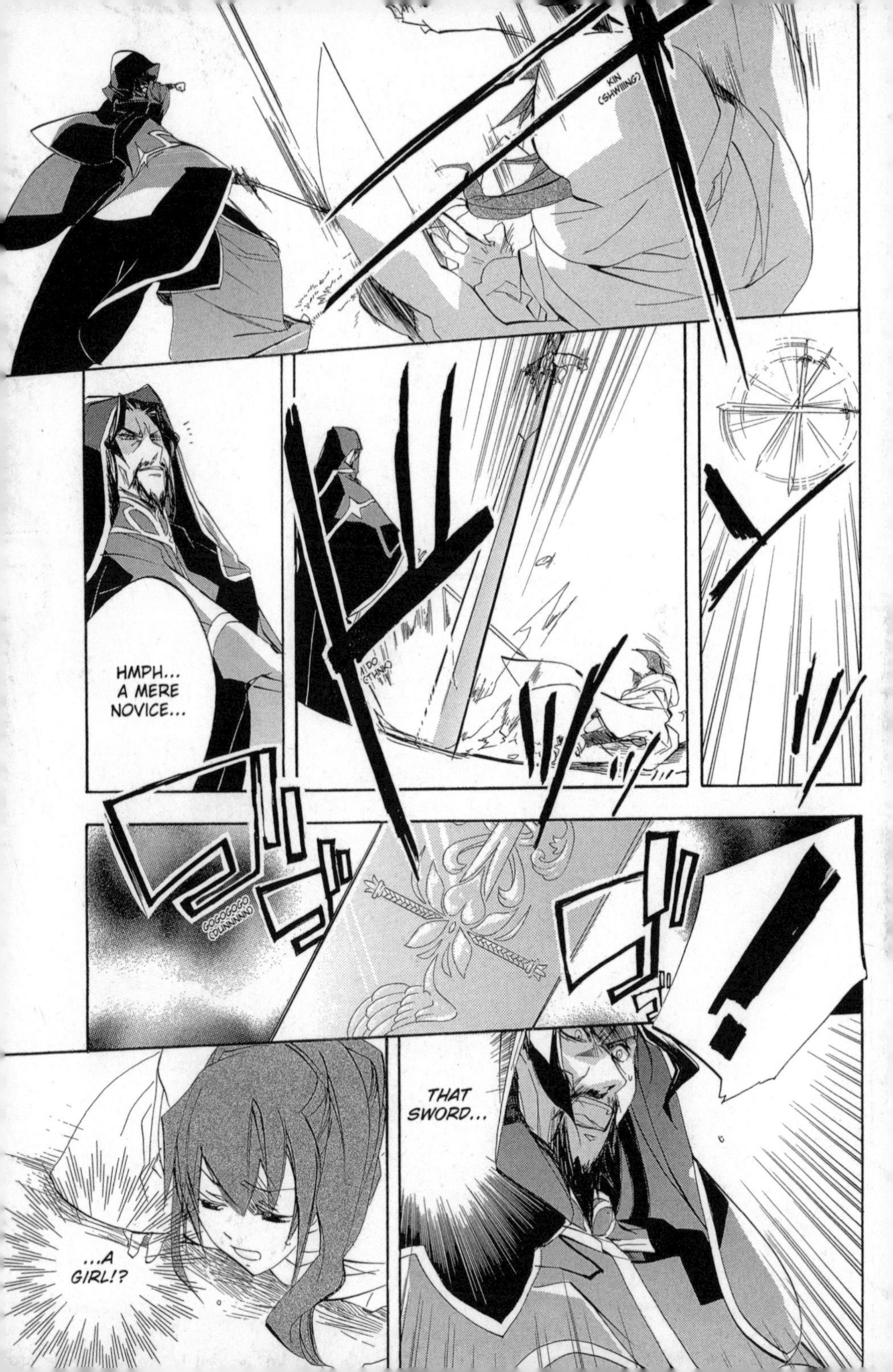
KIN
(SHWIING)
ZA DO
(THNK)
HMPH... A MERE NOVICE...
GOGOGOGO
(DUNNNNN)
THAT SWORD...
...A GIRL!?

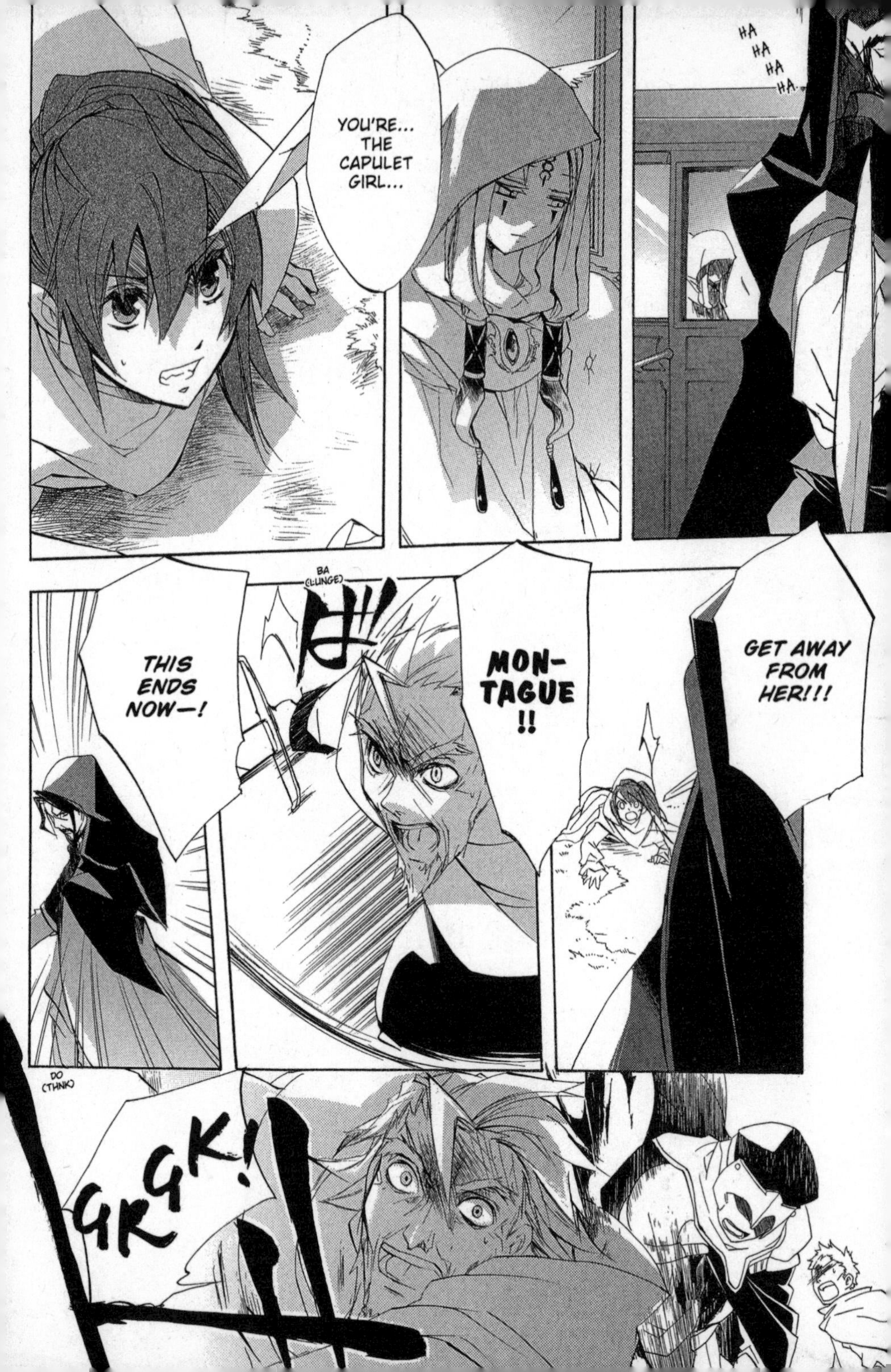
HA HA HA HA.
YOU'RE... THE CAPULET GIRL...
GET AWAY FROM HER!!!
MON-TAGUE !!
BA (LUNGE)
THIS ENDS NOW—!
DO (THNK)
GRGK!

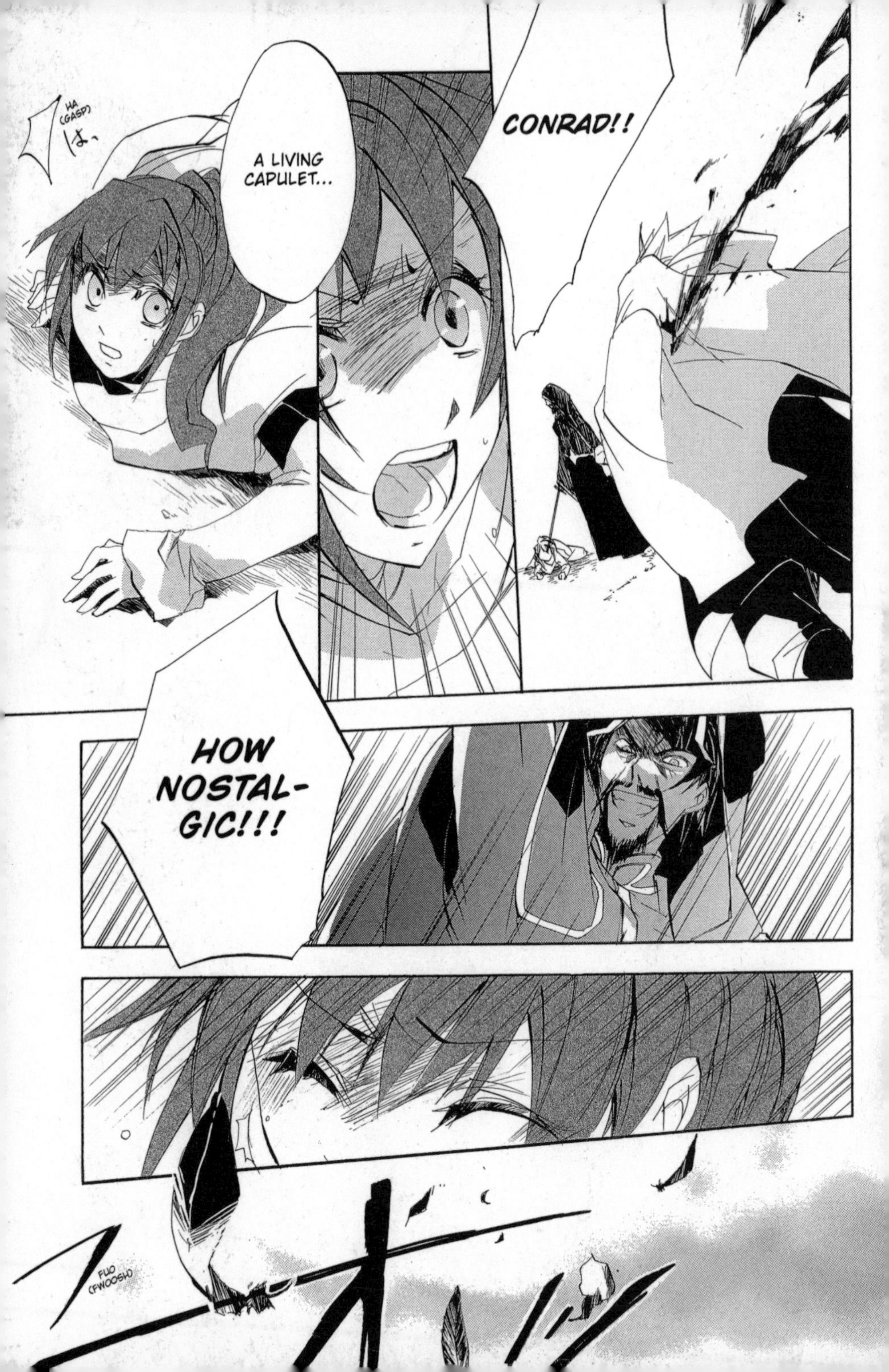
CONRAD!!
A LIVING CAPULET...
HA (GASP)
は、
HOW NOSTAL-GIC!!!
FUO (FWOOSH)

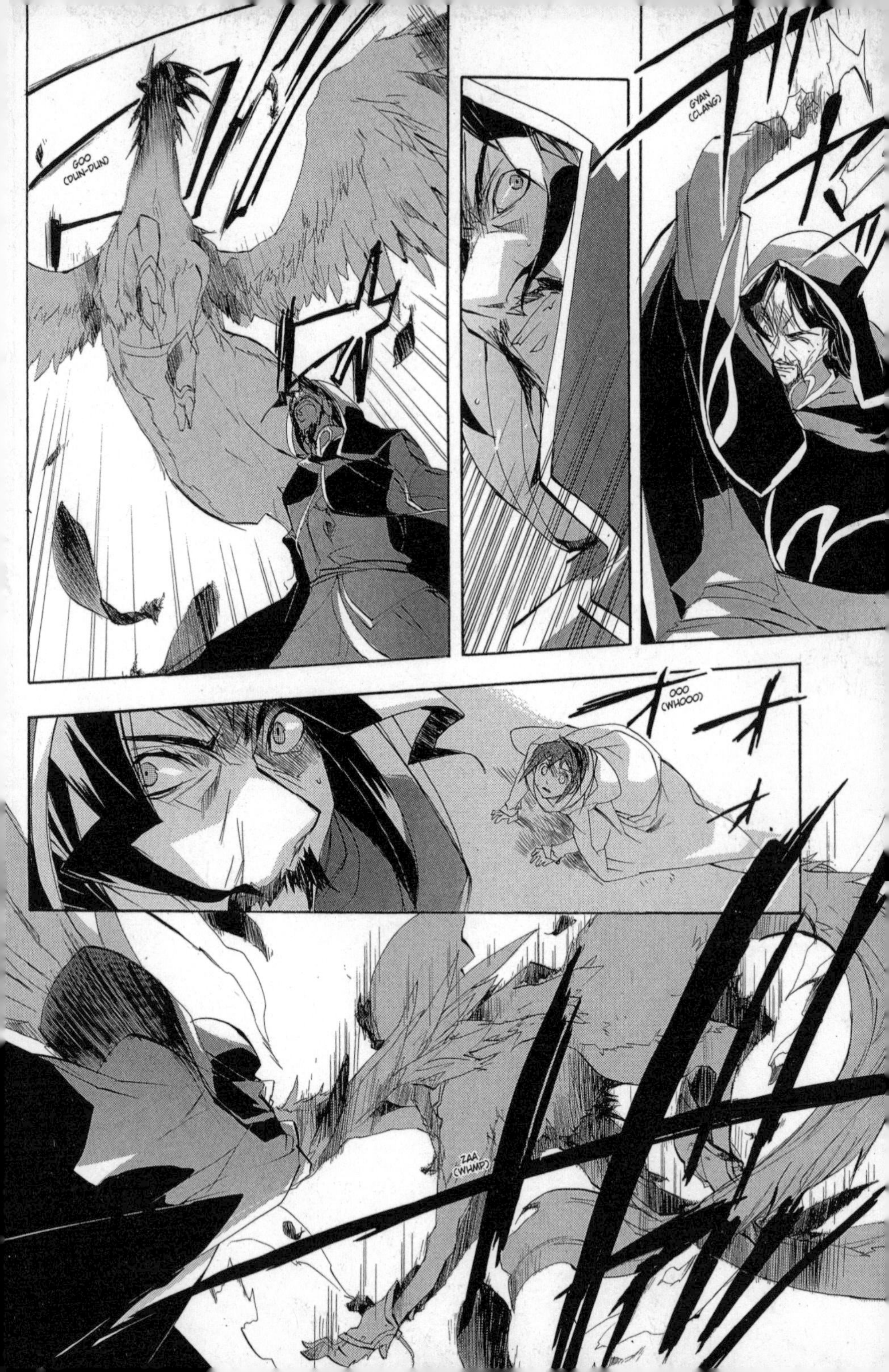
GYAN
(CLANG)
GOO
(DUN-DUN)
OOO
(WHOOO)
ZAA
(WHMP)

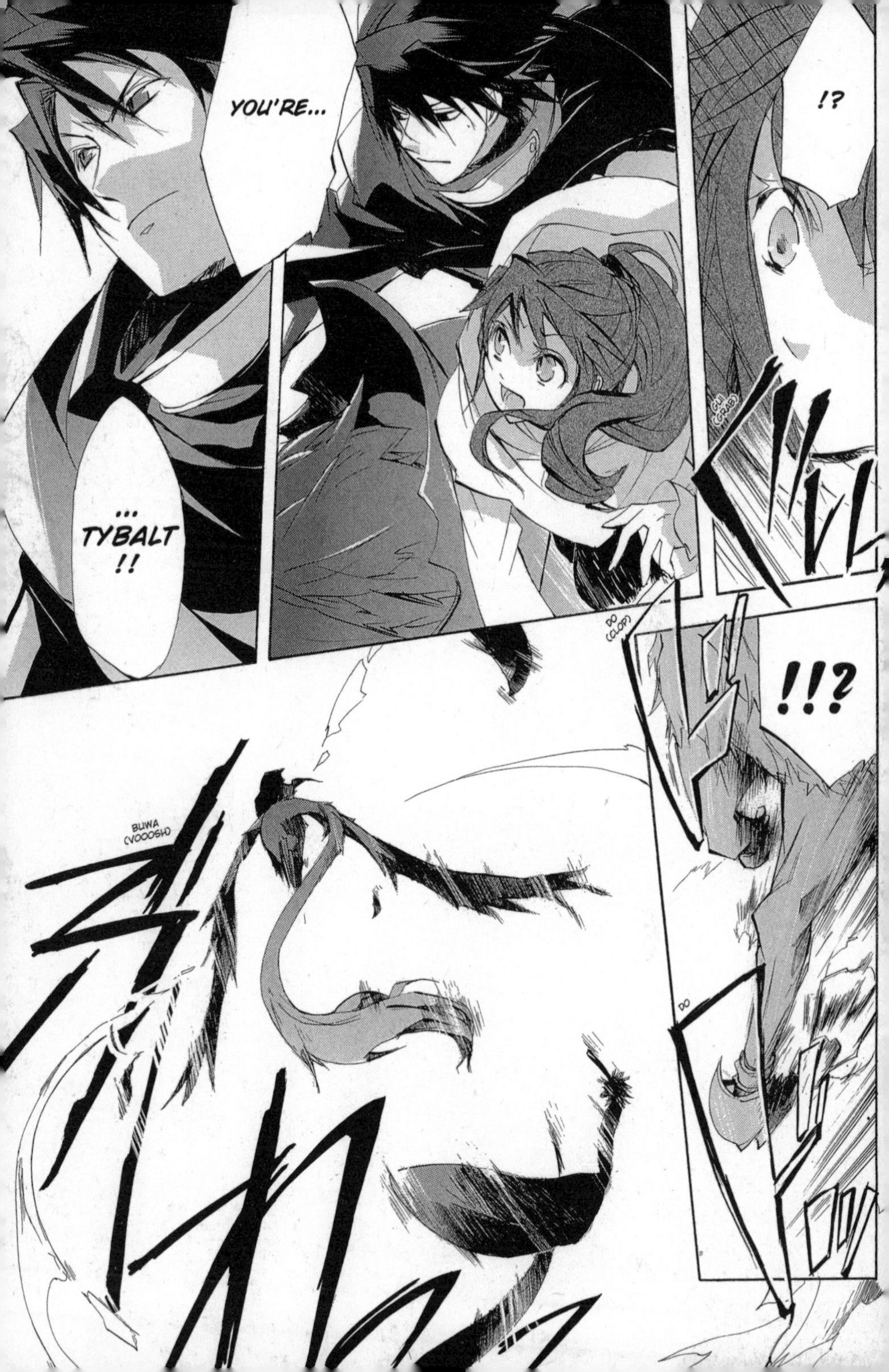
!?
GUI (GRAB)
YOU'RE...
...TYBALT!!
DO (CLOP)
!!?
DO
BUWA (VOOOSH)

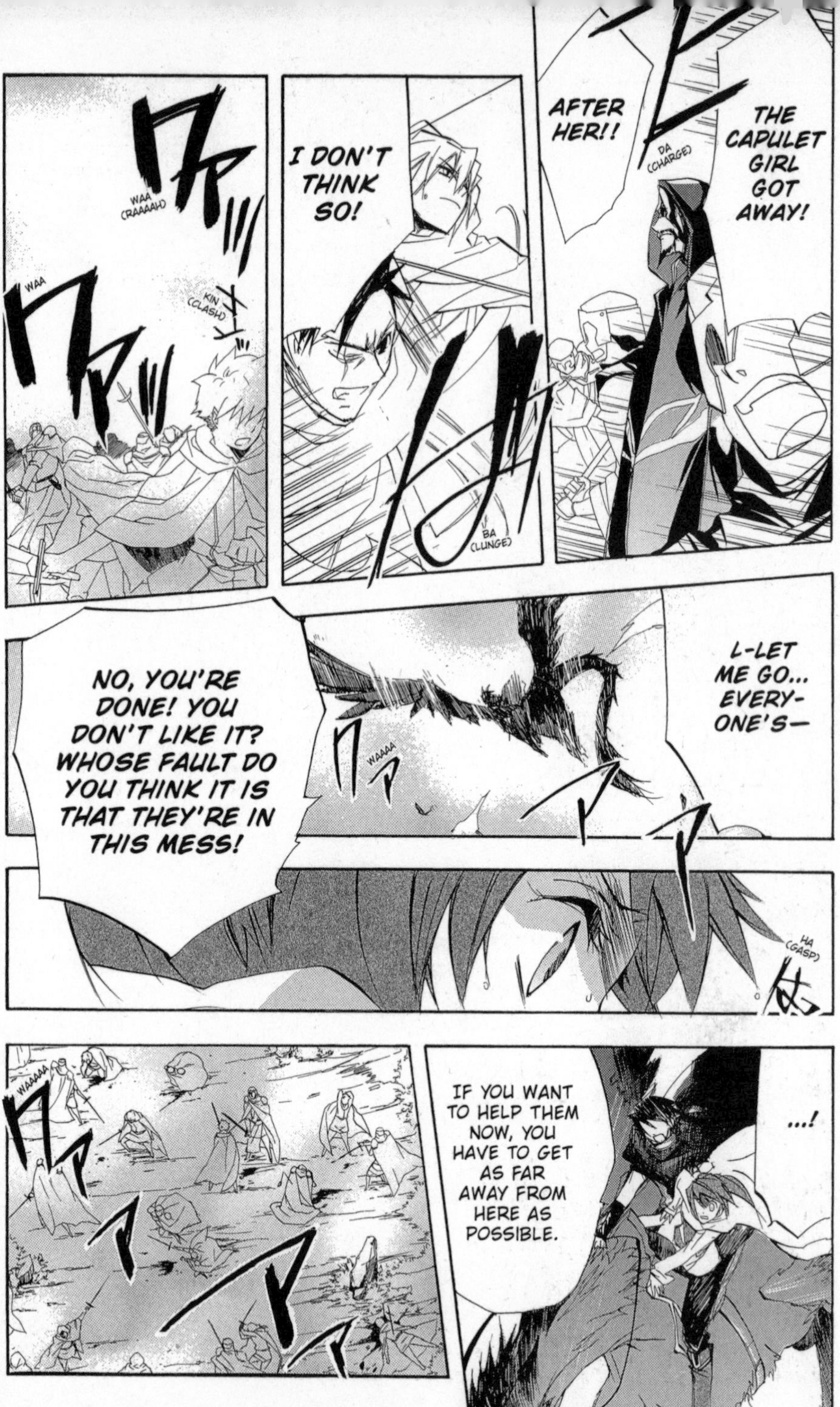
THE CAPULET GIRL GOT AWAY!
AFTER HER!!
DA (CHARGE)
I DON'T THINK SO!
BA (LUNGE)
WAA (RAAAAH)
KIN (CLASH)
WAA
L-LET ME GO... EVERYONE'S—
WAAAA
NO, YOU'RE DONE! YOU DON'T LIKE IT? WHOSE FAULT DO YOU THINK IT IS THAT THEY'RE IN THIS MESS!
HA (GASP)
...!
IF YOU WANT TO HELP THEM NOW, YOU HAVE TO GET AS FAR AWAY FROM HERE AS POSSIBLE.
WAAAAA

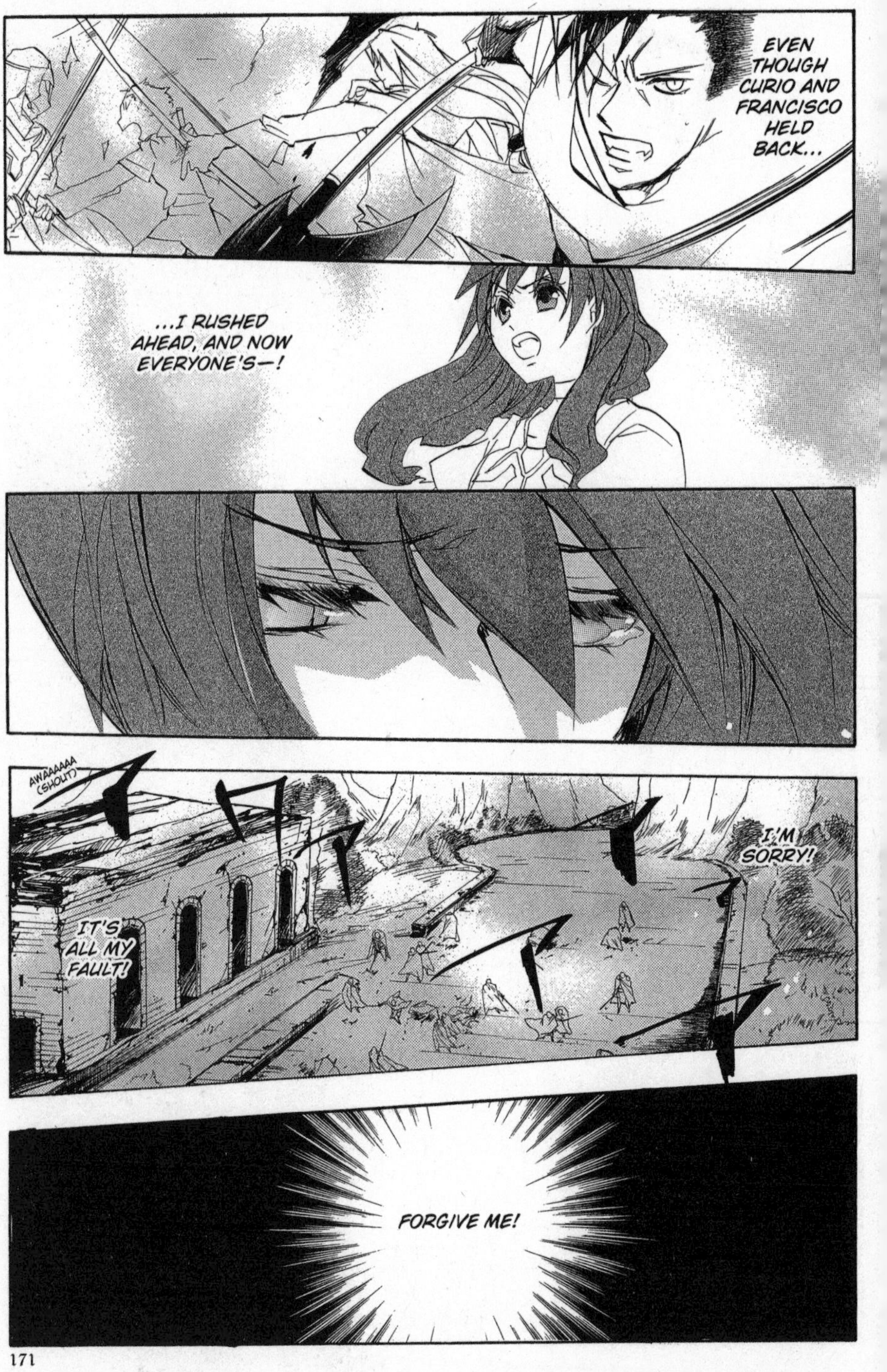
EVEN THOUGH CURIO AND FRANCISCO HELD BACK...
...I RUSHED AHEAD, AND NOW EVERYONE'S—!
I'M SORRY!
AWAAAAAA (SHOUT)
IT'S ALL MY FAULT!
FORGIVE ME!

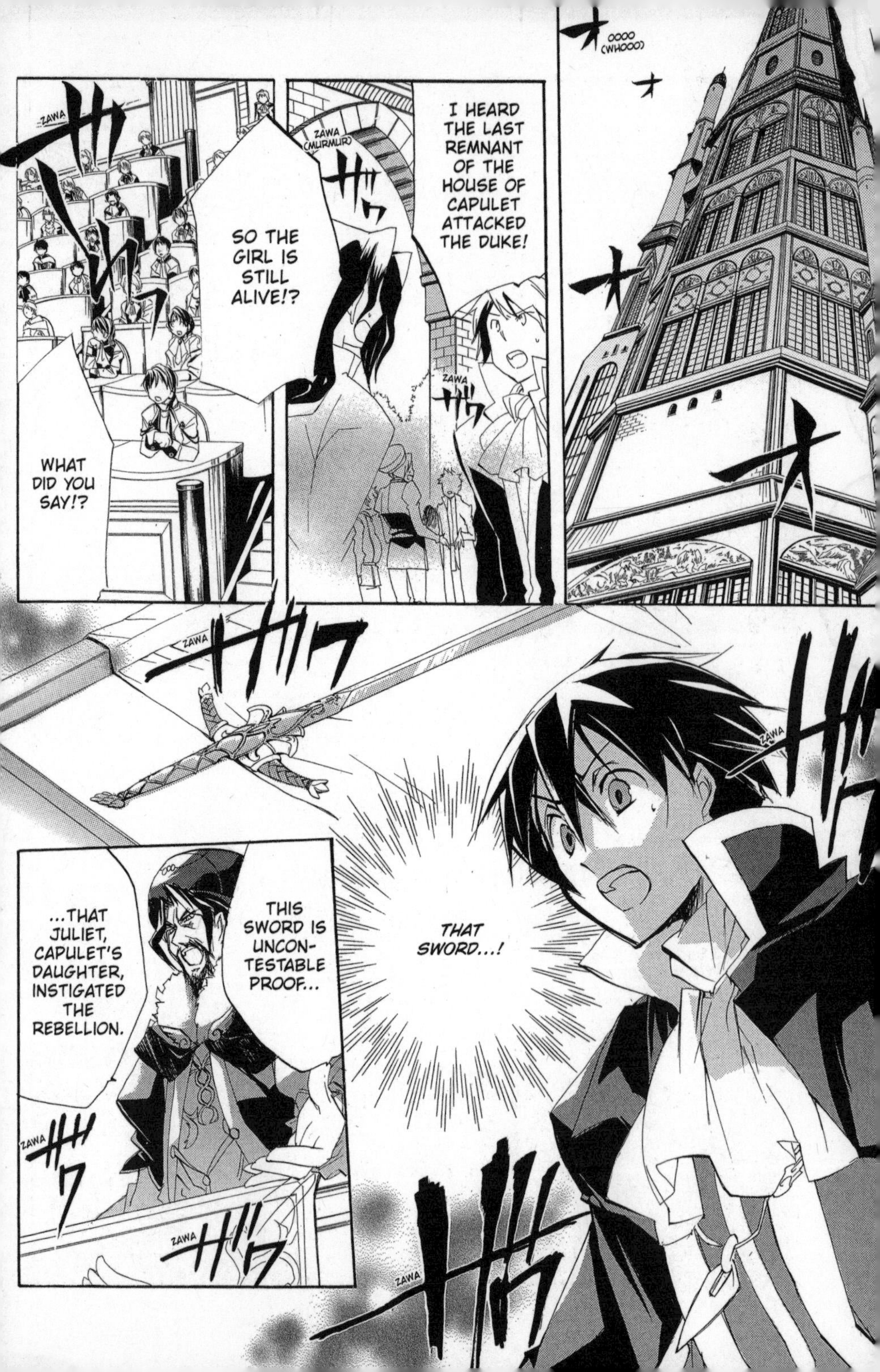
OOOO (WHOOO)
I HEARD THE LAST REMNANT OF THE HOUSE OF CAPULET ATTACKED THE DUKE!
ZAWA (MURMUR)
ZAWA
SO THE GIRL IS STILL ALIVE!?
ZAWA
WHAT DID YOU SAY!?
ZAWA
ZAWA
THAT SWORD...!
THIS SWORD IS UNCONTESTABLE PROOF...
...THAT JULIET, CAPULET'S DAUGHTER, INSTIGATED THE REBELLION.
ZAWA
ZAWA
ZAWA

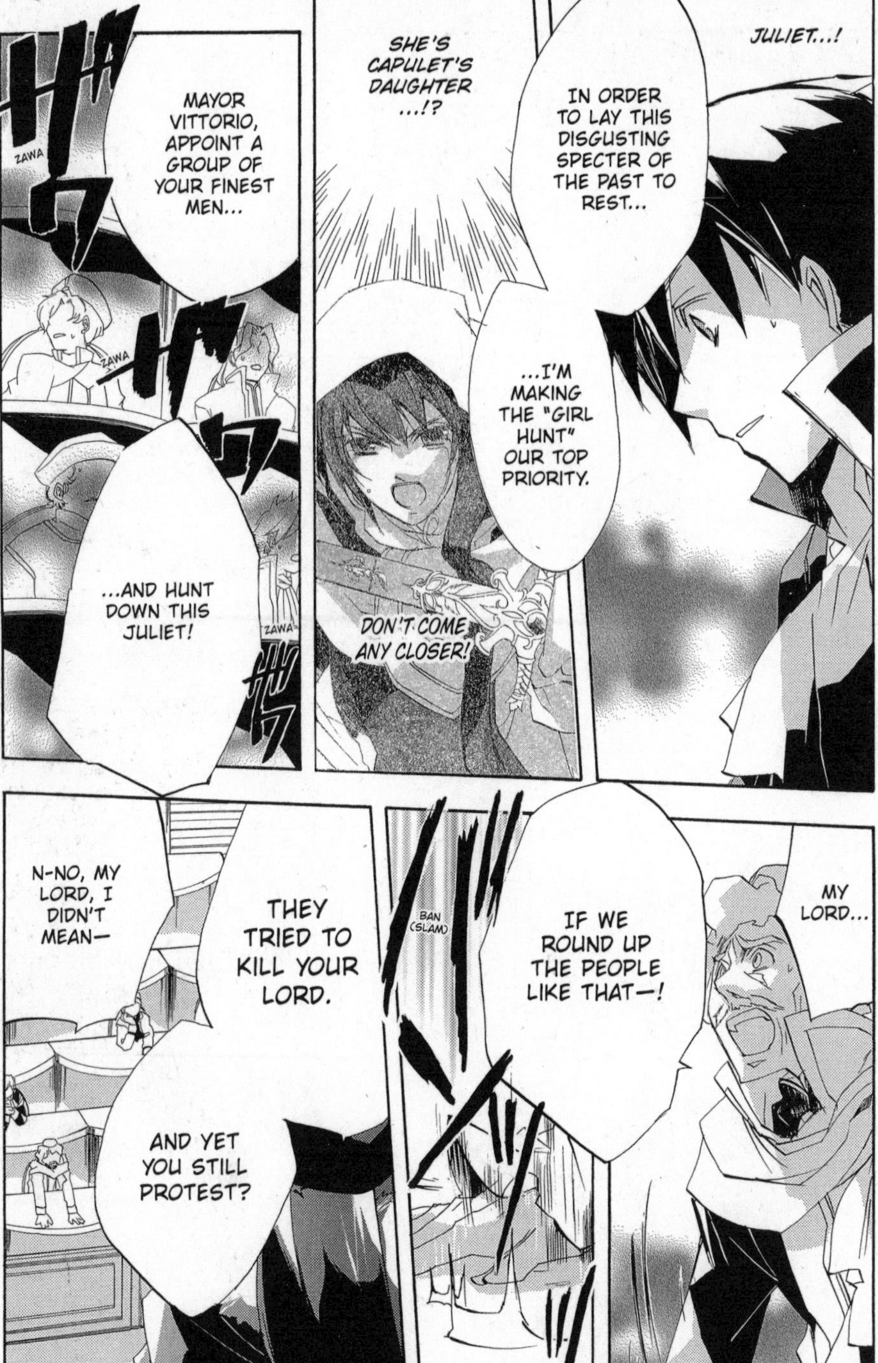
JULIET...!
IN ORDER TO LAY THIS DISGUSTING SPECTER OF THE PAST TO REST...
...I'M MAKING THE "GIRL HUNT" OUR TOP PRIORITY.
SHE'S CAPULET'S DAUGHTER ...!?
DON'T COME ANY CLOSER!
MAYOR VITTORIO, APPOINT A GROUP OF YOUR FINEST MEN...
ZAWA
ZAWA
...AND HUNT DOWN THIS JULIET!
ZAWA
MY LORD...
IF WE ROUND UP THE PEOPLE LIKE THAT—!
BAN (SLAM)
THEY TRIED TO KILL YOUR LORD.
N-NO, MY LORD, I DIDN'T MEAN—
AND YET YOU STILL PROTEST?

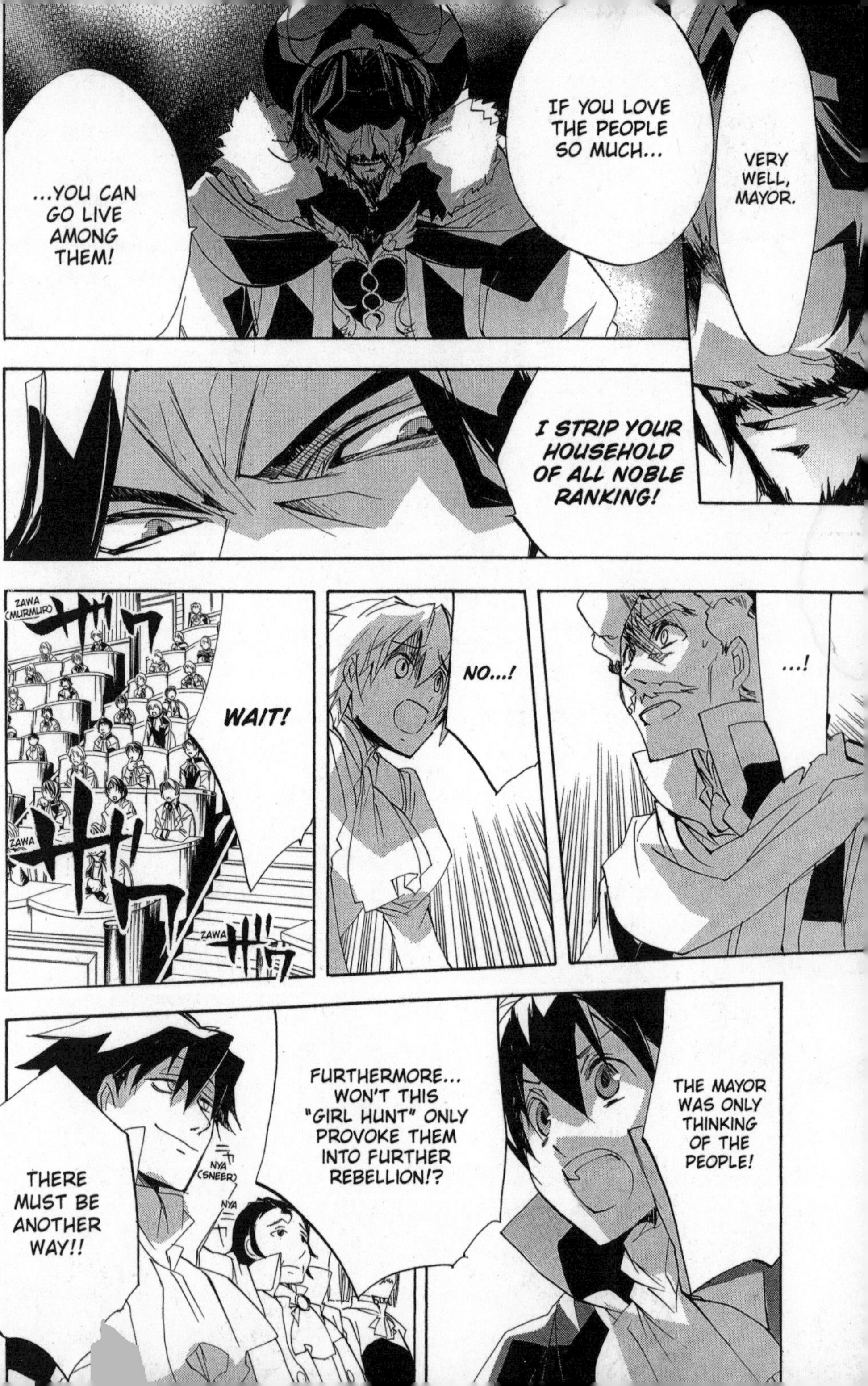
VERY WELL, MAYOR.
IF YOU LOVE THE PEOPLE SO MUCH...
...YOU CAN GO LIVE AMONG THEM!
I STRIP YOUR HOUSEHOLD OF ALL NOBLE RANKING!
...!
NO...!
ZAWA (MURMUR)
WAIT!
ZAWA
ZAWA
THE MAYOR WAS ONLY THINKING OF THE PEOPLE!
FURTHERMORE... WON'T THIS "GIRL HUNT" ONLY PROVOKE THEM INTO FURTHER REBELLION!?
NYA (SNEER)
NYA
THERE MUST BE ANOTHER WAY!!

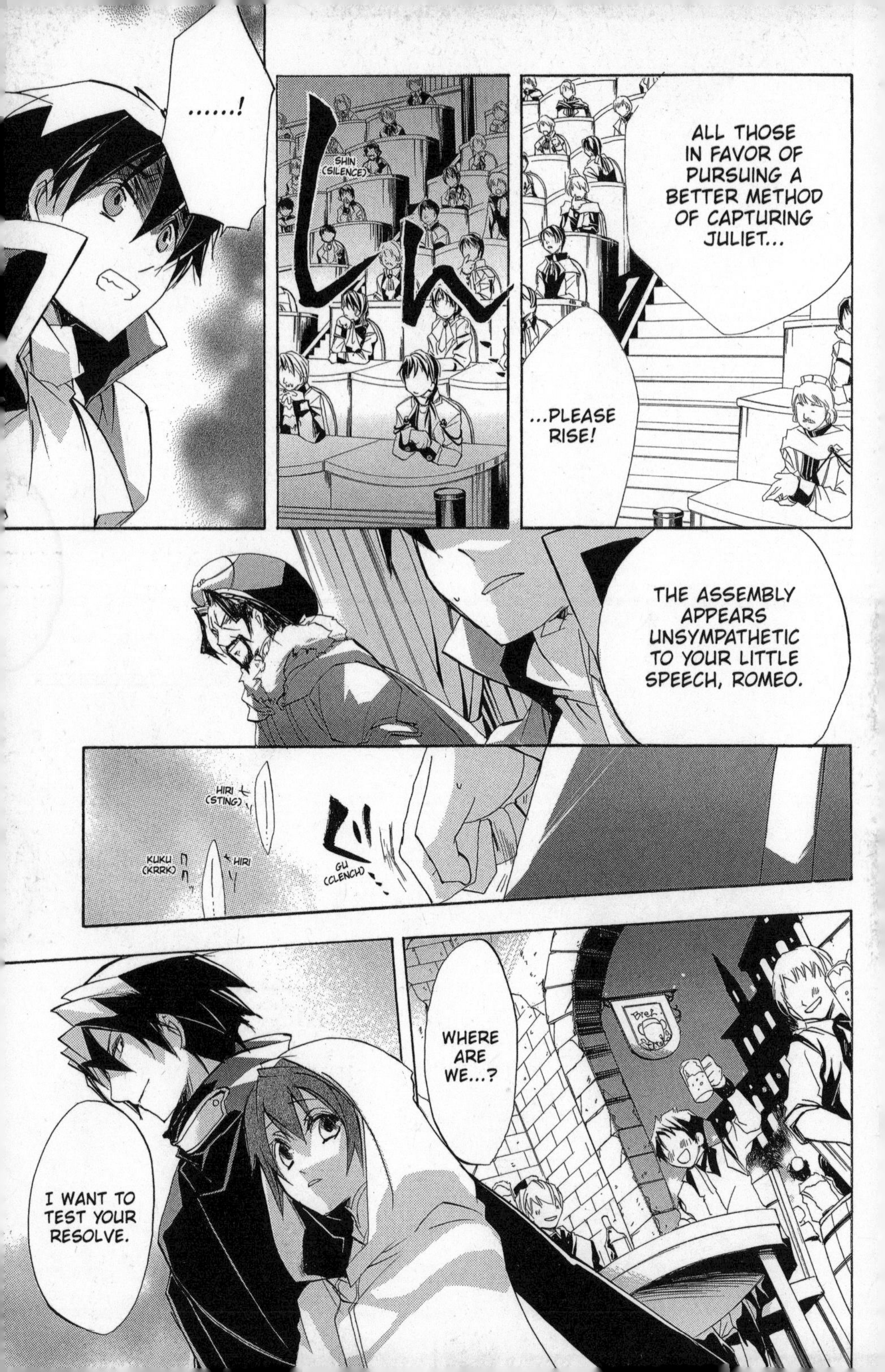
ALL THOSE IN FAVOR OF PURSUING A BETTER METHOD OF CAPTURING JULIET...
...PLEASE RISE!
SHIN (SILENCE)
......!
THE ASSEMBLY APPEARS UNSYMPATHETIC TO YOUR LITTLE SPEECH, ROMEO.
GU (CLENCH)
HIRI (STING)
HIRI
KUKU (KRRK)
WHERE ARE WE...?
I WANT TO TEST YOUR RESOLVE.

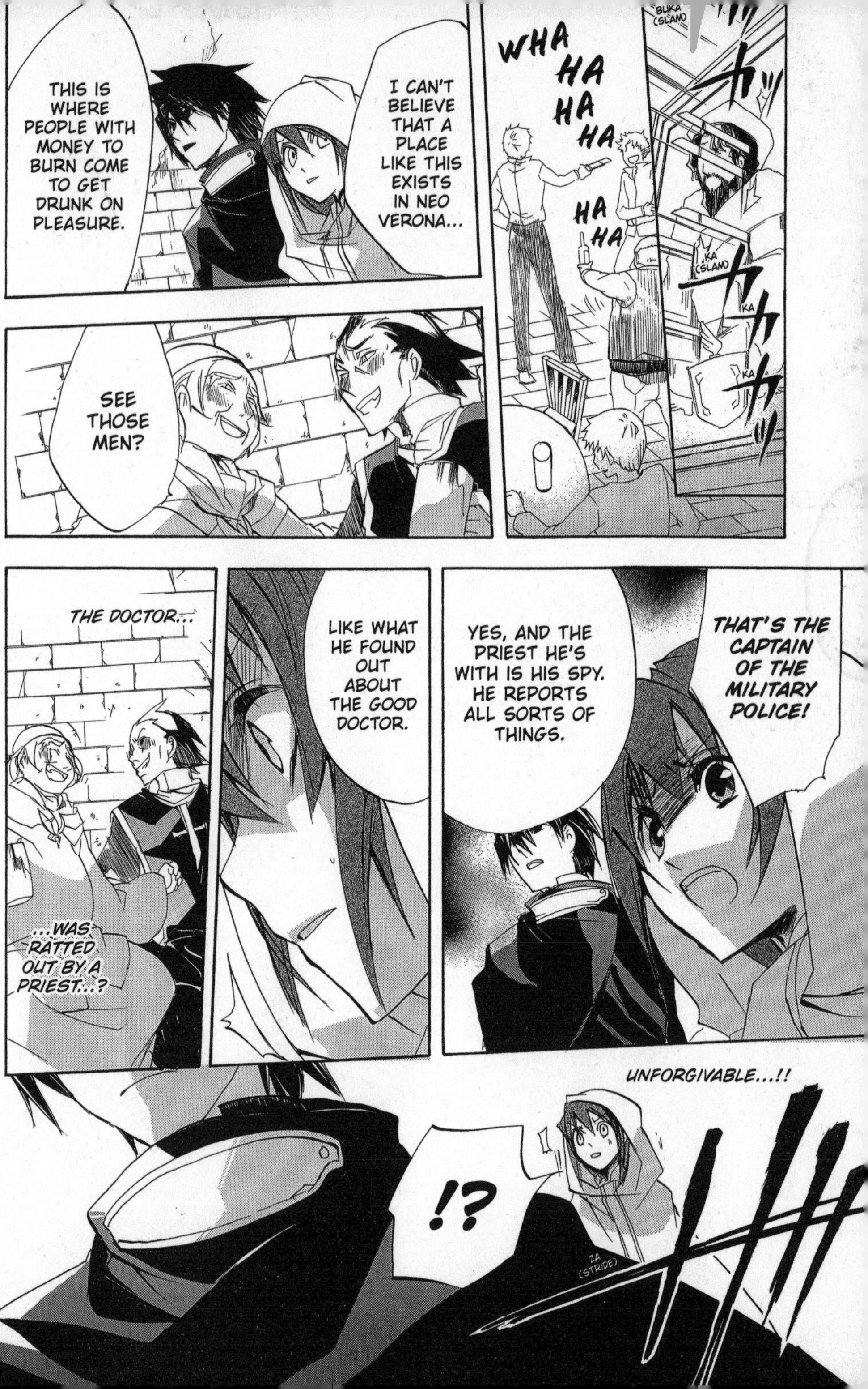
BUKA (SLAM)
WHA HA HA HA HA HA HA
KA (SLAM)
KA
KA
I CAN'T BELIEVE THAT A PLACE LIKE THIS EXISTS IN NEO VERONA...
THIS IS WHERE PEOPLE WITH MONEY TO BURN COME TO GET DRUNK ON PLEASURE.
SEE THOSE MEN?
THAT'S THE CAPTAIN OF THE MILITARY POLICE!
YES, AND THE PRIEST HE'S WITH IS HIS SPY. HE REPORTS ALL SORTS OF THINGS.
LIKE WHAT HE FOUND OUT ABOUT THE GOOD DOCTOR.
THE DOCTOR...
...WAS RATTED OUT BY A PRIEST...?
UNFORGIVABLE...!!
!?
ZA (STRIDE)

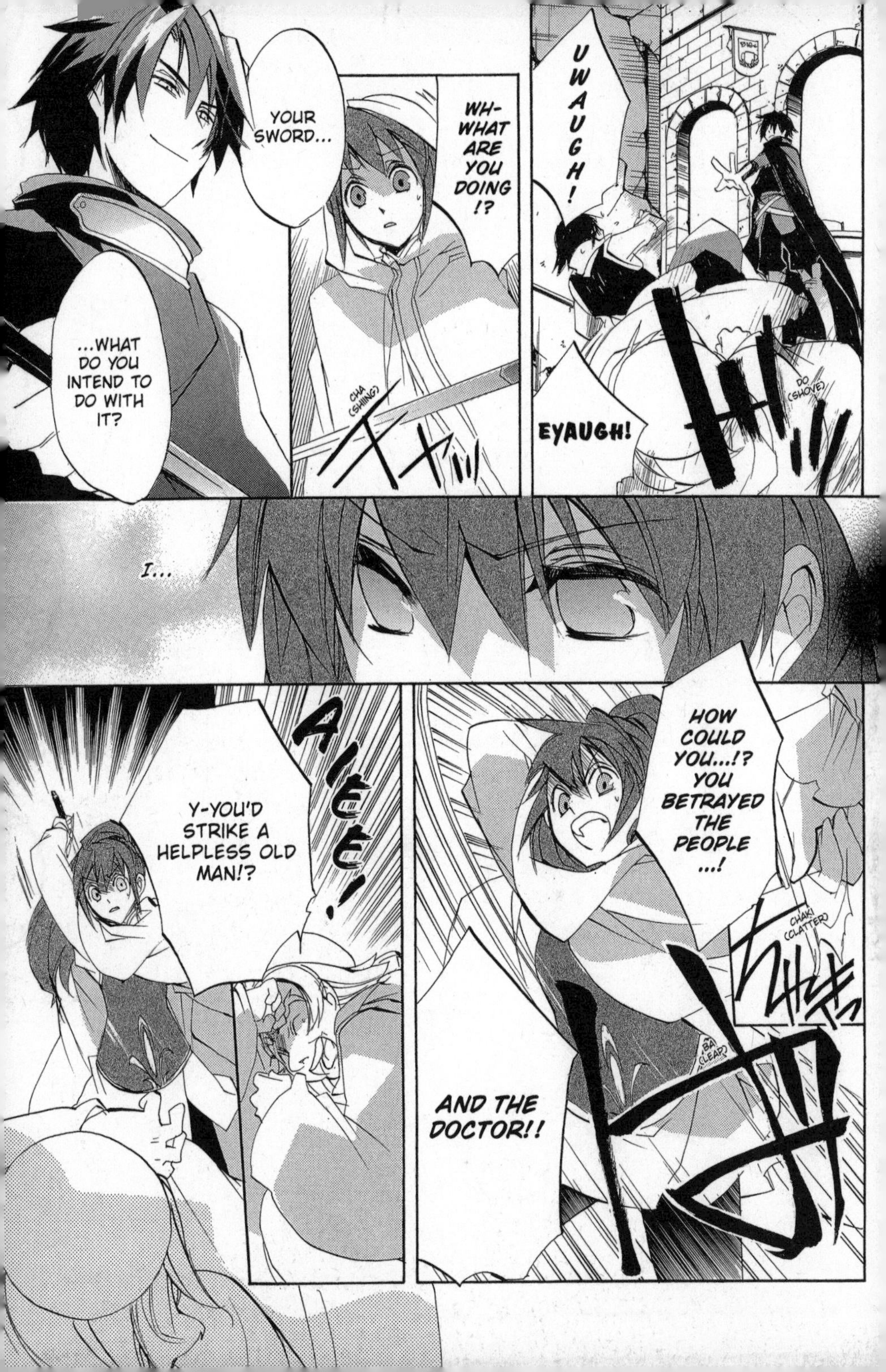
UWAUGH!
DO (SHOVE)
EYAUGH!
WH-WHAT ARE YOU DOING!?
CHA (SHING)
YOUR SWORD...
...WHAT DO YOU INTEND TO DO WITH IT?
I...
HOW COULD YOU...!? YOU BETRAYED THE PEOPLE...!
CHAKI (CLATTER)
BA (LEAP)
AND THE DOCTOR!!
AIEEE!
Y-YOU'D STRIKE A HELPLESS OLD MAN!?

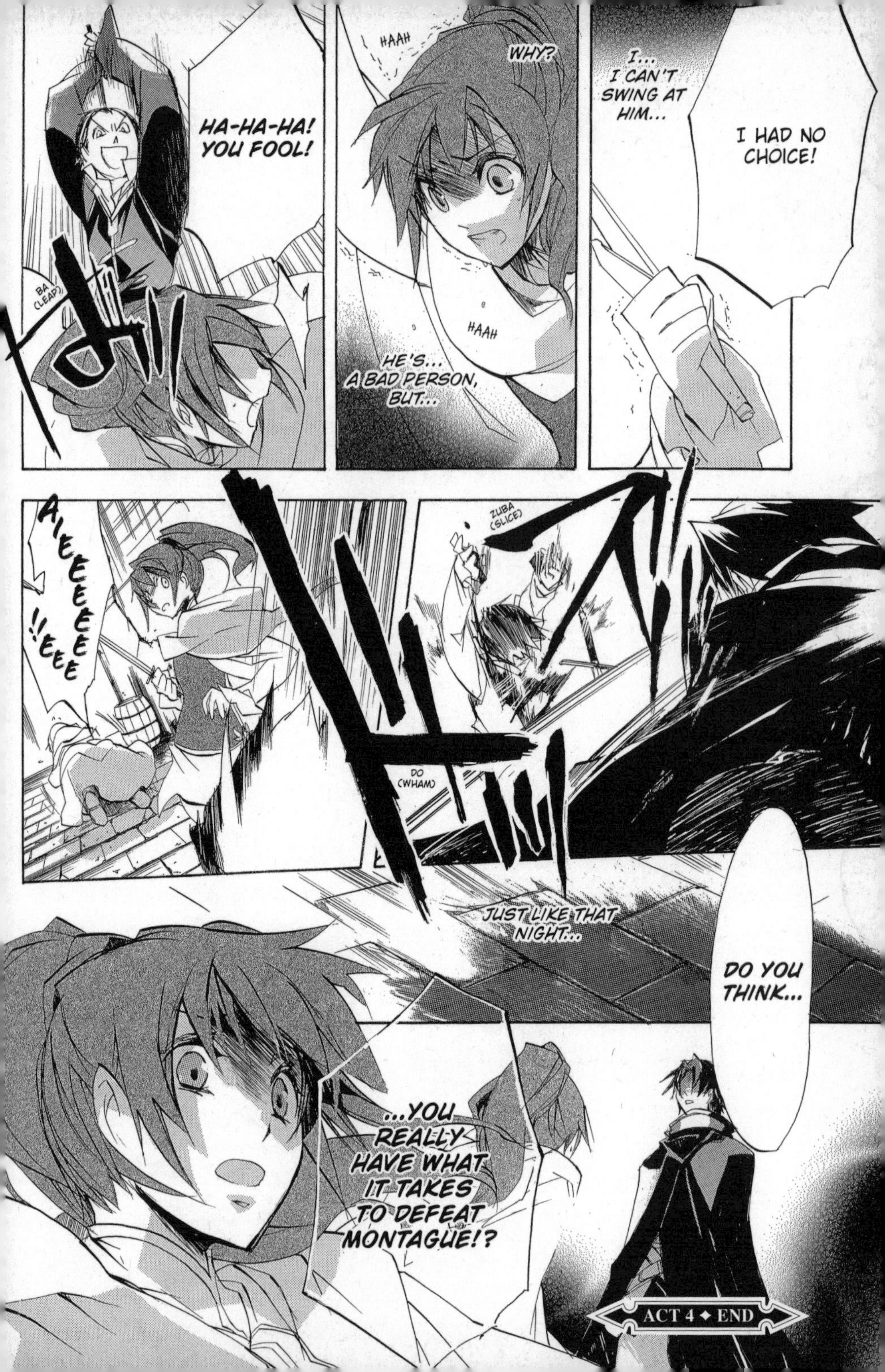
I HAD NO CHOICE!
I... I CAN'T SWING AT HIM...
WHY?
HAAH
HAAH
HE'S... A BAD PERSON, BUT...
HA-HA-HA! YOU FOOL!
BA (LEAP)
ZUBA (SLICE)
DO (WHAM)
AIEEEEEEEEEEEEE!!
JUST LIKE THAT NIGHT...
DO YOU THINK...
...YOU REALLY HAVE WHAT IT TAKES TO DEFEAT MONTAGUE!?
ACT 4 ◆ END

Hitomi Amamiya

"Wow~~~! How lovely~~~!

That's what I yelled out loud when I saw the color title page for Act 1. At that moment, I was so happy to have been able to participate in the manga for *RomiJuli*. What I mean is, I may have been responsible for the novelization, but when I first got the proposal from GONZO-san, I was trembling with fear. (I'm ridiculously bad at revolutions and romance!) And then later, COM-sensei's rough sketches made my heart pound (they were so, so *kawaii!*), and I managed to mumble, "Please tell me if you ever want help writing this (whispered)." I am so grateful to manager Director S-san for contacting me. Yes, it never hurts to ask!

Now, my job...My job is to try to capture the magnificent and sophisticated scenes of the anime *RomeoxJuliet* in a manga. It was a different kind of challenge, trying to envision such a thing...but it was marvelous. All my *RomiJuli*-related synapses just overflowed with an unusual kind of "sad but lovely"dopamine, and I was totally able to stay up for about forty-eight hours straight. (If it had been anything else, I would have fallen asleep right away...)

Hey, how can I say this? I love the anime so much...absolutely love it. I even play the opening theme song on repeat all day, every day. I may even watch my favorite scenes over and over...

And every month I'm blown away by COM-sensei's amazing action and the innocent aura of the two main characters.

Mm...So cute when they flirt...Aww...(Yay!)

Also, I have been working for some time here and there on the novelization... *RomeoxJuliet: Akai Unmei no Deai* (A Kadokawa Beans Paperback Publication) which came out in Japan about the same time as this book. As a story it runs parallel to the anime and manga, but is entirely different. I was extremely happy to take this story on, because I had really been wanting to write some enormous books (← So unlike me!) about pure love and sword-fighting, in order to deliver "love out of the flames of war" to *RomiJuli* fans. (I'm using this afterword to advertise). OHMIGOD — !! You have to see COM-sensei's new illustrations! Romeo is so cool and Juliet is so beautiful, it is soooo mesmerizing...!

And so it would make me very happy if you watch the anime and enjoy the manga.

RomeoxJuliet started in 2007, and I expect it will end next year. Yep, yep.

HITOMI AMAMIYA

AFTERWORD.

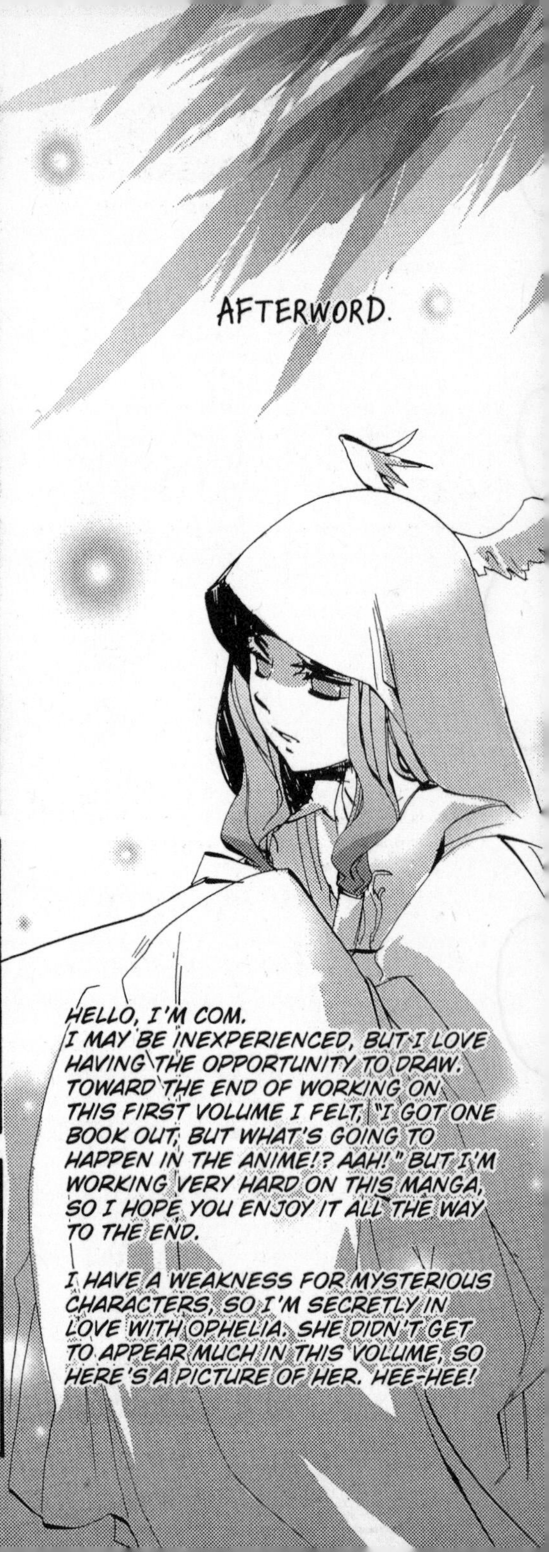

HELLO, I'M COM.
I MAY BE INEXPERIENCED, BUT I LOVE HAVING THE OPPORTUNITY TO DRAW. TOWARD THE END OF WORKING ON THIS FIRST VOLUME I FELT, "I GOT ONE BOOK OUT, BUT WHAT'S GOING TO HAPPEN IN THE ANIME!? AAH!" BUT I'M WORKING VERY HARD ON THIS MANGA, SO I HOPE YOU ENJOY IT ALL THE WAY TO THE END.

I HAVE A WEAKNESS FOR MYSTERIOUS CHARACTERS, SO I'M SECRETLY IN LOVE WITH OPHELIA. SHE DIDN'T GET TO APPEAR MUCH IN THIS VOLUME, SO HERE'S A PICTURE OF HER. HEE-HEE!

FROM THE FIRST EPISODE OF THE ANIME

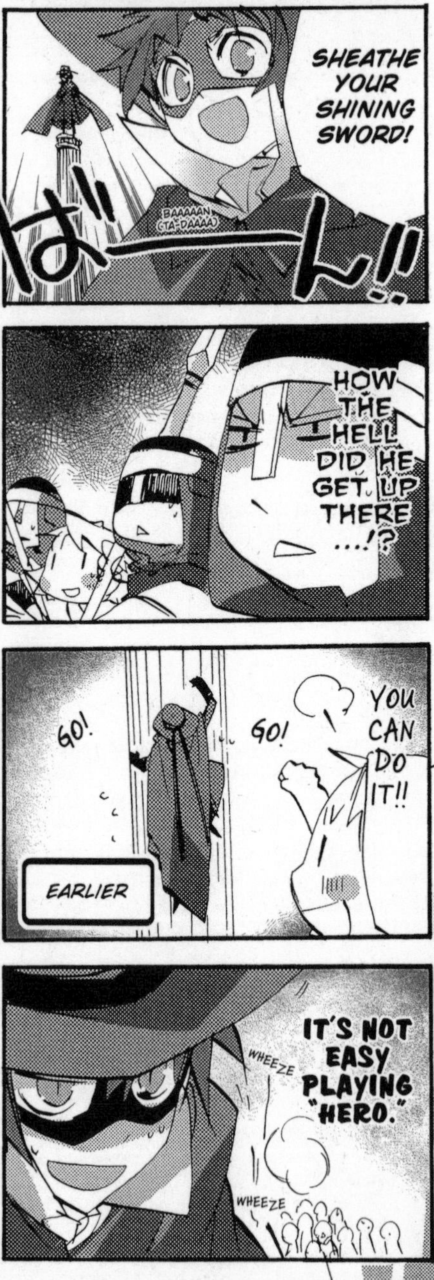
SHEATHE YOUR SHINING SWORD!
ばーーん!!
BAAAAAN (TA-DAAAA)
HOW THE HELL DID HE GET UP THERE ...!?
YOU CAN DO IT!!
GO!
GO!
EARLIER
IT'S NOT EASY PLAYING "HERO."
WHEEZE
WHEEZE

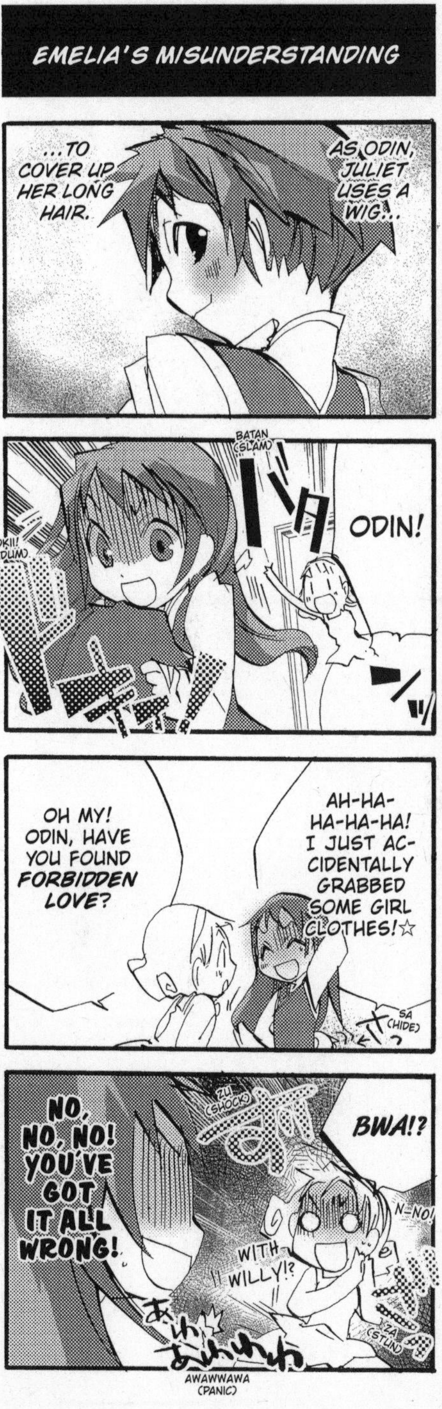
EMELIA'S MISUNDERSTANDING
AS ODIN, JULIET USES A WIG...
...TO COVER UP HER LONG HAIR.
BATAN (SLAM)
ODIN!
DOKI!! (BADUM)
AH-HA-HA-HA-HA! I JUST ACCIDENTALLY GRABBED SOME GIRL CLOTHES!☆
OH MY! ODIN, HAVE YOU FOUND FORBIDDEN LOVE?
SA (HIDE)
BWA!?
ZU (SHOCK)
N-NO!
WITH WILLY!?
NO, NO, NO! YOU'VE GOT IT ALL WRONG!
ZA (STUN)
AWAWWAWA (PANIC)

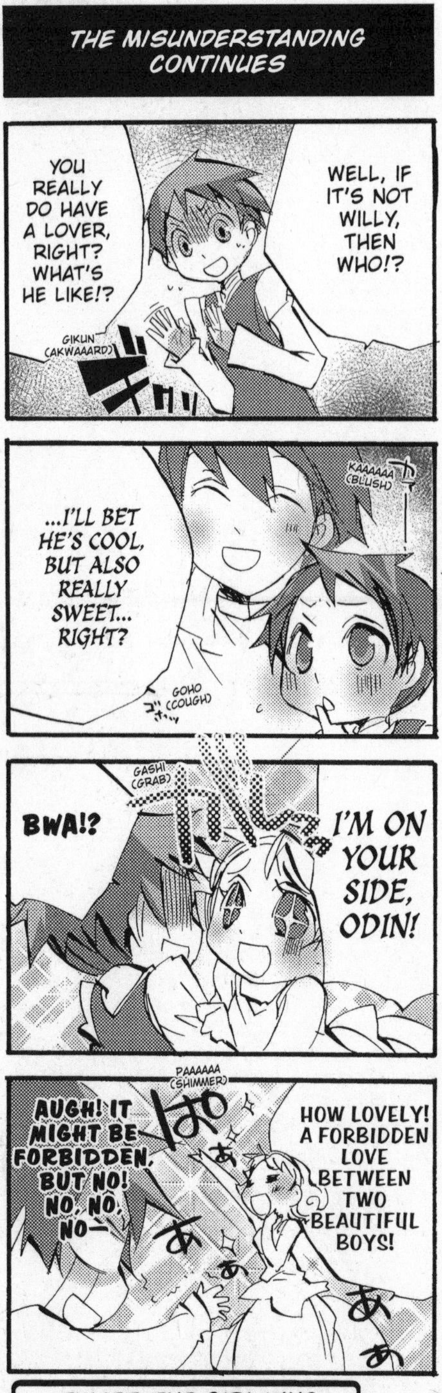
THE MISUNDERSTANDING CONTINUES
WELL, IF IT'S NOT WILLY, THEN WHO!?
YOU REALLY DO HAVE A LOVER, RIGHT? WHAT'S HE LIKE!?
GIKUN (AKWAAARD)
KAAAAAA (BLUSH)
...I'LL BET HE'S COOL, BUT ALSO REALLY SWEET... RIGHT?
GOHO (COUGH)
I'M ON YOUR SIDE, ODIN!
GASHI (GRAB)
BWA!?
HOW LOVELY! A FORBIDDEN LOVE BETWEEN TWO BEAUTIFUL BOYS!
PAAAAAA (SHIMMER)
AUGH! IT MIGHT BE FORBIDDEN, BUT NO! NO, NO, NO–

JULIET, THE GIRL WHO CANNOT EXPLAIN.

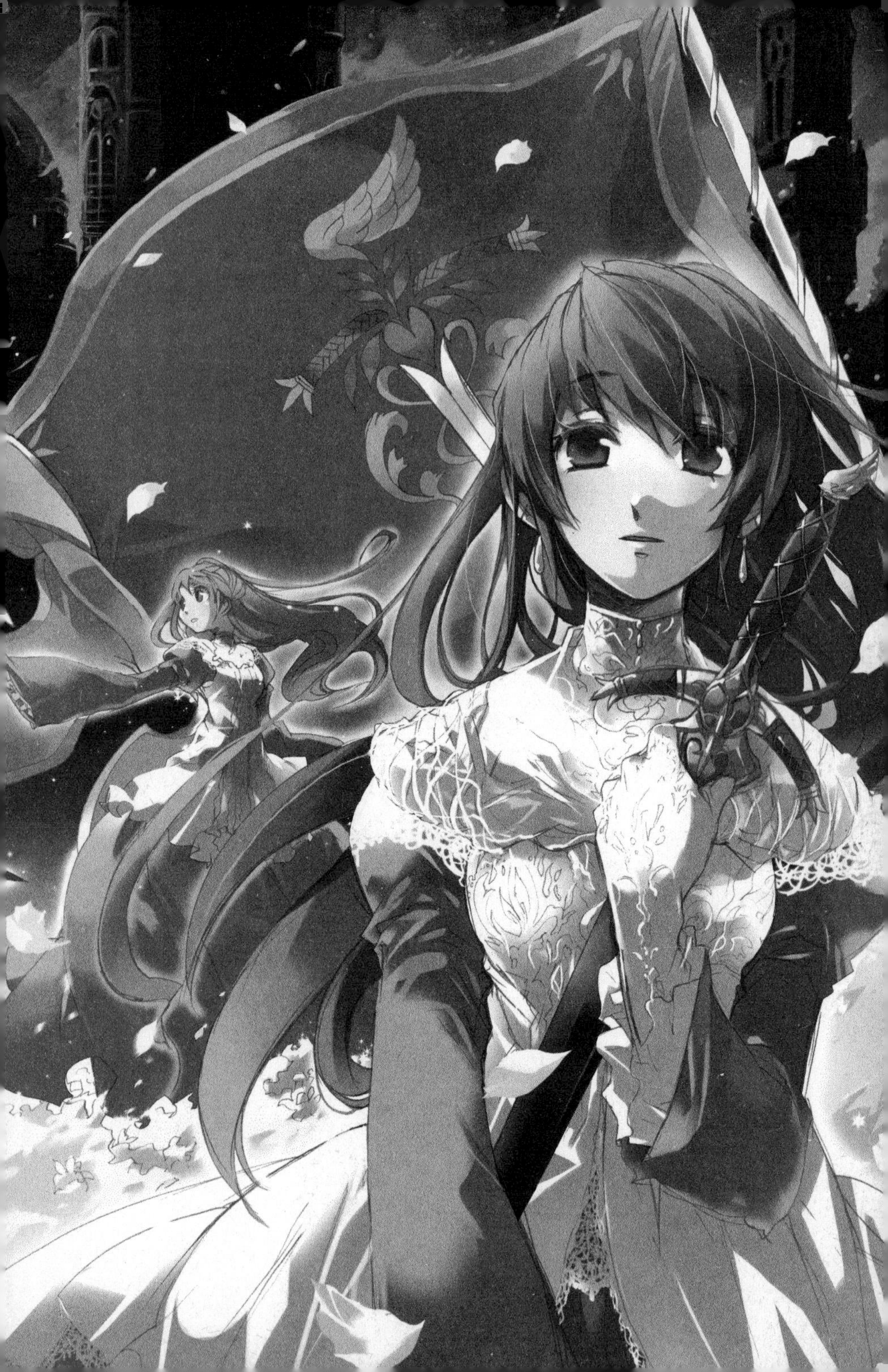

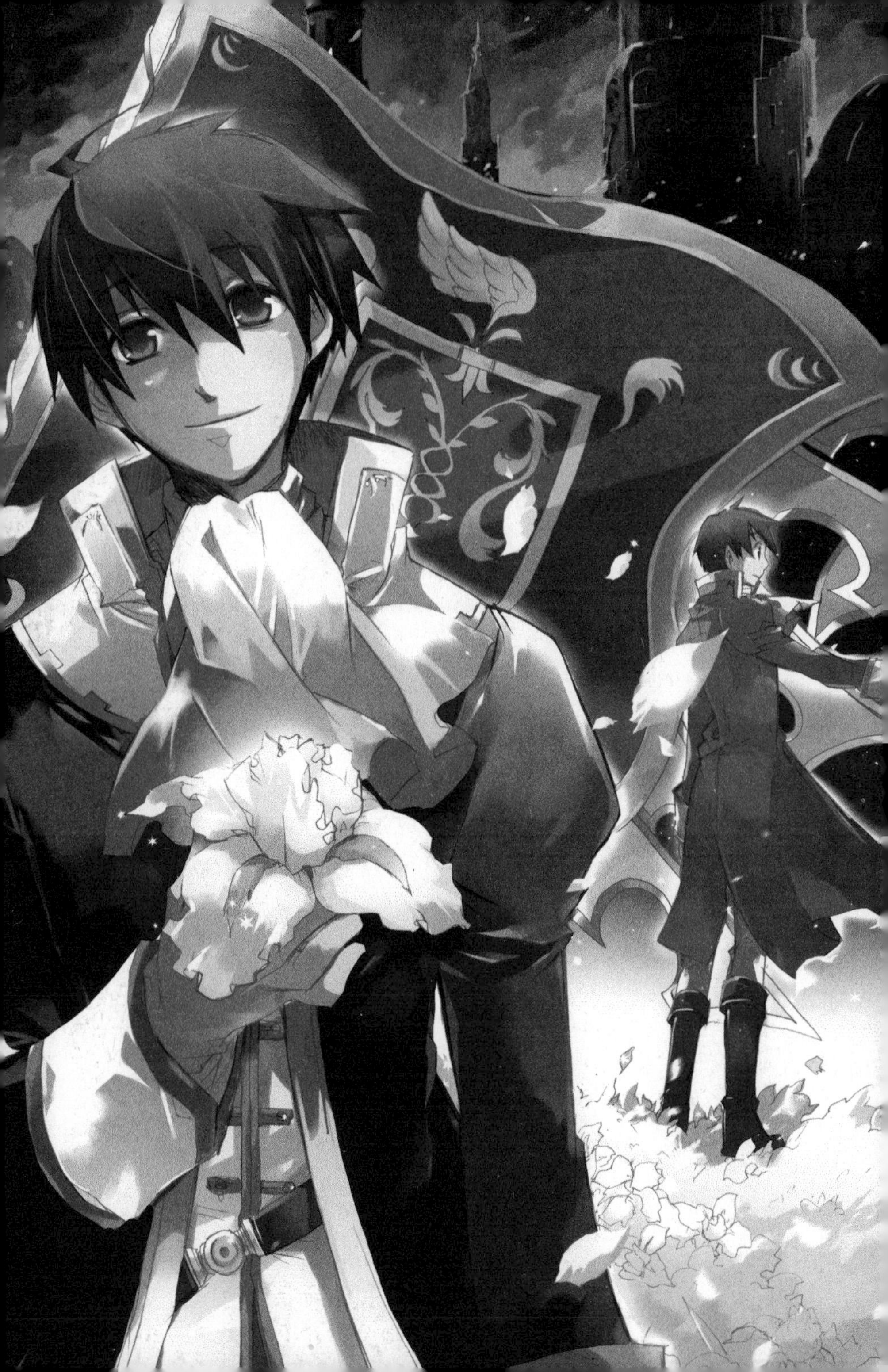

Romeo×Juliet

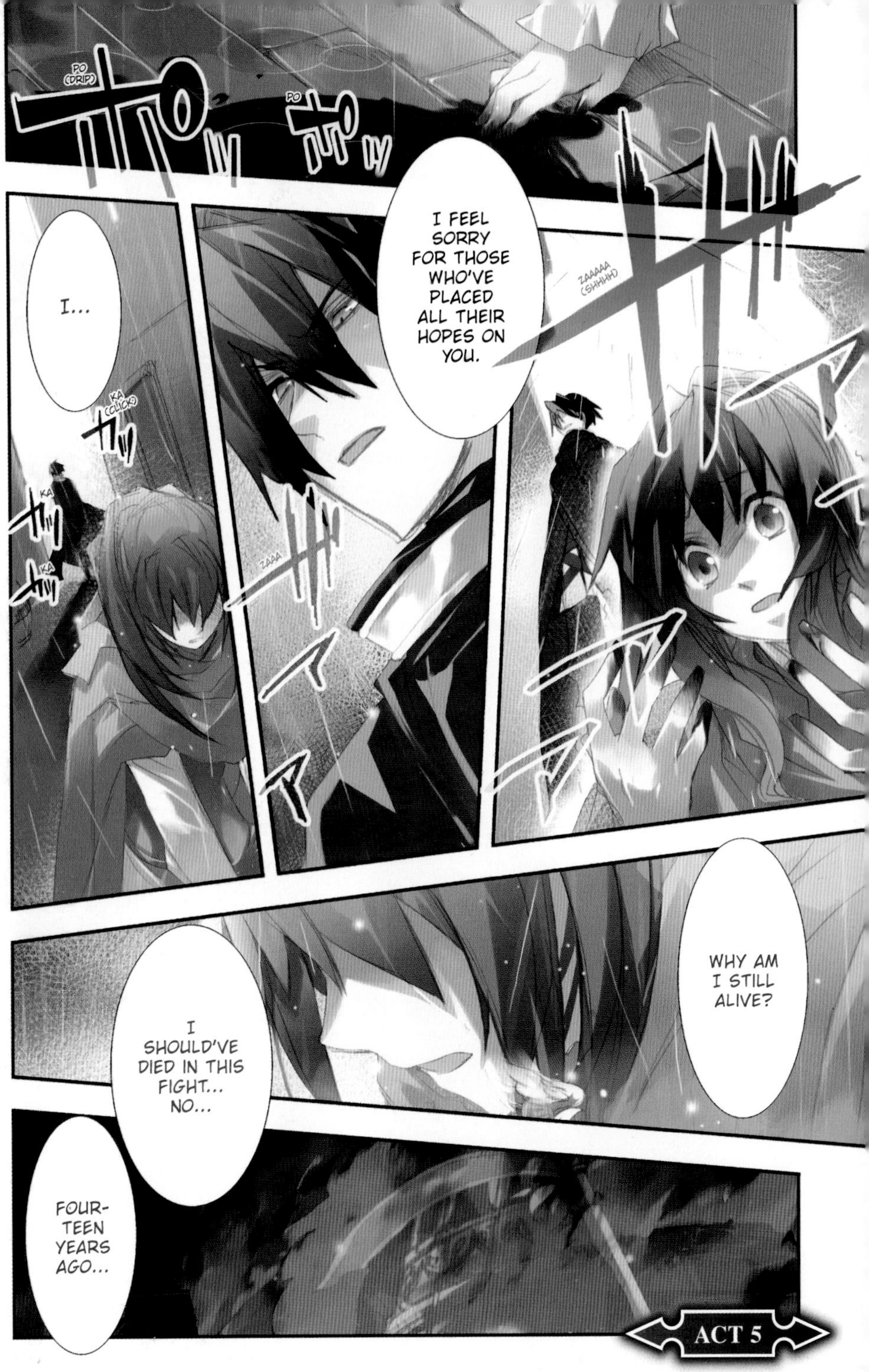
PO
PO (DRIP)
ZAAAAA (SHHHH)
I FEEL SORRY FOR THOSE WHO'VE PLACED ALL THEIR HOPES ON YOU.
ZAAA
I...
KA (CLICK)
KA
KA
WHY AM I STILL ALIVE?
I SHOULD'VE DIED IN THIS FIGHT... NO...
FOUR-TEEN YEARS AGO...
ACT 5

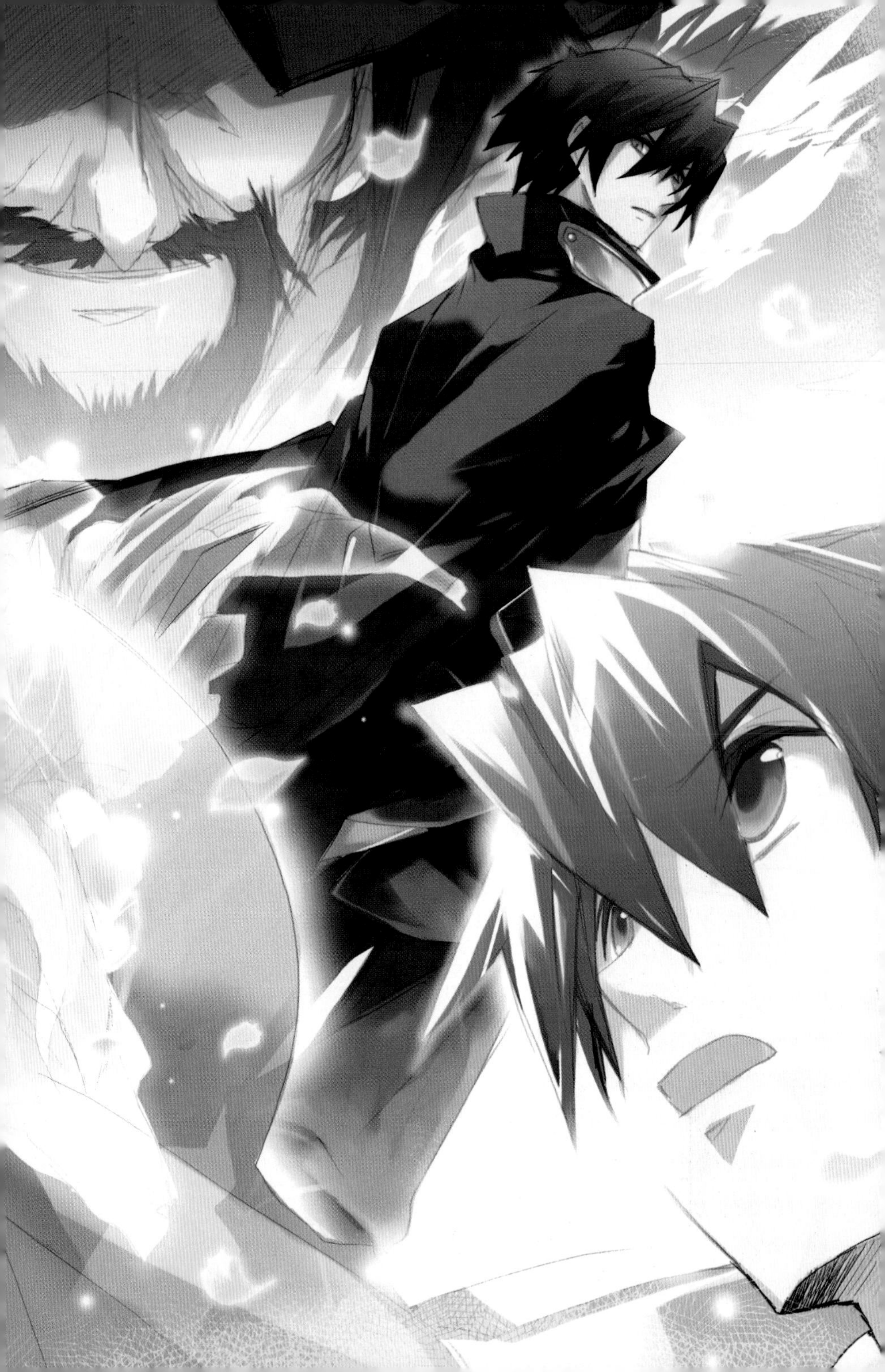

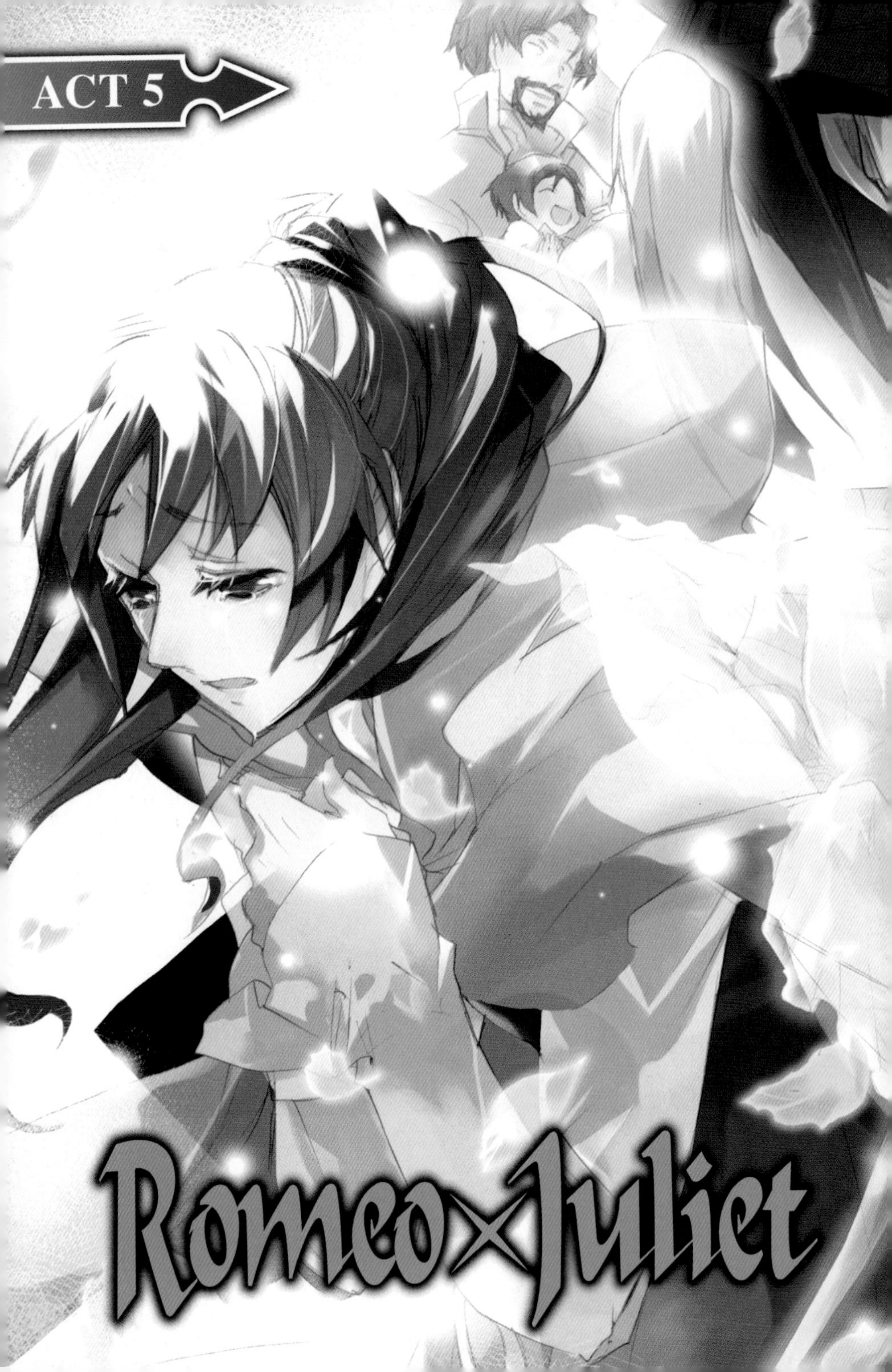
ACT 5
Romeo×Juliet

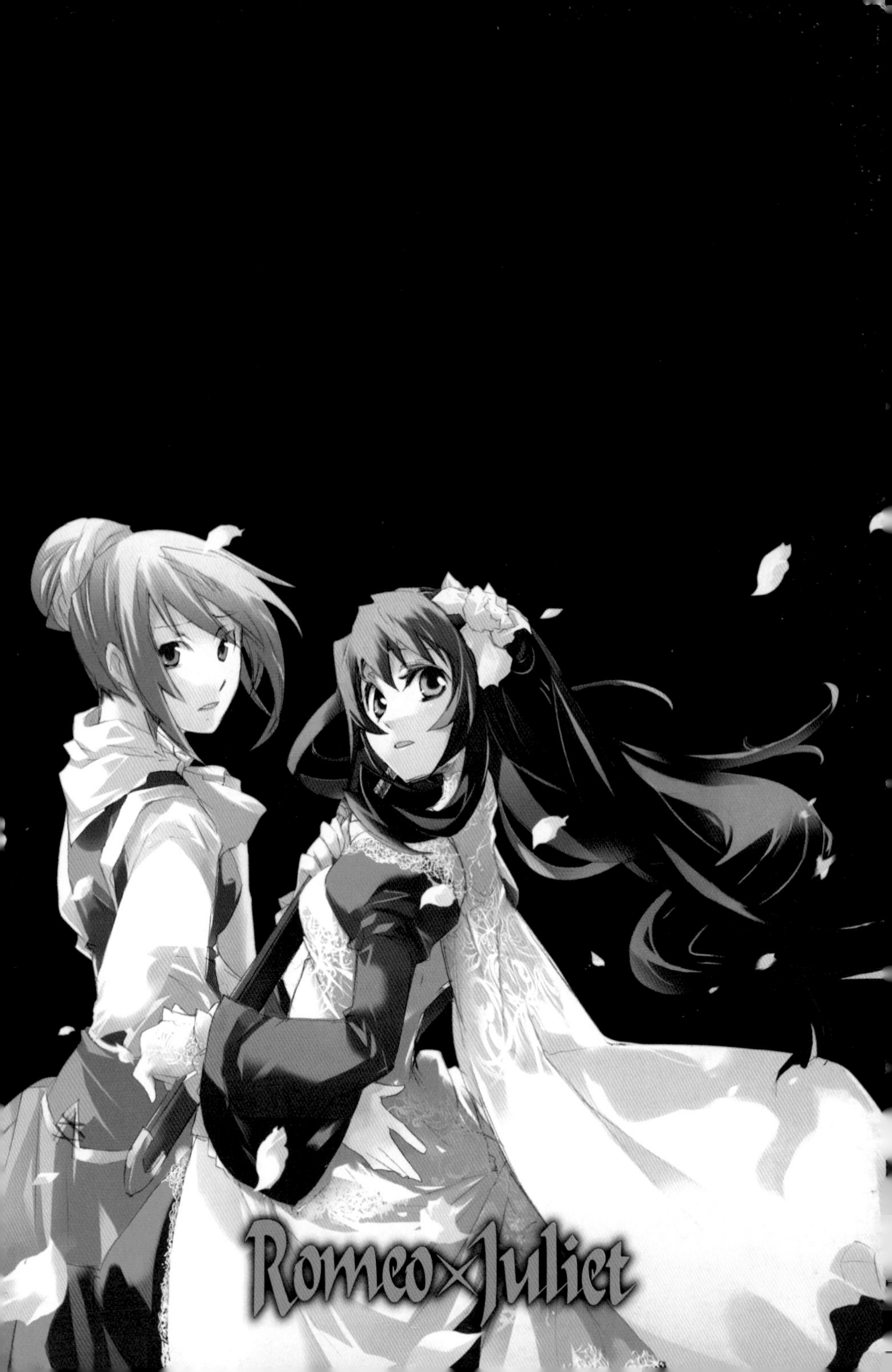
Romeo×Juliet

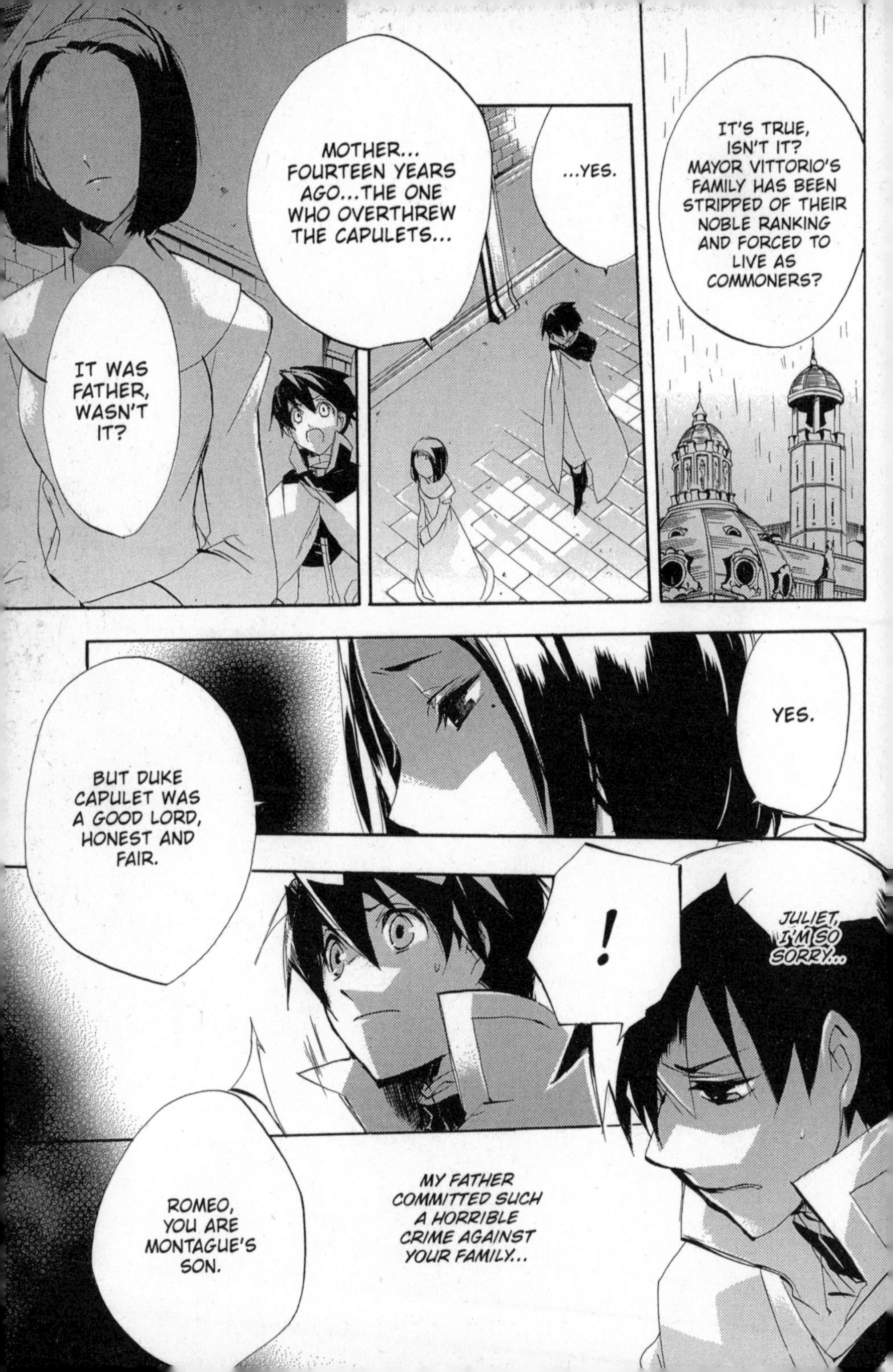
IT'S TRUE, ISN'T IT? MAYOR VITTORIO'S FAMILY HAS BEEN STRIPPED OF THEIR NOBLE RANKING AND FORCED TO LIVE AS COMMONERS?
...YES.
MOTHER... FOURTEEN YEARS AGO...THE ONE WHO OVERTHREW THE CAPULETS...
IT WAS FATHER, WASN'T IT?
YES.
BUT DUKE CAPULET WAS A GOOD LORD, HONEST AND FAIR.
JULIET, I'M SO SORRY...
!
MY FATHER COMMITTED SUCH A HORRIBLE CRIME AGAINST YOUR FAMILY...
ROMEO, YOU ARE MONTAGUE'S SON.

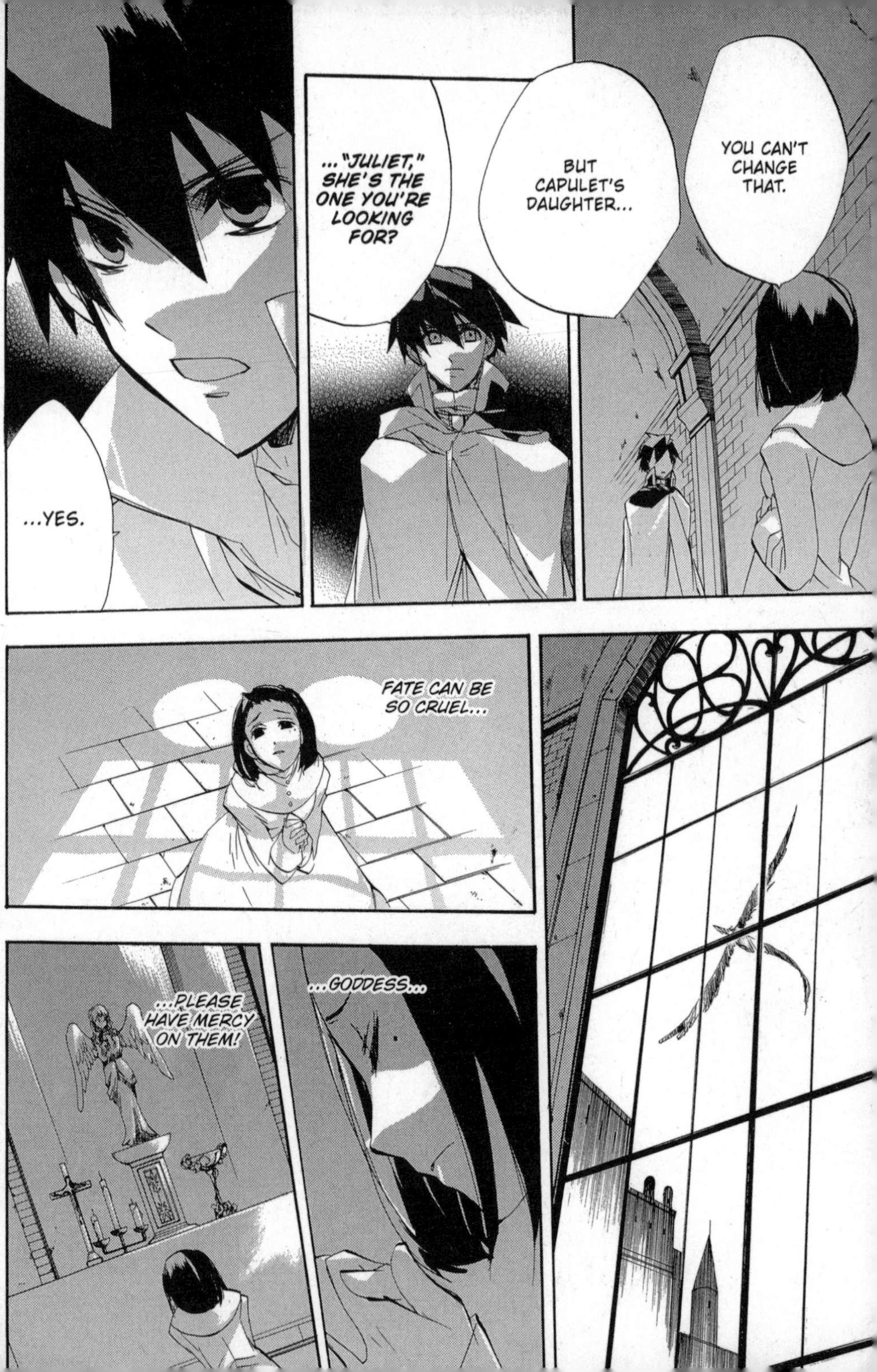
YOU CAN'T CHANGE THAT.
BUT CAPULET'S DAUGHTER...
..."JULIET," SHE'S THE ONE YOU'RE LOOKING FOR?
...YES.
FATE CAN BE SO CRUEL...
...GODDESS...
...PLEASE HAVE MERCY ON THEM!

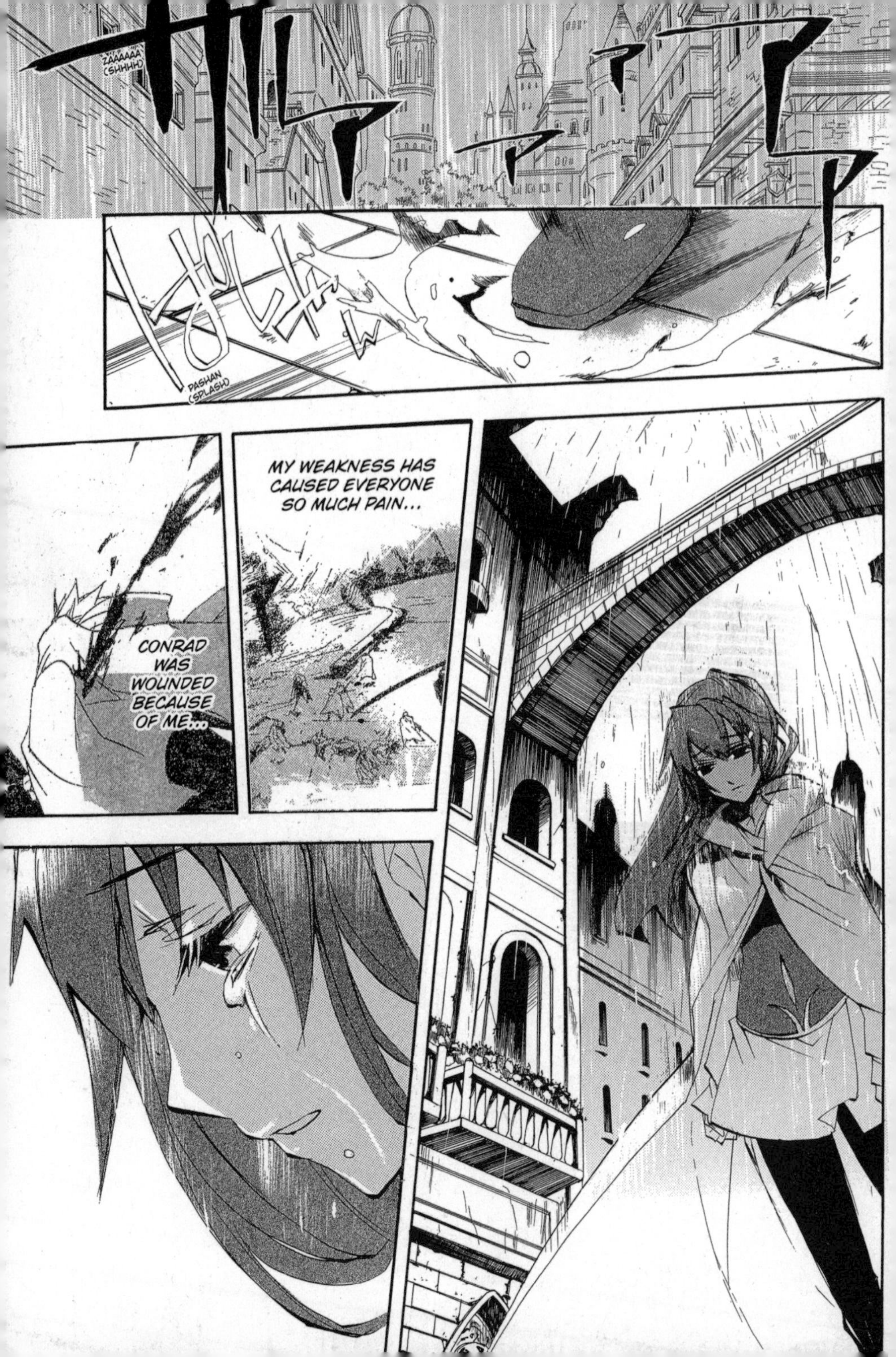
ZAAAAAA (SHHHH)
PASHAN (SPLASH)
MY WEAKNESS HAS CAUSED EVERYONE SO MUCH PAIN...
CONRAD WAS WOUNDED BECAUSE OF ME...

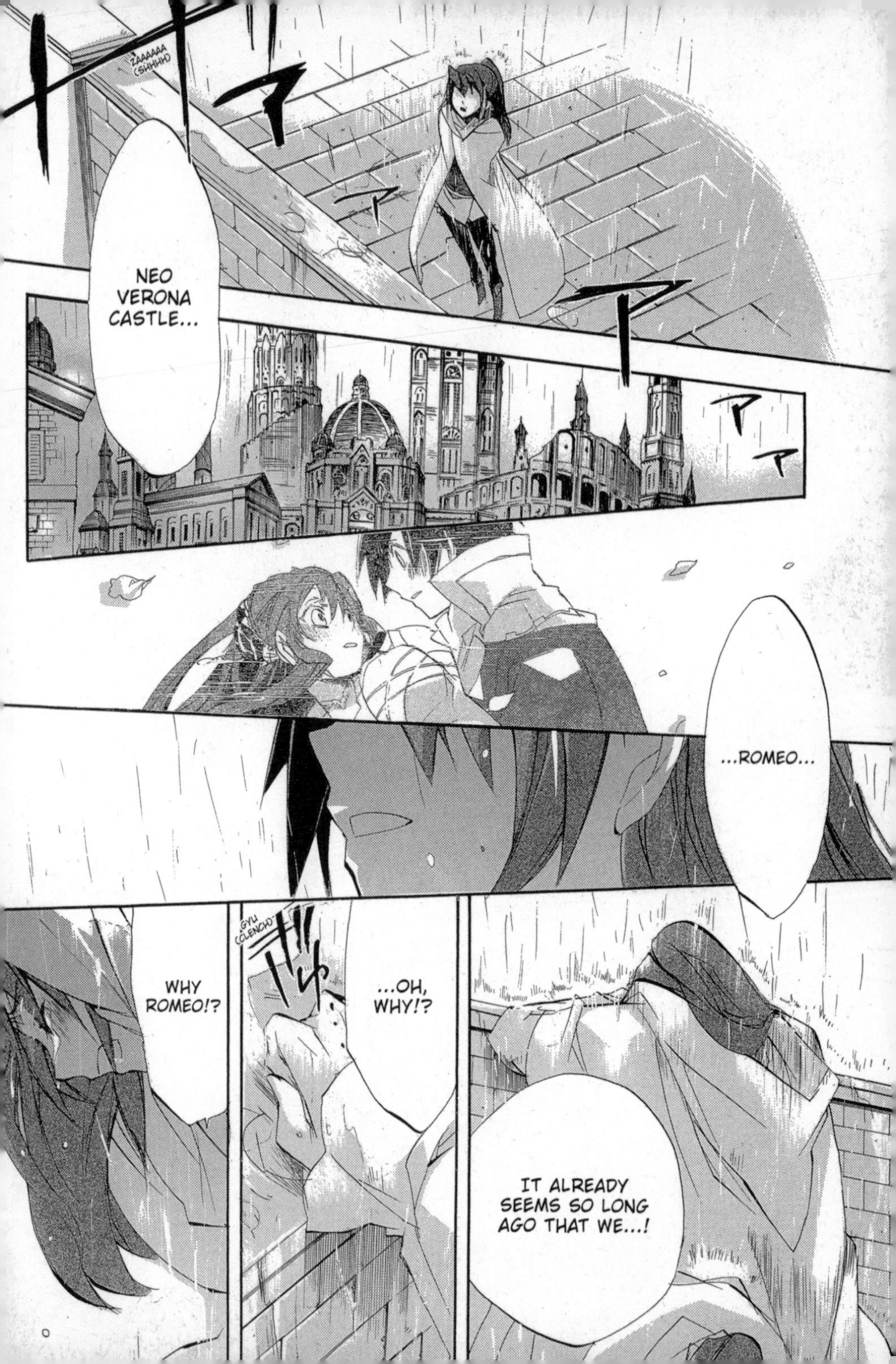
ZAAAAAA (SHHHH)
NEO VERONA CASTLE...
...ROMEO...
IT ALREADY SEEMS SO LONG AGO THAT WE...!
GYU (CLENCH)
...OH, WHY!?
WHY ROMEO!?

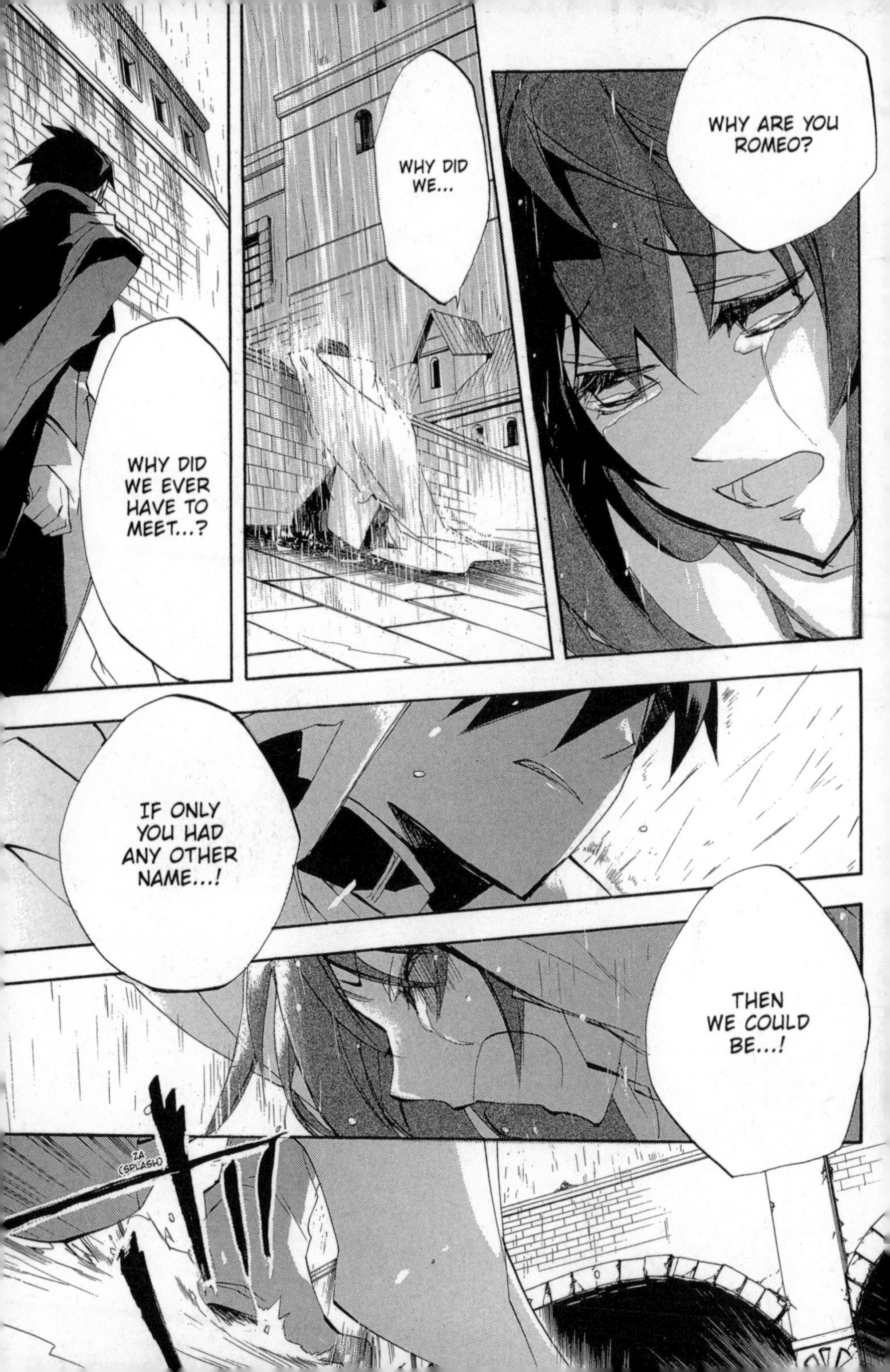
WHY ARE YOU ROMEO?
WHY DID WE...
WHY DID WE EVER HAVE TO MEET...?
IF ONLY YOU HAD ANY OTHER NAME...!
THEN WE COULD BE...!
ZA (SPLASH)

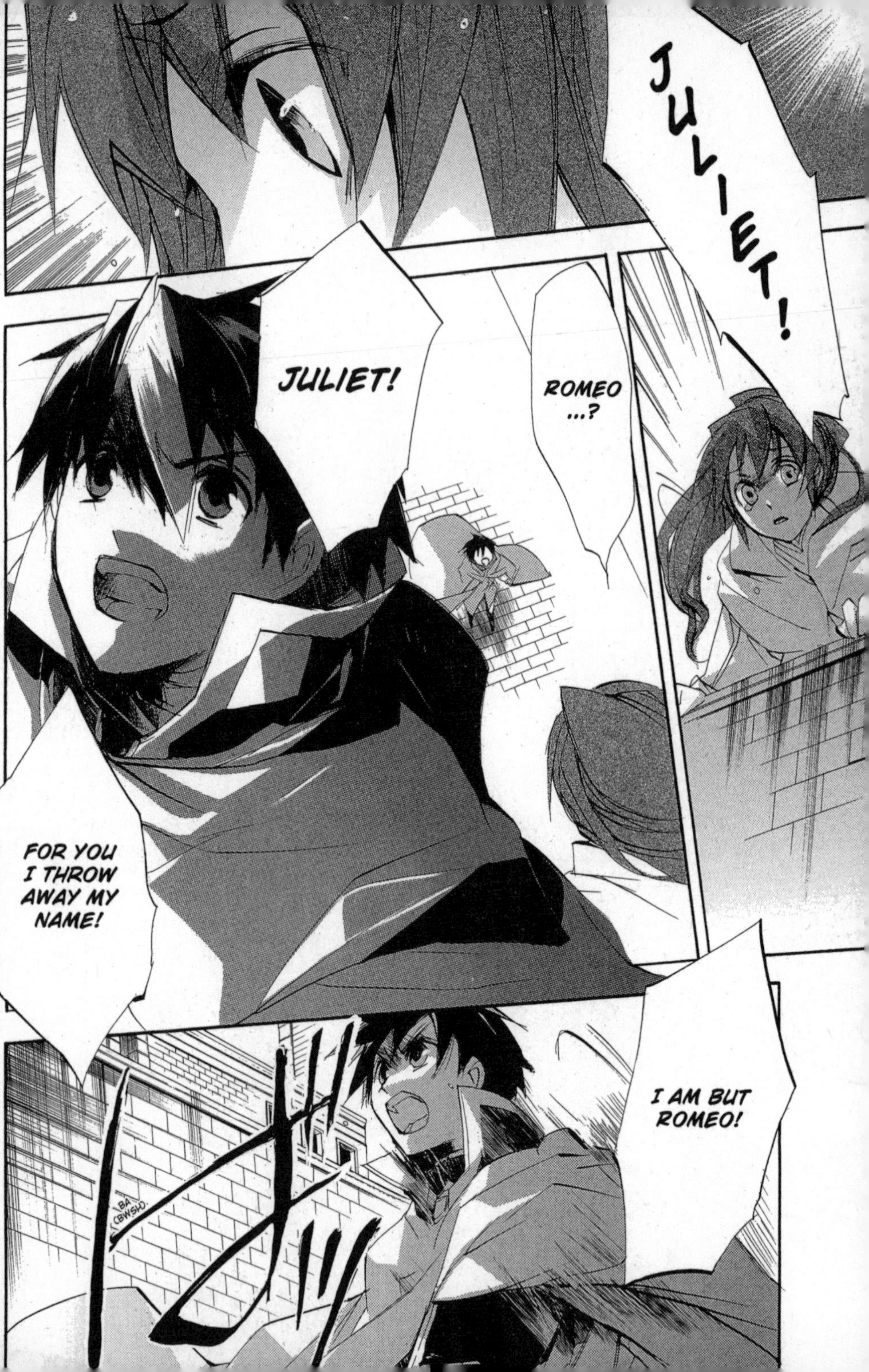
JULIET!
ROMEO ...?
JULIET!
FOR YOU I THROW AWAY MY NAME!
I AM BUT ROMEO!
BA CBWSH.

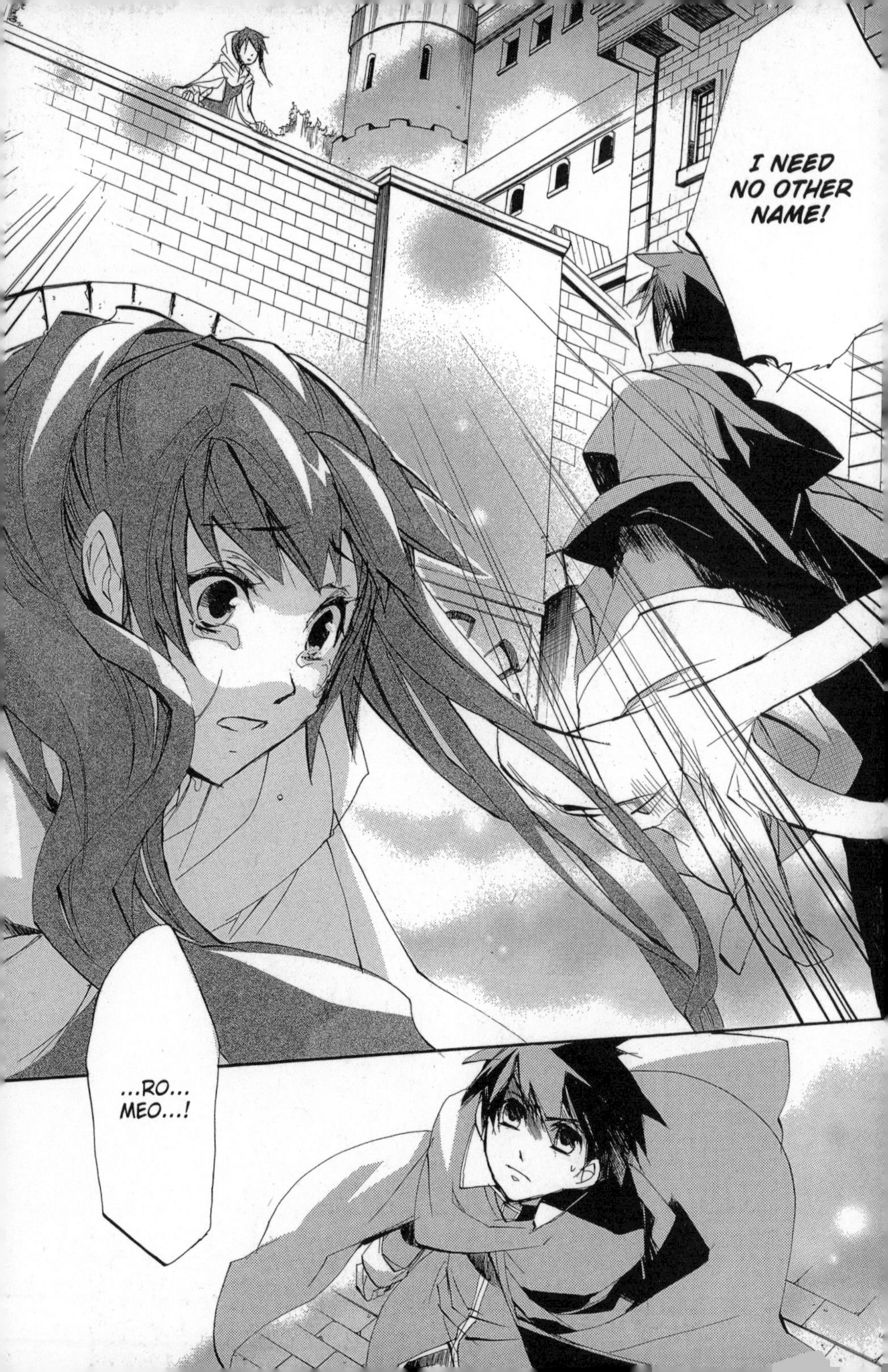
I NEED NO OTHER NAME!
...RO... MEO...!

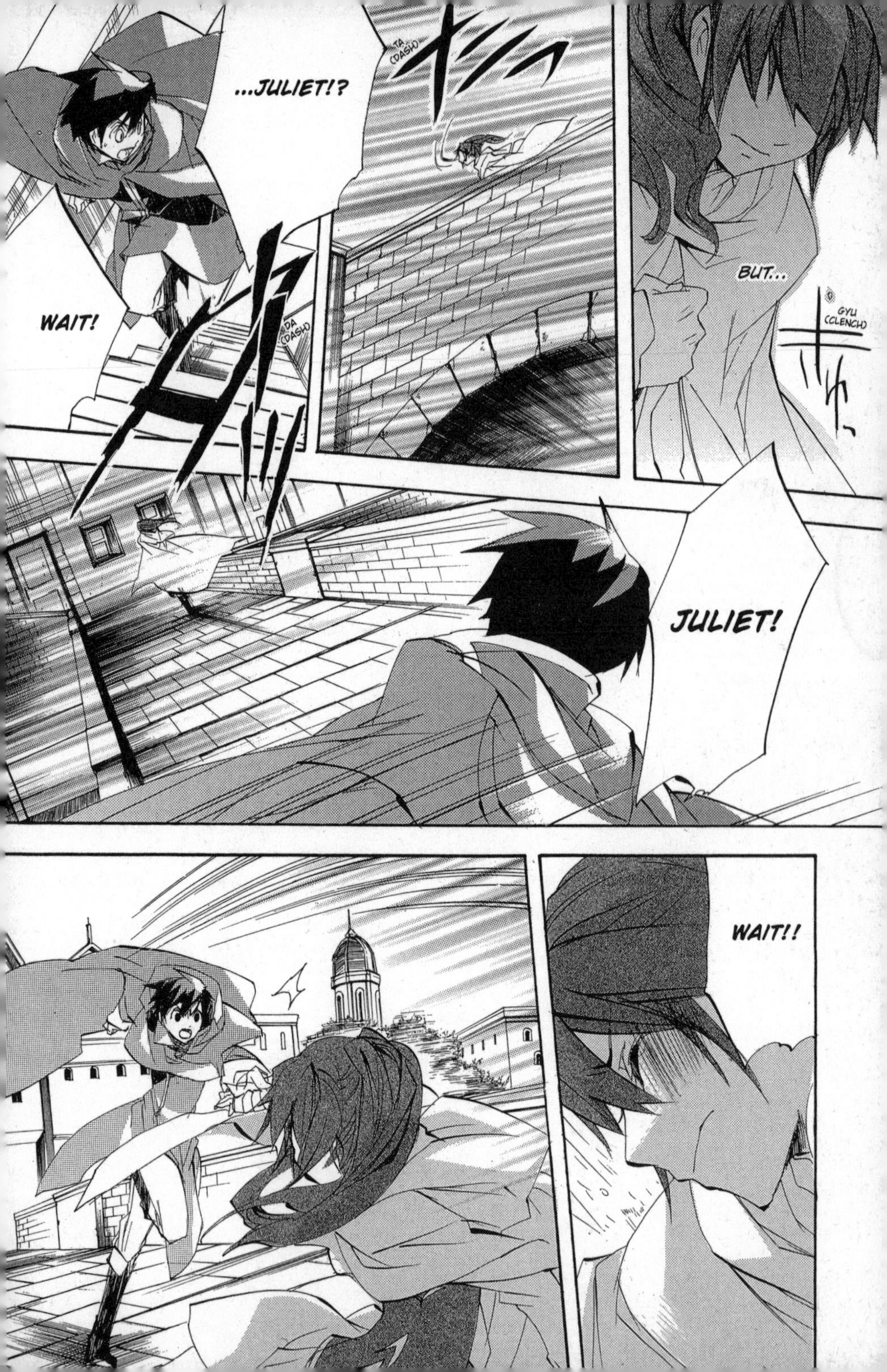
BUT...
GYU (CLENCH)
TA (DASH)
...JULIET!?
DA (DASH)
WAIT!
JULIET!
WAIT!!

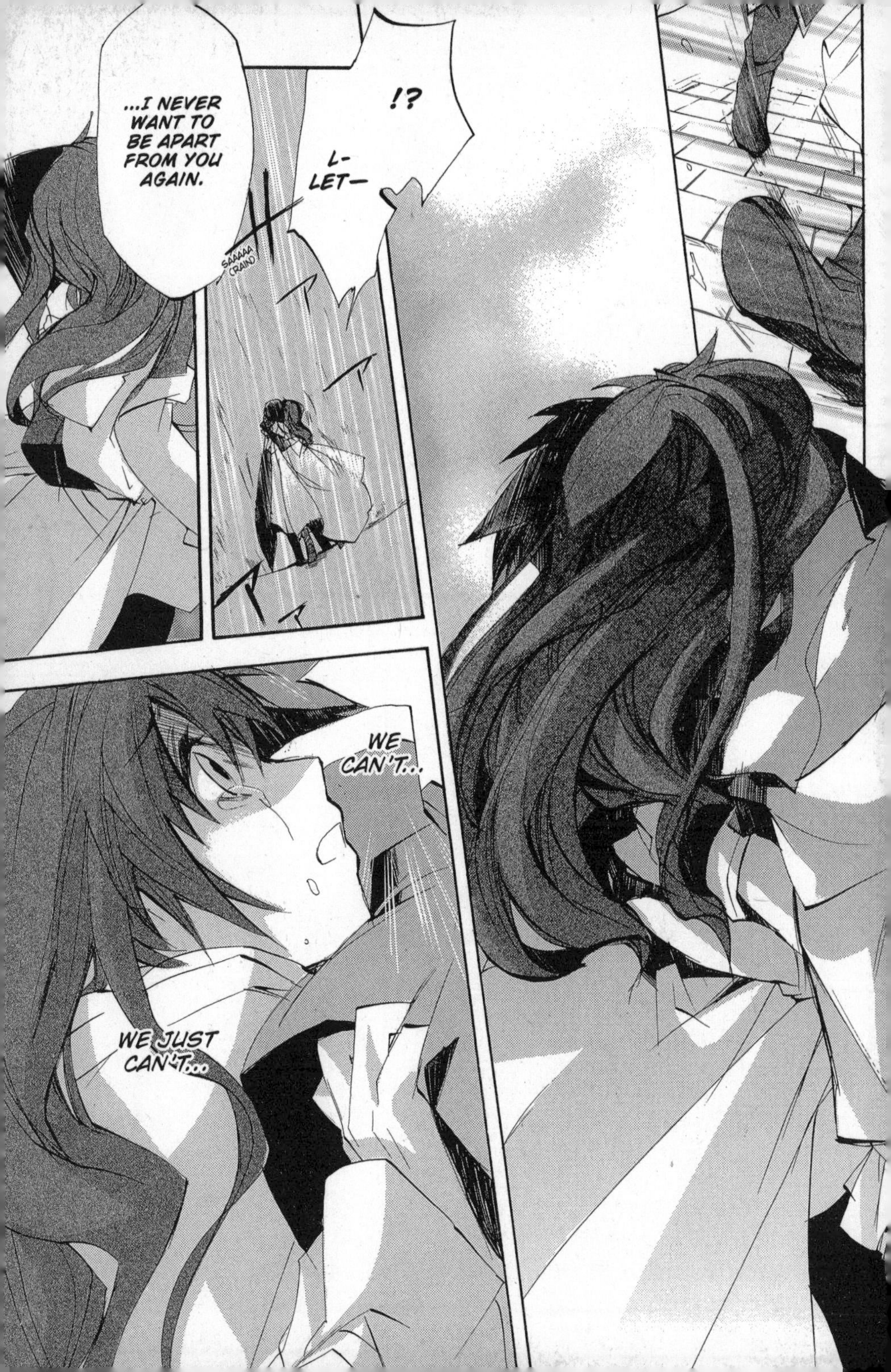
...I NEVER WANT TO BE APART FROM YOU AGAIN.
!?
L- LET—
SAAAAA (RAIN)
WE CAN'T...
WE JUST CAN'T...

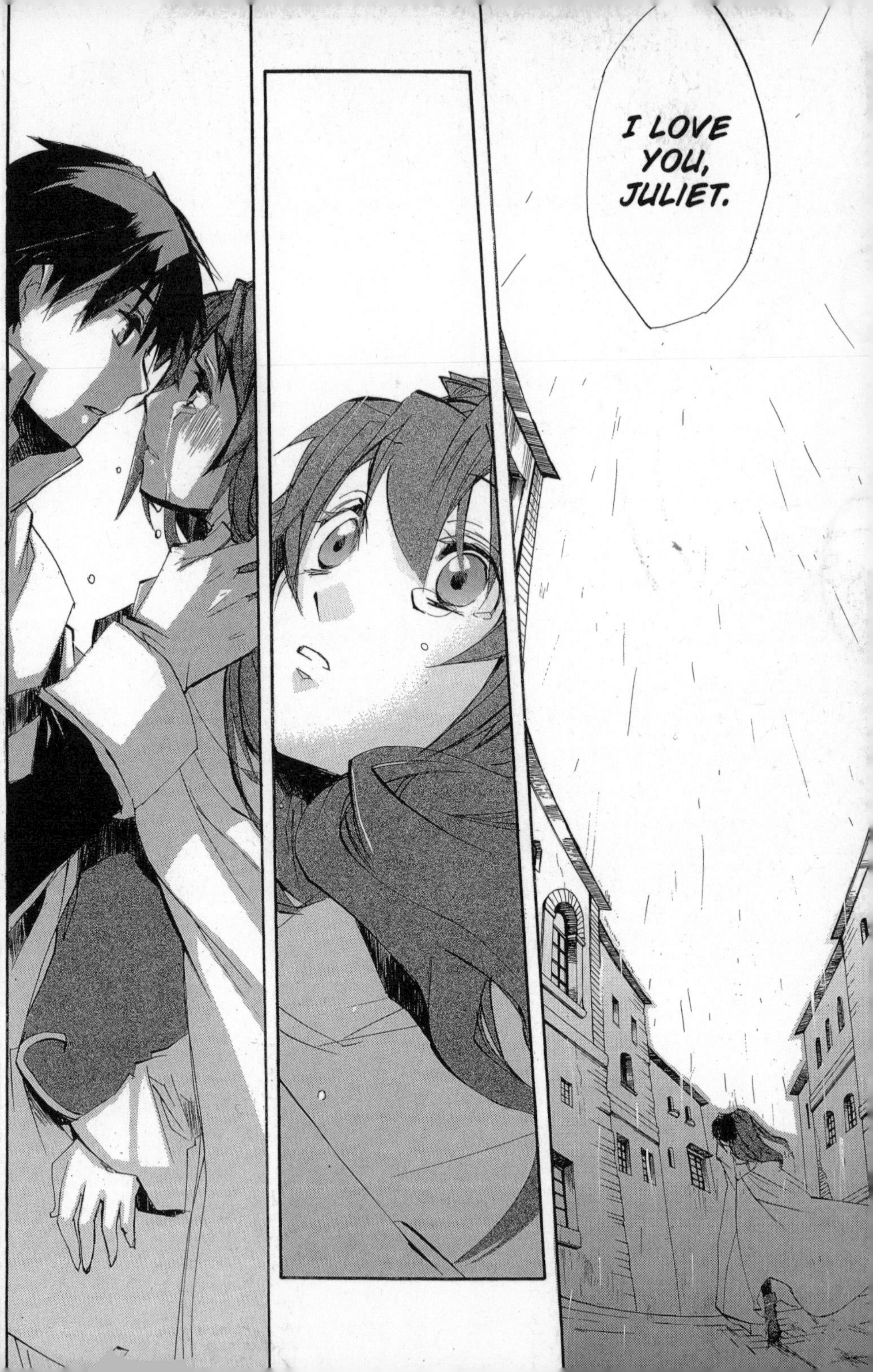
I LOVE YOU, JULIET.

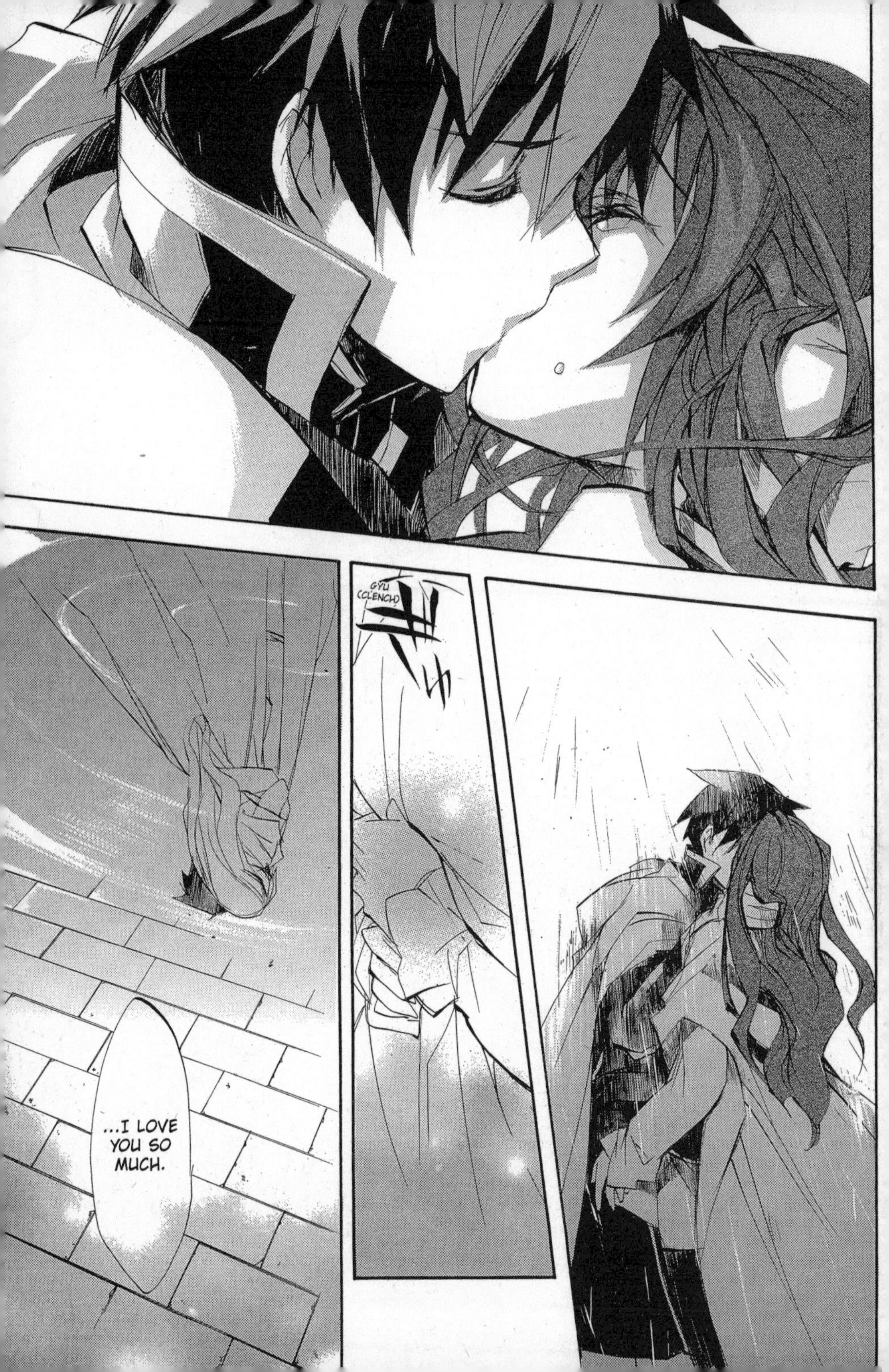
GYU (CLENCH)
...I LOVE YOU SO MUCH.

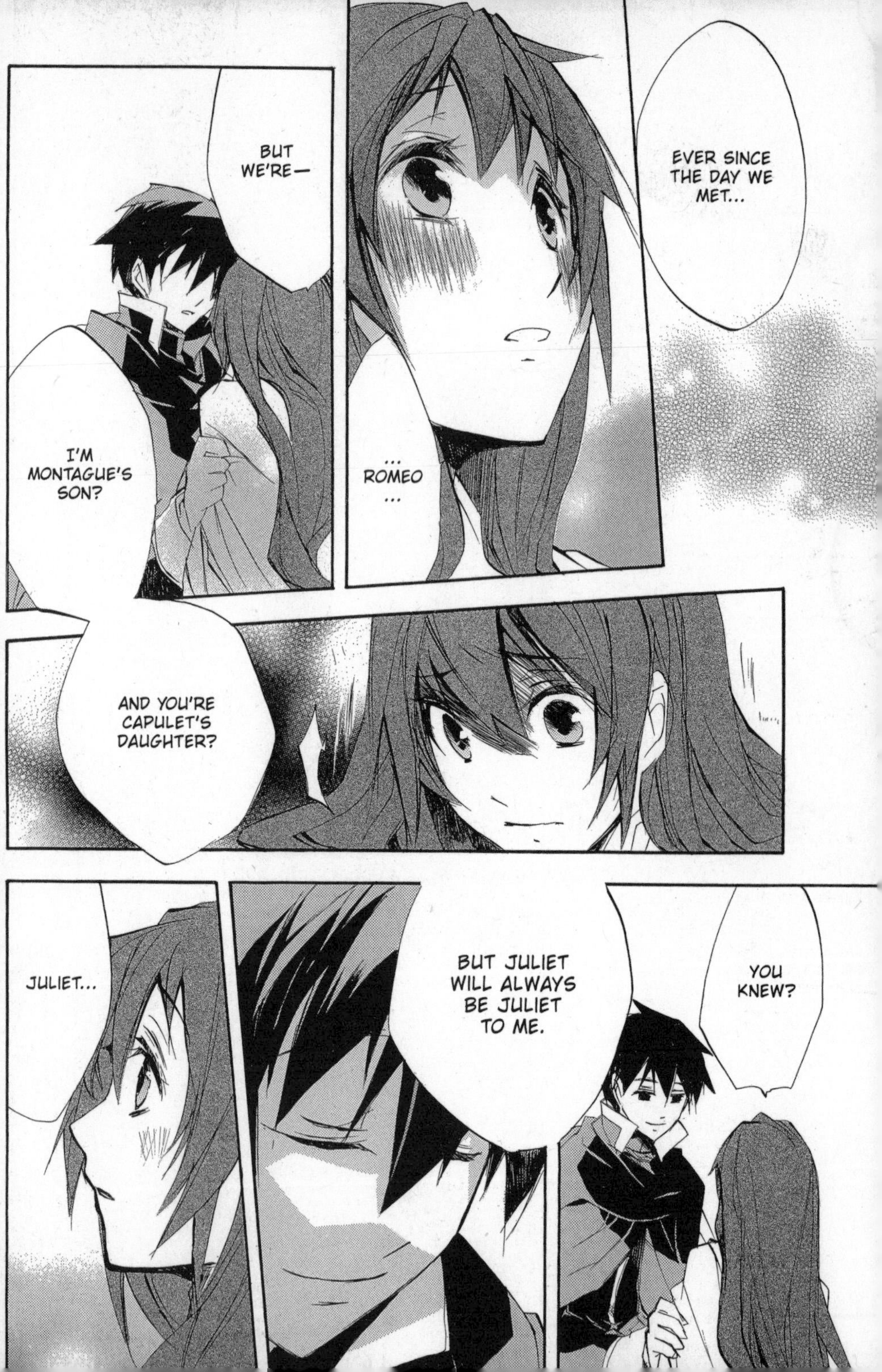
EVER SINCE THE DAY WE MET...
...ROMEO...
BUT WE'RE—
I'M MONTAGUE'S SON?
AND YOU'RE CAPULET'S DAUGHTER?
YOU KNEW?
BUT JULIET WILL ALWAYS BE JULIET TO ME.
JULIET...

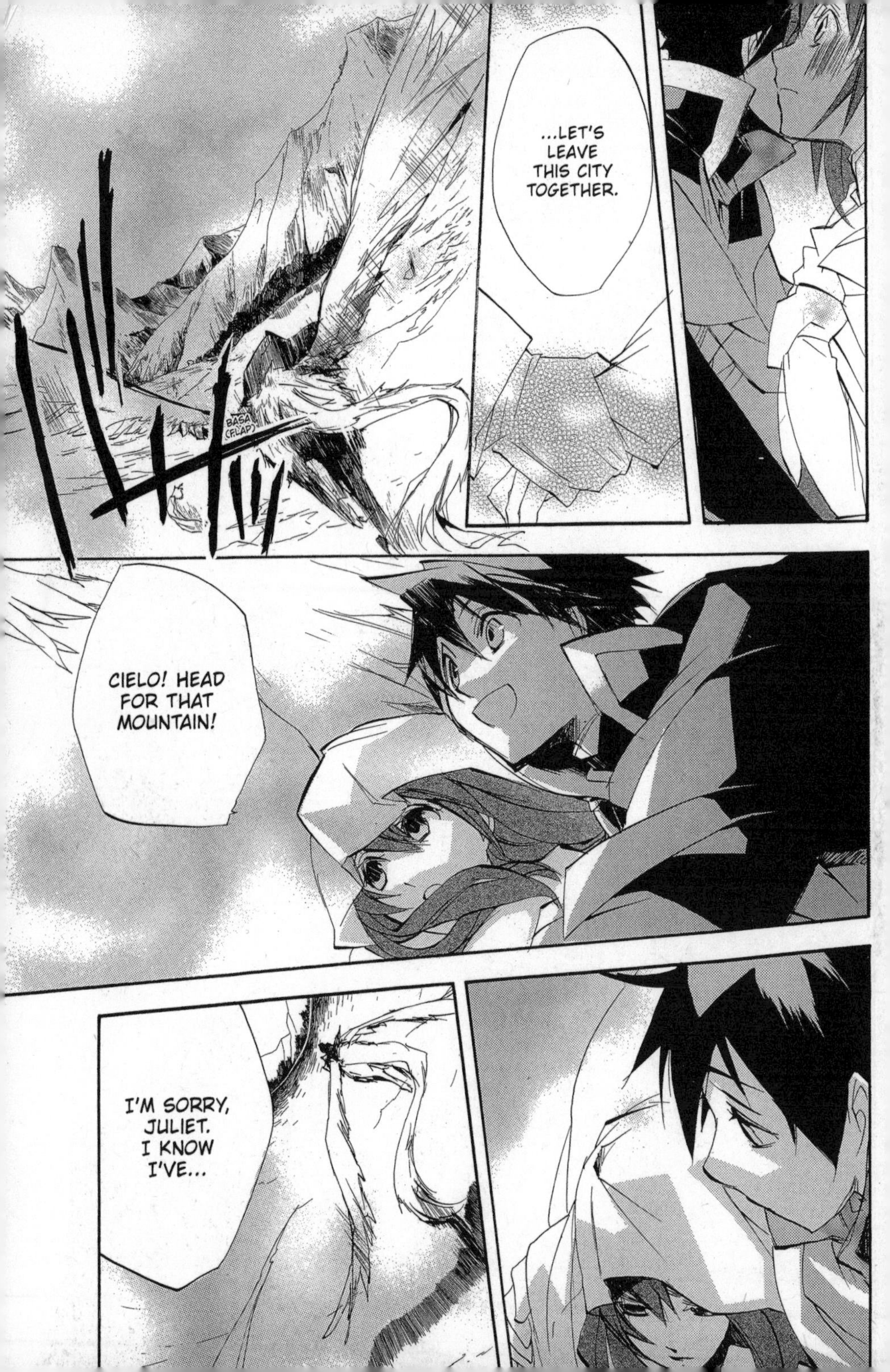
...LET'S LEAVE THIS CITY TOGETHER.
BASA (FLAP)
CIELO! HEAD FOR THAT MOUNTAIN!
I'M SORRY, JULIET. I KNOW I'VE...

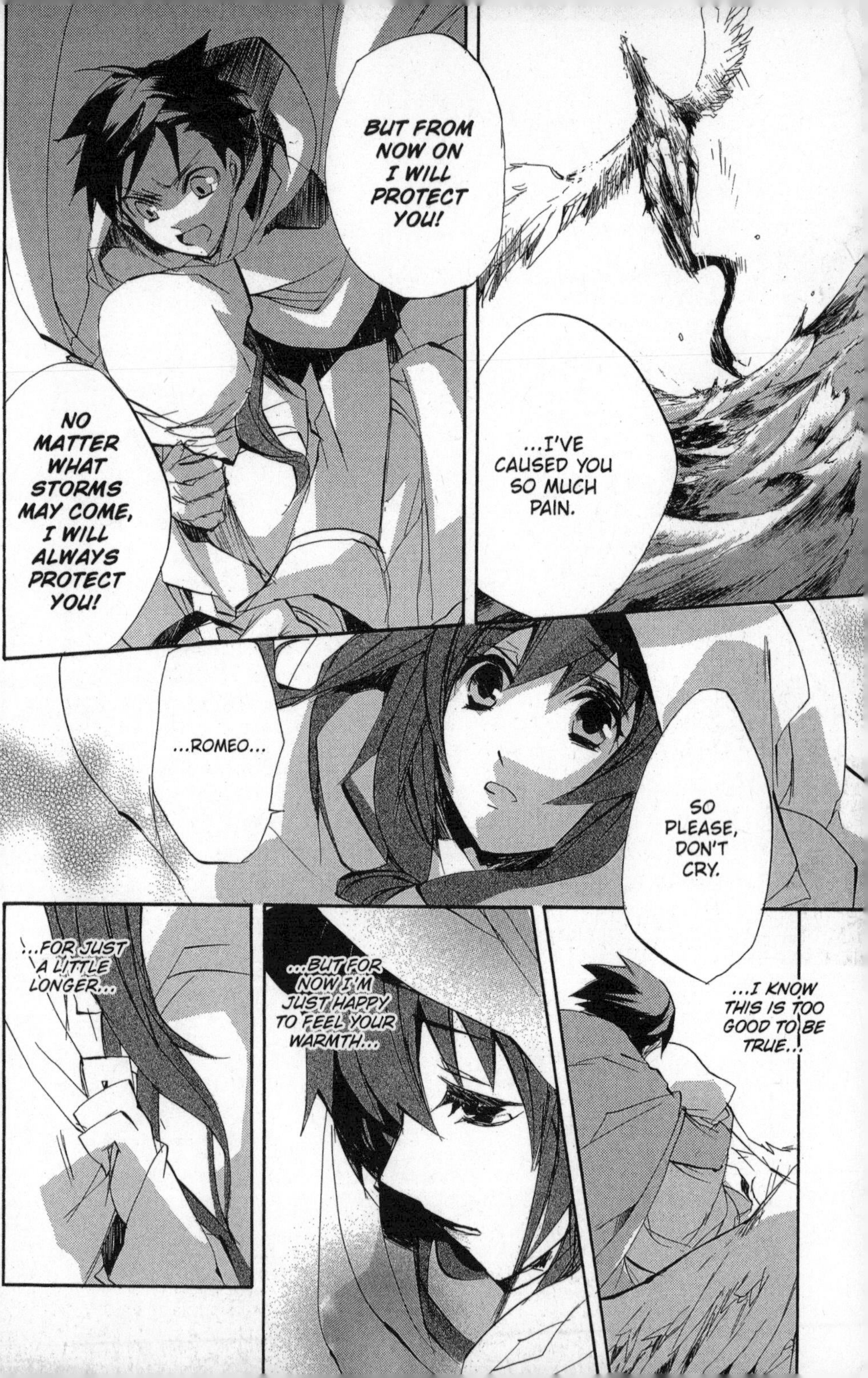
...I'VE CAUSED YOU SO MUCH PAIN.
BUT FROM NOW ON I WILL PROTECT YOU!
NO MATTER WHAT STORMS MAY COME, I WILL ALWAYS PROTECT YOU!
SO PLEASE, DON'T CRY.
...ROMEO...
...I KNOW THIS IS TOO GOOD TO BE TRUE...
...BUT FOR NOW I'M JUST HAPPY TO FEEL YOUR WARMTH...
...FOR JUST A LITTLE LONGER...

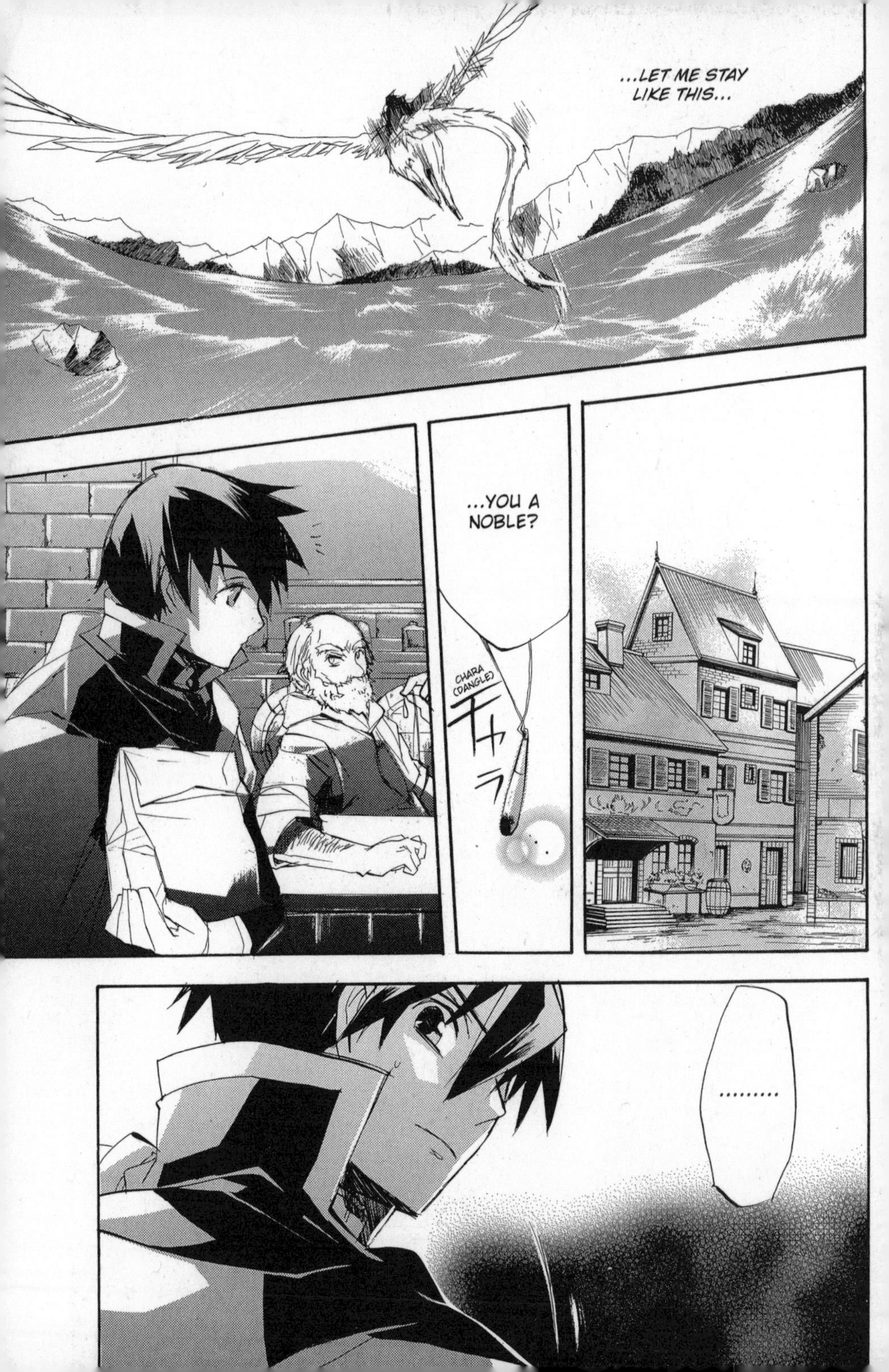
...LET ME STAY LIKE THIS...
...YOU A NOBLE?
CHARA (DANGLE)
チャラ
....

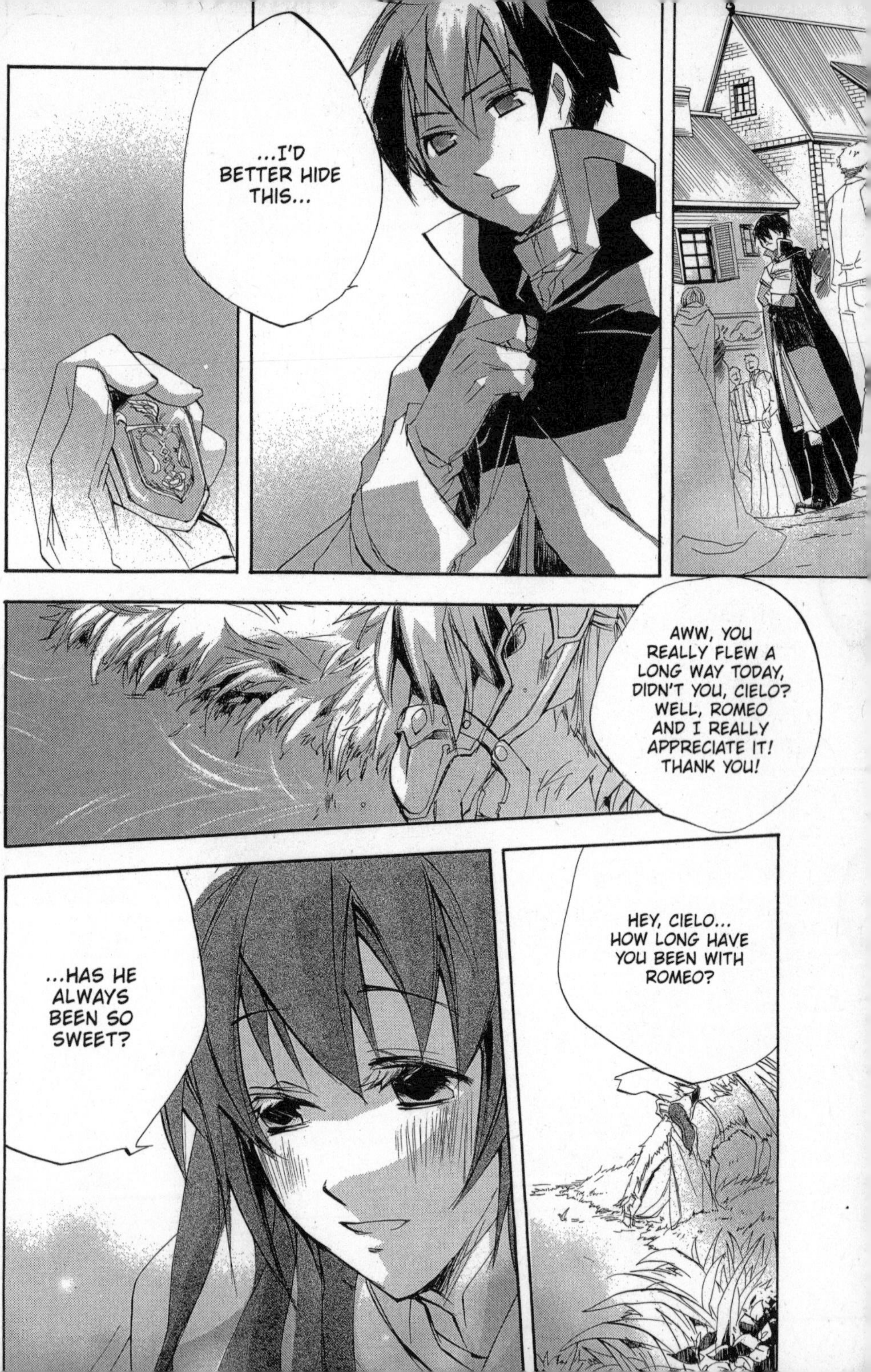
...I'D BETTER HIDE THIS...
AWW, YOU REALLY FLEW A LONG WAY TODAY, DIDN'T YOU, CIELO? WELL, ROMEO AND I REALLY APPRECIATE IT! THANK YOU!
HEY, CIELO... HOW LONG HAVE YOU BEEN WITH ROMEO?
...HAS HE ALWAYS BEEN SO SWEET?

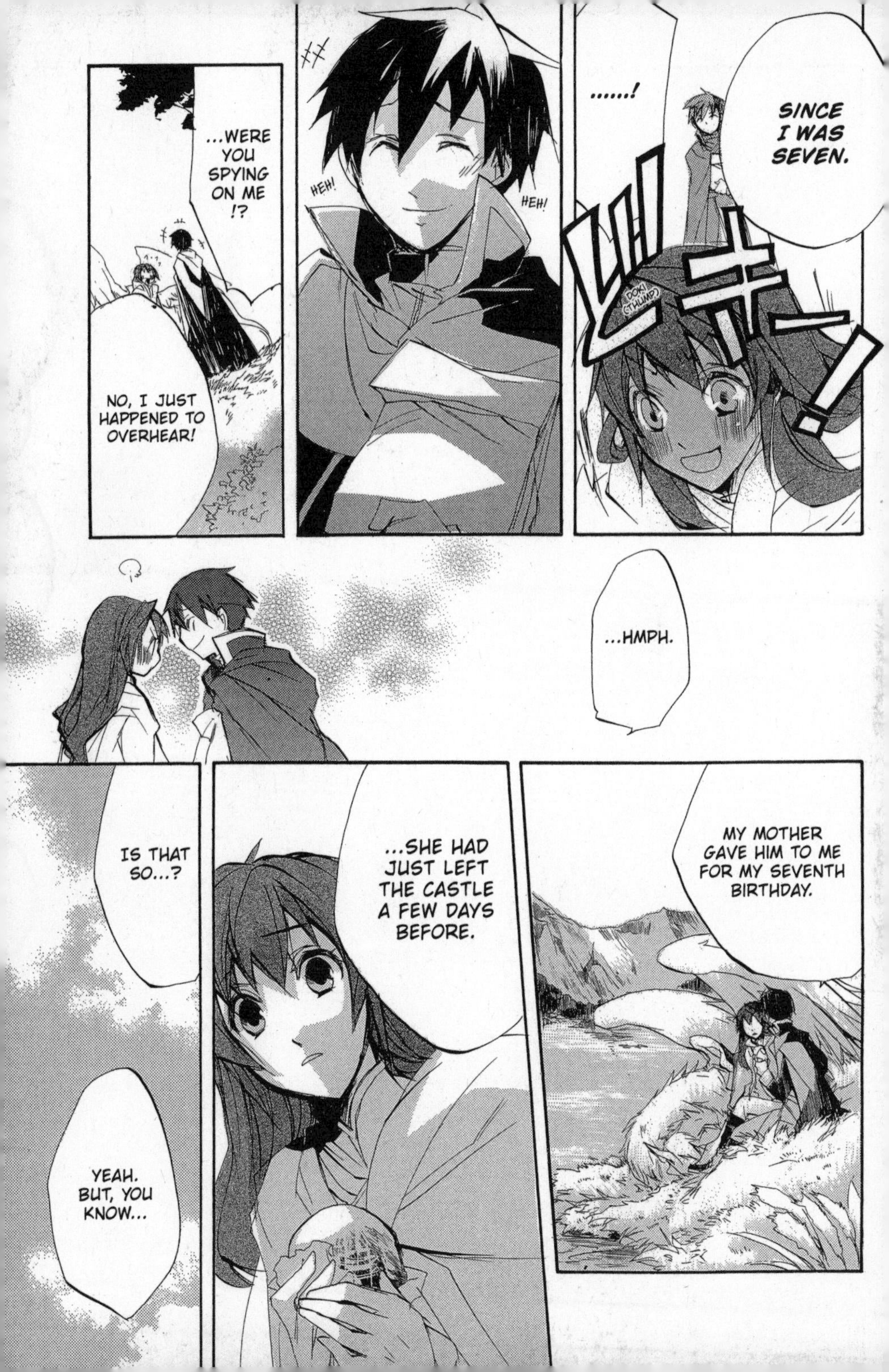
SINCE I WAS SEVEN.
......!
DOKI (THUMP)
HEH!
HEH!
...WERE YOU SPYING ON ME !?
NO, I JUST HAPPENED TO OVERHEAR!
...HMPH.
MY MOTHER GAVE HIM TO ME FOR MY SEVENTH BIRTHDAY.
...SHE HAD JUST LEFT THE CASTLE A FEW DAYS BEFORE.
IS THAT SO...?
YEAH. BUT, YOU KNOW...

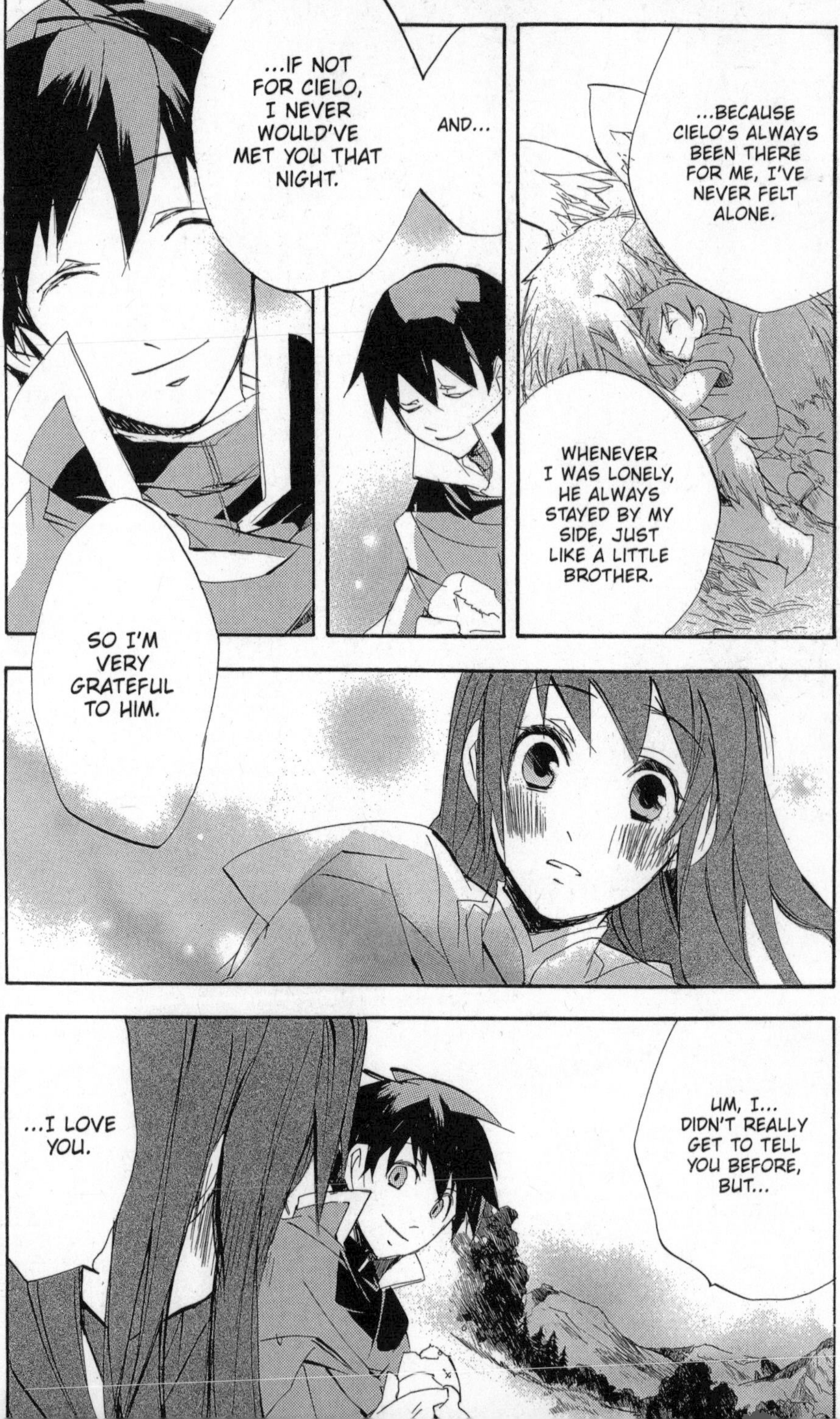
...BECAUSE CIELO'S ALWAYS BEEN THERE FOR ME, I'VE NEVER FELT ALONE.
WHENEVER I WAS LONELY, HE ALWAYS STAYED BY MY SIDE, JUST LIKE A LITTLE BROTHER.
AND...
...IF NOT FOR CIELO, I NEVER WOULD'VE MET YOU THAT NIGHT.
SO I'M VERY GRATEFUL TO HIM.
UM, I... DIDN'T REALLY GET TO TELL YOU BEFORE, BUT...
...I LOVE YOU.

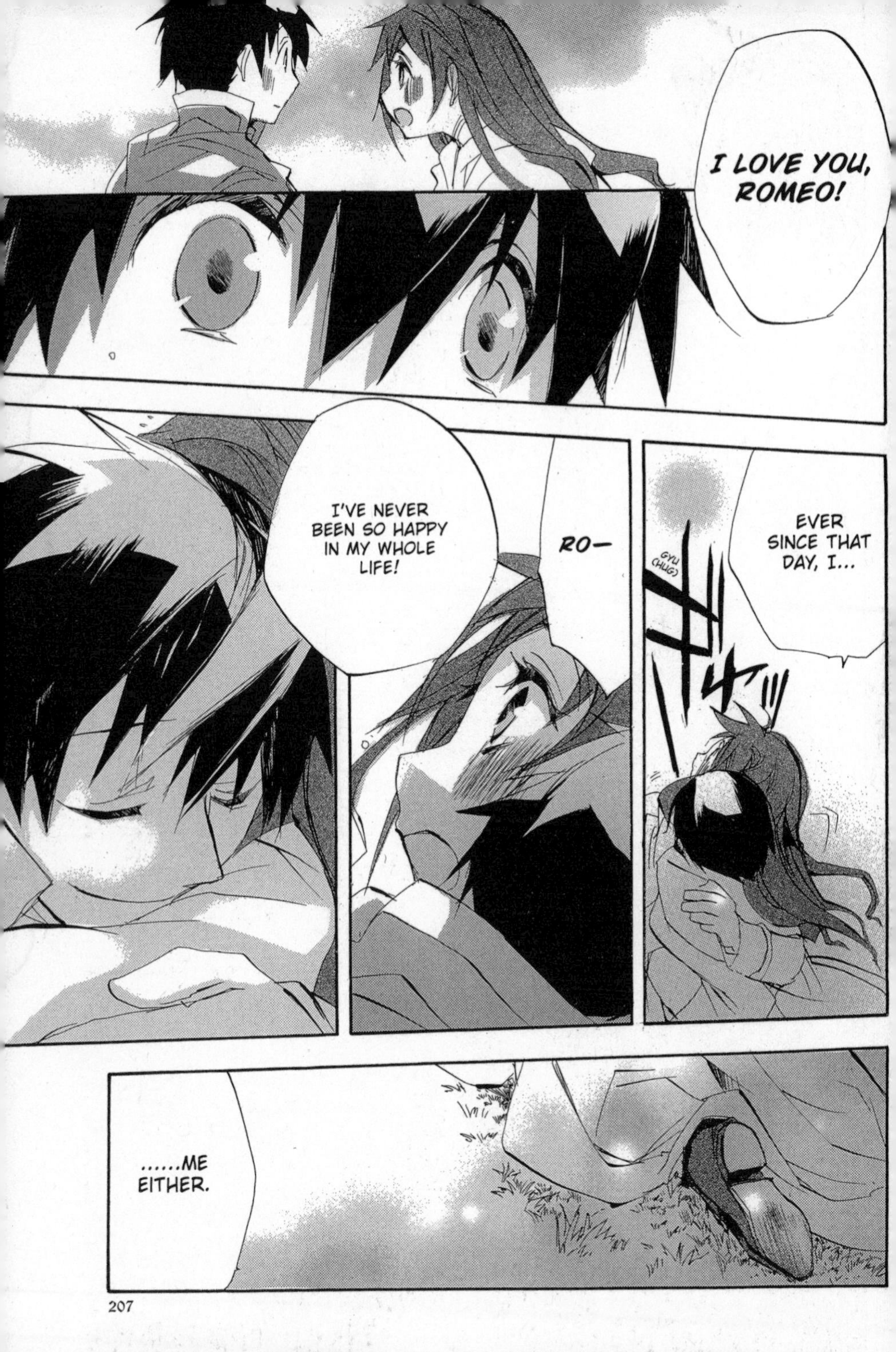
I LOVE YOU, ROMEO!
EVER SINCE THAT DAY, I...
GYU (HUG)
RO—
I'VE NEVER BEEN SO HAPPY IN MY WHOLE LIFE!
......ME EITHER.

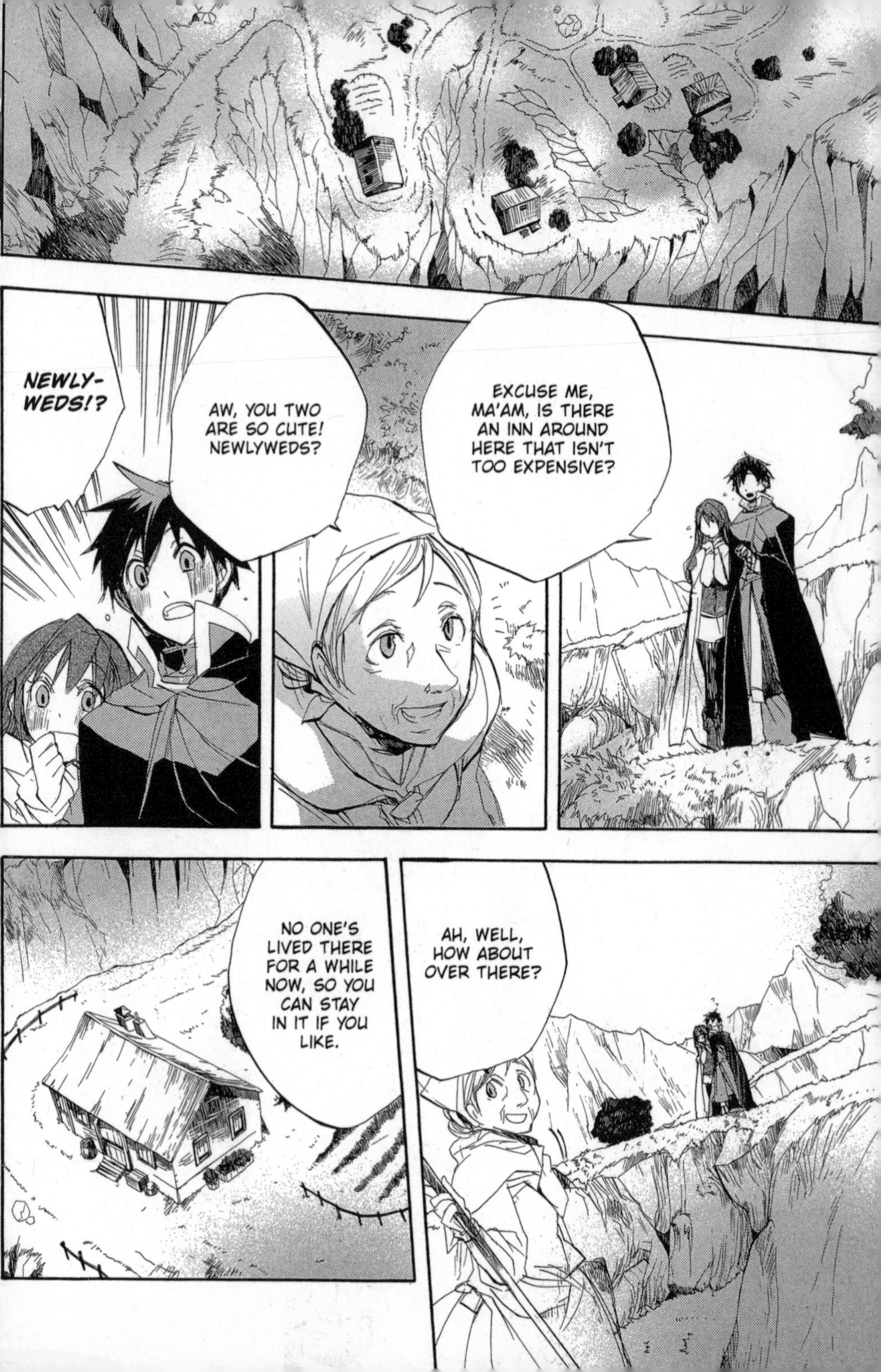
EXCUSE ME, MA'AM, IS THERE AN INN AROUND HERE THAT ISN'T TOO EXPENSIVE?
AW, YOU TWO ARE SO CUTE! NEWLYWEDS?
NEWLY-WEDS!?
AH, WELL, HOW ABOUT OVER THERE?
NO ONE'S LIVED THERE FOR A WHILE NOW, SO YOU CAN STAY IN IT IF YOU LIKE.

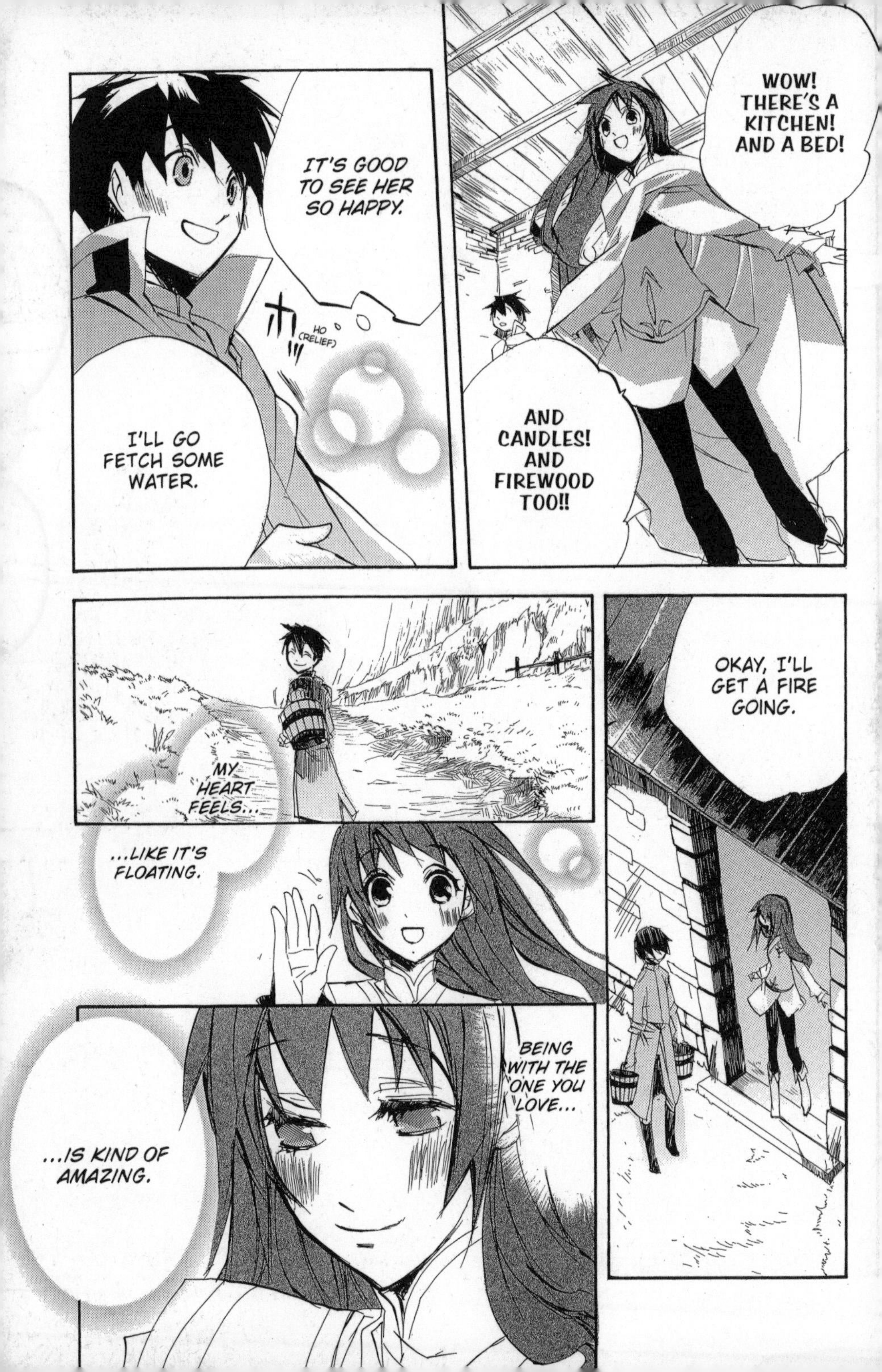
WOW! THERE'S A KITCHEN! AND A BED!
AND CANDLES! AND FIREWOOD TOO!!
IT'S GOOD TO SEE HER SO HAPPY.
HO (RELIEF)
I'LL GO FETCH SOME WATER.
OKAY, I'LL GET A FIRE GOING.
MY HEART FEELS...
...LIKE IT'S FLOATING.
BEING WITH THE ONE YOU LOVE...
...IS KIND OF AMAZING.

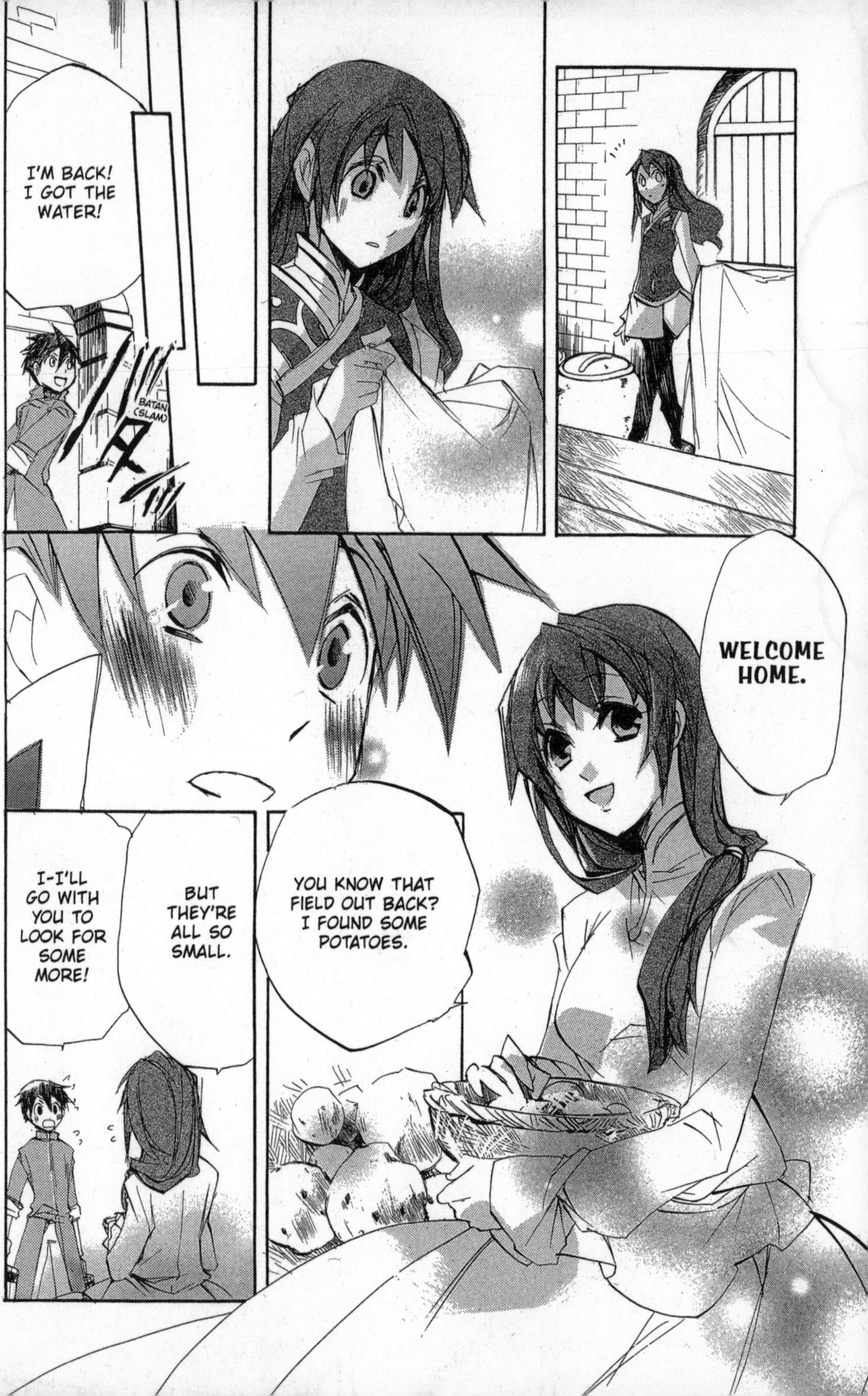
I'M BACK! I GOT THE WATER!
BATAN (SLAM)
WELCOME HOME.
YOU KNOW THAT FIELD OUT BACK? I FOUND SOME POTATOES.
BUT THEY'RE ALL SO SMALL.
I-I'LL GO WITH YOU TO LOOK FOR SOME MORE!

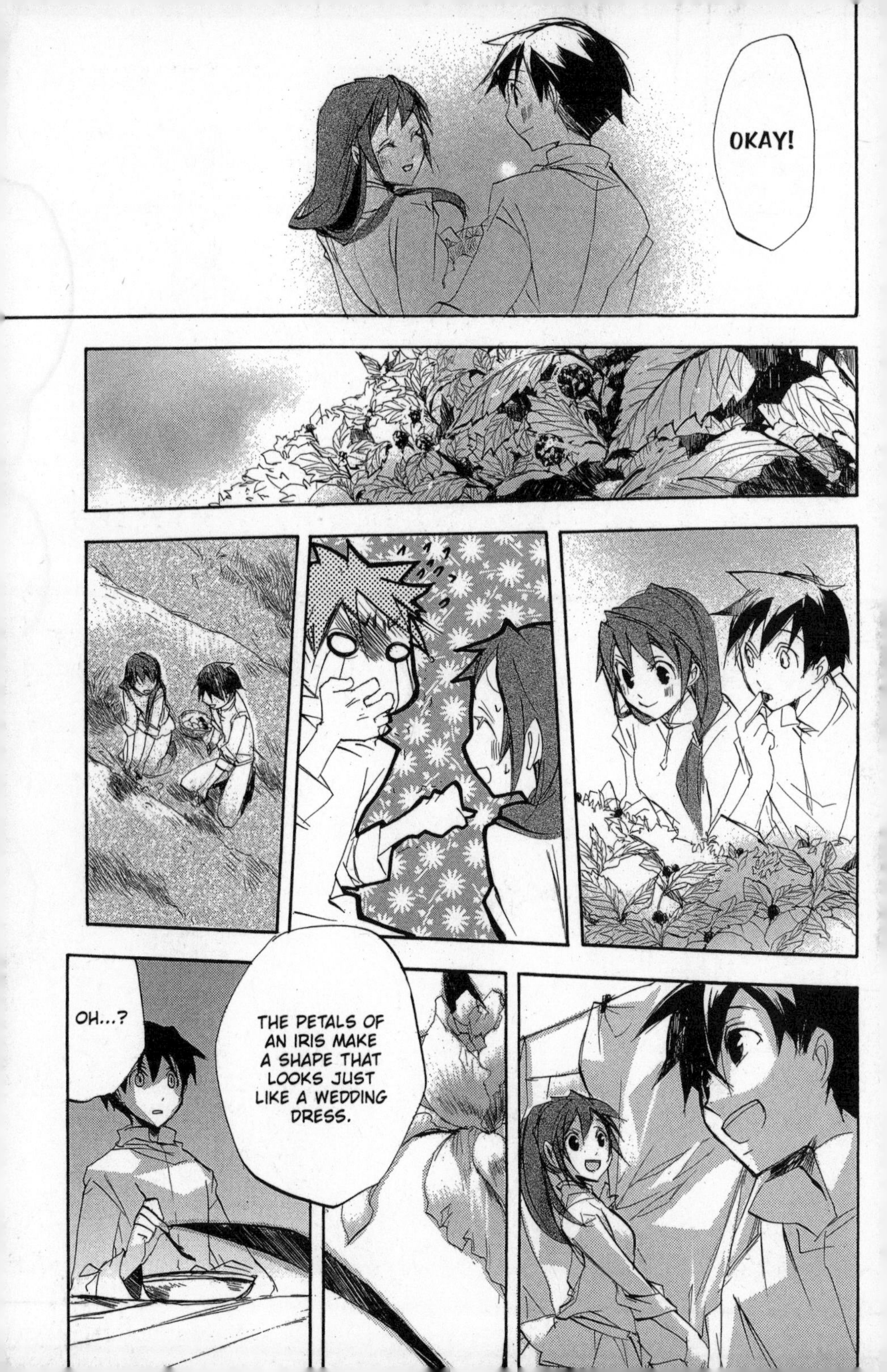
OKAY!
THE PETALS OF AN IRIS MAKE A SHAPE THAT LOOKS JUST LIKE A WEDDING DRESS.
OH...?

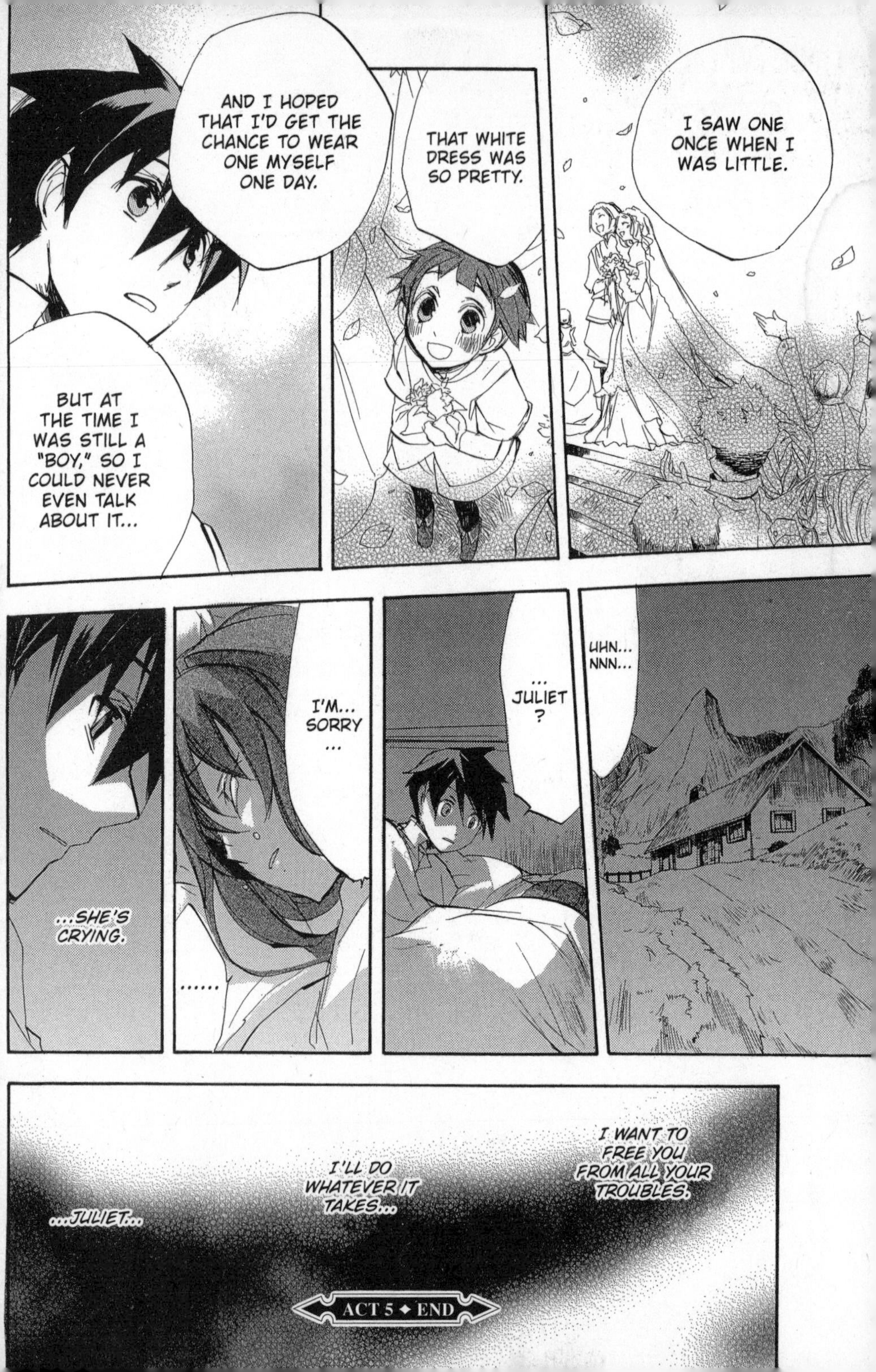
I SAW ONE ONCE WHEN I WAS LITTLE.
THAT WHITE DRESS WAS SO PRETTY.
AND I HOPED THAT I'D GET THE CHANCE TO WEAR ONE MYSELF ONE DAY.
BUT AT THE TIME I WAS STILL A "BOY," SO I COULD NEVER EVEN TALK ABOUT IT...
UHN... NNN...
...JULIET?
I'M... SORRY...
......
...SHE'S CRYING.
I WANT TO FREE YOU FROM ALL YOUR TROUBLES.
I'LL DO WHATEVER IT TAKES...
...JULIET...
ACT 5 ◆ END

ACT 6

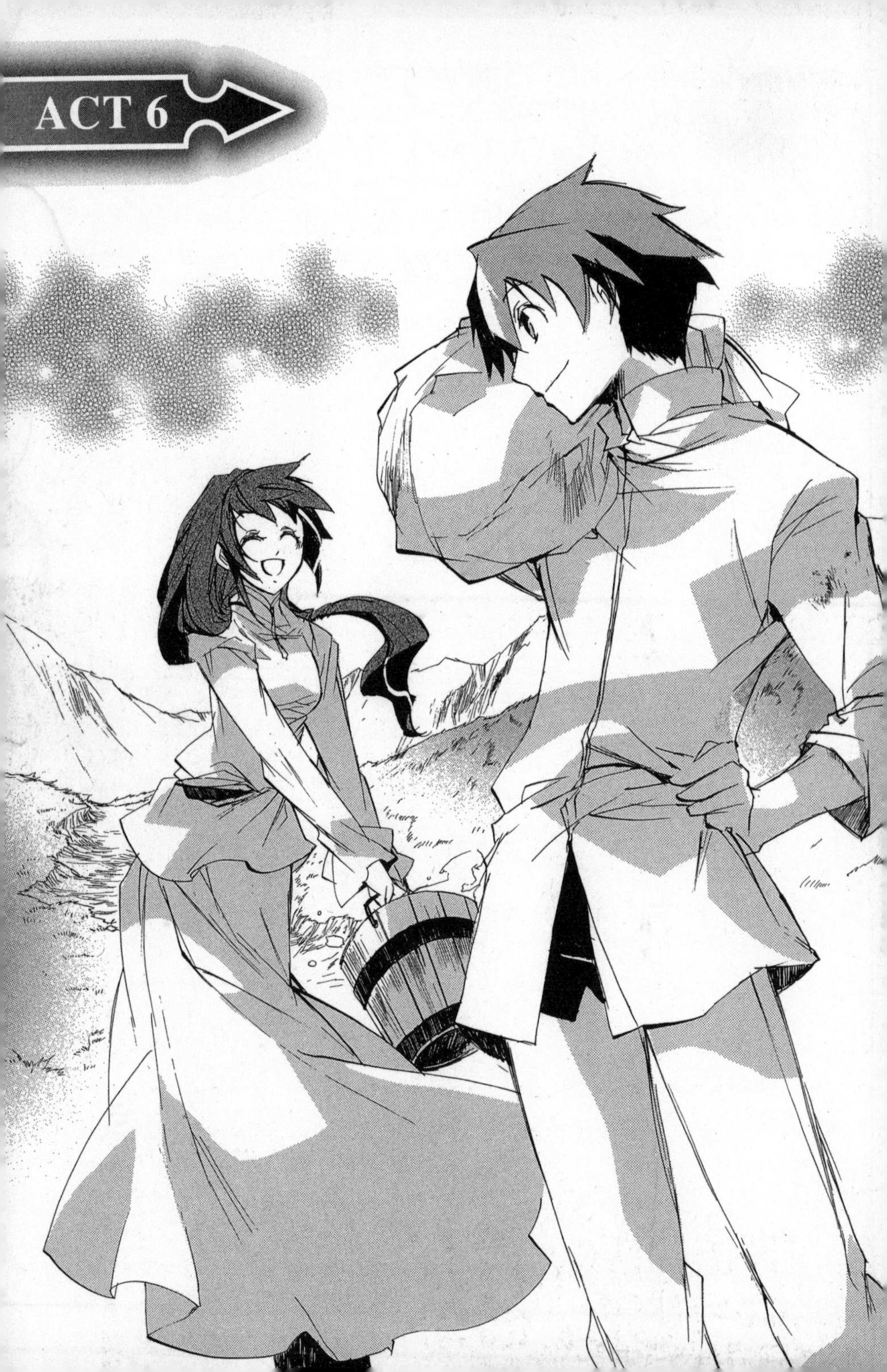

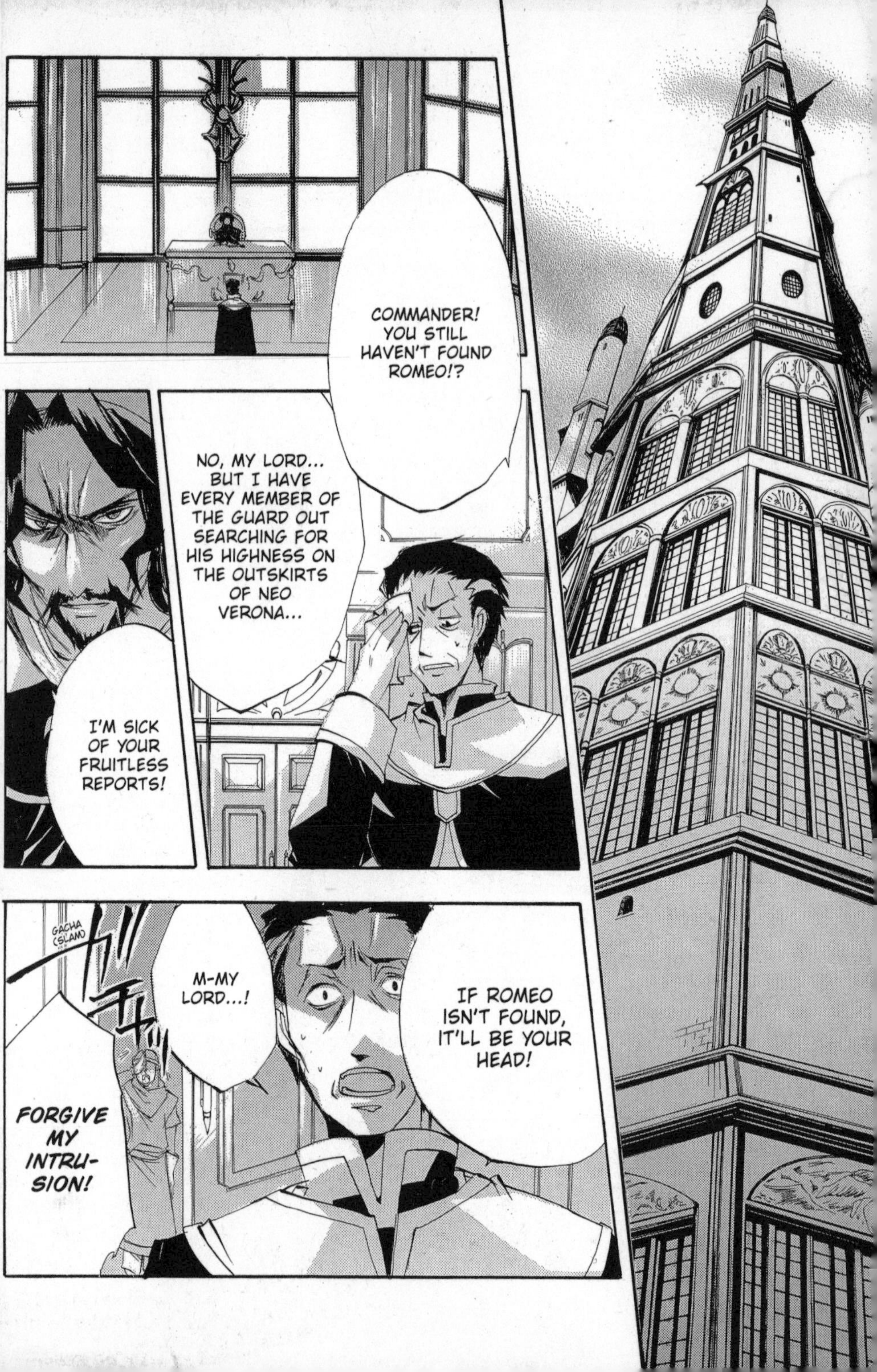
COMMANDER! YOU STILL HAVEN'T FOUND ROMEO!?
NO, MY LORD... BUT I HAVE EVERY MEMBER OF THE GUARD OUT SEARCHING FOR HIS HIGHNESS ON THE OUTSKIRTS OF NEO VERONA...
I'M SICK OF YOUR FRUITLESS REPORTS!
IF ROMEO ISN'T FOUND, IT'LL BE YOUR HEAD!
M-MY LORD...!
GACHA (SLAM)
FORGIVE MY INTRU-SION!

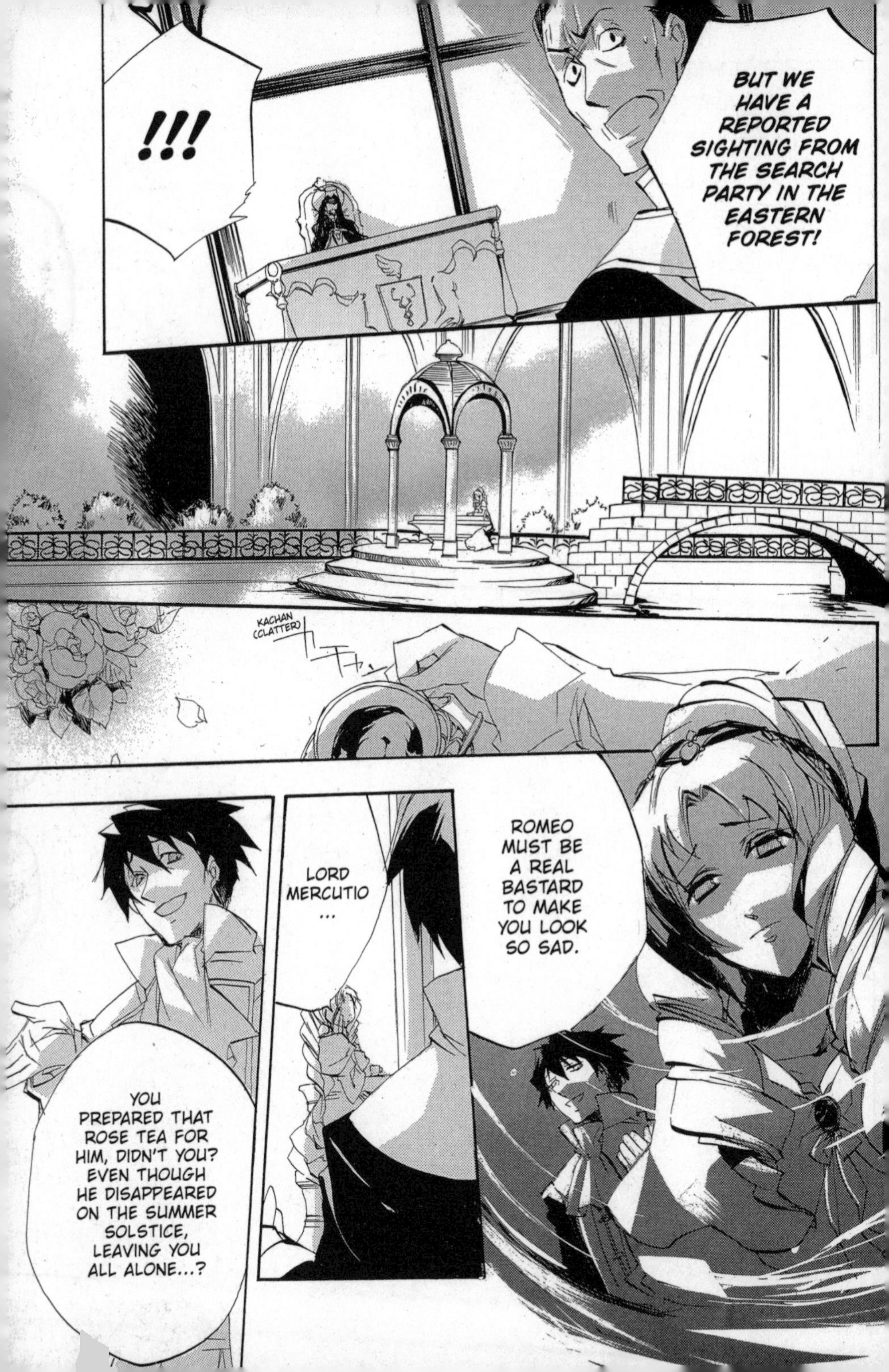
BUT WE HAVE A REPORTED SIGHTING FROM THE SEARCH PARTY IN THE EASTERN FOREST!
!!!
KACHAN (CLATTER)
ROMEO MUST BE A REAL BASTARD TO MAKE YOU LOOK SO SAD.
LORD MERCUTIO ...
YOU PREPARED THAT ROSE TEA FOR HIM, DIDN'T YOU? EVEN THOUGH HE DISAPPEARED ON THE SUMMER SOLSTICE, LEAVING YOU ALL ALONE...?

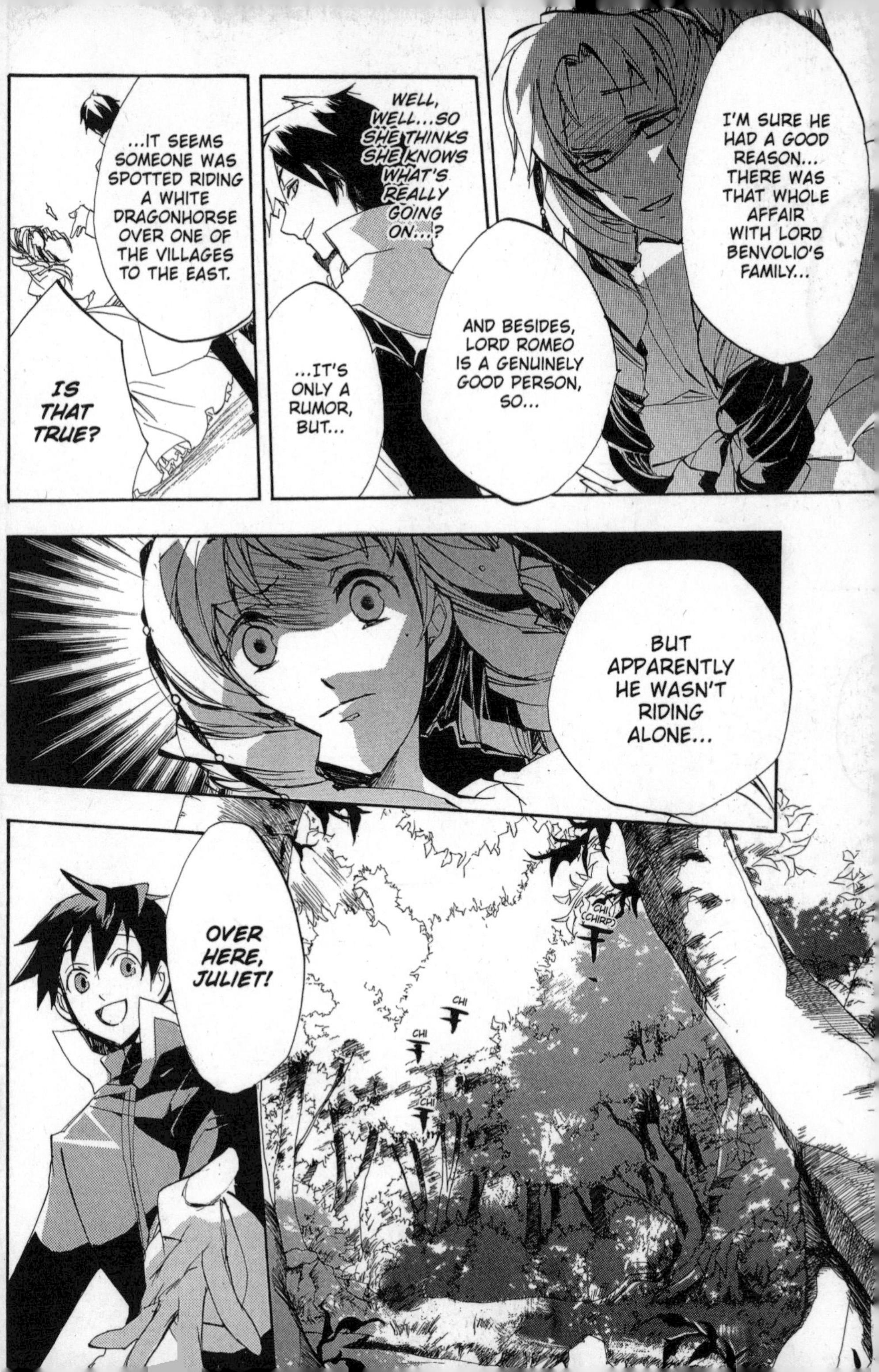
I'M SURE HE HAD A GOOD REASON... THERE WAS THAT WHOLE AFFAIR WITH LORD BENVOLIO'S FAMILY...
AND BESIDES, LORD ROMEO IS A GENUINELY GOOD PERSON, SO...
WELL, WELL...SO SHE THINKS SHE KNOWS WHAT'S REALLY GOING ON...?
...IT'S ONLY A RUMOR, BUT...
...IT SEEMS SOMEONE WAS SPOTTED RIDING A WHITE DRAGONHORSE OVER ONE OF THE VILLAGES TO THE EAST.
IS THAT TRUE?
BUT APPARENTLY HE WASN'T RIDING ALONE...
CHI (CHIRP)
CHI
CHI
CHI
OVER HERE, JULIET!

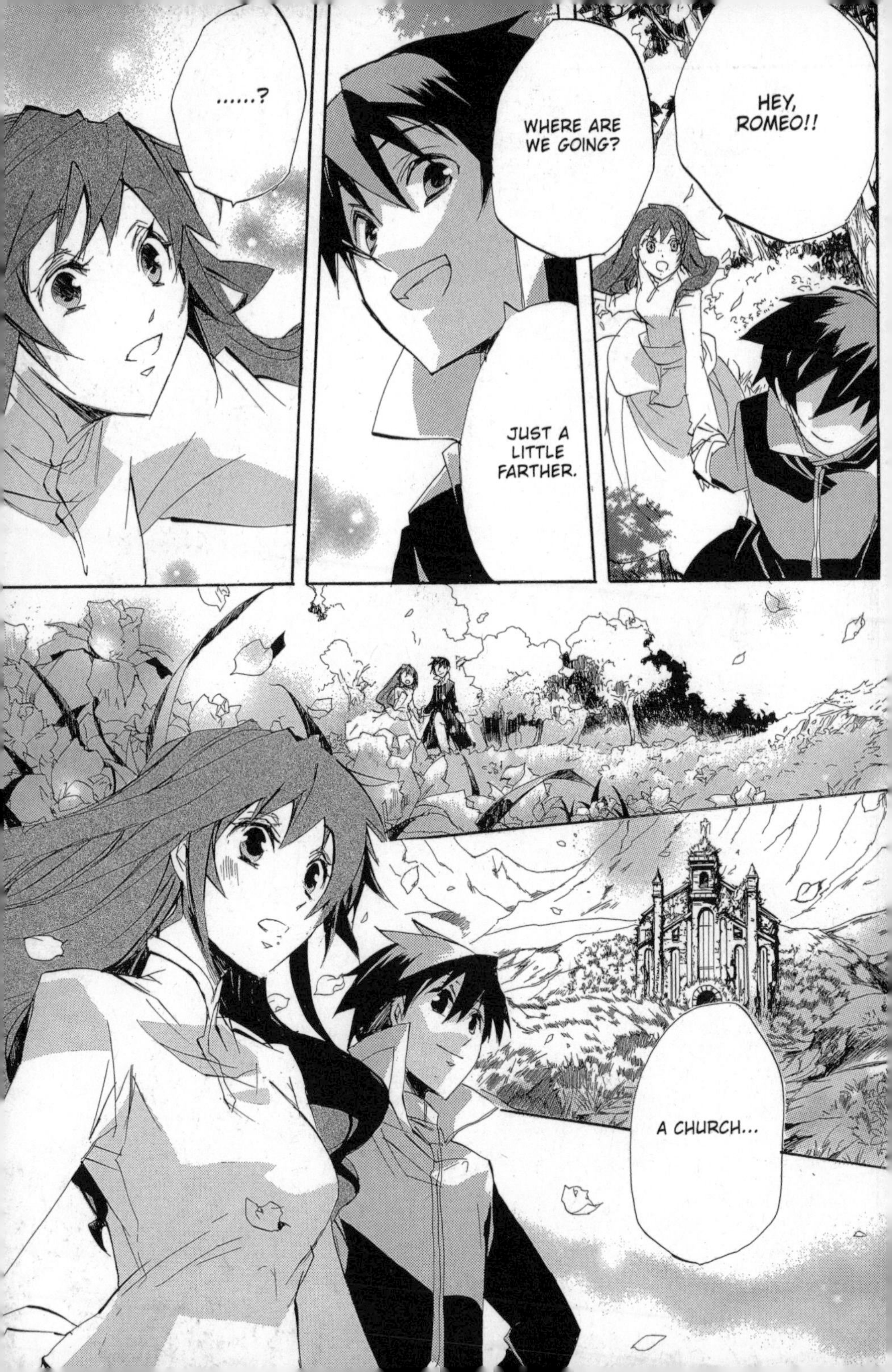
HEY, ROMEO!!
WHERE ARE WE GOING?
JUST A LITTLE FARTHER.
......?
A CHURCH...

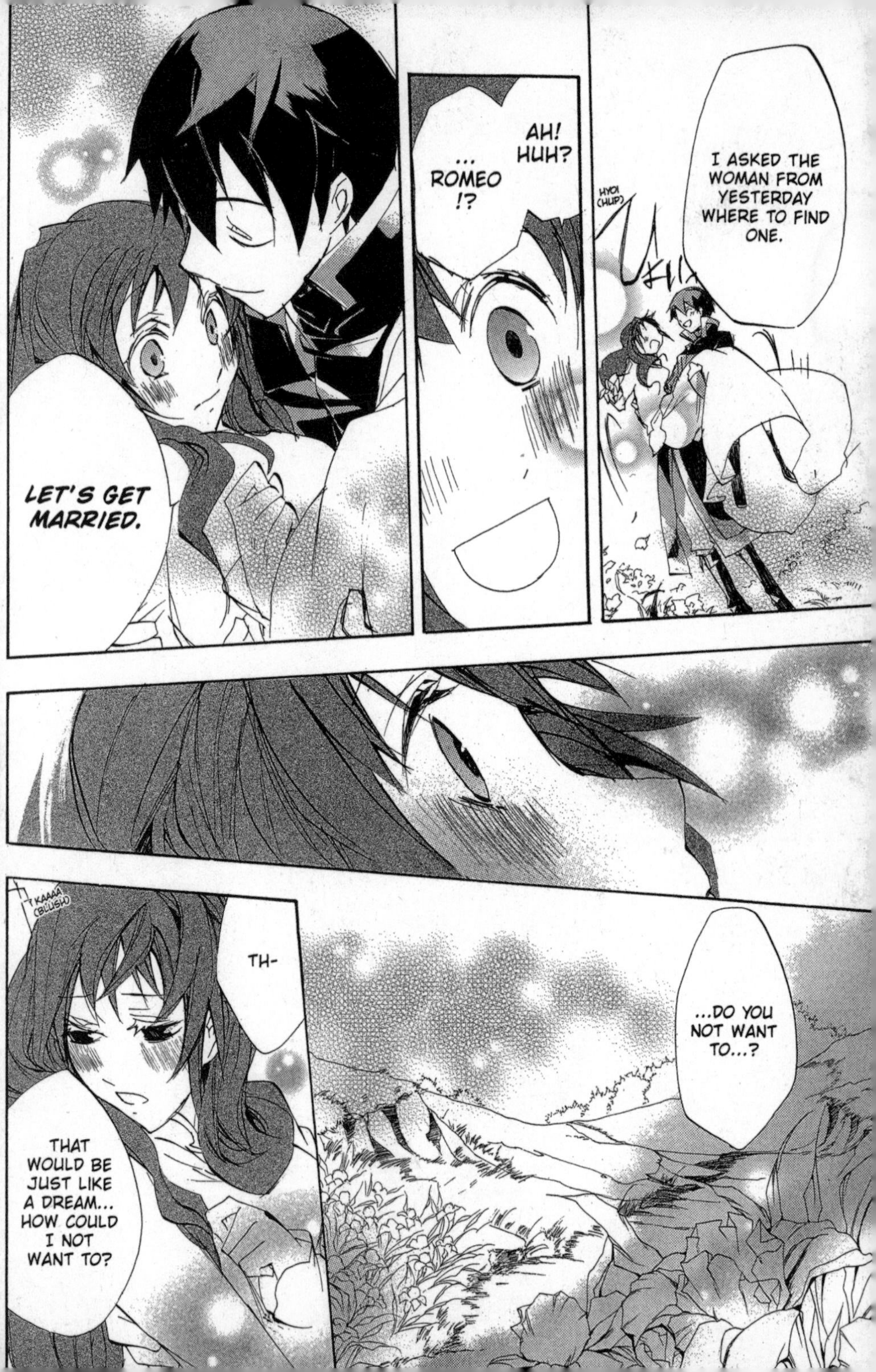
HYOI (HUP)
I ASKED THE WOMAN FROM YESTERDAY WHERE TO FIND ONE.
AH! HUH?
...ROMEO!?
LET'S GET MARRIED.
...DO YOU NOT WANT TO...?
TH-
KAAAA (BLUSH)
THAT WOULD BE JUST LIKE A DREAM... HOW COULD I NOT WANT TO?

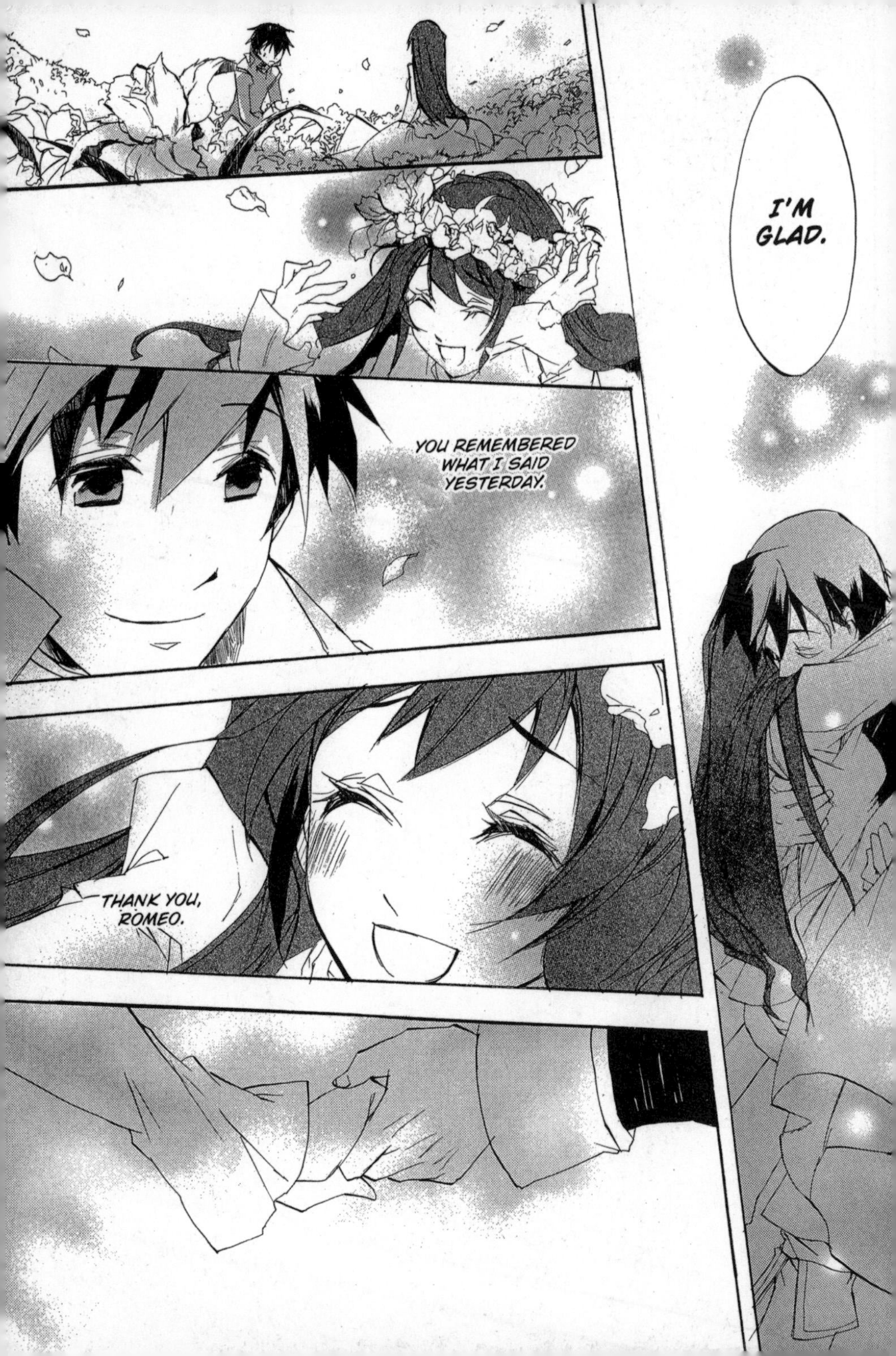
I'M GLAD.
YOU REMEMBERED WHAT I SAID YESTERDAY.
THANK YOU, ROMEO.

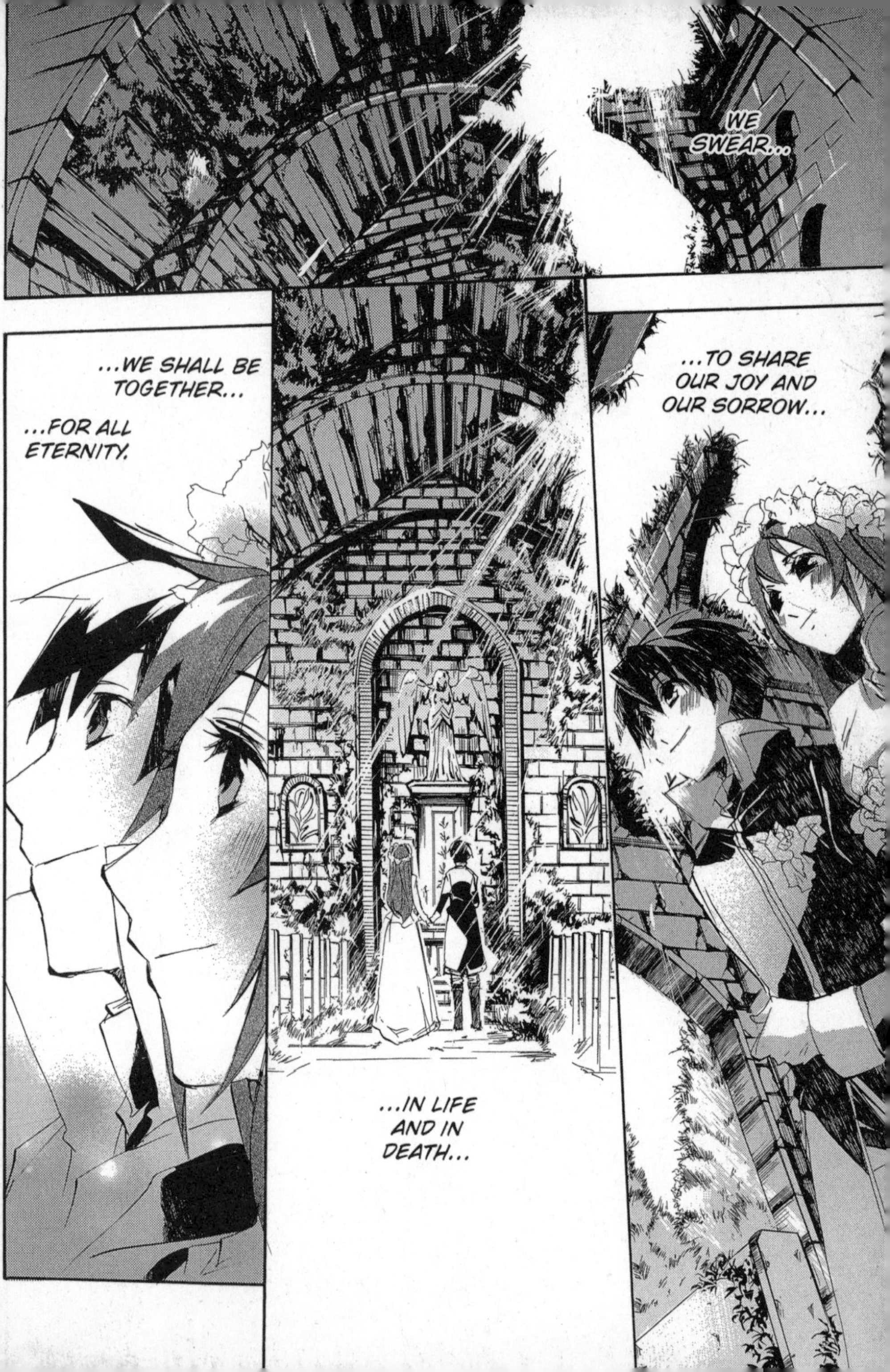
WE SWEAR...
...TO SHARE OUR JOY AND OUR SORROW...
...IN LIFE AND IN DEATH...
...WE SHALL BE TOGETHER...
...FOR ALL ETERNITY.

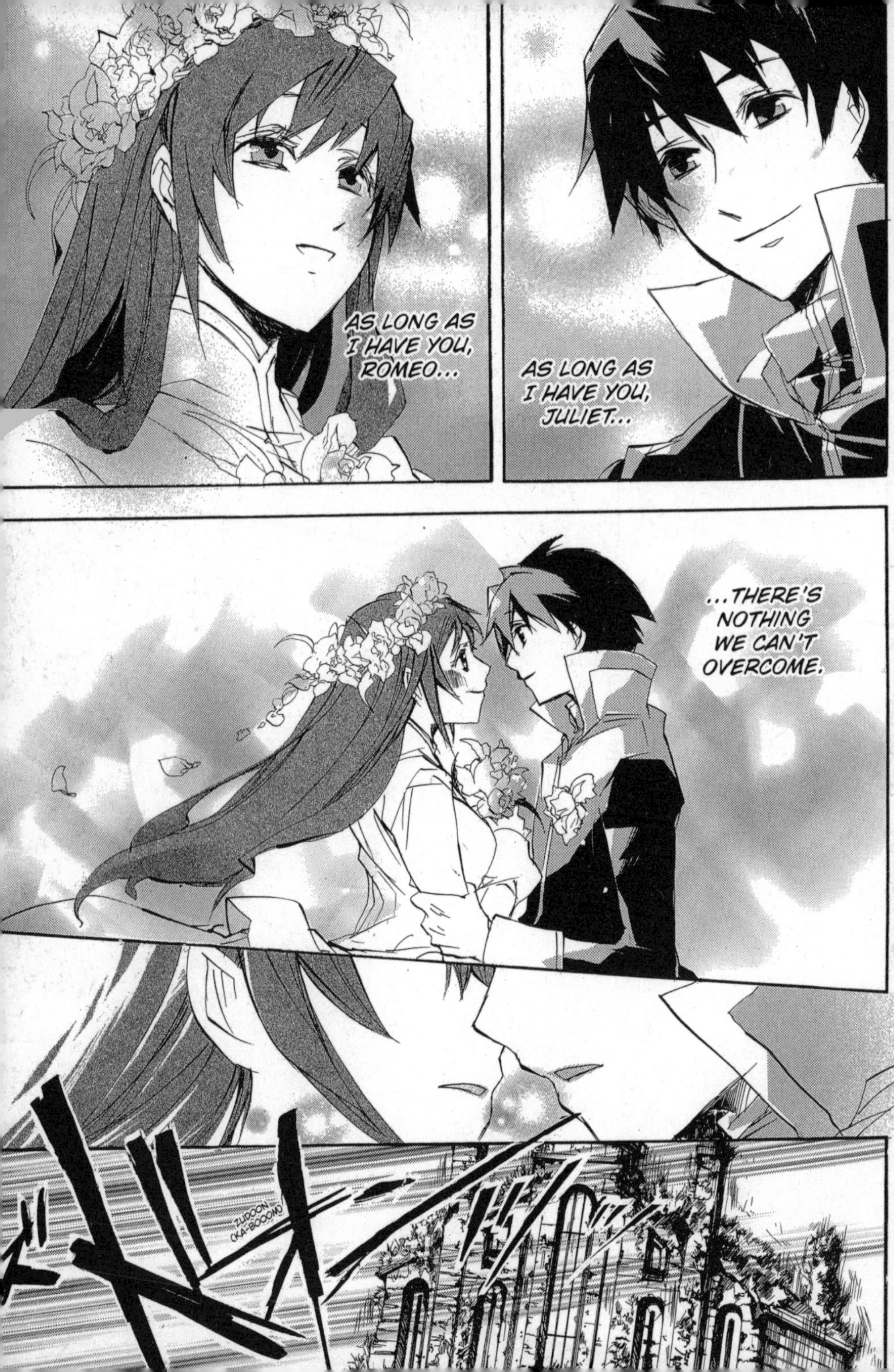
AS LONG AS I HAVE YOU, JULIET...
AS LONG AS I HAVE YOU, ROMEO...
...THERE'S NOTHING WE CAN'T OVERCOME.
ZUDOON (KA-BOOOM)

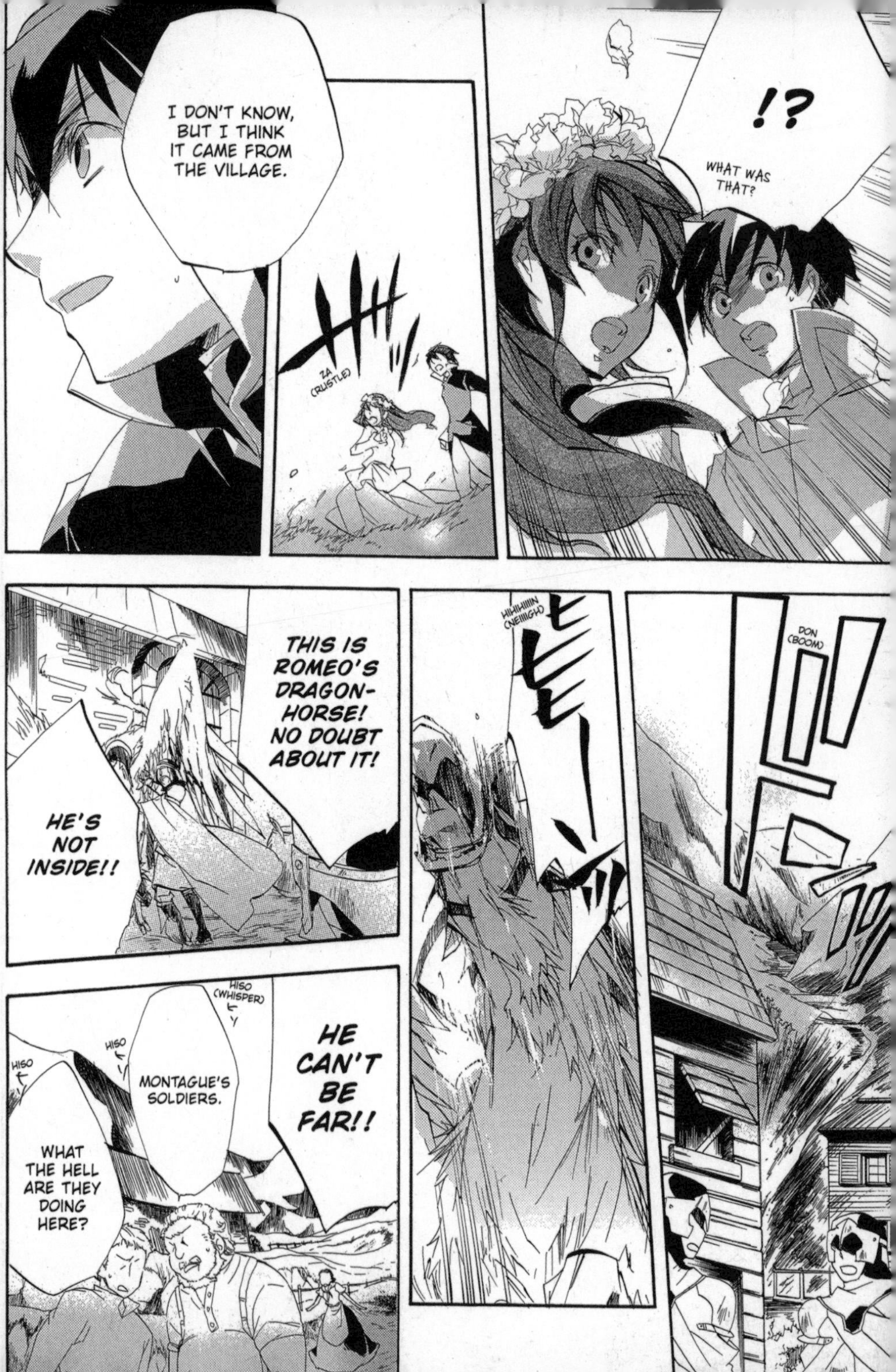
!?
WHAT WAS THAT?
ZA (RUSTLE)
I DON'T KNOW, BUT I THINK IT CAME FROM THE VILLAGE.
DON (BOOM)
HIHIHIIIIN (NEIIIIGH)
THIS IS ROMEO'S DRAGON-HORSE! NO DOUBT ABOUT IT!
HE'S NOT INSIDE!!
HE CAN'T BE FAR!!
HISO (WHISPER)
MONTAGUE'S SOLDIERS.
HISO
HISO
WHAT THE HELL ARE THEY DOING HERE?

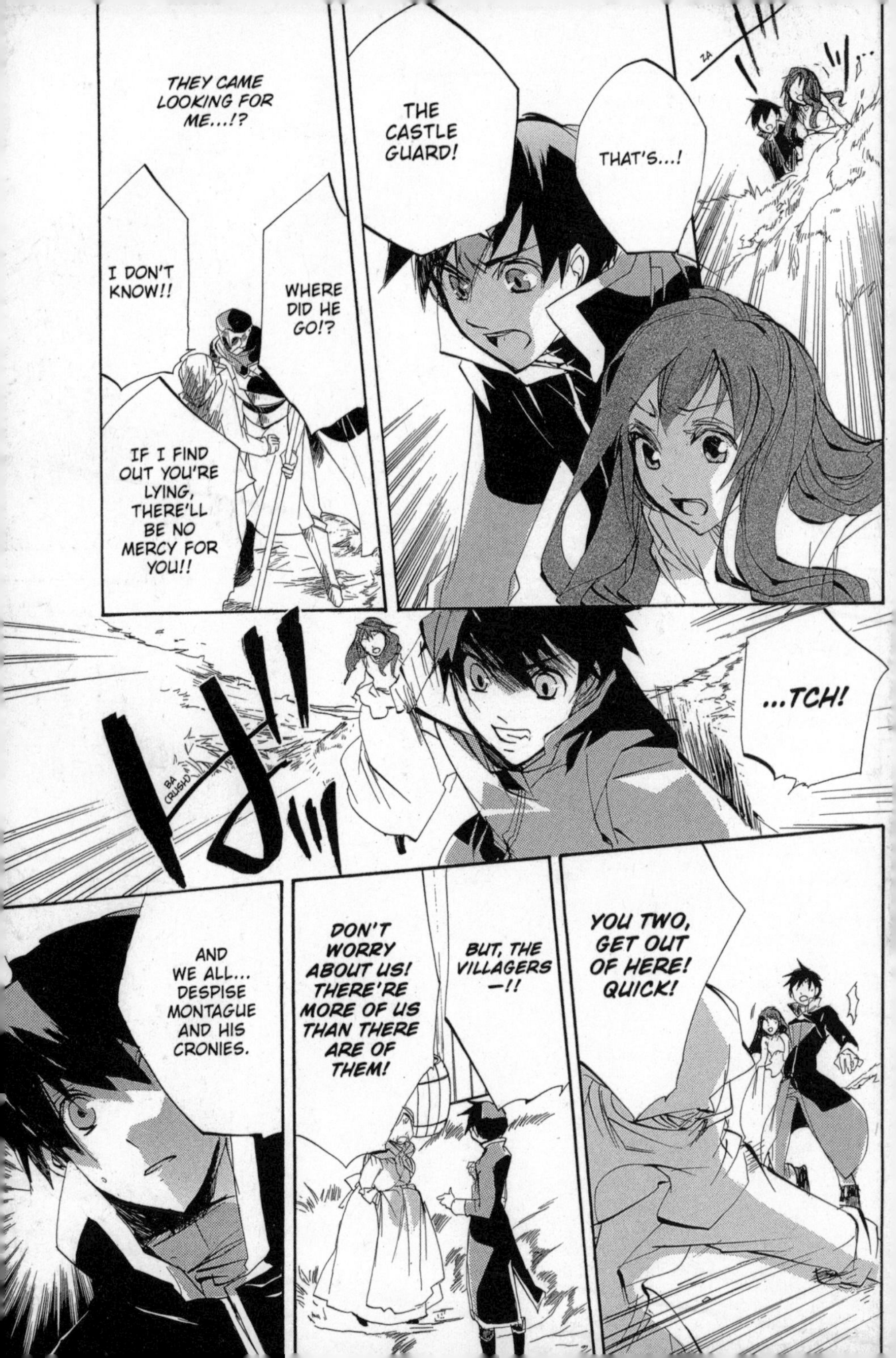
ZA
THAT'S...!
THE CASTLE GUARD!
THEY CAME LOOKING FOR ME...!?
WHERE DID HE GO!?
I DON'T KNOW!!
IF I FIND OUT YOU'RE LYING, THERE'LL BE NO MERCY FOR YOU!!
...TCH!
BA
CRUSHD
YOU TWO, GET OUT OF HERE! QUICK!
BUT, THE VILLAGERS—!!
DON'T WORRY ABOUT US! THERE'RE MORE OF US THAN THERE ARE OF THEM!
AND WE ALL... DESPISE MONTAGUE AND HIS CRONIES.

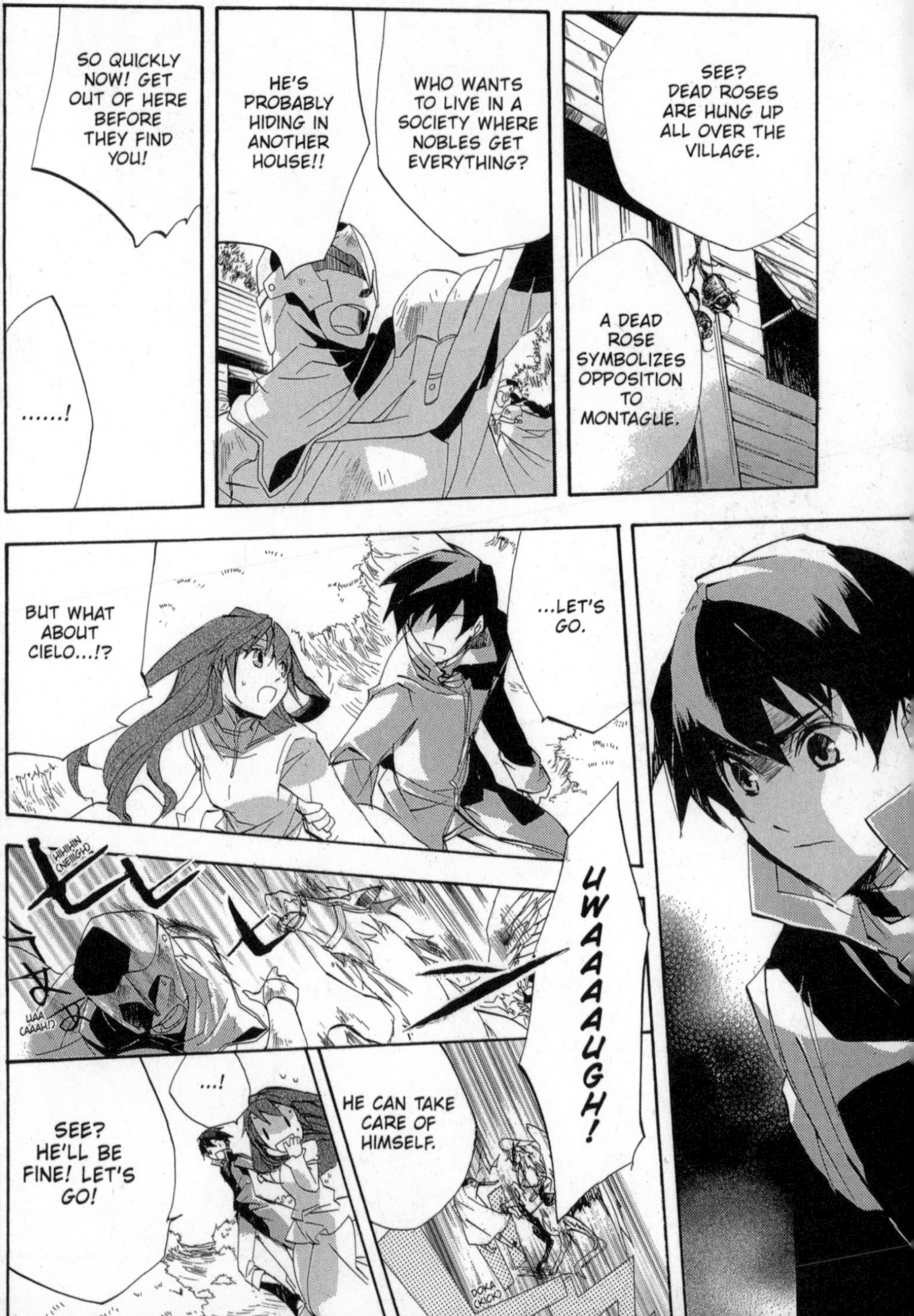
SEE? DEAD ROSES ARE HUNG UP ALL OVER THE VILLAGE.
A DEAD ROSE SYMBOLIZES OPPOSITION TO MONTAGUE.
WHO WANTS TO LIVE IN A SOCIETY WHERE NOBLES GET EVERYTHING?
HE'S PROBABLY HIDING IN ANOTHER HOUSE!!
SO QUICKLY NOW! GET OUT OF HERE BEFORE THEY FIND YOU!
......!
...LET'S GO.
BUT WHAT ABOUT CIELO...!?
UWAAAAAUGH!
HIHIHIN (NEIIIGH)
UAA (AAAH!)
HE CAN TAKE CARE OF HIMSELF.
DOKA (KICK)
...!
SEE? HE'LL BE FINE! LET'S GO!

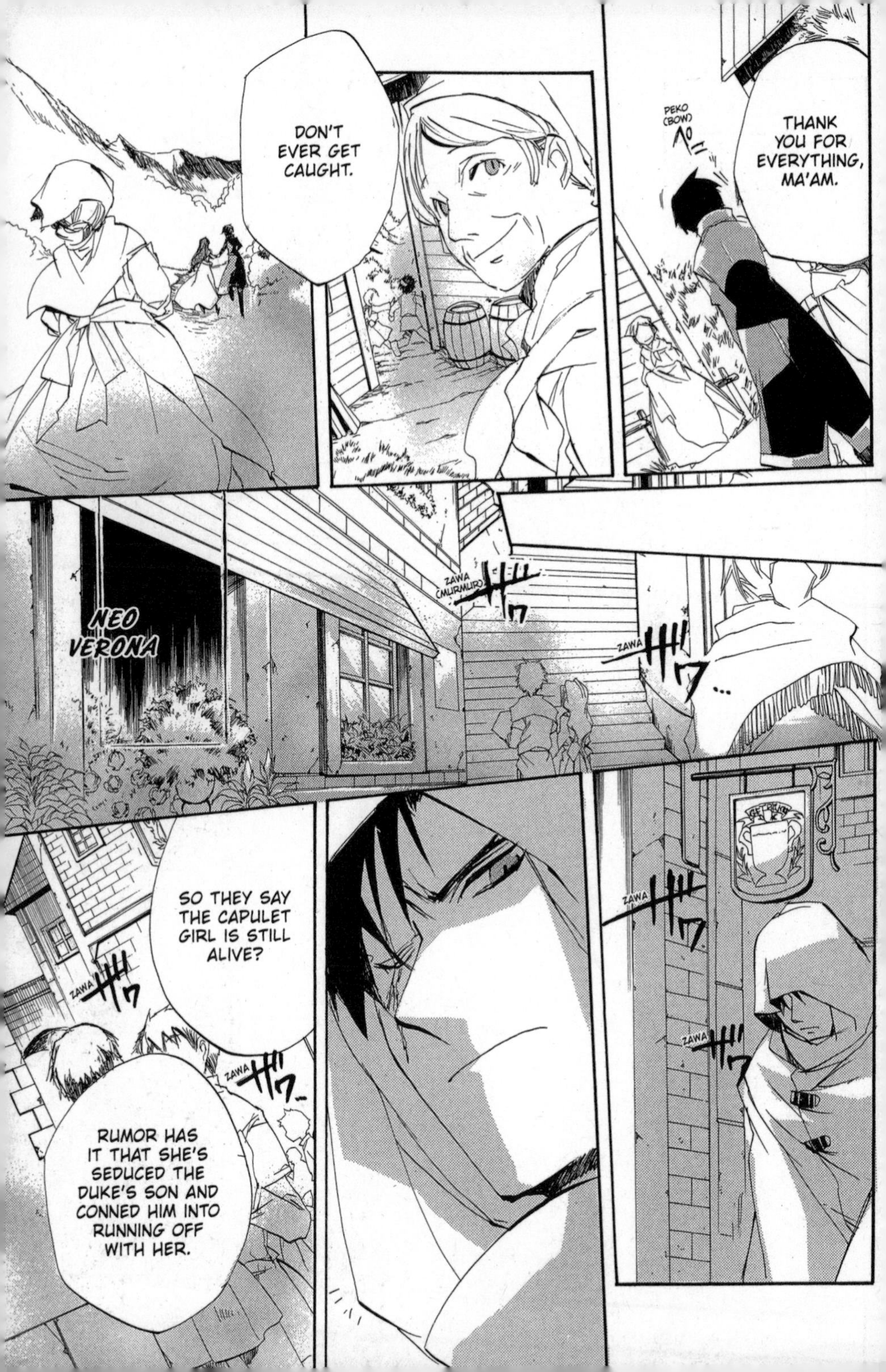
PEKO (BOW)
THANK YOU FOR EVERYTHING, MA'AM.
DON'T EVER GET CAUGHT.
ZAWA
...
ZAWA (MURMUR)
NEO VERONA
ZAWA
ZAWA
SO THEY SAY THE CAPULET GIRL IS STILL ALIVE?
ZAWA
ZAWA
RUMOR HAS IT THAT SHE'S SEDUCED THE DUKE'S SON AND CONNED HIM INTO RUNNING OFF WITH HER.

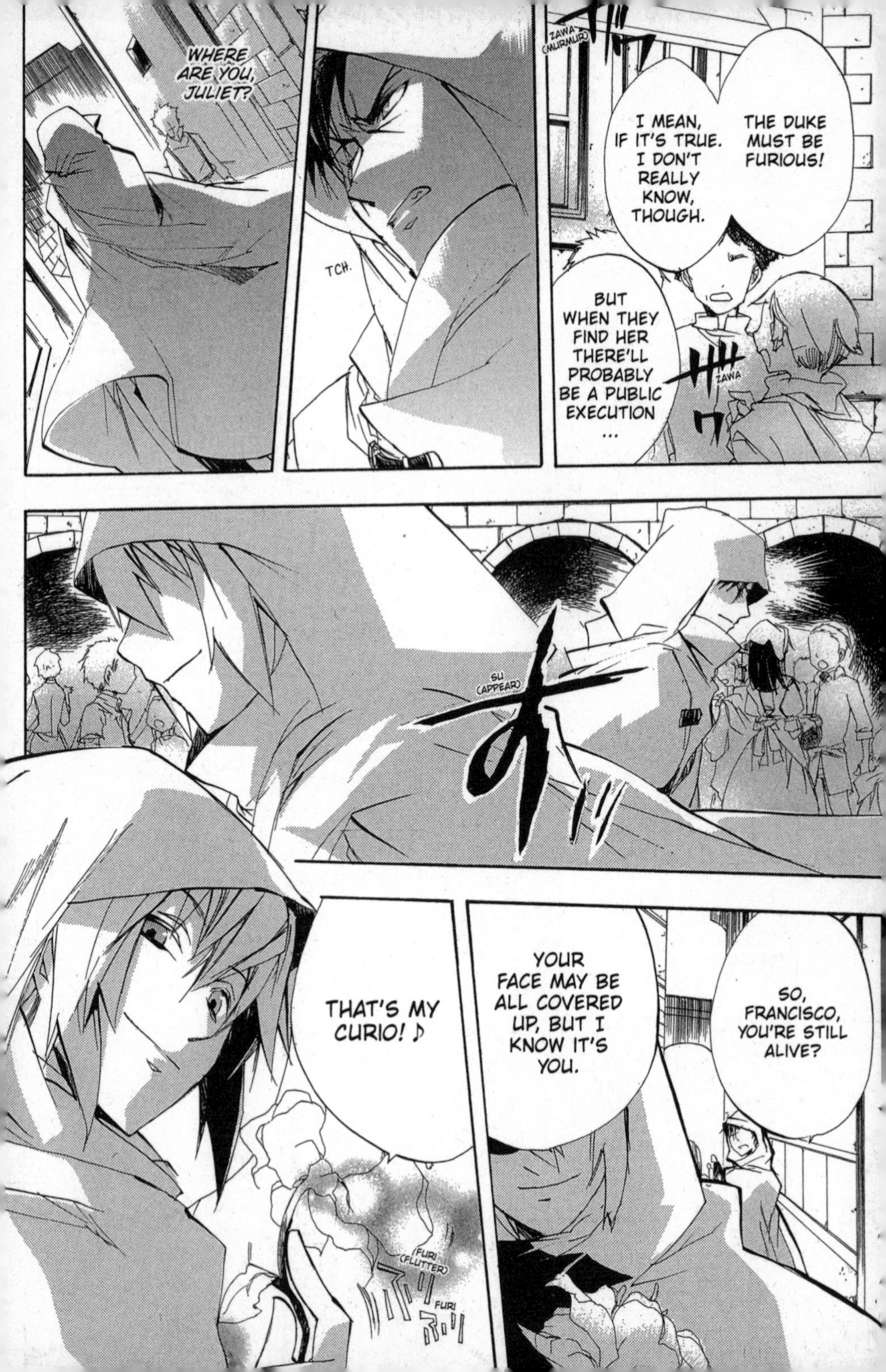
ZAWA (MURMUR)
THE DUKE MUST BE FURIOUS!
I MEAN, IF IT'S TRUE. I DON'T REALLY KNOW, THOUGH.
BUT WHEN THEY FIND HER THERE'LL PROBABLY BE A PUBLIC EXECUTION ...
ZAWA
TCH.
WHERE ARE YOU, JULIET?
SU (APPEAR)
SO, FRANCISCO, YOU'RE STILL ALIVE?
YOUR FACE MAY BE ALL COVERED UP, BUT I KNOW IT'S YOU.
THAT'S MY CURIO! ♪
FURI (FLUTTER)
FURI

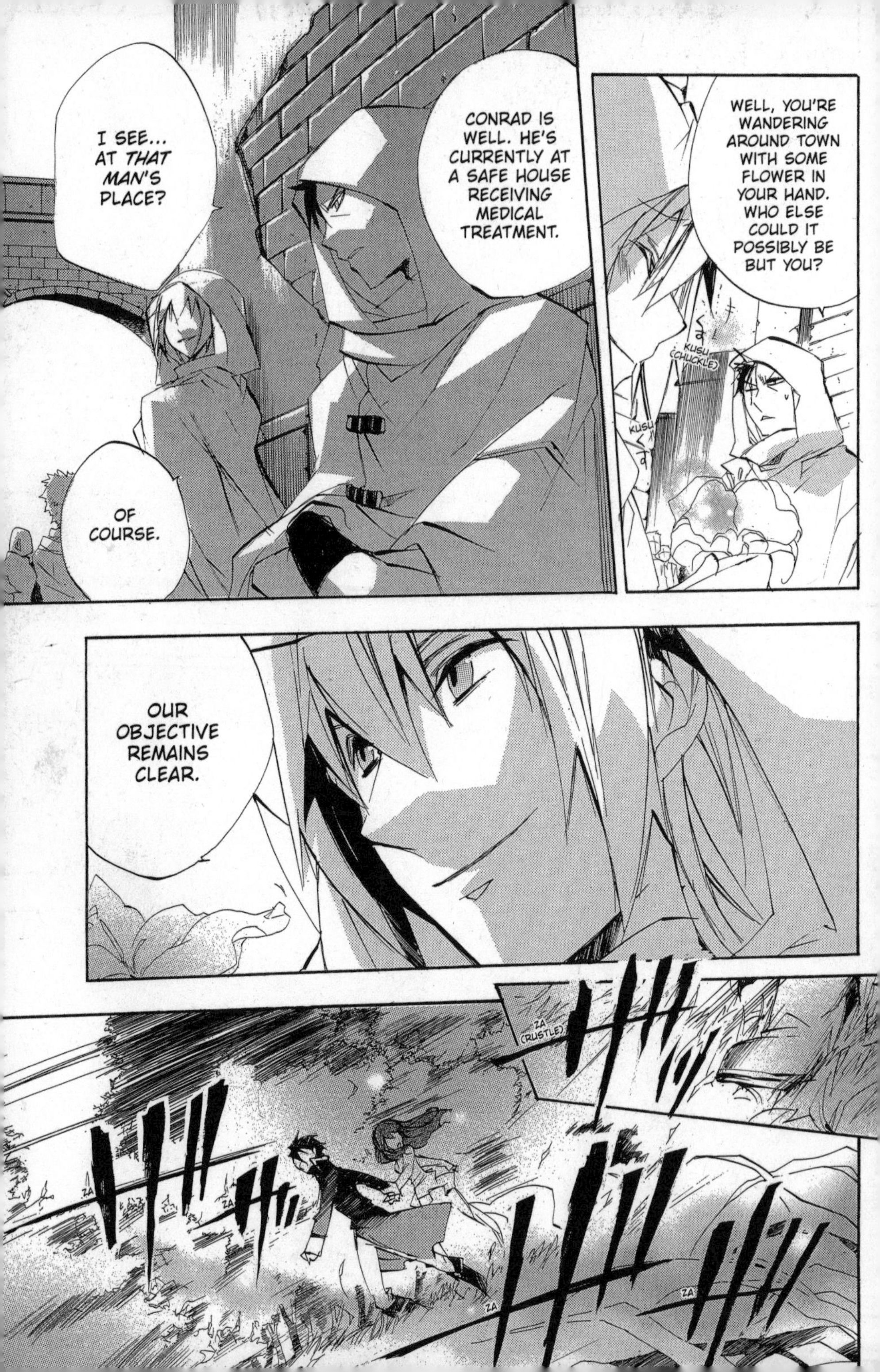
WELL, YOU'RE WANDERING AROUND TOWN WITH SOME FLOWER IN YOUR HAND. WHO ELSE COULD IT POSSIBLY BE BUT YOU?
KUSU (CHUCKLE)
KUSU
CONRAD IS WELL. HE'S CURRENTLY AT A SAFE HOUSE RECEIVING MEDICAL TREATMENT.
I SEE... AT *THAT MAN'S* PLACE?
OF COURSE.
OUR OBJECTIVE REMAINS CLEAR.
ZA (RUSTLE)
ZA
ZA
ZA

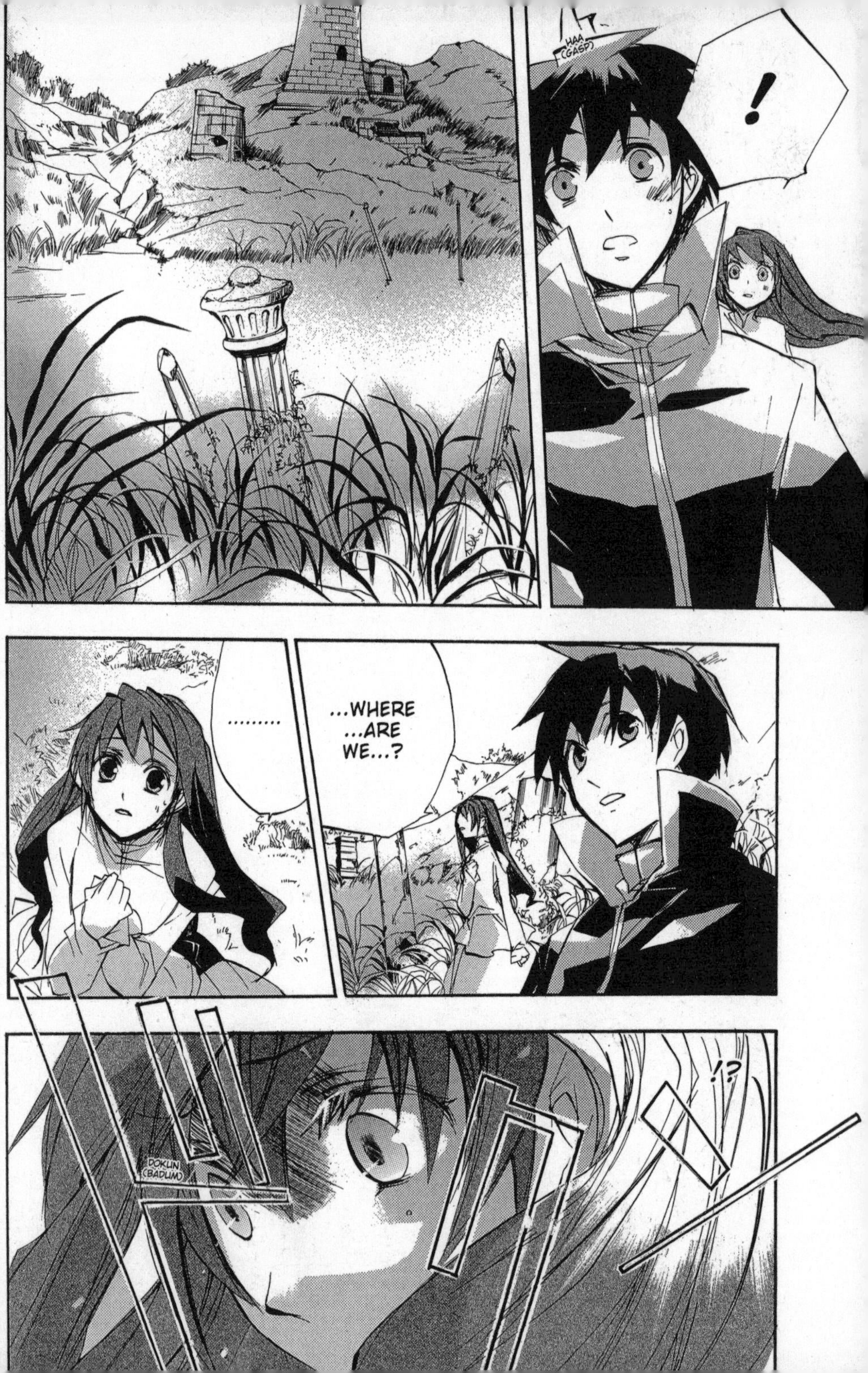
HAA (GASP)
!
...WHERE ...ARE WE...?
....
!?
DOKUN (BADUM)

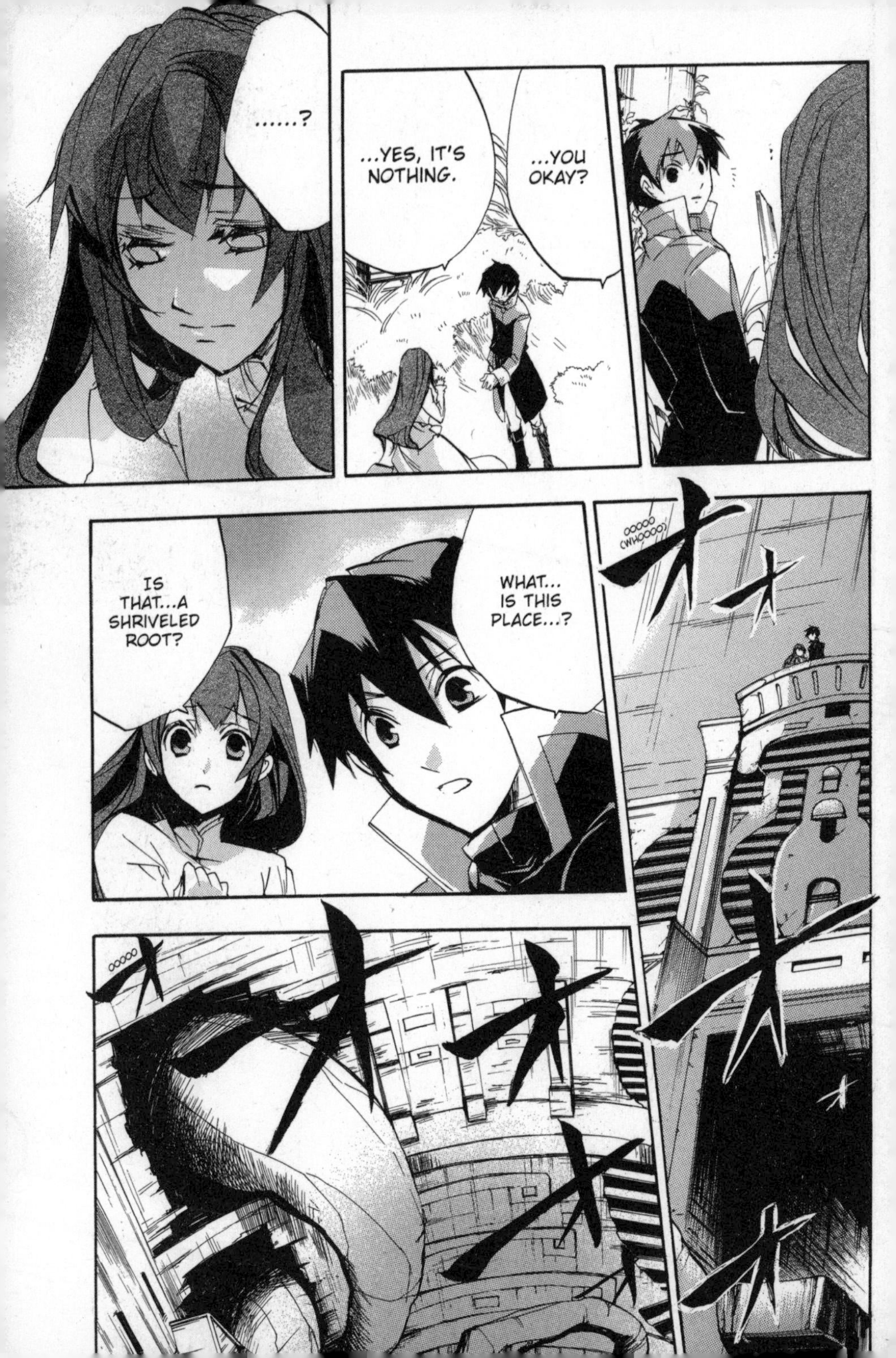
...YOU OKAY?
...YES, IT'S NOTHING.
......?
OOOOO (WHOOOOO)
WHAT... IS THIS PLACE...?
IS THAT...A SHRIVELED ROOT?
OOOOO

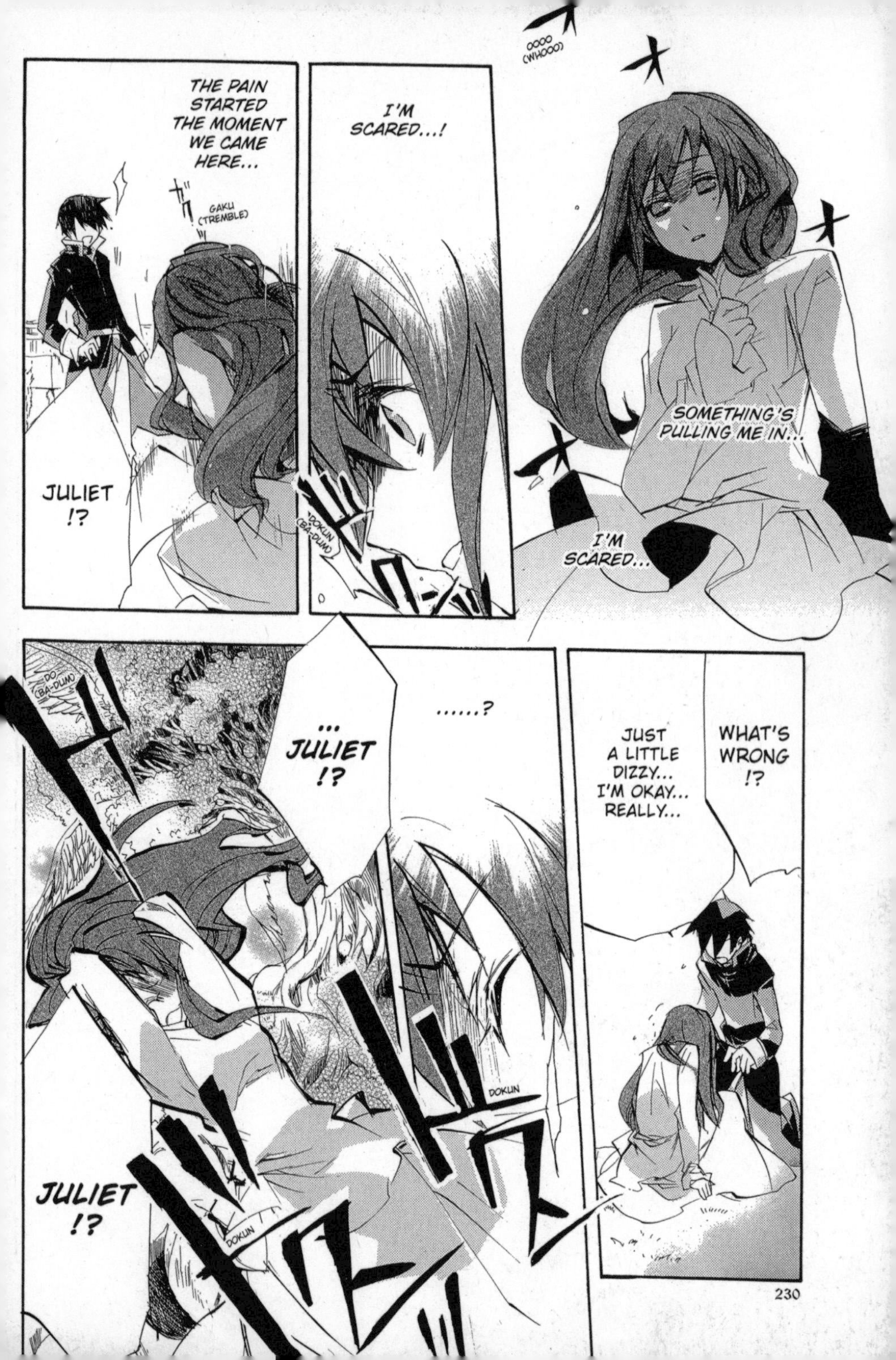
OOOO (WHOOO)
SOMETHING'S PULLING ME IN...
I'M SCARED...
I'M SCARED...!
DOKUN (BA-DUM)
THE PAIN STARTED THE MOMENT WE CAME HERE...
GAKU (TREMBLE)
JULIET !?
WHAT'S WRONG !?
JUST A LITTLE DIZZY... I'M OKAY... REALLY...
......?
...JULIET !?
DO (BA-DUM)
DOKUN
DOKUN
JULIET !?

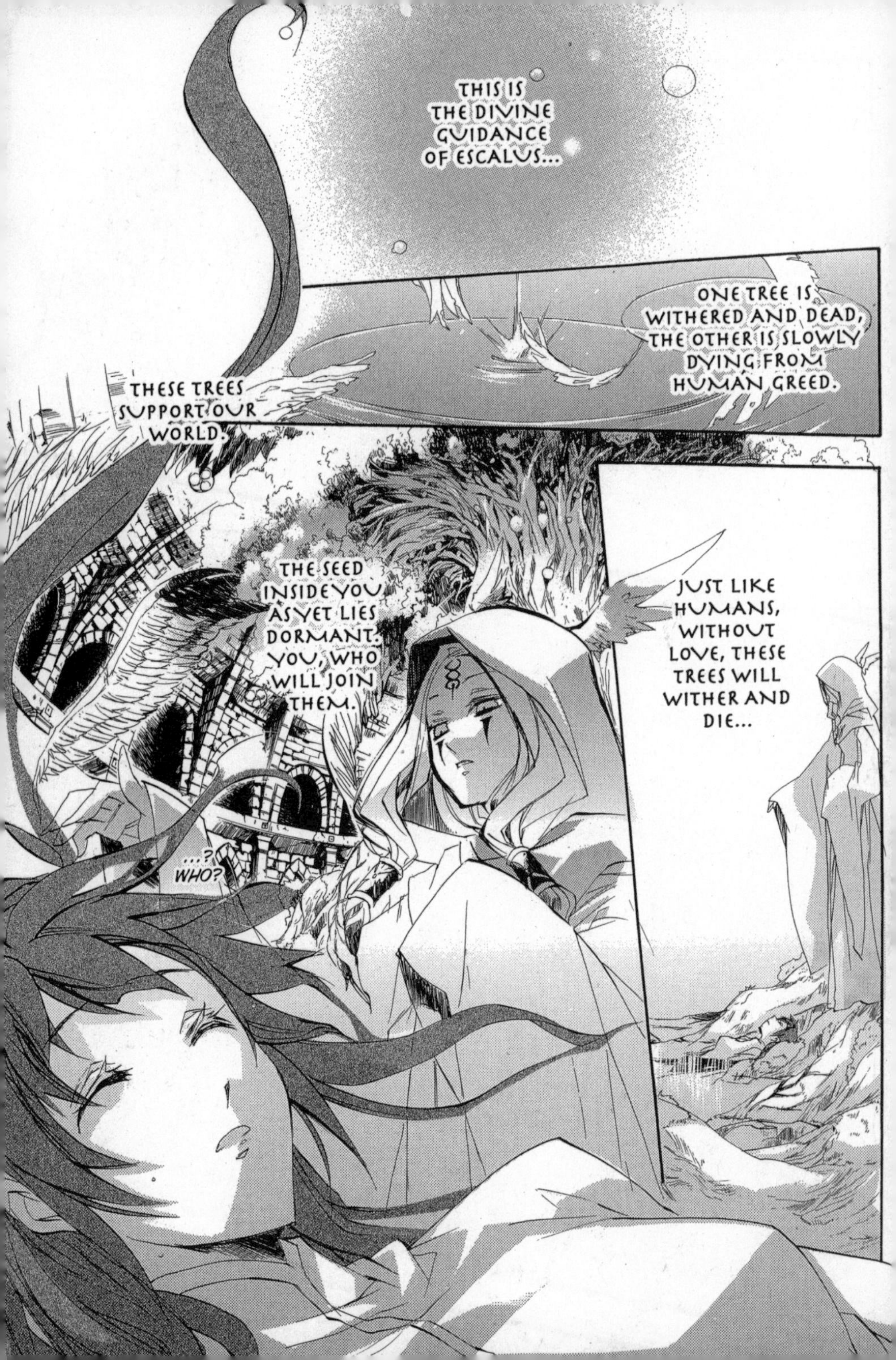
THIS IS THE DIVINE GUIDANCE OF ESCALUS...
ONE TREE IS WITHERED AND DEAD, THE OTHER IS SLOWLY DYING FROM HUMAN GREED.
THESE TREES SUPPORT OUR WORLD.
JUST LIKE HUMANS, WITHOUT LOVE, THESE TREES WILL WITHER AND DIE...
THE SEED INSIDE YOU AS YET LIES DORMANT. YOU, WHO WILL JOIN THEM.
...? WHO?

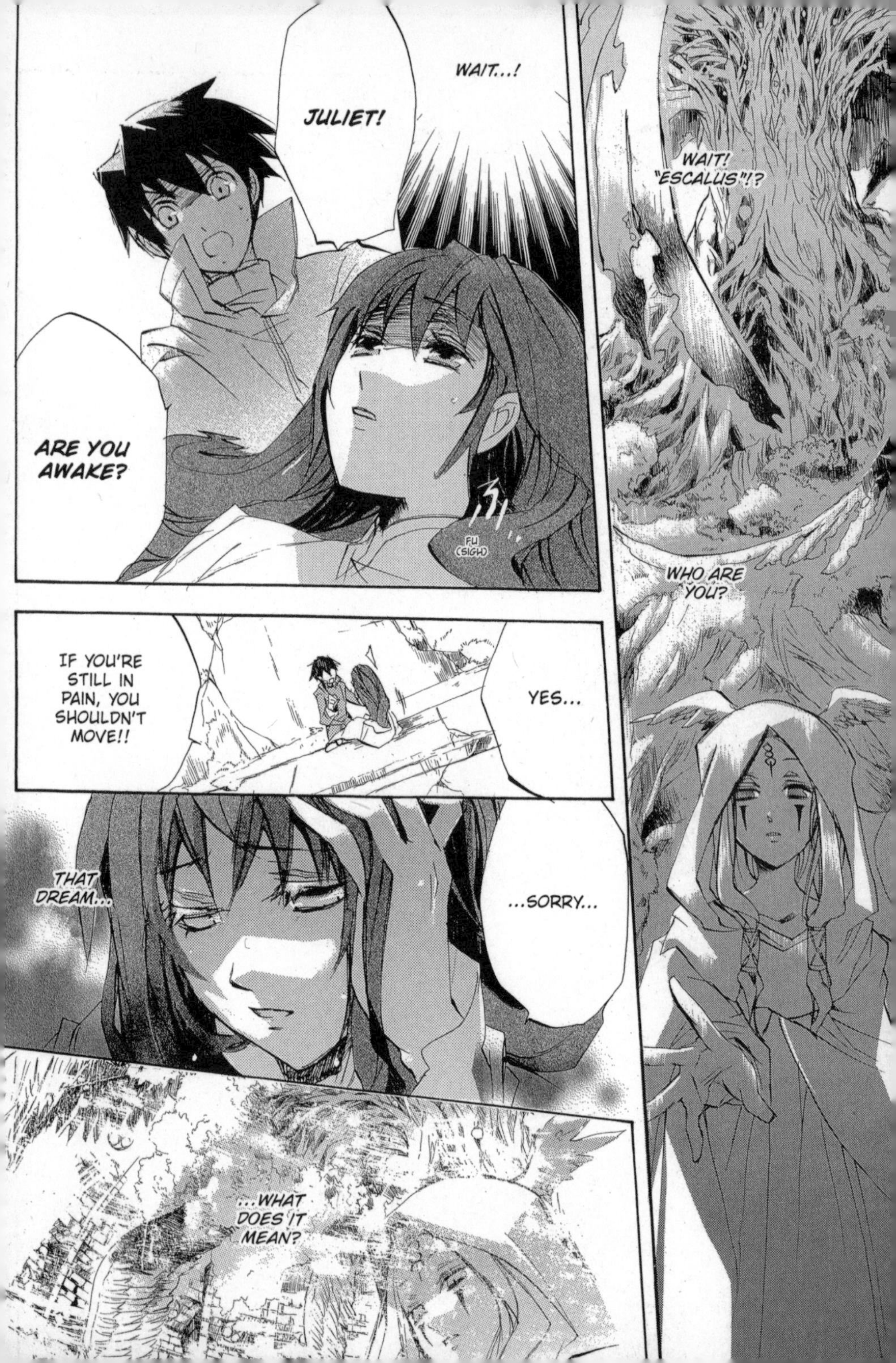
WAIT! "ESCALUS"!?
WHO ARE YOU?
WAIT...!
JULIET!
ARE YOU AWAKE?
FU (SIGH)
YES...
IF YOU'RE STILL IN PAIN, YOU SHOULDN'T MOVE!!
...SORRY...
THAT DREAM...
...WHAT DOES IT MEAN?

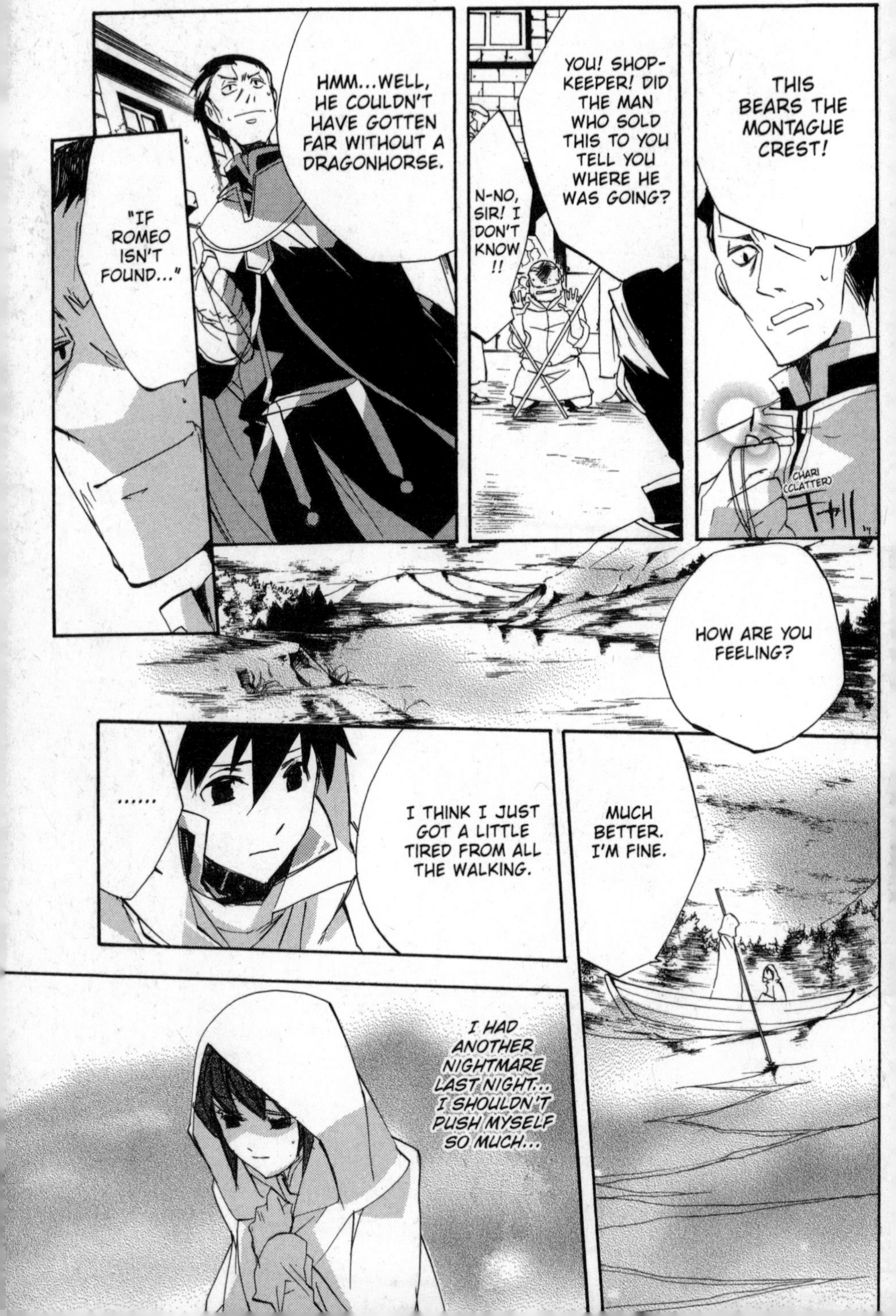
THIS BEARS THE MONTAGUE CREST!
CHARI (CLATTER)
YOU! SHOP-KEEPER! DID THE MAN WHO SOLD THIS TO YOU TELL YOU WHERE HE WAS GOING?
N-NO, SIR! I DON'T KNOW!!
HMM...WELL, HE COULDN'T HAVE GOTTEN FAR WITHOUT A DRAGONHORSE.
"IF ROMEO ISN'T FOUND..."
HOW ARE YOU FEELING?
MUCH BETTER. I'M FINE.
I THINK I JUST GOT A LITTLE TIRED FROM ALL THE WALKING.
......
I HAD ANOTHER NIGHTMARE LAST NIGHT... I SHOULDN'T PUSH MYSELF SO MUCH...

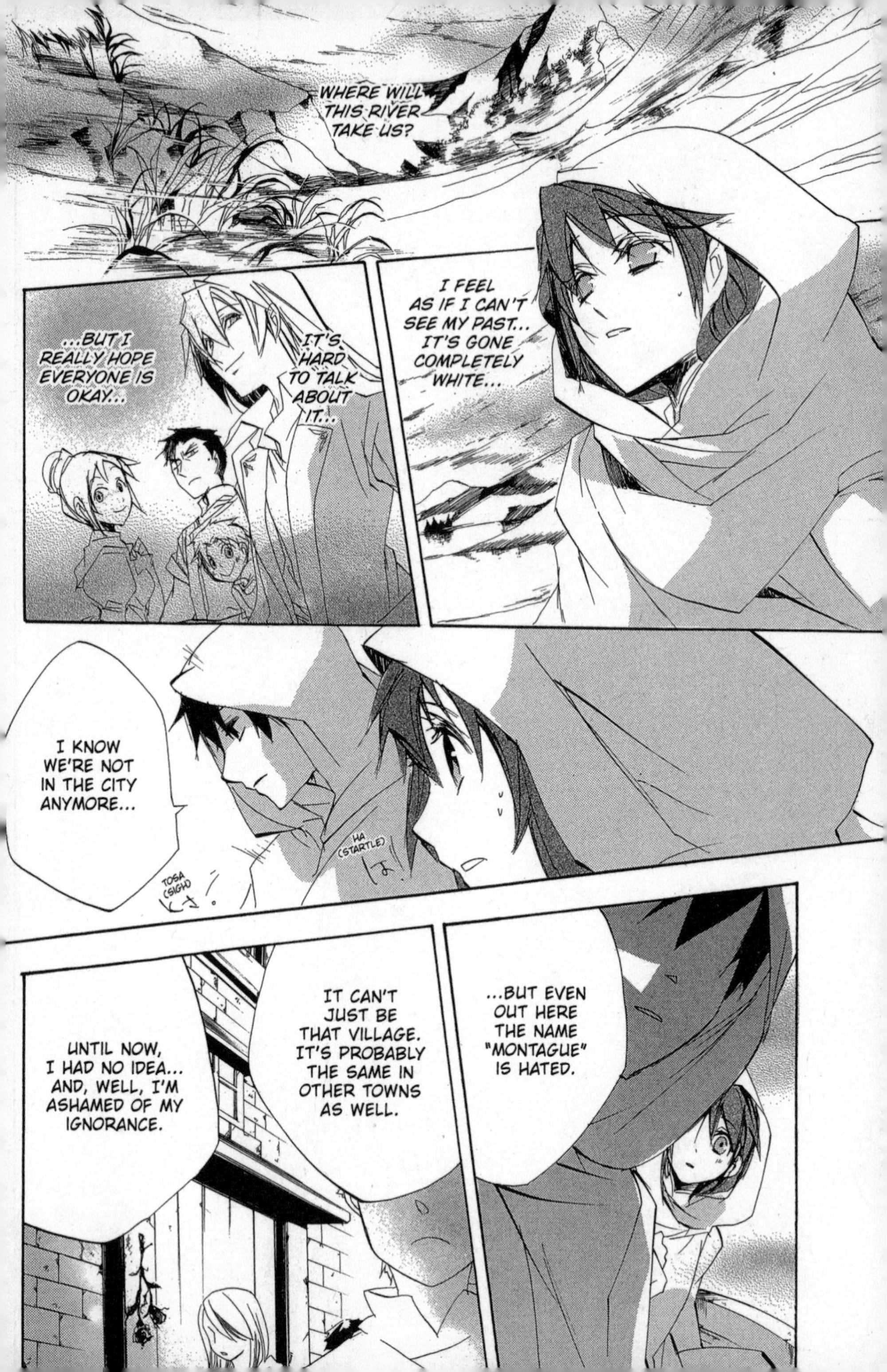
WHERE WILL THIS RIVER TAKE US?
I FEEL AS IF I CAN'T SEE MY PAST... IT'S GONE COMPLETELY WHITE...
IT'S HARD TO TALK ABOUT IT...
...BUT I REALLY HOPE EVERYONE IS OKAY...
I KNOW WE'RE NOT IN THE CITY ANYMORE...
HA (STARTLE)
は
TOSA (SIGH)
とさ。
...BUT EVEN OUT HERE THE NAME "MONTAGUE" IS HATED.
IT CAN'T JUST BE THAT VILLAGE. IT'S PROBABLY THE SAME IN OTHER TOWNS AS WELL.
UNTIL NOW, I HAD NO IDEA... AND, WELL, I'M ASHAMED OF MY IGNORANCE.

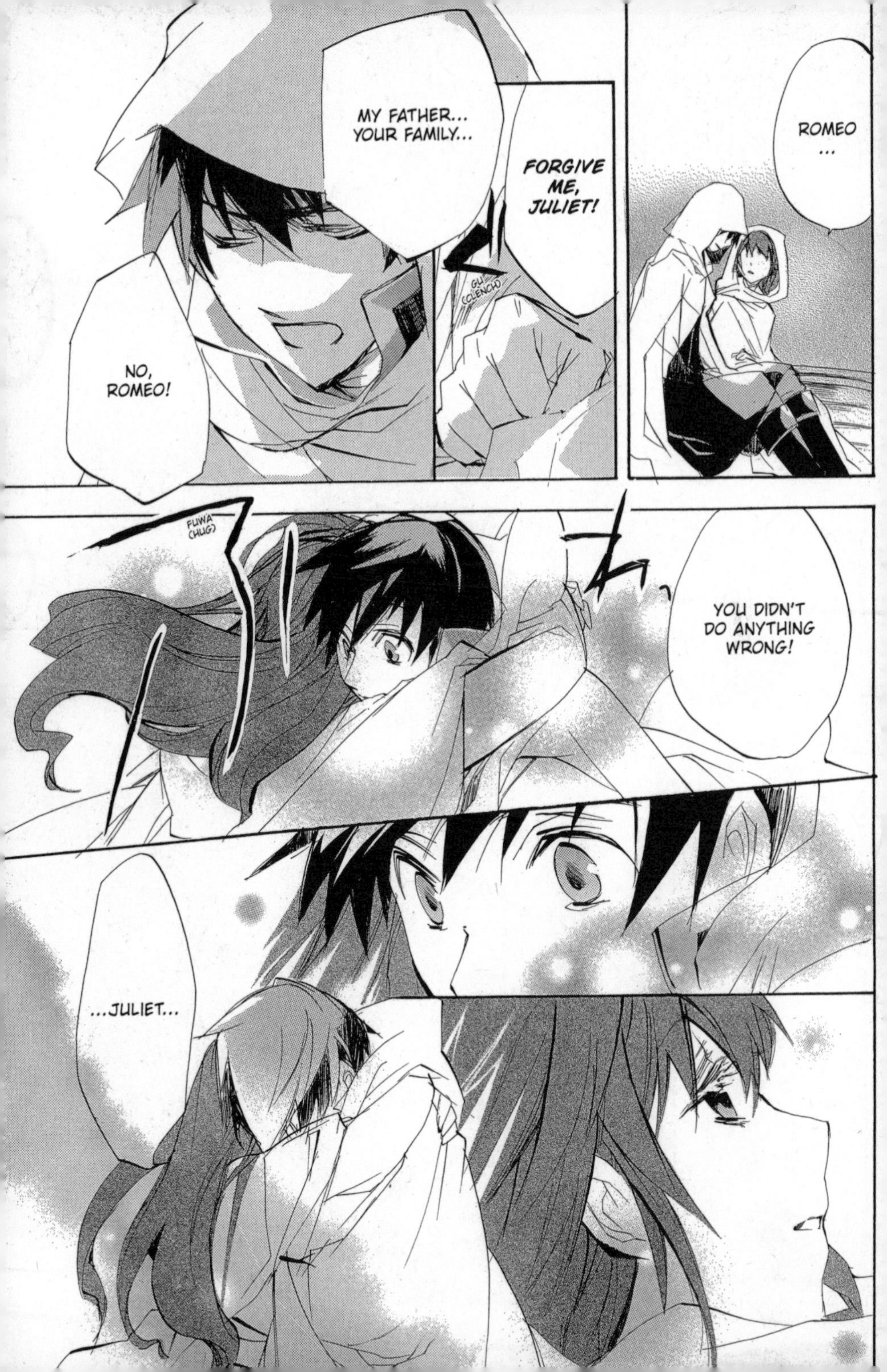
ROMEO ...
MY FATHER... YOUR FAMILY...
FORGIVE ME, JULIET!
GU (CLENCH)
NO, ROMEO!
YOU DIDN'T DO ANYTHING WRONG!
FUWA (HUG)
...JULIET...

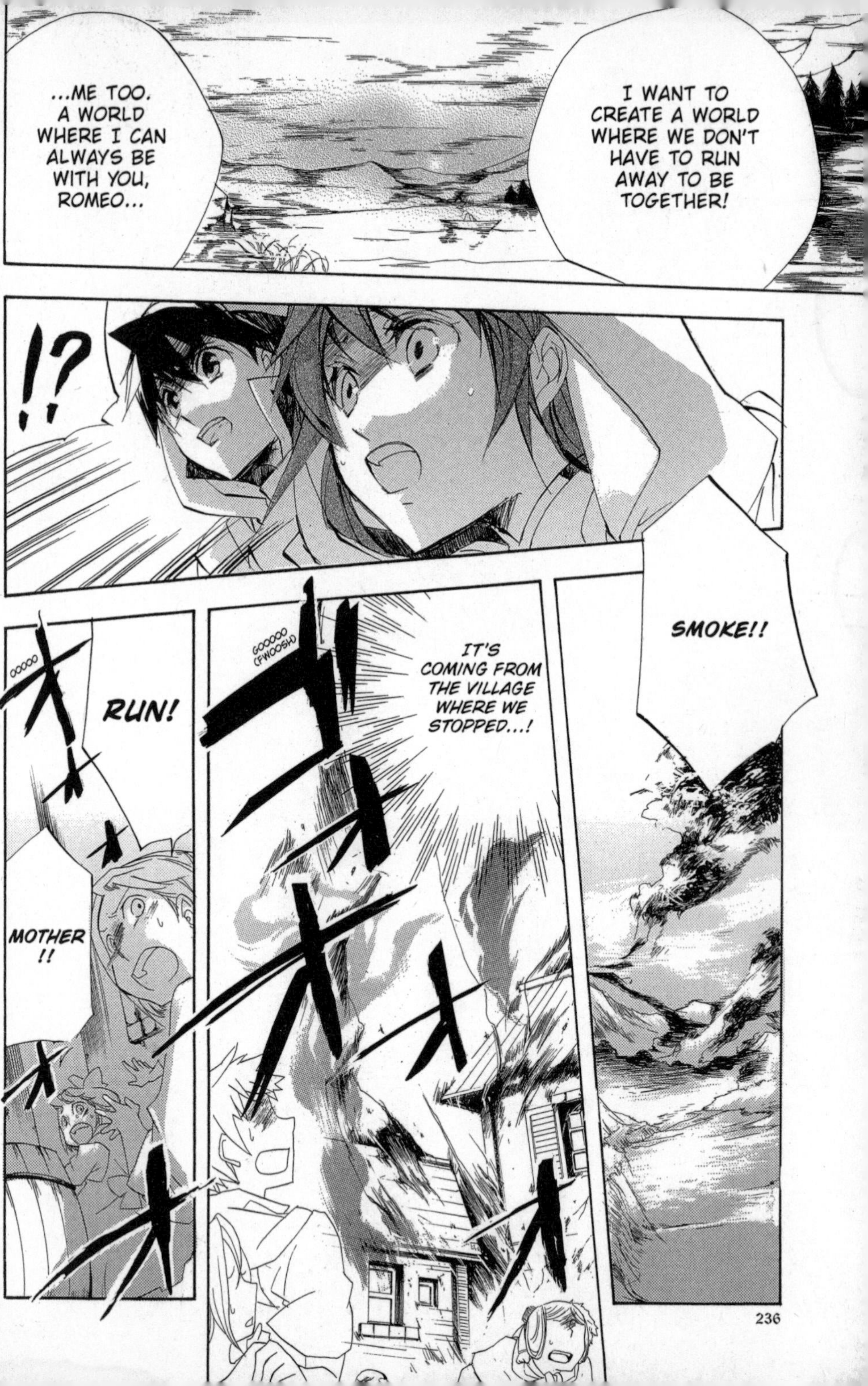
I WANT TO CREATE A WORLD WHERE WE DON'T HAVE TO RUN AWAY TO BE TOGETHER!
...ME TOO. A WORLD WHERE I CAN ALWAYS BE WITH YOU, ROMEO...
!?
SMOKE!!
IT'S COMING FROM THE VILLAGE WHERE WE STOPPED...!
GOOOOO (FWOOSH)
RUN!
OOOOO
MOTHER!!

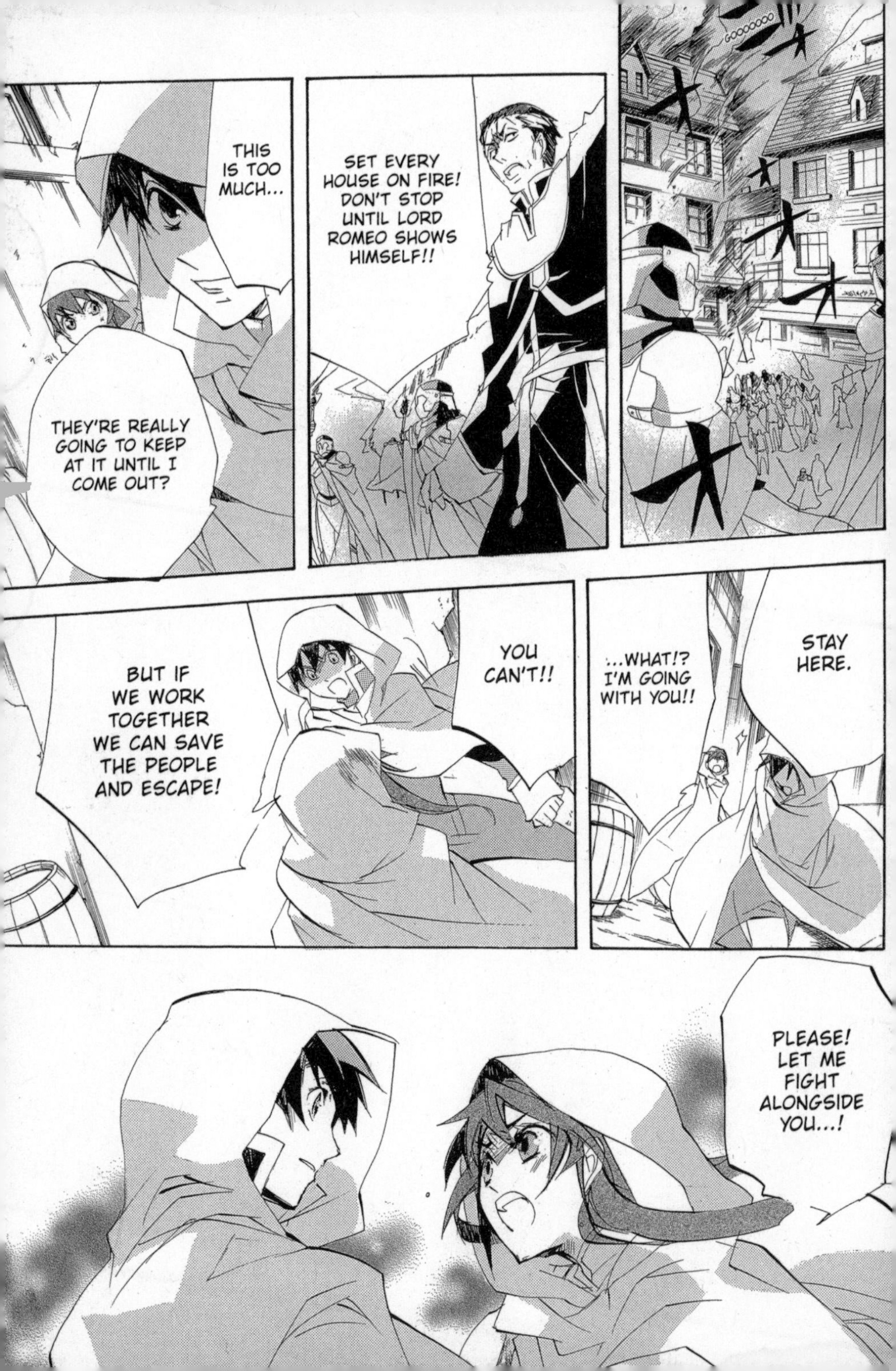
GOOOOOOO
SET EVERY HOUSE ON FIRE! DON'T STOP UNTIL LORD ROMEO SHOWS HIMSELF!!
THIS IS TOO MUCH...
THEY'RE REALLY GOING TO KEEP AT IT UNTIL I COME OUT?
STAY HERE.
...WHAT!? I'M GOING WITH YOU!!
YOU CAN'T!!
BUT IF WE WORK TOGETHER WE CAN SAVE THE PEOPLE AND ESCAPE!
PLEASE! LET ME FIGHT ALONGSIDE YOU...!

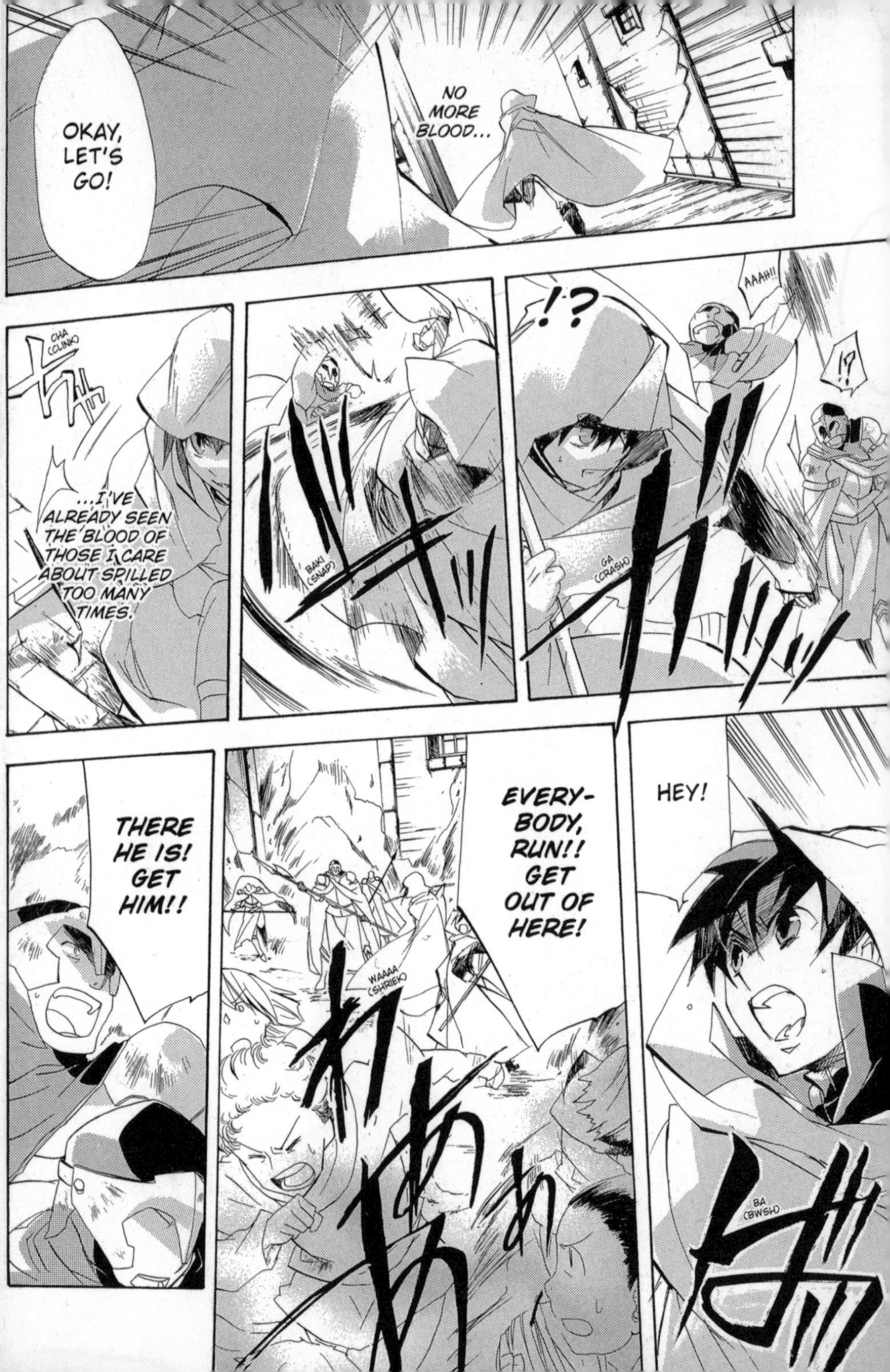

NO MORE BLOOD...
OKAY, LET'S GO!
AAAH!!
!?
!?
GA (CRASH)
BAKI (SNAP)
CHA (CLINK)
...I'VE ALREADY SEEN THE BLOOD OF THOSE I CARE ABOUT SPILLED TOO MANY TIMES.
HEY!
BA (BWSH)
EVERY-BODY, RUN!! GET OUT OF HERE!
WAAAA (SHRIEK)
THERE HE IS! GET HIM!!

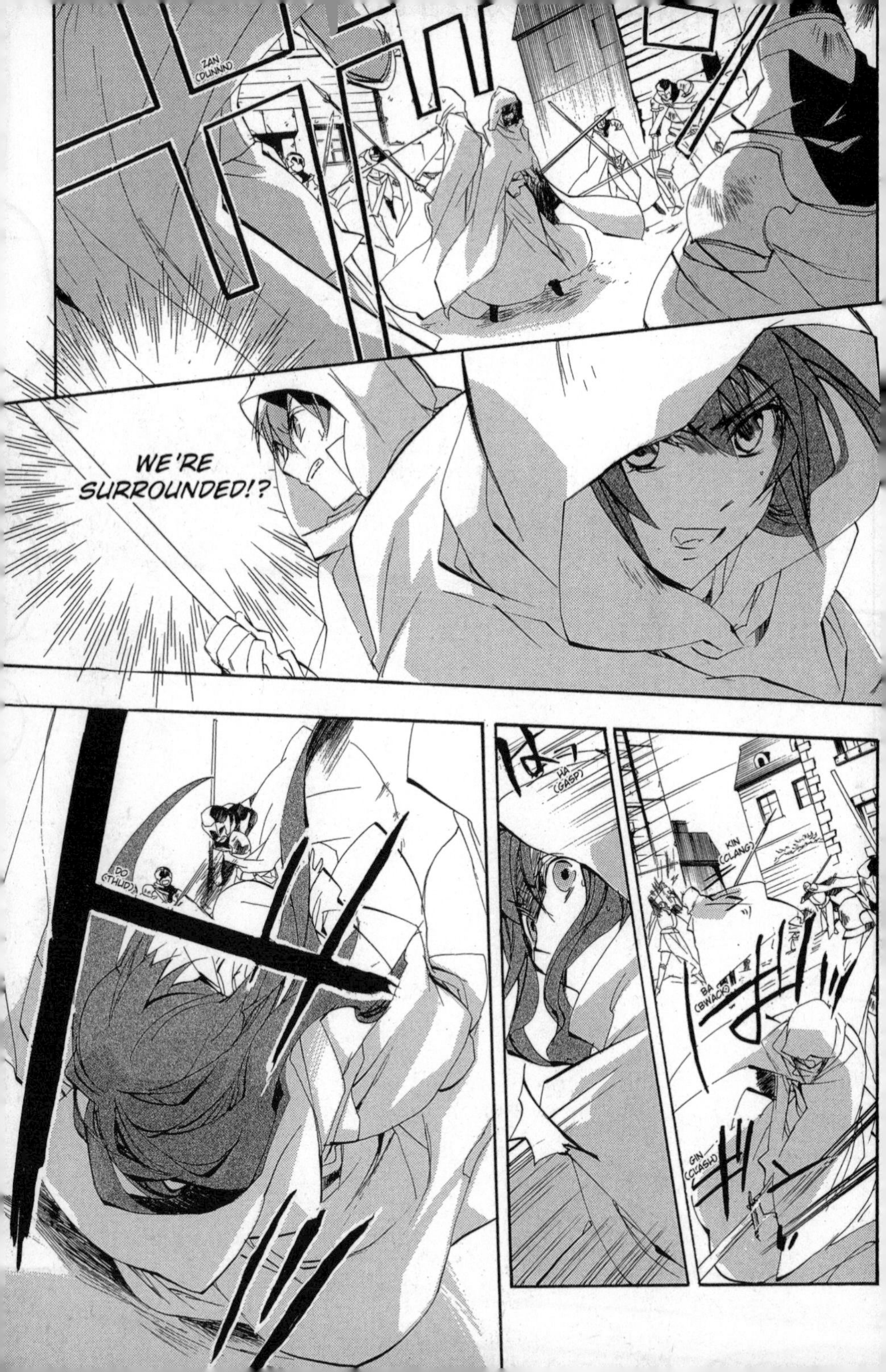
ZAN (DUNNN)
WE'RE SURROUNDED!?
KIN (CLANG)
BA (BWACK)
GIN (CLASH)
HA (GASP)
DO (THUD)

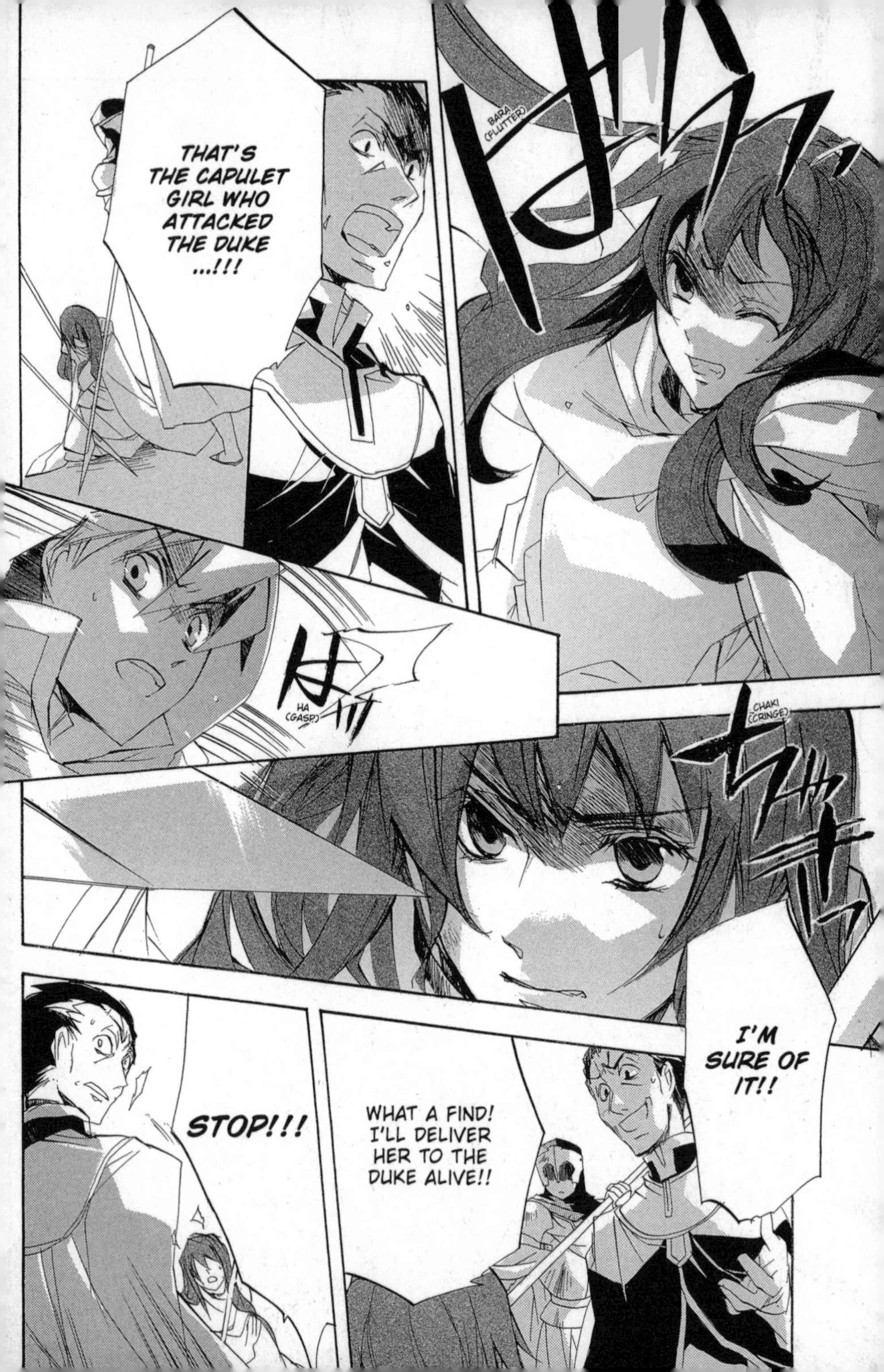
BARA (FLUTTER)
THAT'S THE CAPULET GIRL WHO ATTACKED THE DUKE ...!!!
HA (GASP)
CHAKI (CRINGE)
I'M SURE OF IT!!
WHAT A FIND! I'LL DELIVER HER TO THE DUKE ALIVE!!
STOP!!!

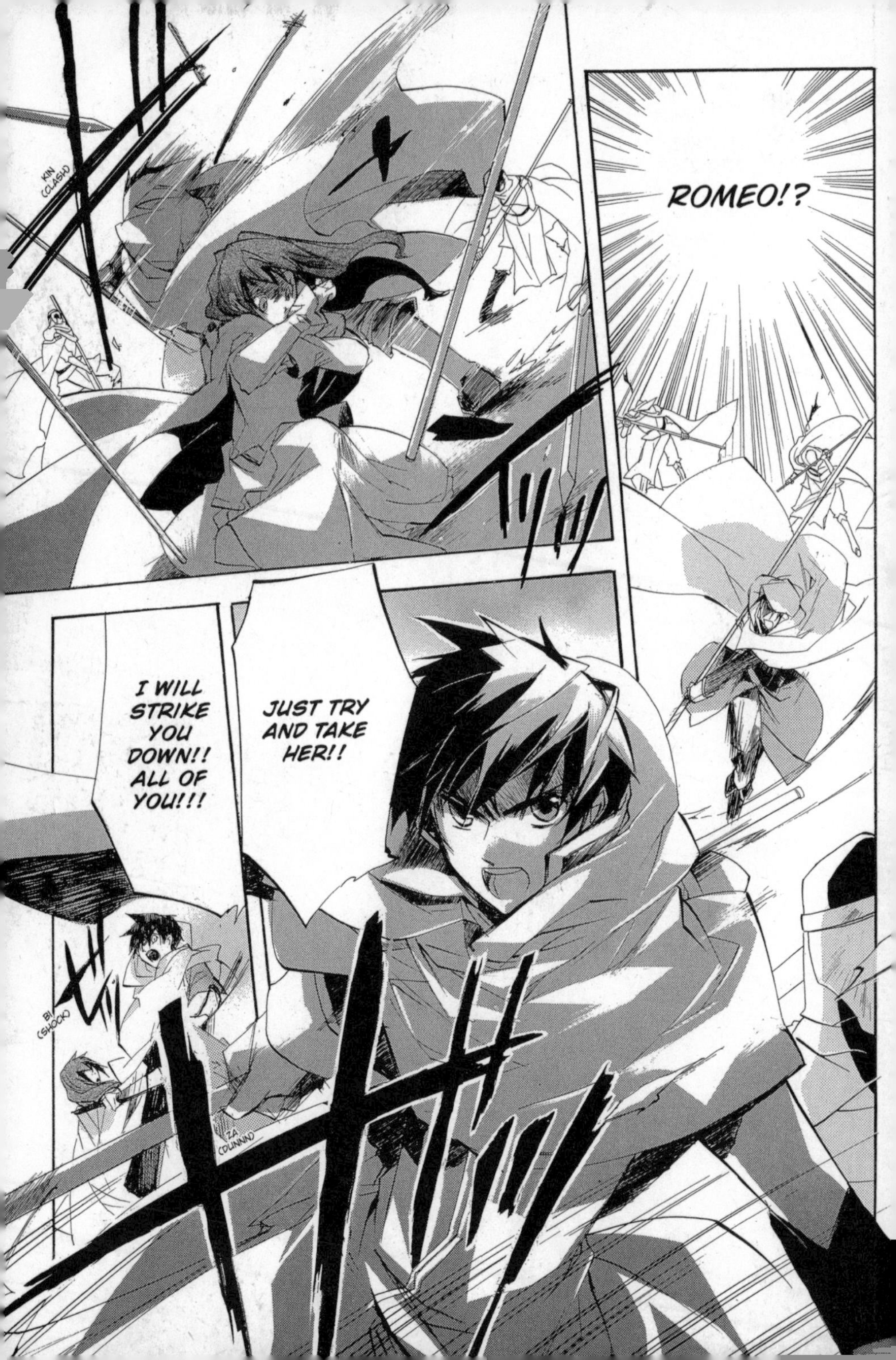
ROMEO!?
KIN (CLASH)
JUST TRY AND TAKE HER!!
I WILL STRIKE YOU DOWN!! ALL OF YOU!!!
BI (SHOCK)
ZA (DUNNN)

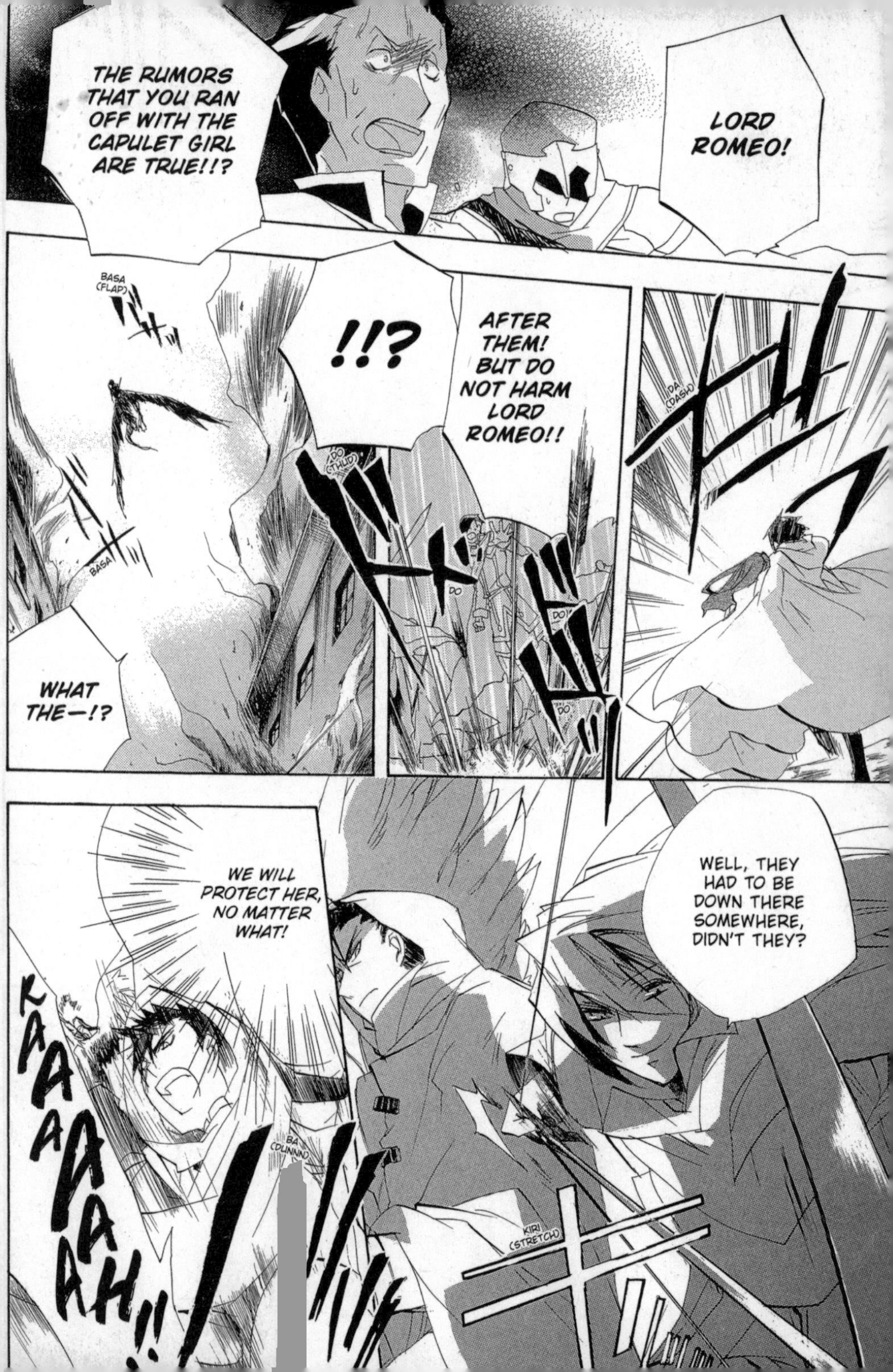
LORD ROMEO!
THE RUMORS THAT YOU RAN OFF WITH THE CAPULET GIRL ARE TRUE!!?
DA (DASH)
AFTER THEM! BUT DO NOT HARM LORD ROMEO!!
DO (THUD)
DO
DO
DO
!!?
BASA (FLAP)
BASA
WHAT THE—!?
WELL, THEY HAD TO BE DOWN THERE SOMEWHERE, DIDN'T THEY?
KIRI (STRETCH)
WE WILL PROTECT HER, NO MATTER WHAT!
BA (DUNNN)
KAAAAAAAAH!!

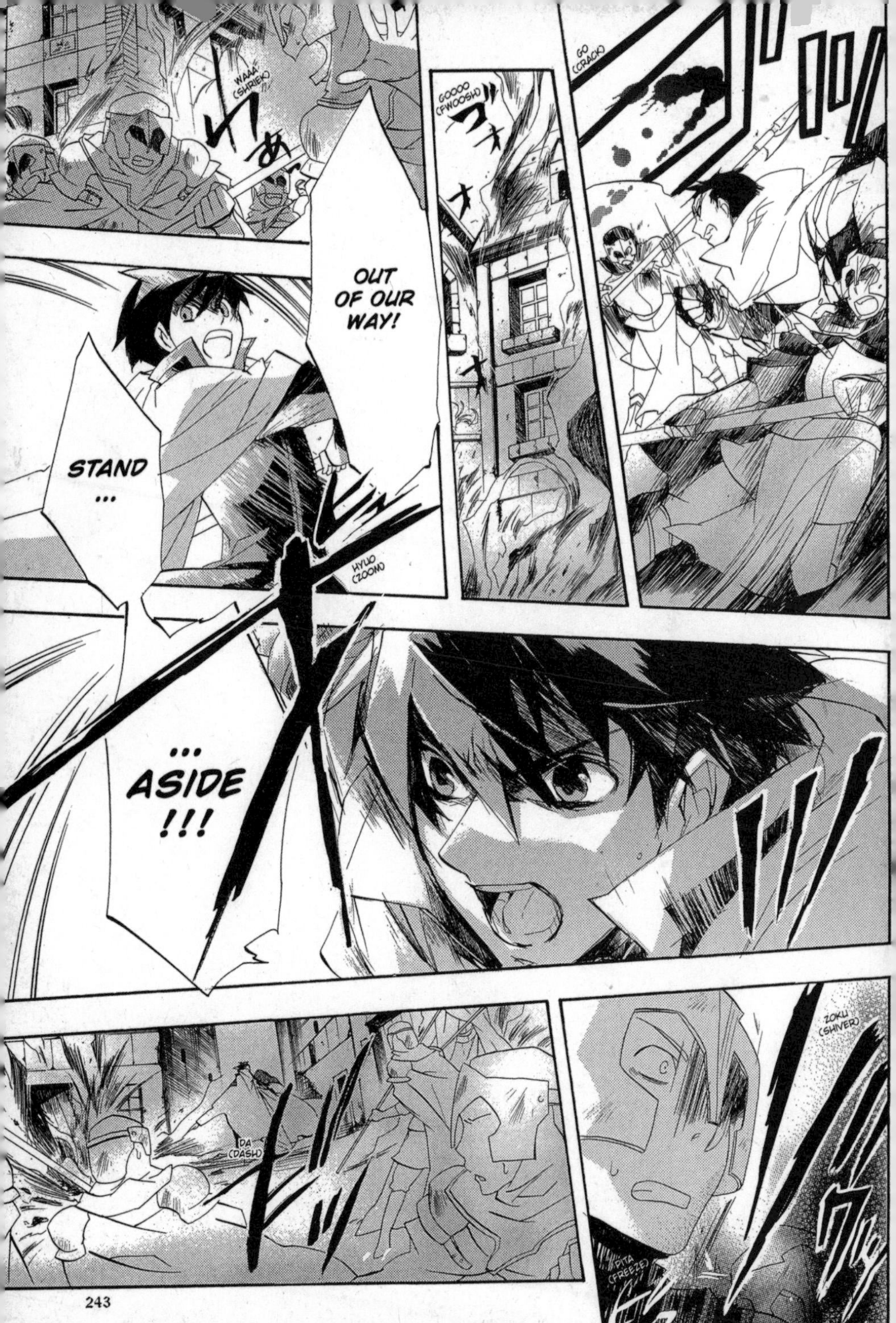
GO (CRACK)
GOOOO (FWOOSH)
WAAA (SHRIEK)
OUT OF OUR WAY!
STAND ...
HYUO (ZOOM)
... ASIDE !!!
ZOKU (SHIVER)
PITA (FREEZE)
DA (DASH)

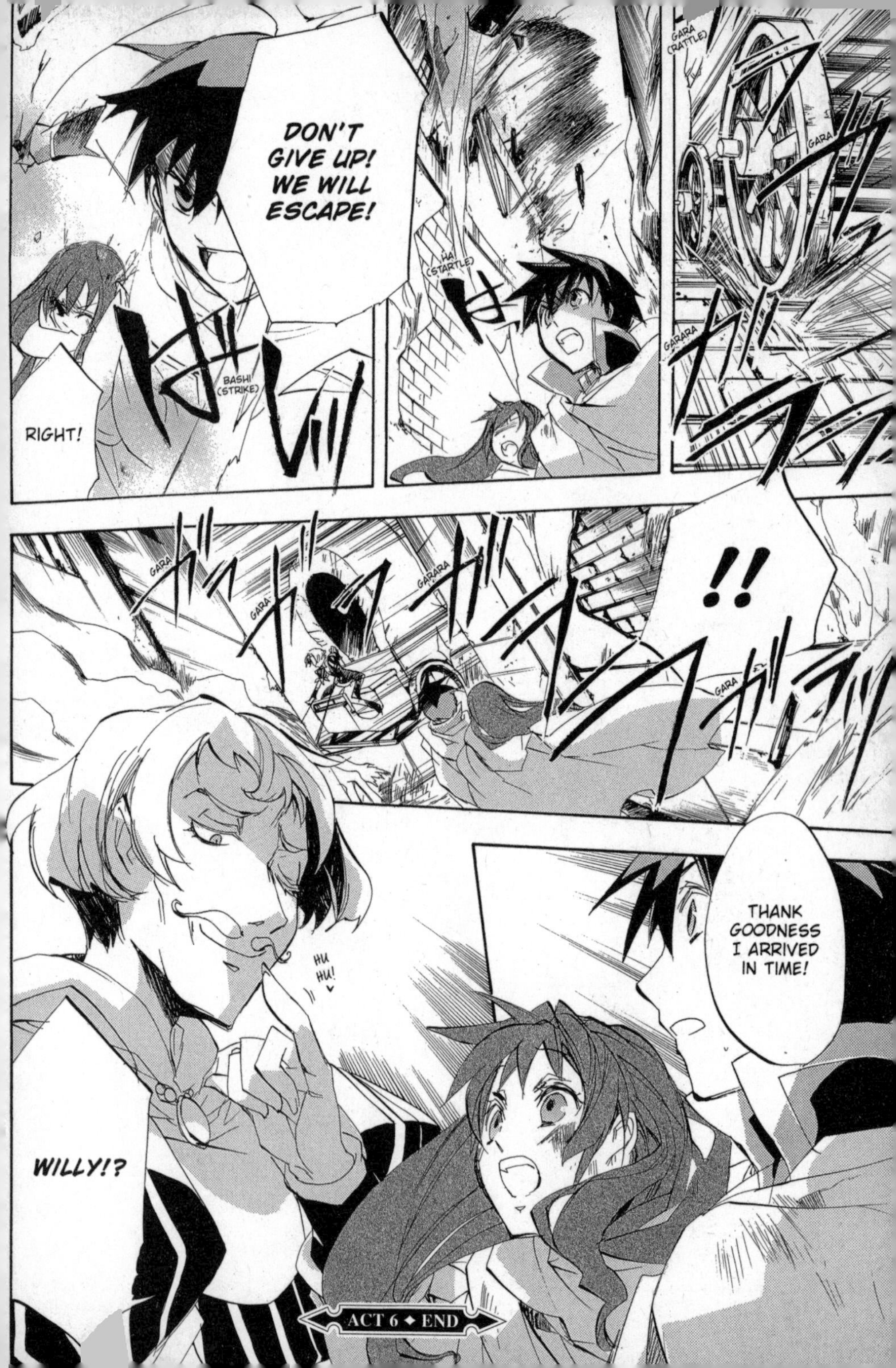
GARA (RATTLE)
GARA
GARARA
HA (STARTLE)
DON'T GIVE UP! WE WILL ESCAPE!
BASHI (STRIKE)
RIGHT!
GARA
!!
GARARA
GARA
GARA
THANK GOODNESS I ARRIVED IN TIME!
HU HU!
WILLY!?
ACT 6 ◆ END

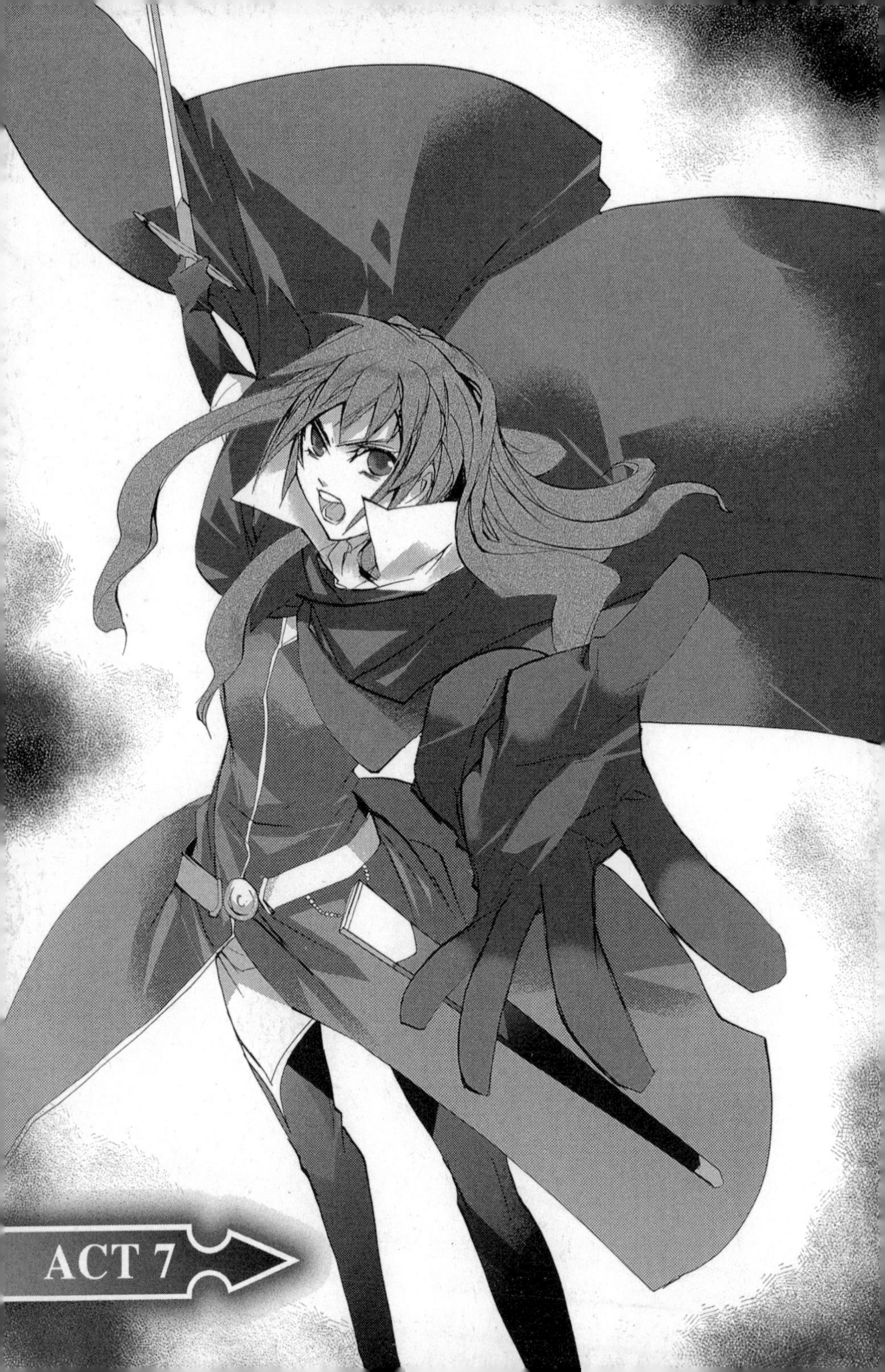
ACT 7

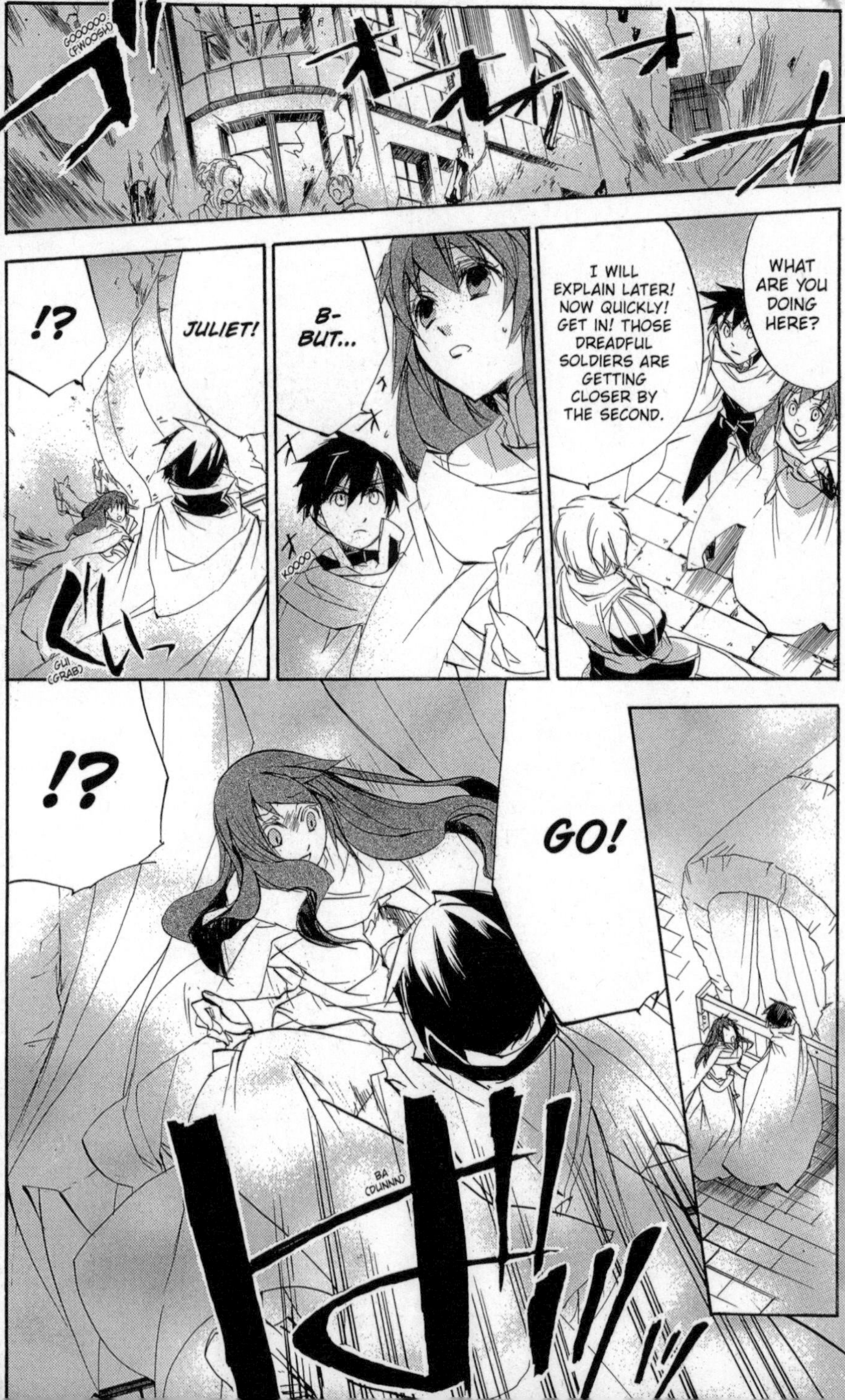
GOOOOOO (FWOOSH)
WHAT ARE YOU DOING HERE?
I WILL EXPLAIN LATER! NOW QUICKLY! GET IN! THOSE DREADFUL SOLDIERS ARE GETTING CLOSER BY THE SECOND.
B-BUT...
KOOOO
JULIET!
!?
GUI (GRAB)
GO!
!?
BA (DUNNN)

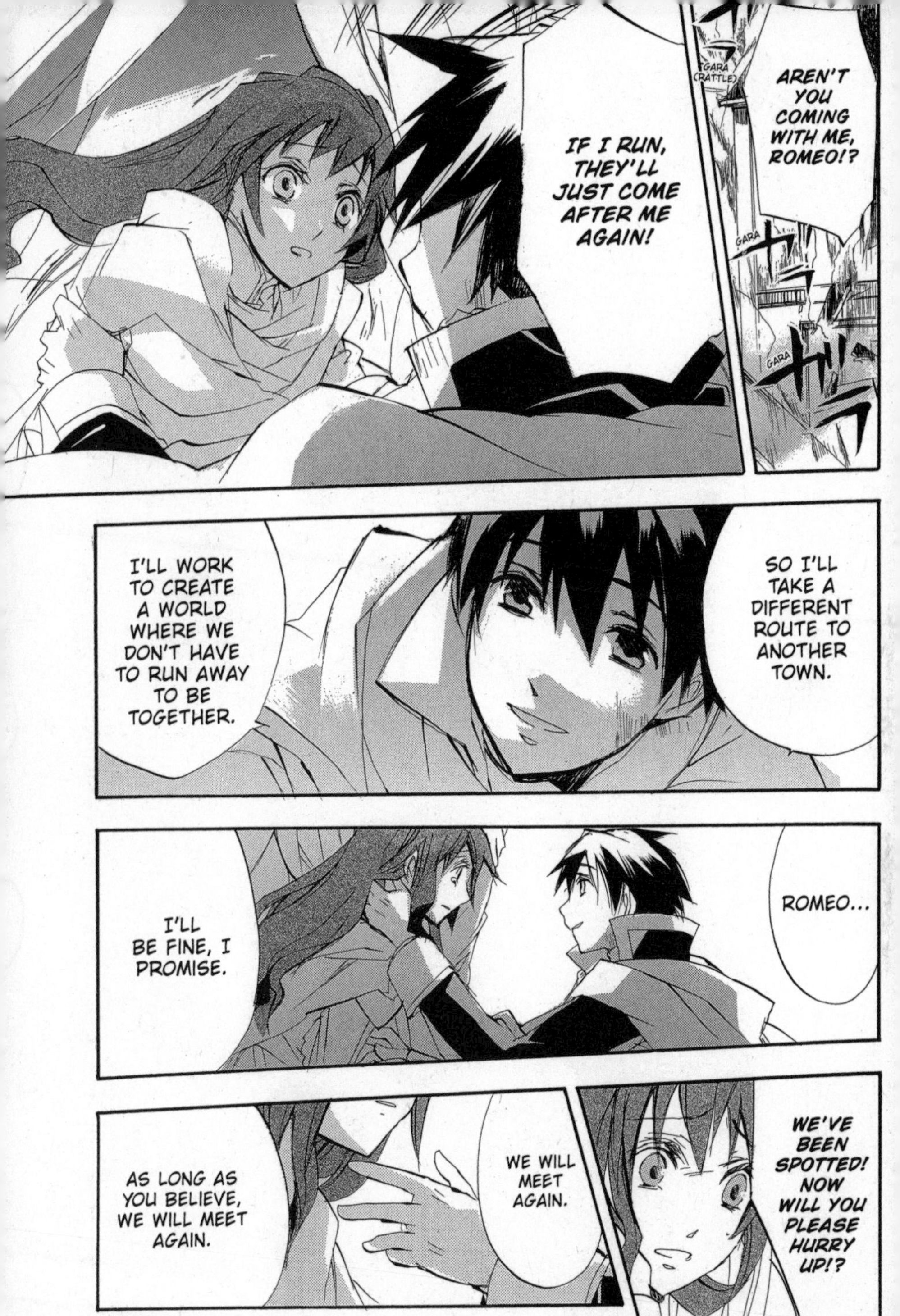
GARA (RATTLE)
AREN'T YOU COMING WITH ME, ROMEO!?
GARA
GARA
IF I RUN, THEY'LL JUST COME AFTER ME AGAIN!
SO I'LL TAKE A DIFFERENT ROUTE TO ANOTHER TOWN.
I'LL WORK TO CREATE A WORLD WHERE WE DON'T HAVE TO RUN AWAY TO BE TOGETHER.
ROMEO...
I'LL BE FINE, I PROMISE.
WE'VE BEEN SPOTTED! NOW WILL YOU PLEASE HURRY UP!?
WE WILL MEET AGAIN.
AS LONG AS YOU BELIEVE, WE WILL MEET AGAIN.

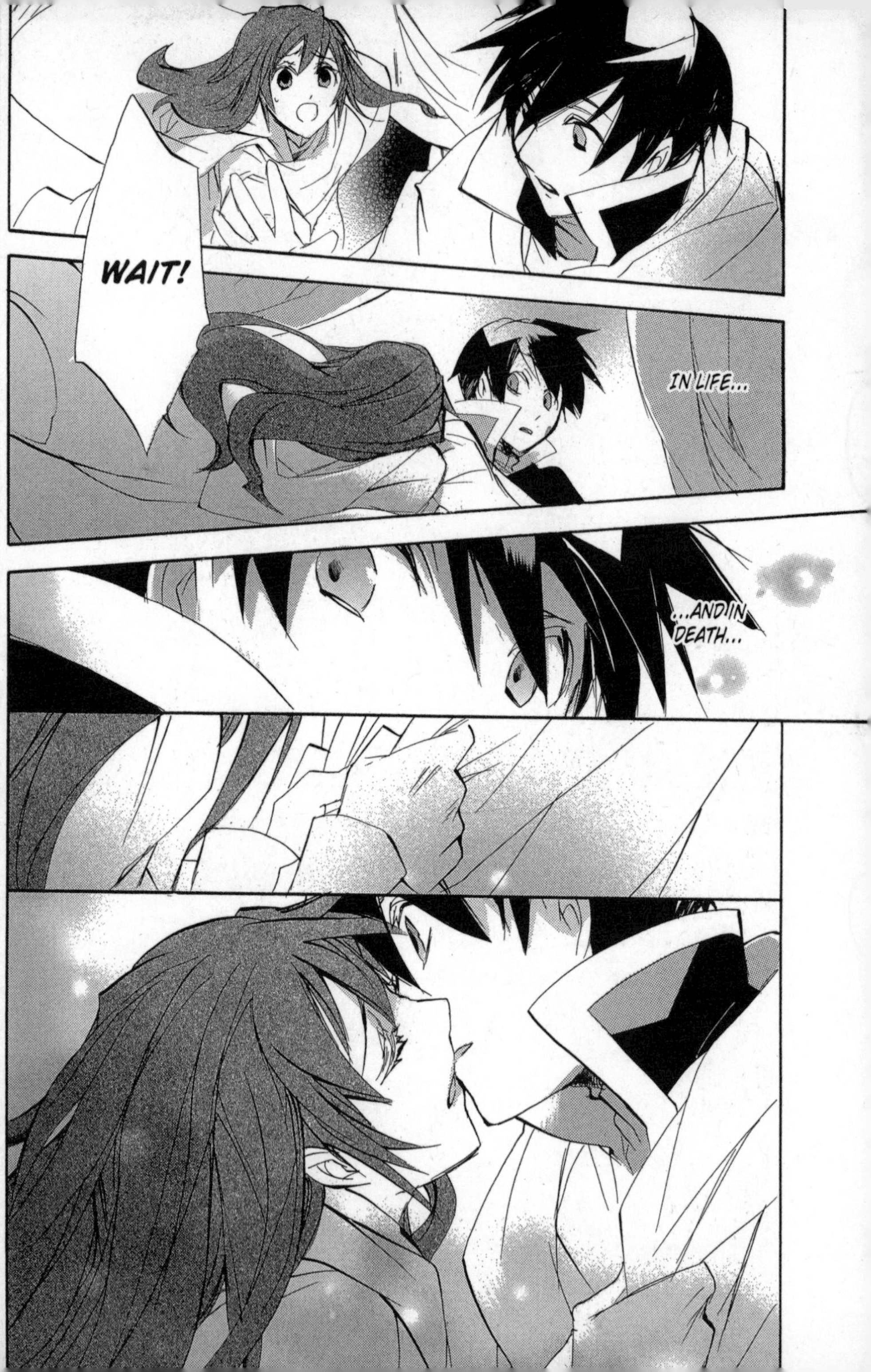
WAIT!
IN LIFE...
...AND IN DEATH...

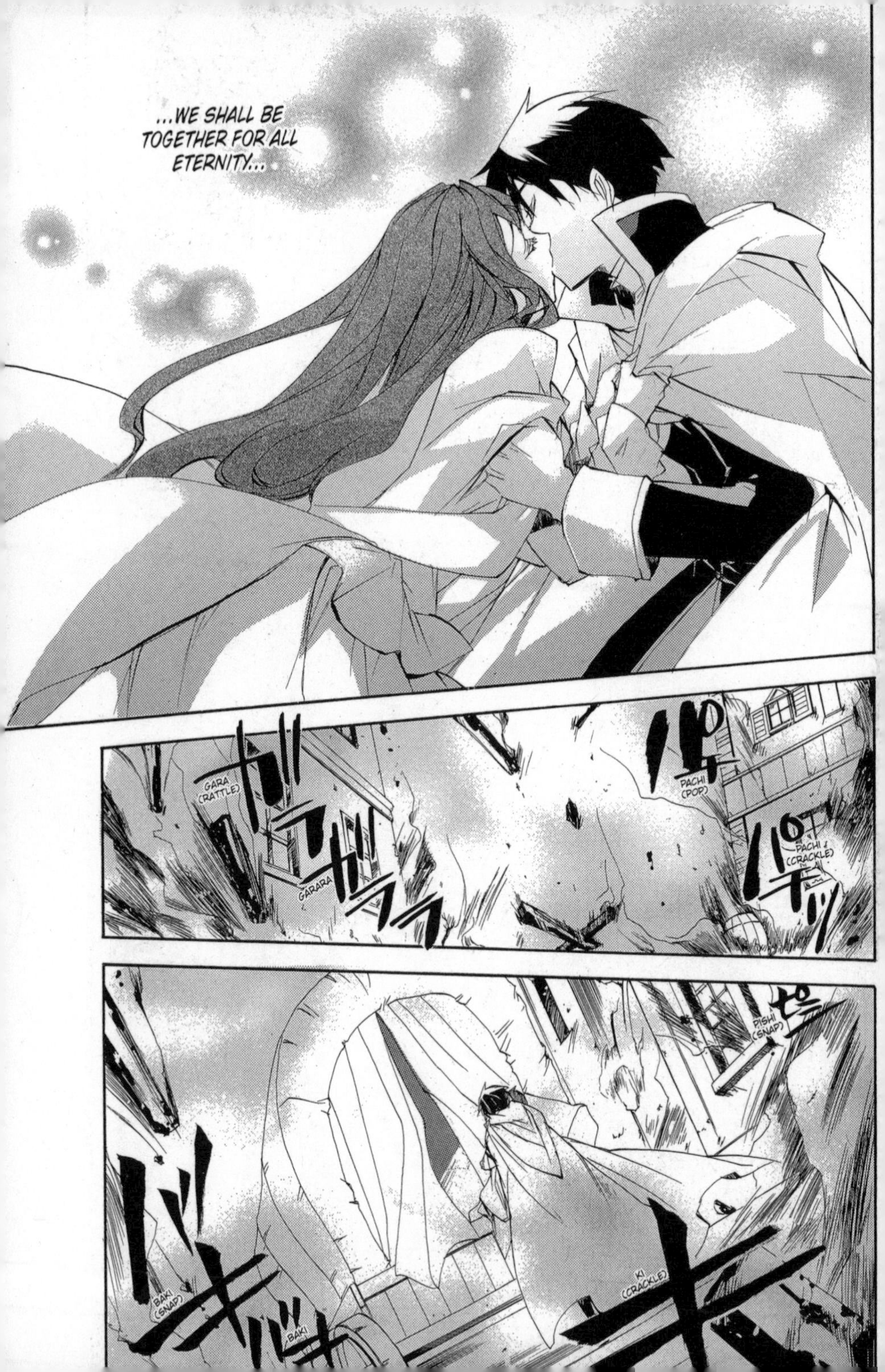
...WE SHALL BE TOGETHER FOR ALL ETERNITY...
PACHI (POP)
PACHI (CRACKLE)
GARA (RATTLE)
GARARA
PISHI (SNAP)
KI (CRACKLE)
BAKI (SNAP)
BAKI

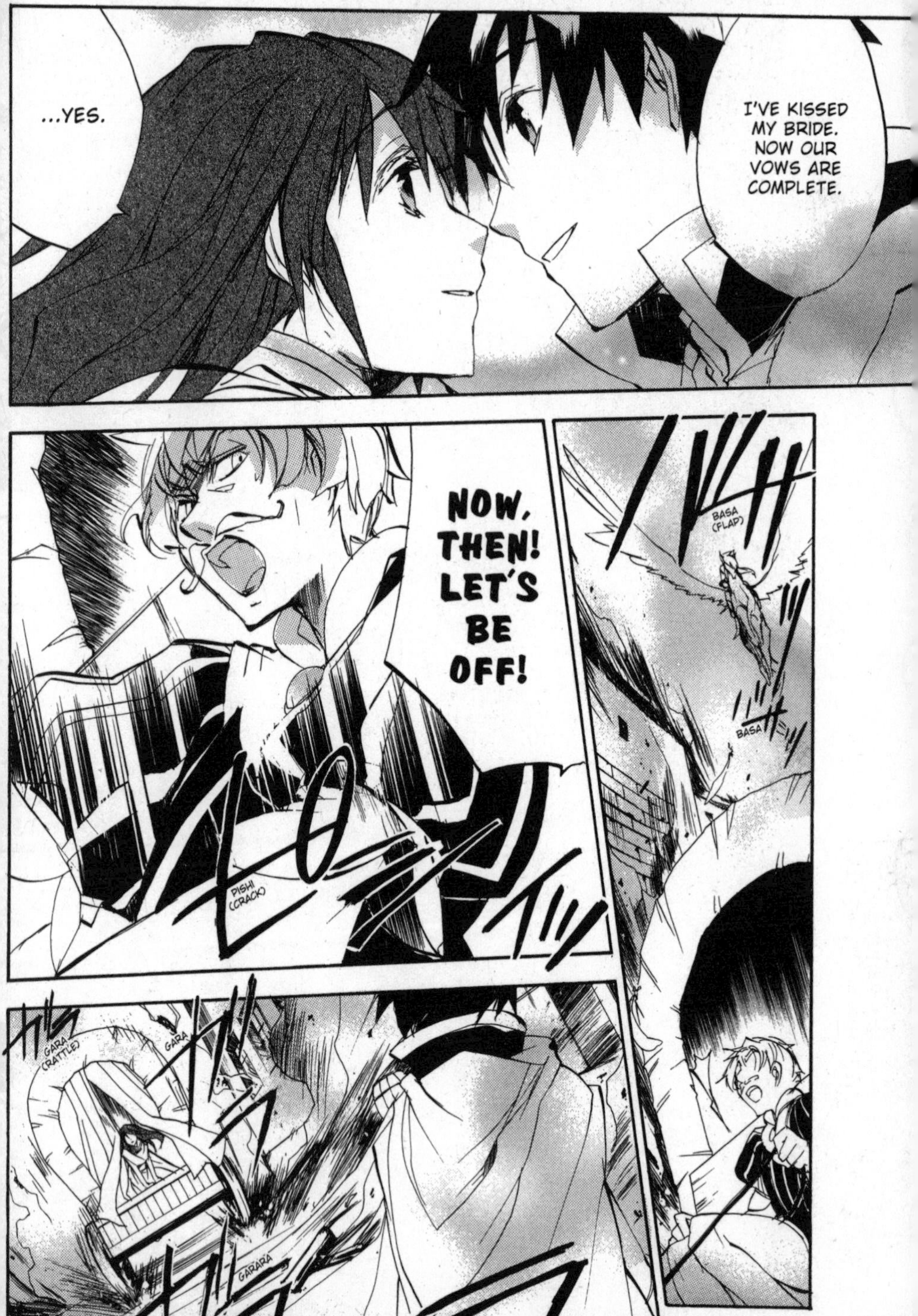
I'VE KISSED MY BRIDE. NOW OUR VOWS ARE COMPLETE.
...YES.
BASA (FLAP)
BASA
NOW, THEN! LET'S BE OFF!
PISHI (CRACK)
GARA (RATTLE)
GARA
GARARA

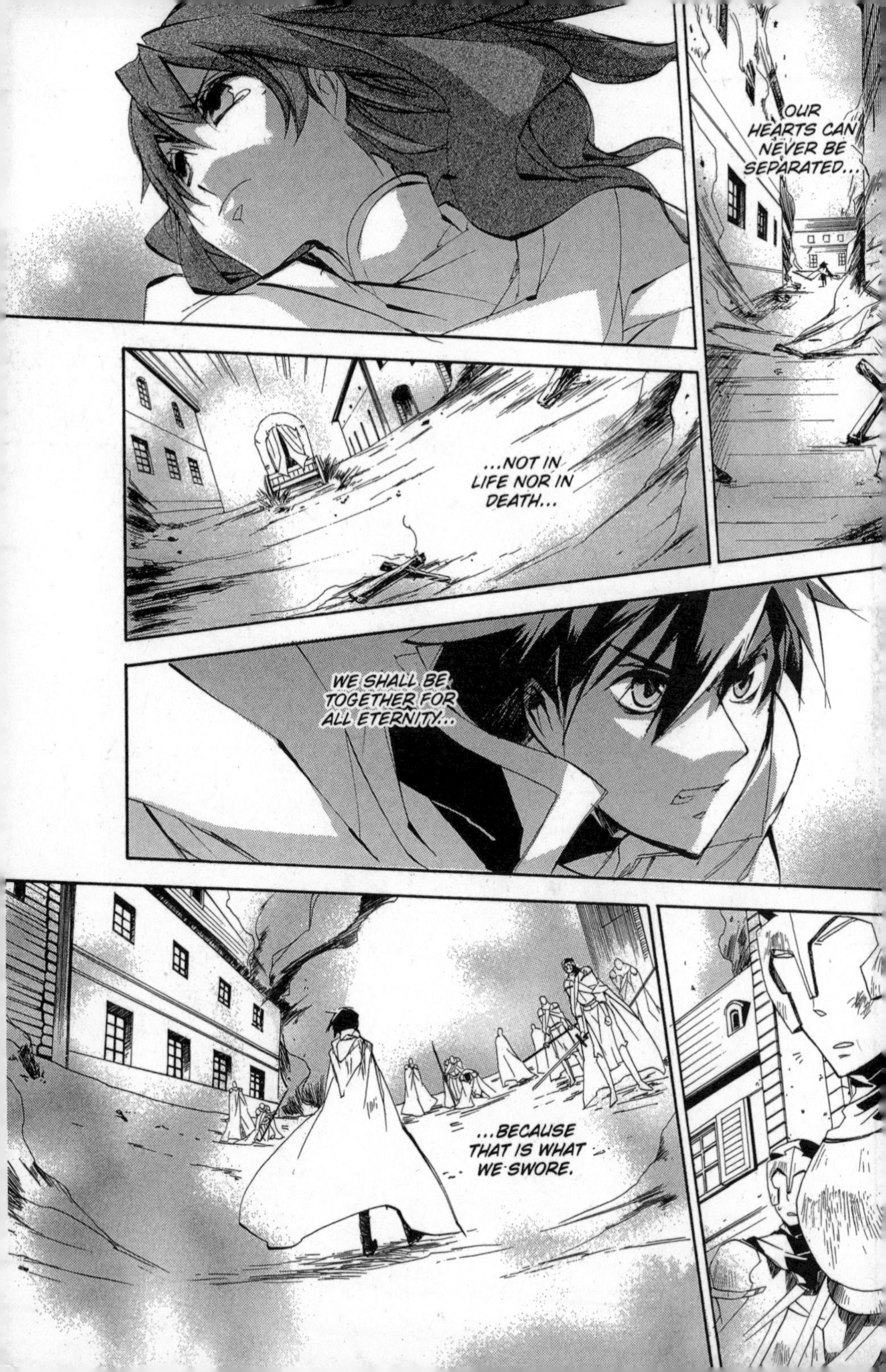
OUR HEARTS CAN NEVER BE SEPARATED...
...NOT IN LIFE NOR IN DEATH...
WE SHALL BE TOGETHER FOR ALL ETERNITY...
...BECAUSE THAT IS WHAT WE SWORE.

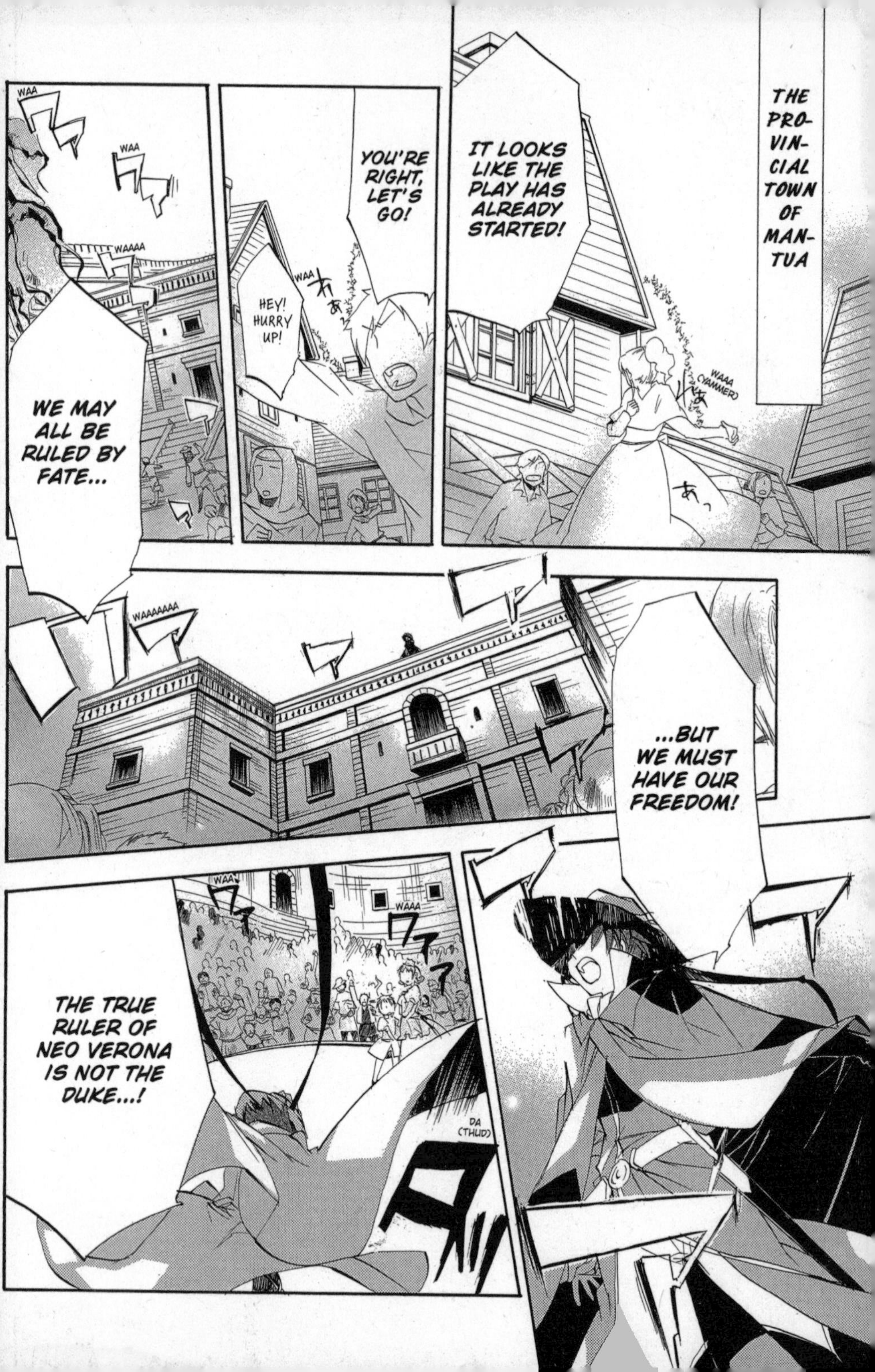
THE PROVINCIAL TOWN OF MANTUA
IT LOOKS LIKE THE PLAY HAS ALREADY STARTED!
WAAA (YAMMER)
YOU'RE RIGHT, LET'S GO!
HEY! HURRY UP!
WAA
WAA
WAA
WAAAA
WE MAY ALL BE RULED BY FATE...
WAAAAAAA
...BUT WE MUST HAVE OUR FREEDOM!
DA (THUD)
WAA
WAAA
THE TRUE RULER OF NEO VERONA IS NOT THE DUKE...!

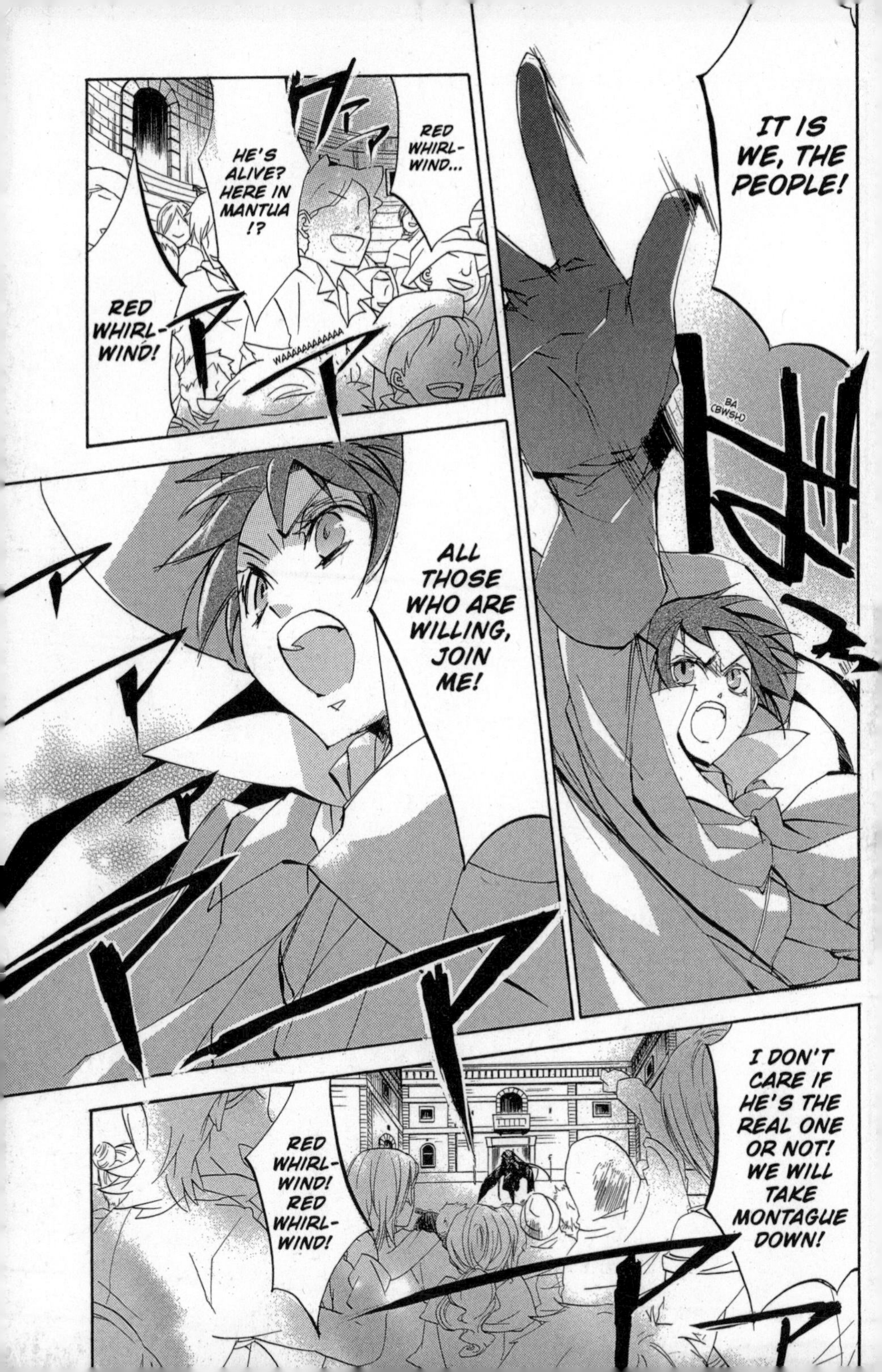
IT IS WE, THE PEOPLE!
BA (BWSH)
RED WHIRLWIND...
HE'S ALIVE? HERE IN MANTUA!?
WAAAAAAAAAAAA
RED WHIRLWIND!
ALL THOSE WHO ARE WILLING, JOIN ME!
I DON'T CARE IF HE'S THE REAL ONE OR NOT! WE WILL TAKE MONTAGUE DOWN!
RED WHIRLWIND! RED WHIRLWIND!

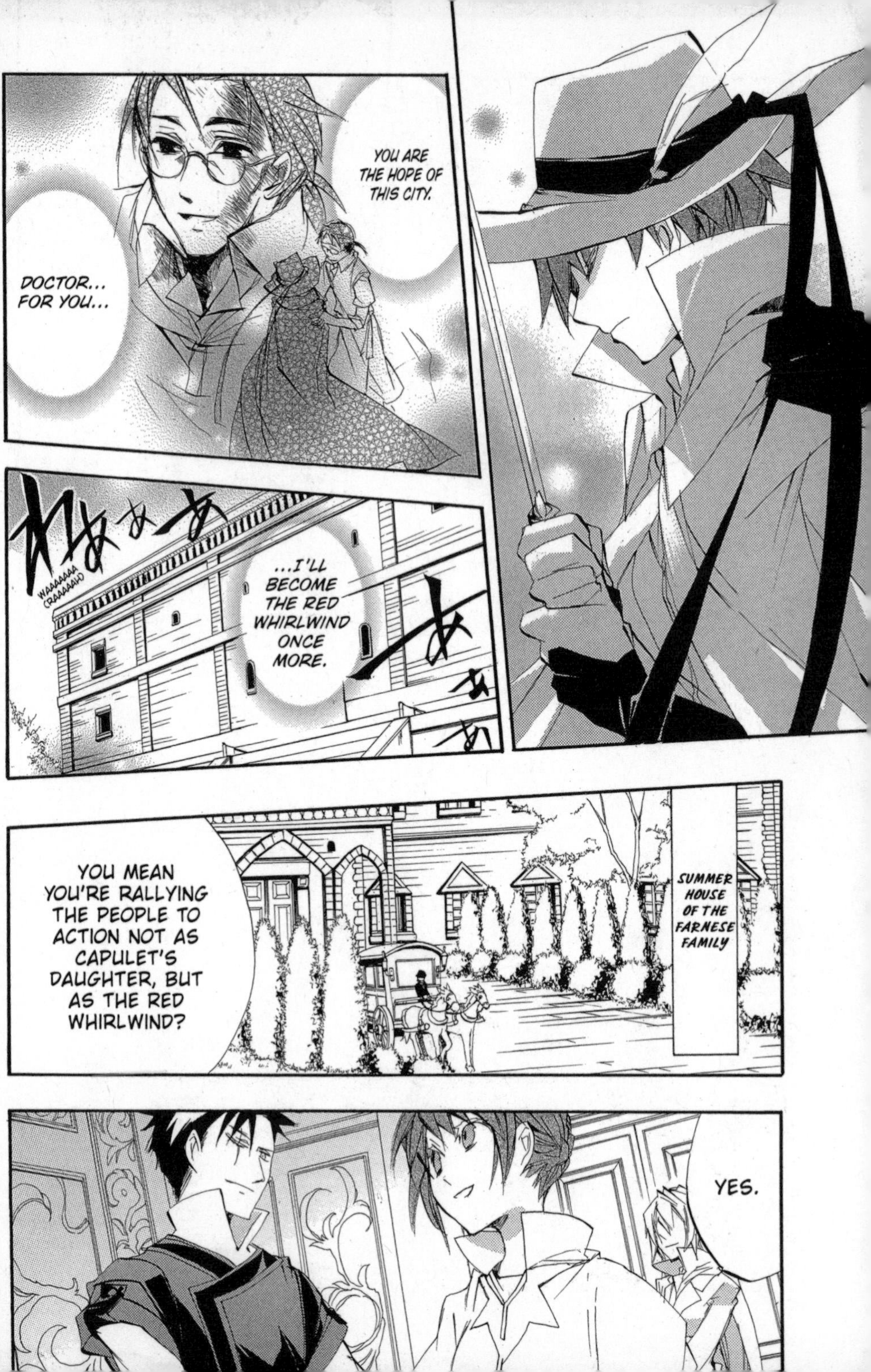
YOU ARE THE HOPE OF THIS CITY.
DOCTOR... FOR YOU...
わぁぁぁあ
WAAAAAAA CRAAAAAHD
...I'LL BECOME THE RED WHIRLWIND ONCE MORE.
SUMMER HOUSE OF THE FARNESE FAMILY
YOU MEAN YOU'RE RALLYING THE PEOPLE TO ACTION NOT AS CAPULET'S DAUGHTER, BUT AS THE RED WHIRLWIND?
YES.

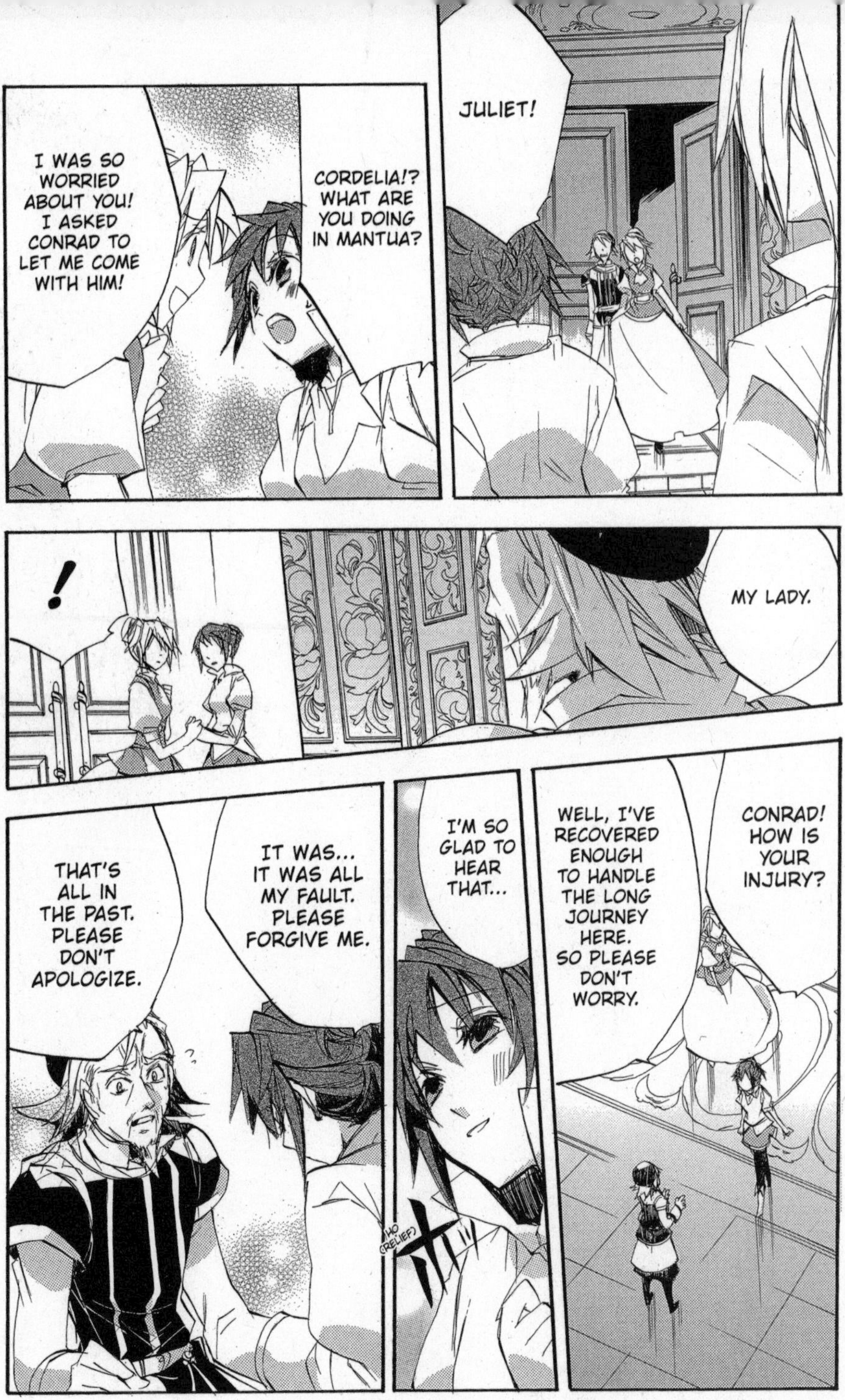
JULIET!
CORDELIA!? WHAT ARE YOU DOING IN MANTUA?
I WAS SO WORRIED ABOUT YOU! I ASKED CONRAD TO LET ME COME WITH HIM!
MY LADY.
!
CONRAD! HOW IS YOUR INJURY?
WELL, I'VE RECOVERED ENOUGH TO HANDLE THE LONG JOURNEY HERE. SO PLEASE DON'T WORRY.
I'M SO GLAD TO HEAR THAT...
HO (RELIEF)
IT WAS... IT WAS ALL MY FAULT. PLEASE FORGIVE ME.
THAT'S ALL IN THE PAST. PLEASE DON'T APOLOGIZE.

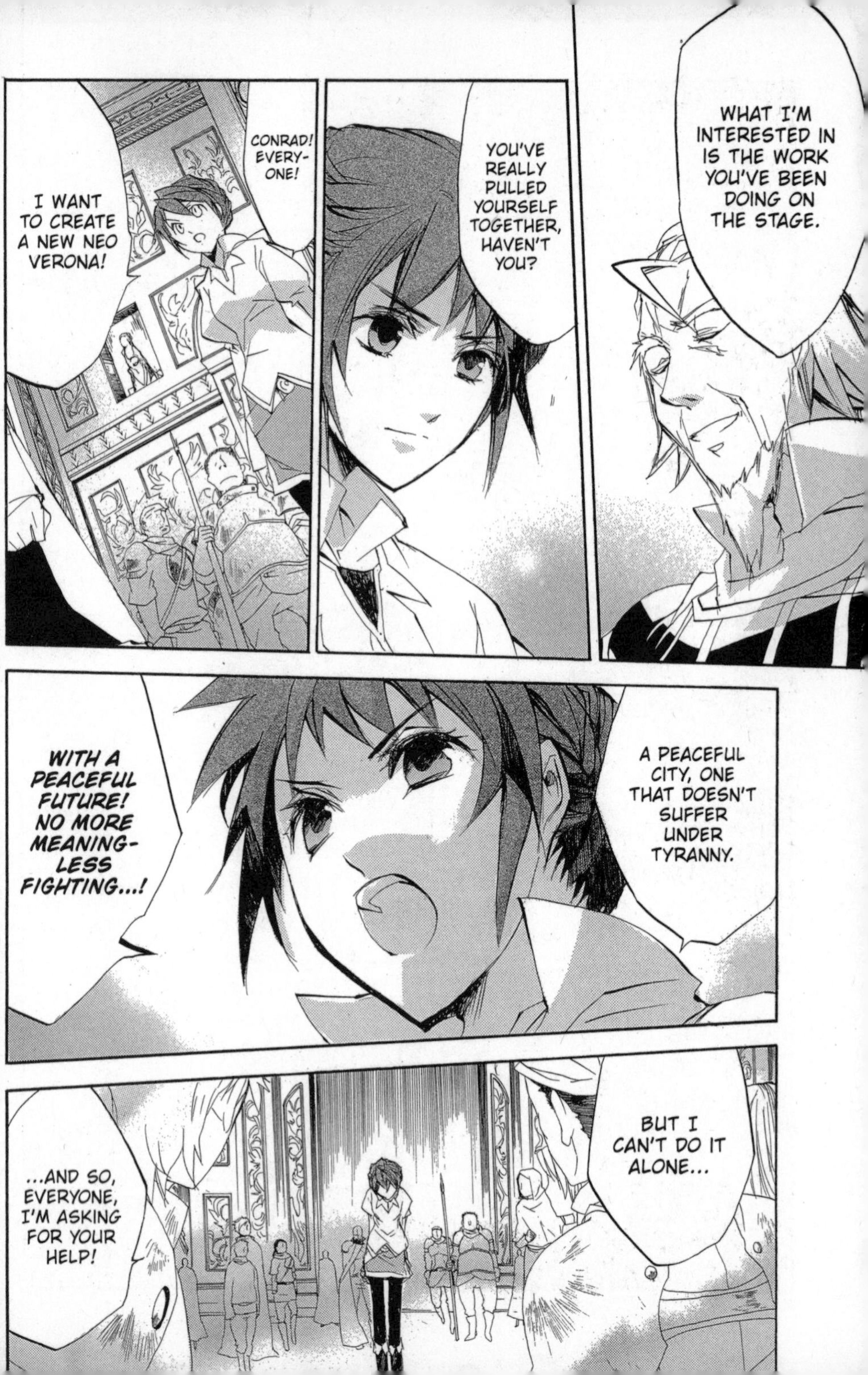
WHAT I'M INTERESTED IN IS THE WORK YOU'VE BEEN DOING ON THE STAGE.
YOU'VE REALLY PULLED YOURSELF TOGETHER, HAVEN'T YOU?
CONRAD! EVERYONE!
I WANT TO CREATE A NEW NEO VERONA!
A PEACEFUL CITY, ONE THAT DOESN'T SUFFER UNDER TYRANNY.
WITH A PEACEFUL FUTURE! NO MORE MEANINGLESS FIGHTING...!
BUT I CAN'T DO IT ALONE...
...AND SO, EVERYONE, I'M ASKING FOR YOUR HELP!

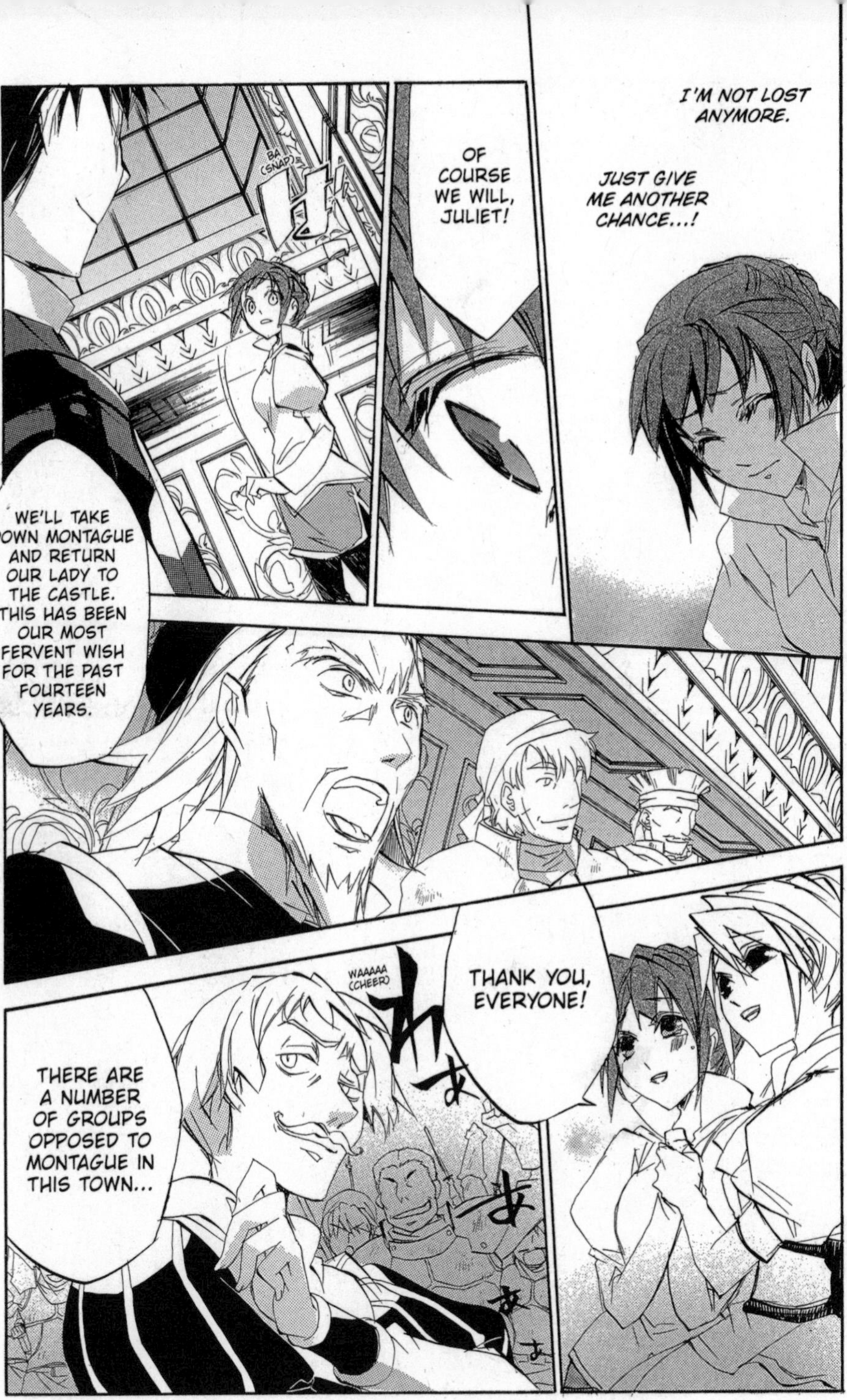
I'M NOT LOST ANYMORE.
JUST GIVE ME ANOTHER CHANCE...!
OF COURSE WE WILL, JULIET!
BA (SNAP)
WE'LL TAKE DOWN MONTAGUE AND RETURN OUR LADY TO THE CASTLE. THIS HAS BEEN OUR MOST FERVENT WISH FOR THE PAST FOURTEEN YEARS.
THANK YOU, EVERYONE!
WAAAAA (CHEER)
THERE ARE A NUMBER OF GROUPS OPPOSED TO MONTAGUE IN THIS TOWN...

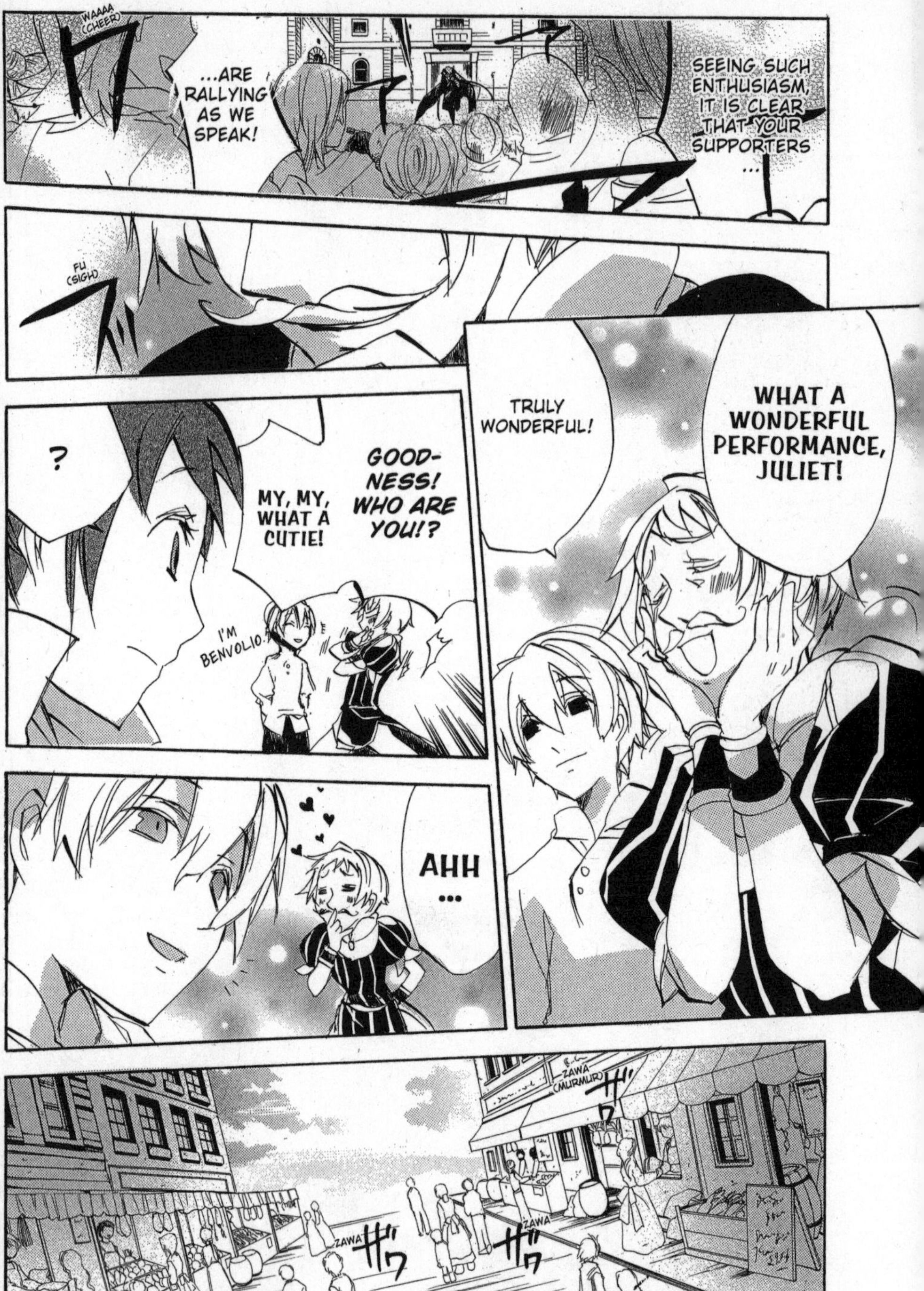
SEEING SUCH ENTHUSIASM, IT IS CLEAR THAT YOUR SUPPORTERS ...
...ARE RALLYING AS WE SPEAK!
WAAAA (CHEER)
FU (SIGH)
WHAT A WONDERFUL PERFORMANCE, JULIET!
TRULY WONDERFUL!
GOOD-NESS! WHO ARE YOU!?
MY, MY, WHAT A CUTIE!
?
I'M BENVOLIO.
AHH ...
ZAWA (MURMUR)
ZAWA
ZAWA

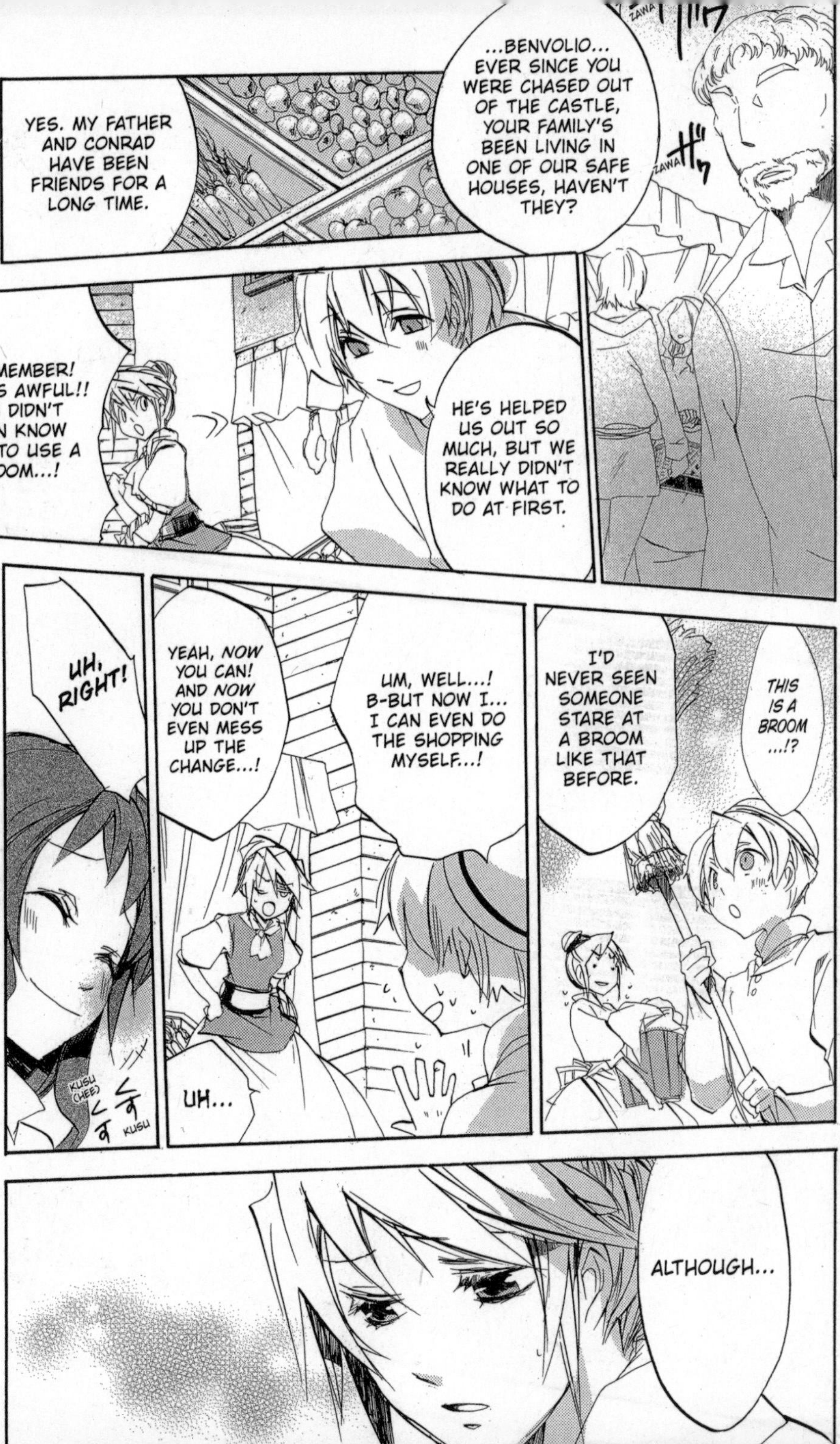
ZAWA
ZAWA
...BENVOLIO... EVER SINCE YOU WERE CHASED OUT OF THE CASTLE, YOUR FAMILY'S BEEN LIVING IN ONE OF OUR SAFE HOUSES, HAVEN'T THEY?
YES. MY FATHER AND CONRAD HAVE BEEN FRIENDS FOR A LONG TIME.
HE'S HELPED US OUT SO MUCH, BUT WE REALLY DIDN'T KNOW WHAT TO DO AT FIRST.
I REMEMBER! IT WAS AWFUL!! YOU DIDN'T EVEN KNOW HOW TO USE A BROOM...!
THIS IS A BROOM ...!?
I'D NEVER SEEN SOMEONE STARE AT A BROOM LIKE THAT BEFORE.
UM, WELL...! B-BUT NOW I... I CAN EVEN DO THE SHOPPING MYSELF...!
YEAH, *NOW* YOU CAN! AND *NOW* YOU DON'T EVEN MESS UP THE CHANGE...!
UH...
UH, RIGHT!
KUSU (HEE) KUSU
ALTHOUGH...

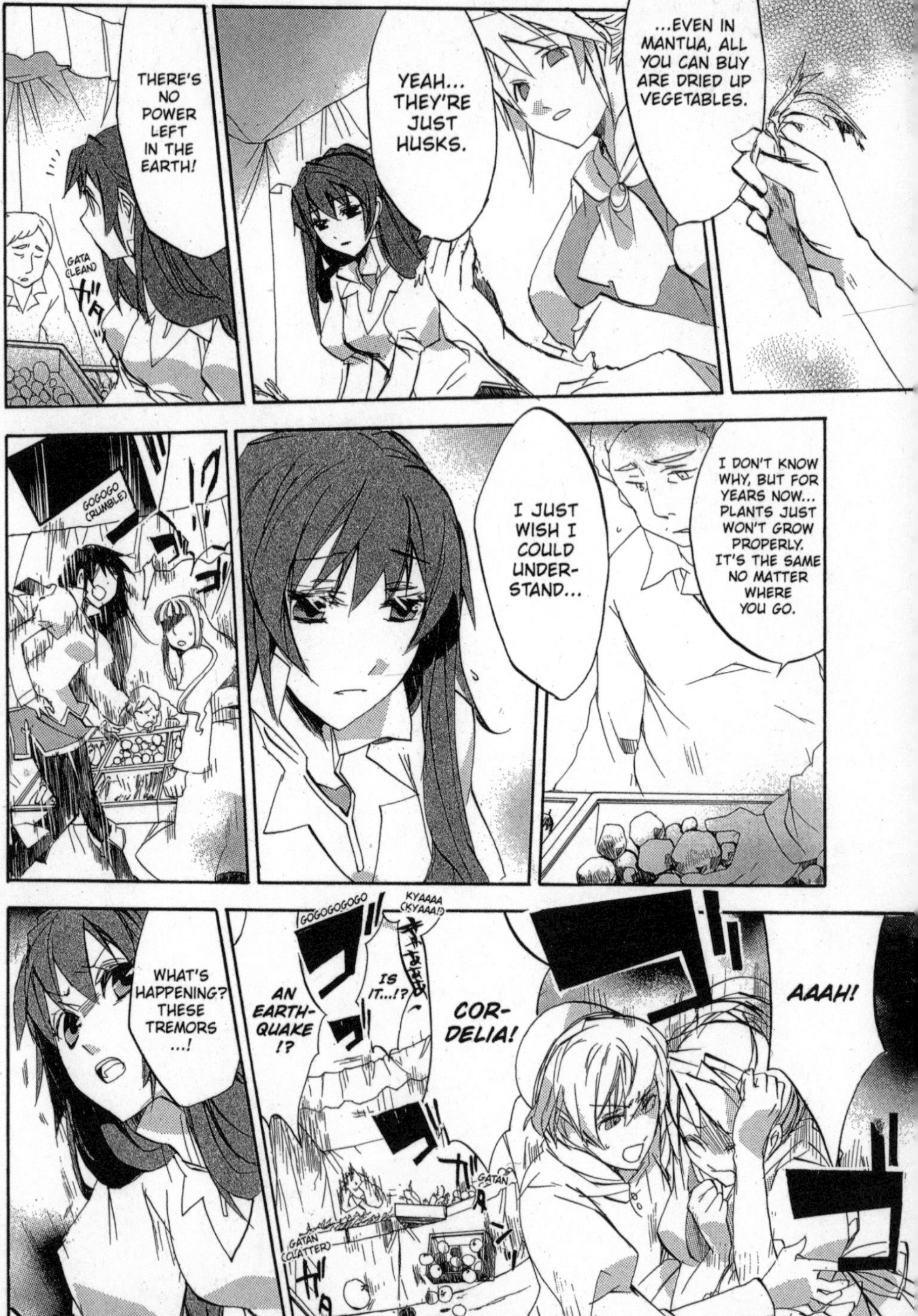

...EVEN IN MANTUA, ALL YOU CAN BUY ARE DRIED UP VEGETABLES.
YEAH... THEY'RE JUST HUSKS.
THERE'S NO POWER LEFT IN THE EARTH!
GATA (LEAN)
I DON'T KNOW WHY, BUT FOR YEARS NOW... PLANTS JUST WON'T GROW PROPERLY. IT'S THE SAME NO MATTER WHERE YOU GO.
I JUST WISH I COULD UNDER-STAND...
GOGOGO (RUMBLE)
AAAH!
COR-DELIA!
KYAAAA (KYAAA!)
IS IT...!?
AN EARTH-QUAKE !?
GOGOGOGOGO
GATAN
GATAN (CLATTER)
WHAT'S HAPPENING? THESE TREMORS ...!

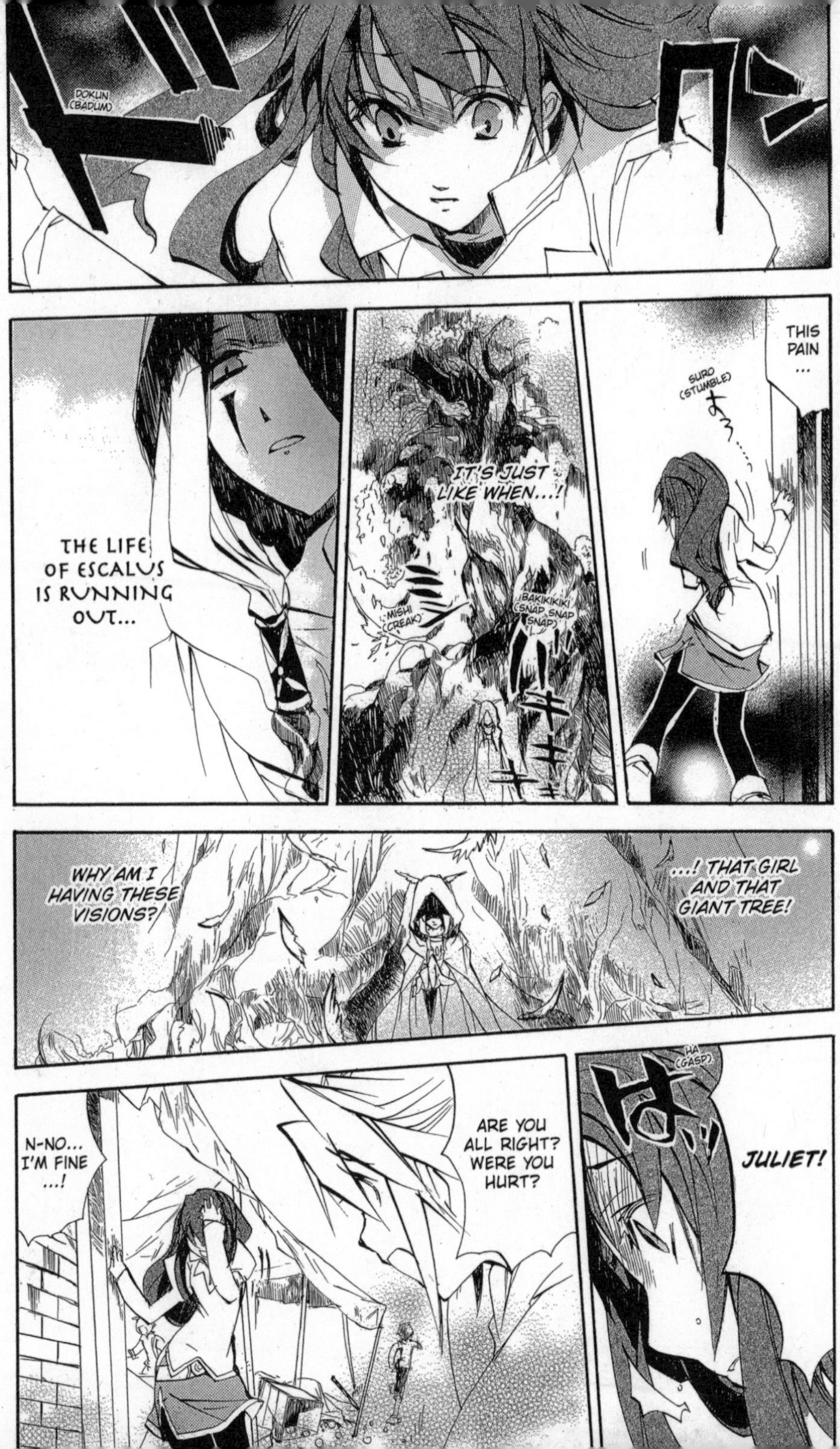
DOKUN (BADUM)
THIS PAIN ...
SURO (STUMBLE)
IT'S JUST LIKE WHEN...!
BAKIKIKIKI (SNAP SNAP SNAP)
MISHI (CREAK)
THE LIFE OF ESCALUS IS RUNNING OUT...
...! THAT GIRL AND THAT GIANT TREE!
WHY AM I HAVING THESE VISIONS?
HA (GASP)
JULIET!
ARE YOU ALL RIGHT? WERE YOU HURT?
N-NO... I'M FINE ...!

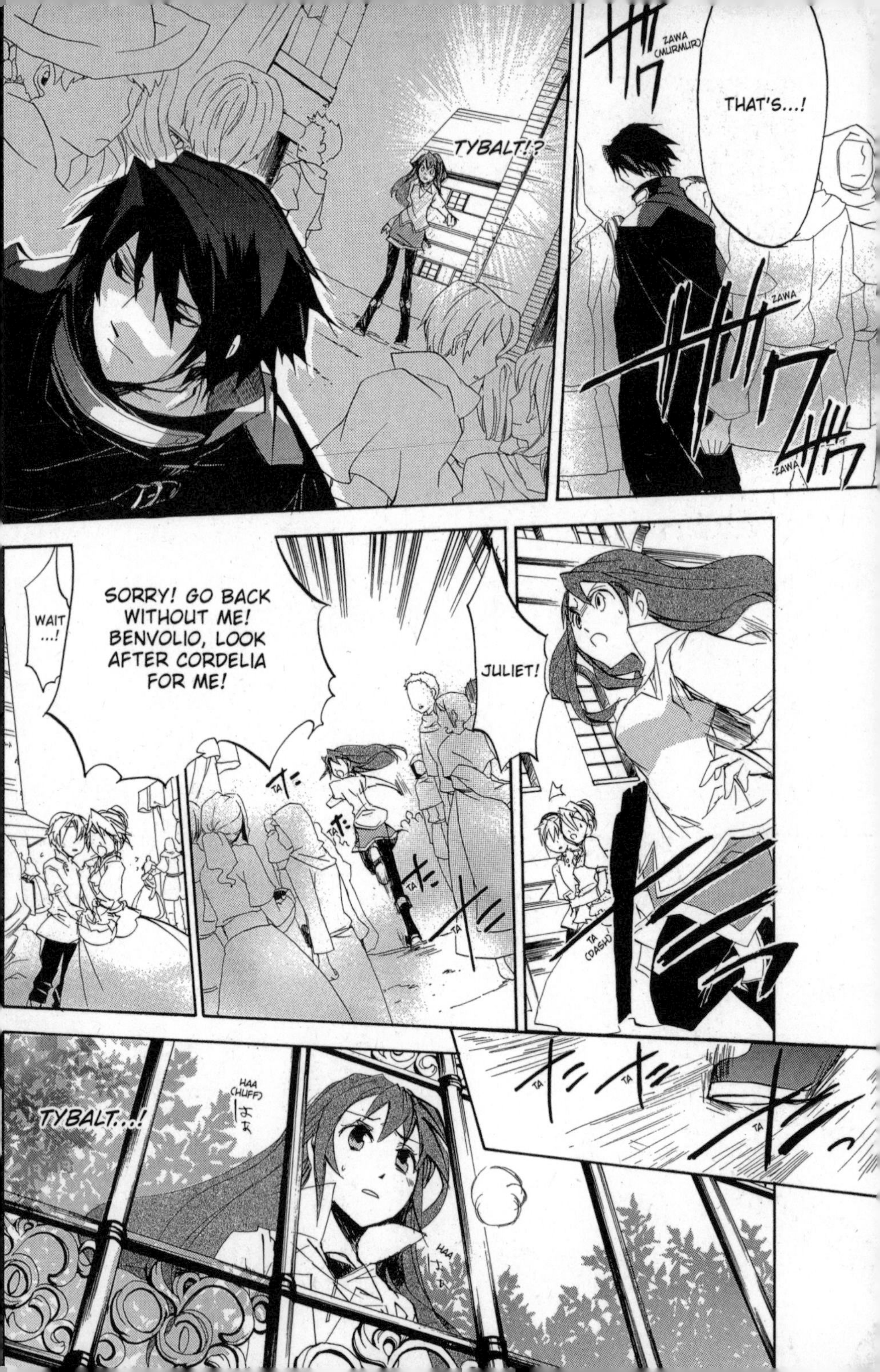
ZAWA (MURMUR)
THAT'S...!
ZAWA
ZAWA
TYBALT!?
JULIET!
TA (DASH)
SORRY! GO BACK WITHOUT ME! BENVOLIO, LOOK AFTER CORDELIA FOR ME!
TA
TA
TA
TA
WAIT ...!
TA
TA
TA
HAA (HUFF)
TYBALT...!
HAA

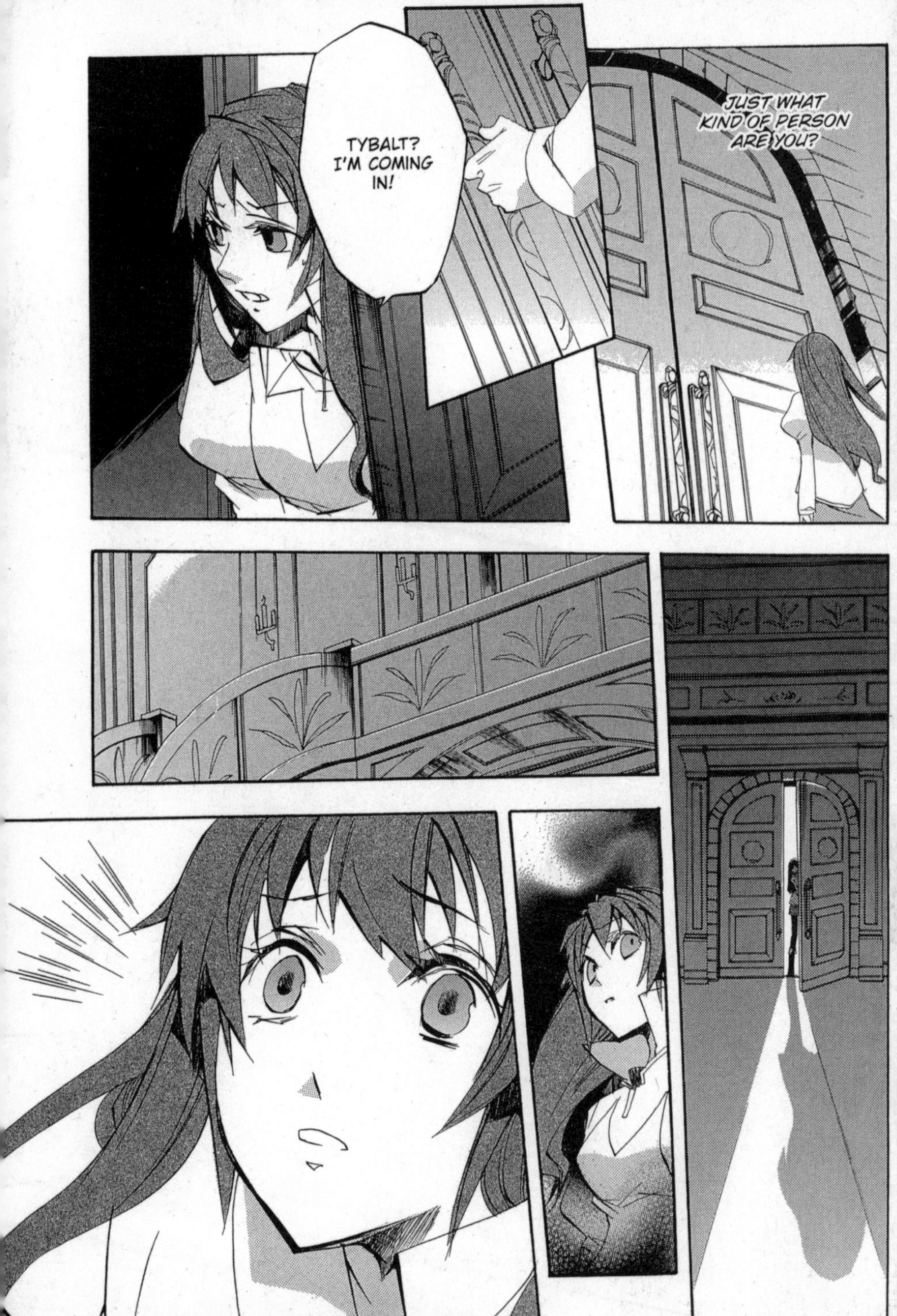
JUST WHAT KIND OF PERSON ARE YOU?
TYBALT? I'M COMING IN!

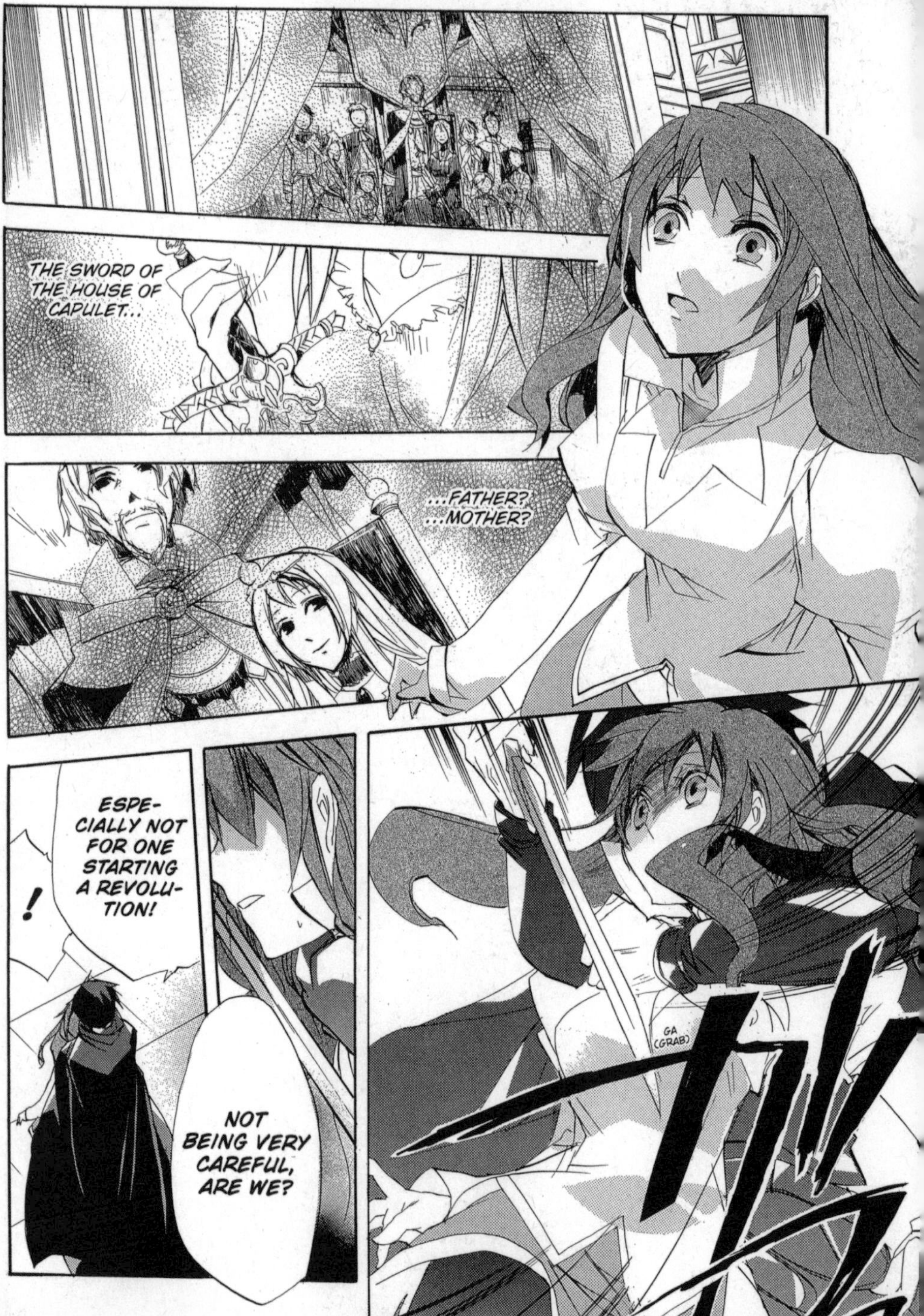
THE SWORD OF THE HOUSE OF CAPULET...
...FATHER? ...MOTHER?
GA (GRAB)
NOT BEING VERY CAREFUL, ARE WE?
ESPECIALLY NOT FOR ONE STARTING A REVOLUTION!
!

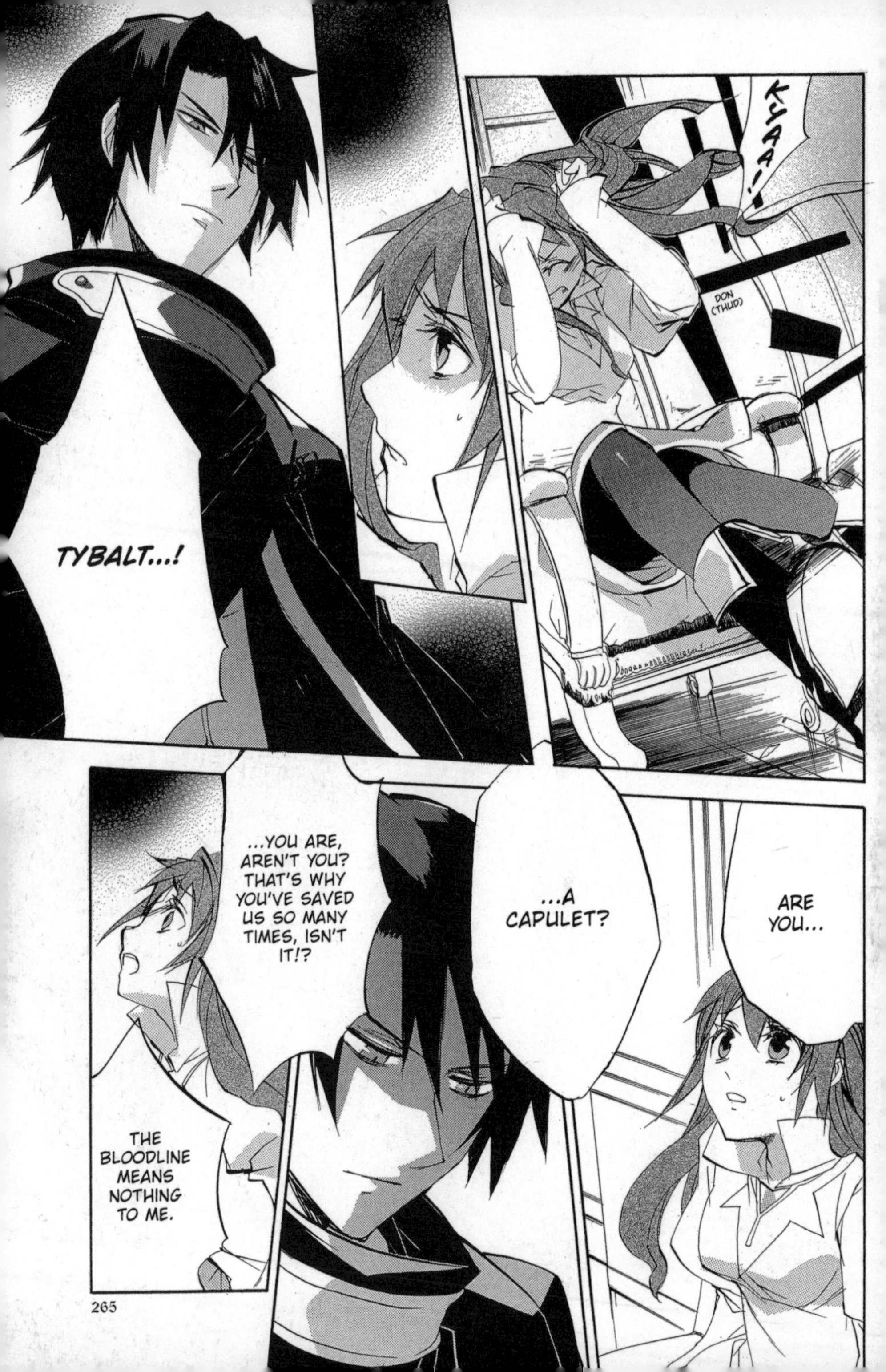
KYAAA!!
DON (THUD)
TYBALT...!
ARE YOU...
...A CAPULET?
...YOU ARE, AREN'T YOU? THAT'S WHY YOU'VE SAVED US SO MANY TIMES, ISN'T IT!?
THE BLOODLINE MEANS NOTHING TO ME.

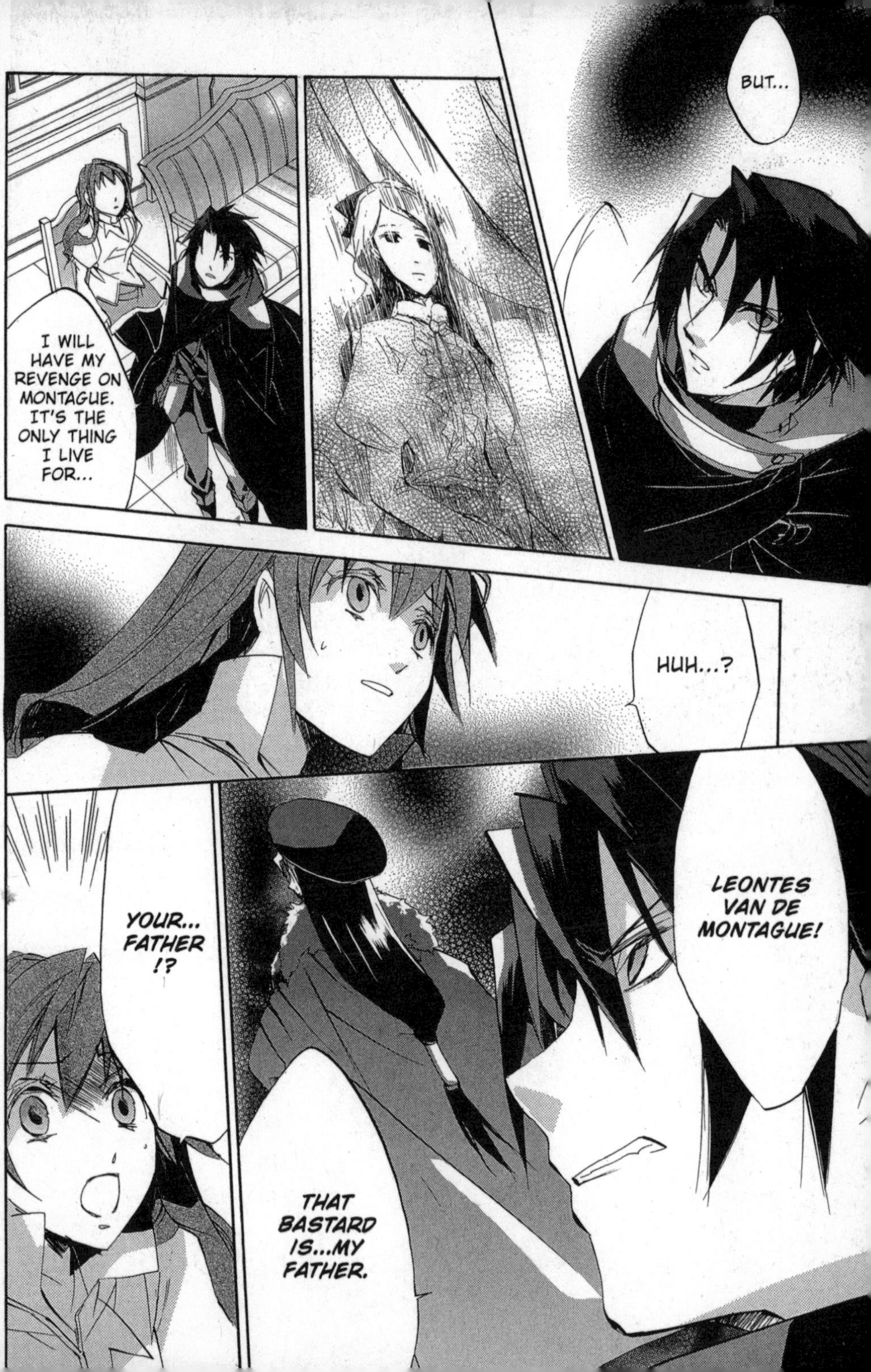
BUT...
I WILL HAVE MY REVENGE ON MONTAGUE. IT'S THE ONLY THING I LIVE FOR...
HUH...?
LEONTES VAN DE MONTAGUE!
THAT BASTARD IS...MY FATHER.
YOUR... FATHER!?

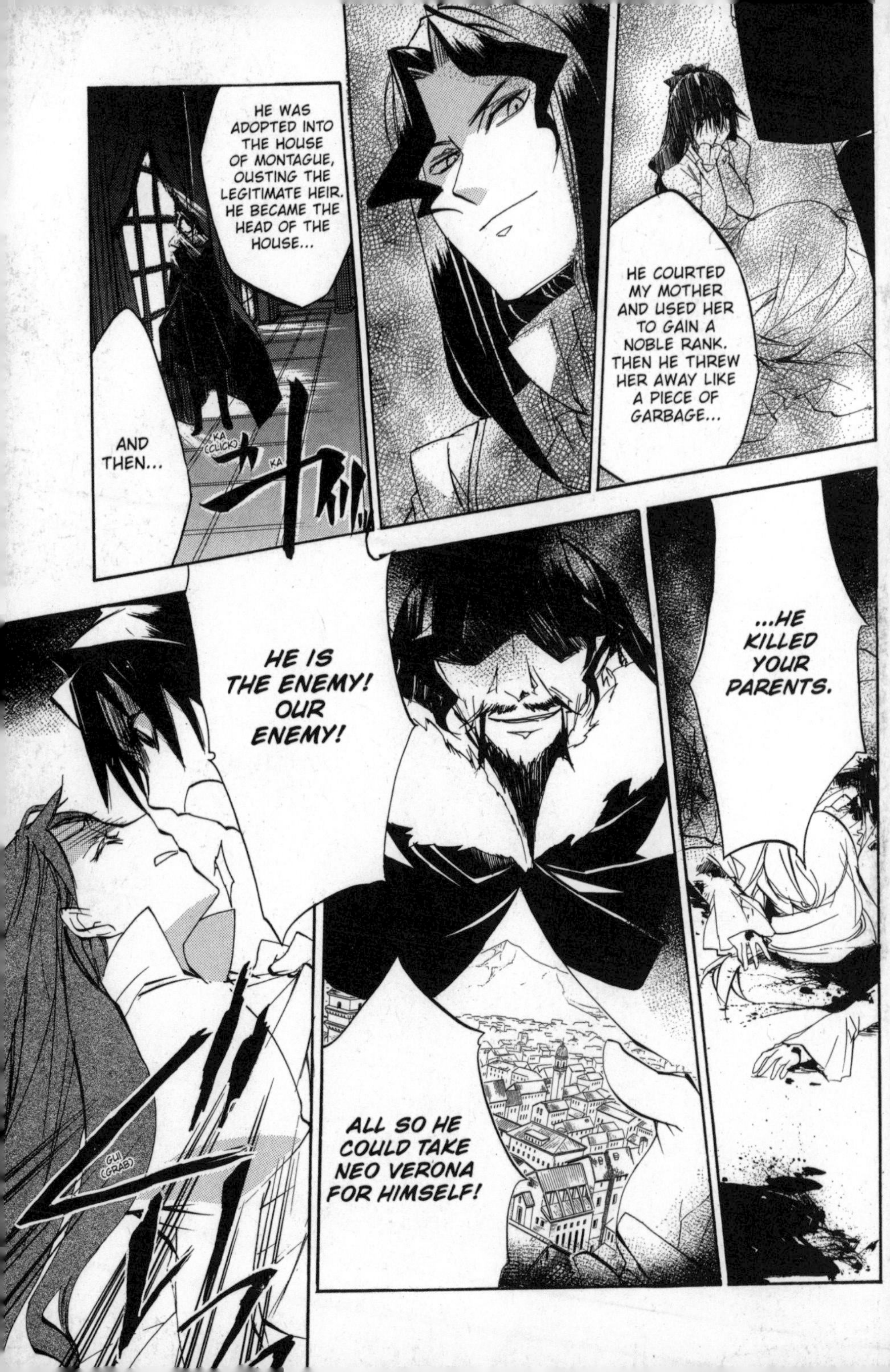
HE COURTED MY MOTHER AND USED HER TO GAIN A NOBLE RANK. THEN HE THREW HER AWAY LIKE A PIECE OF GARBAGE...
HE WAS ADOPTED INTO THE HOUSE OF MONTAGUE, OUSTING THE LEGITIMATE HEIR. HE BECAME THE HEAD OF THE HOUSE...
KA (CLICK)
KA
AND THEN...
...HE KILLED YOUR PARENTS.
ALL SO HE COULD TAKE NEO VERONA FOR HIMSELF!
HE IS THE ENEMY! OUR ENEMY!
GUI (GRAB)

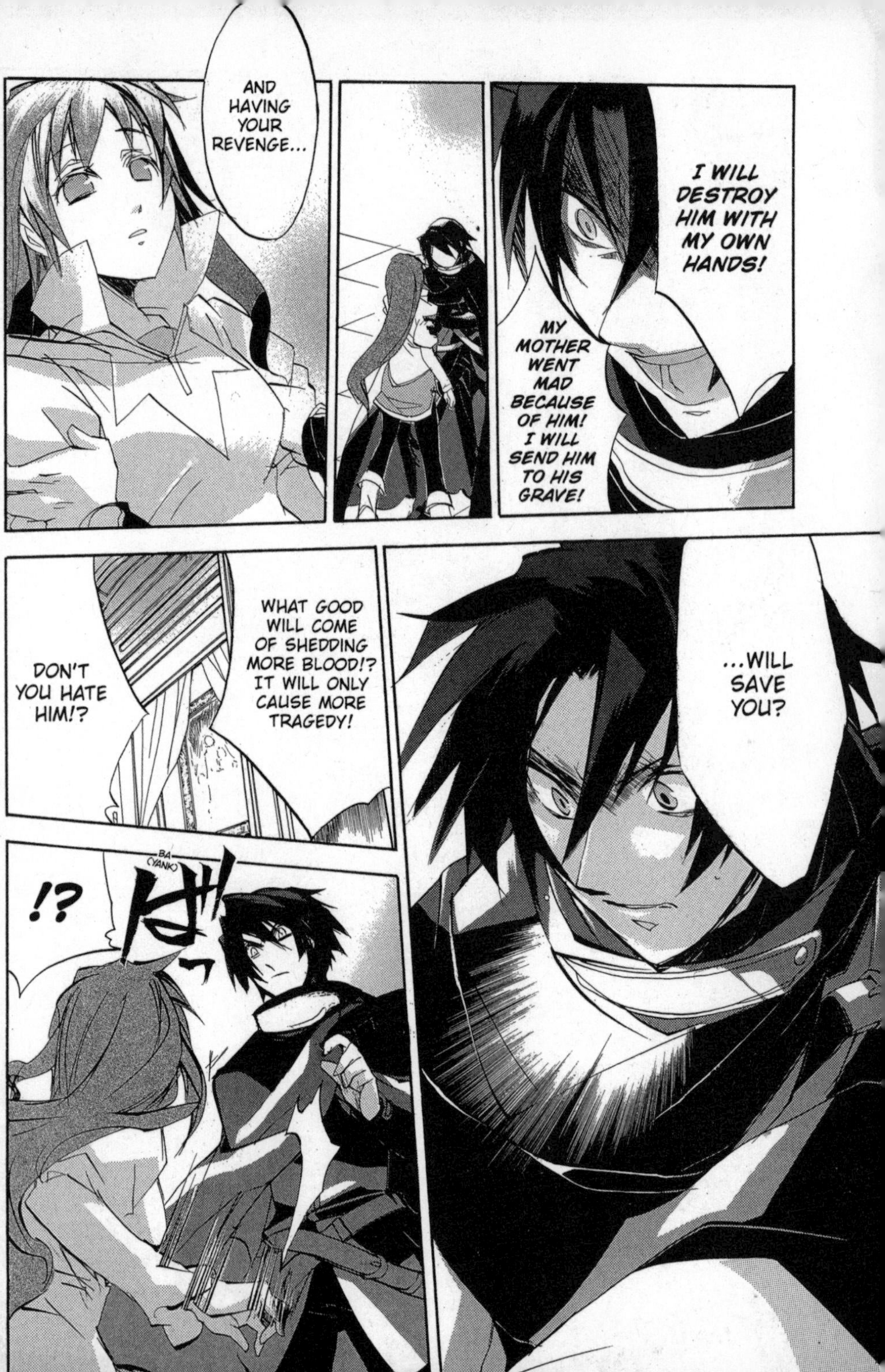
I WILL DESTROY HIM WITH MY OWN HANDS!
MY MOTHER WENT MAD BECAUSE OF HIM! I WILL SEND HIM TO HIS GRAVE!
AND HAVING YOUR REVENGE...
...WILL SAVE YOU?
WHAT GOOD WILL COME OF SHEDDING MORE BLOOD!? IT WILL ONLY CAUSE MORE TRAGEDY!
DON'T YOU HATE HIM!?
BA (YANK)
!?

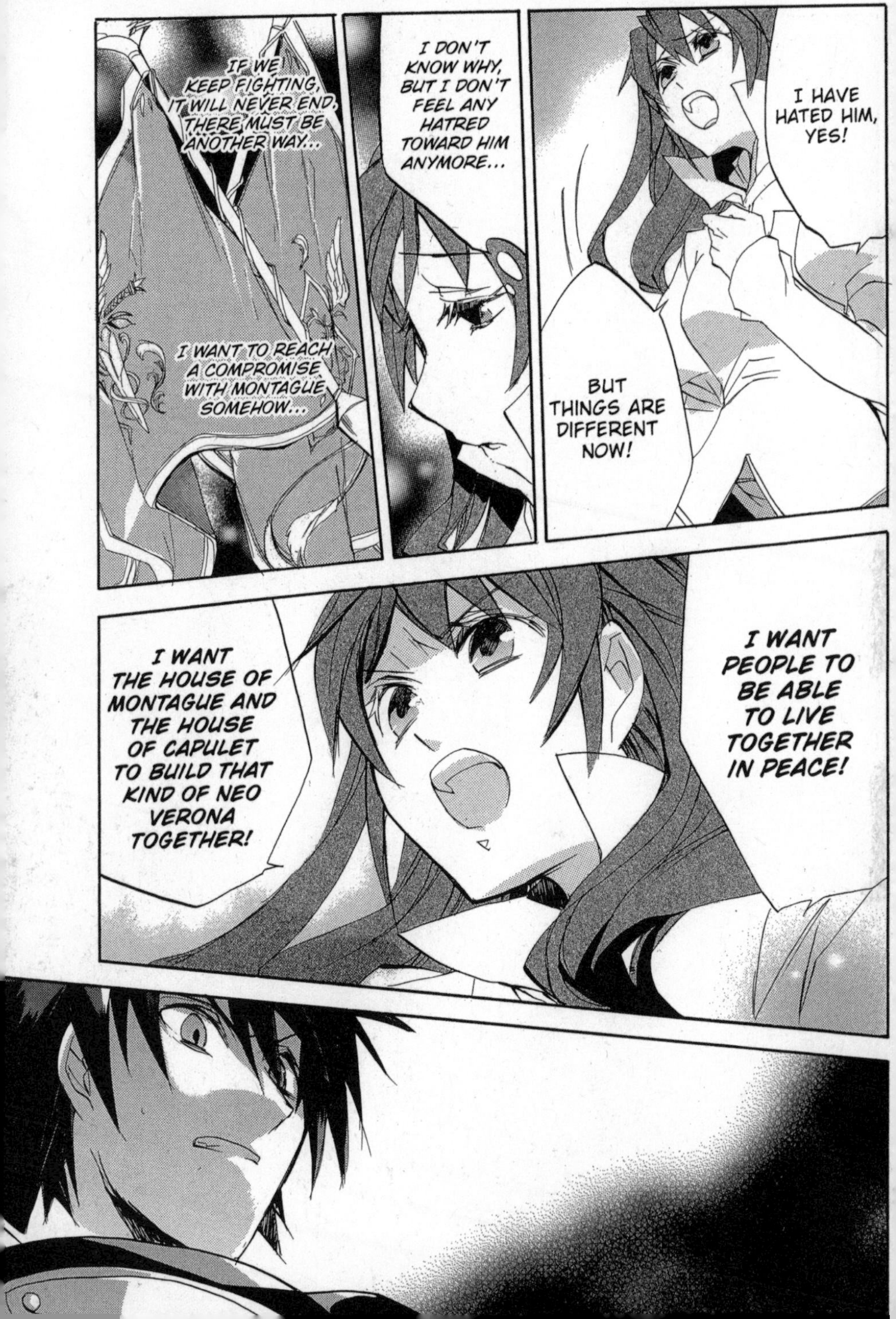

I HAVE HATED HIM, YES!
BUT THINGS ARE DIFFERENT NOW!
I DON'T KNOW WHY, BUT I DON'T FEEL ANY HATRED TOWARD HIM ANYMORE...
IF WE KEEP FIGHTING, IT WILL NEVER END. THERE MUST BE ANOTHER WAY...
I WANT TO REACH A COMPROMISE WITH MONTAGUE SOMEHOW...
I WANT PEOPLE TO BE ABLE TO LIVE TOGETHER IN PEACE!
I WANT THE HOUSE OF MONTAGUE AND THE HOUSE OF CAPULET TO BUILD THAT KIND OF NEO VERONA TOGETHER!

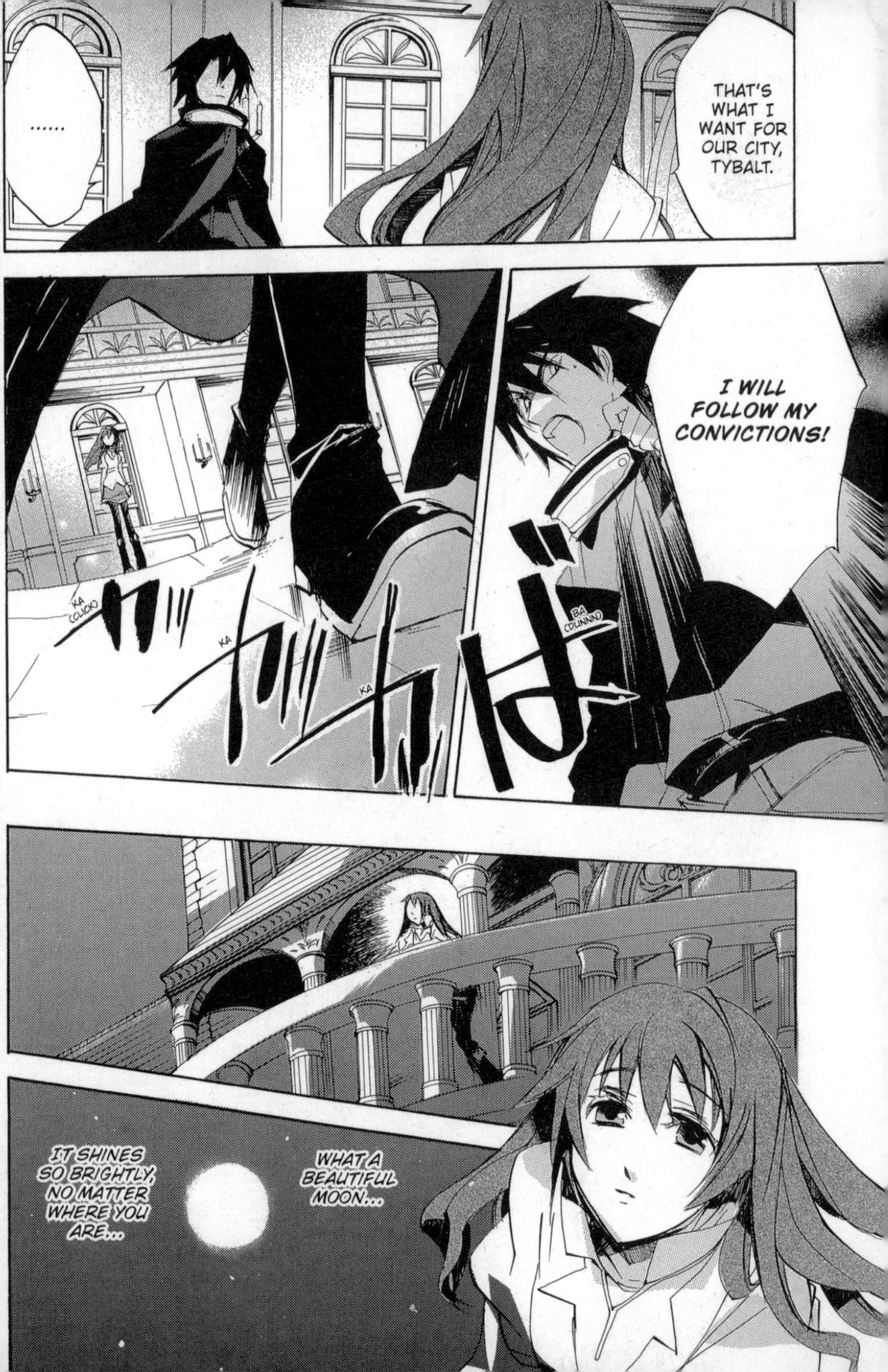
THAT'S WHAT I WANT FOR OUR CITY, TYBALT.
......
I WILL FOLLOW MY CONVICTIONS!
BA (DUNNN)
KA (CLICK)
KA
KA
WHAT A BEAUTIFUL MOON...
IT SHINES SO BRIGHTLY, NO MATTER WHERE YOU ARE...

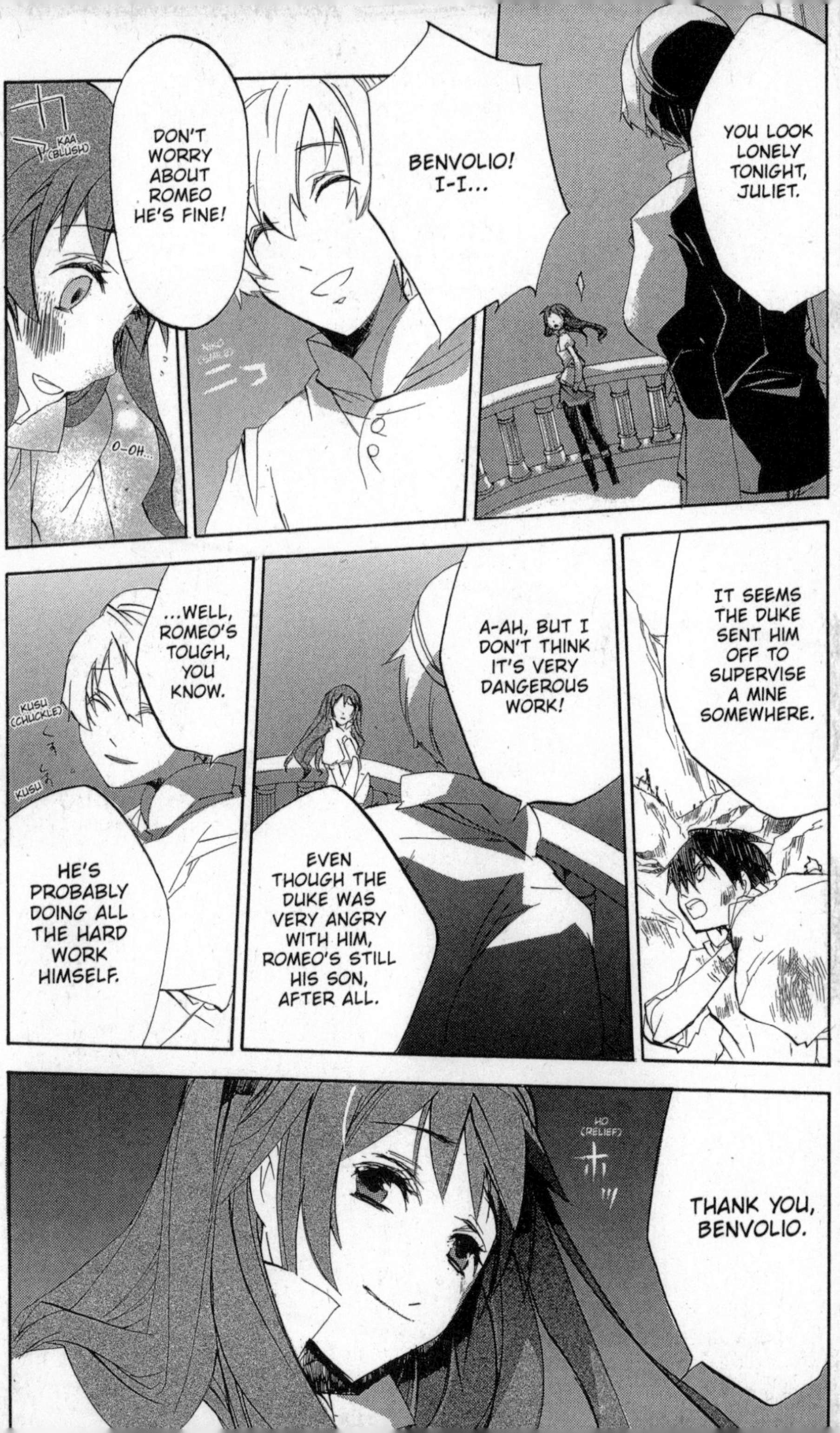
YOU LOOK LONELY TONIGHT, JULIET.
BENVOLIO! I-I...
DON'T WORRY ABOUT ROMEO HE'S FINE!
NIKO (SMILE)
KAA (BLUSH)
O-OH...
IT SEEMS THE DUKE SENT HIM OFF TO SUPERVISE A MINE SOMEWHERE.
A-AH, BUT I DON'T THINK IT'S VERY DANGEROUS WORK!
EVEN THOUGH THE DUKE WAS VERY ANGRY WITH HIM, ROMEO'S STILL HIS SON, AFTER ALL.
...WELL, ROMEO'S TOUGH, YOU KNOW.
KUSU (CHUCKLE)
KUSU
HE'S PROBABLY DOING ALL THE HARD WORK HIMSELF.
HO (RELIEF)
THANK YOU, BENVOLIO.

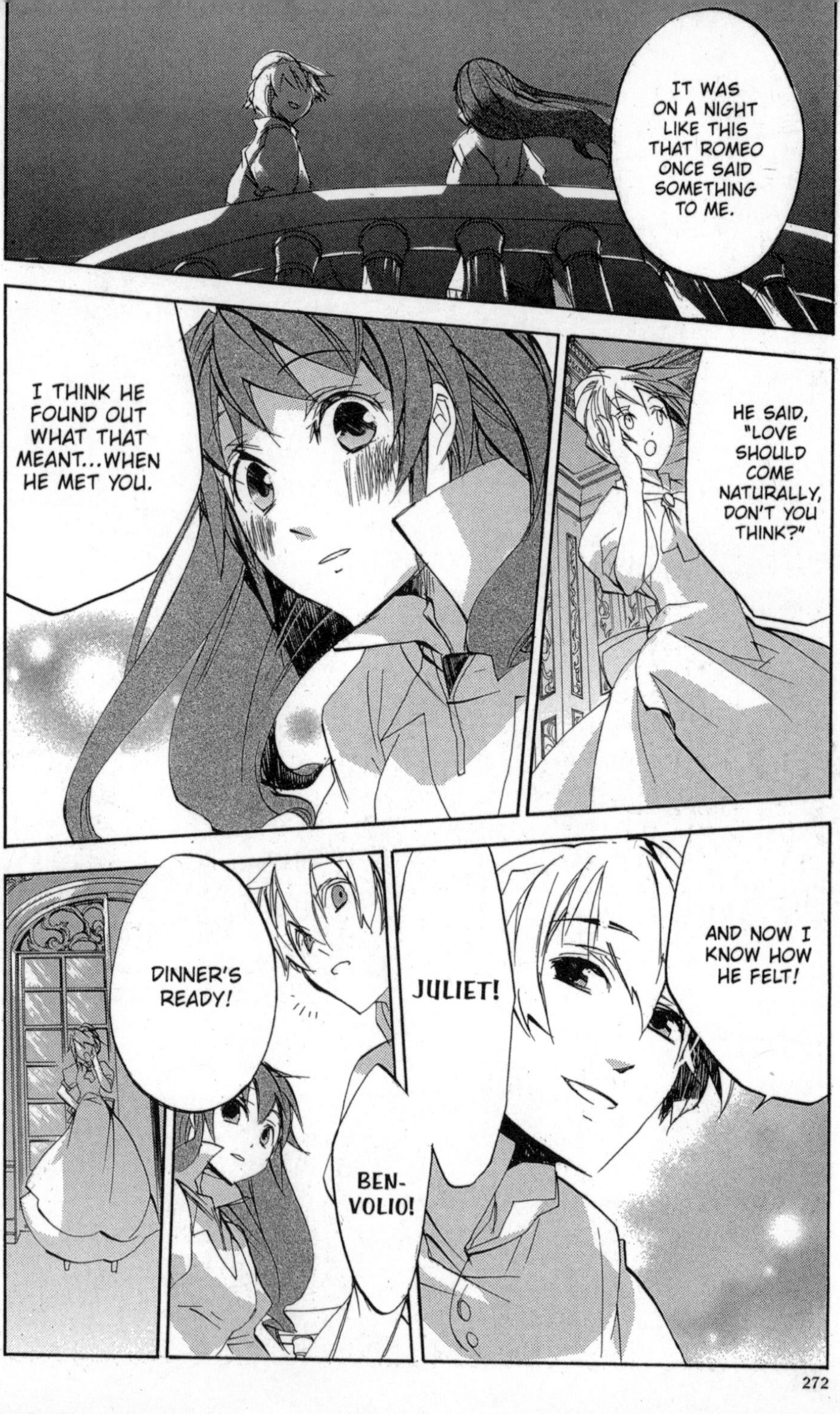
IT WAS ON A NIGHT LIKE THIS THAT ROMEO ONCE SAID SOMETHING TO ME.
HE SAID, "LOVE SHOULD COME NATURALLY, DON'T YOU THINK?"
I THINK HE FOUND OUT WHAT THAT MEANT...WHEN HE MET YOU.
AND NOW I KNOW HOW HE FELT!
JULIET!
BEN-VOLIO!
DINNER'S READY!

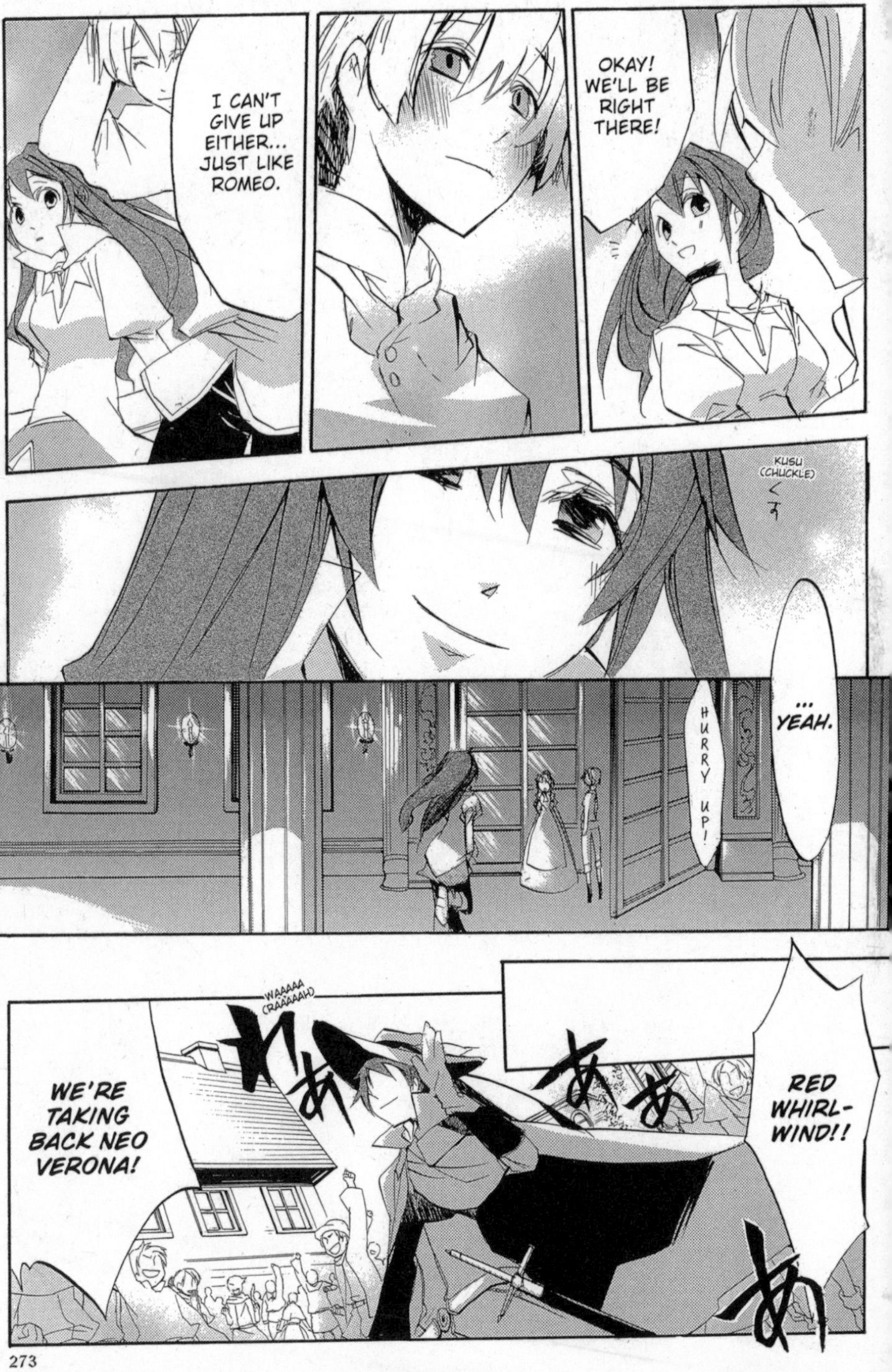
OKAY! WE'LL BE RIGHT THERE!
I CAN'T GIVE UP EITHER... JUST LIKE ROMEO.
KUSU (CHUCKLE)
くす
...YEAH.
HURRY UP!
RED WHIRL-WIND!!
WAAAAA (RAAAAAH)
わあああ
WE'RE TAKING BACK NEO VERONA!

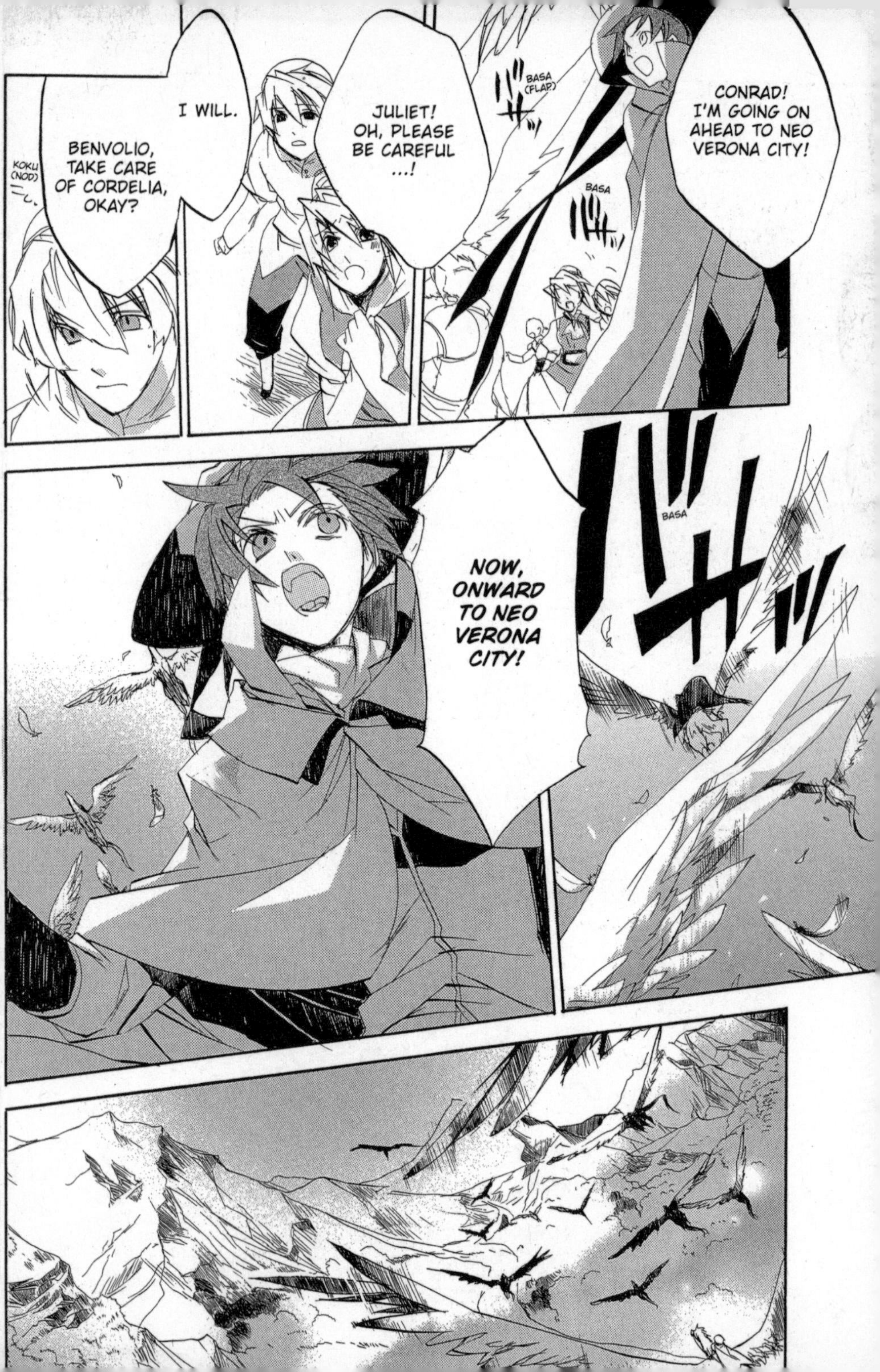
CONRAD! I'M GOING ON AHEAD TO NEO VERONA CITY!
BASA (FLAP)
BASA
JULIET! OH, PLEASE BE CAREFUL ...!
I WILL.
BENVOLIO, TAKE CARE OF CORDELIA, OKAY?
KOKU (NOD)
BASA
NOW, ONWARD TO NEO VERONA CITY!

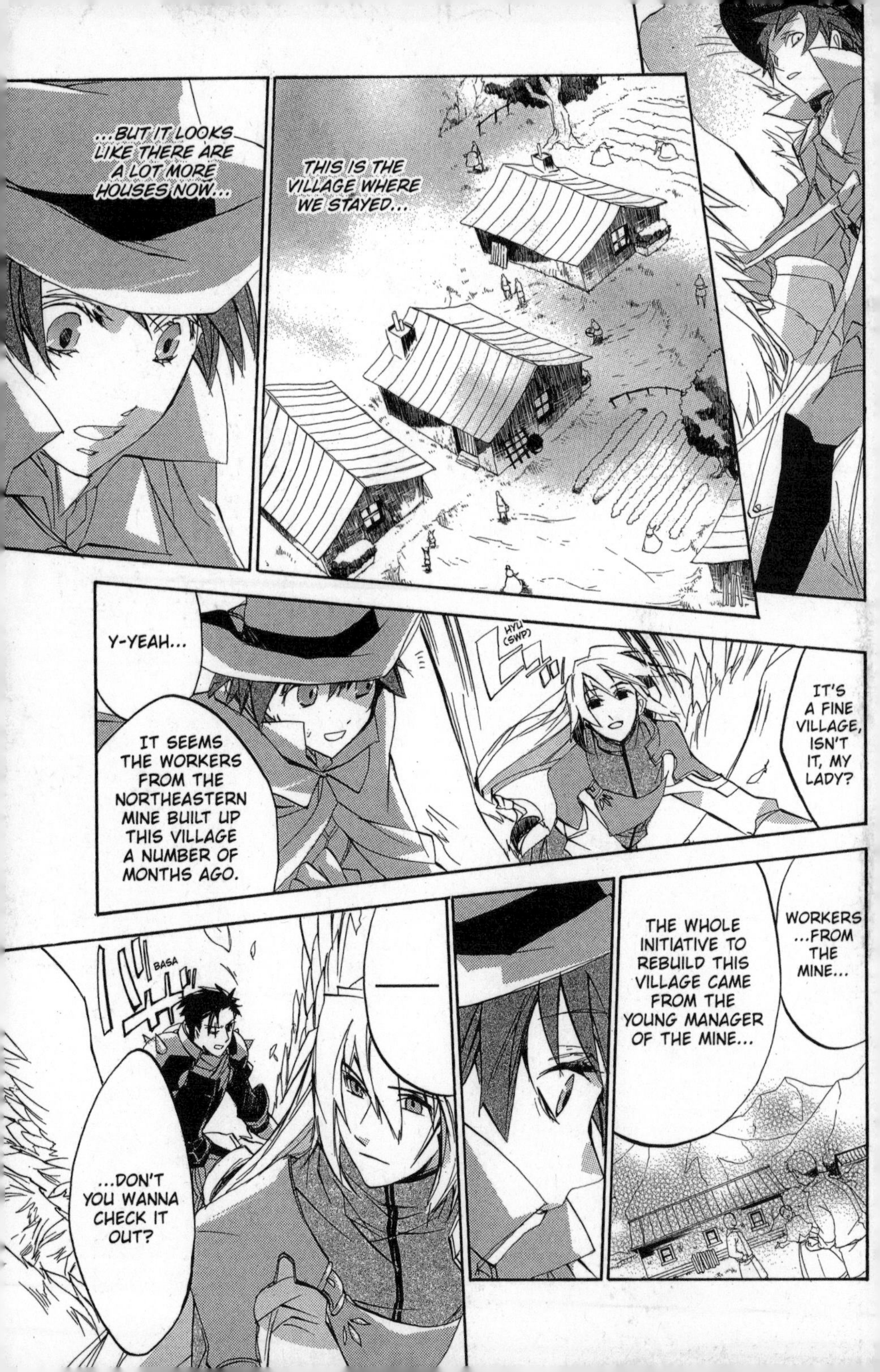
THIS IS THE VILLAGE WHERE WE STAYED...
...BUT IT LOOKS LIKE THERE ARE A LOT MORE HOUSES NOW...
IT'S A FINE VILLAGE, ISN'T IT, MY LADY?
HYU (SWP)
Y-YEAH...
IT SEEMS THE WORKERS FROM THE NORTHEASTERN MINE BUILT UP THIS VILLAGE A NUMBER OF MONTHS AGO.
WORKERS ...FROM THE MINE...
THE WHOLE INITIATIVE TO REBUILD THIS VILLAGE CAME FROM THE YOUNG MANAGER OF THE MINE...
——
BASA
...DON'T YOU WANNA CHECK IT OUT?

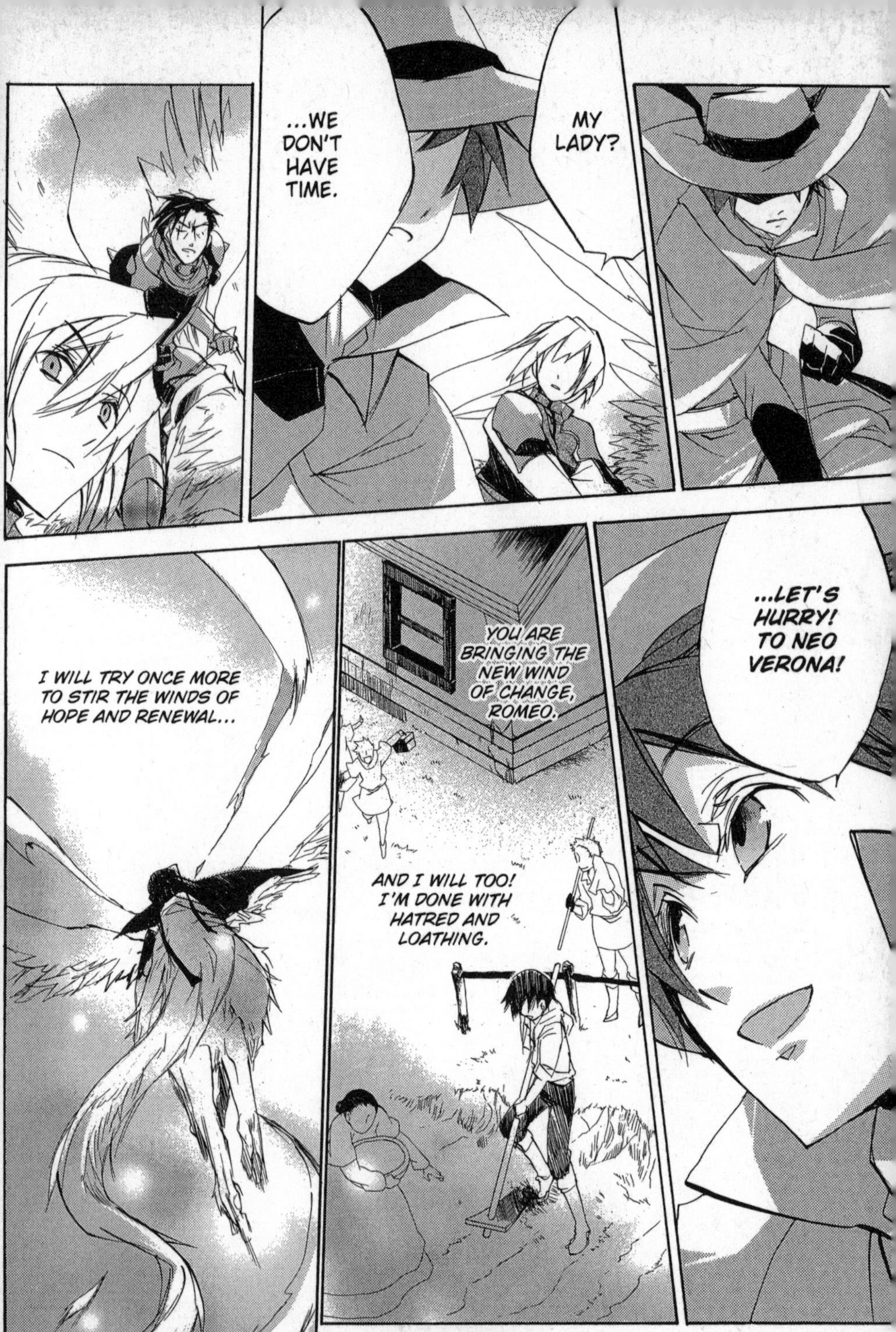
MY LADY?
...WE DON'T HAVE TIME.
...LET'S HURRY! TO NEO VERONA!
YOU ARE BRINGING THE NEW WIND OF CHANGE, ROMEO.
AND I WILL TOO! I'M DONE WITH HATRED AND LOATHING.
I WILL TRY ONCE MORE TO STIR THE WINDS OF HOPE AND RENEWAL...

ACT 7 ◆ END

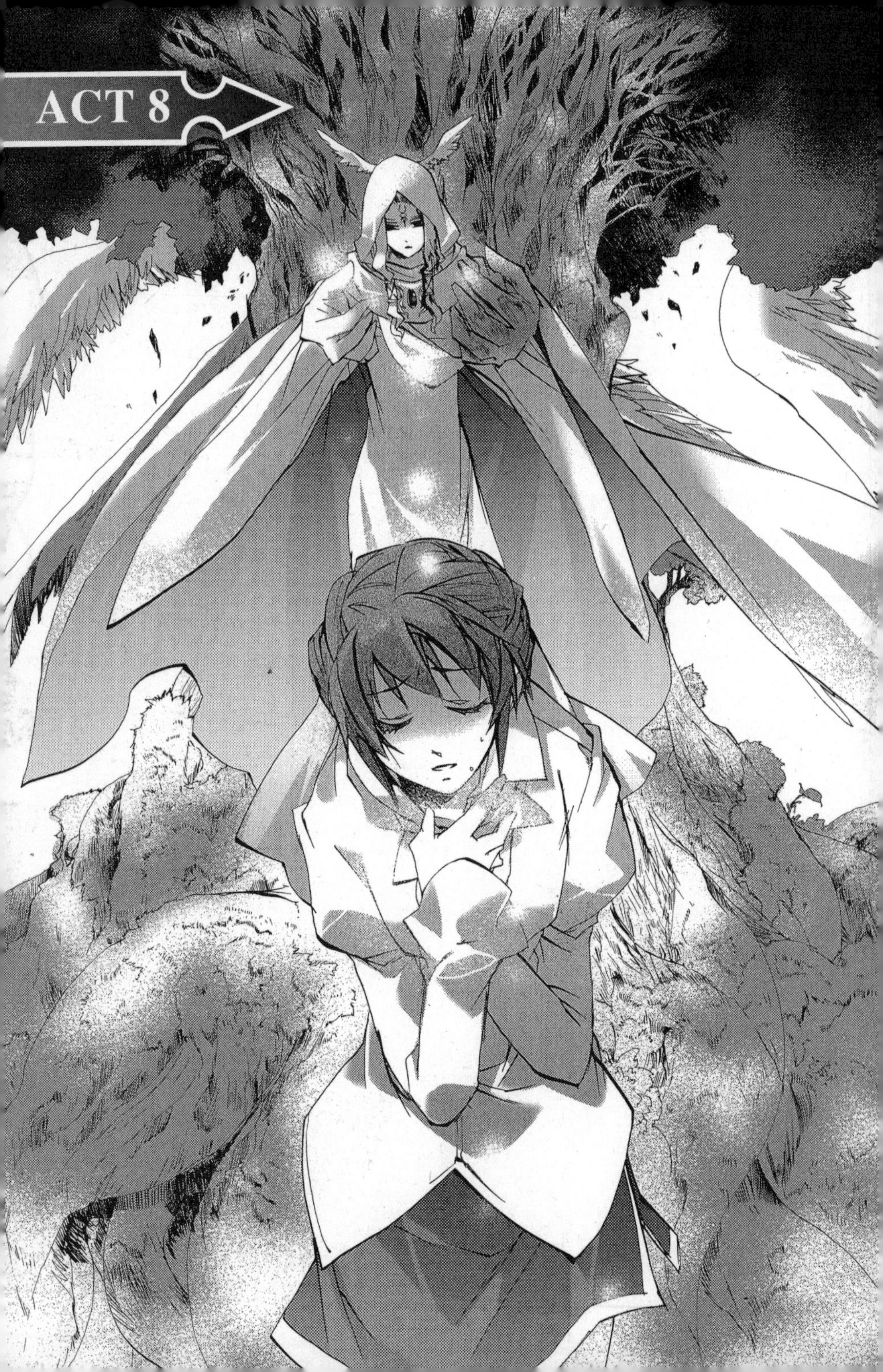
ACT 8

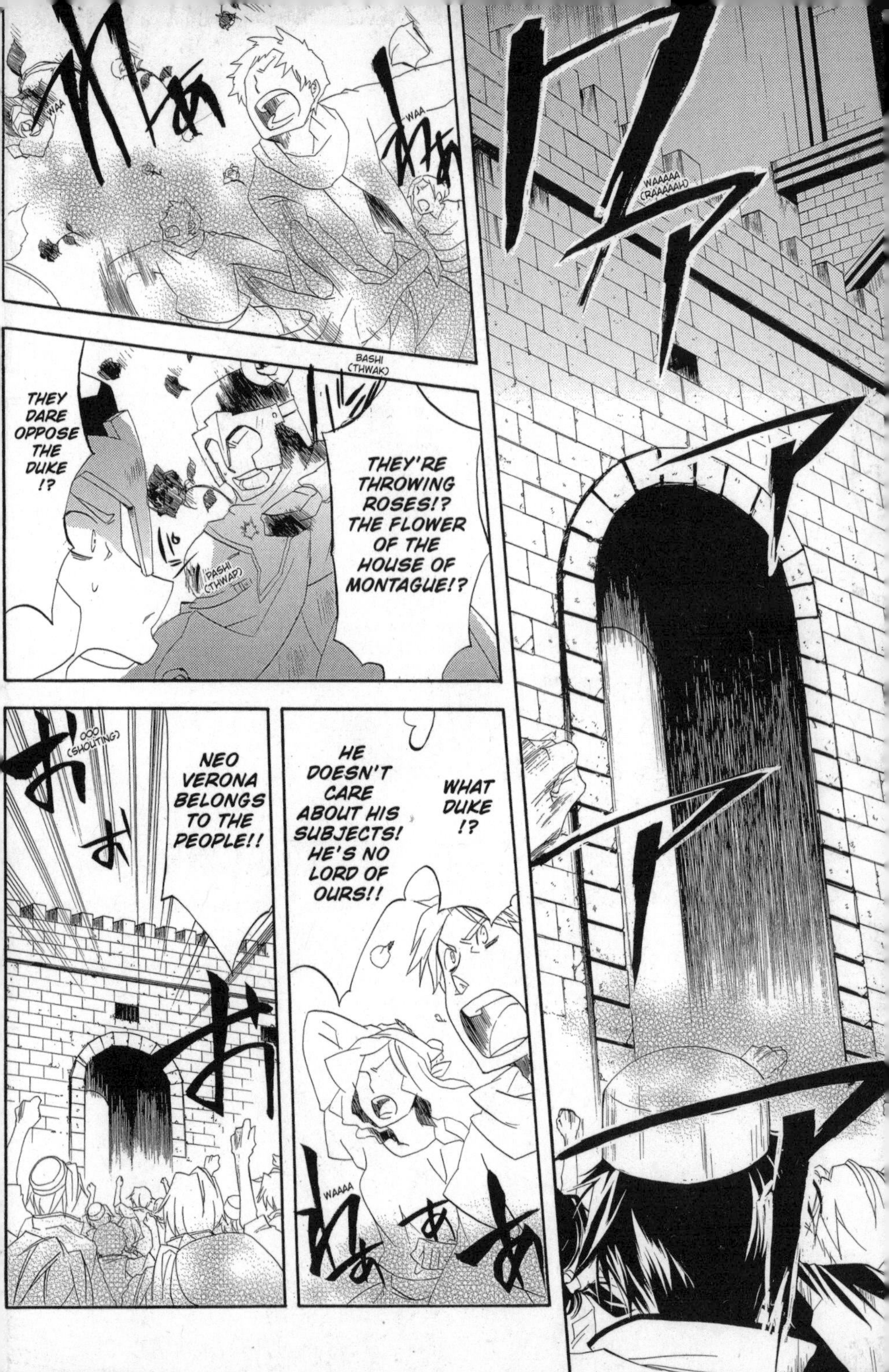
WAAAAA (RAAAAAH)
WAA
WAA
BASHI (THWAK)
THEY'RE THROWING ROSES!? THE FLOWER OF THE HOUSE OF MONTAGUE!?
THEY DARE OPPOSE THE DUKE!?
PASHI (THWAP)
WHAT DUKE!?
HE DOESN'T CARE ABOUT HIS SUBJECTS! HE'S NO LORD OF OURS!!
WAAAA
NEO VERONA BELONGS TO THE PEOPLE!!
OOO (SHOUTING)

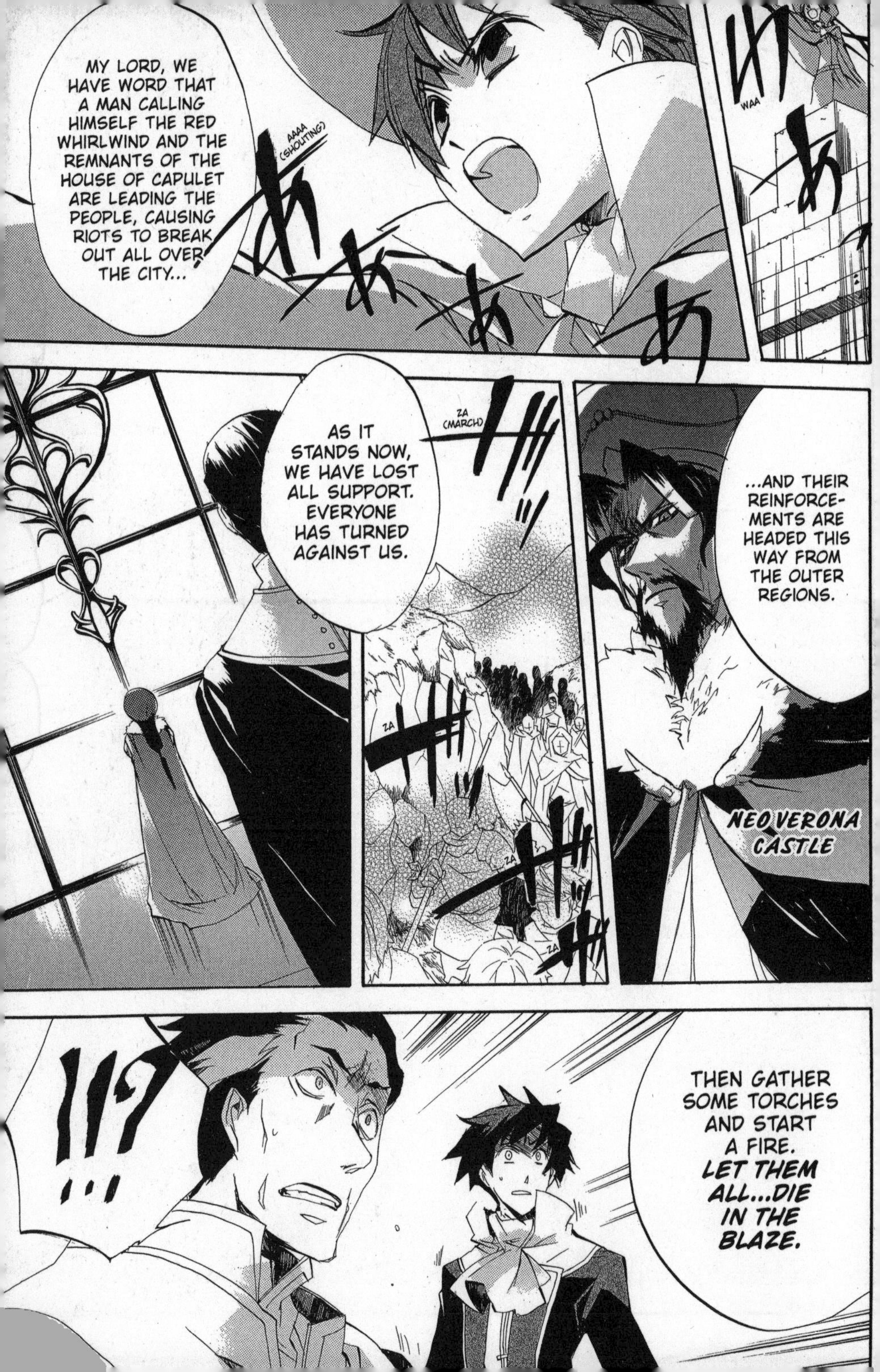
WAA
AAAA (SHOUTING)
MY LORD, WE HAVE WORD THAT A MAN CALLING HIMSELF THE RED WHIRLWIND AND THE REMNANTS OF THE HOUSE OF CAPULET ARE LEADING THE PEOPLE, CAUSING RIOTS TO BREAK OUT ALL OVER THE CITY...
...AND THEIR REINFORCE-MENTS ARE HEADED THIS WAY FROM THE OUTER REGIONS.
NEO VERONA CASTLE
ZA (MARCH)
ZA
ZA
ZA
AS IT STANDS NOW, WE HAVE LOST ALL SUPPORT. EVERYONE HAS TURNED AGAINST US.
THEN GATHER SOME TORCHES AND START A FIRE. LET THEM ALL...DIE IN THE BLAZE.
!!?
!!!

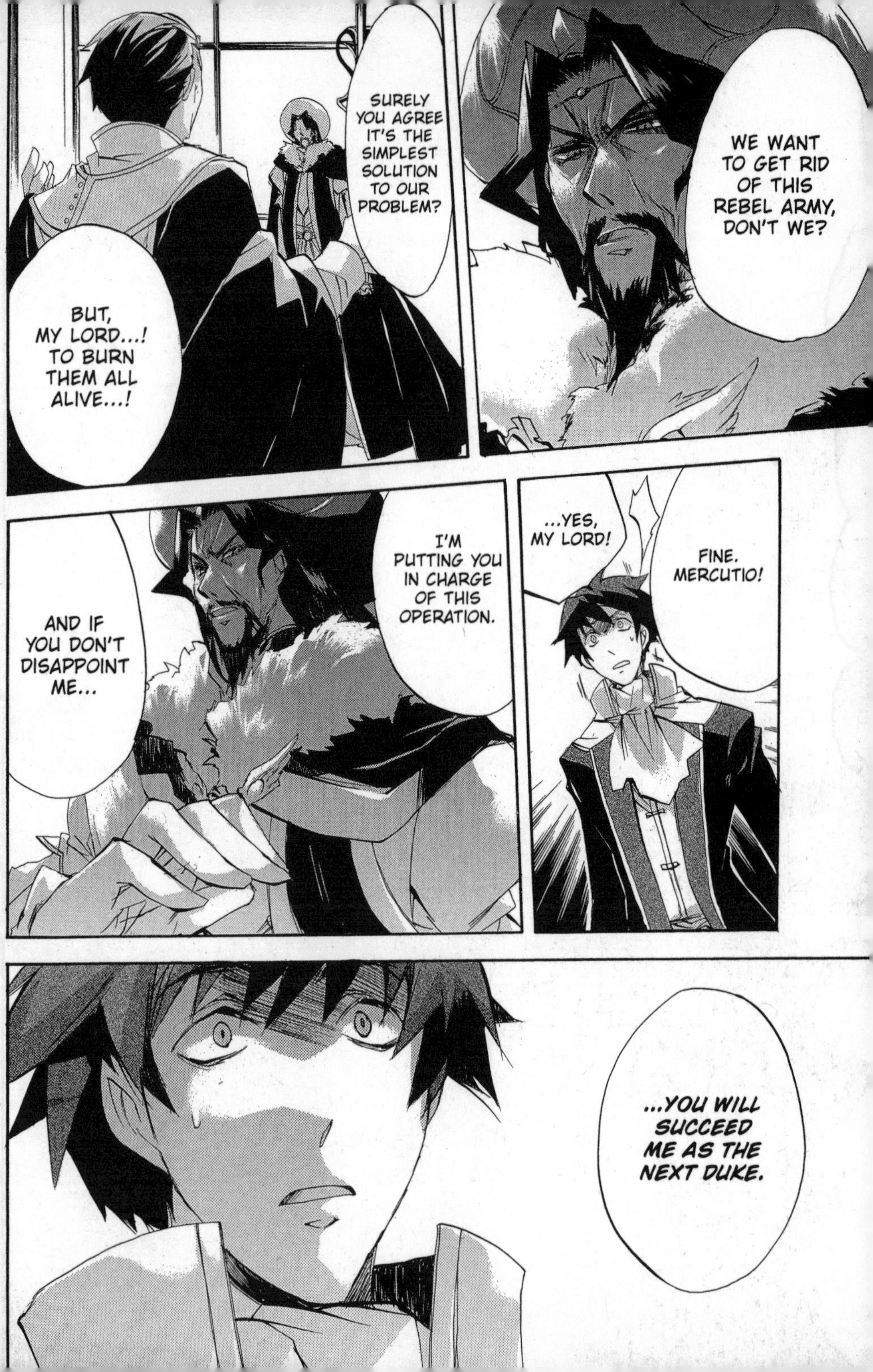
WE WANT TO GET RID OF THIS REBEL ARMY, DON'T WE?
SURELY YOU AGREE IT'S THE SIMPLEST SOLUTION TO OUR PROBLEM?
BUT, MY LORD...! TO BURN THEM ALL ALIVE...!
FINE. MERCUTIO!
...YES, MY LORD!
I'M PUTTING YOU IN CHARGE OF THIS OPERATION.
AND IF YOU DON'T DISAPPOINT ME...
...YOU WILL SUCCEED ME AS THE NEXT DUKE.

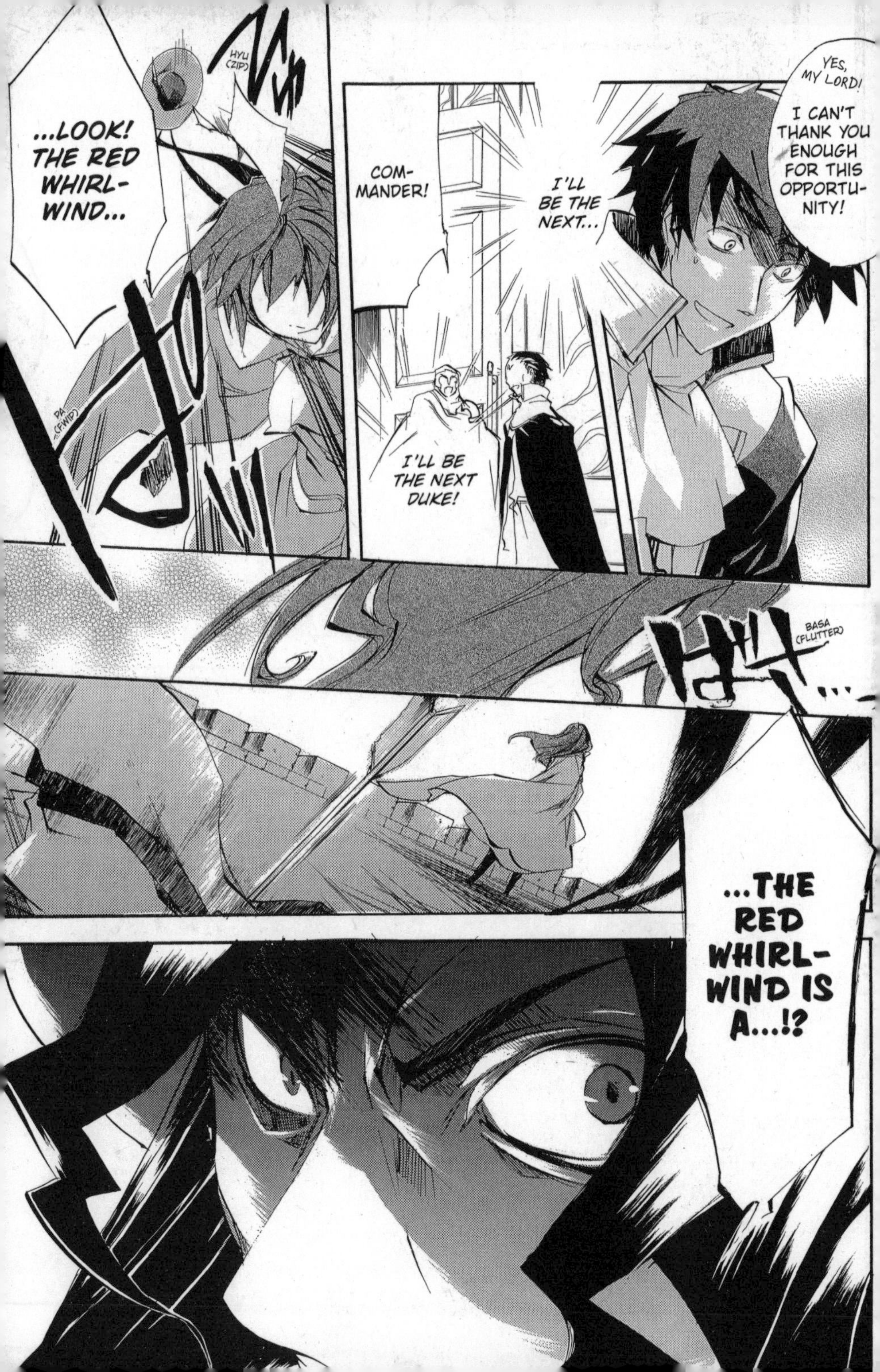

YES, MY LORD!
I CAN'T THANK YOU ENOUGH FOR THIS OPPORTUNITY!
I'LL BE THE NEXT...
COMMANDER!
I'LL BE THE NEXT DUKE!
HYU (ZIP)
...LOOK! THE RED WHIRLWIND...
PA (FWIP)
BASA (FLUTTER)
...THE RED WHIRLWIND IS A...!?

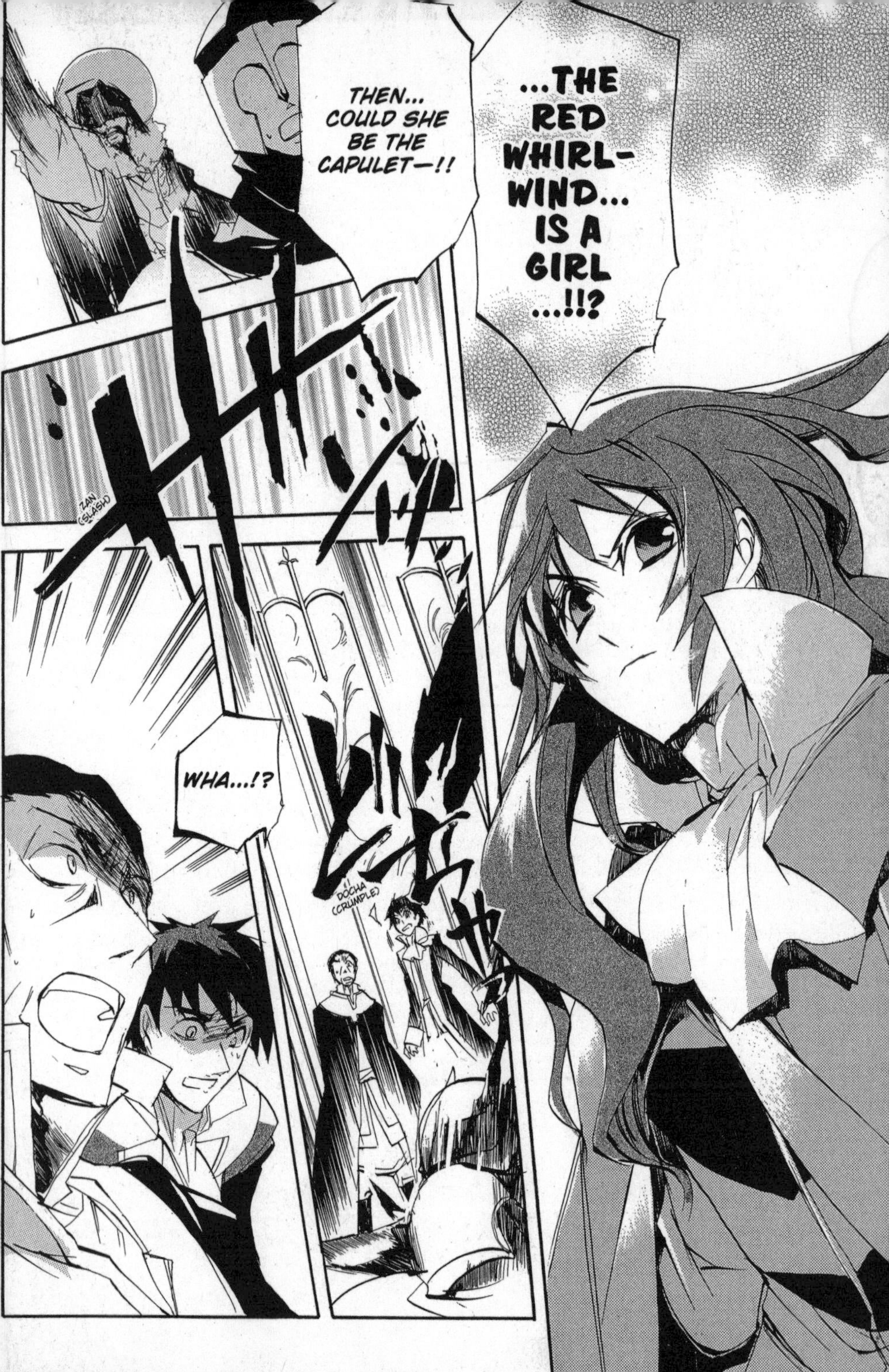
...THE RED WHIRL-WIND... IS A GIRL ...!!?
THEN... COULD SHE BE THE CAPULET—!!
ZAN (SLASH)
DOCHA (CRUMPLE)
WHA...!?

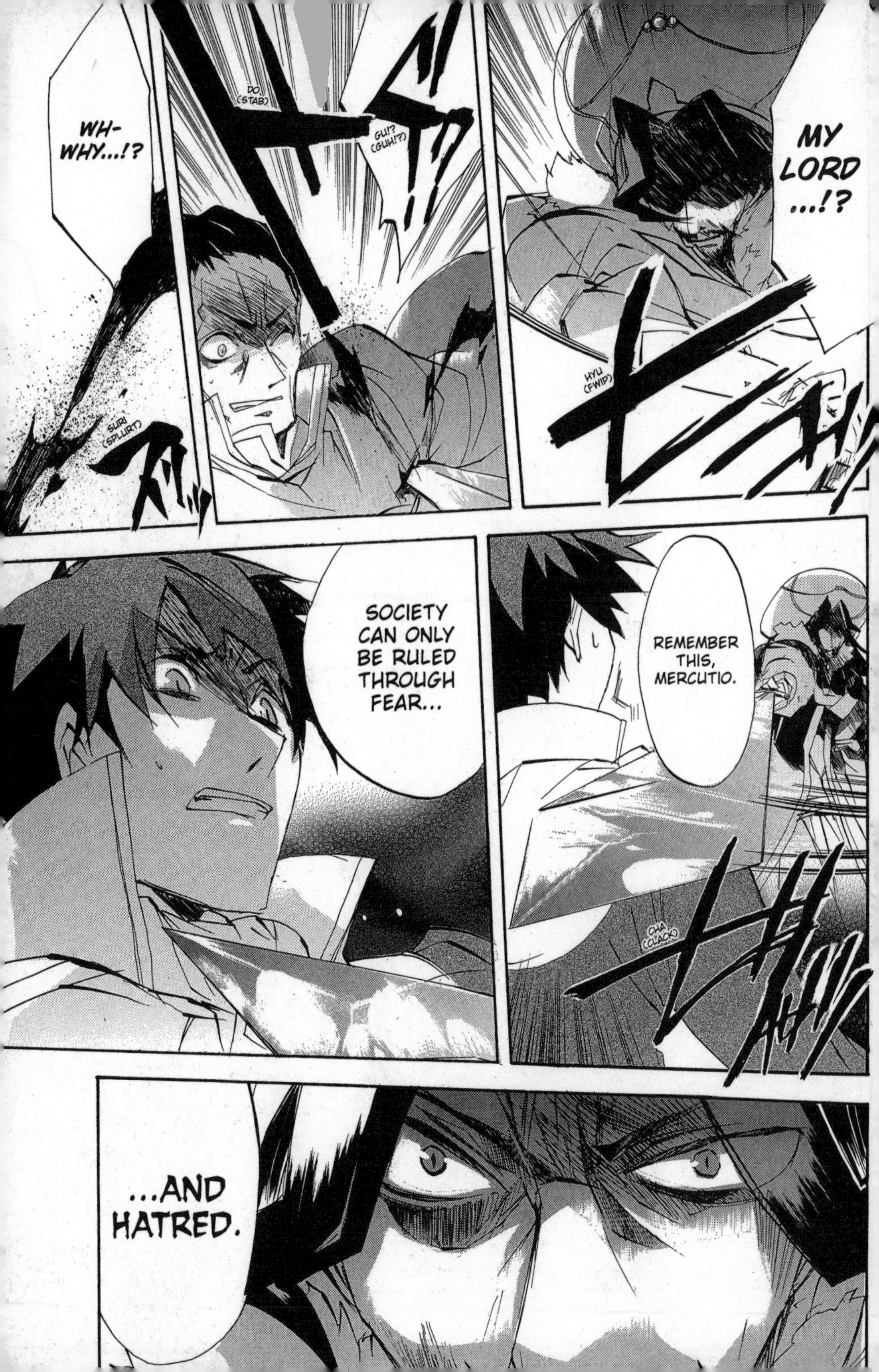
MY LORD ...!?
HYU (FWIP)
DO (STAB)
GU!? (GUH!?)
WH- WHY...!?
SURI (SPLURT)
REMEMBER THIS, MERCUTIO.
CHA (CLACK)
SOCIETY CAN ONLY BE RULED THROUGH FEAR...
...AND HATRED.

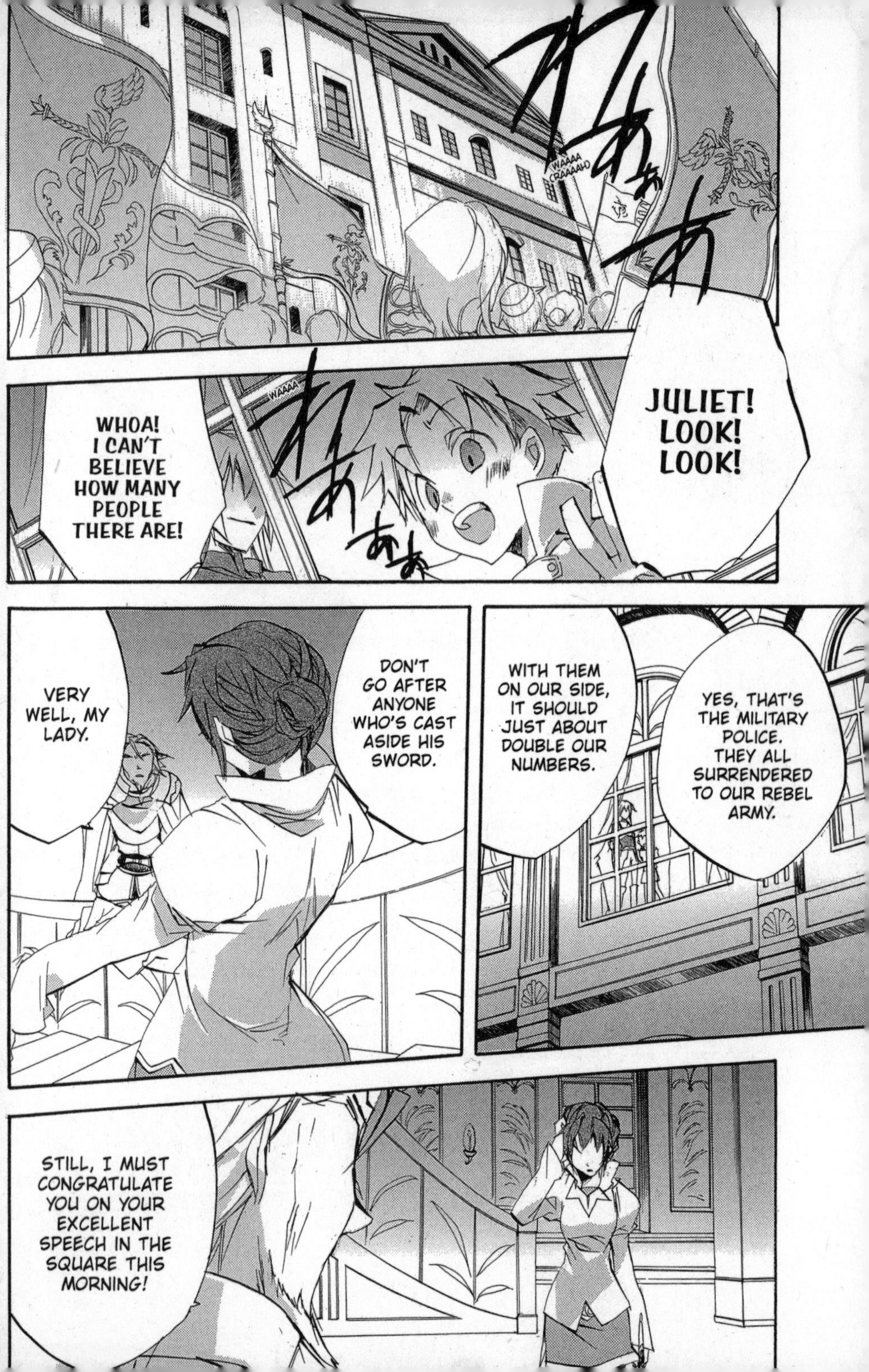
WAAAA CRAAAAH
JULIET! LOOK! LOOK!
WAAAA
WHOA! I CAN'T BELIEVE HOW MANY PEOPLE THERE ARE!
YES, THAT'S THE MILITARY POLICE. THEY ALL SURRENDERED TO OUR REBEL ARMY.
WITH THEM ON OUR SIDE, IT SHOULD JUST ABOUT DOUBLE OUR NUMBERS.
DON'T GO AFTER ANYONE WHO'S CAST ASIDE HIS SWORD.
VERY WELL, MY LADY.
STILL, I MUST CONGRATULATE YOU ON YOUR EXCELLENT SPEECH IN THE SQUARE THIS MORNING!

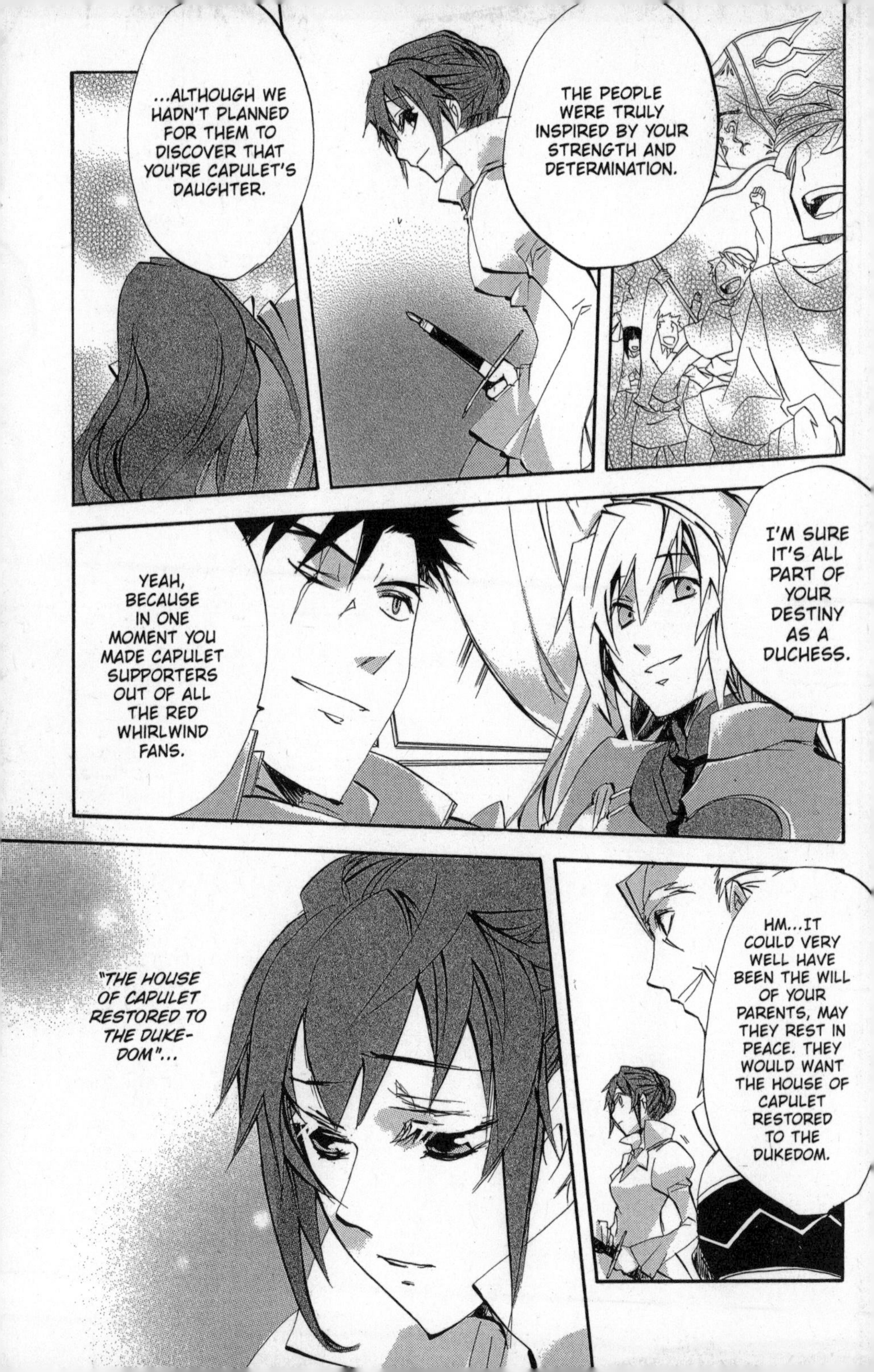
THE PEOPLE WERE TRULY INSPIRED BY YOUR STRENGTH AND DETERMINATION.
...ALTHOUGH WE HADN'T PLANNED FOR THEM TO DISCOVER THAT YOU'RE CAPULET'S DAUGHTER.
I'M SURE IT'S ALL PART OF YOUR DESTINY AS A DUCHESS.
YEAH, BECAUSE IN ONE MOMENT YOU MADE CAPULET SUPPORTERS OUT OF ALL THE RED WHIRLWIND FANS.
HM...IT COULD VERY WELL HAVE BEEN THE WILL OF YOUR PARENTS, MAY THEY REST IN PEACE. THEY WOULD WANT THE HOUSE OF CAPULET RESTORED TO THE DUKEDOM.
"THE HOUSE OF CAPULET RESTORED TO THE DUKE-DOM"...

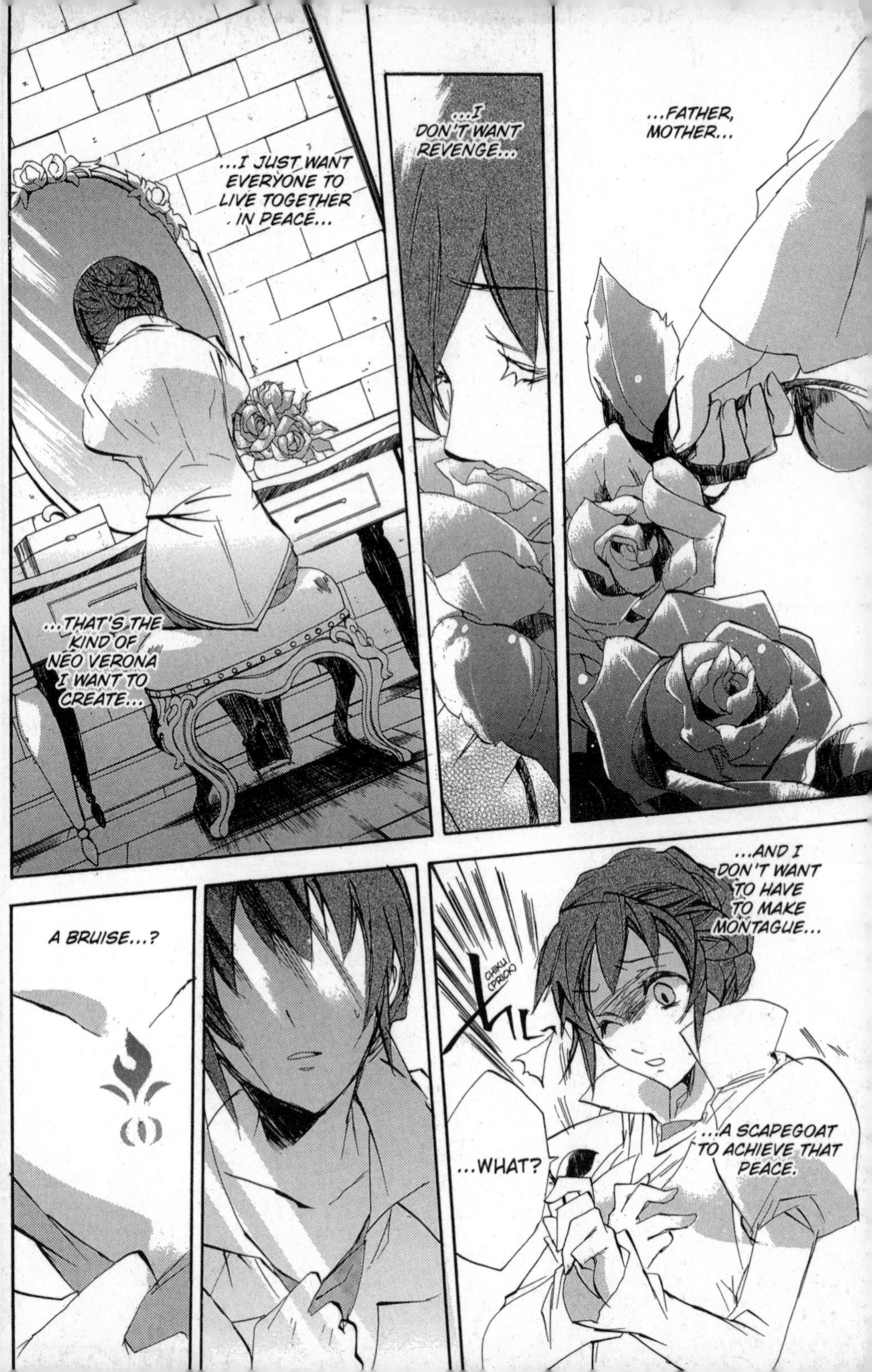
...FATHER, MOTHER...
...I DON'T WANT REVENGE...
...I JUST WANT EVERYONE TO LIVE TOGETHER IN PEACE...
...THAT'S THE KIND OF NEO VERONA I WANT TO CREATE...
...AND I DON'T WANT TO HAVE TO MAKE MONTAGUE...
CHIKU (PRICK)
...A SCAPEGOAT TO ACHIEVE THAT PEACE.
...WHAT?
A BRUISE...?

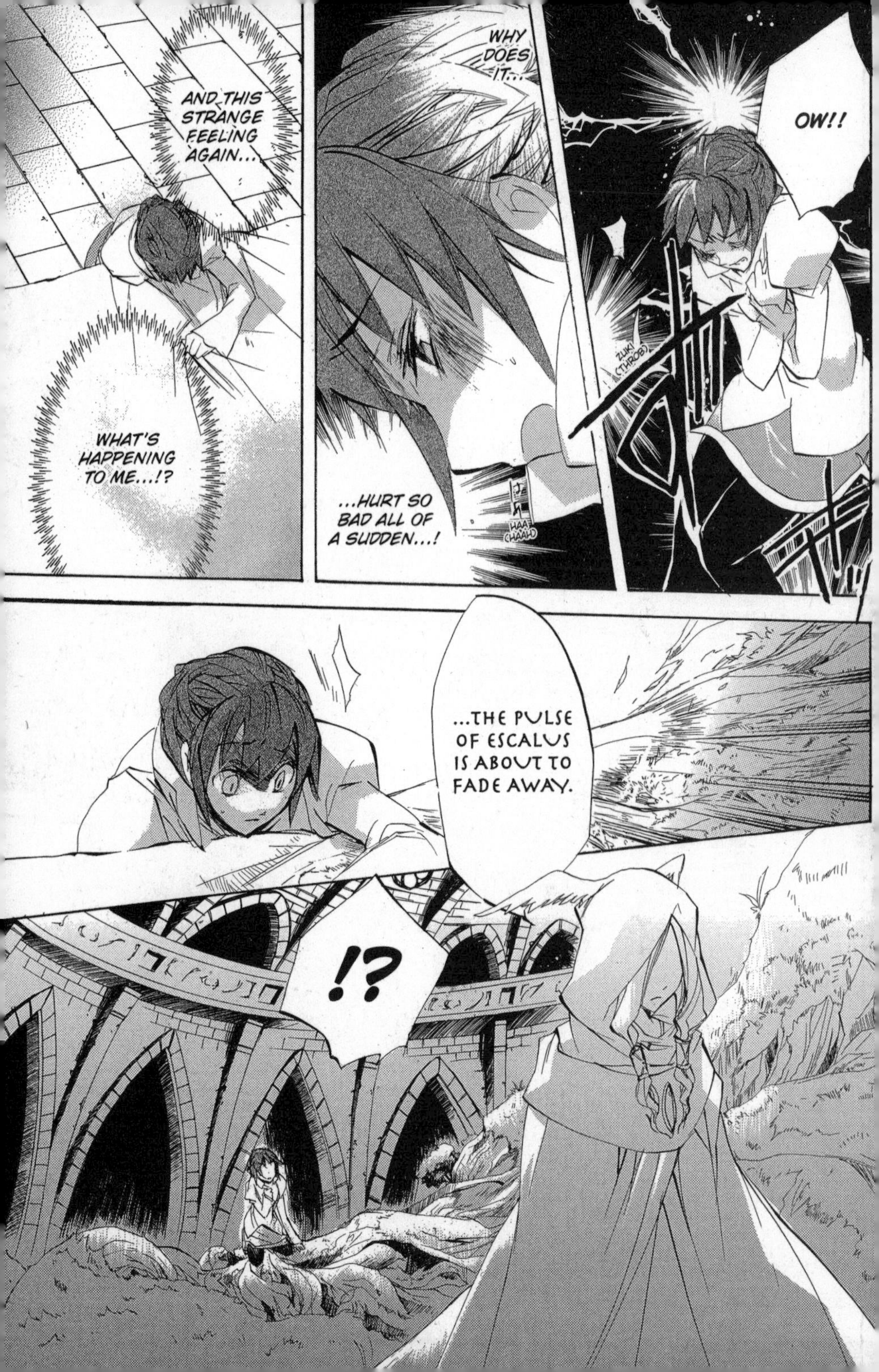
OW!!
ZUKI (THROB)
WHY DOES IT...
...HURT SO BAD ALL OF A SUDDEN...!
HAA (HAAH)
AND THIS STRANGE FEELING AGAIN...
WHAT'S HAPPENING TO ME...!?
...THE PULSE OF ESCALUS IS ABOUT TO FADE AWAY.
!?

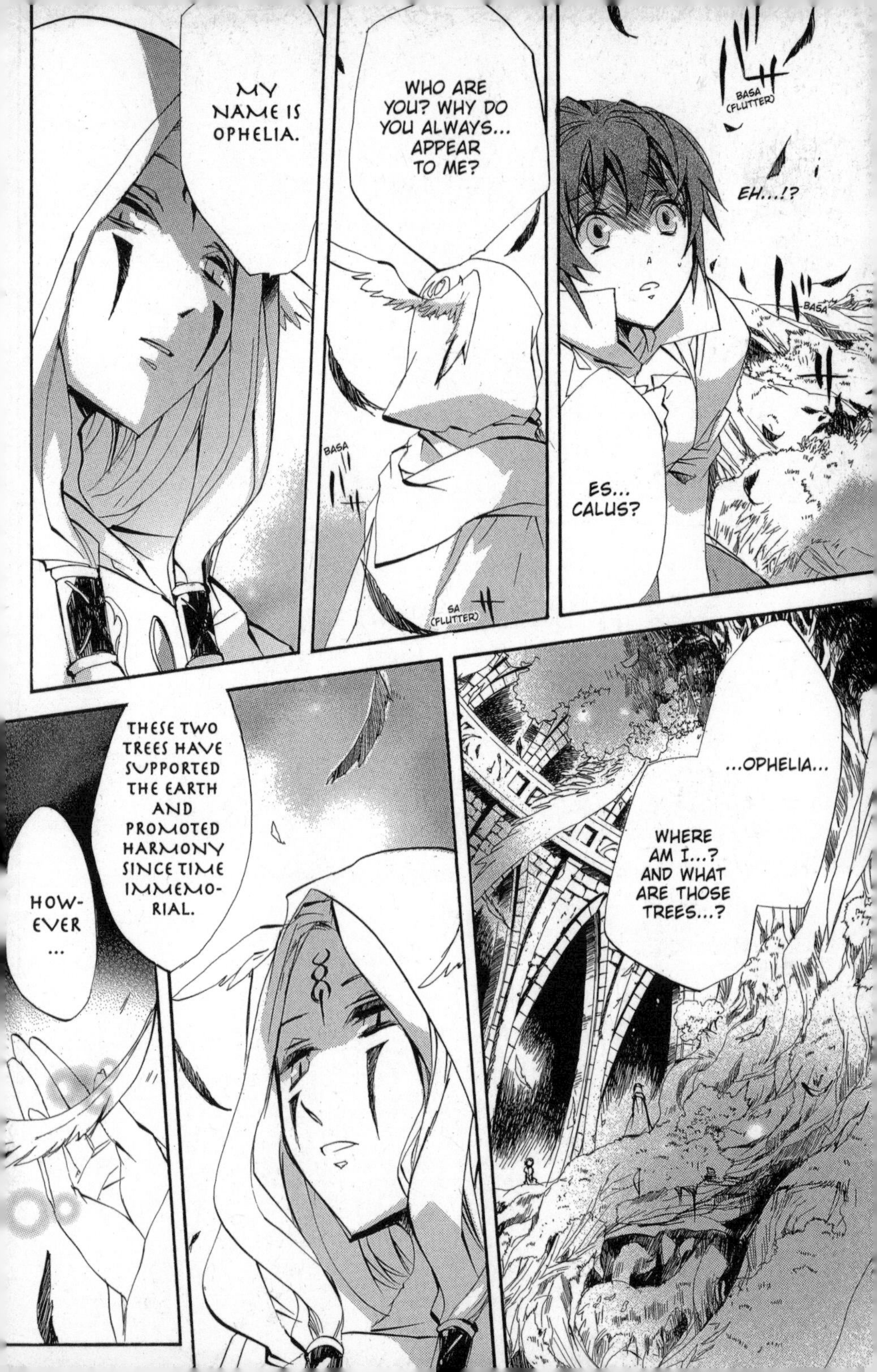
BASA (FLUTTER)
EH...!?
BASA
ES... CALUS?
WHO ARE YOU? WHY DO YOU ALWAYS... APPEAR TO ME?
BASA
SA (FLUTTER)
MY NAME IS OPHELIA.
...OPHELIA...
WHERE AM I...? AND WHAT ARE THOSE TREES...?
THESE TWO TREES HAVE SUPPORTED THE EARTH AND PROMOTED HARMONY SINCE TIME IMMEMO-RIAL.
HOW-EVER ...

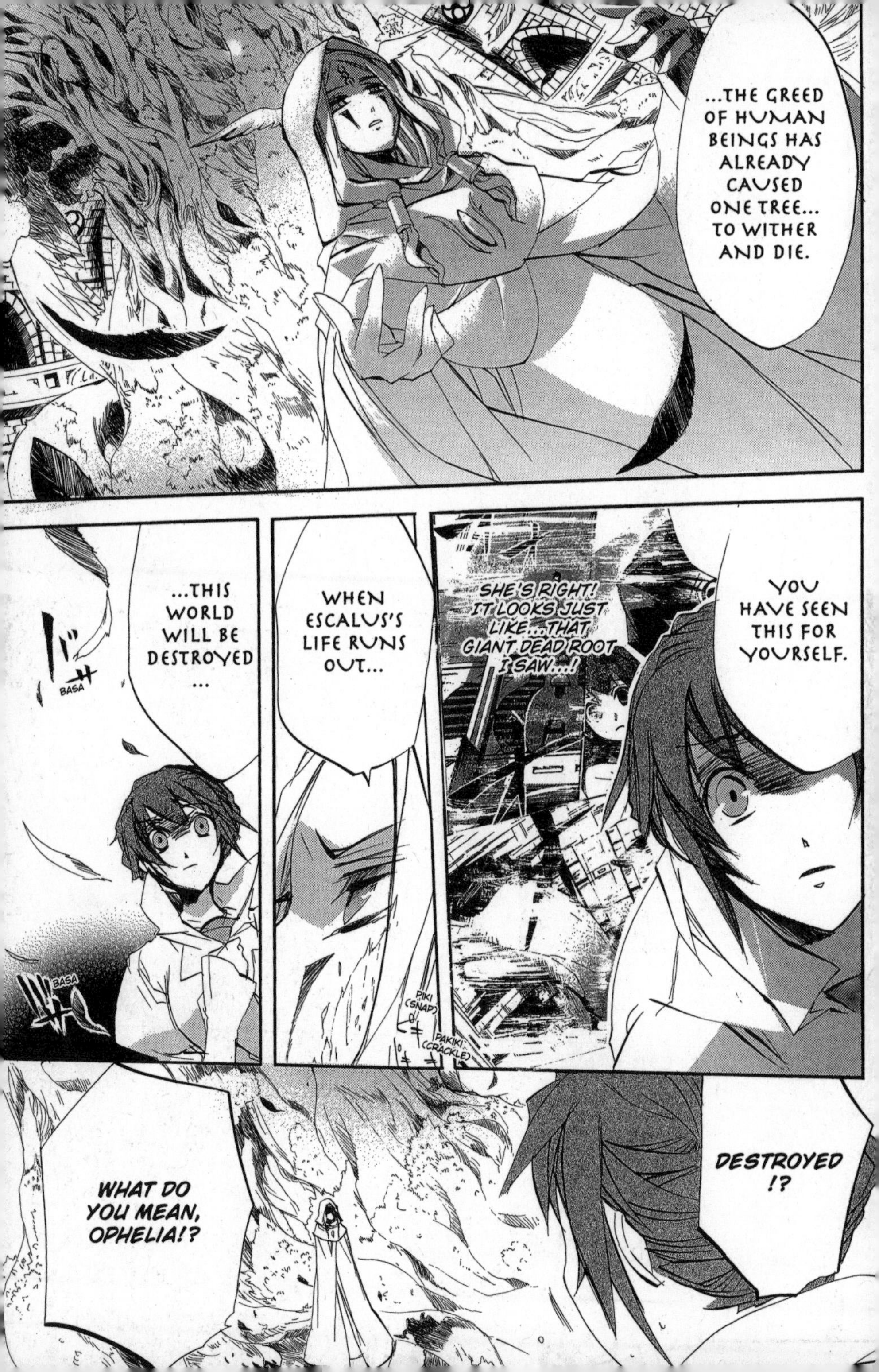
...THE GREED OF HUMAN BEINGS HAS ALREADY CAUSED ONE TREE... TO WITHER AND DIE.
YOU HAVE SEEN THIS FOR YOURSELF.
SHE'S RIGHT! IT LOOKS JUST LIKE... THAT GIANT DEAD ROOT I SAW...!
PAKIKI (CRACKLE)
PIKI (SNAP)
WHEN ESCALUS'S LIFE RUNS OUT...
...THIS WORLD WILL BE DESTROYED ...
BASA
BASA
DESTROYED !?
WHAT DO YOU MEAN, OPHELIA!?

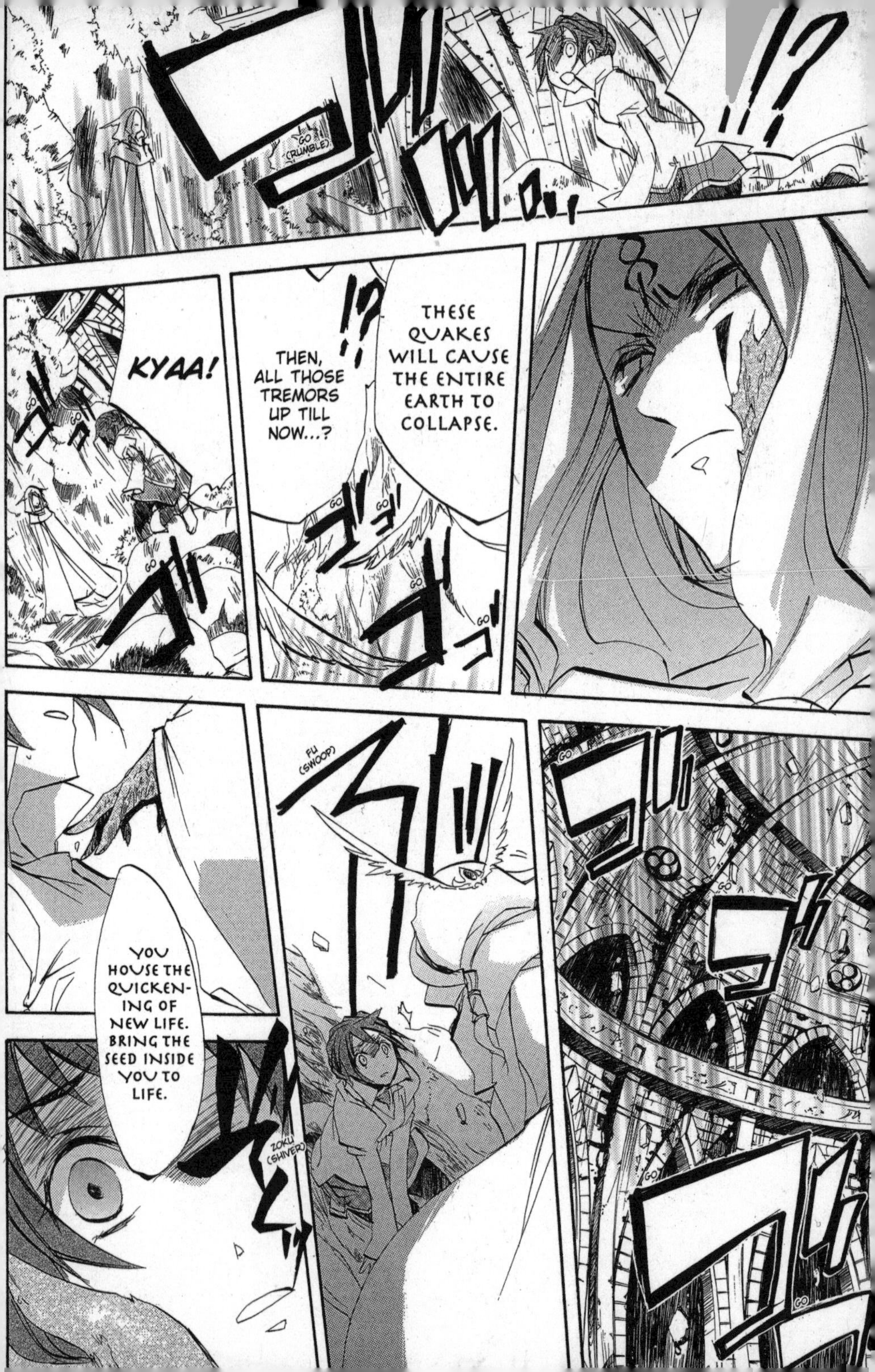
!!?
GO (RUMBLE)
THESE QUAKES WILL CAUSE THE ENTIRE EARTH TO COLLAPSE.
!!?
THEN, ALL THOSE TREMORS UP TILL NOW...?
GO
GO
GO
GO
KYAA!
GO
GO
GO
GO
GO
GO
FU (SWOOP)
ZOKU (SHIVER)
YOU HOUSE THE QUICKEN-ING OF NEW LIFE. BRING THE SEED INSIDE YOU TO LIFE.

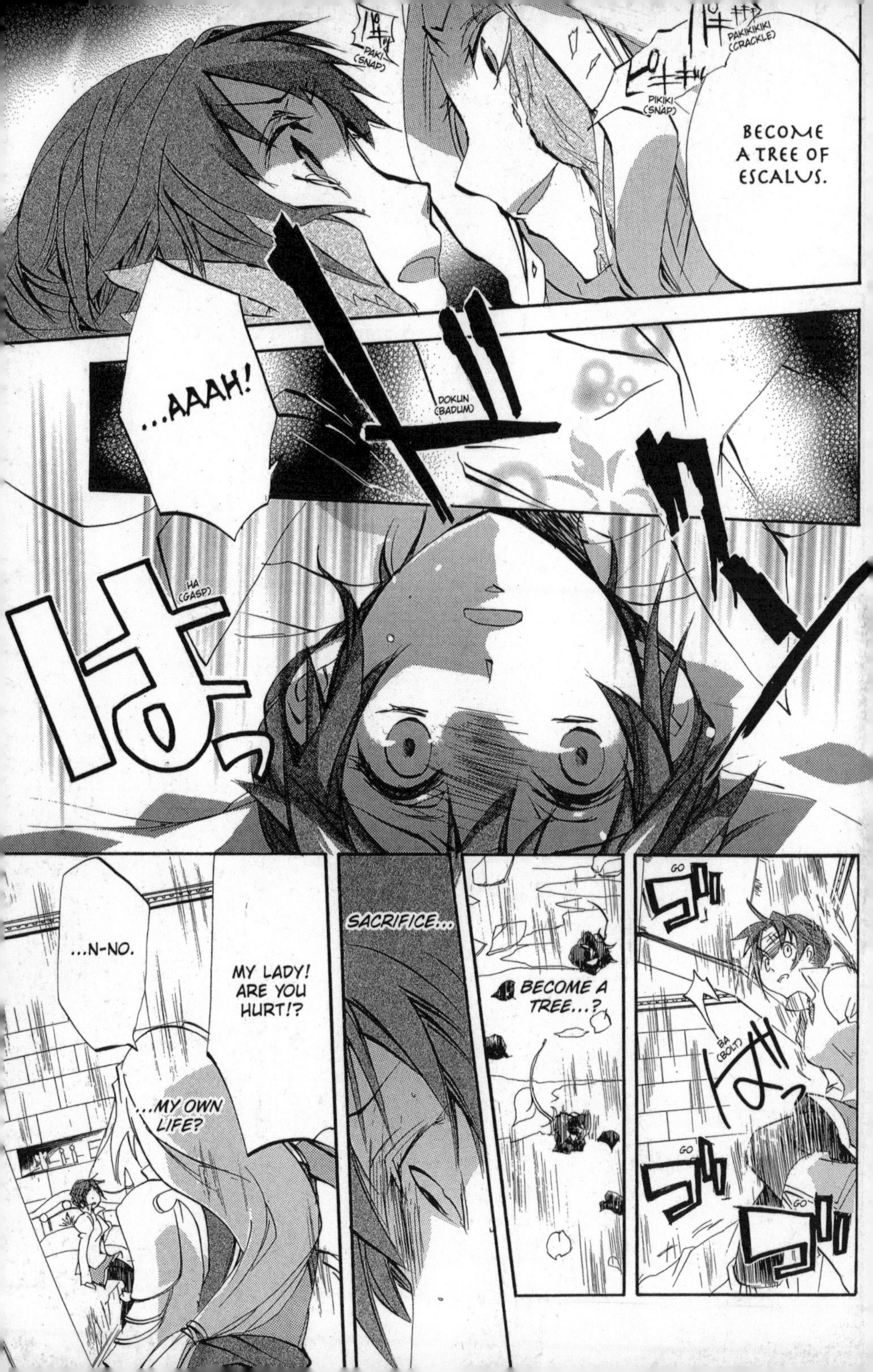
PAKIKIKIKI (CRACKLE)
PIKIKI (SNAP)
BECOME A TREE OF ESCALUS.
PAKI (SNAP)
DOKUN (BADUM)
...AAAH!
HA (GASP)
GO
BA (BOLT)
GO
GO
BECOME A TREE...?
SACRIFICE...
MY LADY! ARE YOU HURT!?
...N-NO.
...MY OWN LIFE?

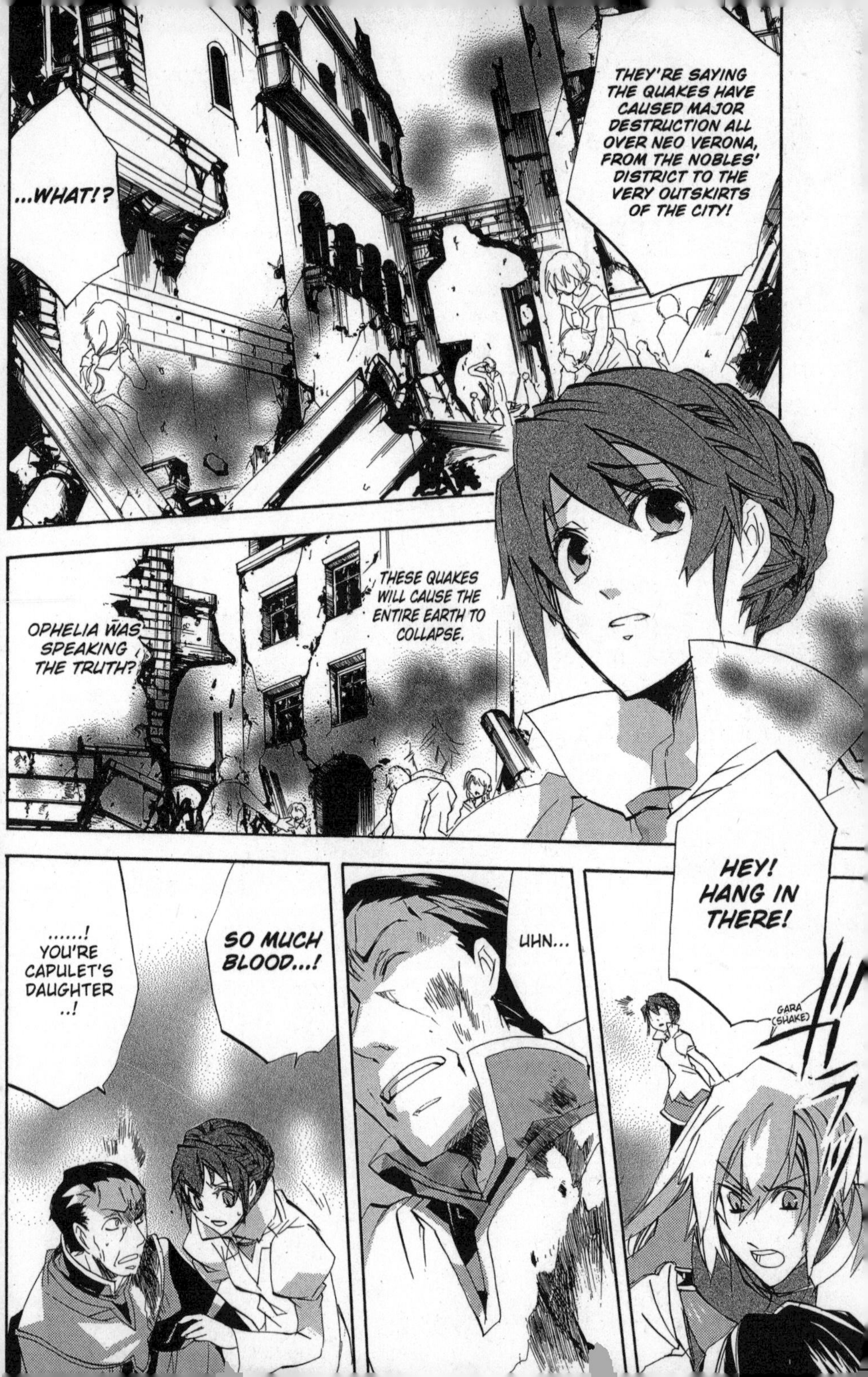
THEY'RE SAYING THE QUAKES HAVE CAUSED MAJOR DESTRUCTION ALL OVER NEO VERONA, FROM THE NOBLES' DISTRICT TO THE VERY OUTSKIRTS OF THE CITY!
...WHAT!?
THESE QUAKES WILL CAUSE THE ENTIRE EARTH TO COLLAPSE.
OPHELIA WAS SPEAKING THE TRUTH?
HEY! HANG IN THERE!
GARA (SHAKE)
UHN...
SO MUCH BLOOD...!
......! YOU'RE CAPULET'S DAUGHTER ..!

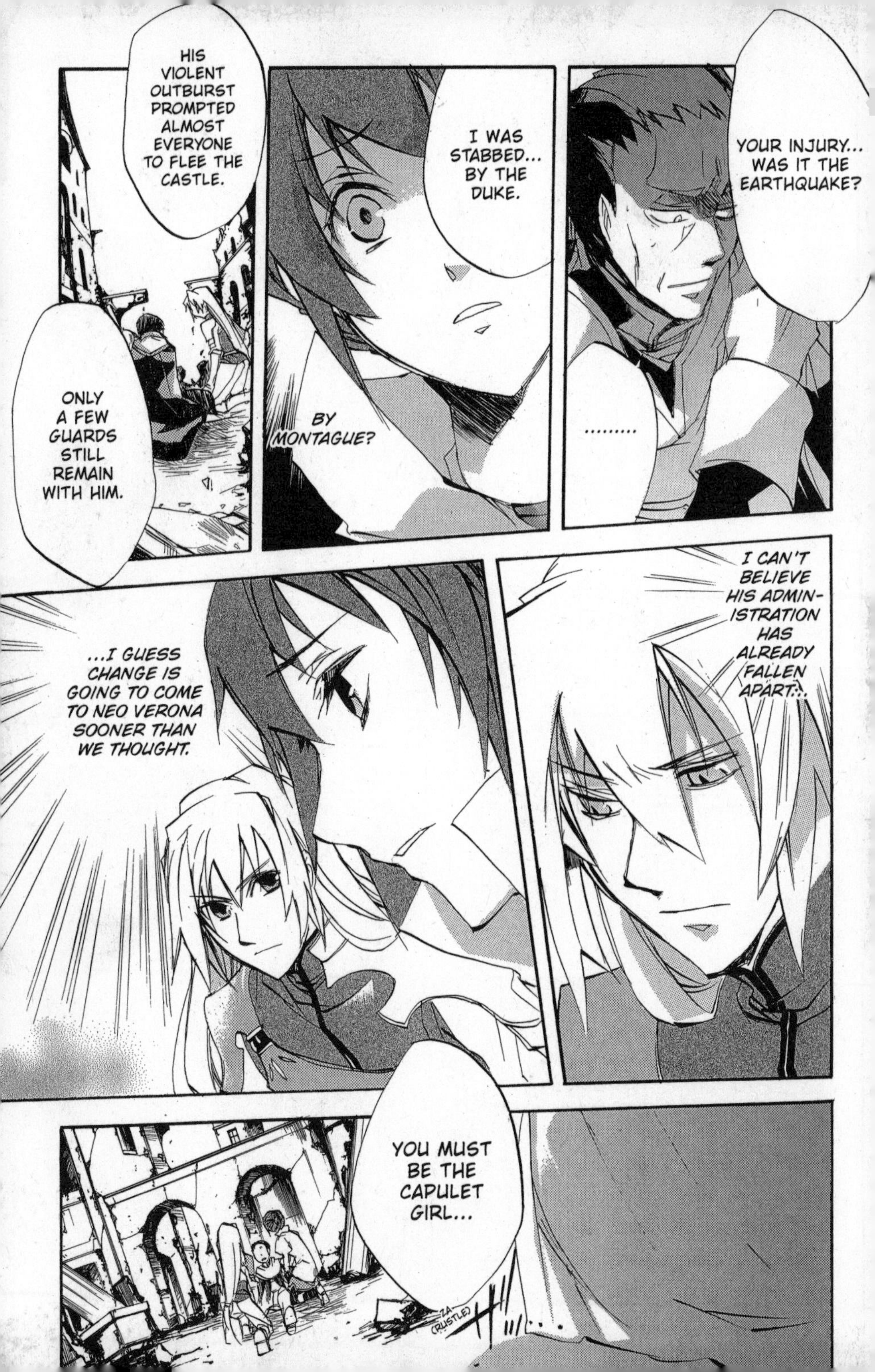
YOUR INJURY... WAS IT THE EARTHQUAKE?
....
I WAS STABBED... BY THE DUKE.
BY MONTAGUE?
HIS VIOLENT OUTBURST PROMPTED ALMOST EVERYONE TO FLEE THE CASTLE.
ONLY A FEW GUARDS STILL REMAIN WITH HIM.
I CAN'T BELIEVE HIS ADMINISTRATION HAS ALREADY FALLEN APART...
...I GUESS CHANGE IS GOING TO COME TO NEO VERONA SOONER THAN WE THOUGHT.
YOU MUST BE THE CAPULET GIRL...
ZA
(RUSTLE)

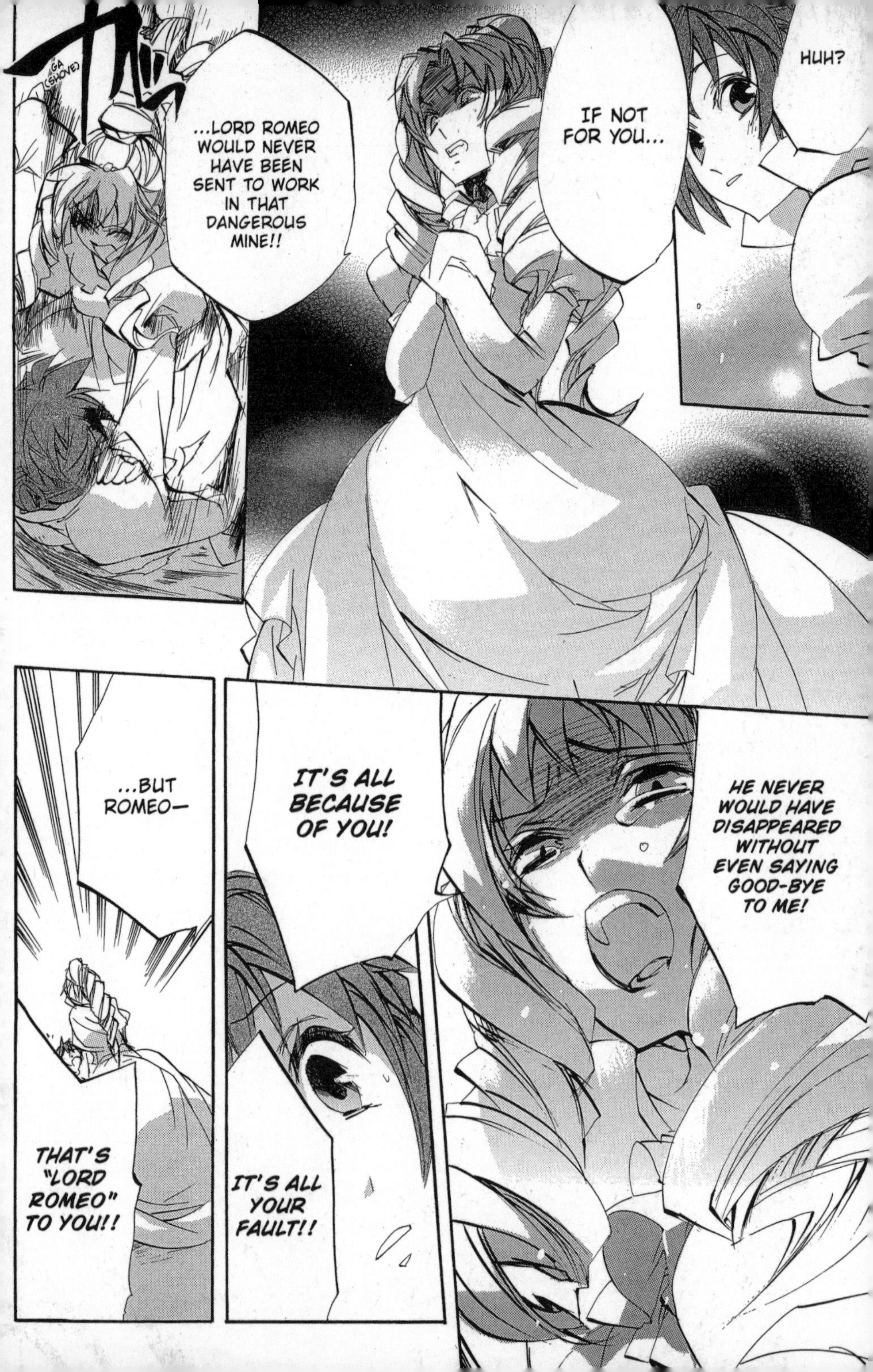
HUH?
IF NOT FOR YOU...
GA (SHOVE)
...LORD ROMEO WOULD NEVER HAVE BEEN SENT TO WORK IN THAT DANGEROUS MINE!!
HE NEVER WOULD HAVE DISAPPEARED WITHOUT EVEN SAYING GOOD-BYE TO ME!
IT'S ALL BECAUSE OF YOU!
IT'S ALL YOUR FAULT!!
...BUT ROMEO—
THAT'S "LORD ROMEO" TO YOU!!

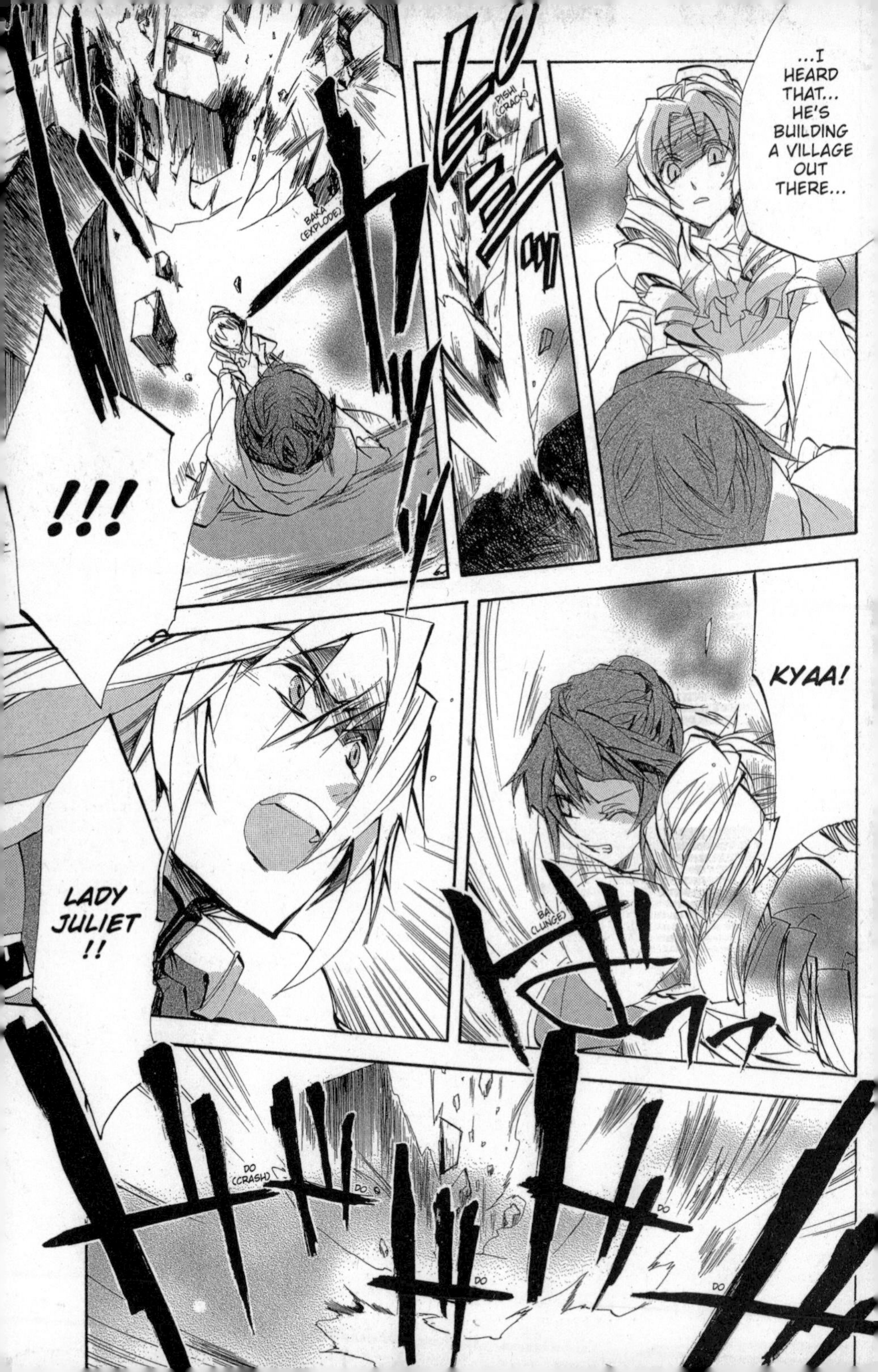
...I HEARD THAT... HE'S BUILDING A VILLAGE OUT THERE...
PISHI (CRACK)
BAKA (EXPLODE)
!!!
KYAA!
BA (LUNGE)
LADY JULIET !!
DO
DO
DO
DO
DO (CRASH)

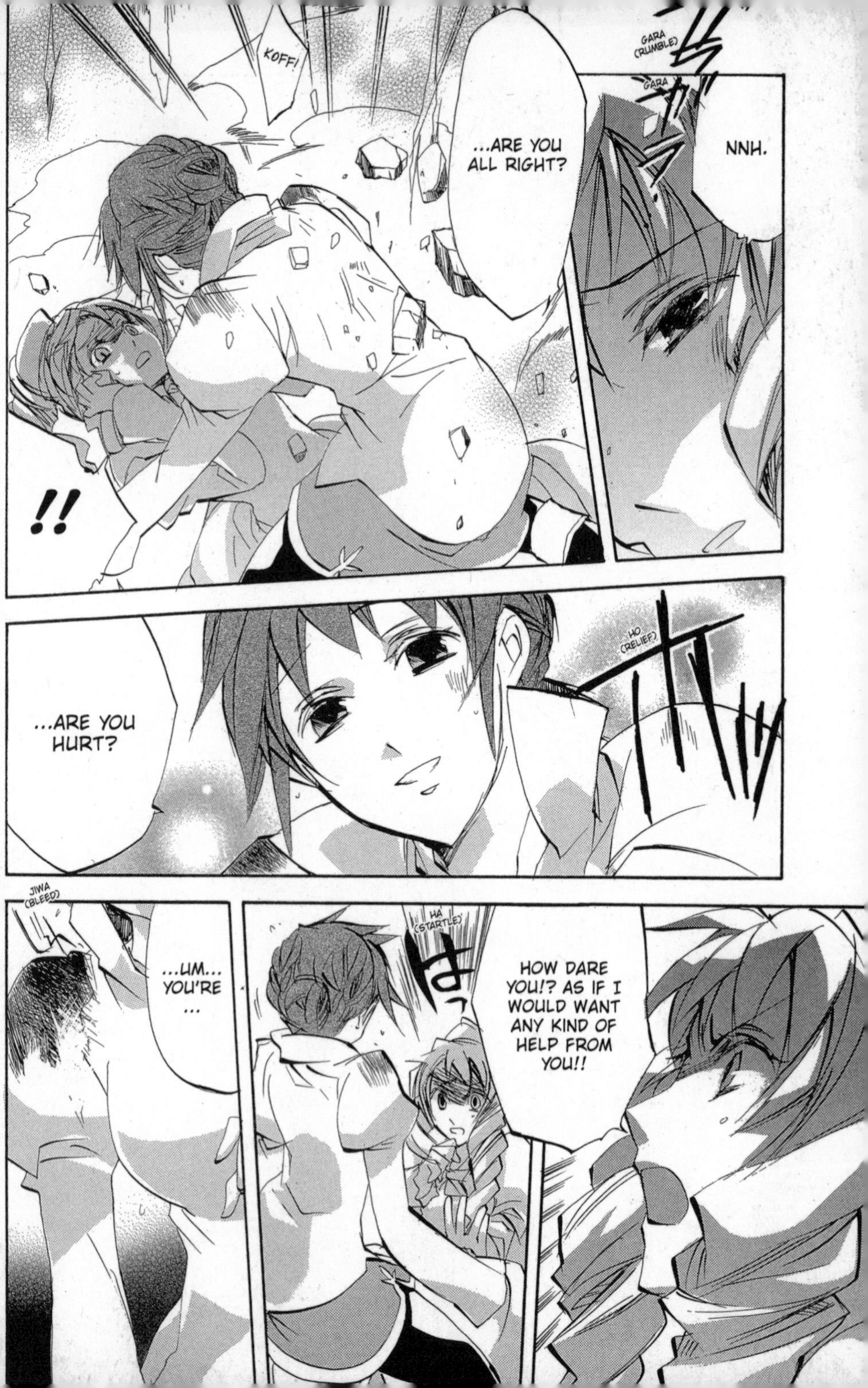
GARA (RUMBLE)
GARA
NNH.
...ARE YOU ALL RIGHT?
KOFF!
!!
HO (RELIEF)
...ARE YOU HURT?
HOW DARE YOU!? AS IF I WOULD WANT ANY KIND OF HELP FROM YOU!!
HA (STARTLE)
JIWA (BLEED)
...UM... YOU'RE ...

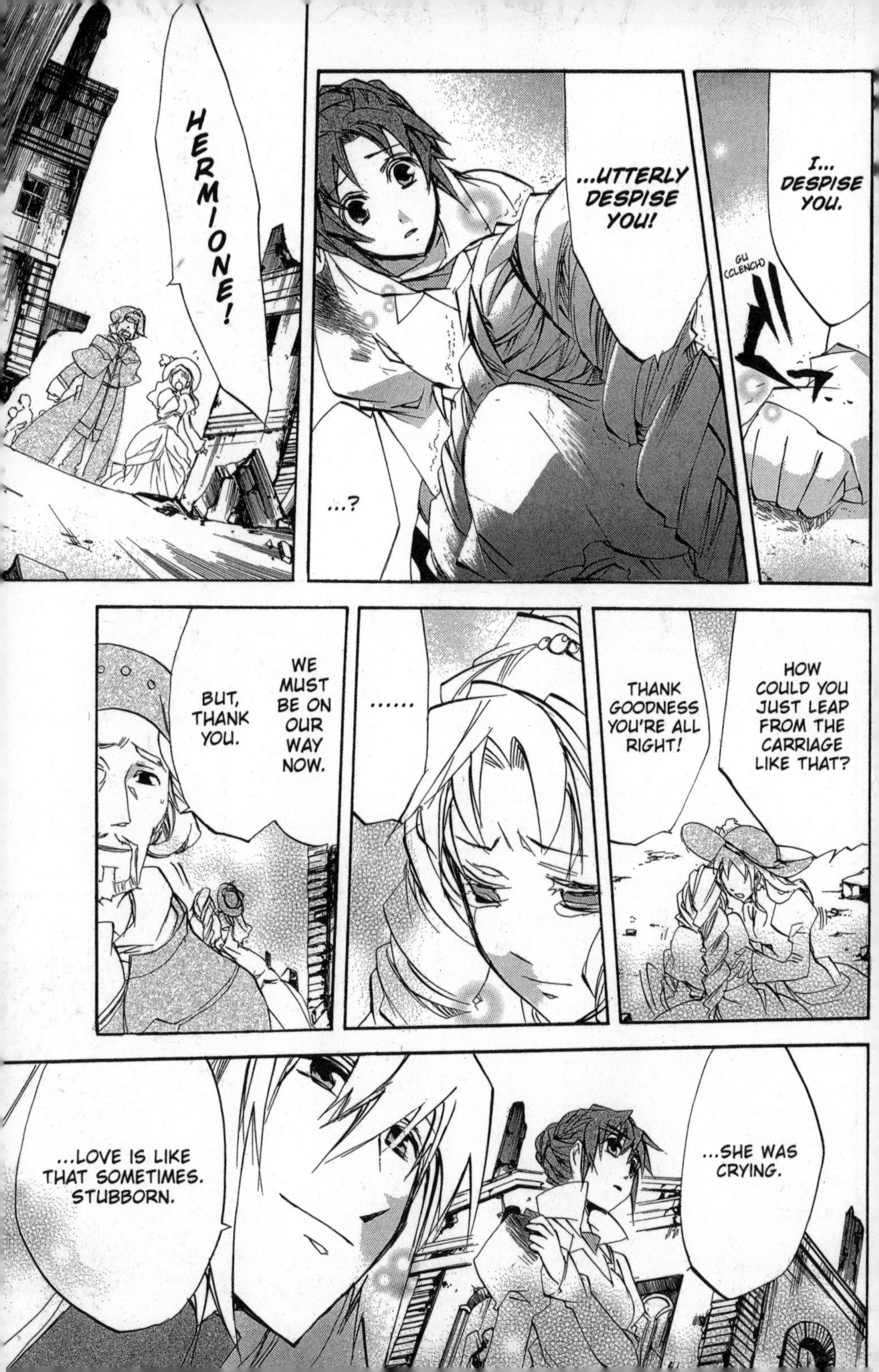
I... DESPISE YOU.
GU (CLENCH)
...UTTERLY DESPISE YOU!
...?
HERMIONE!
HOW COULD YOU JUST LEAP FROM THE CARRIAGE LIKE THAT?
THANK GOODNESS YOU'RE ALL RIGHT!
......
WE MUST BE ON OUR WAY NOW.
BUT, THANK YOU.
...SHE WAS CRYING.
...LOVE IS LIKE THAT SOMETIMES. STUBBORN.

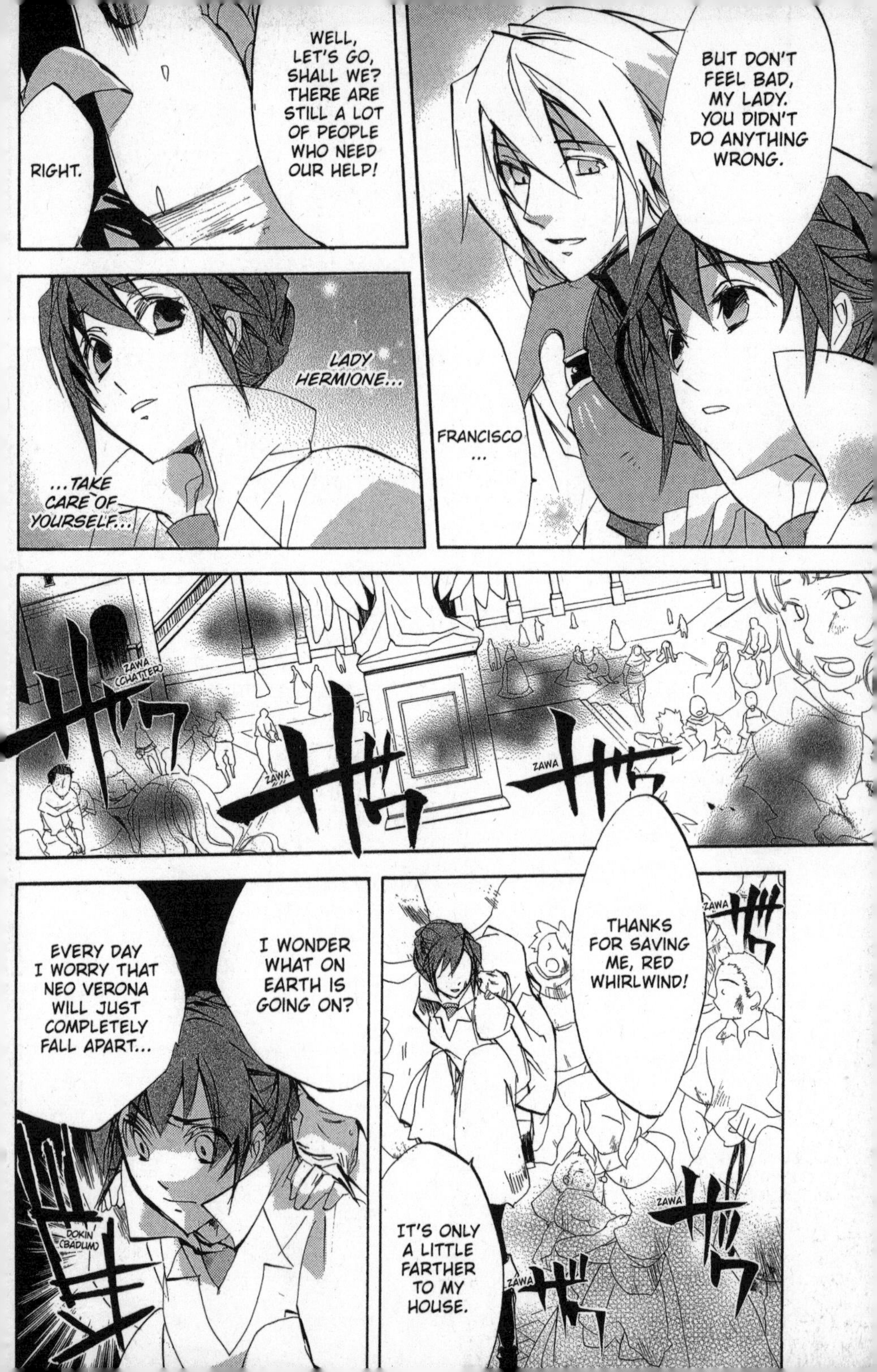
BUT DON'T FEEL BAD, MY LADY. YOU DIDN'T DO ANYTHING WRONG.
FRANCISCO ...
WELL, LET'S GO, SHALL WE? THERE ARE STILL A LOT OF PEOPLE WHO NEED OUR HELP!
RIGHT.
LADY HERMIONE...
...TAKE CARE OF YOURSELF...
ZAWA
ZAWA
ZAWA (CHATTER)
ZAWA
THANKS FOR SAVING ME, RED WHIRLWIND!
ZAWA
IT'S ONLY A LITTLE FARTHER TO MY HOUSE.
ZAWA
I WONDER WHAT ON EARTH IS GOING ON?
EVERY DAY I WORRY THAT NEO VERONA WILL JUST COMPLETELY FALL APART...
DOKIN (BADUM)

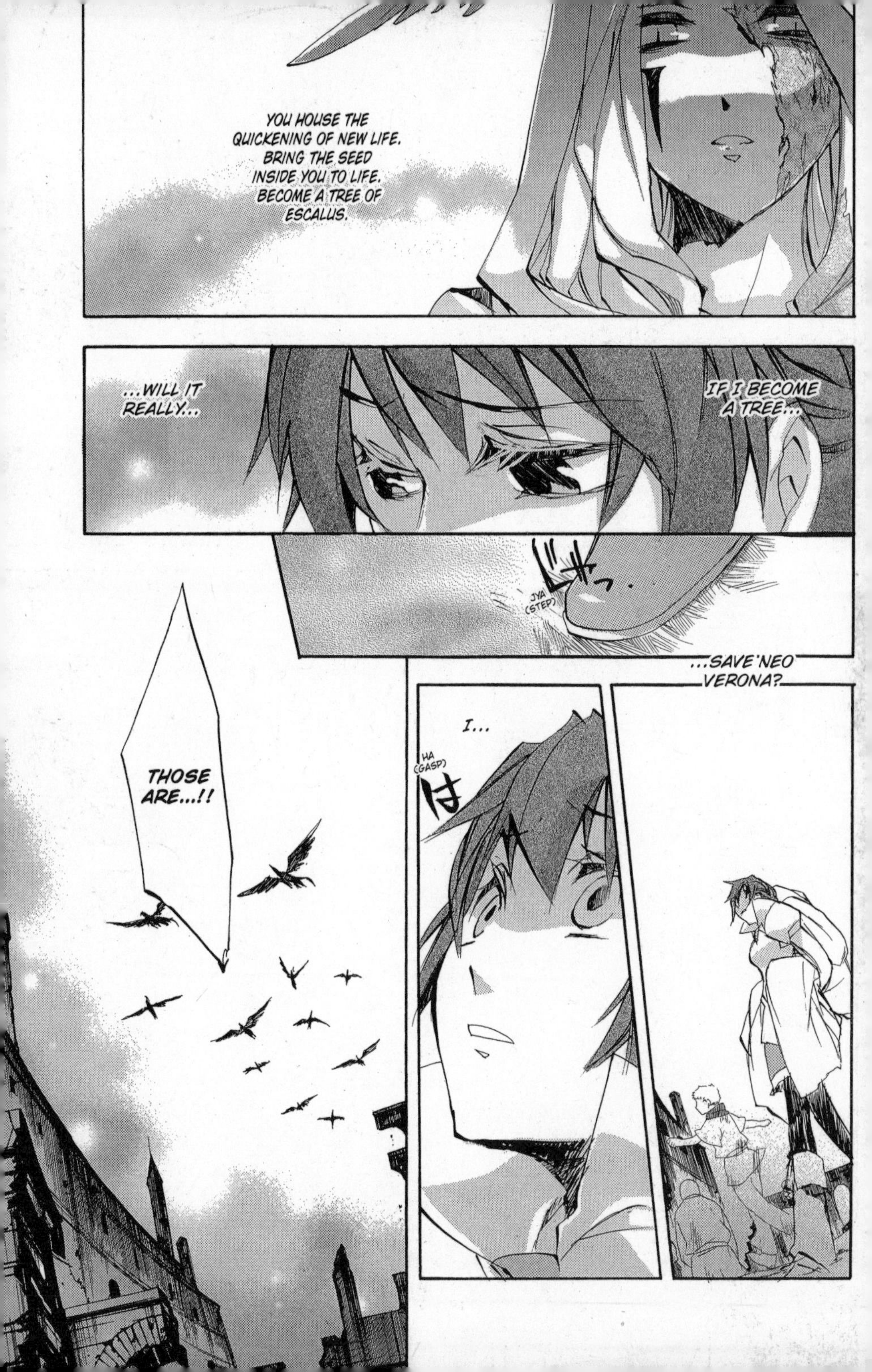
YOU HOUSE THE QUICKENING OF NEW LIFE. BRING THE SEED INSIDE YOU TO LIFE. BECOME A TREE OF ESCALUS.
IF I BECOME A TREE...
...WILL IT REALLY...
じゃっ
JYA (STEP)
...SAVE NEO VERONA?
I...
は
HA (GASP)
THOSE ARE...!!

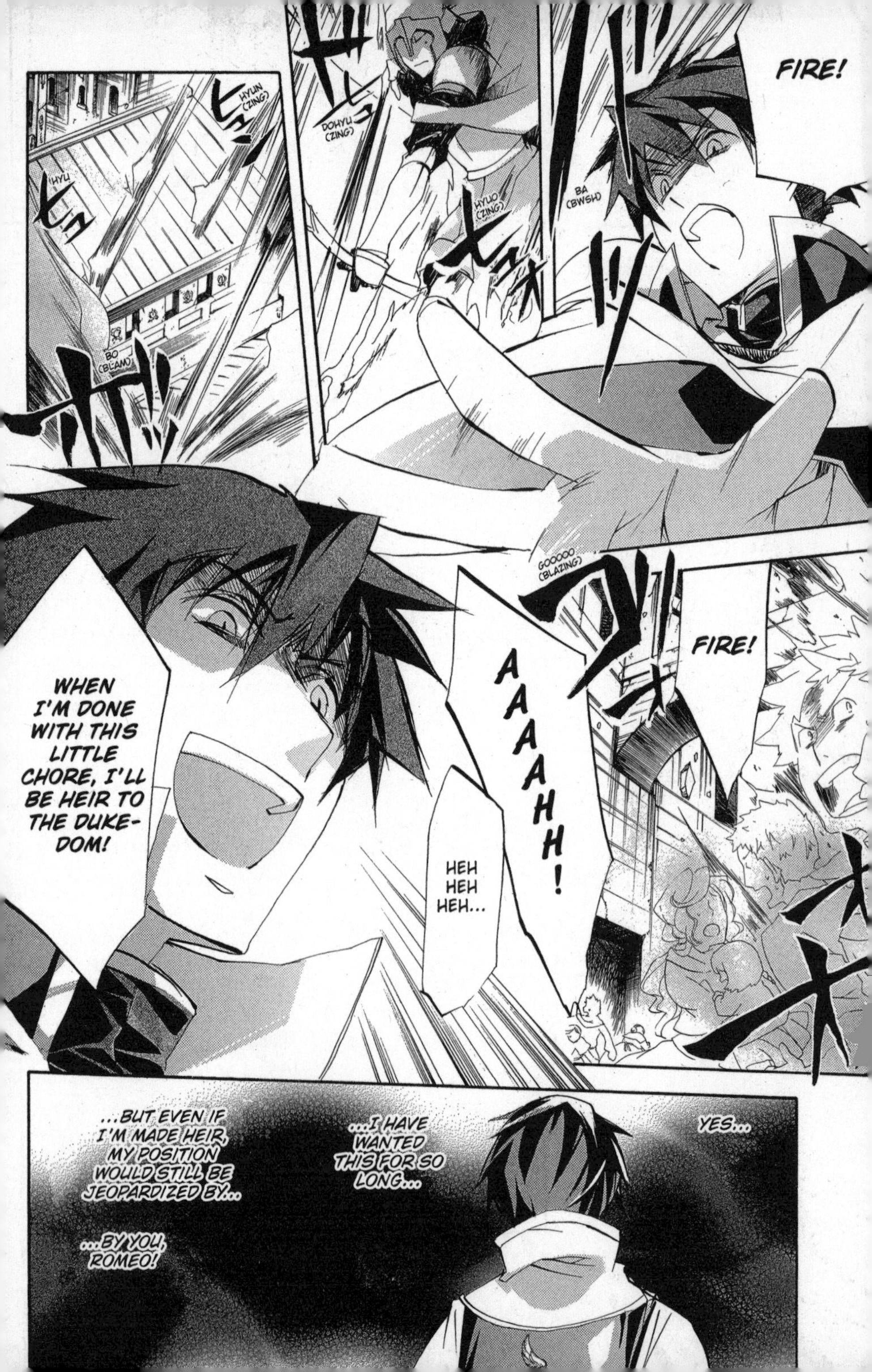

FIRE!
BA (BWSH)
HYUO (ZING)
DOHYU (ZING)
HYUN (ZING)
HYU
BO (BLAM)
FIRE!
GOOOOO (BLAZING)
AAAAAHH!
HEH HEH HEH...
WHEN I'M DONE WITH THIS LITTLE CHORE, I'LL BE HEIR TO THE DUKE-DOM!
YES...
...I HAVE WANTED THIS FOR SO LONG...
...BUT EVEN IF I'M MADE HEIR, MY POSITION WOULD STILL BE JEOPARDIZED BY...
...BY YOU, ROMEO!

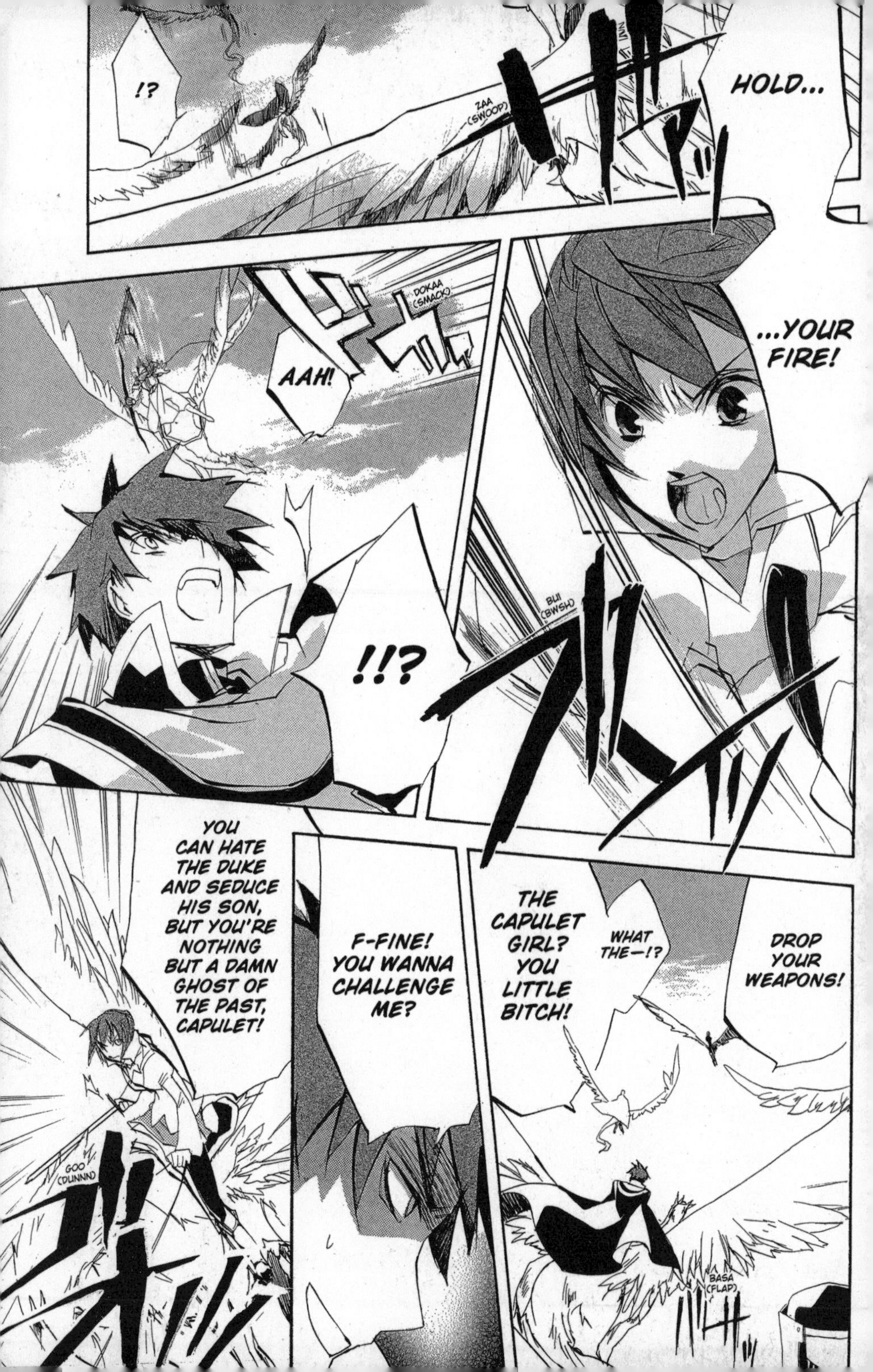
HOLD...
ZAA (SWOOP)
!?
...YOUR FIRE!
BUI (BWSH)
DOKAA (SMACK)
AAH!
!!?
DROP YOUR WEAPONS!
WHAT THE—!?
THE CAPULET GIRL? YOU LITTLE BITCH!
BASA (FLAP)
F-FINE! YOU WANNA CHALLENGE ME?
YOU CAN HATE THE DUKE AND SEDUCE HIS SON, BUT YOU'RE NOTHING BUT A DAMN GHOST OF THE PAST, CAPULET!
GOO (DUNNN)

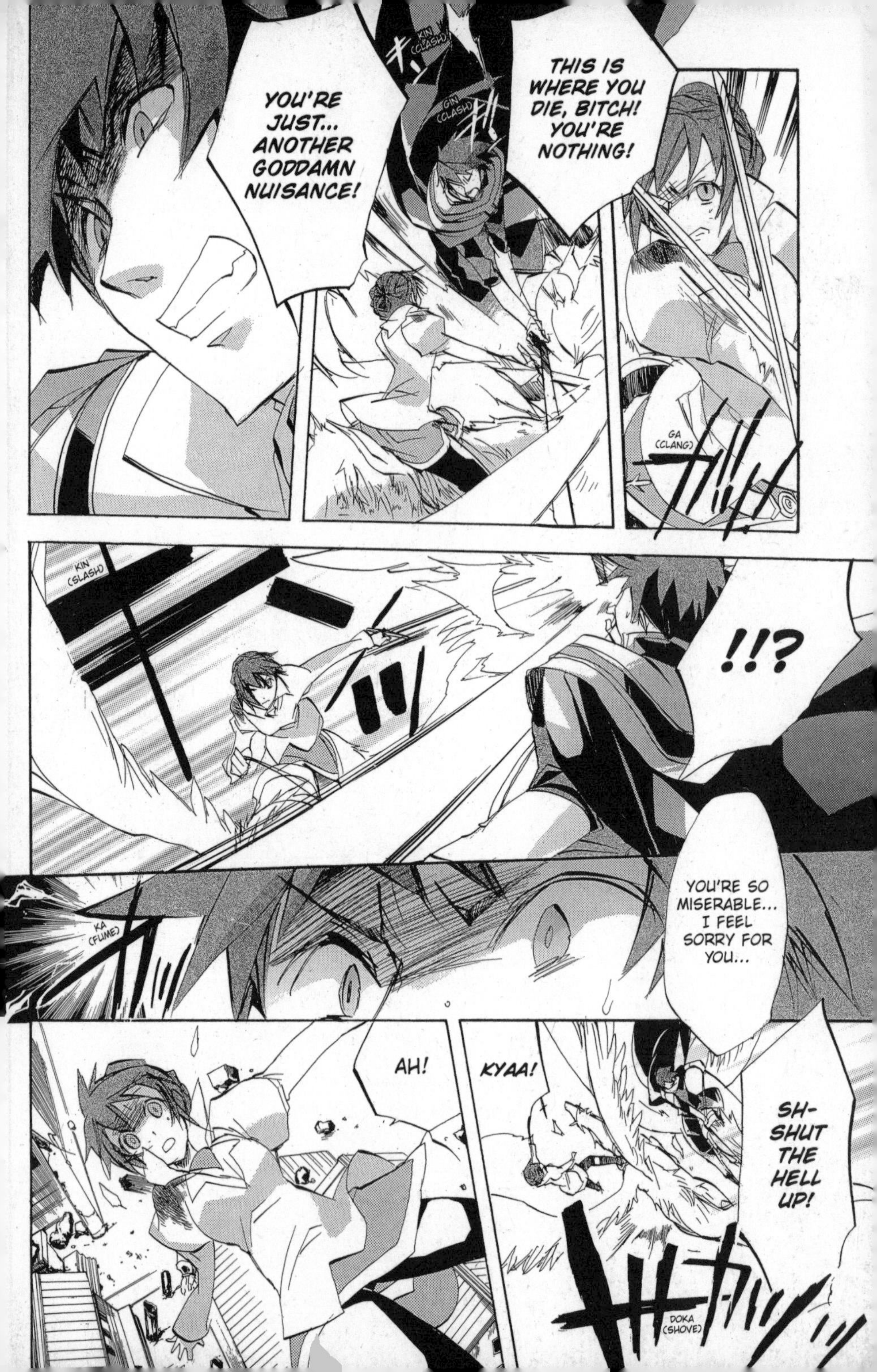
THIS IS WHERE YOU DIE, BITCH! YOU'RE NOTHING!
GA (CLANG)
KIN (CLASH)
GIN (CLASH)
YOU'RE JUST... ANOTHER GODDAMN NUISANCE!
!!?
KIN (SLASH)
YOU'RE SO MISERABLE... I FEEL SORRY FOR YOU...
KA (FUME)
SH-SHUT THE HELL UP!
KYAA!
DOKA (SHOVE)
AH!

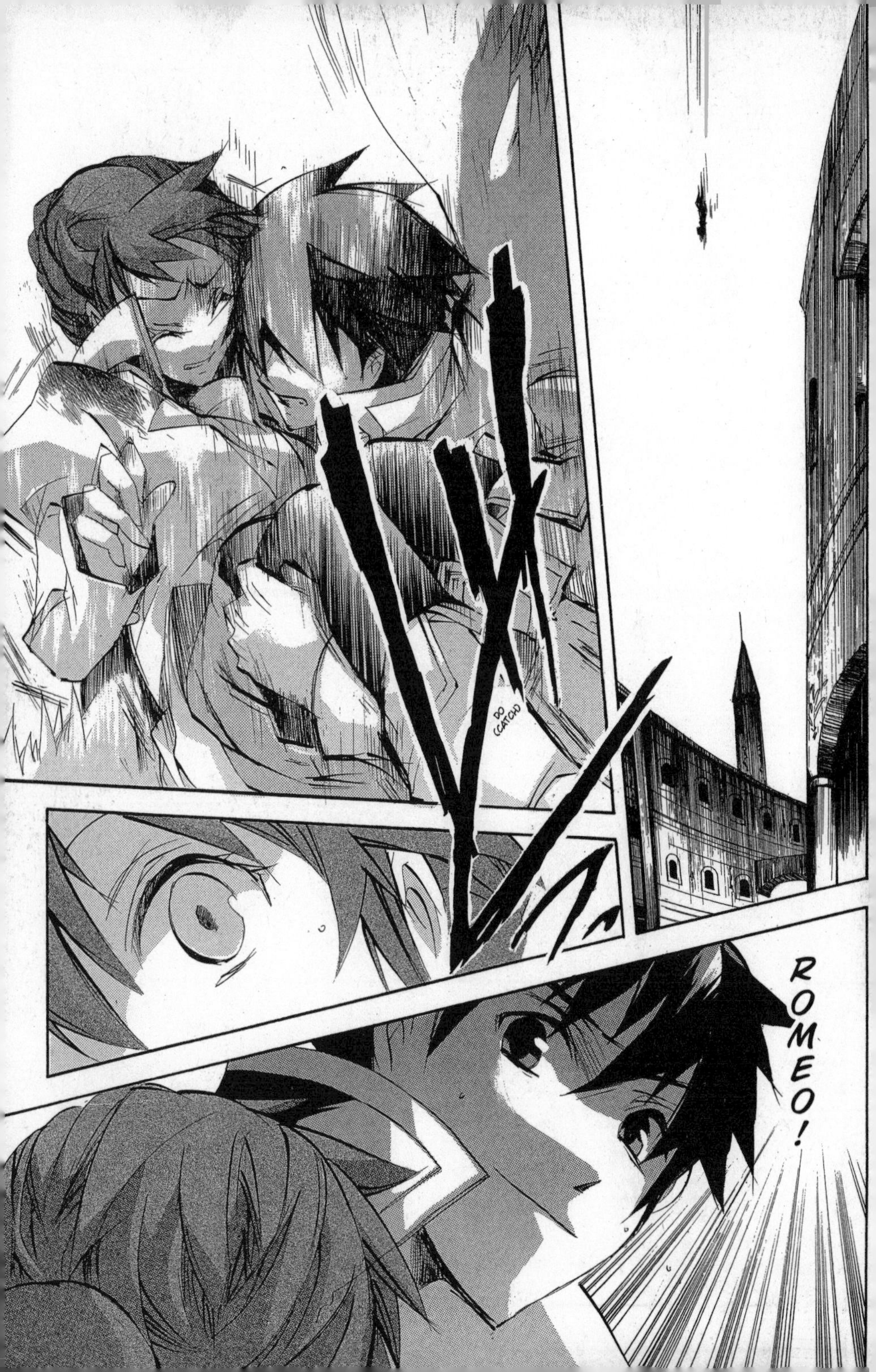
DO
(CATCH)
ROMEO!

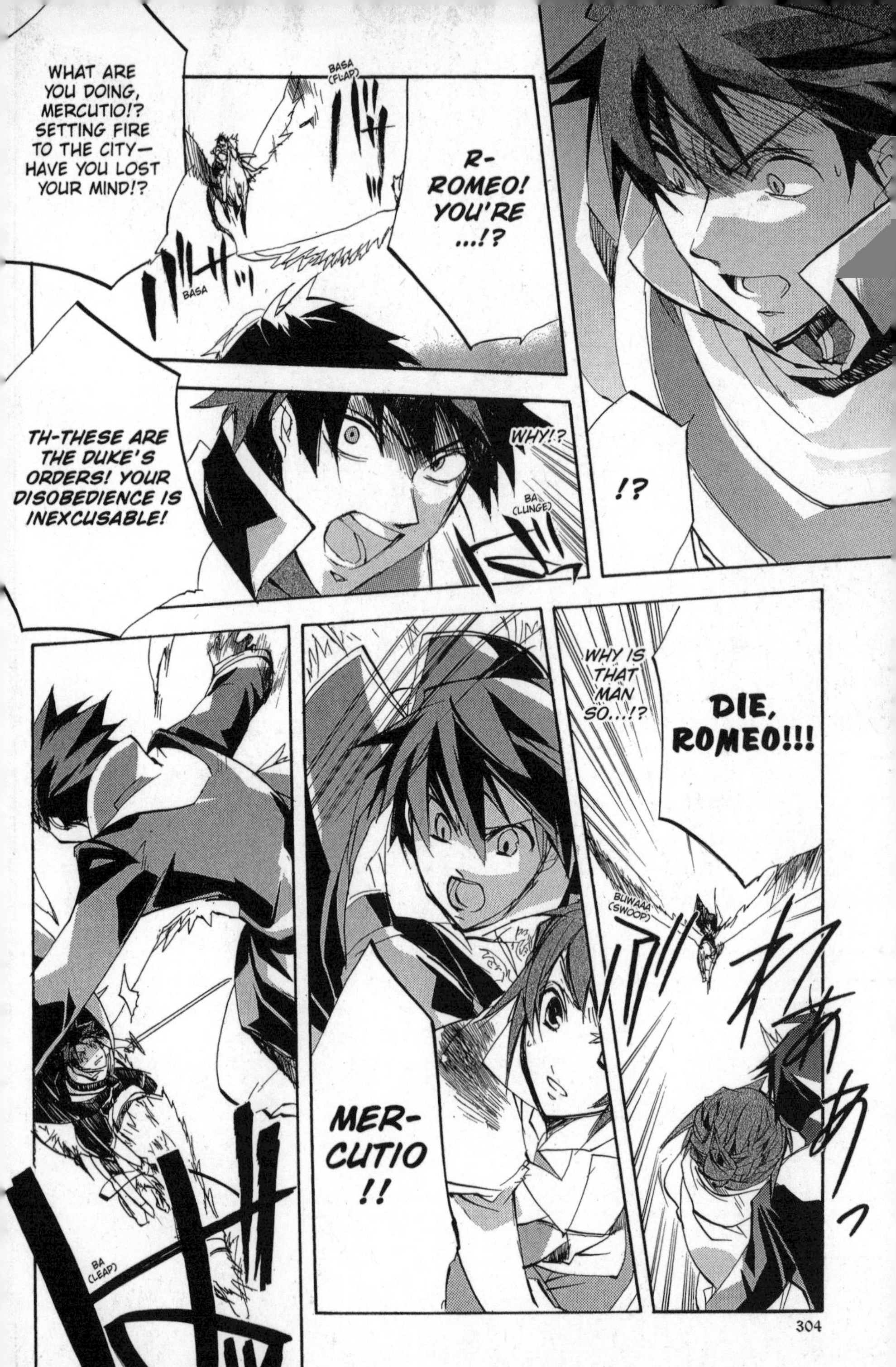
!?
R-ROMEO! YOU'RE ...!?
BASA (FLAP)
WHAT ARE YOU DOING, MERCUTIO!? SETTING FIRE TO THE CITY—HAVE YOU LOST YOUR MIND!?
BASA
WHY!?
BA (LUNGE)
TH-THESE ARE THE DUKE'S ORDERS! YOUR DISOBEDIENCE IS INEXCUSABLE!
WHY IS THAT MAN SO...!?
DIE, ROMEO!!!
BUWAAA (SWOOP)
MER-CUTIO!!
BA (LEAP)

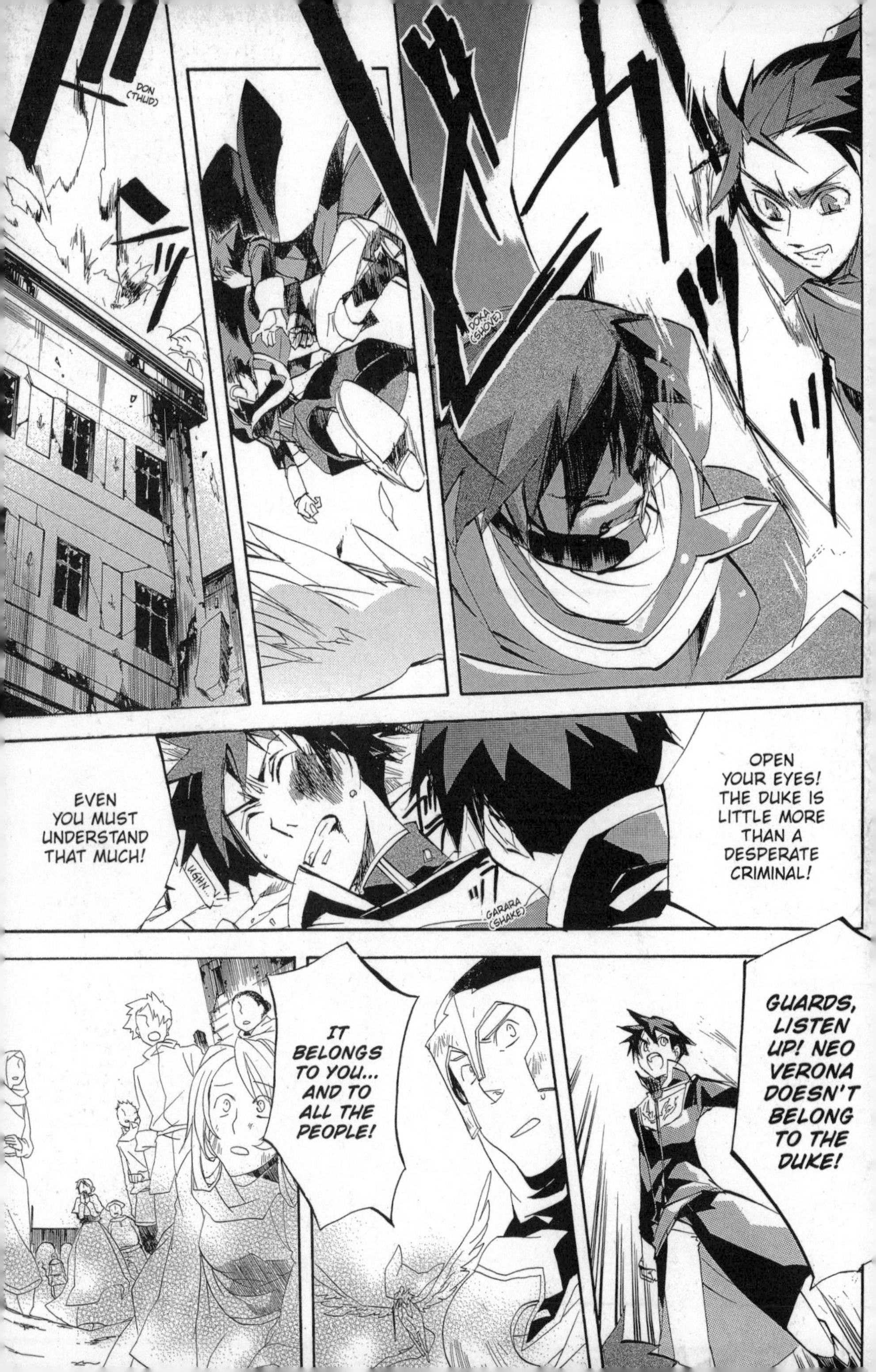
DOKA (SHOVE)
DON (THUD)
OPEN YOUR EYES! THE DUKE IS LITTLE MORE THAN A DESPERATE CRIMINAL!
GARARA (SHAKE)
UGHN...
EVEN YOU MUST UNDERSTAND THAT MUCH!
GUARDS, LISTEN UP! NEO VERONA DOESN'T BELONG TO THE DUKE!
IT BELONGS TO YOU... AND TO ALL THE PEOPLE!

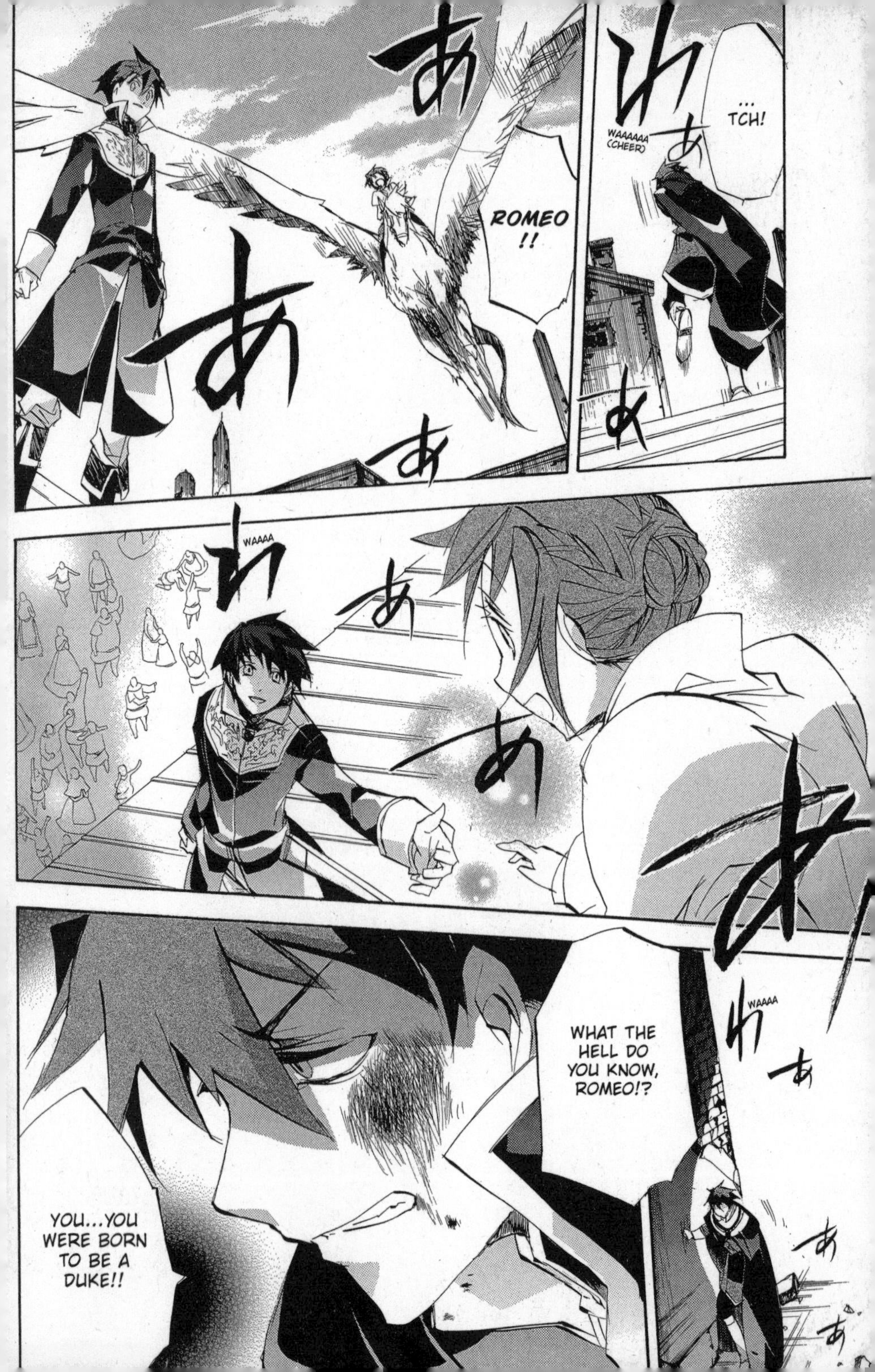
...TCH!
WAAAAAA (CHEER)
ROMEO!!
WAAAA
WAAAA
WHAT THE HELL DO YOU KNOW, ROMEO!?
YOU...YOU WERE BORN TO BE A DUKE!!

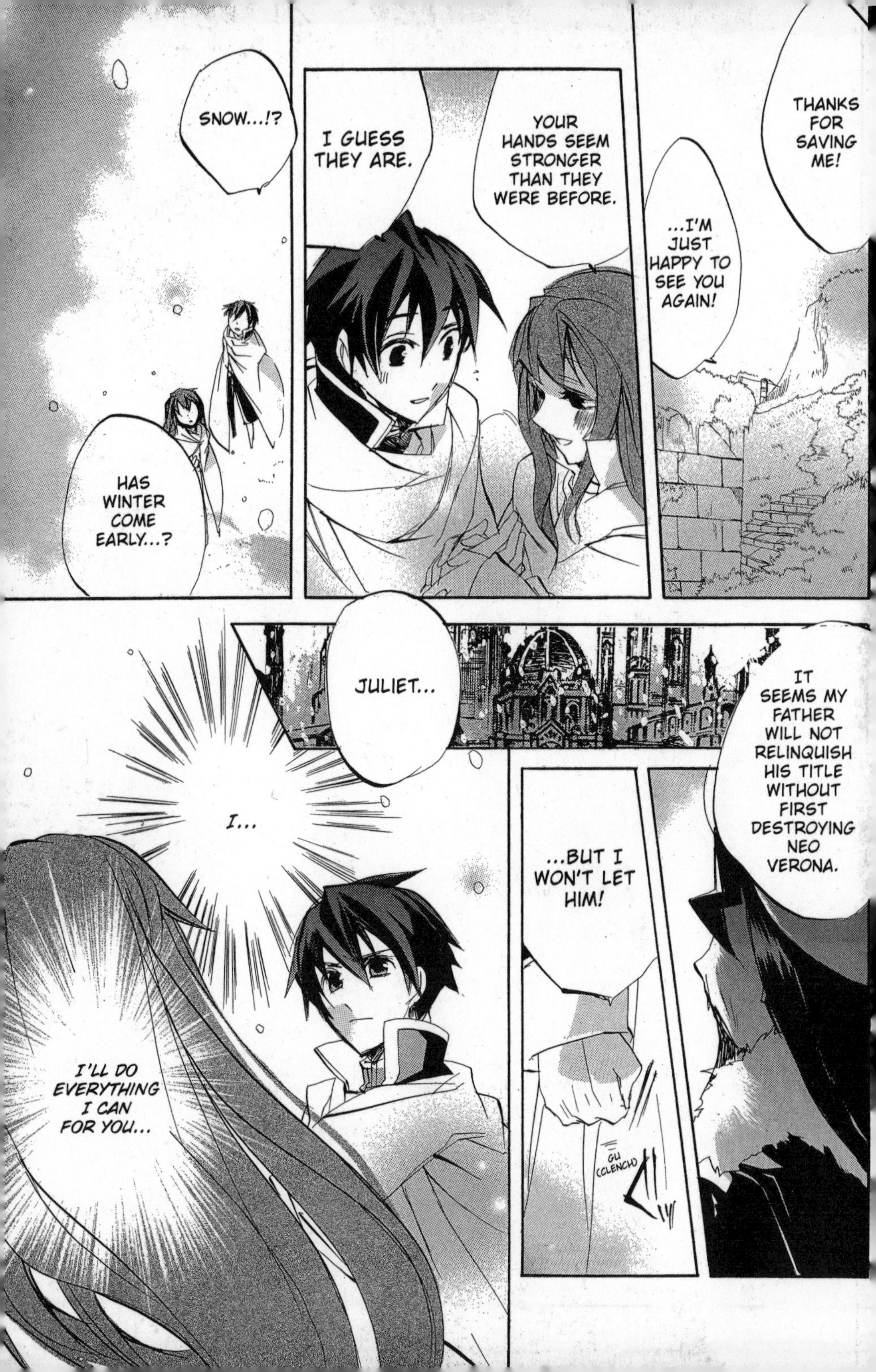
THANKS FOR SAVING ME!
...I'M JUST HAPPY TO SEE YOU AGAIN!
YOUR HANDS SEEM STRONGER THAN THEY WERE BEFORE.
I GUESS THEY ARE.
SNOW...!?
HAS WINTER COME EARLY...?
IT SEEMS MY FATHER WILL NOT RELINQUISH HIS TITLE WITHOUT FIRST DESTROYING NEO VERONA.
JULIET...
...BUT I WON'T LET HIM!
GU (CLENCH)
I...
I'LL DO EVERYTHING I CAN FOR YOU...

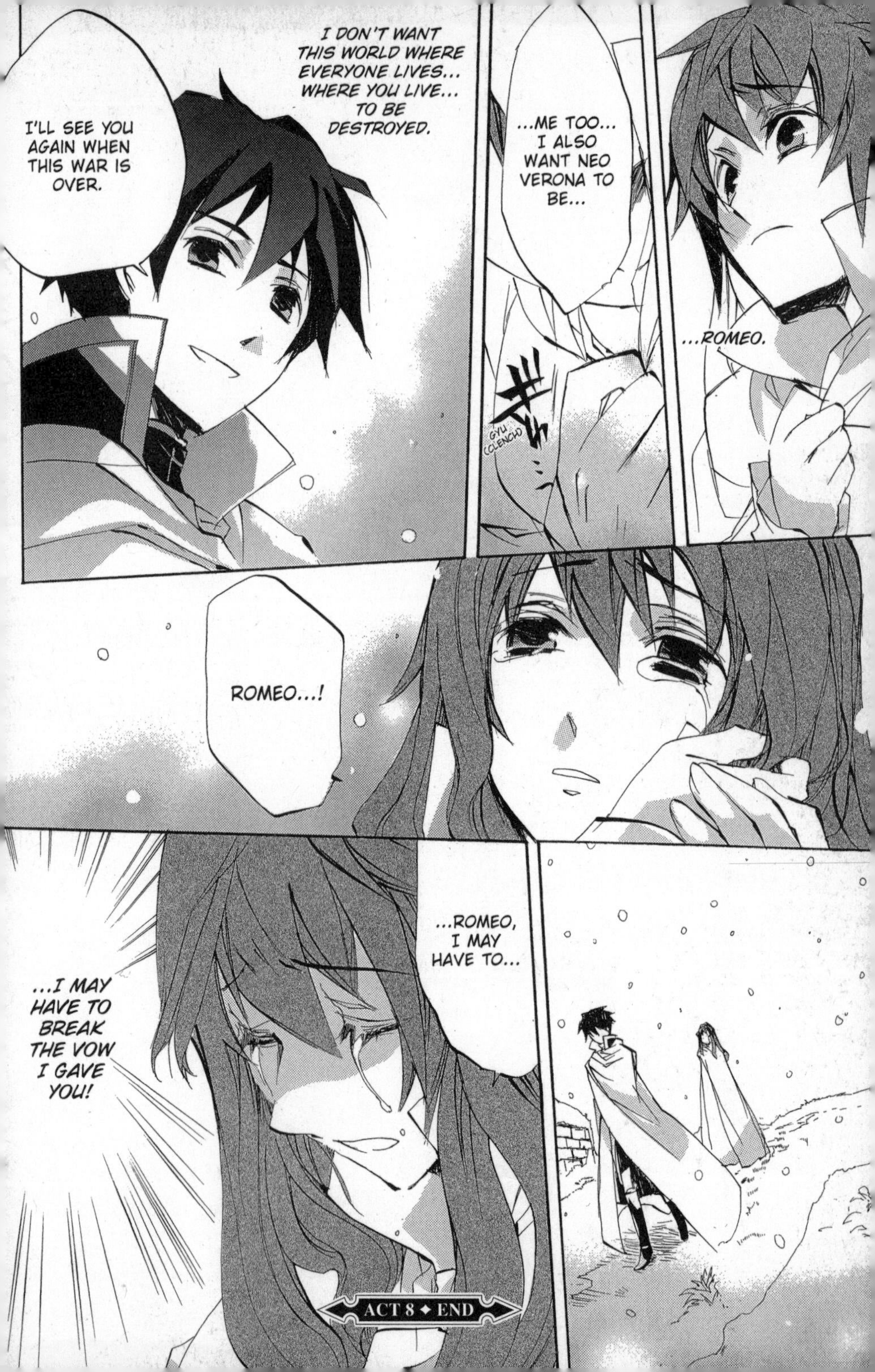
...ROMEO.
...ME TOO... I ALSO WANT NEO VERONA TO BE...
GYU (CLENCH)
I DON'T WANT THIS WORLD WHERE EVERYONE LIVES... WHERE YOU LIVE... TO BE DESTROYED.
I'LL SEE YOU AGAIN WHEN THIS WAR IS OVER.
ROMEO...!
...ROMEO, I MAY HAVE TO...
...I MAY HAVE TO BREAK THE VOW I GAVE YOU!
ACT 8 ◆ END

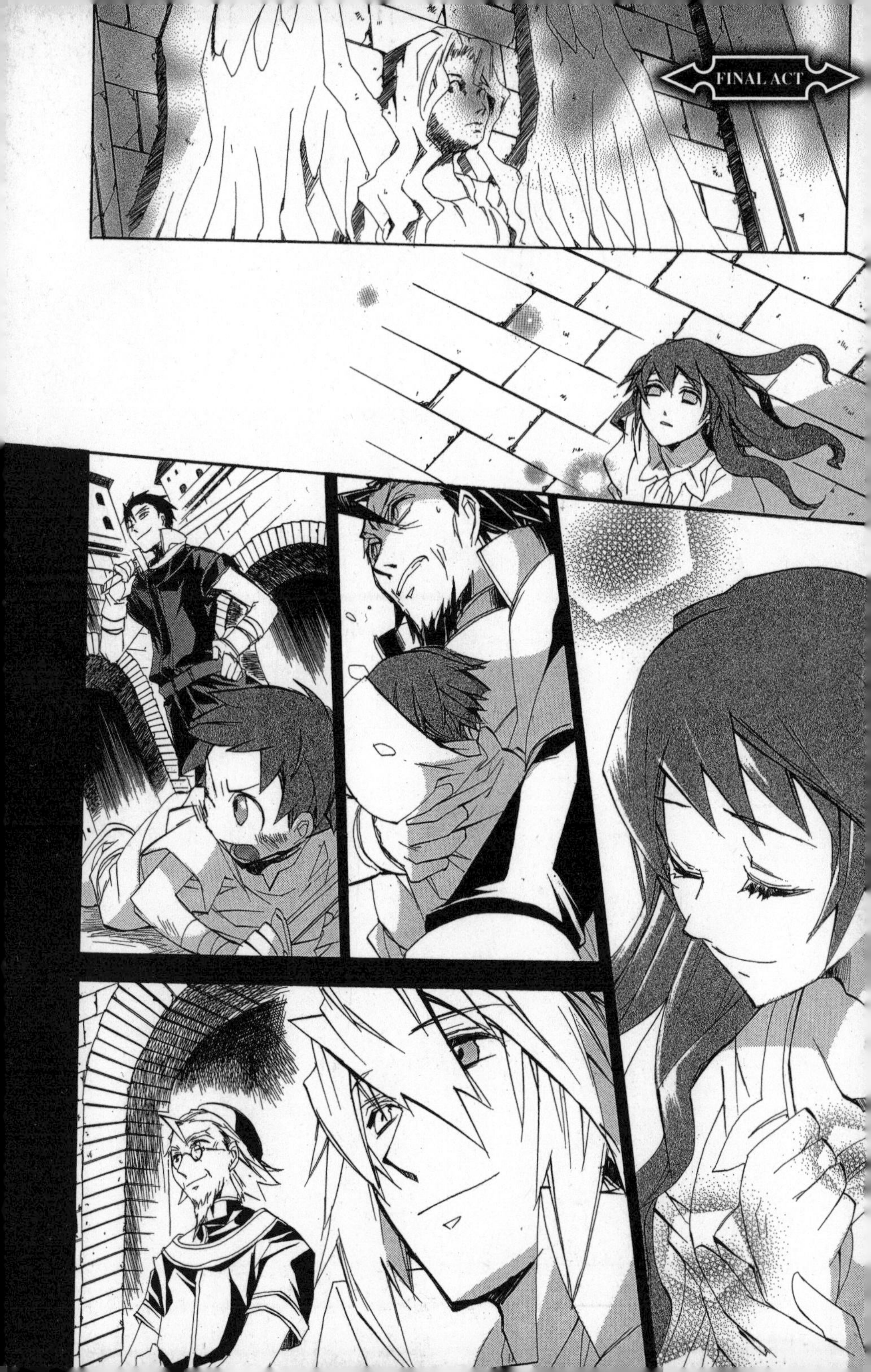
FINAL ACT

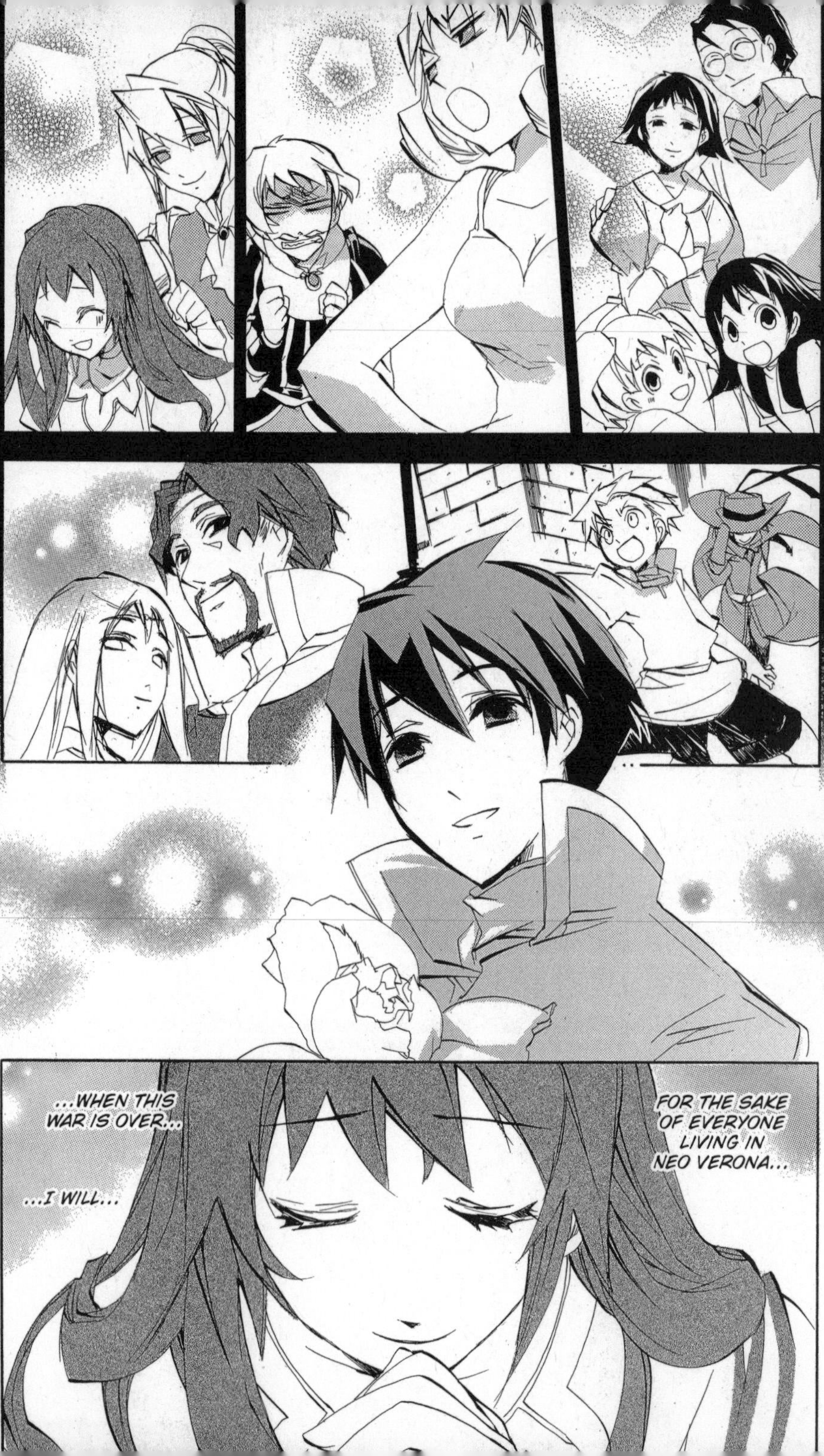
FOR THE SAKE OF EVERYONE LIVING IN NEO VERONA...
...WHEN THIS WAR IS OVER...
...I WILL...

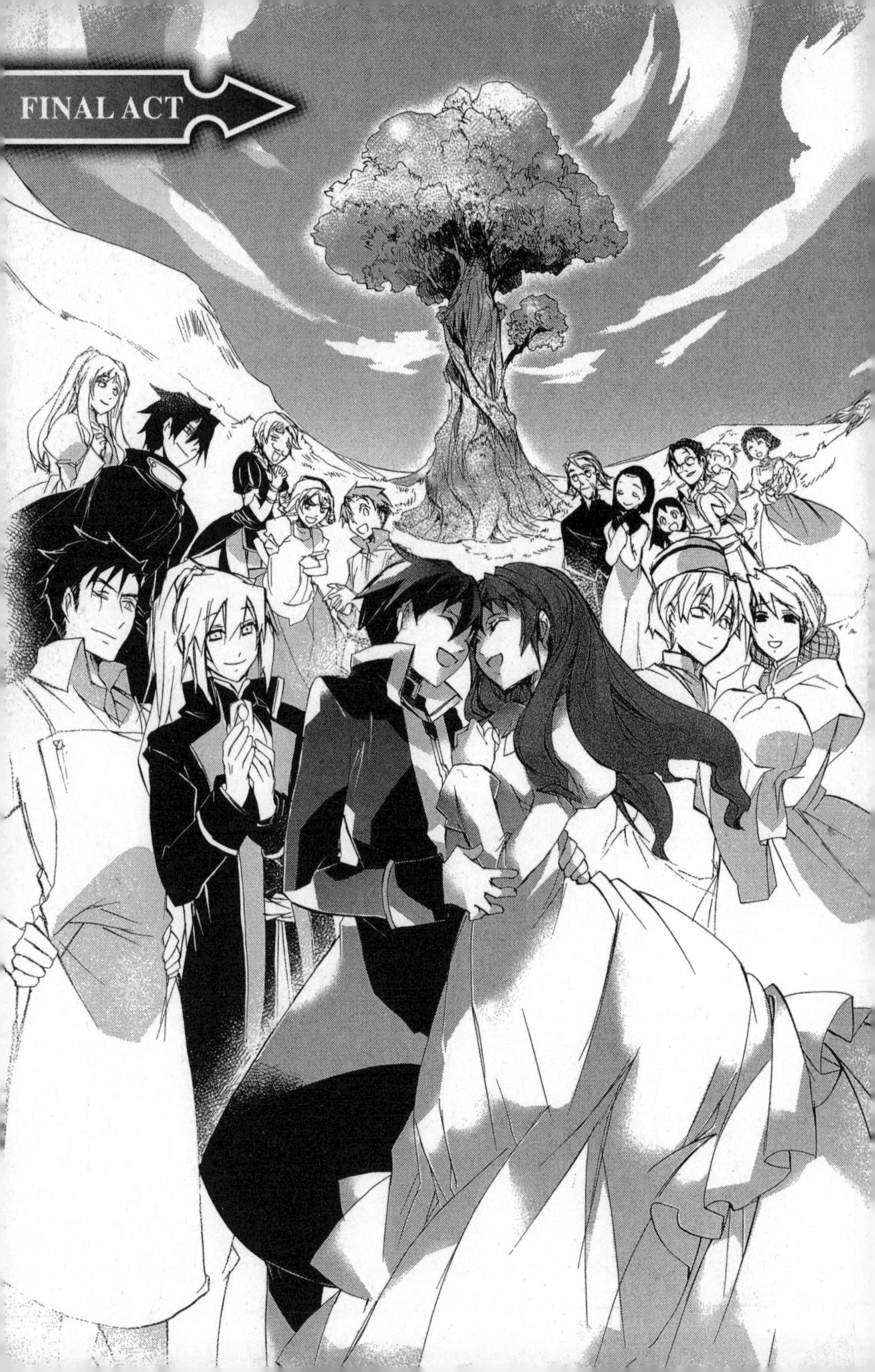
FINAL ACT

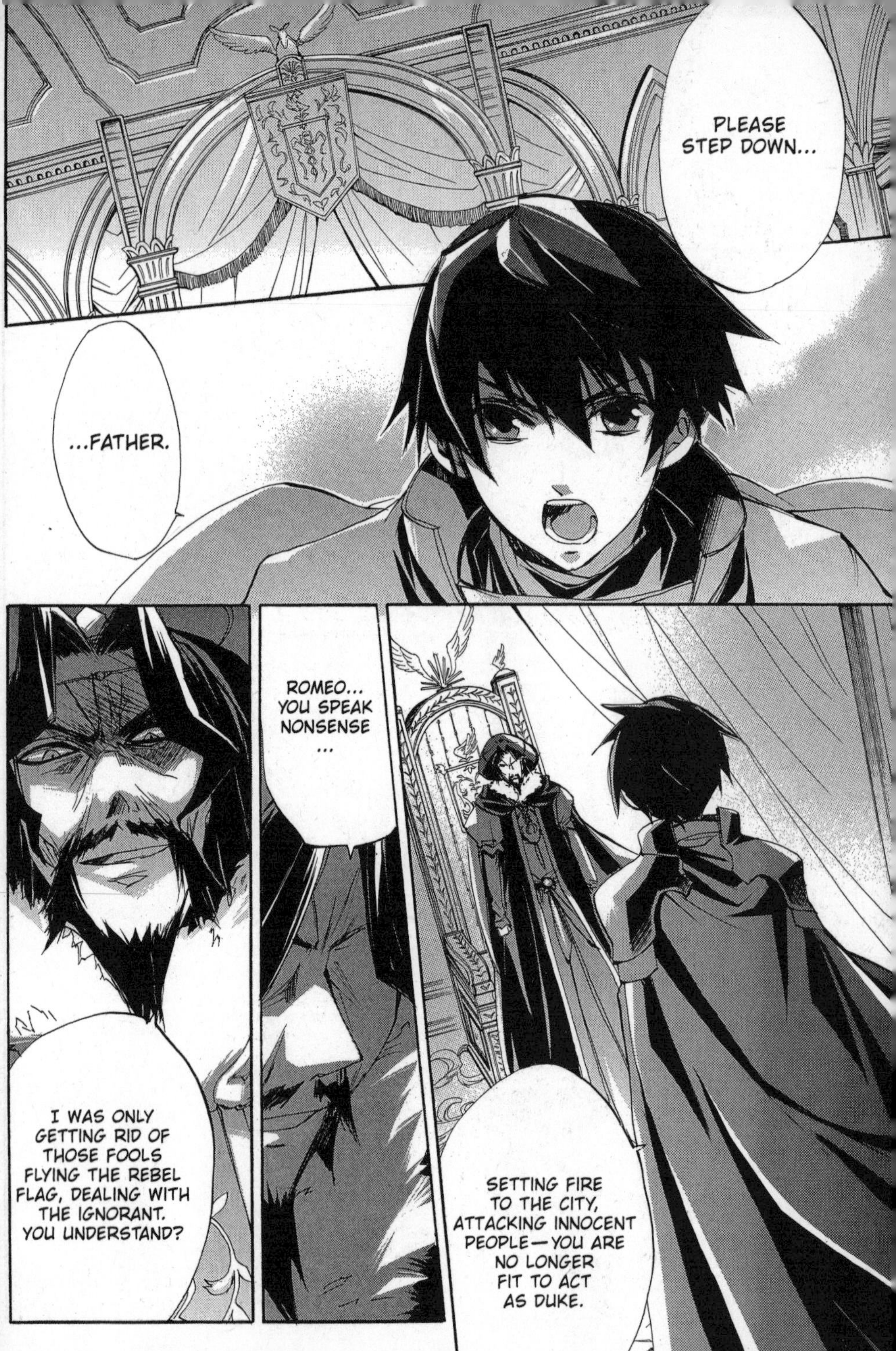
PLEASE STEP DOWN...
...FATHER.
SETTING FIRE TO THE CITY, ATTACKING INNOCENT PEOPLE—YOU ARE NO LONGER FIT TO ACT AS DUKE.
ROMEO... YOU SPEAK NONSENSE...
I WAS ONLY GETTING RID OF THOSE FOOLS FLYING THE REBEL FLAG, DEALING WITH THE IGNORANT. YOU UNDERSTAND?

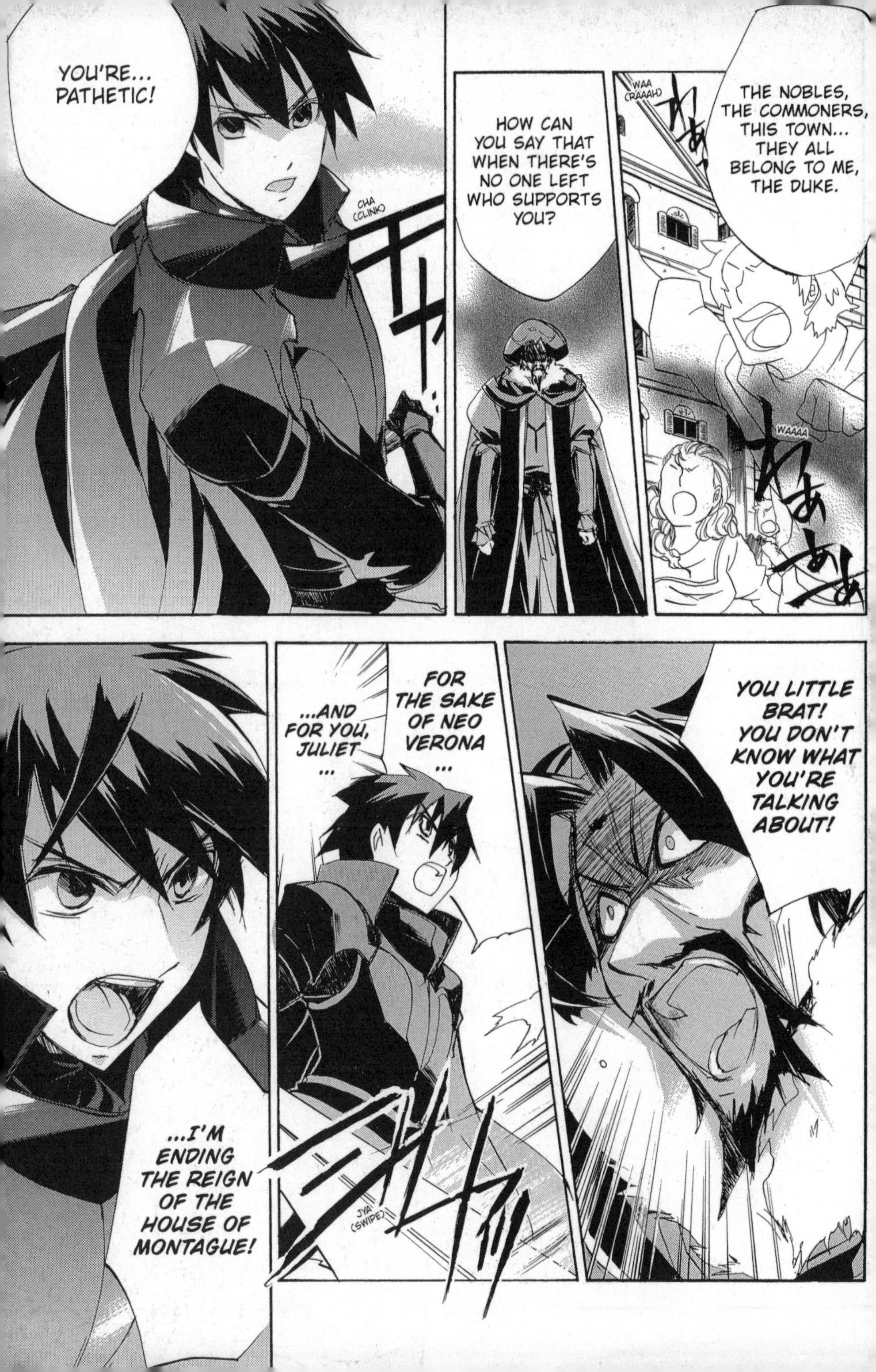
WAA (RAAAH)
THE NOBLES, THE COMMONERS, THIS TOWN... THEY ALL BELONG TO ME, THE DUKE.
WAAAA
HOW CAN YOU SAY THAT WHEN THERE'S NO ONE LEFT WHO SUPPORTS YOU?
YOU'RE... PATHETIC!
CHA (CLINK)
YOU LITTLE BRAT! YOU DON'T KNOW WHAT YOU'RE TALKING ABOUT!
FOR THE SAKE OF NEO VERONA ...
...AND FOR YOU, JULIET ...
JYA (SWIPE)
...I'M ENDING THE REIGN OF THE HOUSE OF MONTAGUE!

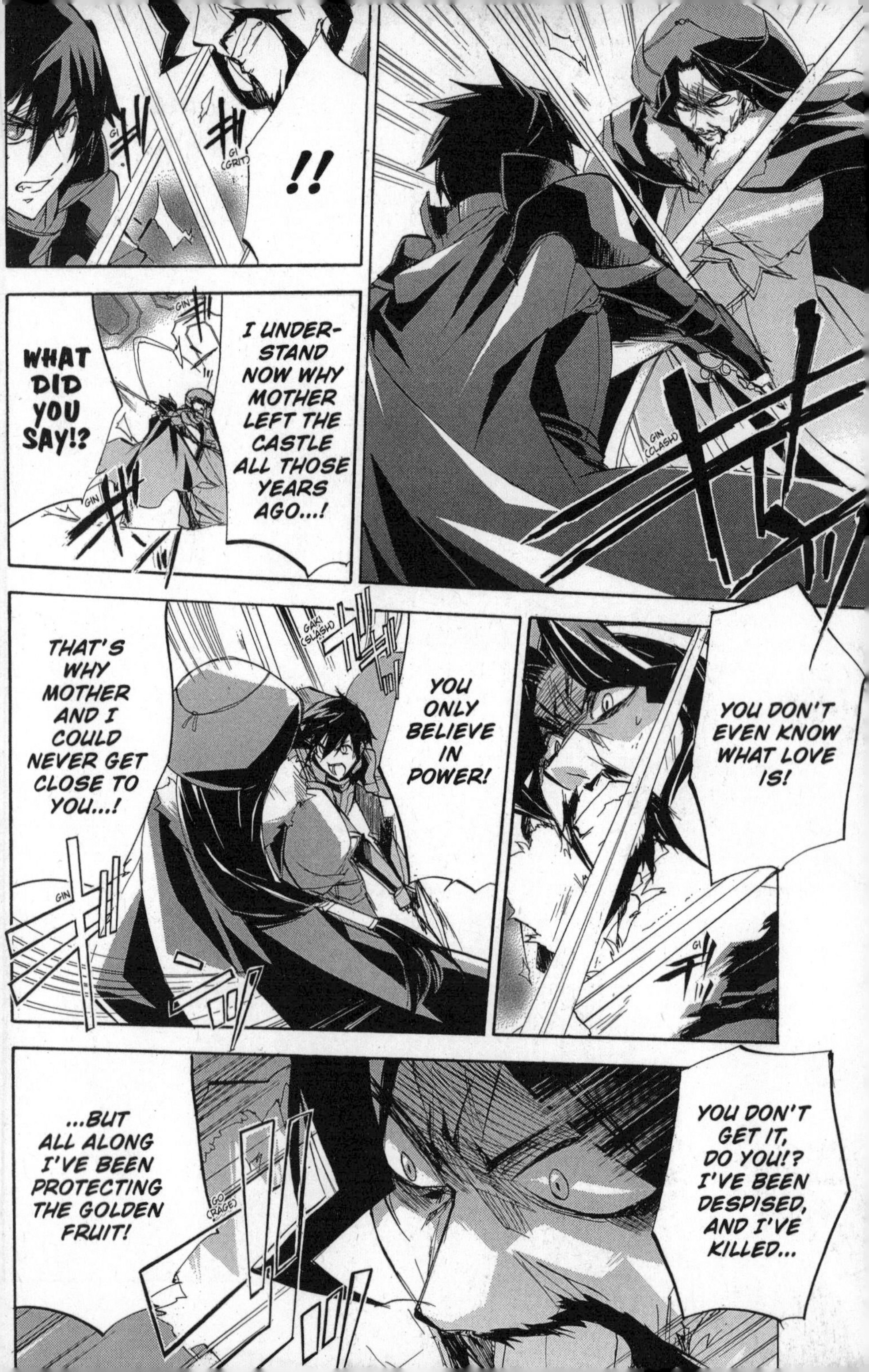
GIN (CLASH)
!!
GI
GI (GRIT)
I UNDER-STAND NOW WHY MOTHER LEFT THE CASTLE ALL THOSE YEARS AGO...!
GIN
WHAT DID YOU SAY!?
GIN
YOU DON'T EVEN KNOW WHAT LOVE IS!
GI
YOU ONLY BELIEVE IN POWER!
GAKI (SLASH)
THAT'S WHY MOTHER AND I COULD NEVER GET CLOSE TO YOU...!
GIN
YOU DON'T GET IT, DO YOU!? I'VE BEEN DESPISED, AND I'VE KILLED...
GO (RAGE)
...BUT ALL ALONG I'VE BEEN PROTECTING THE GOLDEN FRUIT!

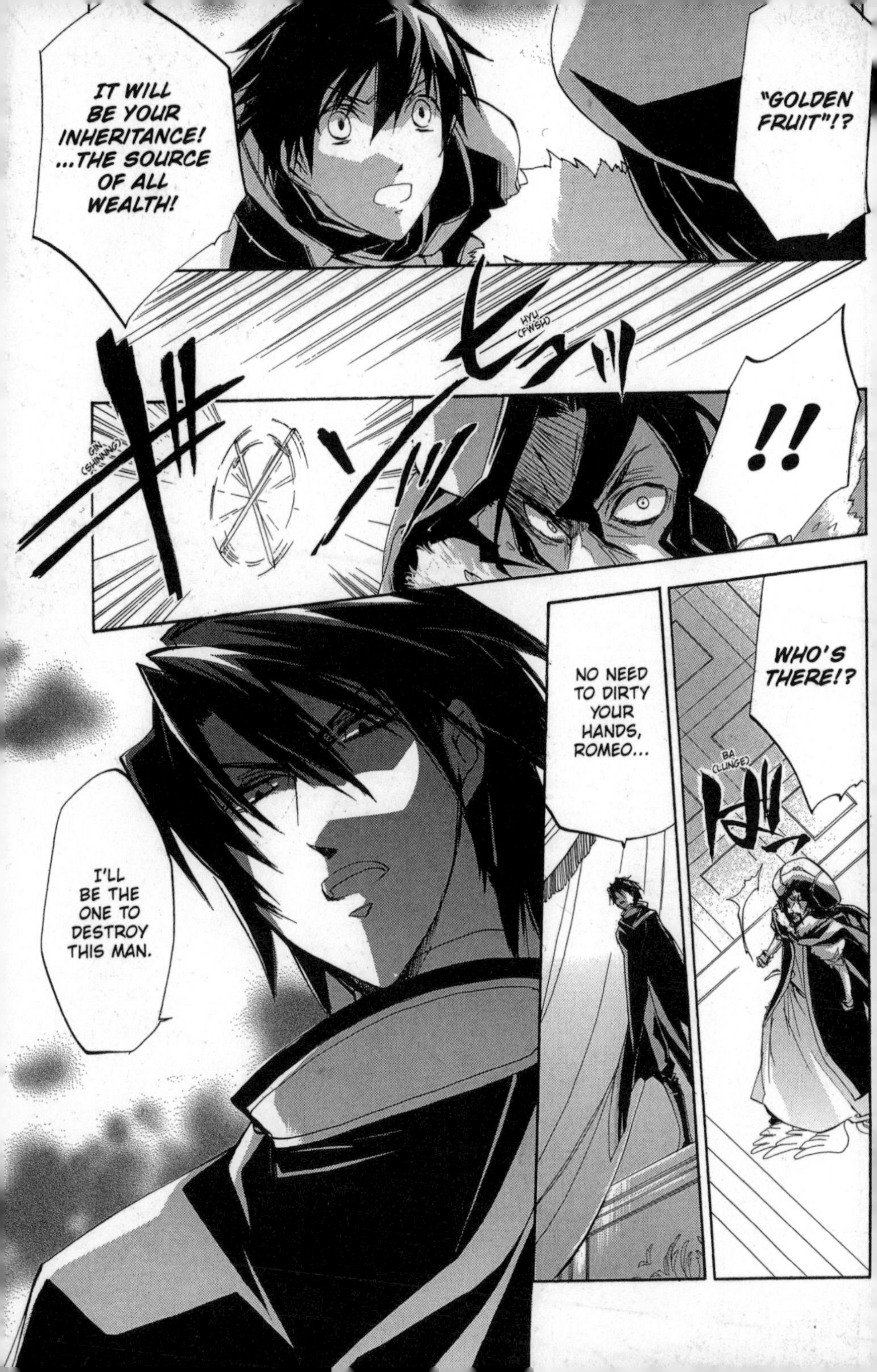
"GOLDEN FRUIT"!?
IT WILL BE YOUR INHERITANCE! ...THE SOURCE OF ALL WEALTH!
HYU (FWSH)
!!
GIN (SHINNNG)
WHO'S THERE!?
BA (LUNGE)
NO NEED TO DIRTY YOUR HANDS, ROMEO...
I'LL BE THE ONE TO DESTROY THIS MAN.

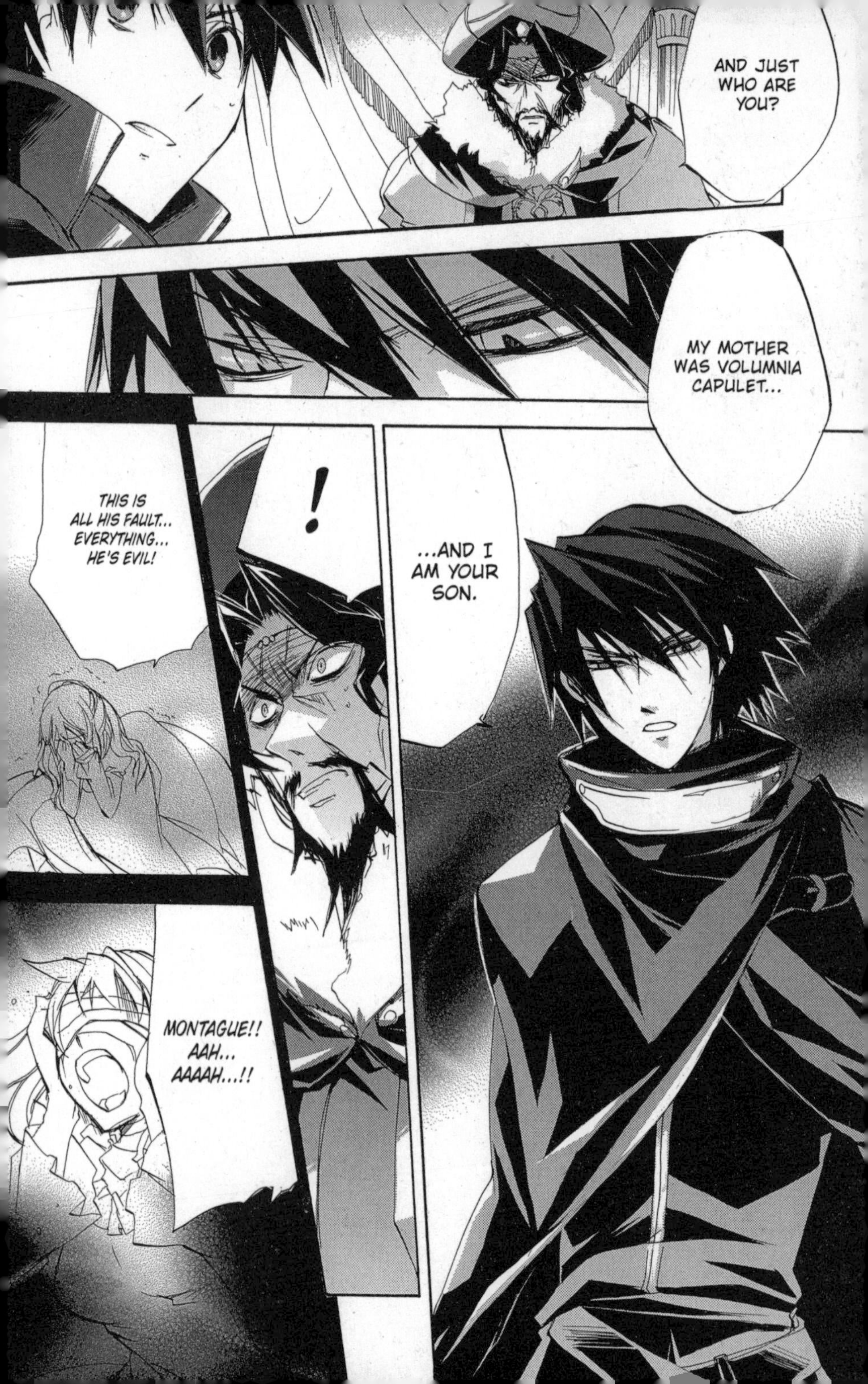
AND JUST WHO ARE YOU?
MY MOTHER WAS VOLUMNIA CAPULET...
...AND I AM YOUR SON.
!
THIS IS ALL HIS FAULT... EVERYTHING... HE'S EVIL!
MONTAGUE!! AAH... AAAAH...!!

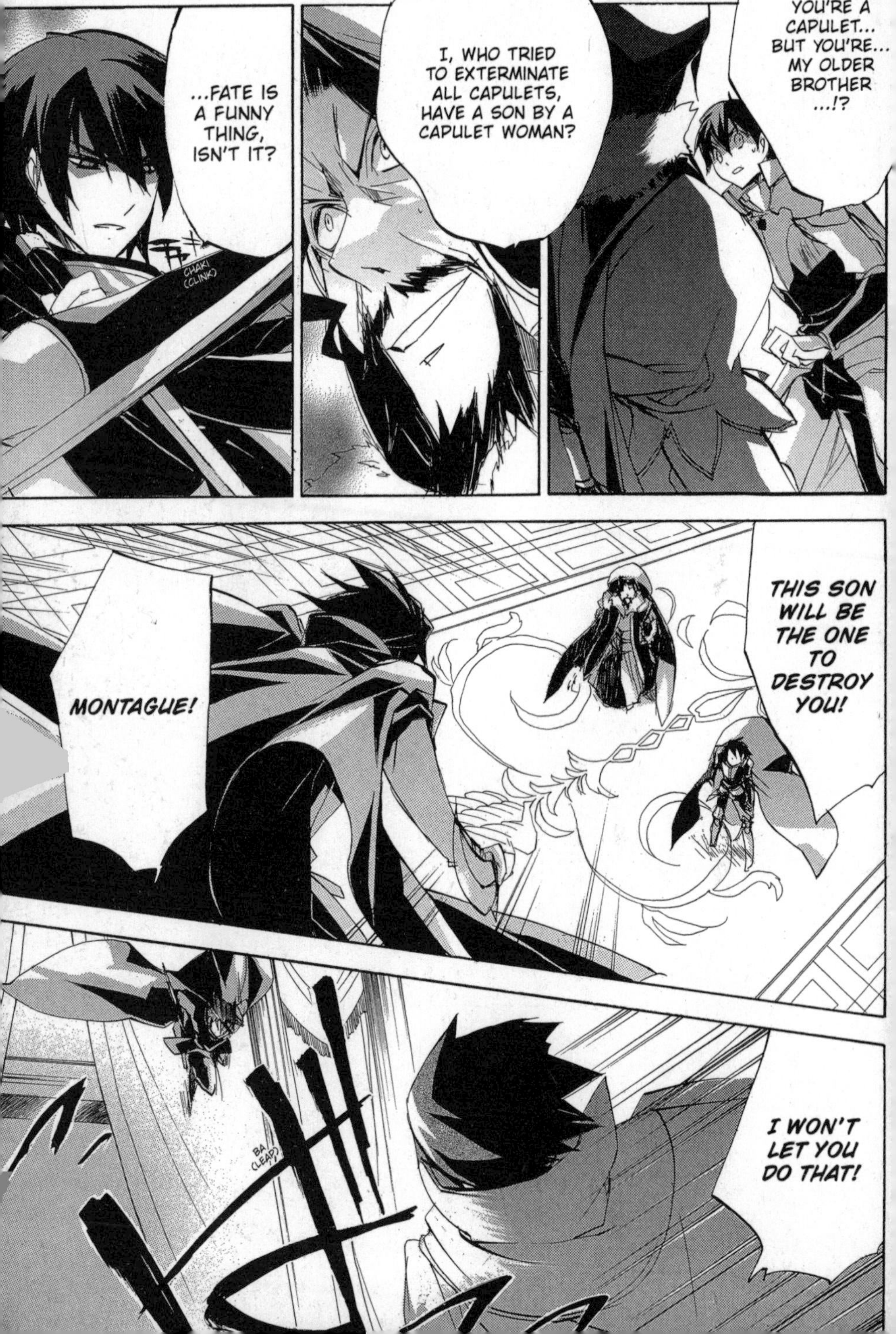
YOU'RE A CAPULET... BUT YOU'RE... MY OLDER BROTHER ...!?
I, WHO TRIED TO EXTERMINATE ALL CAPULETS, HAVE A SON BY A CAPULET WOMAN?
...FATE IS A FUNNY THING, ISN'T IT?
CHAKI (CLINK)
THIS SON WILL BE THE ONE TO DESTROY YOU!
MONTAGUE!
I WON'T LET YOU DO THAT!
BA (LEAP)

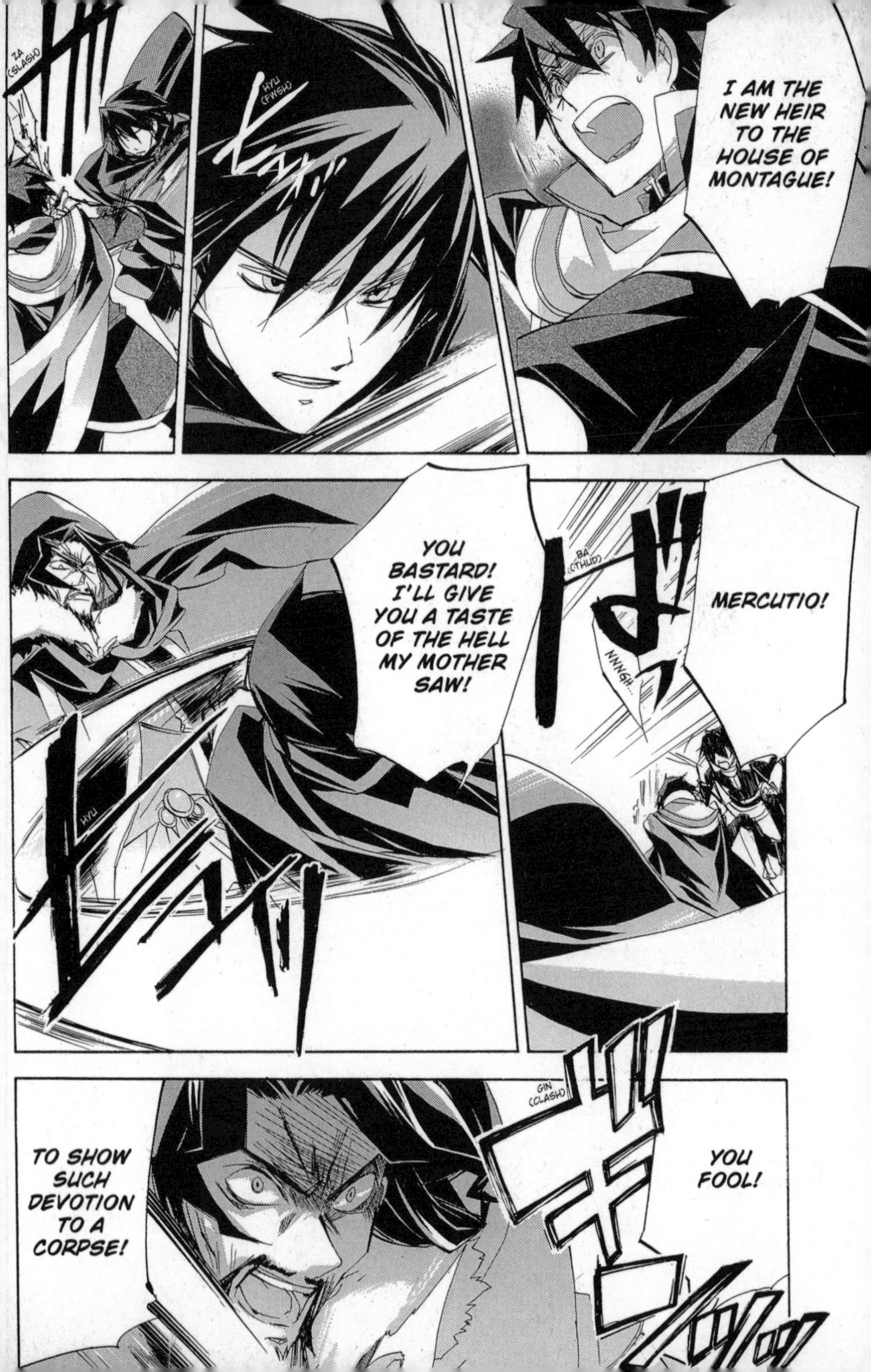
I AM THE NEW HEIR TO THE HOUSE OF MONTAGUE!
HYU (FWSH)
ZA (SLASH)
MERCUTIO!
BA (THUD)
NNNGH...
YOU BASTARD! I'LL GIVE YOU A TASTE OF THE HELL MY MOTHER SAW!
HYU
GIN (CLASH)
YOU FOOL!
TO SHOW SUCH DEVOTION TO A CORPSE!

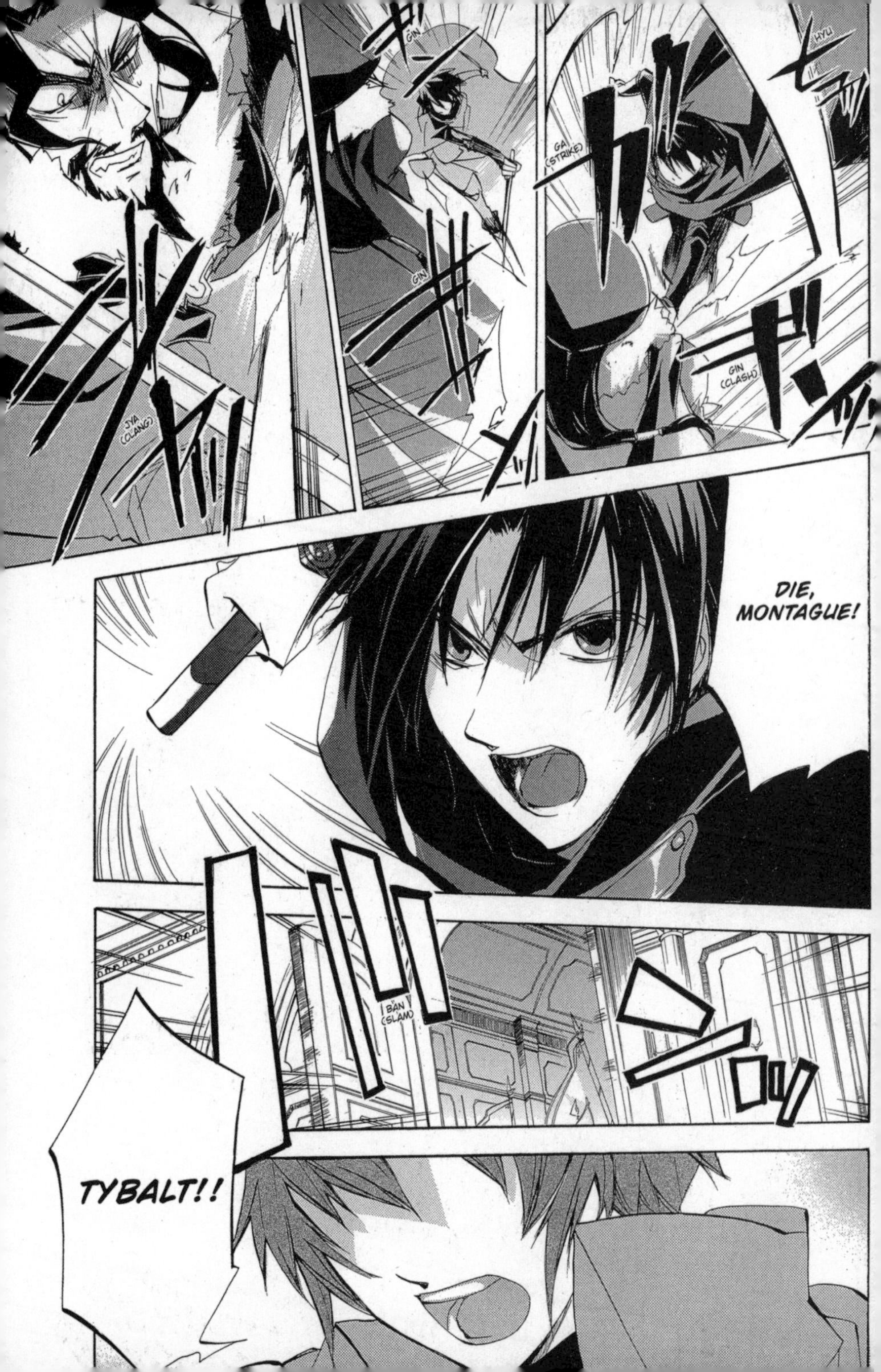
HYU
GA (STRIKE)
GIN (CLASH)
GIN
GIN
JYA (CLANG)
DIE, MONTAGUE!
BAN (SLAM)
TYBALT!!

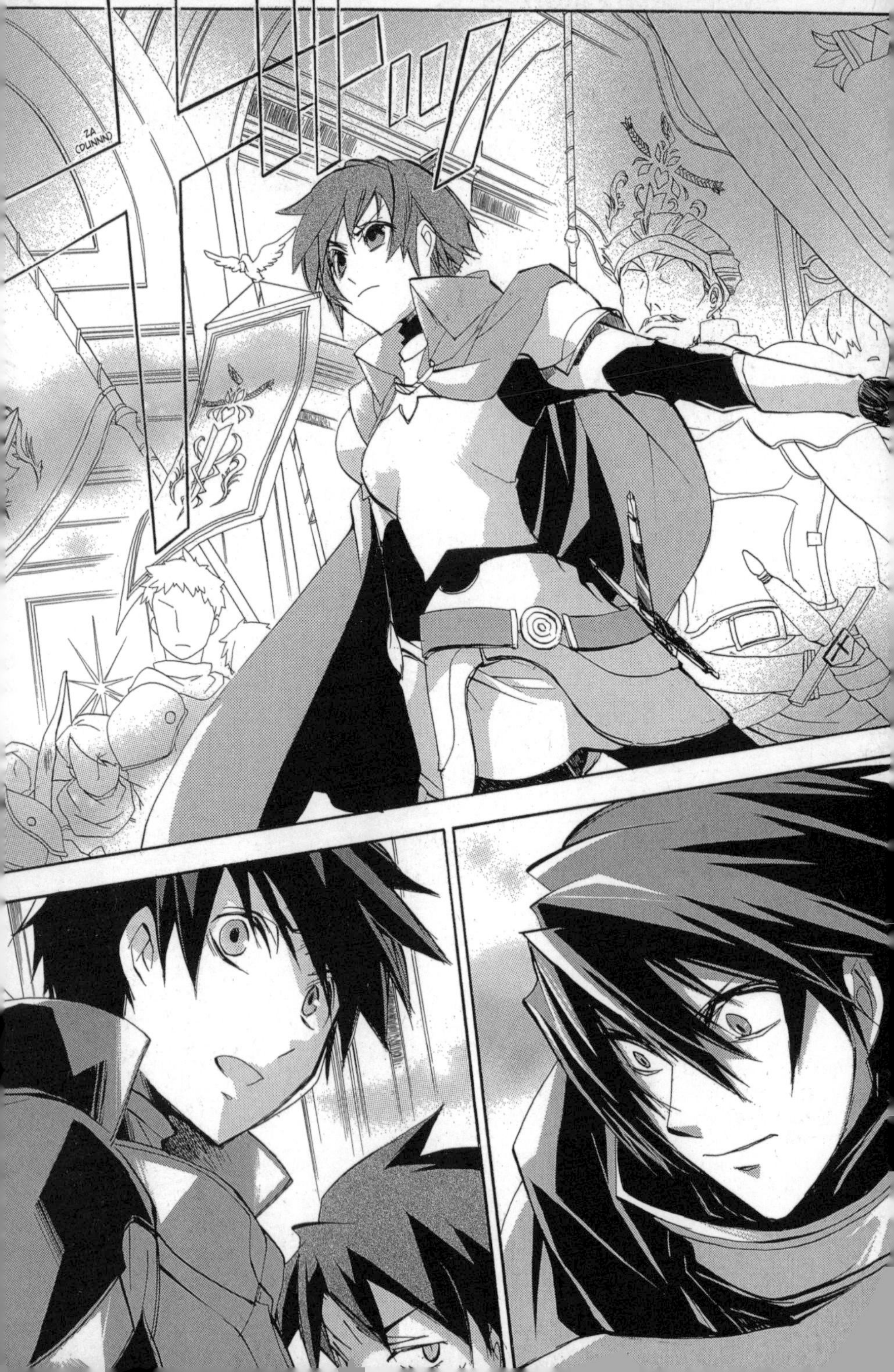
ZA
(DUNNN)

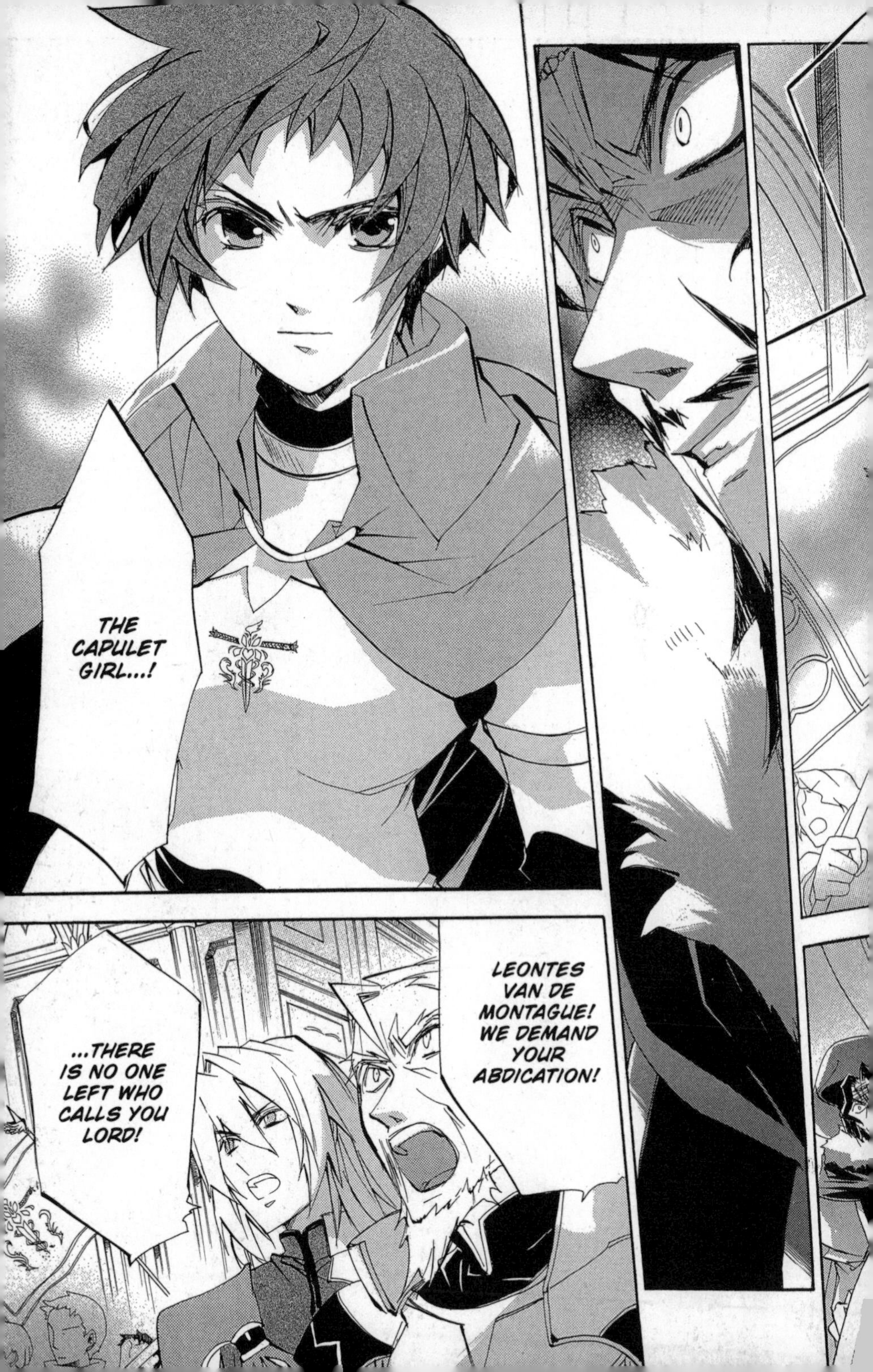
THE CAPULET GIRL...!
LEONTES VAN DE MONTAGUE! WE DEMAND YOUR ABDICATION!
...THERE IS NO ONE LEFT WHO CALLS YOU LORD!

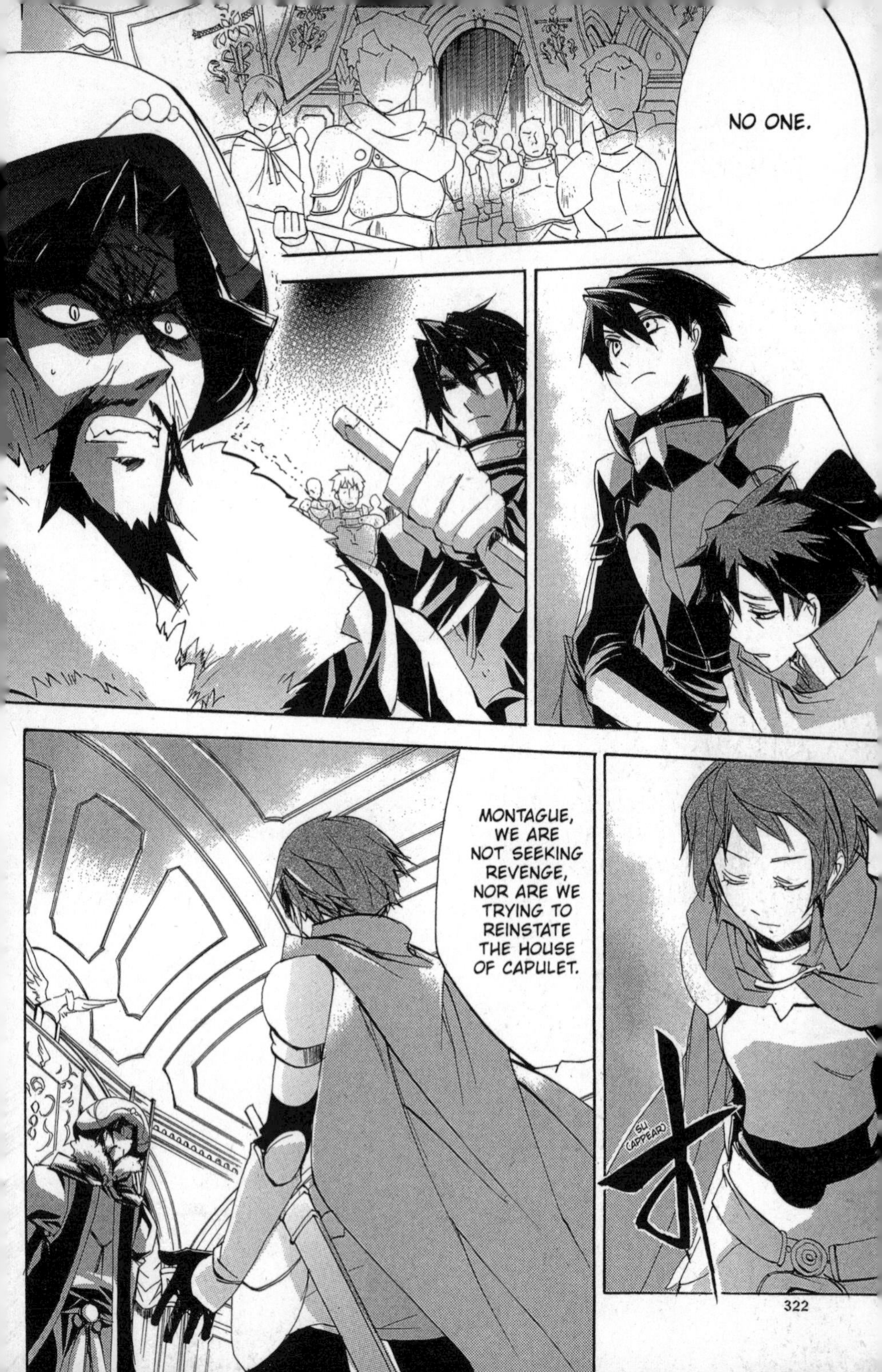
NO ONE.
MONTAGUE, WE ARE NOT SEEKING REVENGE, NOR ARE WE TRYING TO REINSTATE THE HOUSE OF CAPULET.
SU (APPEAR)

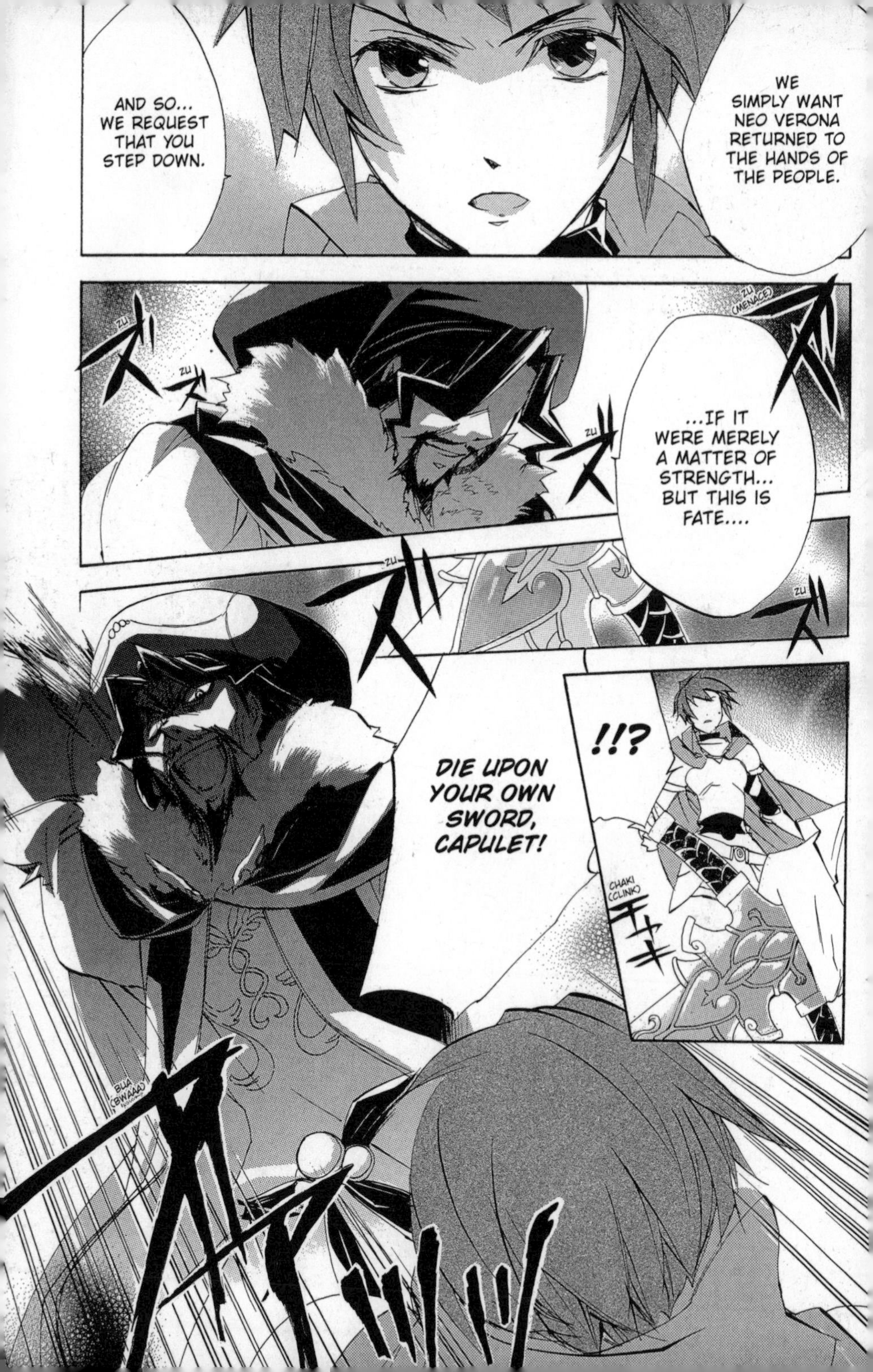
WE SIMPLY WANT NEO VERONA RETURNED TO THE HANDS OF THE PEOPLE.
AND SO... WE REQUEST THAT YOU STEP DOWN.
ZU (MENACE)
ZU
ZU
ZU
...IF IT WERE MERELY A MATTER OF STRENGTH... BUT THIS IS FATE....
ZU
ZU
!!?
CHAKI (CLINK)
DIE UPON YOUR OWN SWORD, CAPULET!
BUA (BWAAA)

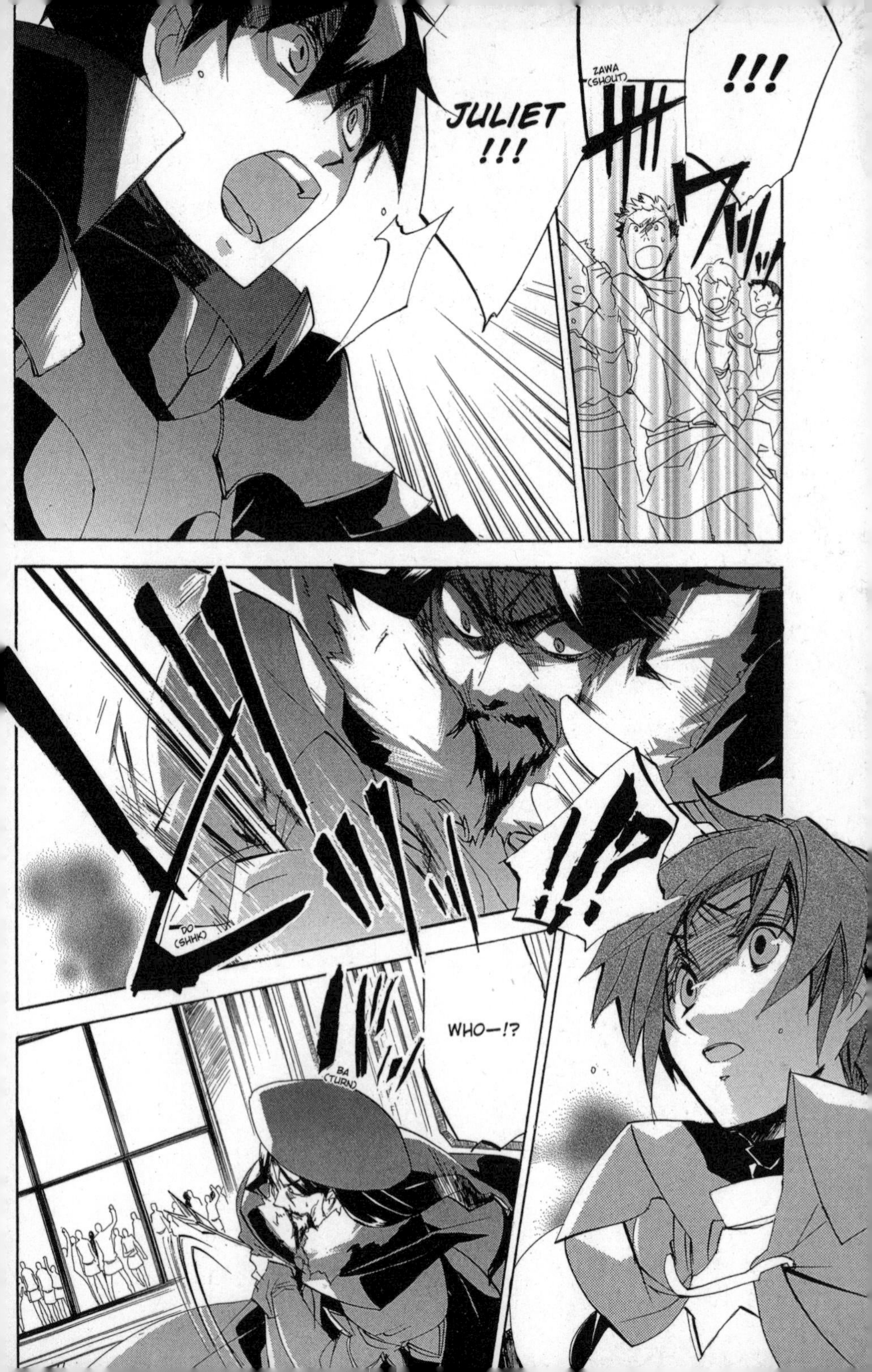
!!!
ZAWA
(SHOUT)
JULIET
!!!
!!?
DO
(SHHK)
WHO—!?
BA
(TURN)

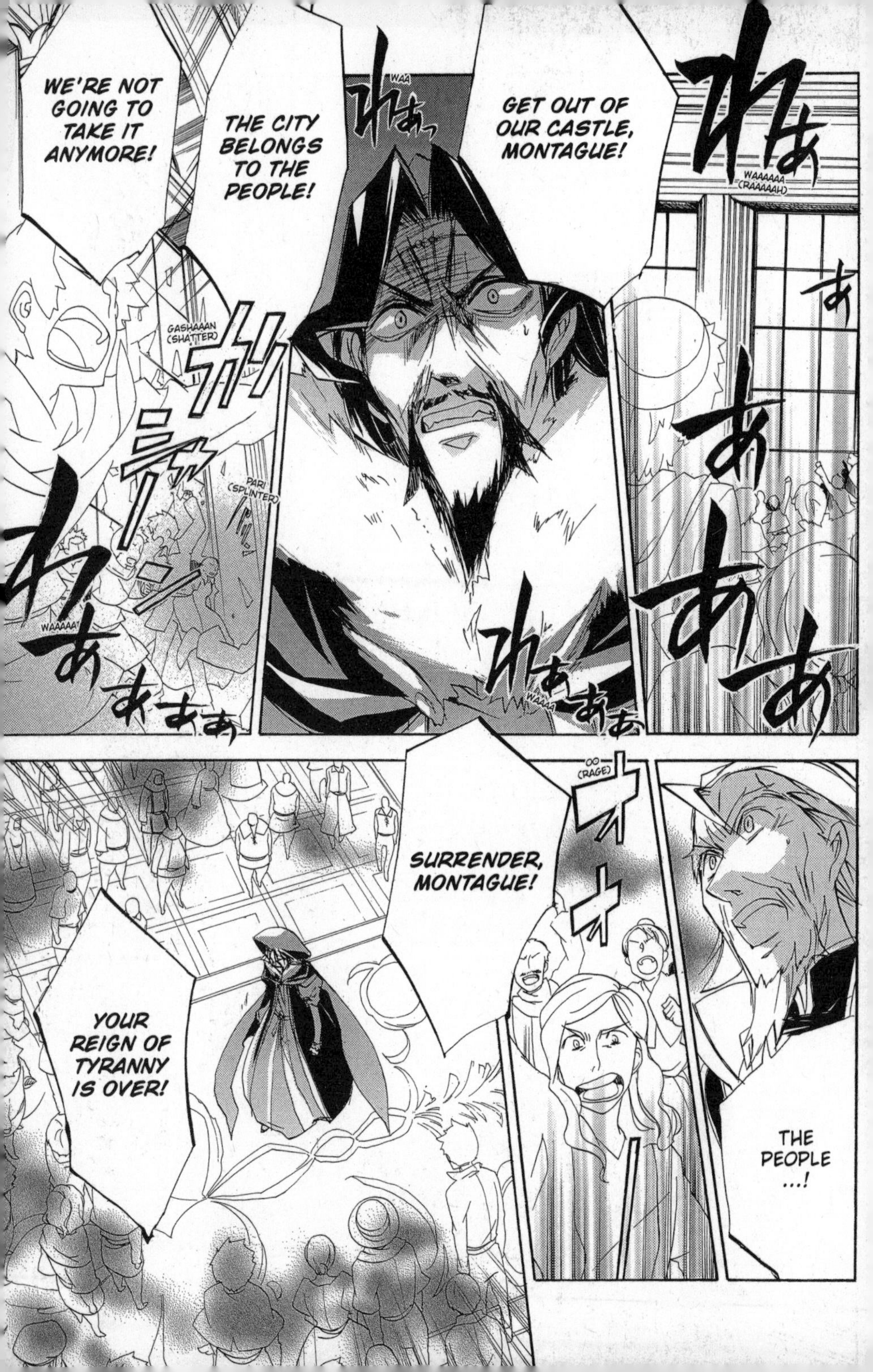

わぁ
WAAAAAA (RAAAAAH)
ああああ
GET OUT OF OUR CASTLE, MONTAGUE!
わぁっ
WAA
わぁああ
WAAAA
THE CITY BELONGS TO THE PEOPLE!
WE'RE NOT GOING TO TAKE IT ANYMORE!
ガシャン
GASHAAAN (SHATTER)
パリ
PARI (SPLINTER)
わぁあああ
WAAAAA!
THE PEOPLE ...!
オオ
OO (RAGE)
SURRENDER, MONTAGUE!
YOUR REIGN OF TYRANNY IS OVER!

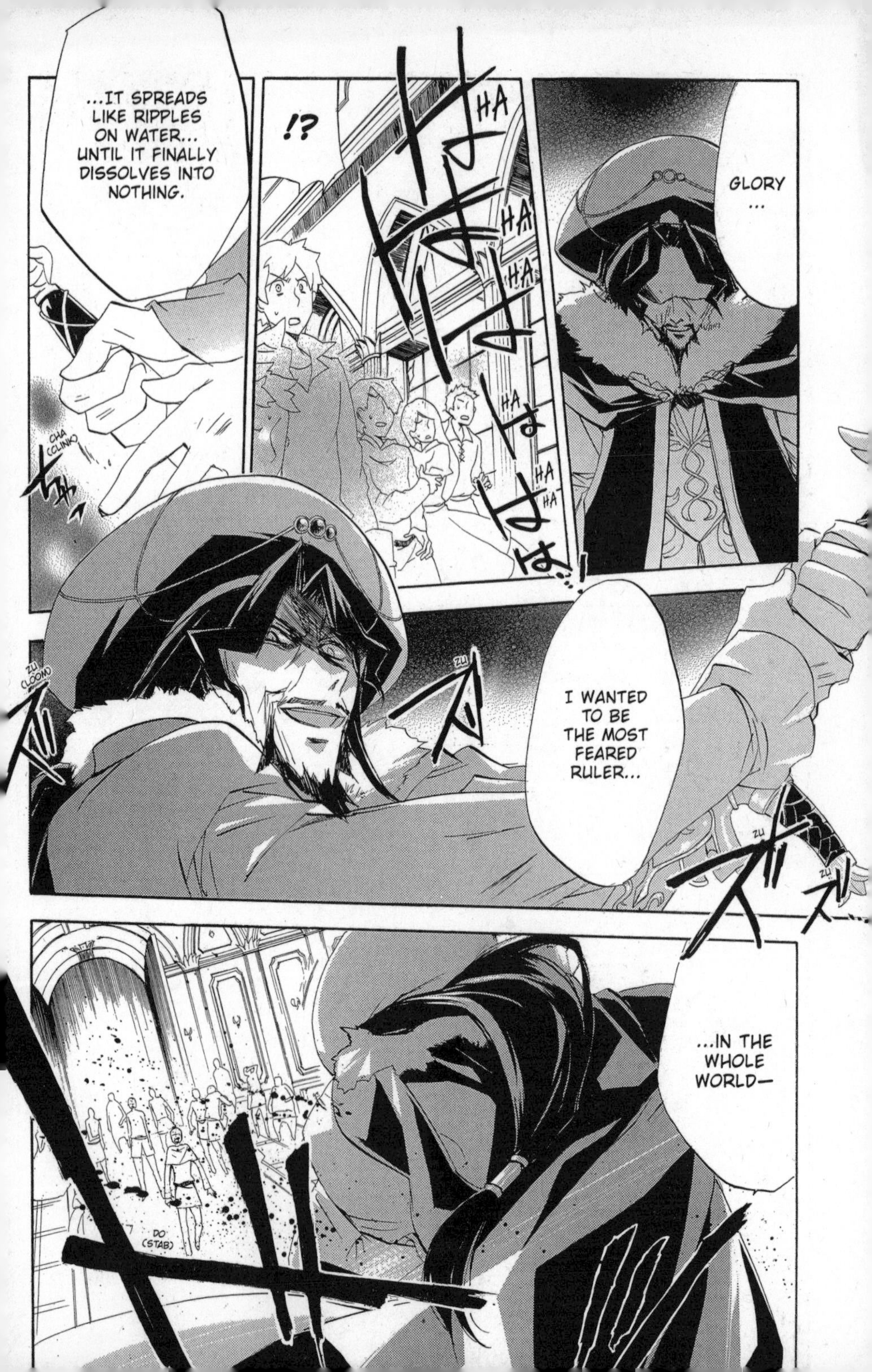
GLORY ...
!?
HA
HA
HA
HA
HA
HA
...IT SPREADS LIKE RIPPLES ON WATER... UNTIL IT FINALLY DISSOLVES INTO NOTHING.
CHA (CLINK)
ZU
ZU
ZU
I WANTED TO BE THE MOST FEARED RULER...
ZU
ZU (LOOM)
...IN THE WHOLE WORLD—
DO (STAB)

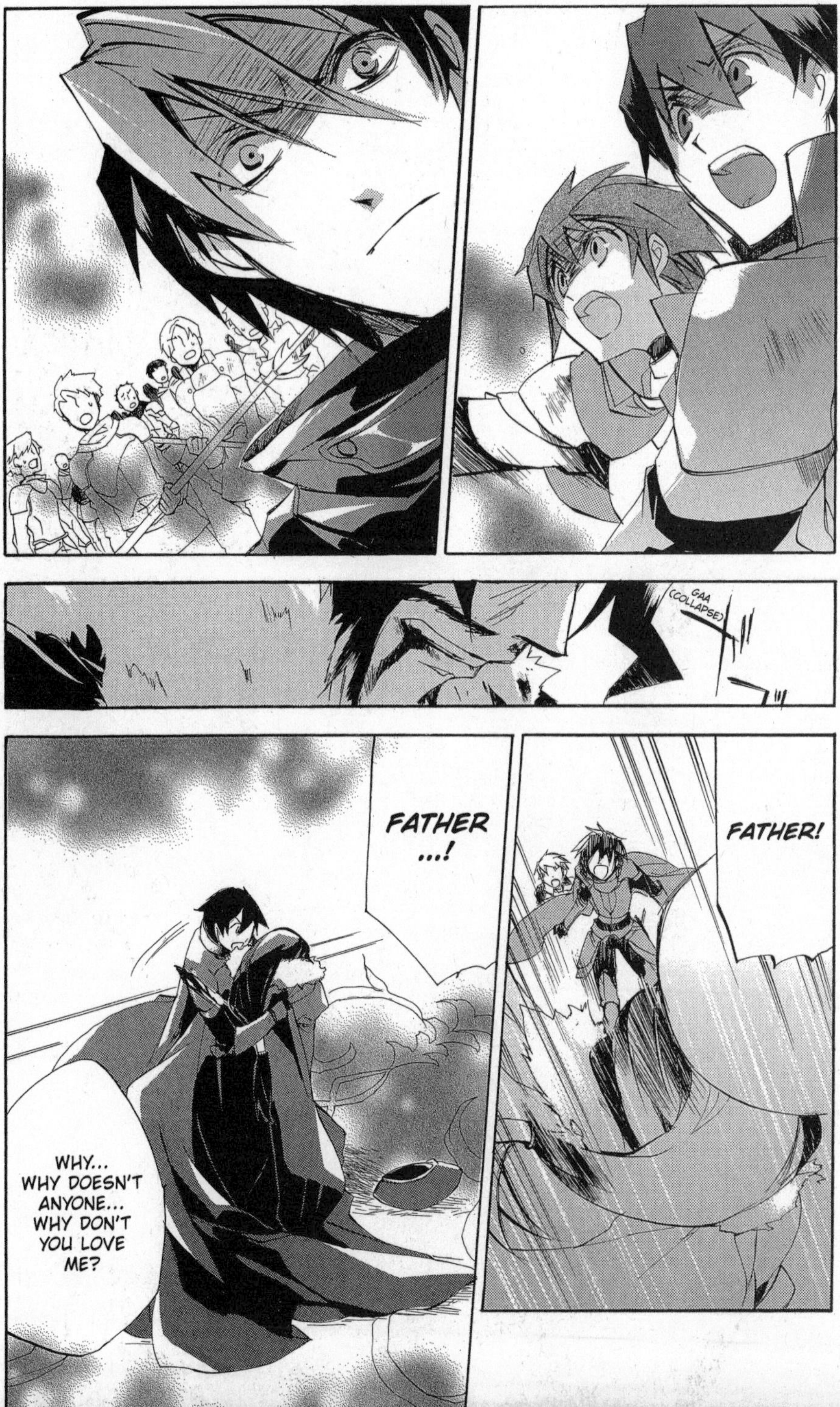
GAA (COLLAPSE)
FATHER!
FATHER ...!
WHY... WHY DOESN'T ANYONE... WHY DON'T YOU LOVE ME?

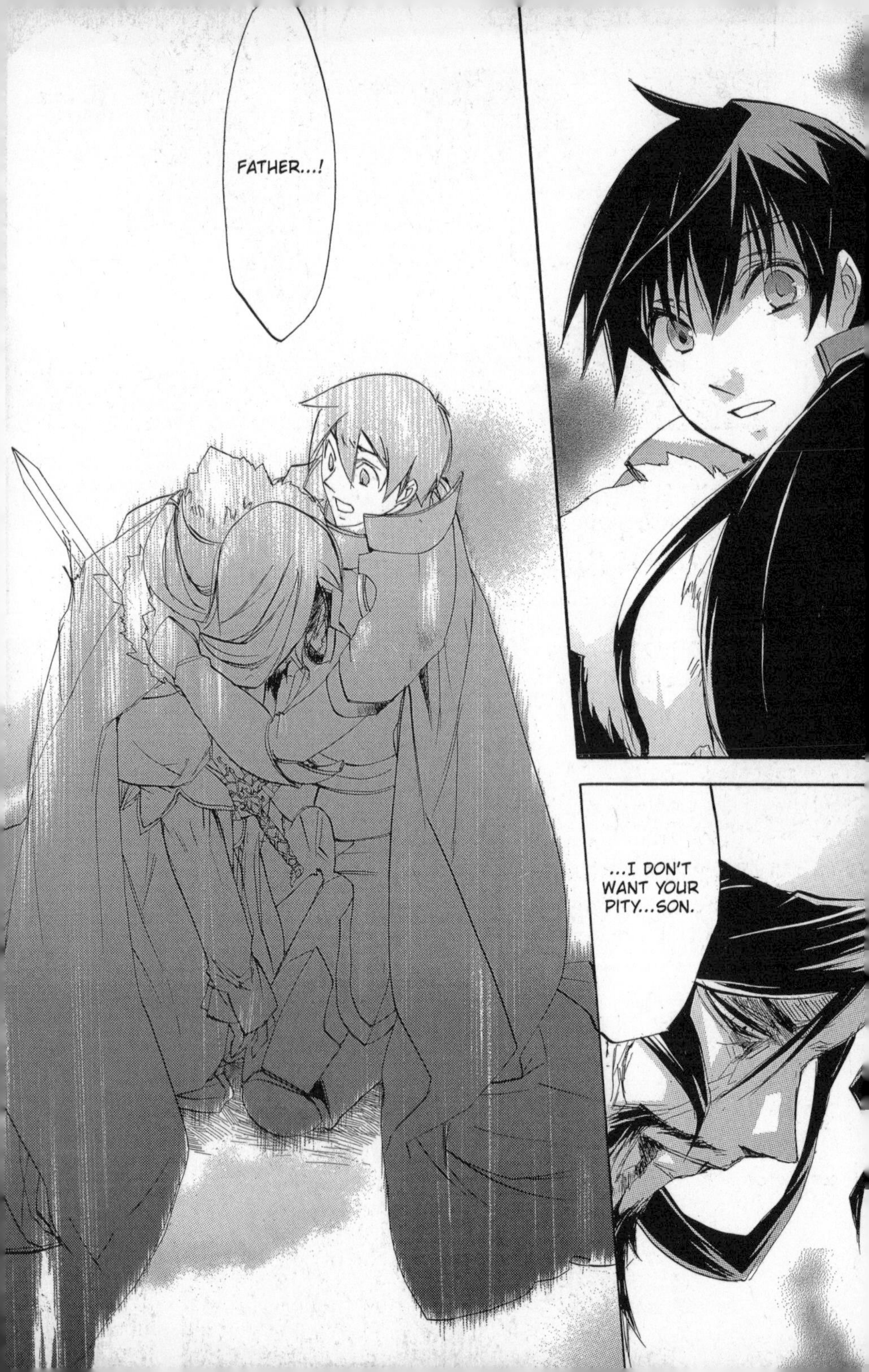
...I DON'T WANT YOUR PITY...SON.
FATHER...!

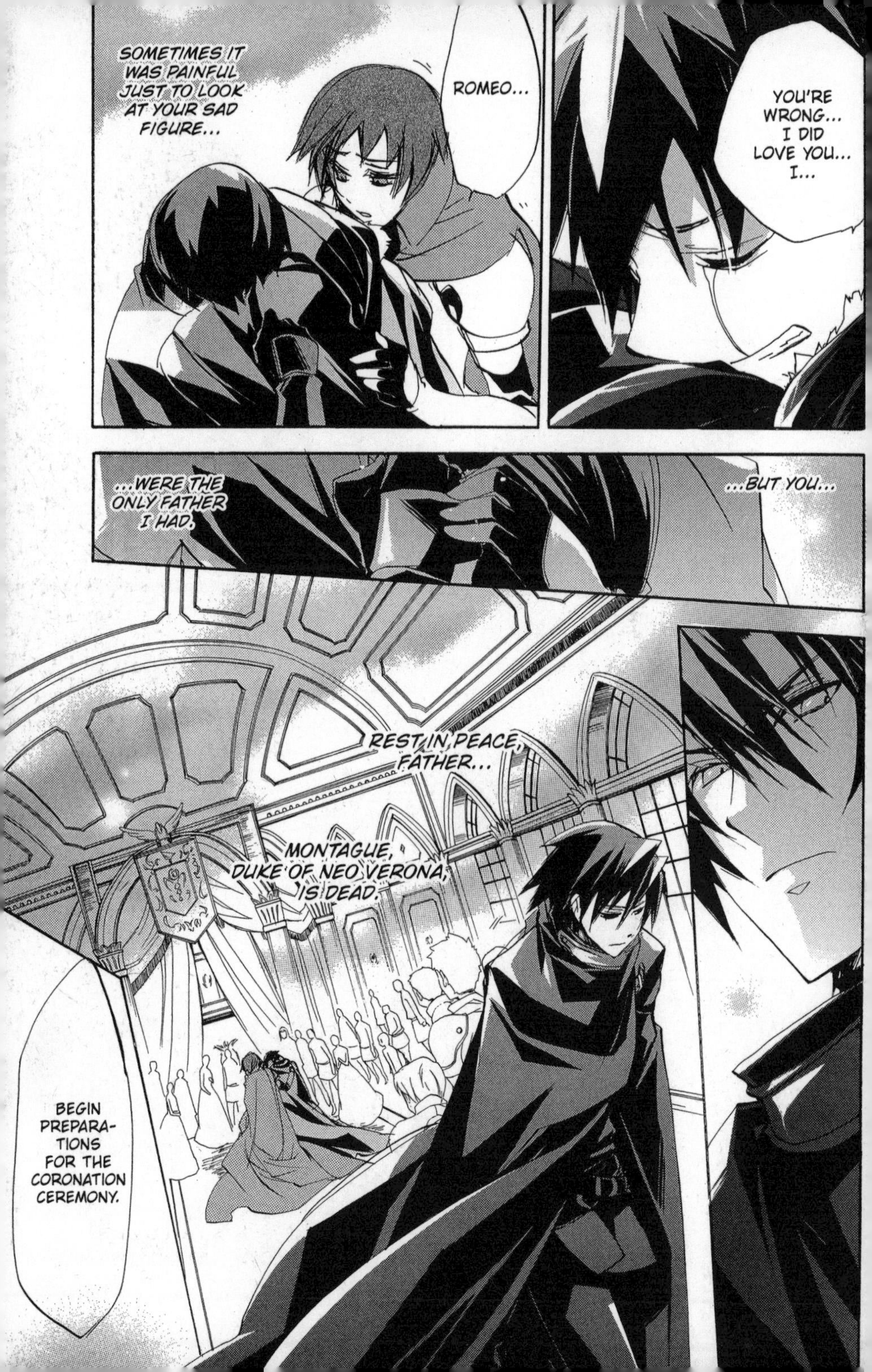
YOU'RE WRONG... I DID LOVE YOU... I...
ROMEO...
SOMETIMES IT WAS PAINFUL JUST TO LOOK AT YOUR SAD FIGURE...
...BUT YOU...
...WERE THE ONLY FATHER I HAD.
REST IN PEACE, FATHER...
MONTAGUE, DUKE OF NEO VERONA, IS DEAD.
BEGIN PREPARATIONS FOR THE CORONATION CEREMONY.

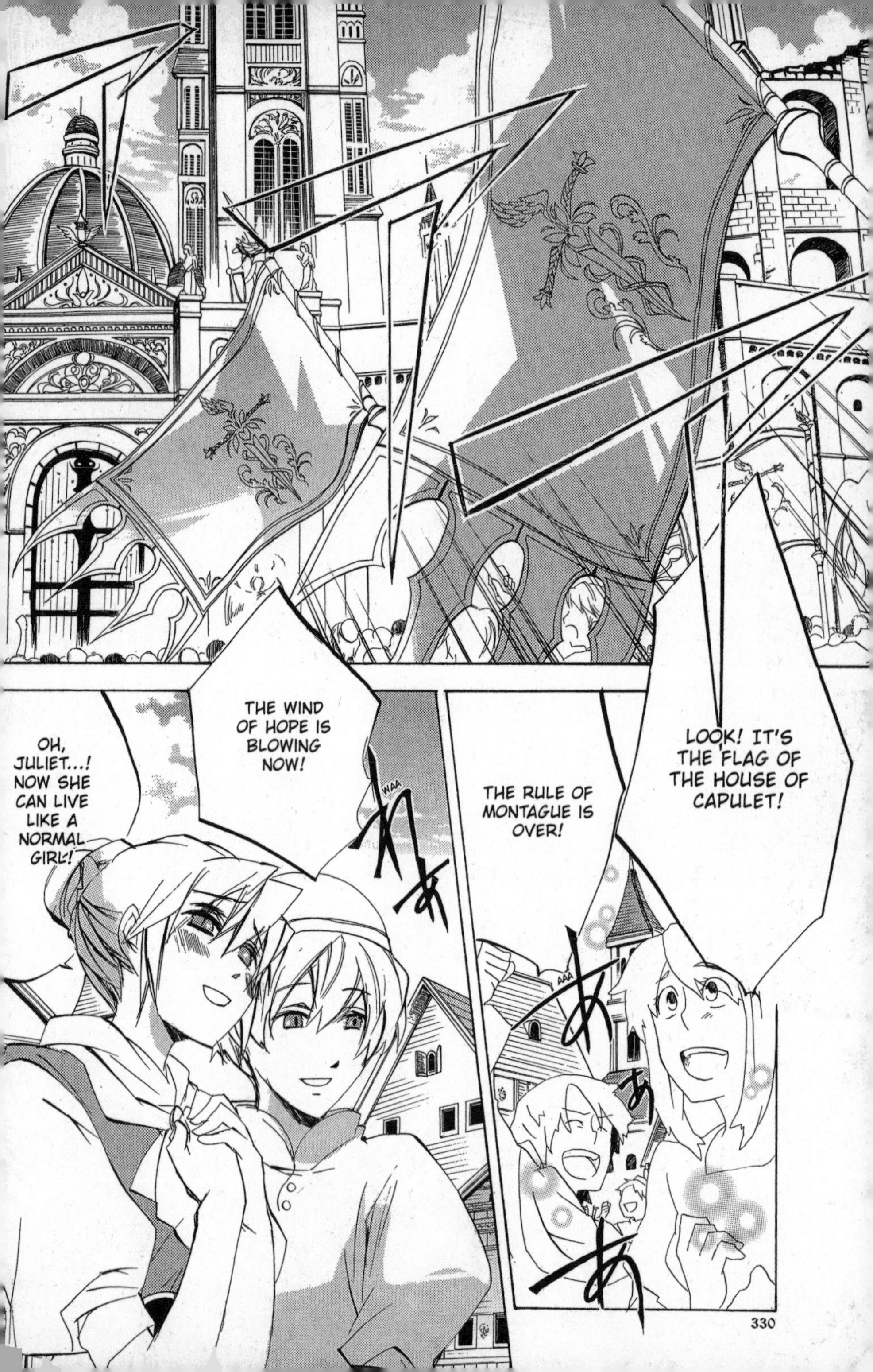
LOOK! IT'S THE FLAG OF THE HOUSE OF CAPULET!
THE RULE OF MONTAGUE IS OVER!
AAA
THE WIND OF HOPE IS BLOWING NOW!
WAA
OH, JULIET...! NOW SHE CAN LIVE LIKE A NORMAL GIRL!

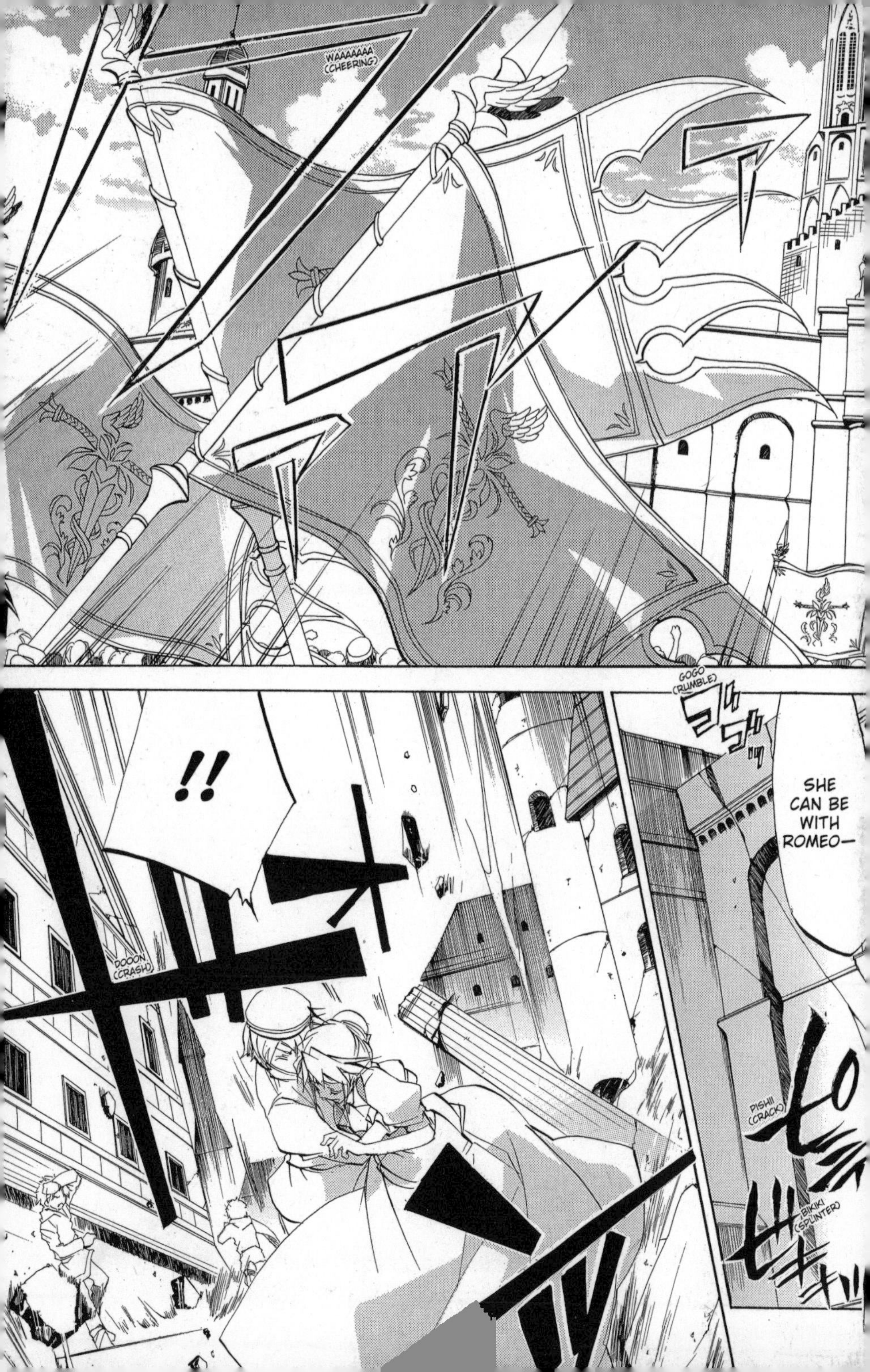
WAAAAAAA
(CHEERING)
GOGO
(RUMBLE)
SHE CAN BE WITH ROMEO—
PISHII
(CRACK)
BIKIKI
(SPLINTER)
!!
DOOON
(CRASH)

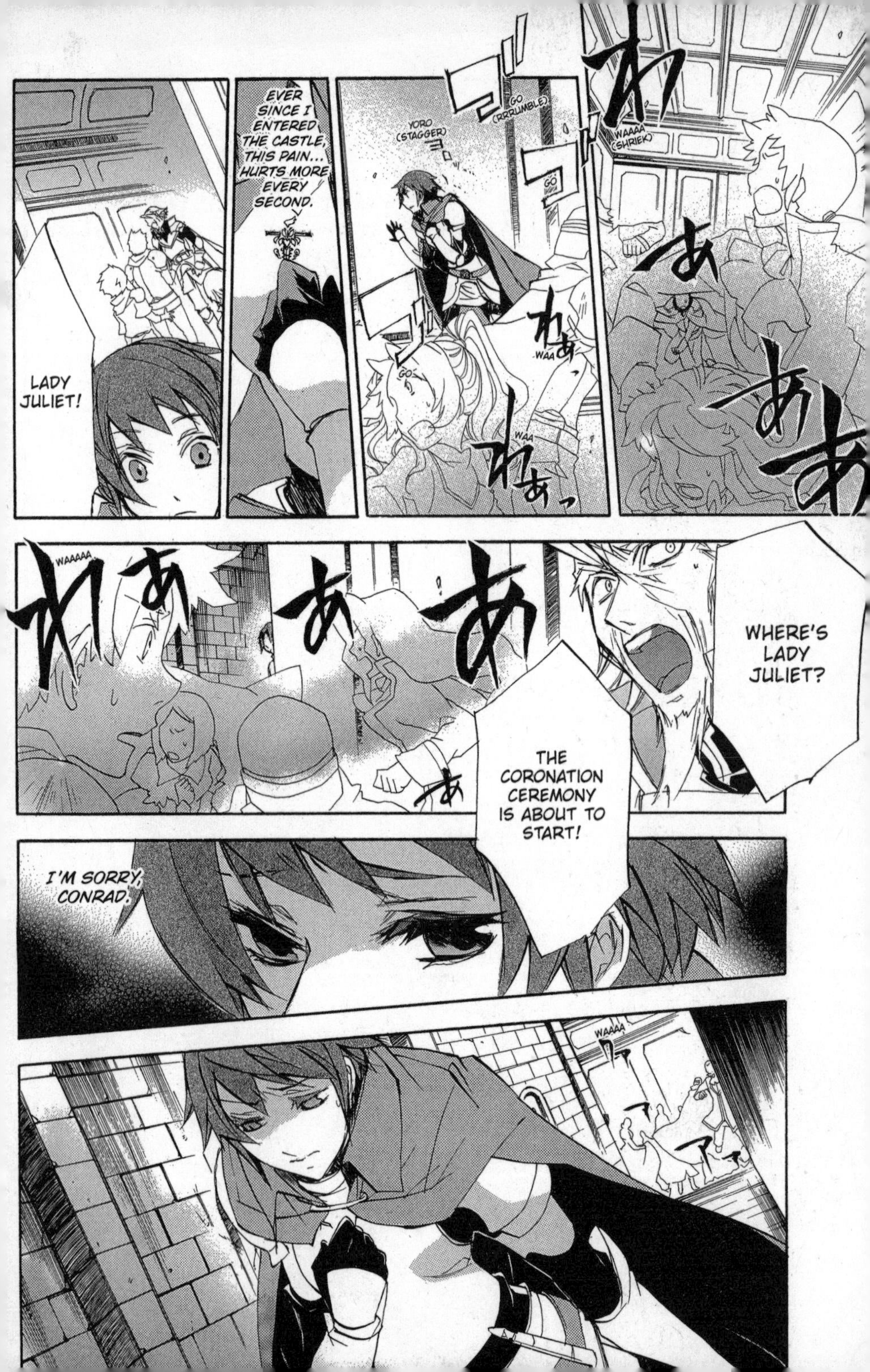

WAAAA (SHRIEK)
GO (RRRUMBLE)
GO
YORO (STAGGER)
WAA
GO
WAA
EVER SINCE I ENTERED THE CASTLE, THIS PAIN... HURTS MORE EVERY SECOND.
LADY JULIET!
WHERE'S LADY JULIET?
THE CORONATION CEREMONY IS ABOUT TO START!
WAAAAA
I'M SORRY, CONRAD.
WAAAA

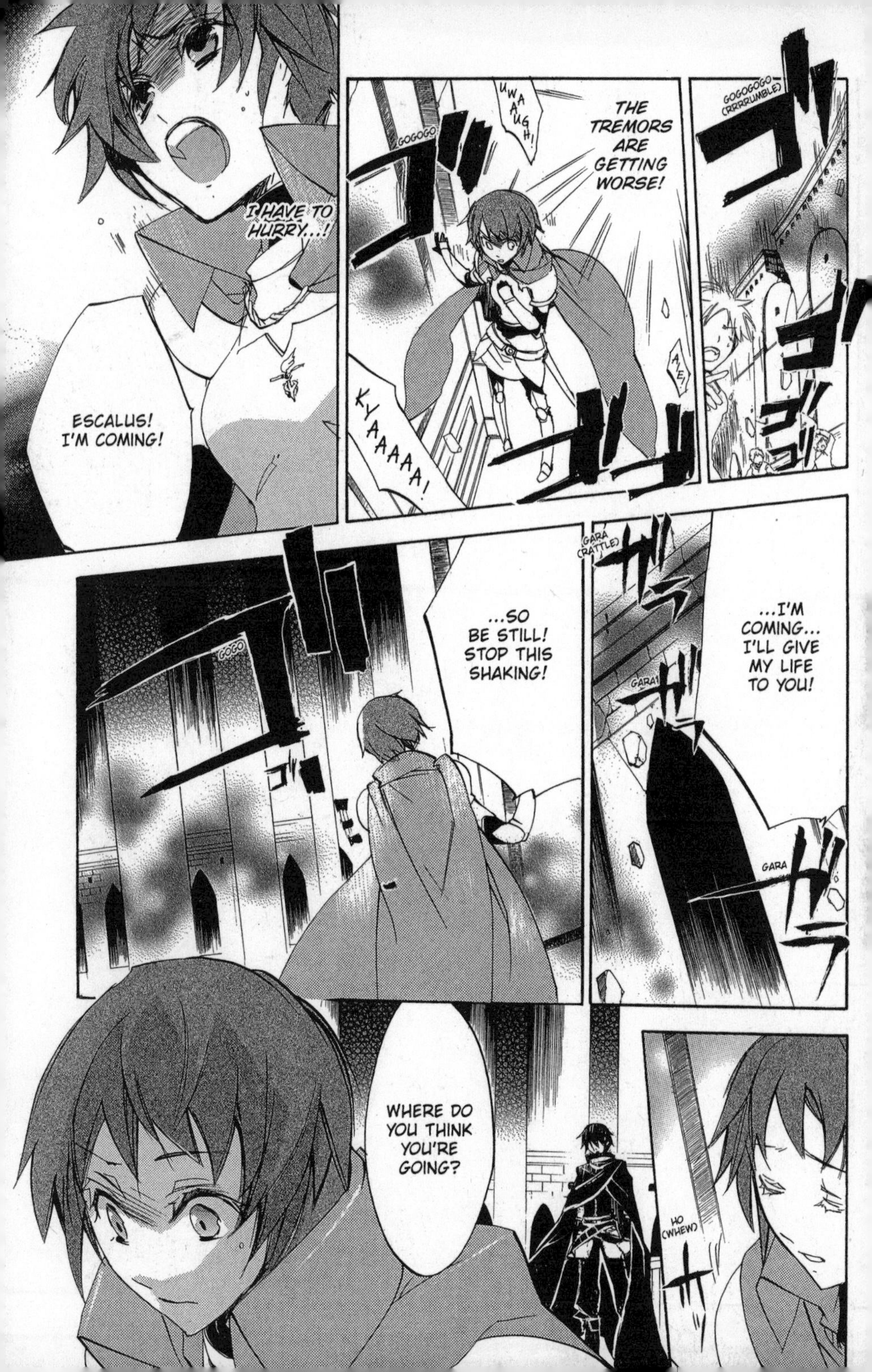
GOGOGOGO (RRRRUMBLE)
AE!
UWAAUGH!
GOGOGO
THE TREMORS ARE GETTING WORSE!
KYAAAAAA!
I HAVE TO HURRY...!
ESCALUS! I'M COMING!
GARA (RATTLE)
GARA
...I'M COMING... I'LL GIVE MY LIFE TO YOU!
GARA
GOGO
...SO BE STILL! STOP THIS SHAKING!
HO (WHEW)
WHERE DO YOU THINK YOU'RE GOING?

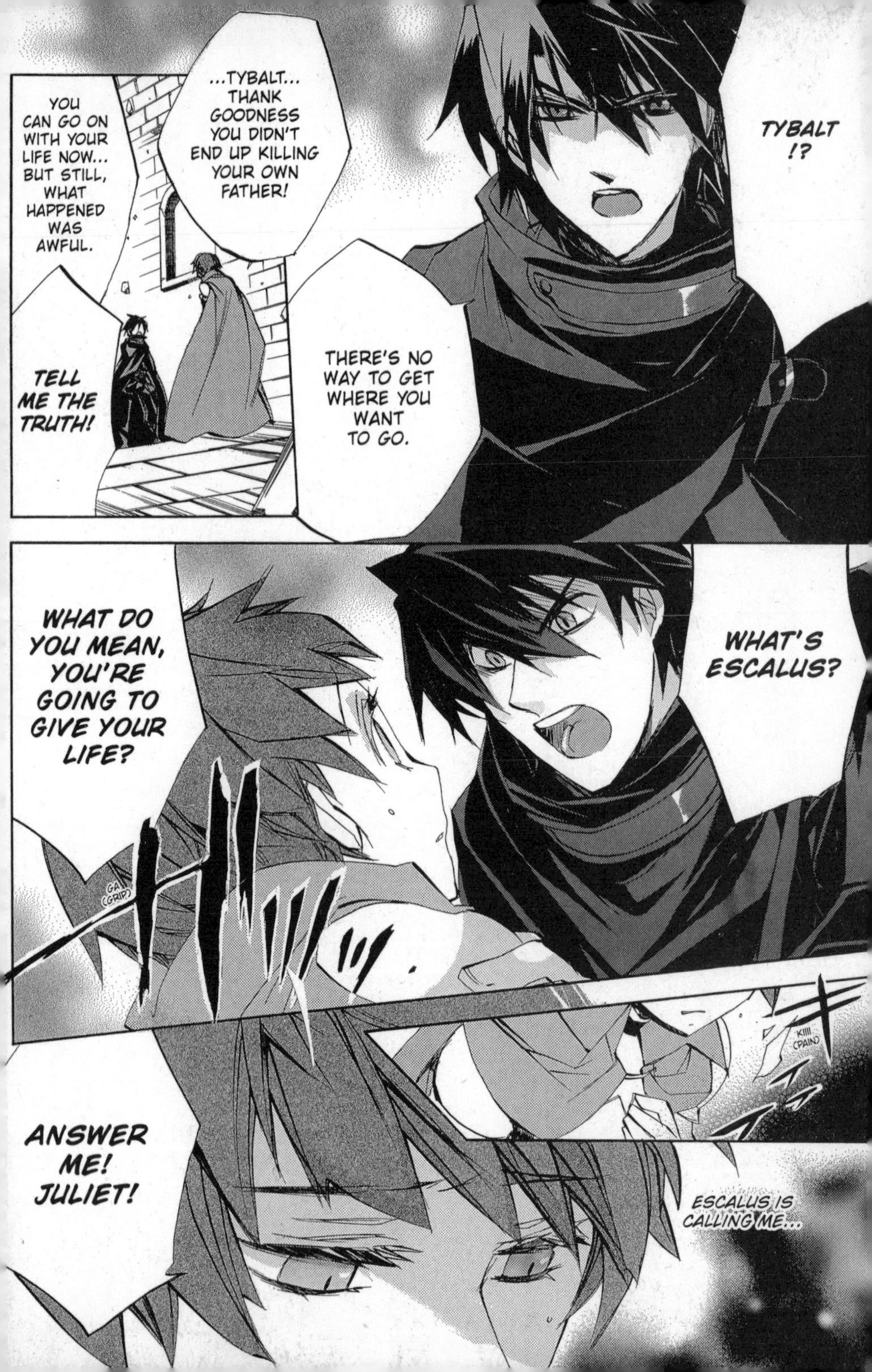

TYBALT !?
...TYBALT... THANK GOODNESS YOU DIDN'T END UP KILLING YOUR OWN FATHER!
YOU CAN GO ON WITH YOUR LIFE NOW... BUT STILL, WHAT HAPPENED WAS AWFUL.
THERE'S NO WAY TO GET WHERE YOU WANT TO GO.
TELL ME THE TRUTH!
WHAT'S ESCALUS?
WHAT DO YOU MEAN, YOU'RE GOING TO GIVE YOUR LIFE?
GA (GRIP)
KIIII (PAIN)
ESCALUS IS CALLING ME...
ANSWER ME! JULIET!

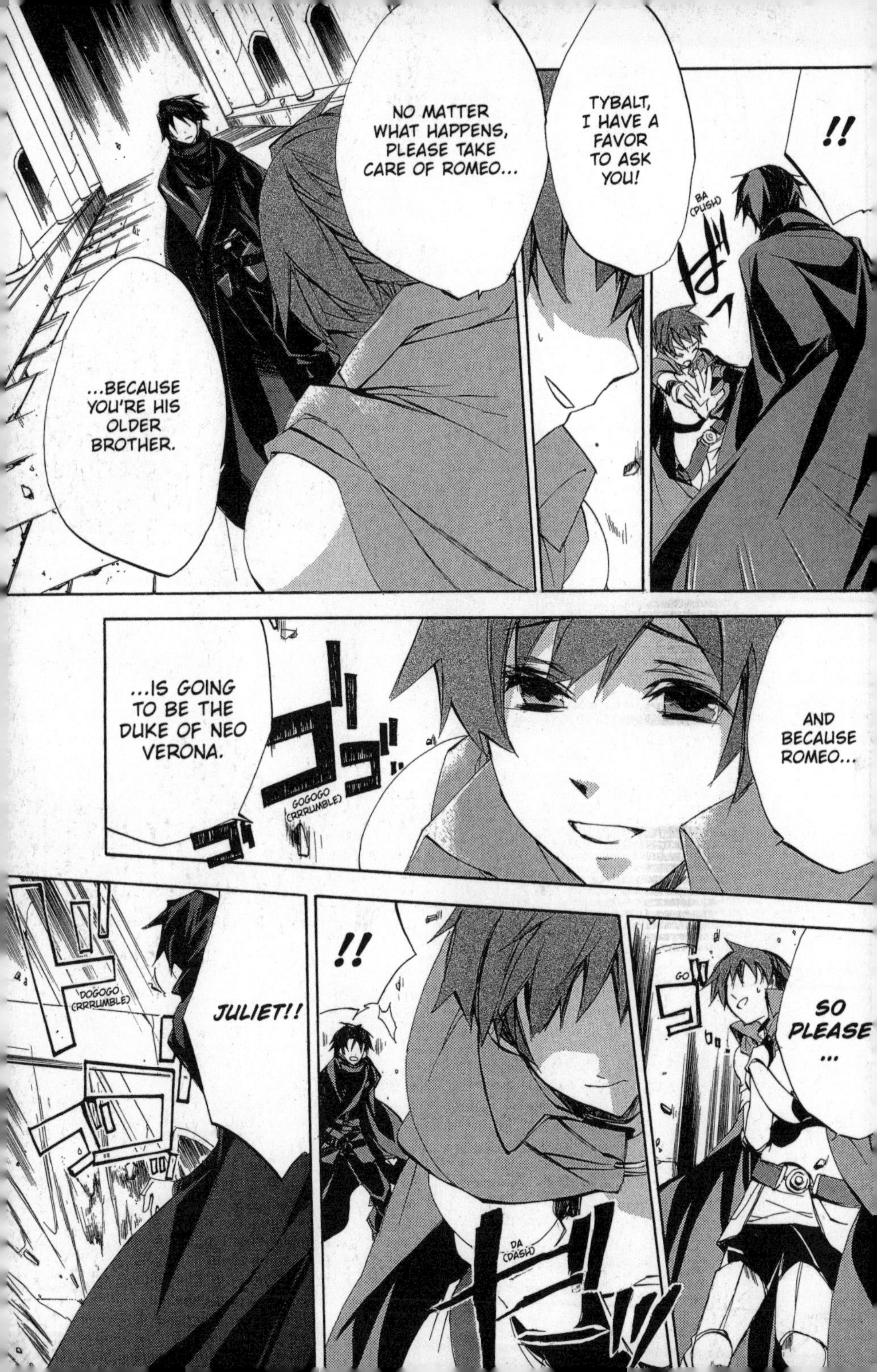
!!
BA (PUSH)
TYBALT, I HAVE A FAVOR TO ASK YOU!
NO MATTER WHAT HAPPENS, PLEASE TAKE CARE OF ROMEO...
...BECAUSE YOU'RE HIS OLDER BROTHER.
AND BECAUSE ROMEO...
GOGOGO (RRRUMBLE)
...IS GOING TO BE THE DUKE OF NEO VERONA.
SO PLEASE ...
GO
DA (DASH)
!!
JULIET!!
DOGOGO (RRRUMBLE)

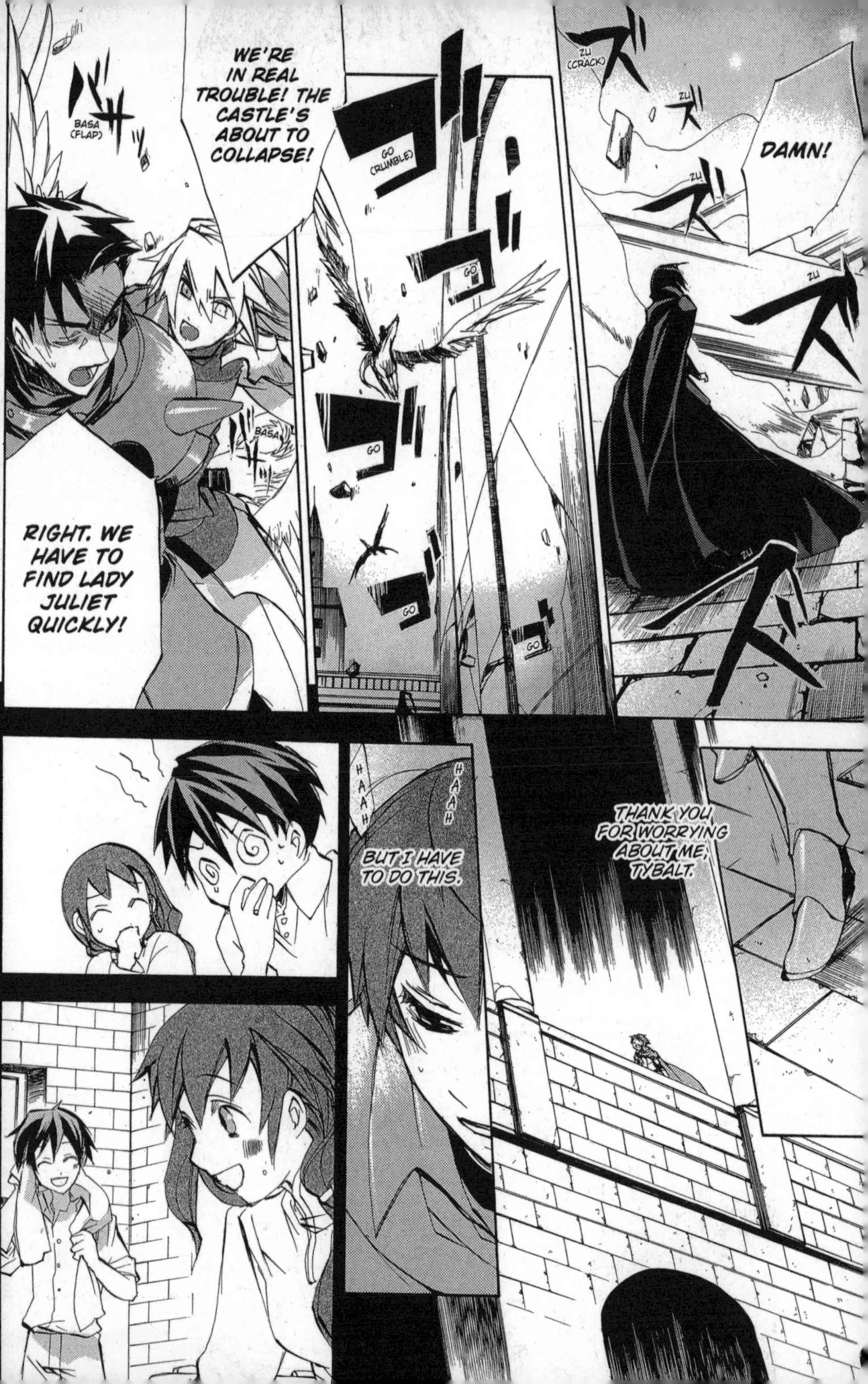
ZU (CRACK)
ZU
DAMN!
ZU
ZU
ZU
GO (RUMBLE)
GO
GO
GO
GO
WE'RE IN REAL TROUBLE! THE CASTLE'S ABOUT TO COLLAPSE!
BASA (FLAP)
BASA
RIGHT. WE HAVE TO FIND LADY JULIET QUICKLY!
THANK YOU FOR WORRYING ABOUT ME, TYBALT.
HAAAH
HAAAH
BUT I HAVE TO DO THIS.

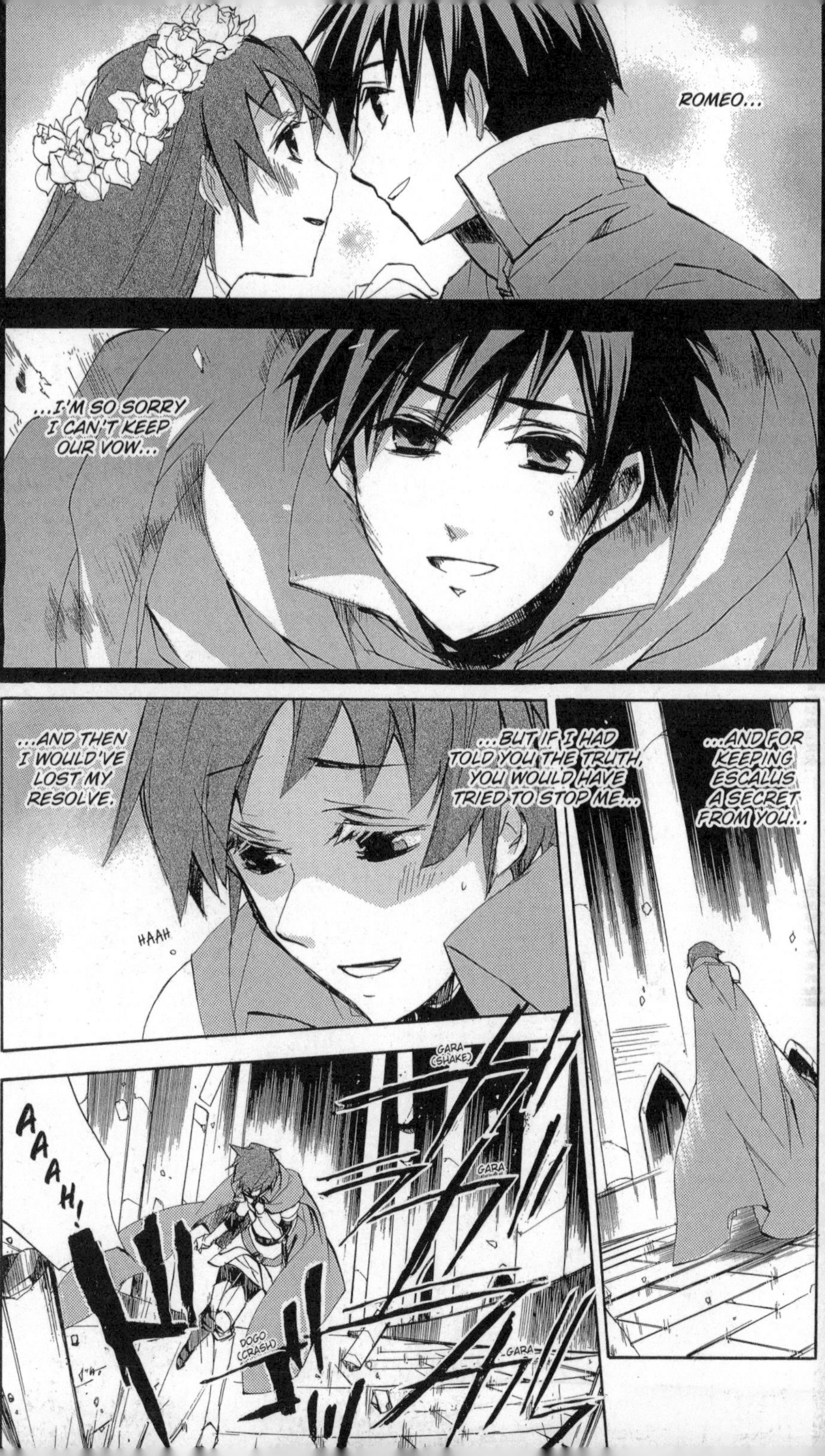
ROMEO...
...I'M SO SORRY I CAN'T KEEP OUR VOW...
...AND FOR KEEPING ESCALUS A SECRET FROM YOU...
...BUT IF I HAD TOLD YOU THE TRUTH, YOU WOULD HAVE TRIED TO STOP ME...
...AND THEN I WOULD'VE LOST MY RESOLVE.
HAAH
GARA (SHAKE)
GARA
AAAAH!
DOGO (CRASH)
GARA

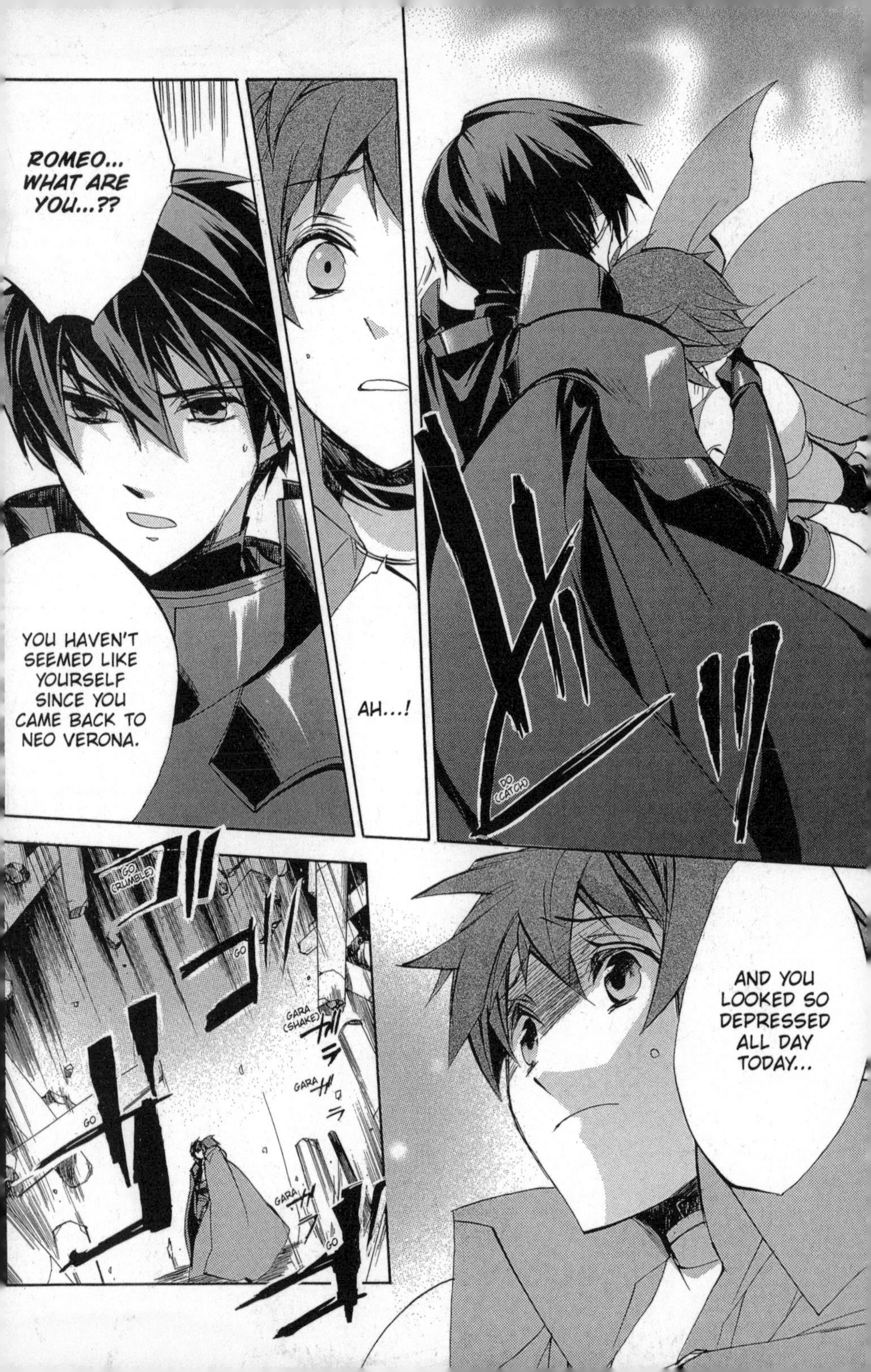
DO (CATCH)
AH...!
ROMEO... WHAT ARE YOU...??
YOU HAVEN'T SEEMED LIKE YOURSELF SINCE YOU CAME BACK TO NEO VERONA.
AND YOU LOOKED SO DEPRESSED ALL DAY TODAY...
GO (RUMBLE)
GO
GARA (SHAKE)
GARA
GO
GARA
GO

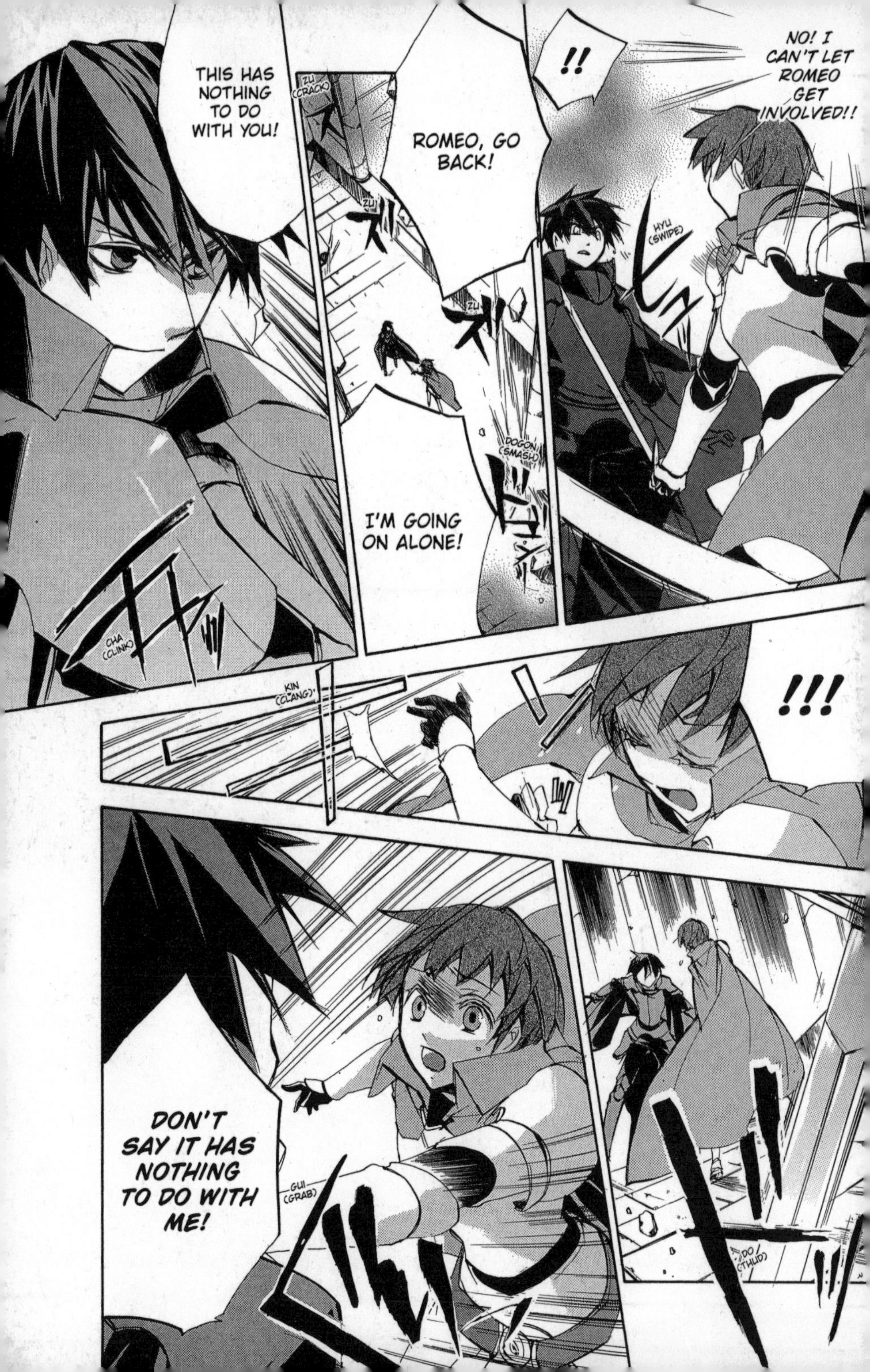
!!
NO! I CAN'T LET ROMEO GET INVOLVED!!
HYU (SWIPE)
ZU (CRACK)
ROMEO, GO BACK!
ZU
ZU
DOGON (SMASH)
I'M GOING ON ALONE!
THIS HAS NOTHING TO DO WITH YOU!
CHA (CLINK)
!!!
KIN (CLANG)
DO (THUD)
DON'T SAY IT HAS NOTHING TO DO WITH ME!
GUI (GRAB)

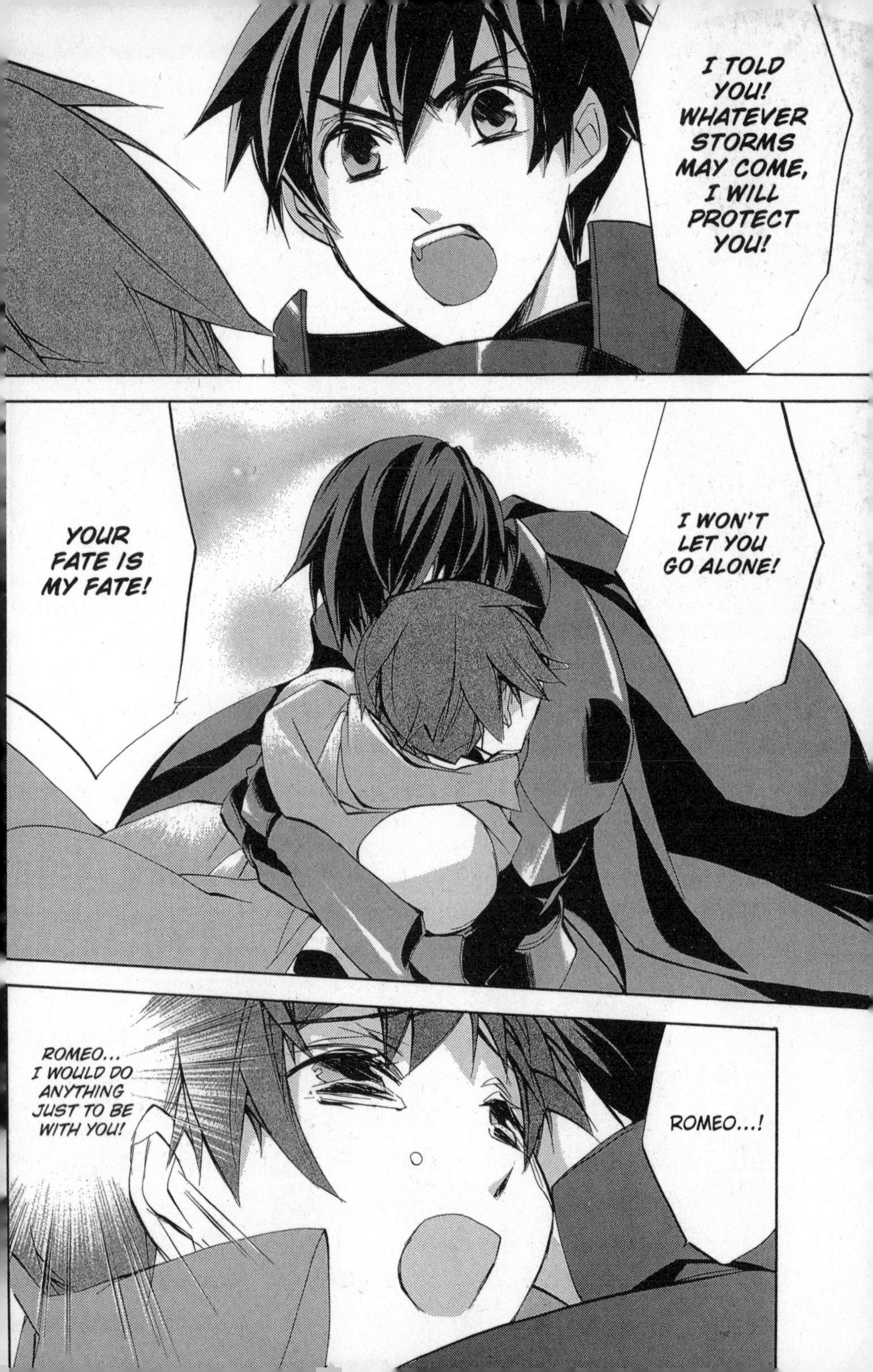
I TOLD YOU! WHATEVER STORMS MAY COME, I WILL PROTECT YOU!
I WON'T LET YOU GO ALONE!
YOUR FATE IS MY FATE!
ROMEO...!
ROMEO... I WOULD DO ANYTHING JUST TO BE WITH YOU!

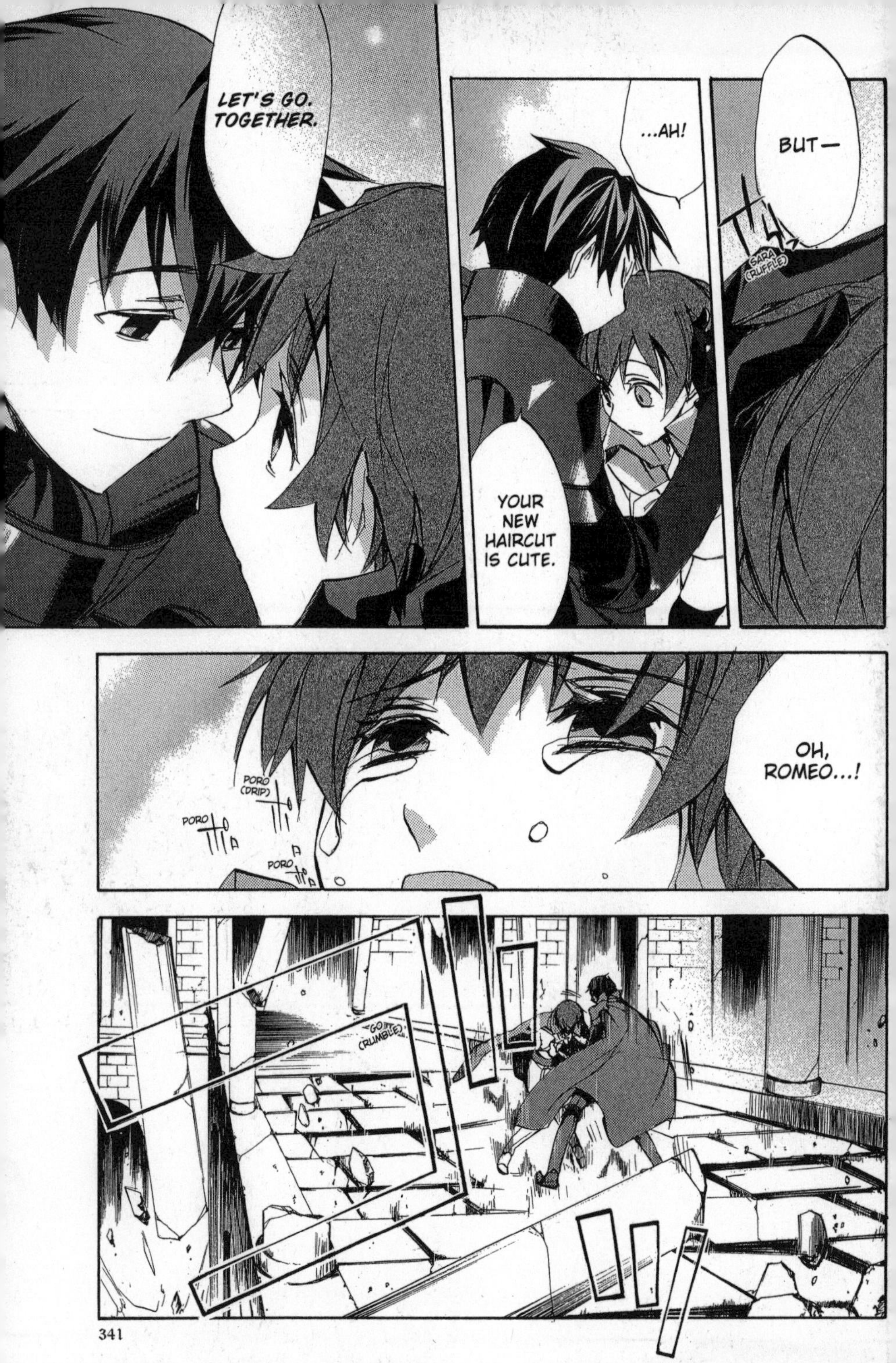
BUT—
SARA (RUFFLE)
...AH!
YOUR NEW HAIRCUT IS CUTE.
LET'S GO. TOGETHER.
OH, ROMEO...!
PORO (DRIP)
PORO
PORO
GO (RUMBLE)

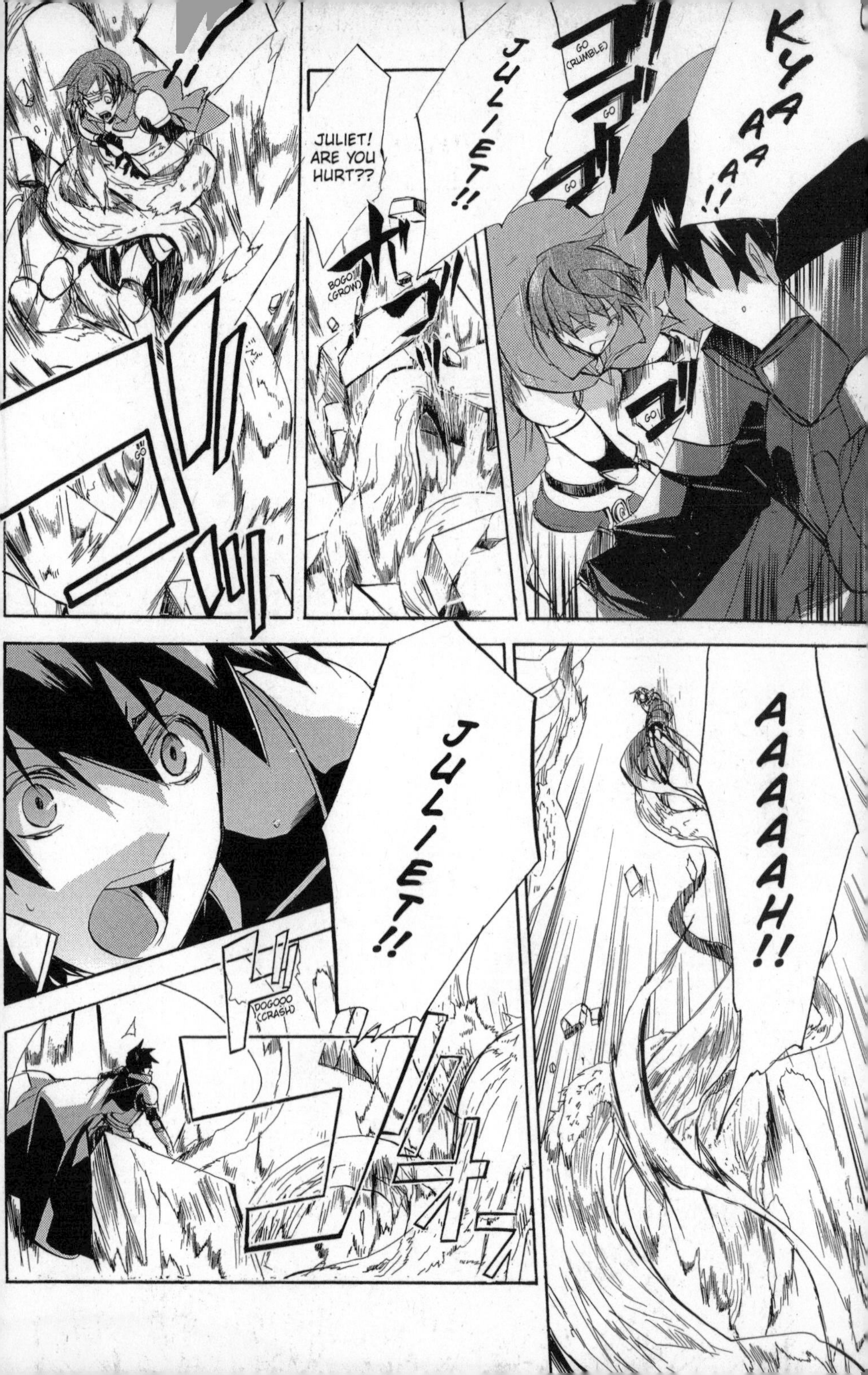
KYAAAAA!!
GO (RUMBLE)
GO
GO
GO
JULIET!!
JULIET! ARE YOU HURT??
BOGO! (GROW)
GO
AAAAAAH!!
JULIET!!
DOGOOO (CRASH)

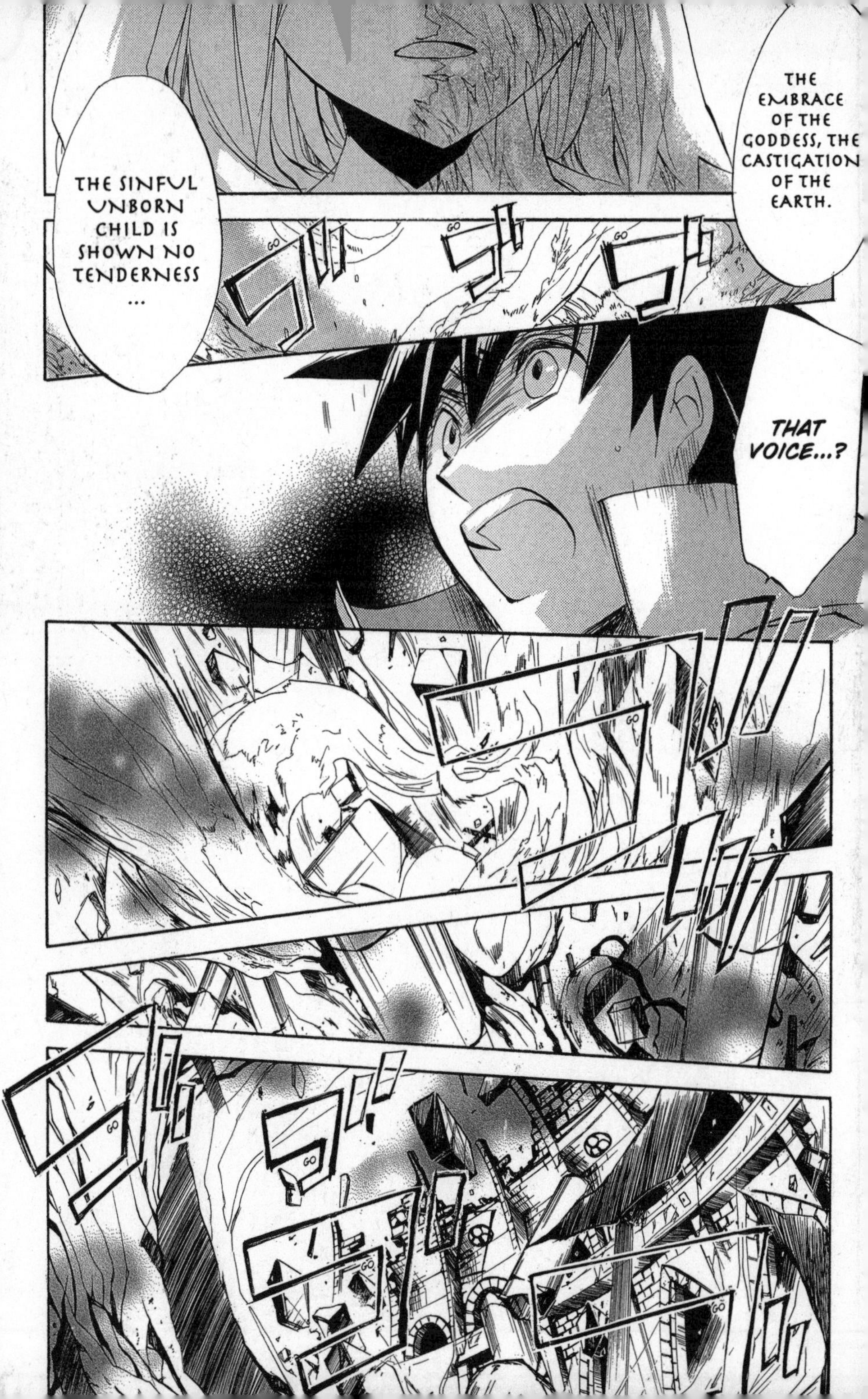
THE EMBRACE OF THE GODDESS, THE CASTIGATION OF THE EARTH.
THE SINFUL UNBORN CHILD IS SHOWN NO TENDERNESS ...
GO
GO
THAT VOICE...?
GO
GO
GO
GO

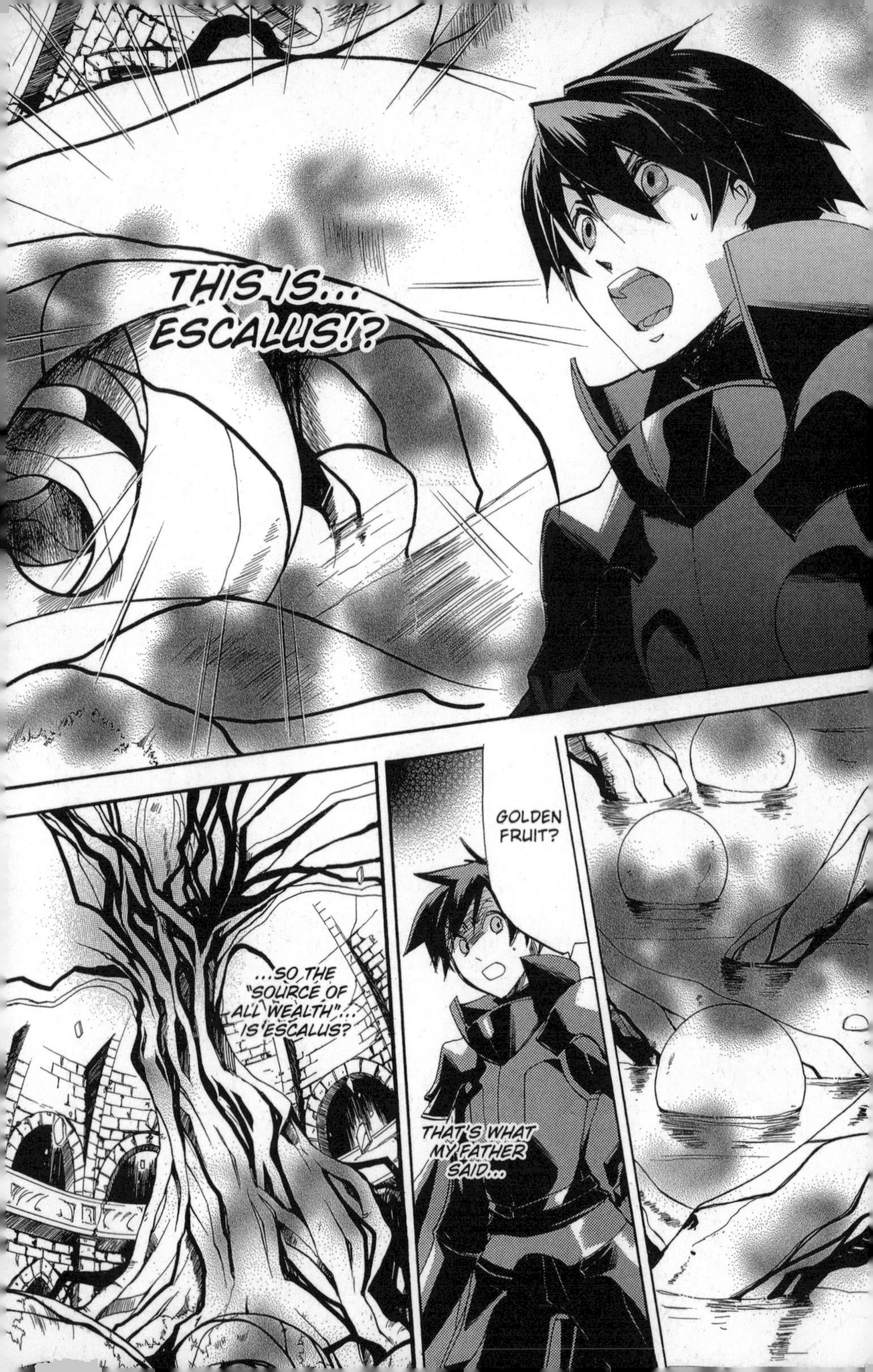
THIS IS... ESCALUS!?
GOLDEN FRUIT?
THAT'S WHAT MY FATHER SAID...
...SO THE "SOURCE OF ALL WEALTH"... IS ESCALUS?

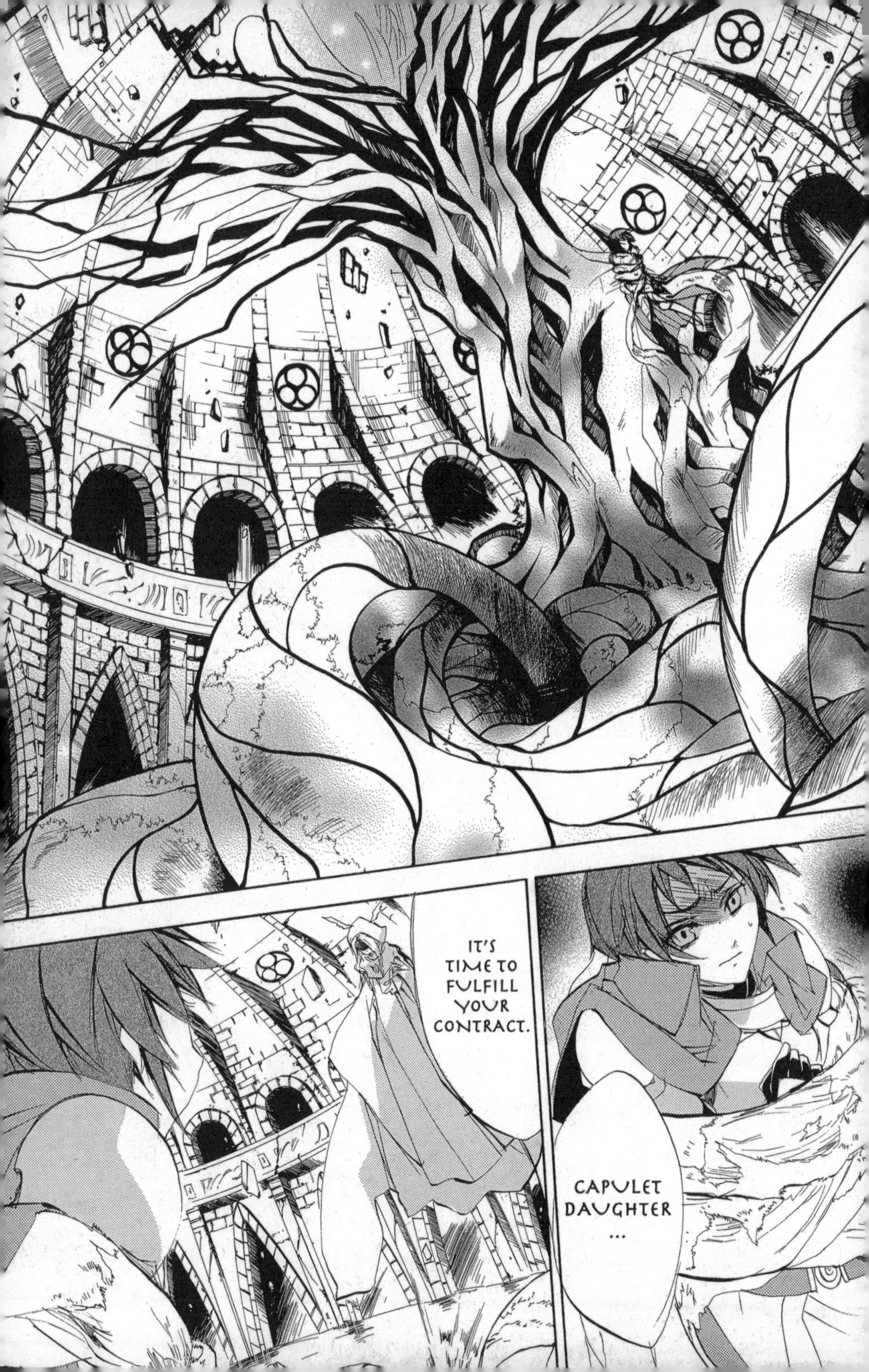
IT'S TIME TO FULFILL YOUR CONTRACT.
CAPULET DAUGHTER ...

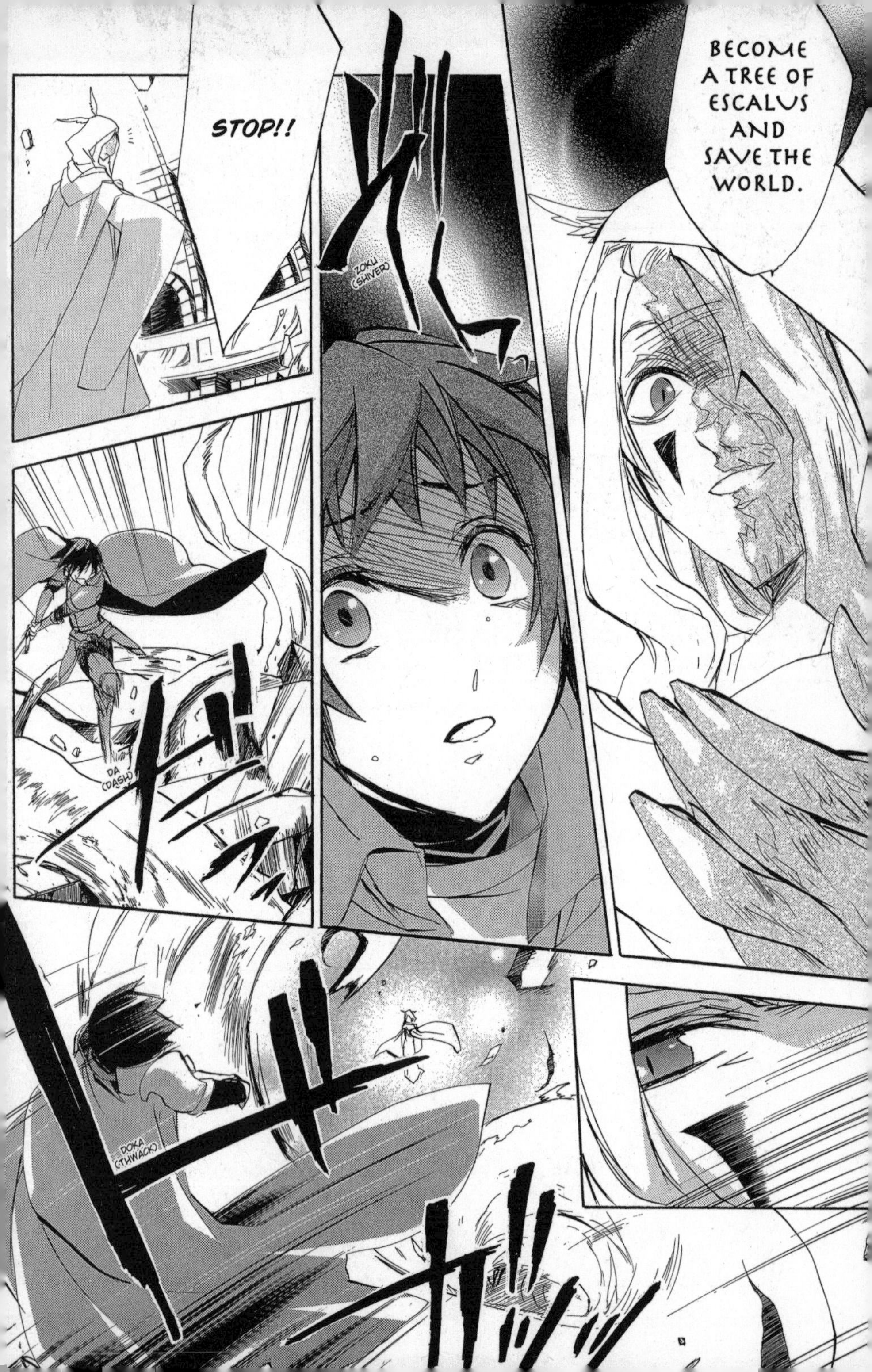
BECOME A TREE OF ESCALUS AND SAVE THE WORLD.
ZOKU (SHIVER)
STOP!!
DA (DASH)
DOKA (THWACK)

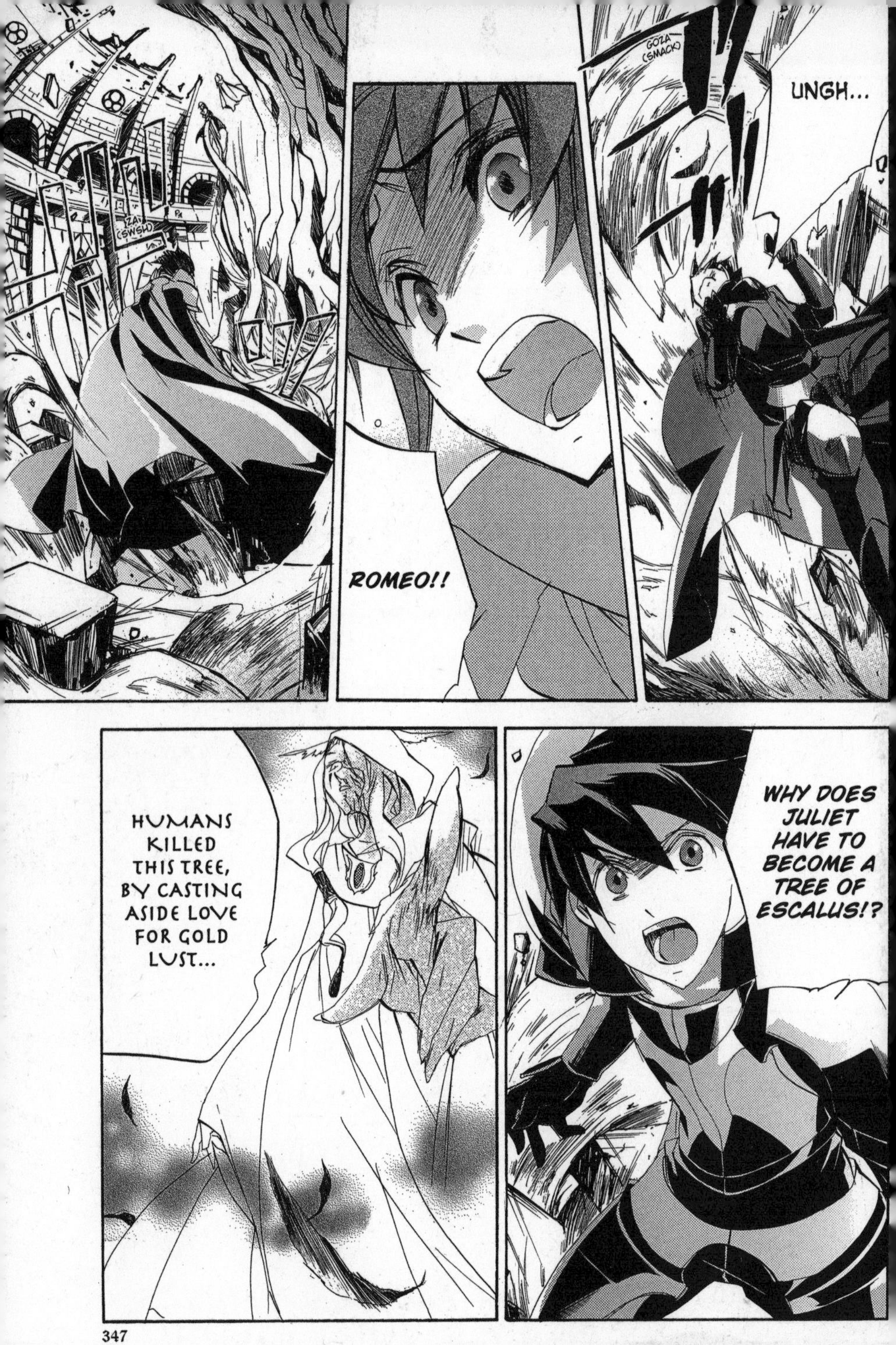
GOZA (SMACK)
UNGH...
ROMEO!!
ZA (SWSH)
WHY DOES JULIET HAVE TO BECOME A TREE OF ESCALUS!?
HUMANS KILLED THIS TREE, BY CASTING ASIDE LOVE FOR GOLD LUST...

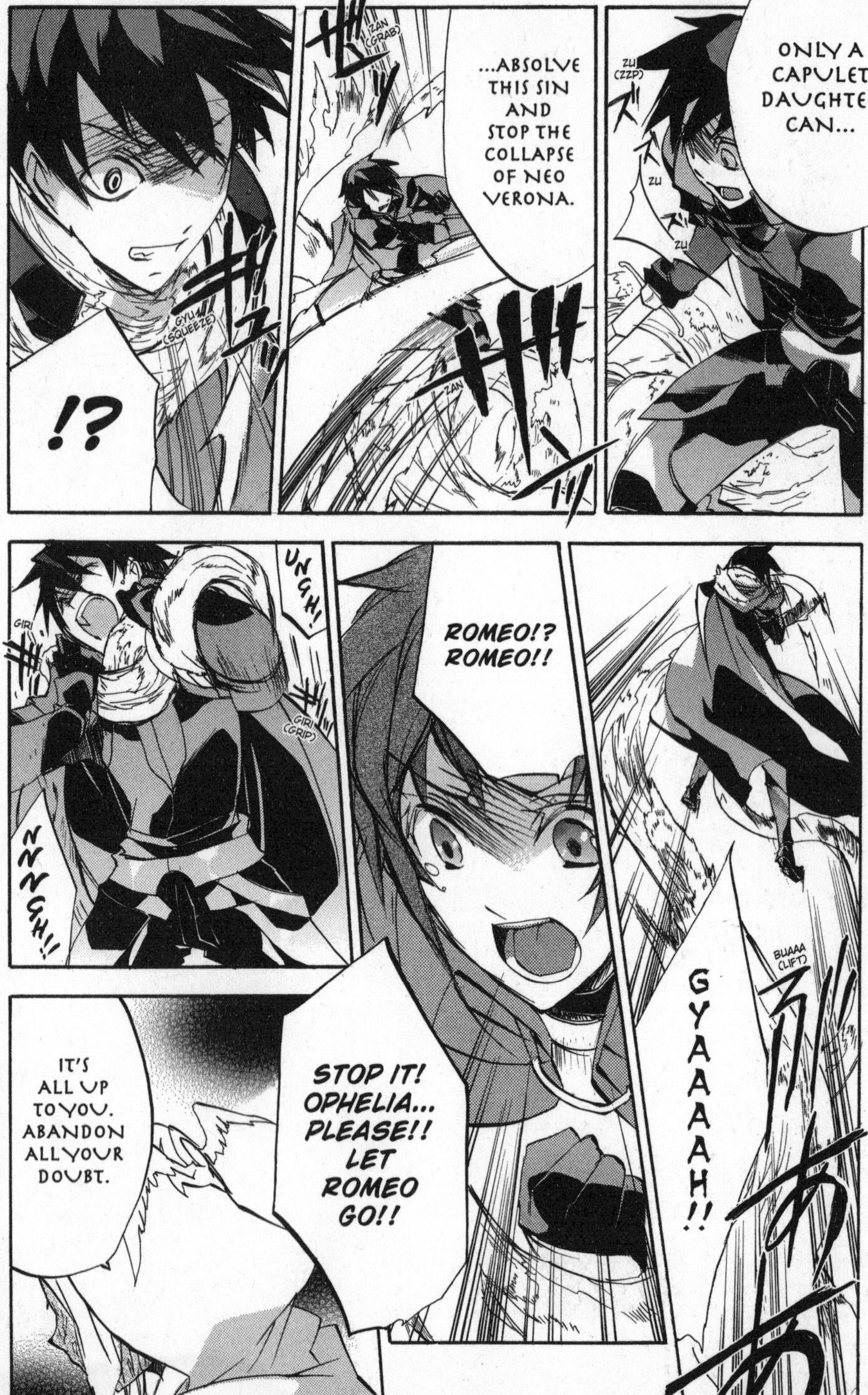
ONLY A CAPULET DAUGHTER CAN...
ZU (ZZP)
ZU
ZU
ZAN (GRAB)
...ABSOLVE THIS SIN AND STOP THE COLLAPSE OF NEO VERONA.
ZAN
GYU (SQUEEZE)
!?
BUAAA (LIFT)
GYAAAAH!!
ROMEO!? ROMEO!!
STOP IT! OPHELIA... PLEASE!! LET ROMEO GO!!
UNGH!
GIRI
GIRI (GRIP)
NNNNGH!!
IT'S ALL UP TO YOU. ABANDON ALL YOUR DOUBT.

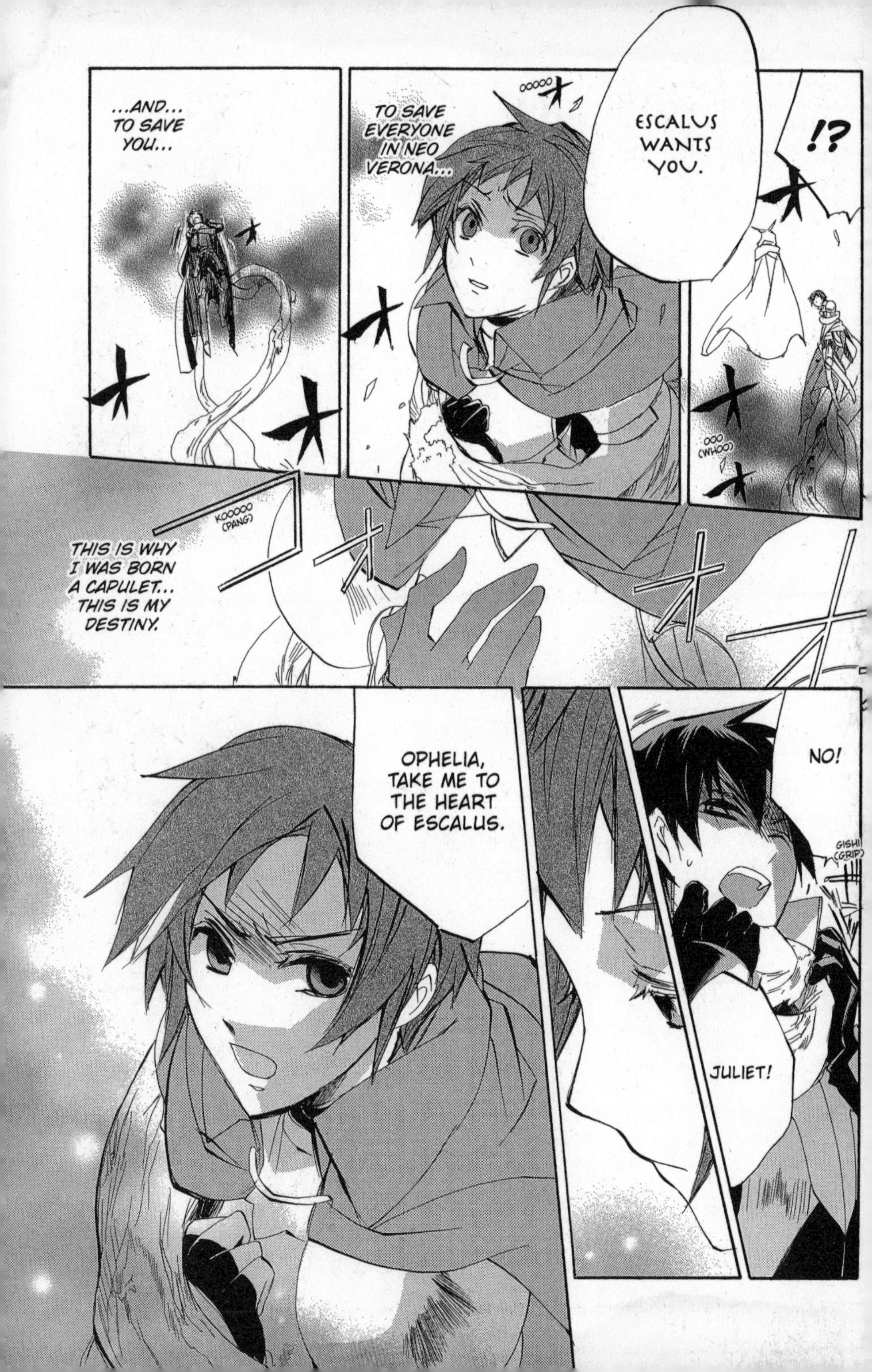
ESCALUS WANTS YOU.
!?
OOO (WHOO)
OOOOO
TO SAVE EVERYONE IN NEO VERONA...
...AND... TO SAVE YOU...
KOOOOO (PANG)
THIS IS WHY I WAS BORN A CAPULET... THIS IS MY DESTINY.
NO!
GISHI (GRIP)
JULIET!
OPHELIA, TAKE ME TO THE HEART OF ESCALUS.

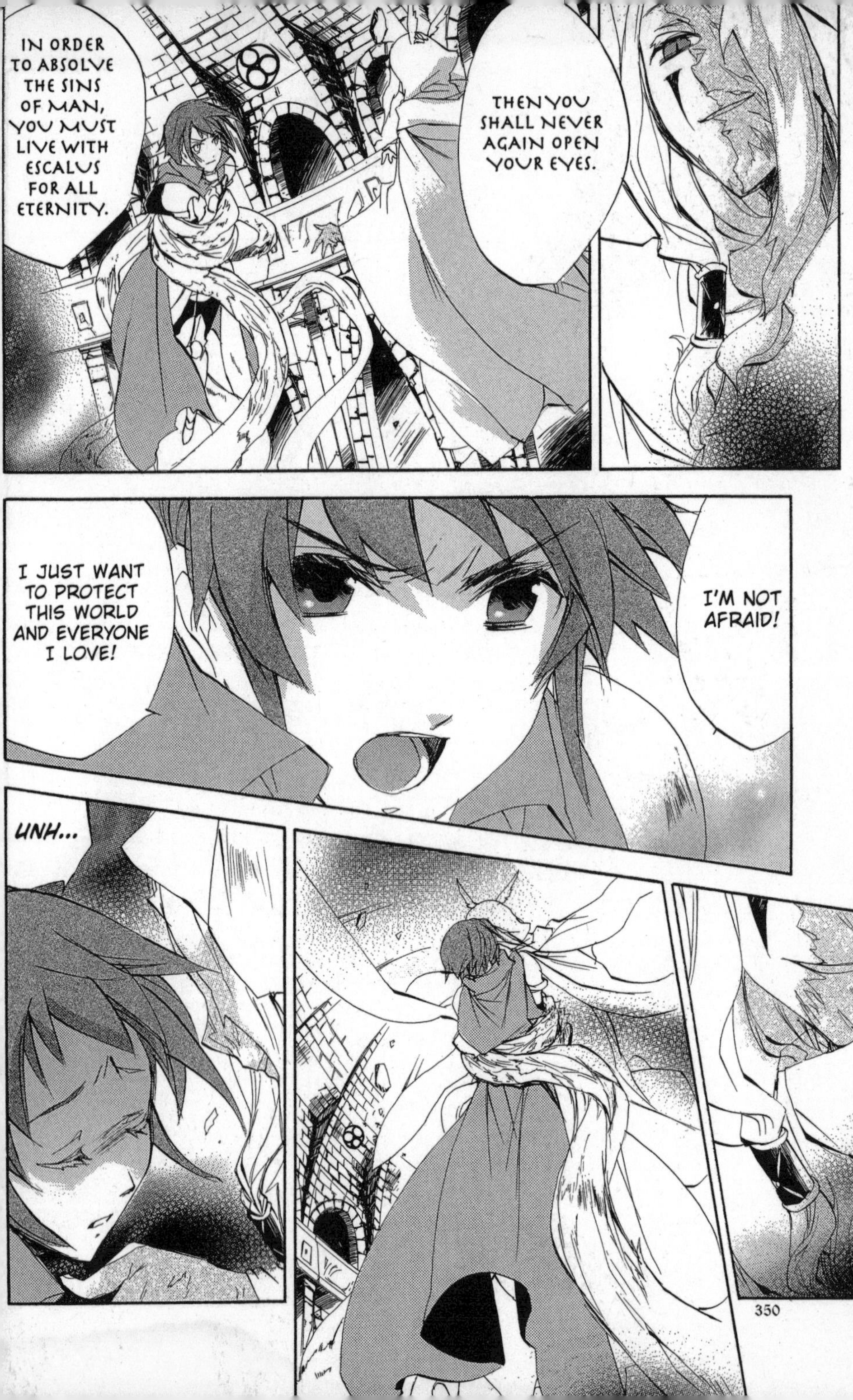
THEN YOU SHALL NEVER AGAIN OPEN YOUR EYES.
IN ORDER TO ABSOLVE THE SINS OF MAN, YOU MUST LIVE WITH ESCALUS FOR ALL ETERNITY.
I'M NOT AFRAID!
I JUST WANT TO PROTECT THIS WORLD AND EVERYONE I LOVE!
UNH...

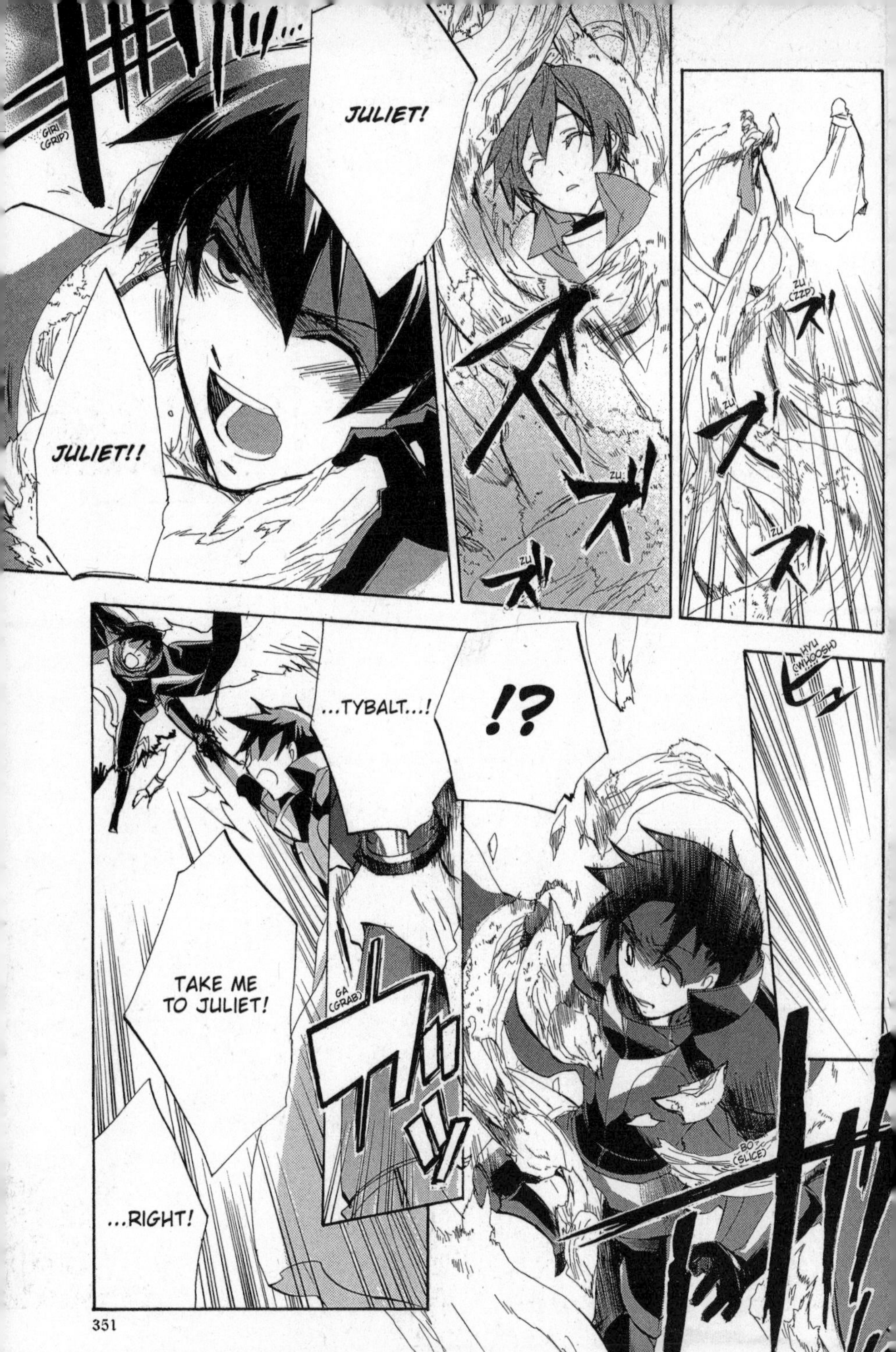
ZU (ZZP)
ZU
ZU
ZU
ZU
ZU
JULIET!
GIRI (GRIP)
JULIET!!
HYU (WHOOSH)
!?
BO (SLICE)
...TYBALT...!
TAKE ME TO JULIET!
GA (GRAB)
...RIGHT!

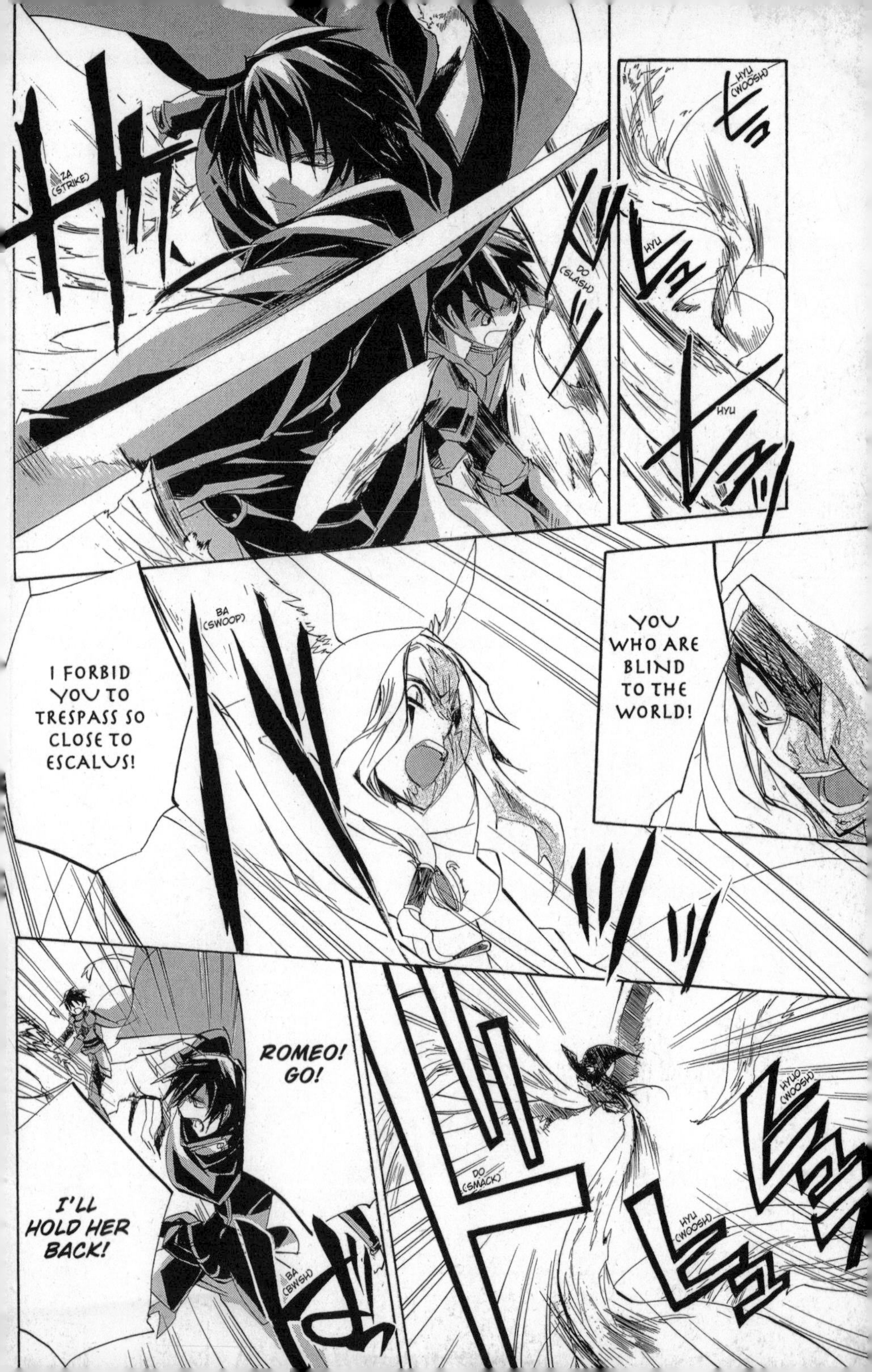
HYU (WOOSH)
HYU
HYU
ZA (STRIKE)
DO (SLASH)
YOU WHO ARE BLIND TO THE WORLD!
BA (SWOOP)
I FORBID YOU TO TRESPASS SO CLOSE TO ESCALUS!
HYUO (WOOSH)
DO (SMACK)
HYU (WOOSH)
ROMEO! GO!
I'LL HOLD HER BACK!
BA (BWSH)

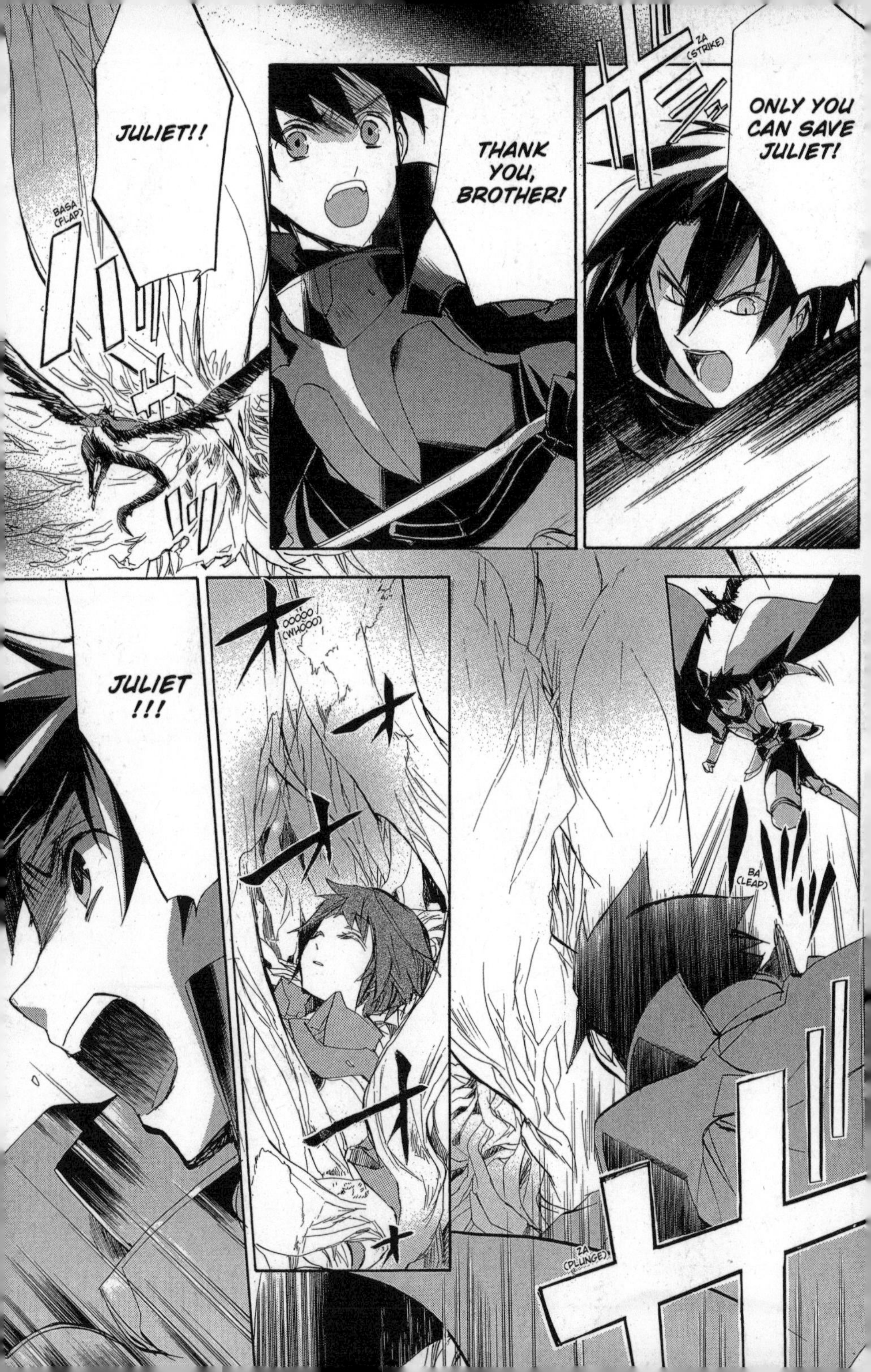
ZA (STRIKE)
ONLY YOU CAN SAVE JULIET!
THANK YOU, BROTHER!
JULIET!!
BASA (FLAP)
BA (LEAP)
ZA (PLUNGE)
OOOOO (WHOOO)
JULIET !!!

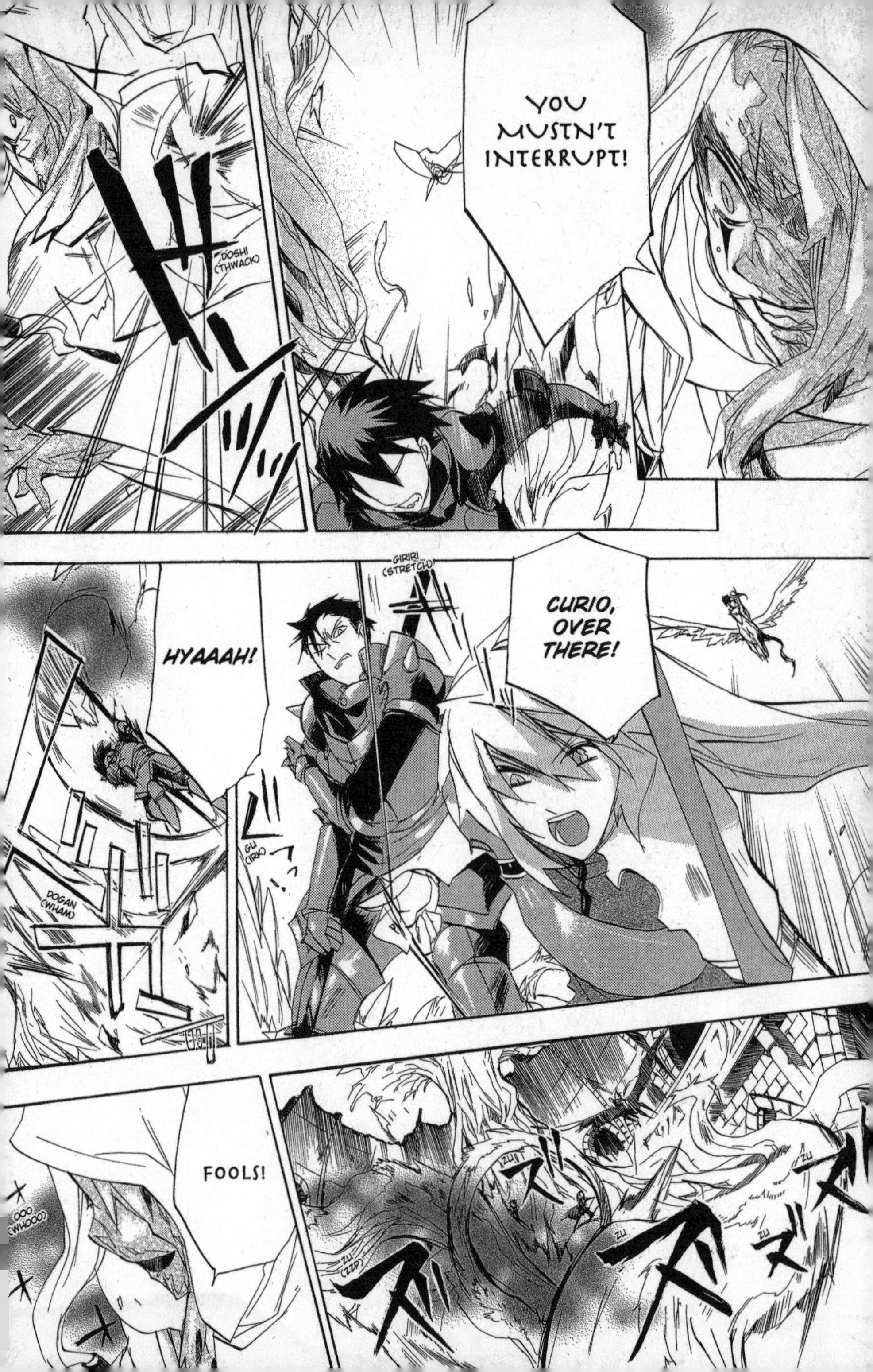
YOU MUSTN'T INTERRUPT!
DOSHI (THWACK)
GIRIRI (STRETCH)
CURIO, OVER THERE!
GU (IRK)
HYAAAH!
DOGAN (WHAM)
ZU
ZU
ZU
ZU (ZZZP)
FOOLS!
OOO (WHOOO)

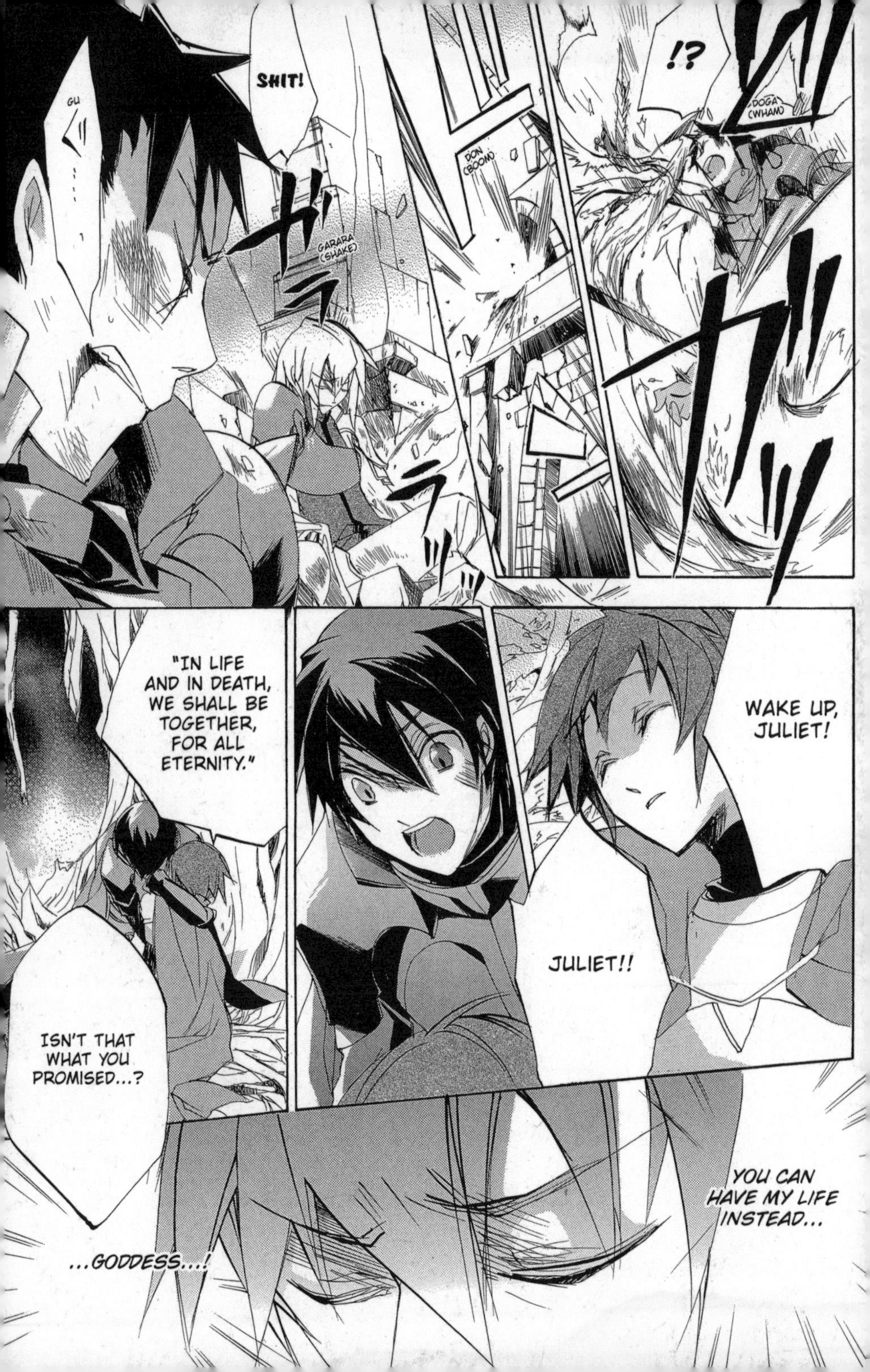
!?
DOGA (WHAM)
DON (BOOM)
SHIT!
GU
GARARA (SHAKE)
WAKE UP, JULIET!
JULIET!!
"IN LIFE AND IN DEATH, WE SHALL BE TOGETHER, FOR ALL ETERNITY."
ISN'T THAT WHAT YOU PROMISED...?
YOU CAN HAVE MY LIFE INSTEAD...
...GODDESS...!

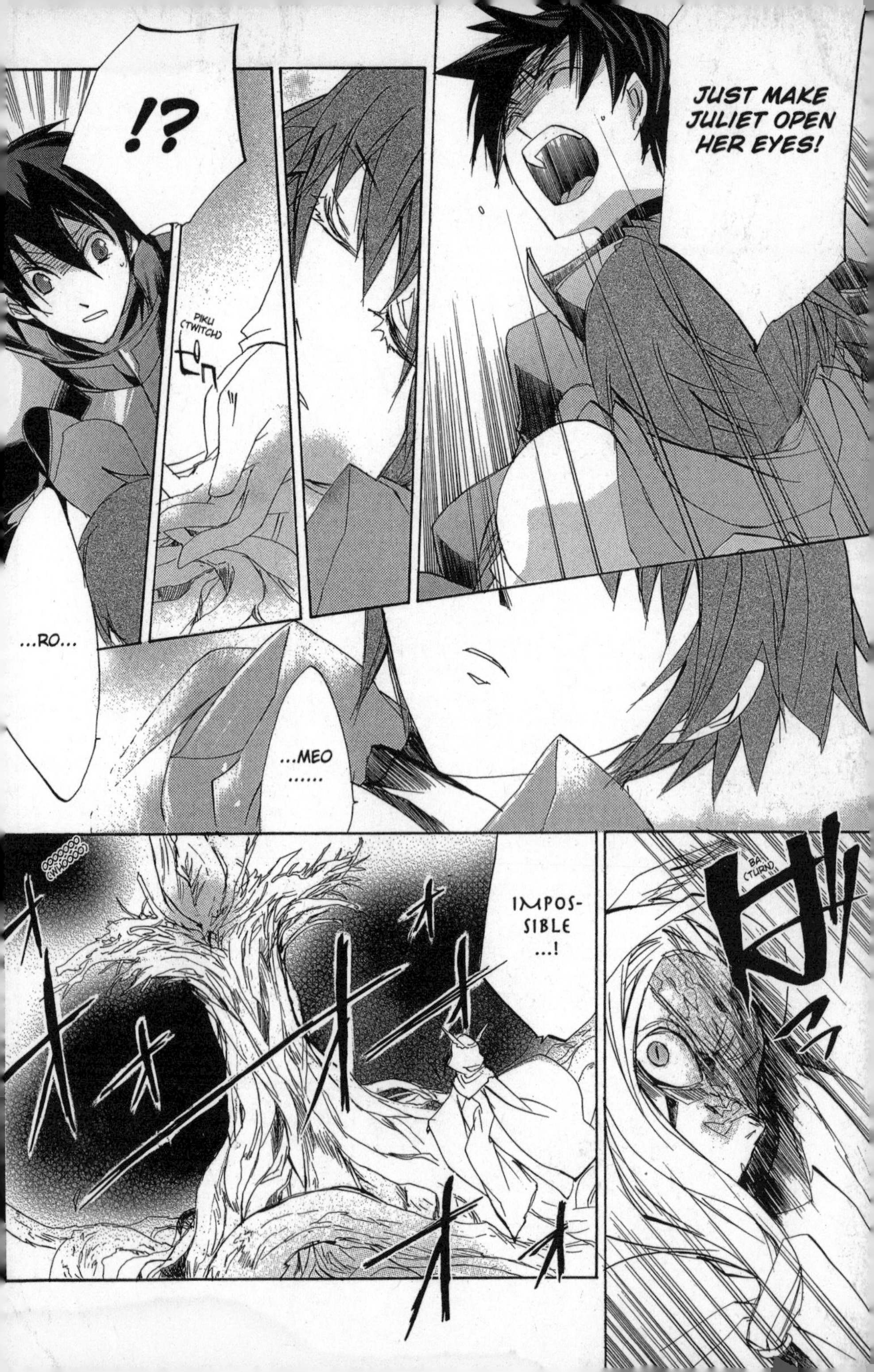
JUST MAKE JULIET OPEN HER EYES!
PIKU (TWITCH)
!?
...RO...
...MEO ......
BA (TURN)
IMPOS-SIBLE ...!
OOOOOOO (WHOOOO)

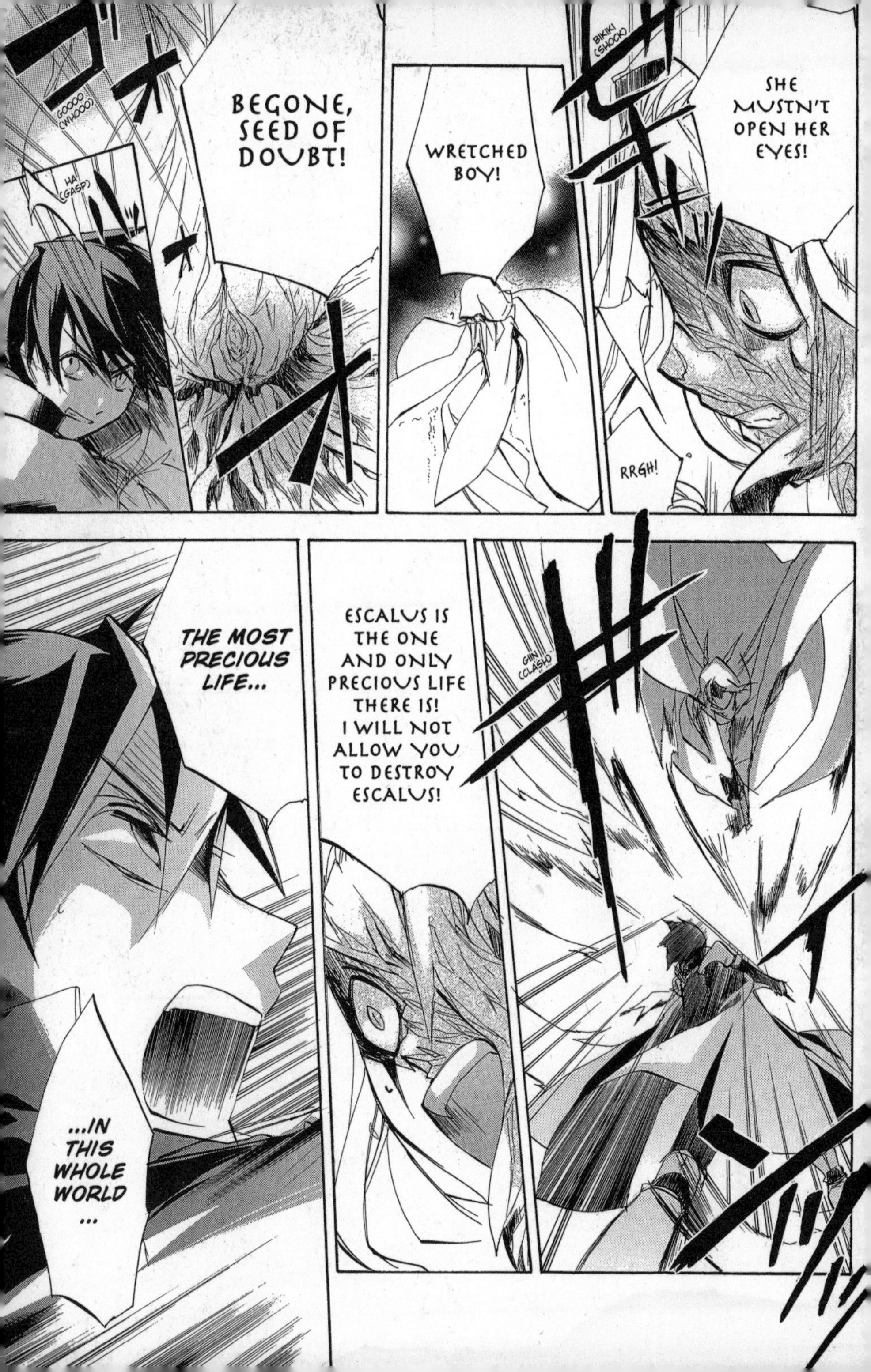
BIKIKI (SHOCK)
SHE MUSTN'T OPEN HER EYES!
RRGH!
WRETCHED BOY!
BEGONE, SEED OF DOUBT!
GOOOO (WHOOO)
HA (GASP)
GIIN (CLASH)
ESCALUS IS THE ONE AND ONLY PRECIOUS LIFE THERE IS! I WILL NOT ALLOW YOU TO DESTROY ESCALUS!
THE MOST PRECIOUS LIFE...
...IN THIS WHOLE WORLD ...

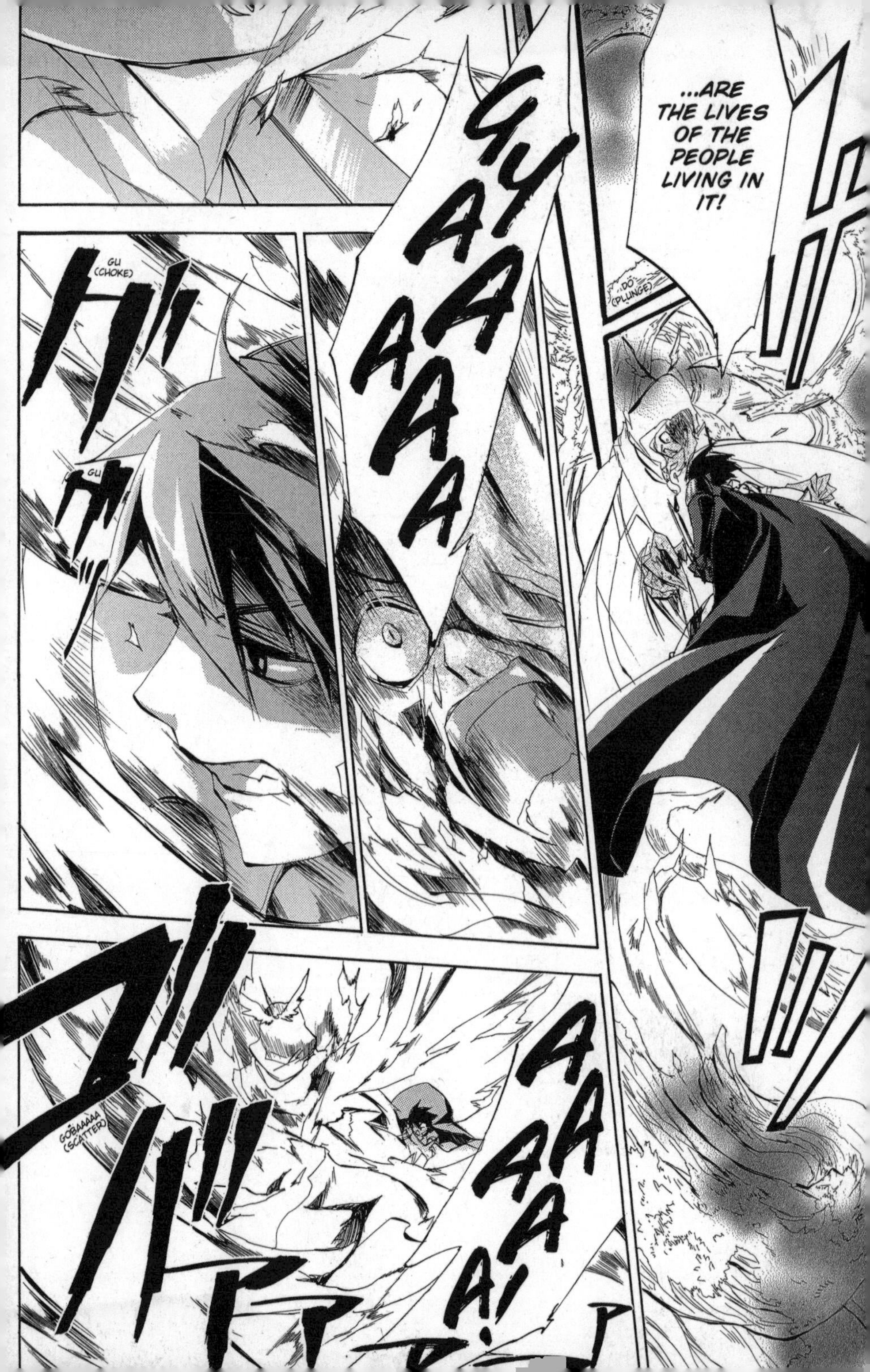
...ARE THE LIVES OF THE PEOPLE LIVING IN IT!
DO (PLUNGE)
GUYAAAAAAA
GU (CHOKE)
GU
AAAAAA!A!
GOBAAAAA (SCATTER)

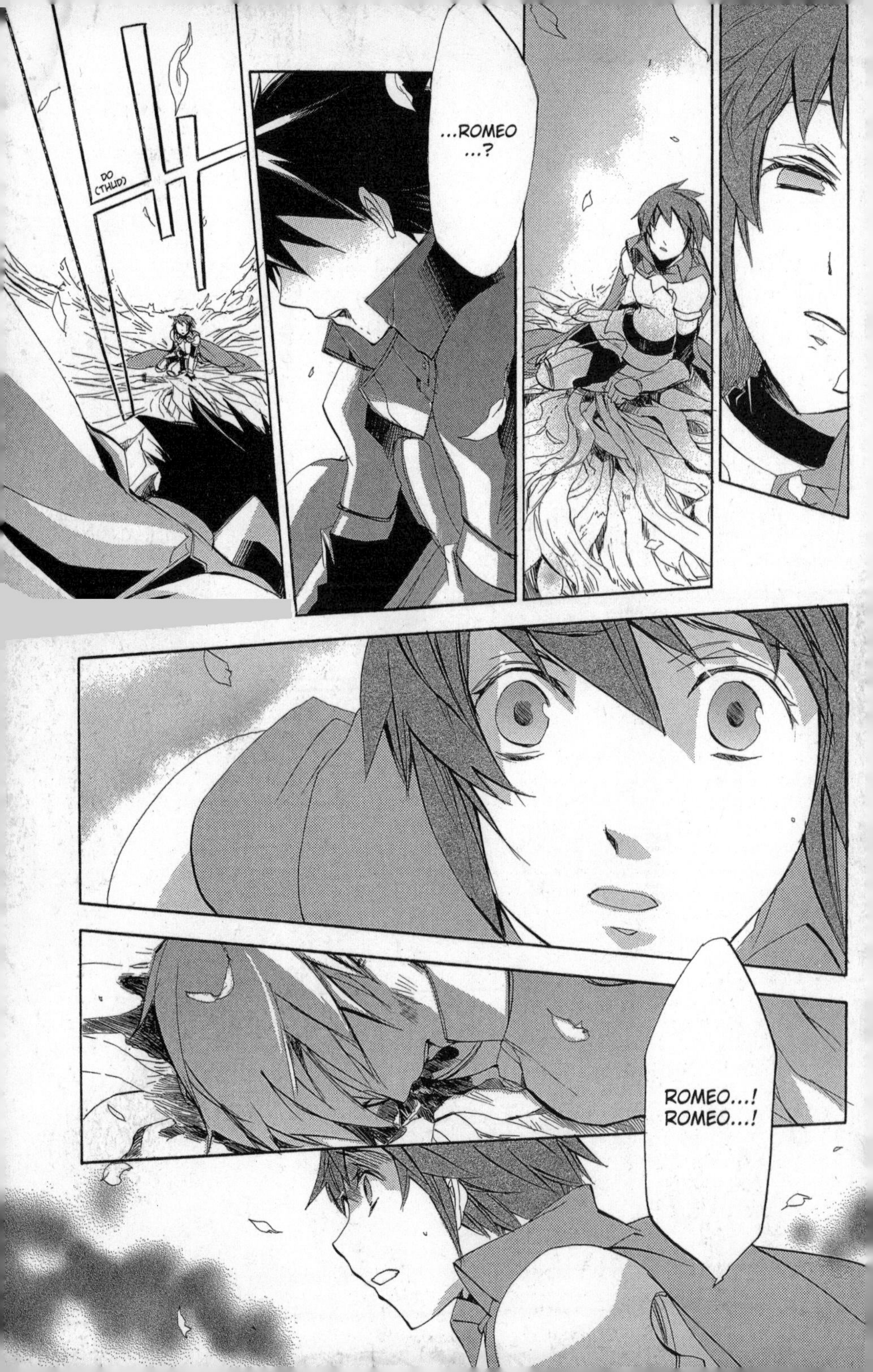
...ROMEO ...?
DO (THUD)
ROMEO...! ROMEO...!

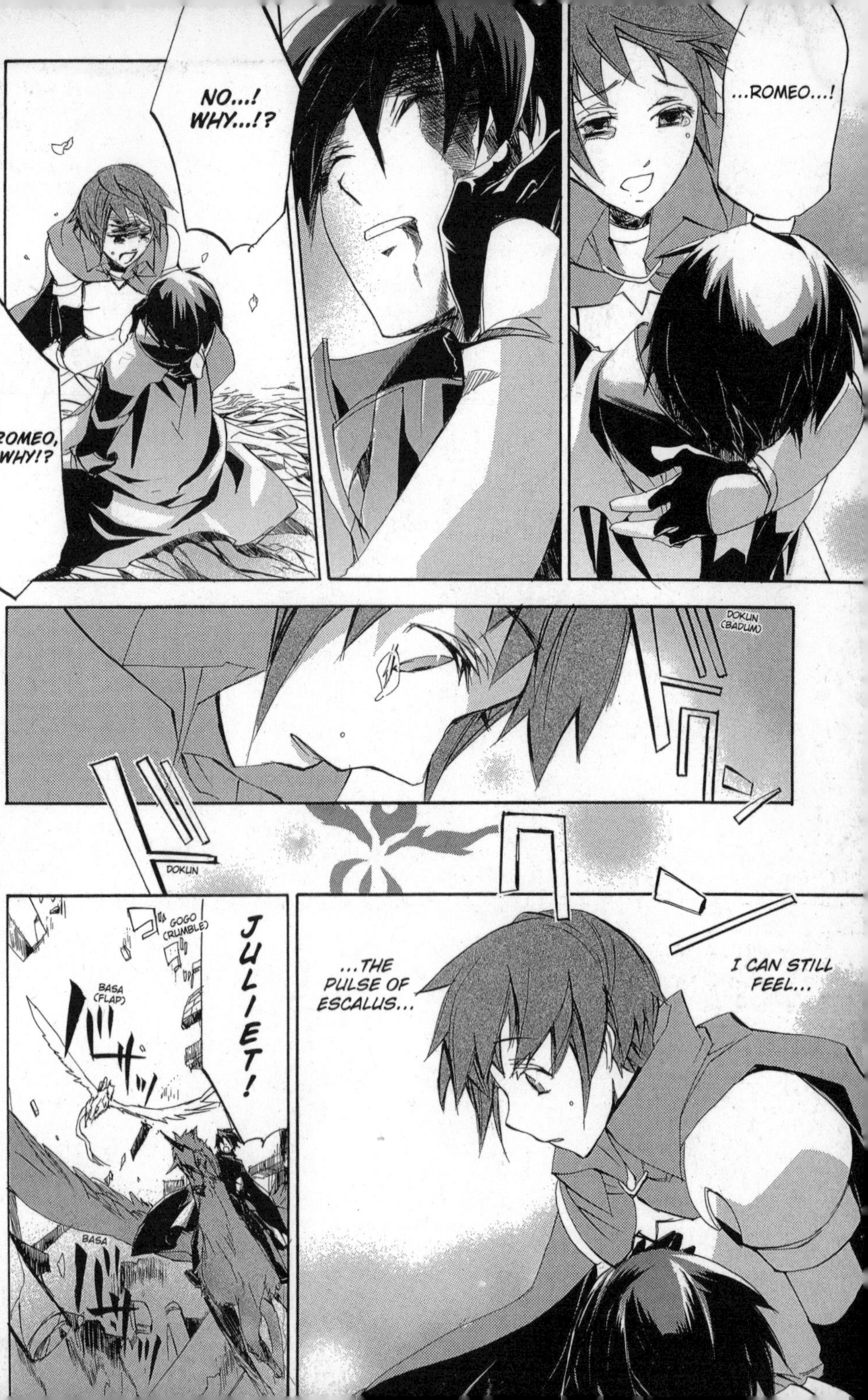
...ROMEO...!
NO...! WHY...!?
ROMEO, WHY!?
DOKUN (BADUM)
DOKUN
I CAN STILL FEEL...
...THE PULSE OF ESCALUS...
JULIET!
GOGO (RUMBLE)
BASA (FLAP)
BASA

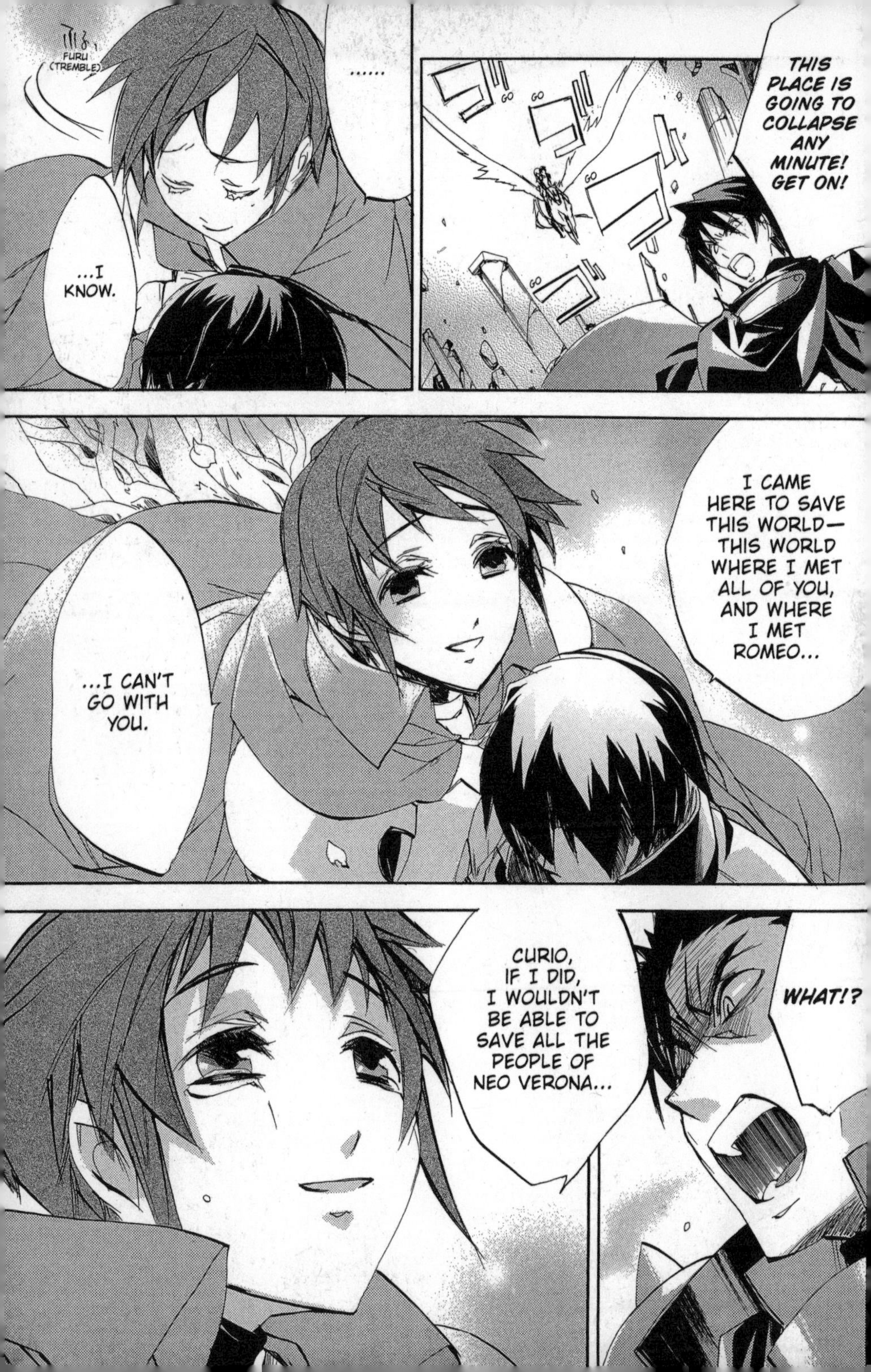

THIS PLACE IS GOING TO COLLAPSE ANY MINUTE! GET ON!
GO GO
GO
GO
FURU (TREMBLE)
......
...I KNOW.
I CAME HERE TO SAVE THIS WORLD— THIS WORLD WHERE I MET ALL OF YOU, AND WHERE I MET ROMEO...
...I CAN'T GO WITH YOU.
WHAT!?
CURIO, IF I DID, I WOULDN'T BE ABLE TO SAVE ALL THE PEOPLE OF NEO VERONA...

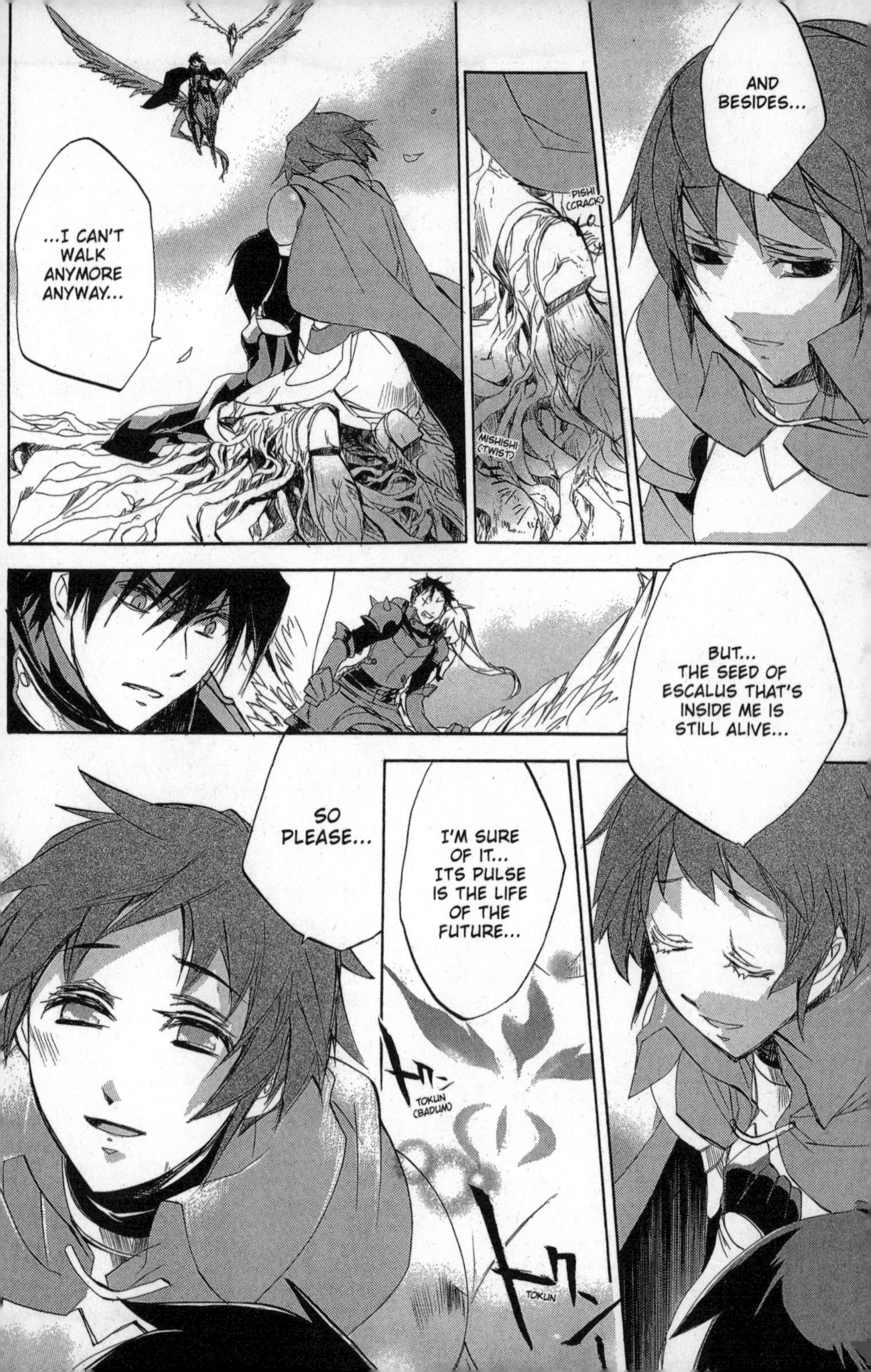
AND BESIDES...
PISHI (CRACK)
MISHISHI (TWIST)
...I CAN'T WALK ANYMORE ANYWAY...
BUT... THE SEED OF ESCALUS THAT'S INSIDE ME IS STILL ALIVE...
I'M SURE OF IT... ITS PULSE IS THE LIFE OF THE FUTURE...
TOKUN (BADUM)
TOKUN
SO PLEASE...

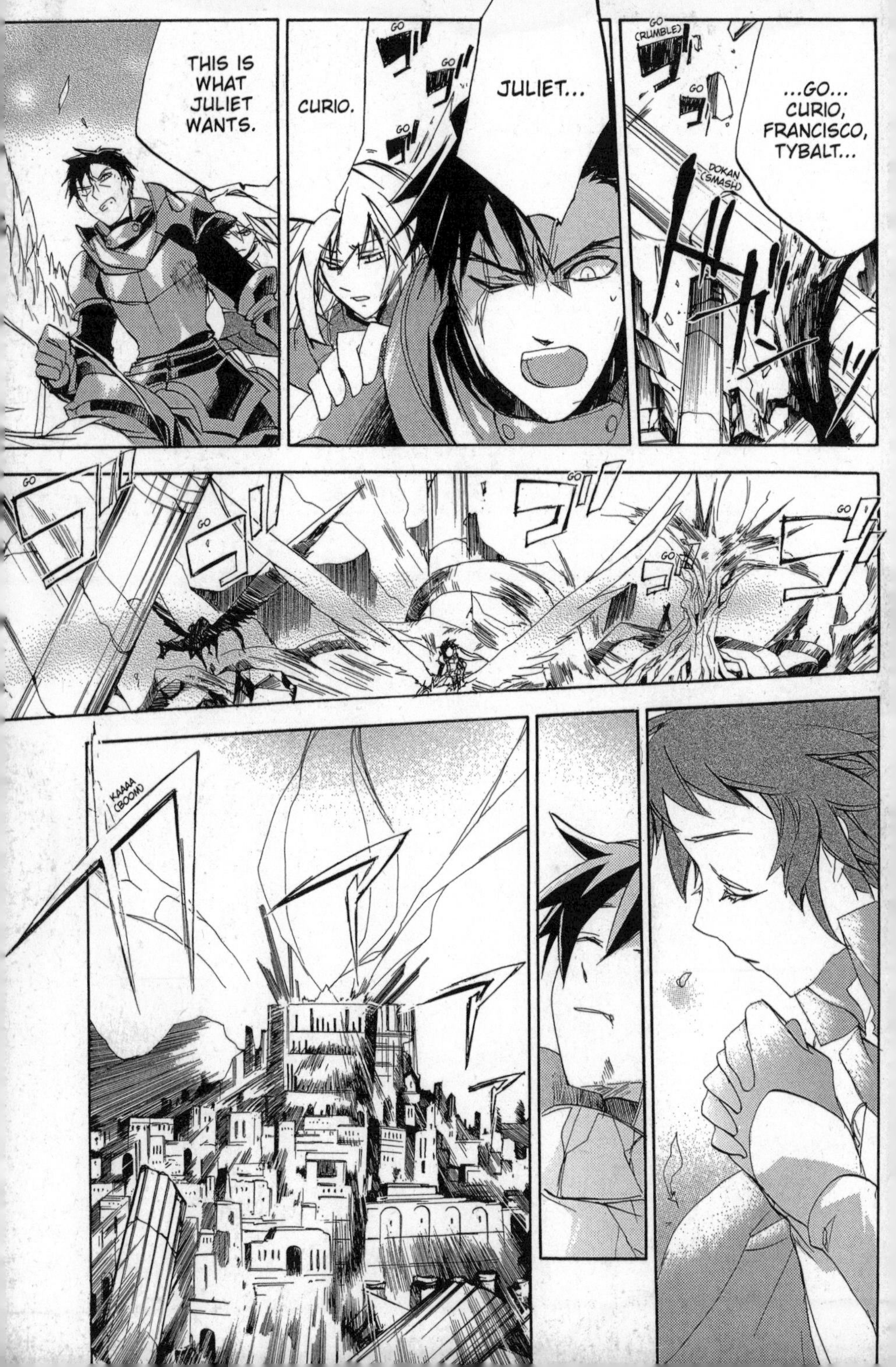
GO
(RUMBLE)
GO
...GO... CURIO, FRANCISCO, TYBALT...
DOKAN
(SMASH)
GO
GO
JULIET...
CURIO.
GO
THIS IS WHAT JULIET WANTS.
GO
GO
GO
GO
GO
KAAAA
(BOOM)

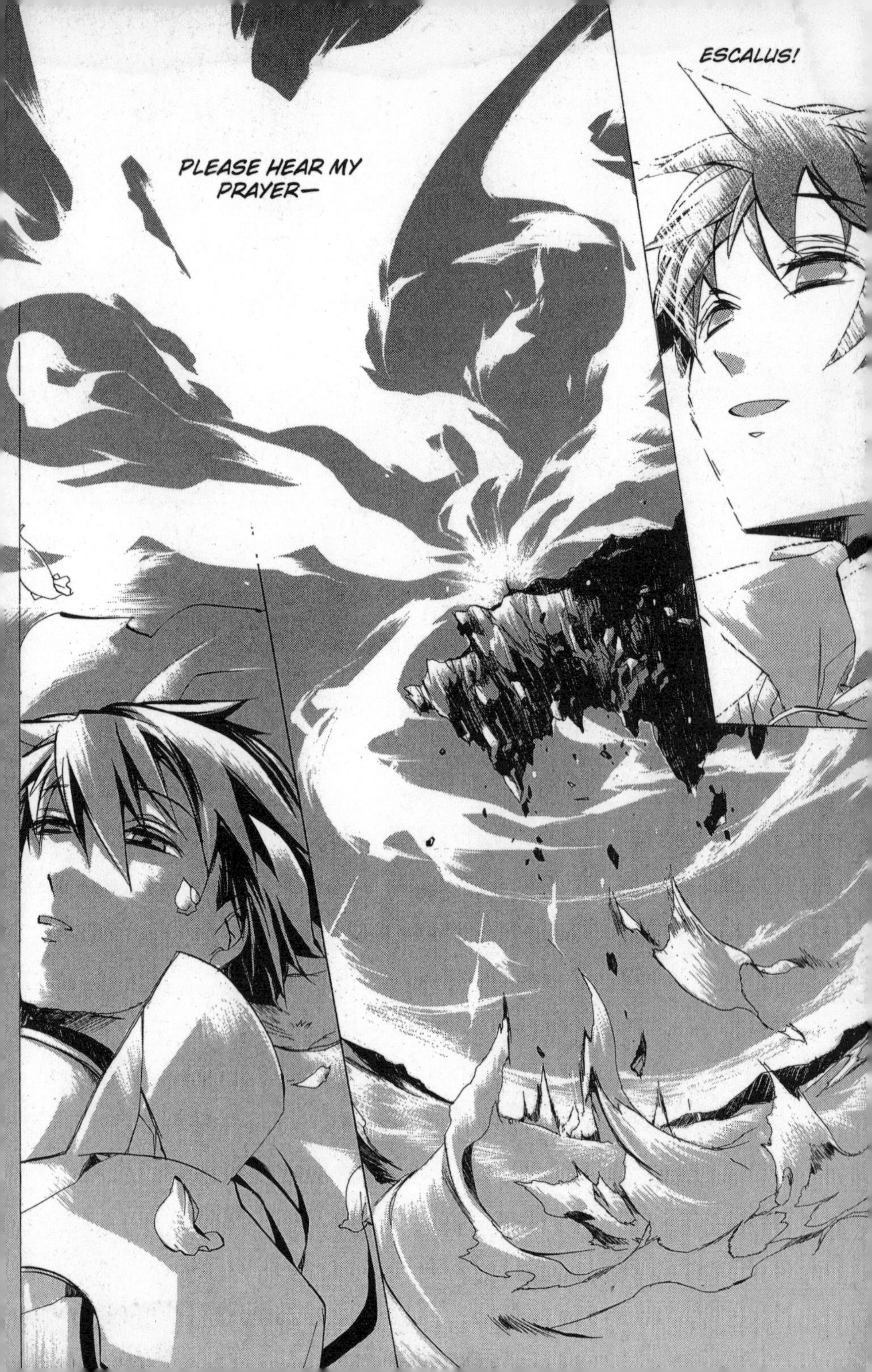
ESCALUS!
PLEASE HEAR MY PRAYER—

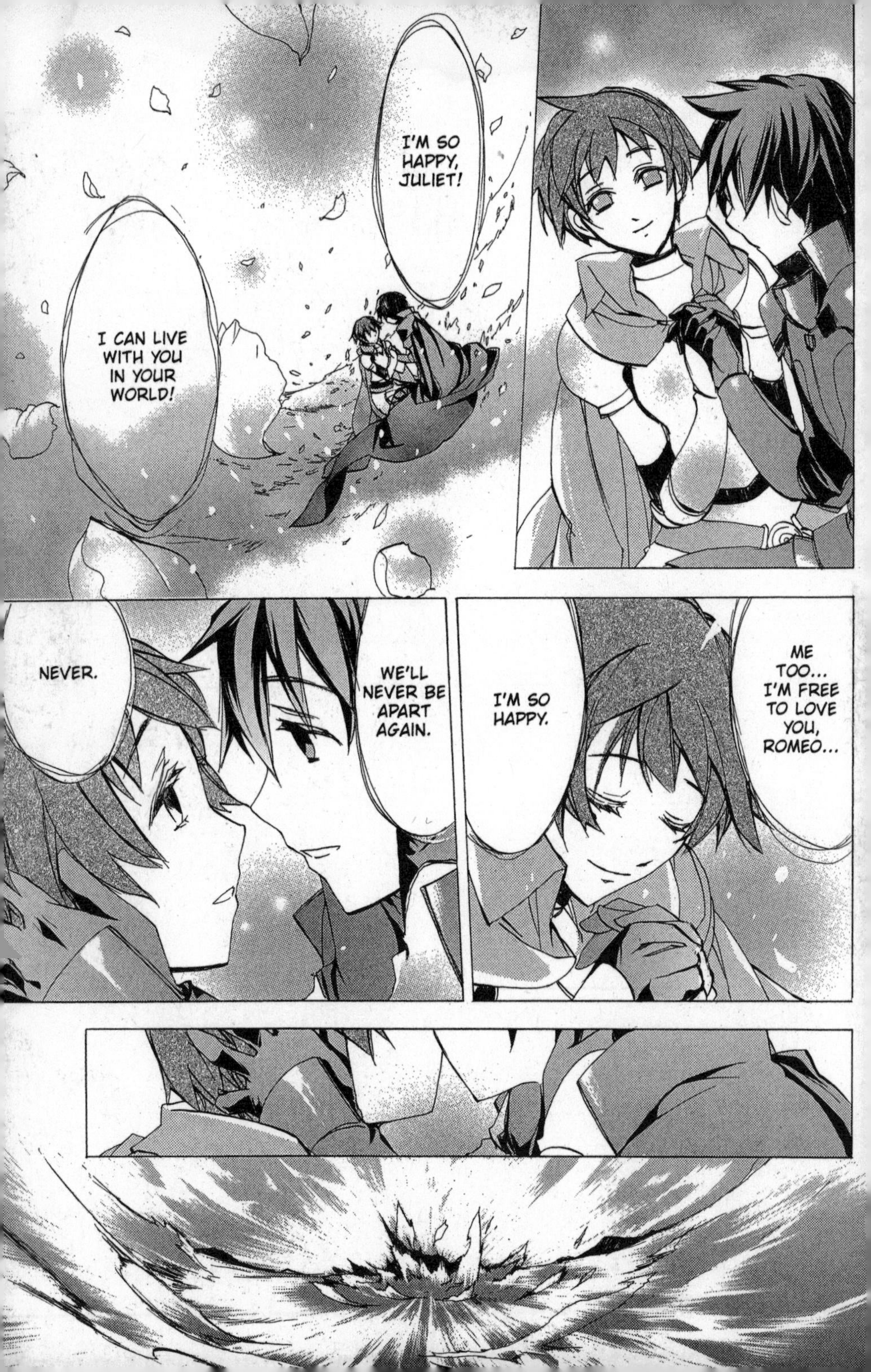
I'M SO HAPPY, JULIET!
I CAN LIVE WITH YOU IN YOUR WORLD!
ME TOO... I'M FREE TO LOVE YOU, ROMEO...
I'M SO HAPPY.
WE'LL NEVER BE APART AGAIN.
NEVER.

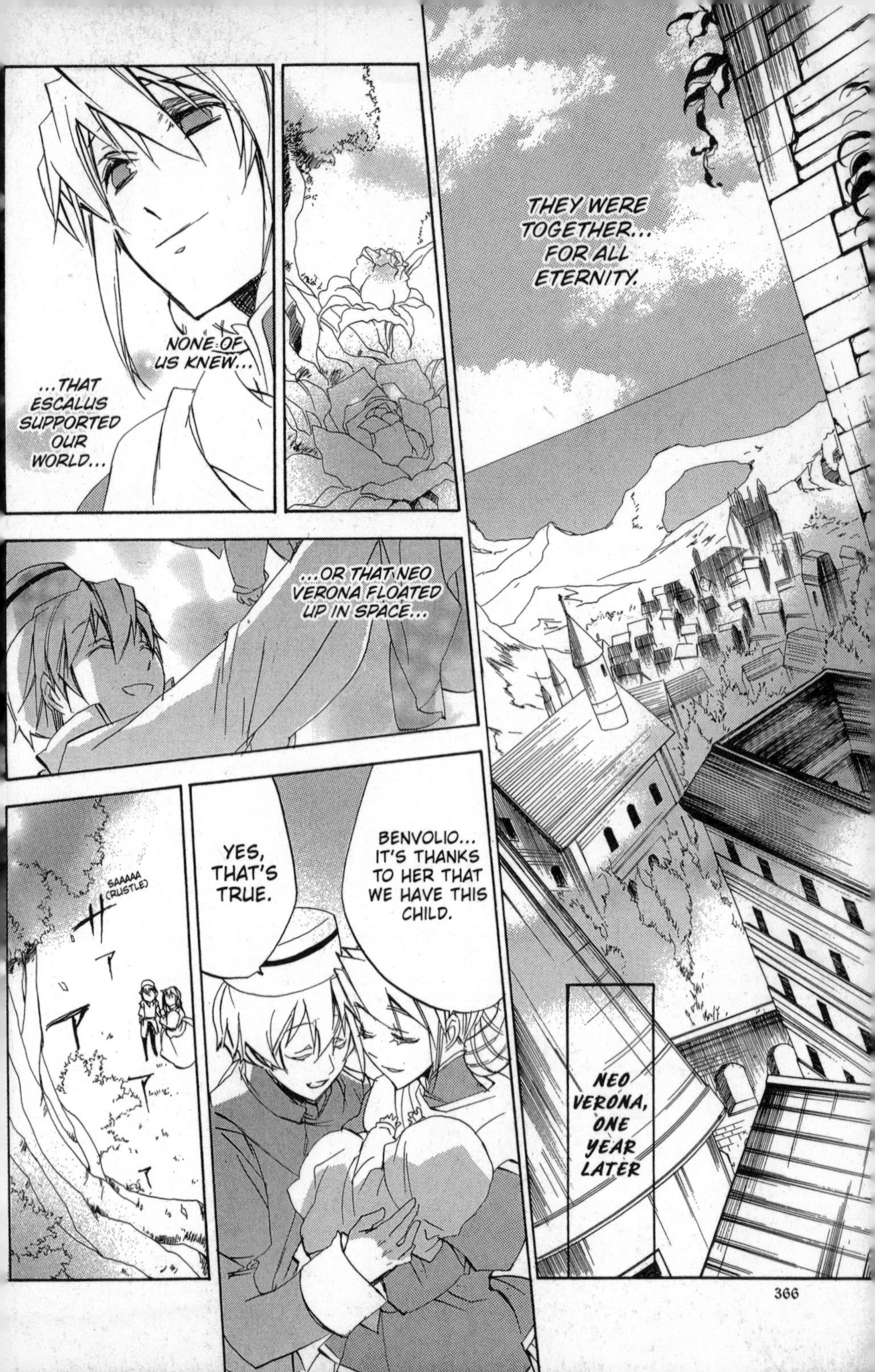
THEY WERE TOGETHER... FOR ALL ETERNITY.
NEO VERONA, ONE YEAR LATER
NONE OF US KNEW...
...THAT ESCALUS SUPPORTED OUR WORLD...
...OR THAT NEO VERONA FLOATED UP IN SPACE...
BENVOLIO... IT'S THANKS TO HER THAT WE HAVE THIS CHILD.
YES, THAT'S TRUE.
SAAAAA (RUSTLE)

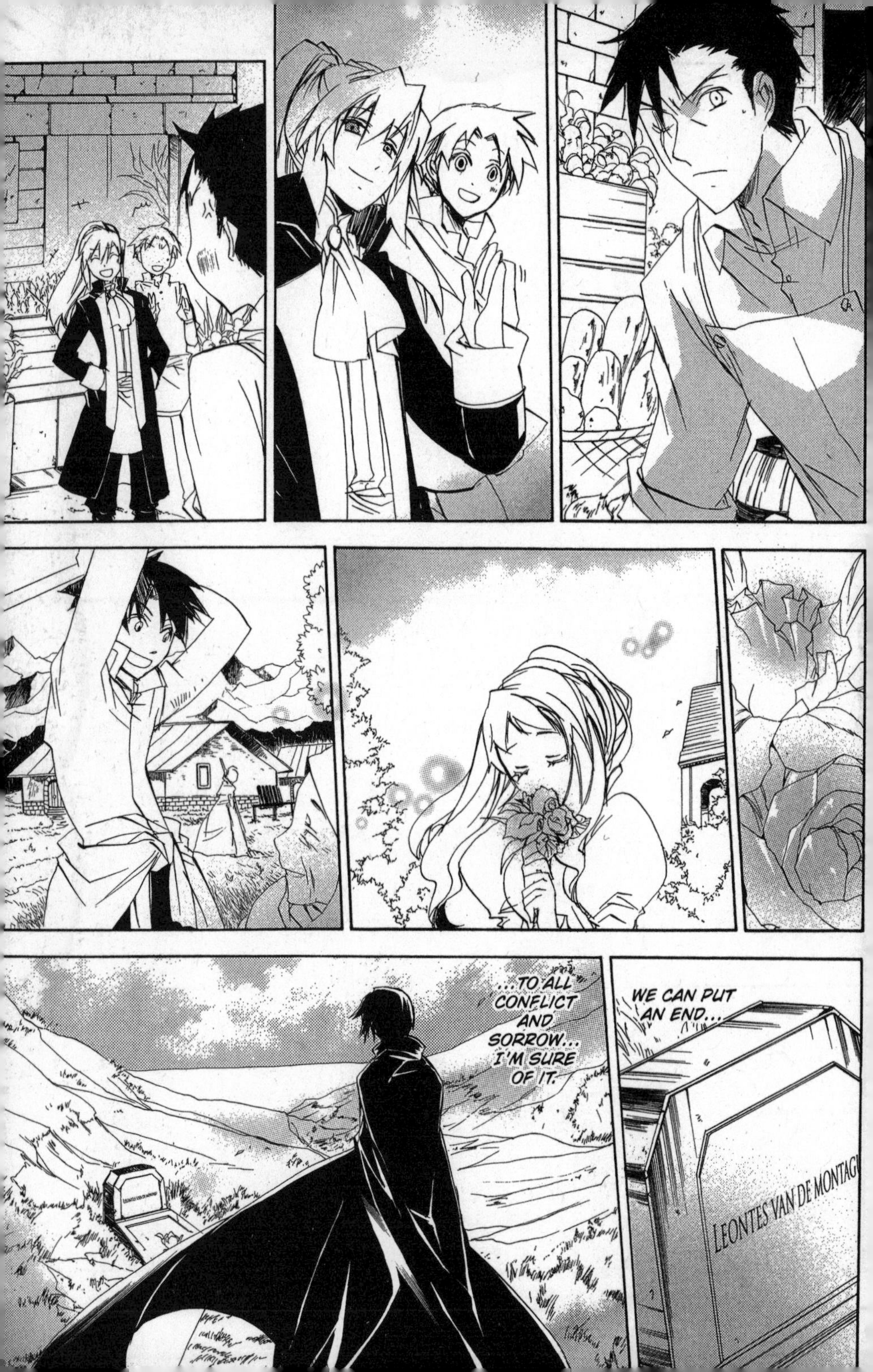
WE CAN PUT AN END...
...TO ALL CONFLICT AND SORROW... I'M SURE OF IT.

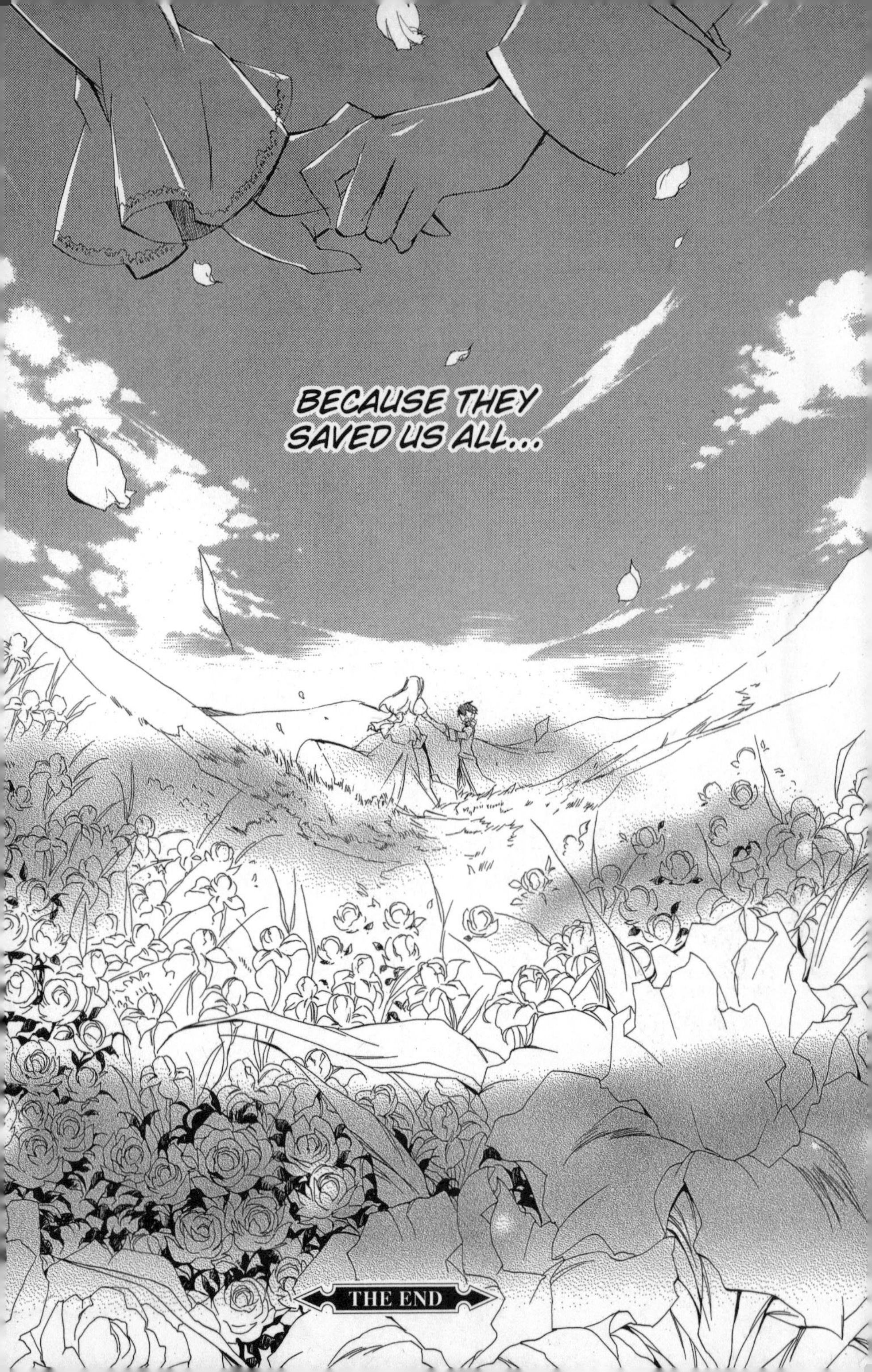
BECAUSE THEY SAVED US ALL...
THE END

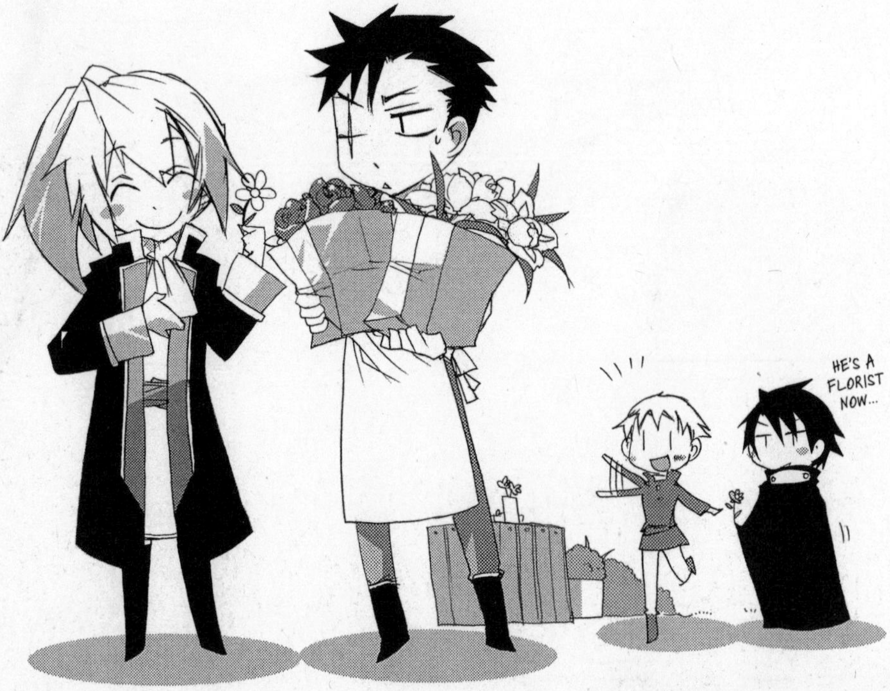
HE'S A FLORIST NOW...

AFTERWORD.

IT WAS ONLY FOR A SHORT TIME, BUT DRAWING THIS WAS DIZZYING AND A LOT OF FUN! IT WAS SUCH AN INVALUABLE EXPERIENCE! THANK YOU VERY, VERY MUCH FOR THIS OPPORTUNITY!

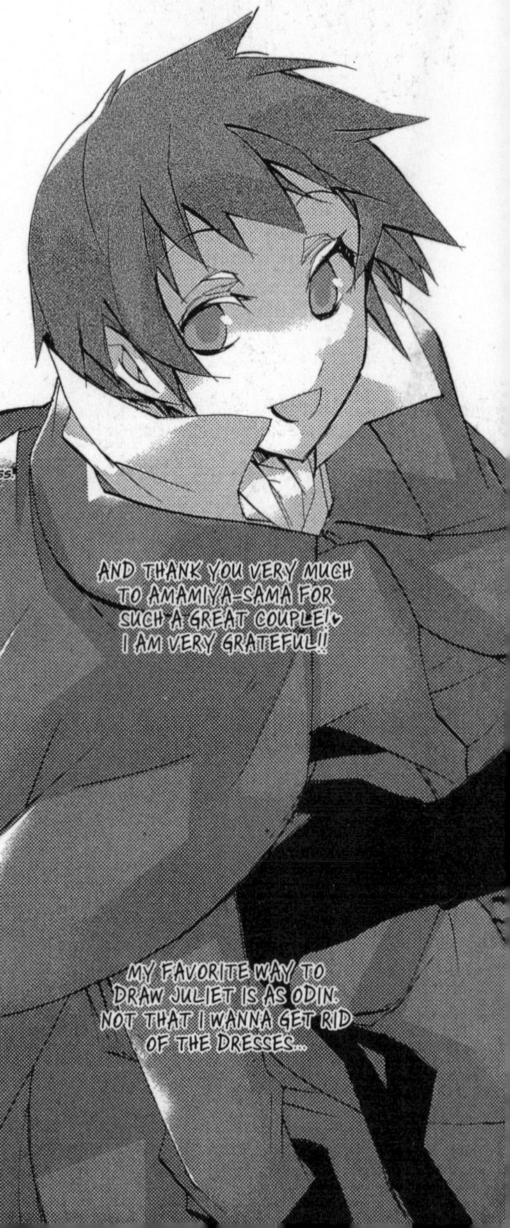
AND THANK YOU VERY MUCH TO AMAMIYA-SAMA FOR SUCH A GREAT COUPLE! I AM VERY GRATEFUL!!
MY FAVORITE WAY TO DRAW JULIET IS AS ODIN. NOT THAT I WANNA GET RID OF THE DRESSES...

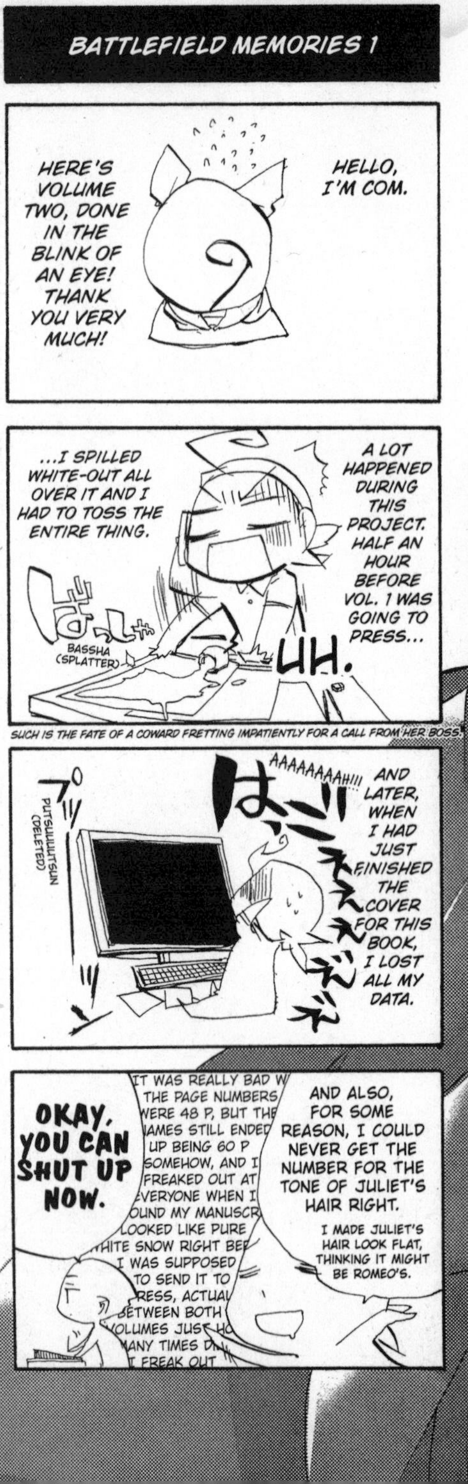
BATTLEFIELD MEMORIES 1
HELLO, I'M COM.
HERE'S VOLUME TWO, DONE IN THE BLINK OF AN EYE! THANK YOU VERY MUCH!
A LOT HAPPENED DURING THIS PROJECT. HALF AN HOUR BEFORE VOL. 1 WAS GOING TO PRESS...
...I SPILLED WHITE-OUT ALL OVER IT AND I HAD TO TOSS THE ENTIRE THING.
BASSHA (SPLATTER)
UH.
SUCH IS THE FATE OF A COWARD FRETTING IMPATIENTLY FOR A CALL FROM HER BOSS.
AND LATER, WHEN I HAD JUST FINISHED THE COVER FOR THIS BOOK, I LOST ALL MY DATA.
AAAAAAAAH!!!
PUTSUUUUTSUN (DELETED)
AND ALSO, FOR SOME REASON, I COULD NEVER GET THE NUMBER FOR THE TONE OF JULIET'S HAIR RIGHT.
I MADE JULIET'S HAIR LOOK FLAT, THINKING IT MIGHT BE ROMEO'S.
IT WAS REALLY BAD W THE PAGE NUMBERS WERE 48 P, BUT THE NAMES STILL ENDED UP BEING 60 P SOMEHOW, AND I FREAKED OUT AT EVERYONE WHEN I OUND MY MANUSCR LOOKED LIKE PURE HITE SNOW RIGHT BE I WAS SUPPOSED TO SEND IT TO RESS, ACTUAL BETWEEN BOTH VOLUMES JUST HO ANY TIMES D I FREAK OUT
OKAY. YOU CAN SHUT UP NOW.

BATTLEFIELD MEMORIES 2

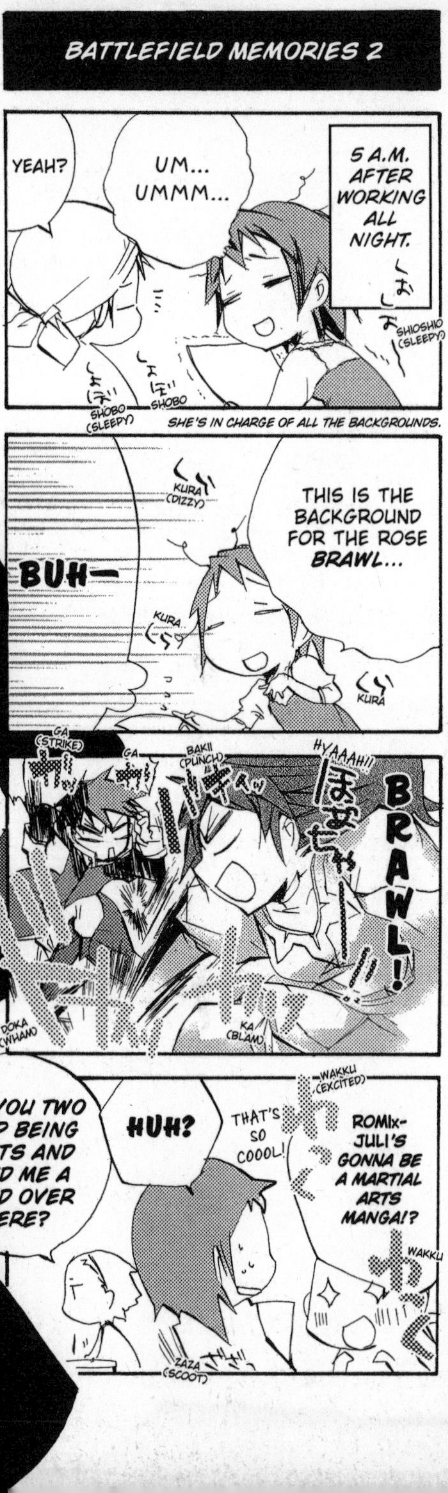
5 A.M. AFTER WORKING ALL NIGHT.
SHIOSHIO (SLEEPY)
UM... UMMM...
YEAH?
SHOBO
SHOBO (SLEEPY)
SHE'S IN CHARGE OF ALL THE BACKGROUNDS.
THIS IS THE BACKGROUND FOR THE ROSE BRAWL...
KURA (DIZZY)
KURA
KURA
BUH—
HYAAAH!!
BRAWL!
BAKII (PUNCH)
GA
GA (STRIKE)
KA (BLAM)
DOKA (WHAM)
ROMIx-JULI'S GONNA BE A MARTIAL ARTS MANGA!?
WAKKU (EXCITED)
WAKKU
THAT'S SO COOOL!
HUH?
CAN YOU TWO STOP BEING IDIOTS AND LEND ME A HAND OVER HERE?
ZAZA (SCOOT)

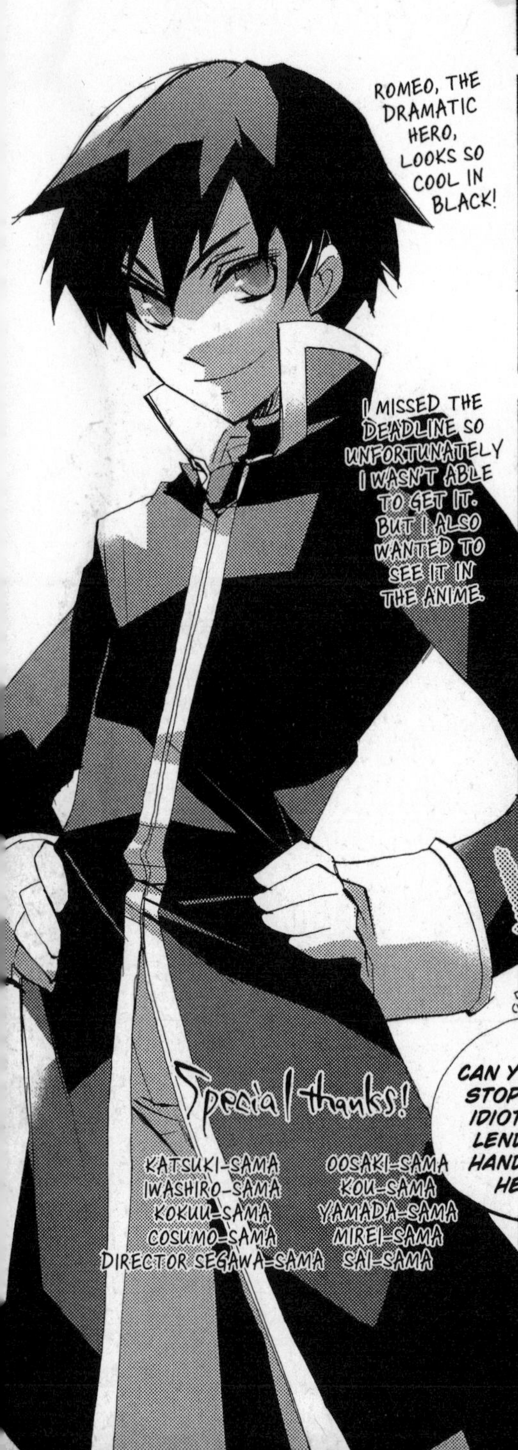
ROMEO, THE DRAMATIC HERO, LOOKS SO COOL IN BLACK!
I MISSED THE DEADLINE SO UNFORTUNATELY I WASN'T ABLE TO GET IT. BUT I ALSO WANTED TO SEE IT IN THE ANIME.
Special thanks!
KATSUKI-SAMA
IWASHIRO-SAMA
KOKUU-SAMA
COSUMO-SAMA
DIRECTOR SEGAWA-SAMA
OOSAKI-SAMA
KOU-SAMA
YAMADA-SAMA
MIREI-SAMA
SAI-SAMA

Hitomi Amamiya

"Red Whirlwind~~~~~! So cool~~~~~!" (Please refer to page two.)

My cry of love for the illustrations was the same every time. I'm kind of in love with Juliet's strength.

Also, I realized something when I finished.

Montague wins the award for perfect attendance! (Whaaaat!?)

He's appeared in every single act...
He's not actually in act 5, but he's right in the middle of the color page and he's huuuuge, bigger than anyone else! And he's really all over the final act, isn't he? I wonder why he's featured so much? Is it because I've secretly been a Montague fan this entire time? Oh well...I like what I like, I guess. Is that weird?

Anyway, my heart was pounding like crazy while this was being serialized, but I emerged unscathed. So when volume two of the manga *RomiJuli* was finally all done, I was very, very happy, and my heart was pounding once again. I want to thank Director Oizaki, who wrote the afterword that follows mine, for all of his hard work. Thank you so much.

And there's also the novelization, *Romeo x Juliet: Shiroi eien no chikai* (available in Japan only). I think this is going to be published soon (it should, anyway...). When it comes out, I hope that you will enjoy it, and thank you for reading.

◆ In the novel you'll be able to see more of COM-sensei's illustrations! They are somewhat different from the manga, of course, and so very beautiful!
◆ And I intend to put in the sort of things you can only do with the printed word which will make you think, "They did what!?"

So...you should...um...definitely...look forward to that. (!?)

And now I would like to thank you, the readers. Thank you so much for enjoying *RomeoxJuliet* with me!

雨宮 ひとみ
HITOMI AMAMIYA

Fumitoshi Oizaki

RomeoxJuliet may be based on an "animation," but just as love itself is a unique experience for each person, it's good that the manga takes on its own dimensions, don't you think?

During the discussions about making *RomeoxJuliet* into a comic, I said I wanted to create *RomeoxJuliet* using all the special techniques that are particular to "manga" as a medium. When I think of it now, I'm so grateful that I had the opportunity to make that request. I feel that there are certain characteristics that make an anime an anime, and then there are certain characteristics that make a manga a manga. A manga made just by tracing the anime wouldn't be interesting at all. I felt that if we could treat the characters and settings from the anime as "raw materials" to be arranged as we liked, then not only would we able to create something new and different, but also the "difference" between the two would be something to appreciate in and of itself.

The result is that the manga edition of *RomixJuli* is a very charming piece of work. Amamiya-san exquisitely arranged and composed the story. When I was reading it, I kept realizing, "Oh! I know this scene!" and, "I know what this is an expansion of!" which was a lot of fun for me as a reader. I also really enjoyed all the cool characters and gorgeous color illustrations drawn by COM-san. I certainly felt the beauty she created was not something that could have been achieved in an anime. For one thing, Juliet couldn't have worn that lovely lace dress! (Hee-hee) Thank you! Thank you both so much!

And finally I would like to thank all the good people at Asuka's editorial department, Amamiya-sama, and COM-sama for all your hard work!!

And I'm sad to say that this marks the end of the anime, the manga, (and soon the novels). However, I hope that you continue to love *RomixJuli* in your hearts for a long time to come.

◆ **Profile:**

Fumitoshi Oizaki.
Born October 15th, Libra, blood type A.
Animator.

Was the animation director for *Final Fantasy: Unlimited*, did character design and was the general animation director for *Kaleido Star*, managed things like character design for *Sgt. Frog*, and directed *RomeoxJuliet*.

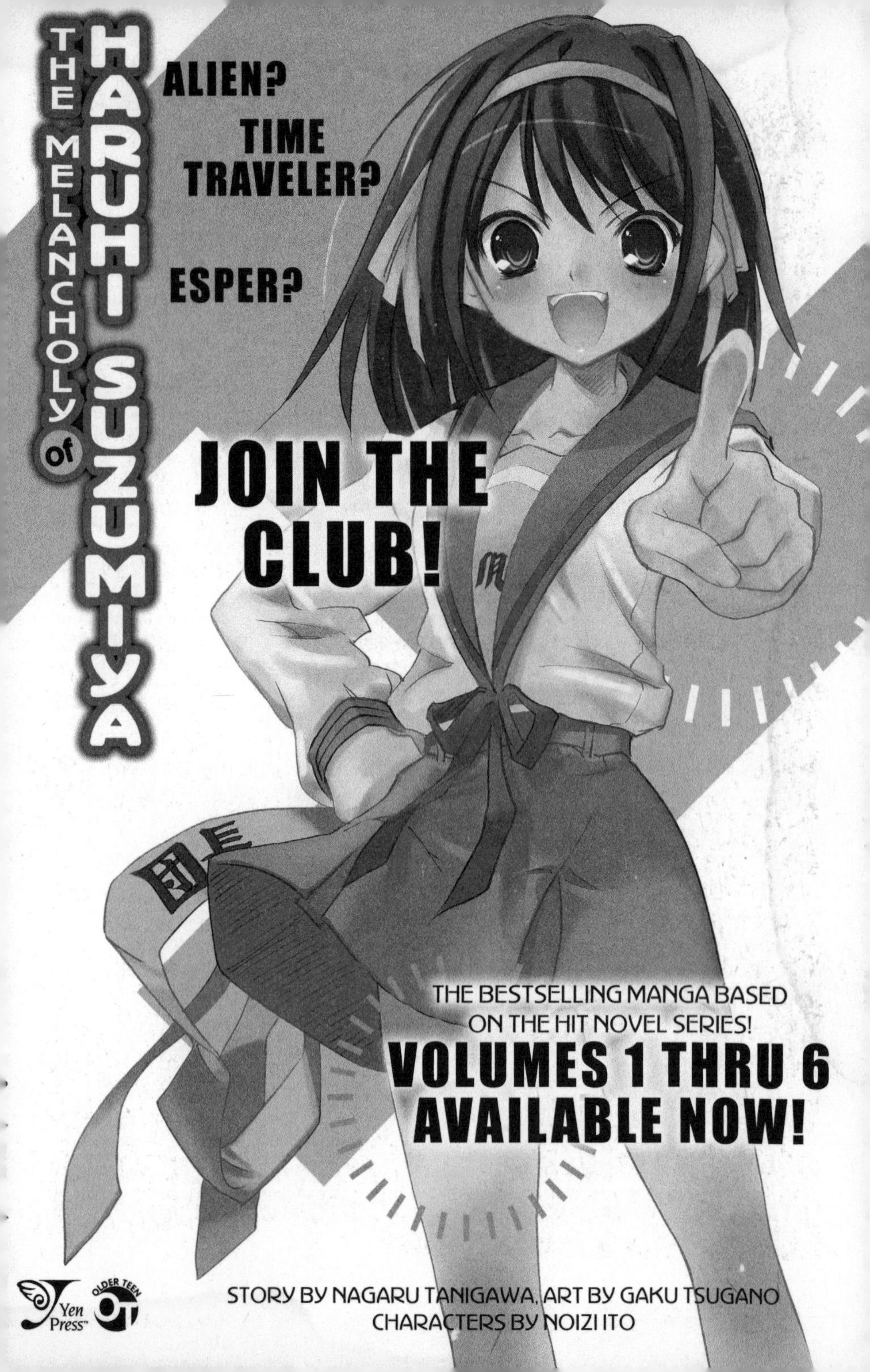
THE MELANCHOLY of HARUHI SUZUMIYA
ALIEN?
TIME TRAVELER?
ESPER?
JOIN THE CLUB!
THE BESTSELLING MANGA BASED ON THE HIT NOVEL SERIES!
VOLUMES 1 THRU 6 AVAILABLE NOW!
Yen Press™
OLDER TEEN OT
STORY BY NAGARU TANIGAWA, ART BY GAKU TSUGANO
CHARACTERS BY NOIZI ITO

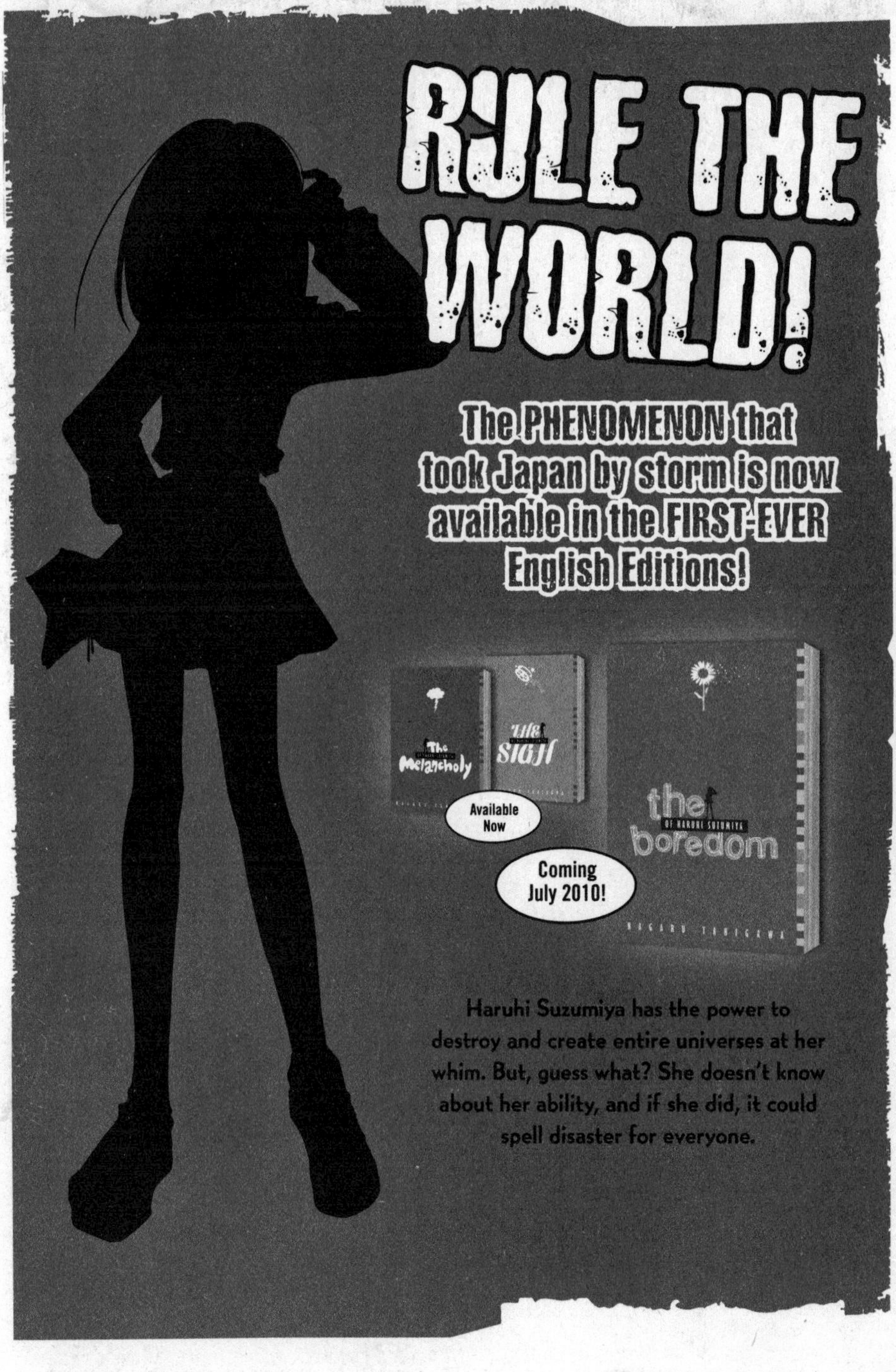
RULE THE WORLD!
The PHENOMENON that took Japan by storm is now available in the FIRST-EVER English Editions!
The Melancholy
The Sigh
Available Now
the boredom
OF HARUHI SUZUMIYA
NAGARU TANIGAWA
Coming July 2010!
Haruhi Suzumiya has the power to destroy and create entire universes at her whim. But, guess what? She doesn't know about her ability, and if she did, it could spell disaster for everyone.

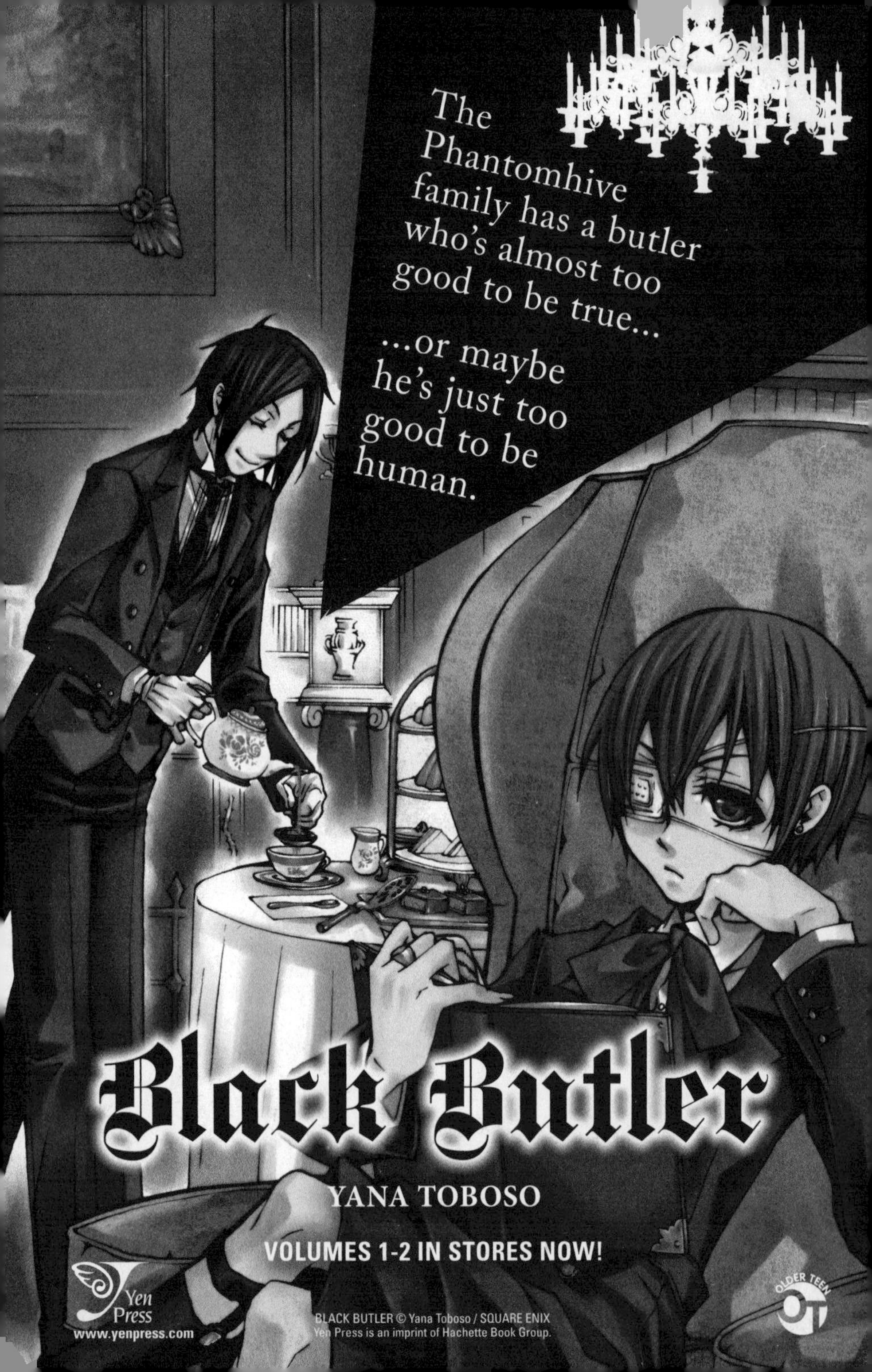
The Phantomhive family has a butler who's almost too good to be true...
...or maybe he's just too good to be human.
Black Butler
YANA TOBOSO
VOLUMES 1-2 IN STORES NOW!
Yen Press
www.yenpress.com
BLACK BUTLER © Yana Toboso / SQUARE ENIX
Yen Press is an imprint of Hachette Book Group.
OLDER TEEN
OT

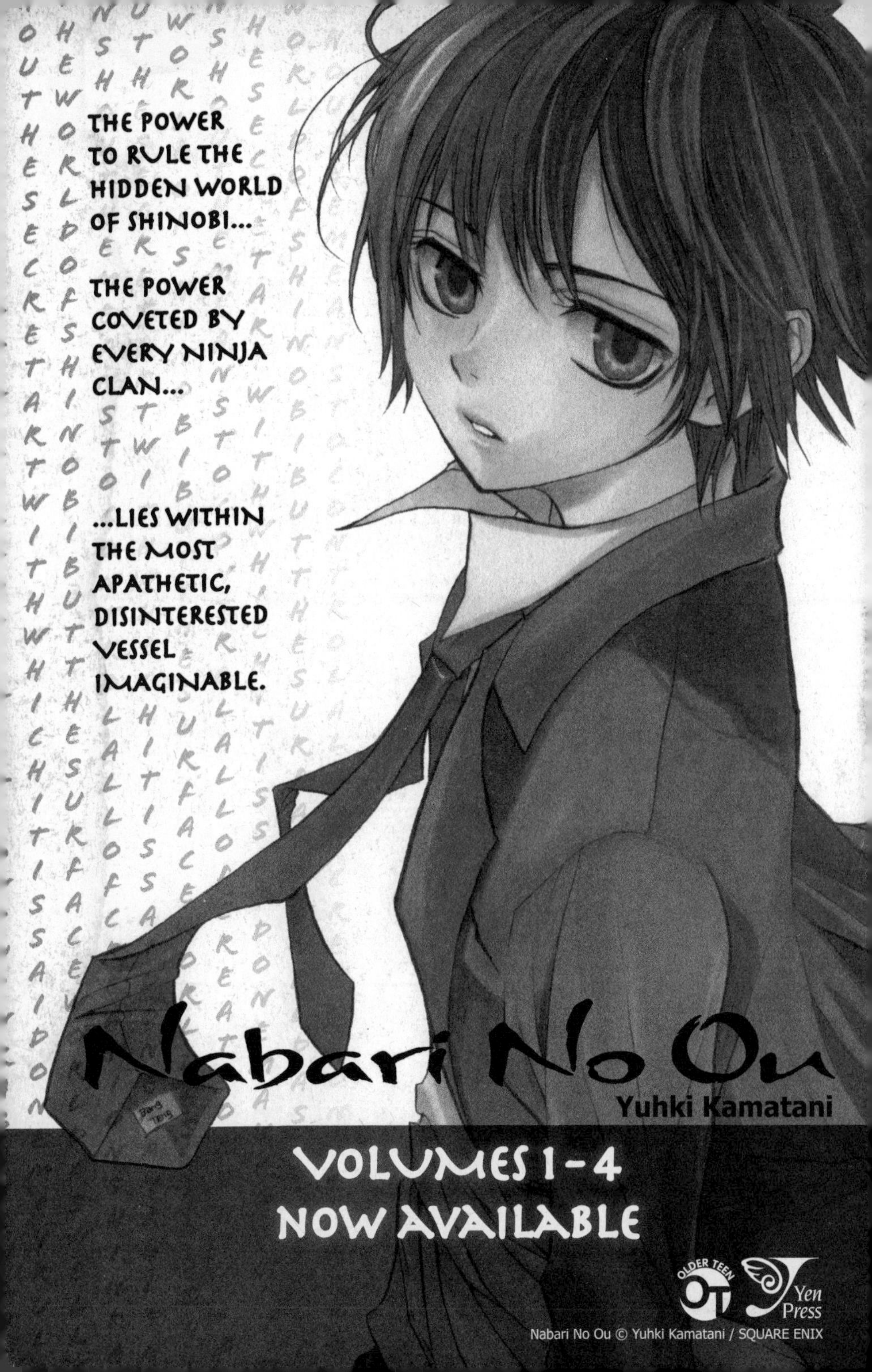
THE POWER TO RULE THE HIDDEN WORLD OF SHINOBI...
THE POWER COVETED BY EVERY NINJA CLAN...
...LIES WITHIN THE MOST APATHETIC, DISINTERESTED VESSEL IMAGINABLE.
Nabari No Ou
Yuhki Kamatani
VOLUMES 1-4
NOW AVAILABLE
OLDER TEEN
OT
Yen Press
Nabari No Ou © Yuhki Kamatani / SQUARE ENIX

𝕽𝖔𝖒𝖊𝖔 x 𝕵𝖚𝖑𝖎𝖊𝖙

ILLUSTRATED BY **COM**
ORIGINAL STORY BY **WILLIAM SHAKESPEARE**
ORIGINAL ANIMATION BY **GONZO** x **SPWT**

Translation: Kate Beckwitt

Lettering: Lys Blakeslee

Romeo x Juliet © COM 2007, 2008 © 2007 GONZO/CBC·GDH·SPWT.
Edited by KADOKAWA SHOTEN
First published in Japan in 2007,2008 by KADOKAWA CORPORATION, Tokyo.
English translation rights arranged with KADOKAWA CORPORATION, Tokyo, through TUTTLE-MORI AGENCY, INC., Tokyo.

Translation © 2010 by Hachette Book Group, Inc.

Yen Press
Hachette Book Group
1290 Avenue of the Americas, New York, NY 10104

www.HachetteBookGroup.com
www.YenPress.com

Yen Press is an imprint of Hachette Book Group, Inc. The Yen Press name and logo are trademarks of Hachette Book Group, Inc.

First Yen Press Edition: July 2010

ISBN: 978-0-316-07328-8

10 9 8 7 6

BVG

Printed in the United States of America